Lecture Notes in Computer Science 1163

Edited by G. Goos, J. Hartmanis and J. van Leeuwen

Advisory Board: W. Brauer   D. Gries   J. Stoer

Springer
Berlin
Heidelberg
New York
Barcelona
Budapest
Hong Kong
London
Milan
Paris
Santa Clara
Singapore
Tokyo

Kwangjo Kim   Tsutomu Matsumoto   (Eds.)

Advances in Cryptology – ASIACRYPT '96

International Conference
on the Theory and Applications
of Cryptology and Information Security
Kyongju, Korea, November 3-7, 1996
Proceedings

Springer

Series Editors

Gerhard Goos, Karlsruhe University, Germany

Juris Hartmanis, Cornell University, NY, USA

Jan van Leeuwen, Utrecht University, The Netherlands

Volume Editors

Kwangjo Kim
Electronics and Telecommunications Research Institute
161 Kajong-dong, Yusong-ku, Taejon 305-350, Korea

Tsutomu Matsumoto
Division of Artificial Environment Systems and
Division of Electrical and Computer Engineering
Yokohama National University
156 Tokiwadai, Hodogaya, Yokohama 240, Japan

Cataloging-in-Publication data applied for
Die Deutsche Bibliothek - CIP-Einheitsaufnahme

Advances in cryptology : proceedings / ASIACRYPT '96,
International Conference on the Theory and Applications of
Cryptology and Information Security, Kyongju, Korea,
November 3 - 7, 1996. Kwangjo Kim ; Tsutomu Matsumoto
(ed.). - Berlin ; Heidelberg ; New York ; Barcelona ; Budapest ;
Hong Kong ; London ; Milan ; Paris ; Santa Clara ; Singapore
;Tokyo : Springer, 1996
  (Lecture notes in computer science ; Vol. 1163)
  ISBN 3-540-61872-4
NE: Kim, Kwangjo [Hrsg.]; ASIACRYPT <1996, Kyongju>; GT

CR Subject Classification (1991): E.3-4, G.2.1, D.4.6,F.2.1-2, C.2, J.1, K.6.5,
K.4.1, K.5.1-2

Mathematics Subject CLassification (1991): 94A60, 11T71, 11YXX, 68P20,
68Q20, 68Q25

ISSN 0302-9743
ISBN 3-540-61872-4 Springer-Verlag Berlin Heidelberg New York

© Springer-Verlag Berlin Heidelberg 1996
Printed in Germany

Typesetting: Camera-ready by author
SPIN 10555455   06/3142 – 5 4 3 2 1 0   Printed on acid-free paper

Preface

ASIACRYPT'96, the conference covering all aspects of theory and applications of cryptology and information security, is held at Kyongju Hilton Hotel situated along the shore of beautiful Pomun Lake Resort in Kyongju, Korea from November 3 to 7, 1996. This is one of the Asiacrypt conferences. In the same series, ASIACRYPT'91 and ASIACRYPT'94 took place in Japan and Australia respectively. ASIACRYPT'96 is sponsored by Korea Institute of Information Security and Cryptology (KIISC), in cooperation with the International Association for Cryptologic Research (IACR) under the patronage of Ministry of Information and Communication (MIC) of Korea.

The 16-member Program Committee organized the scientific program and considered 124 submissions. Of these, 31 were accepted for presentation. The authors' affiliations of the 124 submissions and the 31 accepted papers range over 22 and 14 countries or regions, respectively. In addition, there are three invited talks by Kevin S. McCurley from Sandia National Labs., USA, Shigeo Tsujii from Chou University, Japan, and Jacques Stern from ENS, France. A Rump Session chaired by Thomas A. Berson completes the program.

The submitted version of each paper was sent to all members of the Program Committee and was extensively examined by at least three committee members and/or outside experts. The review process was rigorously blinded and the anonymity of each submission was maintained until the selection was completed. We followed the traditional policy that each member of the Program Committee could be an author of at most one accepted paper.

This is the first time the proceedings is available at the conference in the history of Asiacrypt series. These proceedings contain the revised versions of the 31 contributed talks as well as the 3 papers written by the invited speakers. Comments from the Program Committee were taken into account in the revisions. However, the authors (not the committee) bear full responsibility for the contents of their papers.

We are very grateful to the members of the Program Committee for generously spending so much of their time on the difficult task of selecting the papers. They are : Ross Anderson, Thomas A. Berson, Chin-Chen Chang, Pil Joong Lee, Mitsuru Matsui, Sang Jae Moon, David Naccache, Kaisa Nyberg, Eiji Okamoto, Paul Van Oorschot, Dingyi Pei, Bart Preneel, Moti Yung, and Yuliang Zheng. We also thank the following outside experts who assisted the Program Committee in evaluating various papers : Antoon Bosselaers, Seongtaek Chee, Joan Daemen, Seung-Cheol Goh, Sang-Geun Han, Yuji Ishizuka, Markus Jakobsson, Lars Knudsen, Sangjin Lee, Chae Hoon Lim, Françoise Levy-dit-Vehel, Masahiro Mambo, Serge Mister, Atsuko Miyaji, Hiroshi Miyano, Shiho Moriai, Tim Moses, David M'Raïhi, Takahiko Nakamura, Kazuo Ohta, Motoji Ohmori, Pascal Paillier, Sung Jun Park, Vincent Rijmen, Yasuyuki Sakai, Soo Hak Sung, Michael Wiener, and Kyung-Cheol Yang. We apologize for any omissions in this list.

We would like to appreciate all who have submitted papers to ASIACRYPT'96 and the authors of accepted and invited papers for their on-time preparation of camera-ready manuscripts.

We are pleased to thank Shin Young Lim and Seunghwa Lee for their arrangement of ASIACRYPT'96 official Web page at URL: `http://www.kreonet.re.kr/AC96/AC96.html`. Special thanks also go to Yongdae Kim and Hee Ja Kang for their help with preparation of the various tasks of program co-chairs.

Most of the work by Tsutomu Matsumoto was done while he was away from Yokohama. He would like to thank the Isaac Newton Institute of Cambridge University, U.K., Imre Mojzes of Technical University of Budapest, Hungary, and Thomas Beth of University of Karlsruhe, Germany, for providing convenient working environments.

August 1996   Kwangjo Kim
                                                   Tsutomu Matsumoto

ASIACRYPT'96

Kyongju, November 3 – 7, Korea

International Conference on the Theory and Applications of Cryptology and Information Security

Sponsored by
Korea Institute of Information Security and Cryptology (KIISC)

In cooperation with
The International Association for Cryptologic Research (IACR)

Under the patronage of
Ministry of Information and Communication (MIC), Korea

General Chair
Man Young Rhee (President of KIISC)

Program Committee
Kwangjo Kim (Co-chair, Electronics and Telecommunications Research
                Institute, Korea)
Tsutomu Matsumoto (Co-chair, Yokohama National University, Japan)
Ross Anderson (Cambridge University, UK)
Thomas A. Berson (Anagram Laboratories, USA)
Chin-Chen Chang (National Chung Cheng University, ROC)
Pil Joong Lee (Pohang University of Science and Technology, Korea)
Mitsuru Matsui (Mitsubishi Electric Corporation, Japan)
Sang Jae Moon (Kyungpook National University, Korea)
David Naccache (Gemplus Card International, France)
Kaisa Nyberg (Finnish Defence Forces, Finland)
Eiji Okamoto (Japan Advanced Institute of Science and Technology, Japan)
Paul Van Oorschot (Bell Northern Research, Canada)
Dingyi Pei (Academia Sinica, PROC)
Bart Preneel (Katholieke Universiteit Leuven, Belgium)
Moti Yung (IBM T.J. Watson Research Center, USA)
Yuliang Zheng (Monash University, Australia)

Organizing Committee
Dong Kyoo Kim (Chair, Ajou University, Korea)
Ok-Hwan Byeon (System Engineering Research Institute, Korea)
Kyung Soo Ham (Dongguk University, Korea)
Moon Seog Jun (Soon Sil University, Korea)
Kwangjo Kim (Electronics and Telecommunications Research Institute, Korea)
Kyung-Seok Lee (Korea Institute for Industrial Economics and Trade, Korea)
Sang Jae Moon (Kyungpook National University, Korea)
Kil Hyun Nam (Korea National Defense University, Korea)
Sang Kyu Park (Han Yang University, Korea)
Jae Cheol Ryou (Chung Nam National University, Korea)
Chan Shin (Korea Institute of Information Security and Cryptology, Korea)
Joo Seok Song (Yonsei University, Korea)
Chee Sun Won (Dongguk University, Korea)
Dong Ho Won (Sung Kyun Kwan University, Korea)

Contents

Discrete Log Based Systems

A Message Recovery Signature Scheme Equivalent to DSA over
Elliptic Curves 1
  Atsuko Miyaji (Matsushita, Japan)

Cryptographic Protocols Based on Real-Quadratic A-Fields 15
  Ingrid Biehl, Bernd Meyer (Univ. des Saarlandes, Germany),
  Christoph Thiel (Gesellschaft für Automation und Organisation,
  Germany)

Minding your p's and q's 26
  Ross Anderson (Cambridge Univ., UK),
  Serge Vaudenay (ENS, France)

Authenticated Multi-Party Key Agreement 36
  Mike Just (Carleton Univ., Canada),
  Serge Vaudenay (ENS, France)

Invited Talk 1

Cryptography and the Internet : Lessons and Challenges 50
  Kevin S. McCurley (Sandia National Lab., USA)

Efficient Algorithms

Generating Standard DSA Signatures Without Long Inversion 57
  Arjen K. Lenstra (Citibank, USA)

A Fast Software Implementation for Arithmetic Operations
in $GF(2^n)$ 65
  Erik De Win, Antoon Bosselaers, Servaas Vandenberghe, Peter
  De Gersem, Joos Vandewalle (Katholieke Univ. Leuven, Belgium)

Hash Function and Block Ciphers

Hash Functions Based on Block Ciphers and Quaternary Codes 77
  Lars Knudsen, Bart Preneel (Katholieke Univ. Leuven, Belgium)

Generalized Feistel Networks 91
  Kaisa Nyberg (Finnish Defence Forces, Finland)

On Applying Linear Cryptanalysis to IDEA 105
Philip Hawkes (Univ. of Queensland, Australia),
Luke O'Connor (Distributed Systems Technology Centre, Australia)

Cryptographic Protocols

A Multi-Recastable Ticket Scheme for Electronic Elections 116
Chun-I Fan, Chin-Laung Lei (National Taiwan Univ., Taiwan)

Some Remarks on a Receipt-Free and Universally Verifiable
Mix-Type Voting Scheme 125
Markus Michels, Patrick Horster
(Univ. of Technology Chemnitz-Zwickau, Germany)

Observations on Non-repudiation 133
Jianying Zhou, Dieter Gollmann (Univ. of London, UK)

Signature and Identification

On the Efficiency of One-Time Digital Signatures 145
Daniel Bleichenbacher (Bell Lab., USA),
Ueli Maurer (ETH Zürich, Switzerland)

A Hidden Cryptographic Assumption in No-Transferable
Identification Schemes 159
Kouichi Sakurai (Kyushu Univ., Japan)

Invited Talk 2

Electronic Money and Key Management from Global and Regional
Points of View 173
Shigeo Tsujii (Chuo Univ., Japan)

Visual Secret Sharing

Limiting the Visible Space Visual Secret Sharing Schemes and
Their Application to Human Identification 185
Kazukuni Kobara, Hideki Imai (Univ. of Tokyo, Japan)

Key Distribution

Towards Characterizing When Information-Theoretic Secret Key
Agreement Is Possible 196
Ueli Maurer, Stefan Wolf (ETH Zürich, Switzerland)

Key Sharing Based on the Wire-Tap Channel Type II Concept
with Noisy Main Channel 210
    V. Korjik, D. Kushnir
    (St. Petersburg Univ. of Telecommunications, Russia)

Boolean Functions

Generalization of Higher Order SAC to Vector Output
Boolean Functions 218
    Kaoru Kurosawa, Takashi Satoh
    (Tokyo Institute of Technology, Japan)

On the Correlation Immune Functions and Their Nonlinearity 232
    Seongtaek Chee, Sangjin Lee, Daiki Lee,
    (Electronics and Telecommunications Research Institute, Korea),
    Soo Hak Sung (PaiChai Univ., Korea)

Electronic Cash 1

How to Date Blind Signatures 244
    Masayuki Abe, Eiichiro Fujisaki (NTT, Japan)

Provably Secure Blind Signature Schemes 252
    David Pointcheval, Jacques Stern (ENS, France)

Cost-Effective Payment Schemes with Privacy Regulation 266
    David M'Raïhi (Gemplus, France)

Electronic Cash 2

Mis-representation of Identities in E-Cash Schemes and
How to Prevent it 276
    Agnes Chan (Northeastern Univ., USA),
    Yair Frankel, Philip MacKenzie (Sandia National Lab., USA),
    Yiannis Tsiounis (Northeastern Univ, USA)

"Indirect Discourse Proofs": Achieving Efficient Fair Off-Line
E-cash 286
    Yair Frankel (Sandia National Lab., USA), Yiannis Tsiounis
    (Northeastern Univ, USA), Moti Yung (IBM, USA)

Invited Talk 3

The Validation of Cryptographic Algorithms 301
    Jacques Stern (ENS, France)

Special Signatures

Convertible Group Signatures 311
*Seung Joo Kim (Sung Kyun Kwan Univ., Korea), Sung Jun Park
(KISA, Korea), Dong Ho Won (Sung Kyun Kwan Univ., Korea)*

How to Utilize the Transformability of Digital Signatures
for Solving the Oracle Problem 322
*Masahiro Mambo (JAIST, Japan), Kouichi Sakurai
(Kyushu Univ., Japan), Eiji Okamoto (JAIST, Japan)*

On the Risk of Disruption in Several Multiparty Signature
Schemes 334
*Markus Michels, Patrick Horster
(Univ. of Technology Chemnitz-Zwickau, Germany)*

Stream Ciphers

Correlation Attacks on Cascades of Clock Controlled Shift
Registers 346
*Willi Geiselmann (Univ. of Karlsruhe, Germany),
Dieter Gollmann (Univ. of London, UK)*

Conditional Correlation Attack on Nonlinear Filter Generators 360
*Sangjin Lee, Seongtaek Chee, Sangjoon Park, Sungmo Park
(Electronics and Telecommunications Research Institute, Korea)*

Hard Problems

The Cryptographic Security of the Syndrome Decoding Problem
for Rank Distance Codes 368
Florent Chabaud, Jacques Stern (ENS, France)

A World Wide Number Field Sieve Factoring Record:
on to 512 Bits 382
*James Cowie (Cooperating Systems Co., USA), Bruce Dod-
son (Lehigh Univ., USA), R. Marije Elkenbracht-Huizing (Centrum voor Wiskunde en Informatica, The Netherlands), Arjen K.
Lenstra (Citibank, USA), Peter L. Montgomery (USA), Jörg Zayer
(Germany)*

Author Index 395

A Message Recovery Signature Scheme Equivalent to DSA over Elliptic Curves

Atsuko Miyaji

Multimedia Development Center
Matsushita Electric Industrial Co., LTD.
E-mail : miyaji@isl.mei.co.jp

Abstract. The ElGamal signature([3]) is based on the difficulty of the discrete logarithm problem(DLP). For the ElGamal signature scheme, many variants like the NIST Digital Signature Algorithm(DSA)([10]) and a new signature with a message recovery feature([12]) are proposed. The message recovery feature has the advantage of small signed message length, which is effective especially in applications like identity-based public key system([4]) and the key exchange protocol([2]). However, its security is not widely accepted because it has been only a few years since the scheme was proposed. Even the relative security between the new message recovery scheme and already-existing schemes is scarcely known. In this paper, we make a strict definition of the conception of equivalent classes([14]) between signature schemes. According to this definition, we discuss the security relation between signature schemes. The reason why the Bleichenbacher-attack([1]) works for ElGamal but not for DSA can be also explained well by the conception. We show that an elliptic curve gives the message recovery signature equivalent to DSA. Furthermore we investigate the new attack over elliptic curves and present its new trapdoor generating algorithm. We also show that the trapdoor does not exist in the particular kind of elliptic curves.

1 Introduction

The ElGamal signature([3]) is based on the difficulty of the discrete logarithm problem(DLP). For the ElGamal signature schemes, many variants like the NIST Digital Signature Algorithm(DSA)([10]) are proposed, any of which does not have a message recovery feature. Recently new variants with the message recovery feature are proposed([12]), which have an advantage of smaller signed message length. Therefore they are effective especially in applications like identity-based public key system([4]) and the key exchange protocol([2]). However, the new signatures have stood only for a few years, so its security is not widely accepted. Therefore we would construct an ElGamal-type message recovery signature whose security is proved to be equivalent to a widely known signature like ElGamal or DSA with some criterion. A conception is proposed to investigate the security relation between signature schemes([14]). The conception is useful, but it need to be discussed more strictly.

In this paper, we make a strict definition of the conception of equivalent classes between signature schemes. According to this definition, we discuss the security relation between signature schemes. The reason why a new attack([1]), called Bleichenbacher-attack, works for ElGamal but not for DSA can be also explained well by the conception. We found that the relation between modulo-p arithmetic and modulo q-arithmetic is important for the equivalences between ElGamal-type signatures, where $\mathbb{F}_p = GF(p)$ is an underlying field and q is the order of a basepoint. We know the ElGamal-type signatures can be also constructed on an elliptic curve([6, 7]), which have a good feature that they can be implemented in smaller size than finite fields([5]). We also know they have another remarkable feature that elliptic curve signatures can choose various modulo-q arithmetics on an underlying field $\mathbb{F}_p$. By using the feature, we show that the message recovery signature on a special elliptic curve is strongly equivalent to DSA on it. Furthermore we investigate how Bleichenbacher-attack is applied on elliptic curve signatures. As for Bleichenbacher-attack, a trapdoor generating algorithm is an important factor: whoever knows a trapdoor for a signature can generate a user's valid signature on any message. However, a trapdoor generating algorithm over elliptic curves has not been known. We present a new trapdoor generating algorithm over elliptic curves. We also show that the elliptic curve, which constructs the message recovery signature equivalent to DSA, does not have the trapdoor.

This paper is organized as follows. Section 2 summarizes ElGamal, DSA and message recovery signature. Section 3 discusses the conception of security equivalence and some equivalent classes based on it. Section 4 investigates the security equivalent classes of signatures defined on elliptic curve, and also shows an elliptic curve gives the message recovery signature equivalent to DSA. Section 5 presents a new trapdoor generating algorithm over elliptic curves.

2   ElGamal, DSA and message recovery signature

This section summarizes ElGamal, DSA, and the message recovery signature called MR in this paper. We assume that in any signature schemes, the trusted authority uses system parameters, that are a large prime p, a large prime factor q of $p - 1$ and a basepoint $g \in \mathbb{F}_p = GF(p) = \{0, \ldots, p-1\}$ whose order is q. These system parameters are known to all users. The signer Alice has a secret key x_A and publishes its corresponding public key $y_A = g^{x_A} \pmod{p}$. The original ElGamal signature([3]) uses a generator of $\mathbb{F}_p^* = \{1, \ldots, p-1\}$ as a basepoint. However for practical purposes([17, 14]), we use the above basepoint in $\mathbb{F}_p$. Here we summarize how each signature scheme is defined for $m \in \mathbb{F}_p^*$, where m is typically the hashed value of a message but in the case of using the message recovery feature m is a message with redundancy.

ElGamal
Alice chooses a random number $k \in \mathbb{F}_q^*$, and computes $r_1 = g^k \pmod{p}$ and $r_1' = r_1 \pmod{q}$. Then she computes $s \in \mathbb{F}_q^*$ from

$$sk = m + r_1' x_A \pmod{q}. \tag{1}$$

Here if $s = 0$, then she chooses the random number k again. Of course such a probability is negligibly small. Then the triplet $(m; (r_1, s))$ constitutes the signed message. The signature verification is done by checking that $(r_1, s) \in \mathbb{F}_p^* \times \mathbb{F}_q^*$ and the next equation,

$$r_1^s = g^m y_A^{r_1'} \pmod{p}. \tag{2}$$

We make the sign $+$ of r_1' in Equation (1) coincide with that of DSA since the following discussion holds regardless of signs.

DSA

Alice chooses a random number $k \in \mathbb{F}_q^*$, and computes $r_1 = g^k \pmod{p}$ and $r_1' = r_1 \pmod{q}$. Then she computes $s \in \mathbb{F}_q^*$ from Equation (1). Here if $r_1' = 0$ or $s = 0$, then she chooses the random number k again. Then the triplet $(m; (r_1', s))$ constitutes the signed message. The signature verification is done by checking $(r_1', s) \in \mathbb{F}_q^* \times \mathbb{F}_q^*$ and the next equation,

$$r_1' = (g^{m/s} y_A^{r_1'/s} \pmod{p}) \pmod{q}. \tag{3}$$

Here we summarize Bleichenbacher-attack([1]) over ElGamal.

Bleichenbacher-attack:

   Assume that a forger knows $\beta \in \mathbb{F}_p^*$ such as $\beta = 0 \pmod{q}$ and $\beta^t = g \pmod{p}$ for a known $t \in \mathbb{F}_q^*$. For $\forall m \in \mathbb{F}_p^*$, he sets $r_1 = \beta$ and $s = tm \pmod{q}$. Then (r_1, s) is a valid signature on m since $g^m y_A^{r_1} r_1^{-s} = g^m g^{-tm/t} = 1$.

   For a given $\mathbb{F}_p$ and g, it would be difficult to find the above β. However, an authority can generate $\mathbb{F}_p$ and g with a trapdoor β by repeating a natural trial([1]): first set $\mathbb{F}_p$, a large prime $q|p-1$, and $p-1 = qn$, next find $\beta = lq$ ($l \in \{1, \cdots, n-1\}$) such that the order of β is q, then set a basepoint $g = \beta^t$ for $1 < t < q-1$. Generally, n is sufficiently large, so this algorithm may work well. Apparently the existence of the trapdoor β cannot be recognized easily. In the case of DSA-signature, such $r_1 = \beta$ is already removed. Therefore DSA is strong against the attack.

MR

MR can be derived from ElGamal by adding the message-mask equation (4) and replacing m (resp. r_1') by 1 (resp. r_2') in Equation (1). To sign a message $m \in \mathbb{F}_p^*$, Alice chooses a random number $k \in \mathbb{F}_q^*$, and computes $r_1 = g^k \pmod{p}$, and

$$r_2 = m^{-1} r_1 \pmod{p}. \tag{4}$$

Then she sets $r_2' = r_2 \pmod{q}$, and computes $s_m \in \mathbb{F}_q^*$ from

$$s_m k \equiv 1 + r_2' x_A \pmod{q}. \tag{5}$$

Here if $r_2 = 0$ or $s_m = 0$, then she chooses the random number k again. Then the signature is given by (r_2, s_m). The message can be recovered by checking $(r_2, s_m) \in \mathbb{F}_p^* \times \mathbb{F}_q^*$ and computing a recovery equation

$$m = g^{1/s_m} y_A^{r_2'/s_m} r_2^{-1} \pmod{p}. \tag{6}$$

Another message-mask equation $r_2 = mr_1^{-1}$ (mod p) and other signature equations are also proposed in [14]. The following discussion also holds for the message-mask equation and the signature equations in almost the same way.

3 Security equivalent classes

A conception of equivalent classes between signature schemes was proposed([14]), which is based on an idea of transformability. However, the relation between transformability of signature schemes and the security equivalence is not known. In this section, we will discuss the relation and will make a strict definition of this conception based on transformability.

Let S1 and S2 be two signature schemes, and I be a common public information necessary for verifying these signatures. Then in order to forge a valid Alice's S1- or S2-signature for a given m without the knowledge of her secret key, we have to solve the next two problems, $\text{Pr\_S1}(I, m)$ or $\text{Pr\_S2}(I, m)$ respectively, where

$\text{Pr\_S1}(I, m)$ is the problem that on input I and m, outputs a valid S1-signature $S1(m)$ of Alice,
$\text{Pr\_S2}(I, m)$ is the problem that on input I and m, outputs a valid S2-signature $S2(m)$ of Alice.

Then the next proposition shows that the equivalence between $\text{Pr\_S1}(I, m)$ and $\text{Pr\_S2}(I, m)$ is related with transformability between two signatures S1 and S2.

Proposition 1. *(1) If any S1-signature can be transformed into an S2-signature by a function f in (expected) time polynomial in the size of public information for verifying S1-signature without knowledge of the secret key, then $\text{Pr\_S2}(I, m)$ is (expected) polynomial-time reducible to $\text{Pr\_S1}(I, m)$.*
(2) If any S1-signature can be transformed into an S2-signature by a function f in (expected) time polynomial in the size of public information for verifying S1-signature, and vice versa, without knowledge of the secret key, then $\text{Pr\_S1}(I, m)$ and $\text{Pr\_S2}(I, m)$ are equivalent with respect to the (expected) polynomial-time Turing reducibility.

Proof. (1) For input I and m, output $\text{Pr\_S2}(I, m) := f(\text{Pr\_S1}(I, m))$. Since f runs in a (expected) polynomial-time, $\text{Pr\_S2}(I, m)$ is (expected) polynomial-time reducible to $\text{Pr\_S1}(I, m)$.
(2) It follows immediately from the discussion of (1).

From Proposition 1, we define "strong equivalence" between signature schemes as follows.

Definition 2. Two signature schemes S1 and S2 are called strongly equivalent if any S1-signature can be transformed into an S2-signature in (expected) time polynomial in the size of public information for verifying S1-signature, and vice versa, without knowledge of the secret key.

Note that the transitive law holds in strong equivalences: for three signature schemes S1, S2 and S3, if S1 and S2, and, S2 and S3 are strongly equivalent respectively, then S1 and S3 are strongly equivalent. In order to show that two signature schemes are strongly equivalent, we must show that any signature for a scheme can be transformed into another and vice versa. In [14], DSA and ElGamal were erroneously said to be strongly equivalent since they did not investigate ElGamal signatures that are not transformed into DSA signatures. The following theorem will show the correct relation between ElGamal and DSA and explain well why Bleichenbacher-attack works for ElGamal but not for DSA.

Theorem 3. *Any DSA signature can be transformed in time polynomial in $|p|$ to an ElGamal signature without knowledge of the secret key, but some ElGamal signatures cannot be transformed. (i.e. DSA and ElGamal are not strongly equivalent.) If we add the condition of $r_1 \neq 0 \pmod q$ both to the signature generation and verification of ElGamal, then ElGamal is strongly equivalent to DSA.*

Proof. Let $(r_1', s) \in \mathbb{F}_q^* \times \mathbb{F}_q^*$ be a DSA signature on $m \in \mathbb{F}_p^*$. First set

$$r_1 = g^{m/s} y_A^{r_1'/s} \pmod p.$$

Then (r_1, s) is an ElGamal signature on m since $(r_1, s) \in \mathbb{F}_p^* \times \mathbb{F}_q^*$.

On the other hand, let $(r_1, s) \in \mathbb{F}_p^* \times \mathbb{F}_q^*$ with $q | r_1$ be an ElGamal signature on $m \in \mathbb{F}_p^*$. Then the signature cannot be transformed explicitly to DSA signature since $r_1' = r_1 \pmod q = 0$. Therefore ElGamal is not strongly equivalent to DSA. Apparently if the condition of $r_1 \neq 0 \pmod q$ is added to both the signature generation and verification of ElGamal, then the ElGamal signature which cannot be transformed to DSA is removed. Therefore it is strongly equivalent to DSA.

For practical purposes, it might be insignificant to remove the case of $r_1 = 0 \pmod q$ from ElGamal-signatures. Importantly, the conception of *strong equivalence* is effective in discussing how attacks exist. Theorem 3 says that ElGamal removed the case of $r_1 = 0 \pmod q$ is strongly equivalent to DSA and strong against Bleichenbacher-attack also.

The relation between MR and DSA is correctly pointed out not to be strongly equivalent([14]). Here we summarize why MR is not strongly equivalent to DSA. We can make r_2 of MR-signature transform into r_1' of DSA-signature. But s_m of MR cannot be transformed into s of DSA by the following reason. The signature equation is computed on the modulo-q arithmetic, while the message-mask equation (4) in MR is computed on the modulo-p arithmetic. Therefore the next relation between the modulo-p arithmetic and the modulo-q arithmetic, that is

$$(m^{-1} r_1 \pmod p) \pmod q \neq m^{-1} r_1 \pmod q, \tag{7}$$

reduces non-equivalences. By the same reason, MR and ElGamal are not strongly equivalent.

To sum up, the relative security of MR to DSA or ElGamal is not known at this moment. Especially it has been only a few years since MR was proposed, so its security is not widely accepted. If a message recovery signature is shown to be strongly equivalent to a widely known signature scheme like DSA, it would be safe to say that its security is guaranteed by DSA.

4 Aspect of elliptic curves in signature schemes

The ElGamal-type signatures can be constructed in other groups, as long as DLP is hard. So ElGamal, DSA, and MR can be also constructed on an elliptic curve, which are called ECElG, ECDSA, and ECMR respectively in this paper.

Elliptic curves, chosen suitably, can be implemented in smaller size than finite fields since the most serious attacks defined on finite fields cannot be applied to elliptic curves([11]). Furthermore there is a remarkable difference in conditions of the order q of a basepoint between elliptic curves and finite fields. In the case of finite fields, q is limited to a divisor of $p - 1$. On the other hand, in the case of elliptic curves $E/\mathbb{F}_p$, q is chosen randomly in the range determined by Hasse's theorem([18]): $p + 1 - 2\sqrt{p} \leq \#E(\mathbb{F}_p) \leq p + 1 + 2\sqrt{p}$. For example, we can choose a basepoint $G \in E(\mathbb{F}_p)$ with the order $q \geq p$, which is impossible in the case of finite fields. In the previous section, we saw that the relation between the modulo-p arithmetic and the modulo-q arithmetic is important for the equivalence between signature schemes. Therefore such characteristics might be suitably used on signature schemes.

We assume that the trusted authority chooses an elliptic curve $E/\mathbb{F}_p$(p is a large prime) and a basepoint $G \in E(\mathbb{F}_p)$ with a large prime order q. The signer Alice has a secret key x_A and publishes the corresponding public key $Y_A = x_A G$. Here we summarize how each signature scheme is defined for a message $m \in \mathbb{F}_p^*$. The following discussion also holds in the case of $E/\mathbb{F}_{2^r}$.

ECElG
Alice chooses a random number $k \in \mathbb{F}_q^*$, and computes

$$R_1 = kG, \tag{8}$$

in E. Then she sets $r_1' = x(R_1) \pmod{q}$ and computes $s \in \mathbb{F}_q^*$ from Equation (1), where $x(R_1)$ denotes the x-coordinate of R_1. Here if either $x(R_1) = 0$ or $s = 0$, then she chooses the random number k again. Then the triplet $(m; (R_1, s))$ constitutes the signed message. The signature verification is done by checking $x(R_1) \in \mathbb{F}_p^*$, $s \in \mathbb{F}_q^*$, and the next equation in E,

$$sR_1 = mG + r_1' Y_A, \tag{9}$$

where $r_1' = x(R_1) \pmod{q}$.

ECDSA
Alice chooses a random number $k \in \mathbb{F}_q^*$, computes Equation (8), and sets

$$r_1' = x(R_1) \pmod{q}. \tag{10}$$

Then she computes $s \in \mathbb{F}_q^*$ from Equation (1). Here if either $r_1' = 0$ or $s = 0$, then she chooses the random number k again. Then the triplet $(m; (r_1', s))$ constitutes the signed message. The signature verification is done by checking $r_1', s \in \mathbb{F}_q^*$ and the next equation,

$$r_1' = x(\frac{m}{s}G + \frac{r_1'}{s}Y_A) \pmod{q}. \tag{11}$$

ECMR

Alice chooses a random number $k \in \mathbb{F}_q^*$, and computes Equation (8). Then she sets

$$r_2 = m^{-1}x(R_1) \pmod{p}, \tag{12}$$

$r_2' = r_2 \pmod{q}$ and computes $s_m \in \mathbb{F}_q^*$ from Equation (5). Here if either $r_2 = 0$ or $s_m = 0$, then she chooses the random number k again. Then the signature is given by (r_2, s_m). The message can be recovered, after checking $r_2 \in \mathbb{F}_p^*$ and $s_m \in \mathbb{F}_q^*$, by computing the recovery equation:

$$m = x(\frac{1}{s_m}G + \frac{r_2'}{s_m}Y_A)r_2^{-1} \pmod{p}. \tag{13}$$

4.1 Equivalences among ECElG, ECDSA and ECMR

We discuss the strong equivalent classes between elliptic curve signature schemes. The equivalent classes are different according to the choice of elliptic curves. In this section, we deal with elliptic curves except for a special elliptic curve $E/\mathbb{F}_p$ with p-elements([8, 9]). For elliptic curves dealt in this section, the order q of G is always different from p from Hasse's theorem. As for the special elliptic curve, we will discuss in the next section.

Theorem 4. *(i) Any ECDSA signature can be transformed in time polynomial in $|p|$ to an ECElG signature without knowledge of the secret key.*
(ii) If $q > p$, then ECElG is strongly equivalent to ECDSA.
If $q < p$, then there exists ECElG that is not strongly equivalent to ECDSA.
(iii) If $p \neq q$, ECMR is not strongly equivalent to either ECDSA or ECElG.

Proof. (i) Let (r_1', s) be an ECDSA signature on $m \in \mathbb{F}_p^*$. First compute

$$R_1 = \frac{m}{s}G + \frac{r_1'}{s}Y_A,$$

in E. Then (R_1, s) is an ECElG signature on m. In fact, (R_1, s) satisfies $x(R_1) \in \mathbb{F}_p^*$ and $s \in \mathbb{F}_q^*$ since $r_1' = x(R_1) \pmod{q}$ satisfies $r_1' \neq 0$.
(ii) Let (R_1, s) be an ECElG signature on $m \in \mathbb{F}_p^*$. First set $r_1' = x(R_1) \pmod{q}$. In the case of $q > p$, $x(R_1)$ satisfies $1 \leq x(R_1) \leq p - 1 < q$. So $r_1' = x(R_1)$. Therefore $(r_1's)$ is an ECDSA signature on m. Thus ECElG is strongly equivalent to ECDSA.
   On the other hand, in the case of $q < p$, there exists an elliptic curve $E/\mathbb{F}_p$ with $E(\mathbb{F}_p) \ni R_1$ such as $x(R_1) \neq 0$ and $q|x(R_1)$. In the same way as Theorem 3,

a signature with R_1 cannot be transformed into an ECDSA signature. Therefore for $E/\mathbb{F}_p$ with $E(\mathbb{F}_p) \ni R_1$ such as $x(R_1) \neq 0$ and $q|x(R_1)$, ECElG is not strongly equivalent to ECDSA.

(iii) From the assumption of E, the order q is different from p. Therefore in the same way as the case of finite fields, the next relation between the modulo-p arithmetic and the modulo-q arithmetic, that is

$$(m^{-1}x(R_1) \pmod{p}) \pmod{q} \neq m^{-1}x(R_1) \pmod{q}, \qquad (14)$$

reduces non-equivalences.

We can construct $E/\mathbb{F}_p$ and G with $q > p$, on which ECElG is strongly equivalent to ECDSA, since constraint of the order q is loose for elliptic curves. Furthermore we will show that ECElG, ECDSA, and ECMR on a special elliptic curve $E/\mathbb{F}_p$ are all strongly equivalent each other in the next section.

4.2   Message recovery signature equivalent to ECDSA

We deal with an elliptic curve $E/\mathbb{F}_p$ which has p-elements over $\mathbb{F}_p$, denoted E_p in this paper. Such an elliptic curve can be constructed as easily as the other elliptic curve([8, 9]). Then the system parameters are: an elliptic curve $E_p/\mathbb{F}_p$, a basepoint $G \in E_p(\mathbb{F}_p)$ whose order is p. For the equivalences among ECElG, ECDSA, and ECMR on $E_p/\mathbb{F}_p$, we have the next result.

Theorem 5. *Let $E_p/\mathbb{F}_p$ be an elliptic curve with $\#E_p(\mathbb{F}_p) = p$. For signature schemes on E_p, ECElG, ECDSA, and ECMR are strongly equivalent each other.*

Proof. We show the next two facts,

(i) ECElG is strongly equivalent to ECDSA,

(ii) ECMR is strongly equivalent to ECDSA.

Then from the transitive law, ECElG, ECDSA, and ECMR are strongly equivalent each other.

(i) Any ECDSA signature can be transformed into an ECElG from Theorem 4. On the other hand, let (R_1, s) be an ECElG signature on a message $m \in \mathbb{F}_p^*$. We set $r_1' = x(R_1)$. Then (r_1', s) is a DSA signature since $r_1' \neq 0$. Thus ECElG is strongly equivalent to ECDSA.

(ii) Let (r_1', s) be an ECDSA signature on $m \in \mathbb{F}_p^*$. We set

$$R_1 = \frac{m}{s}G + \frac{r_1'}{s}Y_A, \quad r_2 = m^{-1}r_1' \pmod{p}, \text{ and } s_m = s/m \pmod{p}.$$

Then $x(R_1) = r_1'$ and $(r_2, s_m) \in \mathbb{F}_p^* \times \mathbb{F}_p^*$ since $(r_1', s) \in \mathbb{F}_p^* \times \mathbb{F}_p^*$, and m is recovered as follows,

$$m = x(\frac{1}{s_m}G + \frac{r_2}{s_m}Y_A)r_2^{-1} \pmod{p}.$$

So (r_2, s_m) is an ECMR signature. Conversely, let (r_2, s_m) be an ECMR signature on $m \in \mathbb{F}_p^*$. We compute

$$R_1 = \frac{1}{s_m}G + \frac{r_2}{s_m}Y_A,$$

and recover $m = x(R_1)r_2^{-1} \pmod{p}$. Then we set $s = ms_m \pmod{p}$ and $r_1' = x(R_1)$. Then $(r_1', s) \in \mathbb{F}_p^* \times \mathbb{F}_p^*$ since $r_2 = m^{-1}x(R_1) \pmod{p} \neq 0$. So (r_1', s) is an ECDSA signature. Thus ECMR is strongly equivalent to ECDSA.

ElGamal-type signature requires two modulo arithmetics. One is modulo-p arithmetic in underlying field $\mathbb{F}_p$. The other is modulo-q arithmetic for the order q of a basepoint. In ElGamal-type signature, the two modulo arithmetics are not independent. In fact a result of modulo-p arithmetic is the input for the next modulo-q arithmetic. In the case of a finite field, the relation between these two modulo arithmetics, as we see in Equation (7), makes the equivalences among signature schemes impossible. On the other hand, in the case of elliptic curves the order q is chosen randomly in the range determined by Hasse's theorem. Therefore there exists the above $E_p/\mathbb{F}_p$ with p elements. For such an elliptic curve, two modulo arithmetics are the same. This is why ECElG, ECDSA, and ECMR are strongly equivalent each other. This is an advantage of elliptic curves over finite fields.

4.3   Summary of known facts on elliptic curves

As a concluding remark of Section 4, we present the next known facts on elliptic curves $E/\mathbb{F}_p$, including this paper's result.

(A) If $E/\mathbb{F}_p$ is supersingular, then the elliptic curve discrete logarithm problem(EDLP) is vulnerable to MOV-reduction([11]): EDLP is reduced to in probabilistic polynomial time to DLP.

(B) If $E/\mathbb{F}_p$ is a prime-order elliptic curve, then some equivalences of cryptosystems based on EDLP are proved: the problems of breaking the Diffie-Hellman's key exchange scheme denoted by DH_E, the ElGamal's public-key cryptosystems denoted by EG_E, and the Shamir's 3-pass key-transmission scheme([19]) denoted by $3PASS_E$ are all equivalent([16]).

(C) If $E/\mathbb{F}_p$ and G with the order q satisfies $q \geq p$, ECElG is strongly equivalent to ECDSA. Especially in the case of $E/\mathbb{F}_p$ and G with the order q satisfies $q = p$, ECElG, ECDSA, and ECMR are strongly equivalent each other(Theorem 4 and 5).

As for (A), an elliptic curve $E/\mathbb{F}_p$ is supersingular if and only if $\#E(\mathbb{F}_p) = p + 1(p \geq 5)$, where $\#E(\mathbb{F}_p) = p + 1$ is a composite number. As for (C), from Hasse's theorem an elliptic curve with $q \geq p$ is limited to a prime-order elliptic curve, that is $\#E(\mathbb{F}_p) = q \geq p$. To sum up, in the case of a prime-order elliptic curve with $\#E(\mathbb{F}_p) \geq p$, it has been known that such an elliptic curve is not supersingular, that some problems of cryptosystems based on EDLP are equivalent, and that ECDSA and ECELG are strongly equivalent. Furthermore, in the case of en elliptic curve with $\#E(\mathbb{F}_p) = p$, it has been also known that ECDSA,

ECElG and ECMR are strongly equivalent each other. Figure 1 presents the relations among (A), (B), and (C).

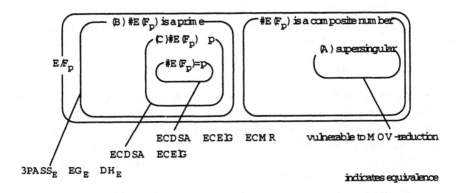

Fig. 1. Known facts on Elliptic curves over $\mathbb{F}_p (p \geq 5)$

In the case of $E/\mathbb{F}_{2^r}$, the order $\#E(\mathbb{F}_{2^r})$ of a supersingular elliptic curve is not necessarily a composite number though the facts (A), (B), and (C) hold. Therefore in the case of a prime-order elliptic curve with $\#E(\mathbb{F}_{2^r}) \geq 2^r$, it has been known that some problems of cryptosystems based on EDLP are equivalent, and that ECDSA and ECElG are strongly equivalent. We often construct elliptic curves by using Weil-conjecture: lifting E over a lower field, for example $E/\mathbb{F}_2$ or $E/\mathbb{F}_{2^2}$, to $E/\mathbb{F}_{2^r}$. However, in such a way we cannot construct a prime-order elliptic curve $E/\mathbb{F}_{2^r}$ since $\#E(\mathbb{F}_{2^r})$ is always divisible by the lifted $\#E(\mathbb{F}_2)$ or $\#E(\mathbb{F}_{2^2})$ respectively.

5   Bleichenbacher-attack over elliptic curves

We saw in Section 3 that Bleichenbacher-attack indicates the security relation between ElGamal and DSA:(i) ElGamal is not strongly equivalent to DSA and vulnerable to Bleichenbacher-attack, (ii) ElGamal removed the case of $r_1 = 0$ (mod q) from the signatures is strongly equivalent to DSA and strong against Bleichenbacher-attack. As for elliptic curves, from Theorem 4 and 5, we saw that if $q \geq p$, then ECElG is always strongly equivalent to ECDSA, and if $q < p$, then there exists ECElG that is not strongly equivalent to ECDSA. Does Bleichenbacher-attack also indicate the security relation well? We also saw in Section 2 that a trapdoor algorithm is one of the important factors for Bleichenbacher-attack. The conception of a trapdoor might be used for a constructive purpose such as Key-Escrow system. Therefore we take interest in a technique of constructing a trapdoor algorithm over elliptic curves.

This section will investigate how Bleichenbacher-attack is applied to ECElG and also present a new trapdoor algorithm by using another feature of elliptic curves.

Bleichenbacher-attack against ECElG is as follows. Assume that a forger knows $B \in E(\mathbb{F}_p)$ such as $x(B) \in \mathbb{F}_p^*$, $x(B) = 0 \pmod q$, and $tB = G$ for a known $t \in \mathbb{F}_q^*$. For $m \in \mathbb{F}_p^*$, he sets $R_1 = B$ and $s = tm \pmod q$. Then (R_1, s) is a valid signature on m since

$$mG + x(R_1)Y_A - sR_1 = mG - tm/tG = \mathcal{O}.$$

In the case of ECDSA, such $R_1 = B$ is removed from the signatures. Therefore ECDSA is strong against the attack. In the case of ECElG, Theorem 4 and 5 say that the above B exists if and only if ECElG is not strongly equivalent to DSA. Therefore Bleichenbacher-attack also indicates the security relation between ECElG and ECDSA: ECElG is vulnerable to Bleichenbacher-attack if and only if ECElG is not strongly equivalent to ECDSA.

In the case of elliptic curves, a natural-trial trapdoor algorithm to generate $E/\mathbb{F}_p$ and G with a trapdoor B would be as follows: first set $E/\mathbb{F}_p$ and a large prime $q|\#E(\mathbb{F}_p)$, next find $B \in E(\mathbb{F}_p)$ such that the order of B is q, $x(B) \in \mathbb{F}_p^*$ and $x(B) = 0 \pmod q$, then set a basepoint $G = tB$ for $1 < t < q - 1$.

The above natural-trial trapdoor algorithm over elliptic curves seems to be more difficult than that over finite fields in Section 2 by the following reason. Usually in elliptic curves, we take p and q whose sizes are almost the same and smaller than finite fields([5]). Therefore for a fixed elliptic curve there are few points with the x-coordinate divisible by q. This is why the natural-trial algorithm seems not to be practical. Here we show a new algorithm generating the trapdoor over elliptic curves by using another feature that there exist many isomorphic elliptic curves for any elliptic curve.

Algorithm generating a trapdoor over elliptic curves
1. Choose an elliptic curve $E/\mathbb{F}_p$ and $R \in E(\mathbb{F}_p)$ with a prime order $q < p$ such that q is a quadratic residue modulo p, and that $x(R) = 1$, that is

$$E : \quad y^2 = x^3 + ax + b \ (a, b \in \mathbb{F}_p), \quad R = (1, r_y).$$

Here we set $u \in \mathbb{F}_p$ such that $u^2 = q \pmod p$.
2. Choose $1 < t < q$ and computes

$$tR = G = (g_x, g_y).$$

Then the order of G is q since t is relatively prime to q.
3. Define an isomorphism φ from E to E_q as follows

$$\varphi : \quad E(\mathbb{F}_p) \ni (x, y) \rightarrow (qx, uqy) \in E_q(\mathbb{F}_p),$$

where $E_q/\mathbb{F}_p : y^2 = x^3 + aq^2x + bq^3$. Then the elliptic curve E_q, and a basepoint $\varphi(G)$ have a trapdoor $\varphi(R)$.

We show the above elliptic curve has a trapdoor. Since φ is isomorphism and

$\varphi(\mathcal{O}) = \mathcal{O}$, φ is homomorphism([18]). So E_q, $\varphi(G) = (qg_x, uqg_y)$, and $\varphi(R) = (q, uqr_y)$ satisfy that:

1. both the order of $\varphi(R)$ and $\varphi(G)$ are q;
2. $t\varphi(R) = \varphi(G)$;
3. the x-coordinate of $\varphi(R)$ is q, that is $x(\varphi(R)) = 0 \pmod{q}$.

This means that $\varphi(R)$ is a trapdoor of the elliptic curve E_q and the basepoint $\varphi(G)$.

Note that the existence of the trapdoor cannot be recognized easily by E_q and $\varphi(G)$. The coefficients of E_q are not necessarily divisible by q since the coefficients aq^2 and bq^3 are represented by modulo p. Furthermore if we choose a suitable t such as $qg_x, uqg_y > p$, then both x- and y-coordinate of $\varphi(G)$ are not necessarily divisible by q since they are represented by modulo p.

We discuss the running time of the above trapdoor generating algorithm. The above Algorithm requires only the next three conditions (adding to an original algorithm generating elliptic curves for ECElG, ECDSA, ECMR, etc): q is a quadratic residue modulo p, $x(R) = 1$, and $q < p$. The first and the third conditions are easy to be satisfied. The second condition also seems not to be so difficult since an algorithm generating elliptic curves with a basepoint of a small coordinate, implemented easily, is reported([9]). Therefore the above trapdoor generating algorithm is expected to be more practical than the natural-trial algorithm.

6 Conclusion

In this paper, we have investigated the next two facts:

(1) we have strictly analyzed strong equivalences between signature schemes. We have explained why Bleichenbacher-attack works for ElGamal but not for DSA, and shown that ElGamal removed the case of $r_1 = 0 \pmod{q}$ from the signatures is strongly equivalent to DSA and strong against Bleichenbacher-attack. We have discussed that the relation between modulo-p arithmetic and modulo q-arithmetic is important for the equivalences between ElGamal-type signatures. We have focussed our attention on elliptic curves which have a good feature, in addition to smaller size, that elliptic curve signatures can choose various modulo-q arithmetics on an underlying field $\mathbb{F}_p$. By using this feature, we have shown that ECElG is strongly equivalent to ECDSA on a prime-order elliptic curve $E/\mathbb{F}_p$ with $\#E(\mathbb{F}_p) = q \geq p$. Furthermore we have shown that ECElG, ECDSA, and ECMR on an elliptic curve $E_p/\mathbb{F}_p$ with $\#E_p(\mathbb{F}_p) = p$ are all strongly equivalent each other. Therefore such an elliptic curve $E_p/\mathbb{F}_p$ can construct a message recovery signature whose security is guaranteed by a widely known signature, ECDSA and ECElG.

(2) we have investigated how Bleichenbacher-attack is applied to ECElG. We have shown that Bleichenbacher-attack reflects the relation between ECElG and ECDSA: Bleichenbacher-attack works only for such ECElG that is not strongly equivalent to ECDSA. We have also presented a new trapdoor generating algorithm against the attack by using another feature of elliptic curves.

Acknowledgements

The author would like to thank Hiroki Shizuya for helpful conversations. The author is grateful to Daniel Bleichenbacher, Markus Michels, and Rainer A. Rueppel for sending me papers. The author wishes to thank Makoto Tatebayashi for helpful advice.

References

1. D. Bleichenbacher, "Generating ElGamal signatures without knowing the secret key" to appear in *Advances in Cryptology-Proceedings of EUROCRYPT'96*.
2. W. Diffie and M. Hellman, "New directions in cryptography" *IEEE Trans. Inform. Theory*, Vol. IT-22 (1976), 644-654.
3. T. ElGamal, "A public key cryptosystem and a signature scheme based on discrete logarithms", *IEEE Trans. Inform. Theory*, Vol. IT-31 (1985), 469-472.
4. C. G. Günther, "An identity-based key-exchange protocol", *Advances in Cryptology-Proceedings of Eurocrypt'89*, Lecture Notes in Computer Science, **434**(1990), Springer-Verlag, 29-37.
5. G. Harper, A. Menezes and S. Vanstone, "Public-key cryptosystems with very small key lengths", *Advances in Cryptology-Proceedings of Eurocrypt'92*, Lecture Notes in Computer Science, **658**(1993), Springer-Verlag, 163-173.
6. N. Koblitz, "Elliptic curve cryptosystems", *Mathematics of Computation*, **48**(1987), 203-209.
7. V. S. Miller, "Use of elliptic curves in cryptography", *Advances in Cryptology-Proceedings of Crypto'85*, Lecture Notes in Computer Science, **218**(1986), Springer-Verlag, 417-426.
8. A. Miyaji, "On ordinary elliptic curves", *Advances in Cryptology-Proceedings of ASIACRYPT'91*, Lecture Notes in Computer Science, **739**(1993), Springer-Verlag, 460-469.
9. A. Miyaji, "Elliptic curve over F_p suitable for cryptosystems", *Advances in Cryptology-Proceedings of AUSCRYPT'92*, Lecture Notes in Computer Science, **718**(1993), Springer-Verlag, 479-491.
10. "Proposed federal information processing standard for digital signature standard (DSS)", *Federal Register*, v. 56, n. 169, 30 Aug 1991, 42980-42982.
11. A. Menezes, T. Okamoto and S. Vanstone, "Reducing elliptic curve logarithms to logarithms in a finite field", *Proceedings of the 22nd Annual ACM Symposium on the Theory of Computing*, 80-89, 1991.
12. K. Nyberg and R. A. Rueppel, "A new signature scheme based on the DSA giving message recovery", *Proceedings of 1st ACM Conference on Computer and Communications Security*, 1993.
13. K. Nyberg and R. A. Rueppel, "Message recovery for signature schemes based on the discrete logarithm problem", *Advances in Cryptology-Proceedings of Eurocrypt'94*, Lecture Notes in Computer Science, **950**(1995), Springer-Verlag, 182-193.
14. K. Nyberg and R. A. Rueppel, "Message recovery for signature schemes based on the discrete logarithm problem", *Designs Codes and Cryptography*, **7**(1996), 61-81.
15. R. Rivest, A. Shamir and L. Adleman, "A method for obtaining digital signatures and public-key cryptosystems", *Communications of the ACM*, vol.21, No.2(1978), 120-126.

16. K. Sakurai and H. Shizuya, "Relationships among the computational powers of breaking Discrete Log cryptosystems", *Advances in Cryptology-Proceedings of Eurocrypt'95*, Lecture Notes in Computer Science, **921**(1995), Springer-Verlag, 341-355.

17. C. P. Schnorr, "Efficient identification and signatures for smart cards", *Advances in cryptology-Proceedings of Crypto'89*, Lecture Notes in Computer Science, **435**(1989), Springer-Verlag, 239-252.

18. J. H. Silverman, *The Arithmetic of Elliptic Curves*, GTM106, Springer-Verlag, New York, 1986.

19. A. Shamir, R. Rivest and L. Adleman, "Mental Poker", MIT/LCS, TM-125, (Feb. 1979).

Cryptographic Protocols Based on
Real-Quadratic A-fields
(Extended Abstract)

Ingrid Biehl[1] and Bernd Meyer[1] and Christoph Thiel[2]

[1] Universität des Saarlandes, Fachbereich 14, Im Stadtwald, Gebäude 36,
66123 Saarbrücken, Germany, email: {ingi,bmeyer}@cs.uni-sb.de
[2] Gesellschaft für Automation und Organisation mbH, Euckenstraße 12, 81369
München, Germany, email: thieloph@cs.uni-sb.de

Abstract. In [7] and [3] the difficulty of the Discrete-Logarithm problem
in the cycle of reduced principal ideals in a real-quadratic number field
was used as basis for the construction of secure cryptographic protcols.
In [14] a Diffie-Hellman key exchange variant based on a real-quadratic
congruence function fields is presented. We generalize and extend these
results by investigating real-quadratic A-fields. We define the Distance
problem, the Discrete-Logarithm problem and the Diffie-Hellman problem in the cycle of reduced principal ideals in real-quadratic A-fields and
discuss their difficulty. We show that with respect to probabilistic polynomial time reductions the Distance problem and the Discrete-Logarithm
problem are equivalent and are at least as difficult as the Diffie-Hellman
problem. Moreover we introduce the problem of computing square roots
of reduced principal ideals in real-quadratic A-fields as another computationally difficult problem. In real-quadratic number fields this again is
at least as difficult as the integer factorization problem. In congruence
function fields the problem of computing square roots is supposed to
be even more difficult than in number fields. We present a secure bit
commitment scheme based on the difficulty of the square root problem
and an oblivious transfer protocol based on the Diffie-Hellman problem.
These protocols are important since they may serve as components for
the construction of more sophisticated cryptographic protocols.

1 Introduction

The *Discrete-Logarithm problem (DL-problem)* in the multiplicative group
$GF(p)^*$ of prime fields $GF(p)$ of characterisic $p > 0$ as well as the *integer factorization problem* are well-studied infeasible problems which are the basis for the
security of a lot of cryptographic primitives as bit commitment and oblivious
transfer and of more sophisticated cryptographic protocols.

Gordon [12] has shown that under some reasonable assumptions the DL-
problem in $GF(p)^*$ can be solved in subexponentiell time. The same expected
running time was formerly proved by Buhler, Lenstra and Pomerance in [8] for
the integer factorization problem. The algorithm which is used in both cases is
called the *number field sieve*. Intensive implementatory work now shows that

these theoretical results lead to impressive results in practice (see [2], [5] and [15]). Since further improvements in that area are conceivable as was pointed out in [4] it is important to investigate other intractable problems which may serve as basis for secure cryptographic protocols. In [7] and [4] the infrastructure of the cycles of reduced ideals in real-quadratic number fields was used to construct a variant of the Diffie-Hellman key exchange protocol respectively to create a signature scheme based on the ElGamal signature scheme. In [14] real-quadratic congruence function fields are used by means of very similar techniques as in [7] to implement another Diffie-Hellman key exchange variant. This means that the infrastructure of the cycle of reduced principal ideals in both the real-quadratic number fields and the real-quadratic congruence function fields is used for the construction of cryptographic systems in [7], [4] and [14].

In this paper we generalize and extend these results of [7], [4] and [14]. The set of real-quadratic number fields and the set of real-quadratic congruence function fields form together the set of the so-called *real-quadratic A-fields* (see [22]). Thus it may not wonder that a lot of techniques which are useful in one of these types of fields can be adapted in the other type too. For that reason we present a uniform treatment of the cryptographic use of both types here.

In Sect. 2 we introduce definitions and facts concerning these fields which are essential in the following. We explain the algorithms for efficient computing with reduced principal ideals in these *real-quadratic A-fields* in Sect. 4. In Sect. 5 we present cryptographic protocols. Generalising [4] we argue that cryptographic protocols which use the difficulty of the Diffie-Hellman problem in $GF(p)^*$ as guarantee for their security can be modified by use of reduced principal ideals in a real-quadratic A-field. Thus we can for example construct an *oblivious transfer protocol* based on the difficulty of the *Diffie-Hellman problem (DH-problem)* in the cycle of reduced principal ideals. To achieve this one can for example modify an oblivious transfer scheme presented in [9]. Moreover we introduce the problem of computing the *Square-Root (SR-problem)* of a reduced principal ideal as a difficult problem in real-quadratic A-fields and explicitly explain a *bit commitment scheme* based on this problem. In Sect. 3 we show that the presented DL-problem is at least as difficult as to compute the *regulator* of the A-field. In the case of real-quadratic number fields one can show that this again is at least as difficult as the integer factorization problem. In real-quadratic congruence function fields it is unknown how difficult the problem of calculating the regulator is. No relationship to some well-studied problem as the integer factorization problem is shown so far. Nevertheless this problem is expected to be infeasible too. We also can give strong evidence that the DH-problem and the SR-problem are intractable in both cases too.

By means of these basic cryptographic protocols more complicated protocols can be realised. We give an example for such a higher protocol. Since the basic protocols based on the reduced principal ideals are at least as secure as the well-known analogues based on the integer DL-problem and on the integer factorization problem, one may have even higher confidence in the security of these more complicated protocols.

2 Real-quadratic A-fields

Andre Weil defines in [22] an *A-field* to be either a finite algebraic extension of $\mathbb{Q}$ or a finitely generated extension of a finite prime field $\mathbb{F}_q$ of degree of transcendency 1 over $\mathbb{F}_q$. Thus if we consider a real-quadratic A-field K it is of the form $K = k(\sqrt{D})$. There are two cases: In the first case it is $k = \mathbb{Q}$ and D is a squarefree positive rational integer which satisfies $D \equiv 0, 1 \bmod 4$. Then K is a *real-quadratic number field.* In the second case we have $k = \mathbb{F}_q(x)$, where q is an odd prime, x is a transcendental element in K, D is a squarefree polynomial of even degree and its leading coefficient is a square in $\mathbb{F}_q^*$. Fields of that type are called *real-quadratic congruence function fields.*

The *ring of integers* $\mathcal{O}$ in K is $\mathbb{Z} + \frac{D+\sqrt{D}}{2}\mathbb{Z}$ if K is a real-quadratic number field and it is $\mathbb{F}_q[x][\sqrt{D}]$ if K is a real-quadratic congruence function field. Elements $\alpha \in K$ can be represented in the form $\frac{x+y\sqrt{D}}{2z}$ with $x, y, z \in \mathbb{Z}$, $z > 0$ and $\gcd(x, y, z) = 1$ if K is a number field. If K is a congruence function field α has the form $u + v\sqrt{D}$ with $u, v \in \mathbb{F}_q(x)$. These representations are called *standard representation.* As pointed out in [6], [3] and [13] for a lot of elements in K this standard representation may be of exponential size in $\deg(D)$ where $\deg(D) = \log(|D|)$ in the number field case. (The definition of deg can be found in the following.) But a *compact representation* was presented in these articles which needs polynomially many bits of storage. Moreover polynomial time algorithms for the manipulation of elements in this representation were presented. In the following we assume all elements in K to be represented in this compact representation.

An *integral ideal* A is an additive subgroup of $\mathcal{O}$ such that $\alpha A \subseteq A$ for all $\alpha \in \mathcal{O}$. Ideals A, B of $\mathcal{O}$ are called *equivalent* if there is $\alpha \in K^*$ with $A = \alpha B$. We say α is a *generator of A relatively to B*. The equivalence classes are called *ideal classes.* A is called *principal ideal* and α is called *generator of A*, if $B = \mathcal{O}$. One can show that for $A = \alpha B$ the set of all generators of A relative to B is $\{\nu\alpha : \nu \text{ is a unit of } \mathcal{O}\}$. Moreover there is a unique unit $\varepsilon > 1$ in $\mathcal{O}$ such that any unit ν in $\mathcal{O}$ can be represented as $\nu = \pm\mu\varepsilon^\ell$ with $\ell \in \mathbb{Z}$, where μ is a unit of the ring k. Thus the generators of A relatively to B can be written as $\alpha' = \pm\mu\varepsilon^\ell\alpha$ with $\ell \in \mathbb{Z}$.

One can show that K is a subfield of $\mathbb{F}_q((1/x))$ if K is a real-quadratic congruence function field. Then one can consider elements of K as Laurent series in the variable $1/x$. (See [14].) For a non-zero element $\alpha = \sum_{i=-\infty}^{m} c_i x^i \in k((1/x))$ with $c_m \neq 0$ we define the *degree of α* as $deg(\alpha) = m$. If K is a real-quadratic number field then we define $deg(\alpha) = \log|\alpha|$. Moreover we set $\deg(0) = -\infty$. The positive rational integer $R = \deg(\varepsilon)$ is called the *regulator* of $\mathcal{O}$. Due to the definition of the degree for all generators α, α' of an ideal A relative to an ideal B we have $\deg(\alpha') = \deg(\alpha) + kR$ for some $k \in \mathbb{Z}$. The residue class $\deg(\alpha) + R\mathbb{Z}$ is called *distance from A to B* and is denoted by $\delta(A, B)$. The *minimal distance between A and B* is the minimal value in $\delta(A, B)$ and is denoted by $\delta^*(A, B)$. Obviously it is $0 \leq \delta^*(A, B) < R$. If $B = \mathcal{O}$ then we briefly write $\delta(A)$ and $\delta^*(A)$. Note that in the number field case $\delta^*(A, B)$ is a nonnegative real number and in the congruence function field case it is a nonnegative rational integer.

For each ideal there is a *standard representation.* (See [3] and [14].) In each ideal class one is interested in the *reduced ideals* which have a special normalized form. Given an ideal in standard representation one can by means of a polynomial time algorithm REDUCE find an equivalent reduced ideal in standard representation. Typically there are several reduced ideals in an ideal class. One can show that the set of reduced ideals in an ideal class is finite. See [3] and [14] for precise definitions of reduced ideals.

In cryptosystems based on real-quadratic A-fields the analogue of the finite field $\mathbb{F}_p$ used in classical cryptosystems is the set of reduced principal ideals $\mathcal{R}$. Shanks [17] discovered for real-quadratic number fields that $\mathcal{R}$ resembles a cyclic group. The same observation holds for real-quadratic congruence function fields too. On a cycle of circumpherence R fix a point for $\mathcal{O}$. Then $B \in \mathcal{R}$ corresponds to a point on that cycle whose *distance* from $\mathcal{O}$ is $\delta^*(B)$. The set $\mathcal{R}$ forms a cyclic graph. In that graph, each reduced principal ideal B has a *left neighbor* left(B) and a *right neighbor* right(B). According to the ordering given by δ^*, left(B) is the reduced principal ideal with maximal distance from $\mathcal{O}$ which is less than $\delta^*(B)$ and right(B) respectively is the reduced principal ideal with minimal distance from $\mathcal{O}$ which is greater that $\delta^*(B)$. Both left and right neighbor can be computed in time polyomial in $\deg(D)$. The distance between neighbors is at most $\deg(D)/2$. In the congruence function field case it is a rational integer (see [13]). In real-quadratic number fields the distance generally is not a rational integer and can be very small. But the distance between a reduced principal ideal A and right(right(A)) is at least 1.

Multiplication for ideals can be defined and there is a polynomial time algorithm for multiplication.

Finally, given an ideal A we define A^{-1} to be its inverse. This *fractional ideal* can be computed in polynomial time too.

3 Difficult Problems in the Cycle of Reduced Principal Ideals

We have to explain exponentiation in $\mathcal{R}$. Informally the mth power $(m \in \mathbb{R}_{>0})$ of a reduced principal ideal A with distance $d = \delta^*(A)$ is the reduced principal ideal B which is nearest to $d * m$.

In the number field case one has to deal with high precision approximations of the distance values. This causes for example in the Diffie-Hellman variant by [7] one additional round of communication that is not necessary in the original Diffie-Hellman protocol. Thus in [4] instead of dealing with ideals, pairs consisting of an ideal and a small correction term were introduced. This approach can be used in all real-quadratic A-fields: We associate with $k \in \mathbb{R}$ a pair (A, a) consisting of the nearest reduced principal ideal A to k and a high precision approximation a of the distance from k to A. That *nearest ideal* is defined by the property that there is $\alpha \in \mathcal{O}$ with $(1/\alpha)\mathcal{O} = A$ such that $|\deg(\alpha) - k| < |\deg(\alpha') - k|$ for all $\alpha' \in \mathcal{O}$. The distance from k to A is $a = \deg(\alpha) - k$. In case that A is not uniquely determined by those conditions we make A unique by requiring a to be positive. In the congruence function field case all distances are rational integers. Thus we need no high precision approximation for the distance between A and k. We call (A, a) the *ideal-correction representation of k (ic-representation)*. By means of techniques used to compute the compact representation of elements in K as explained in [3] one can construct polynomial time algorithms for the computation of the ic-representation of some given k. (See algorithm NEAREST in [3].)

Given a pair (A, a) one can verify in polynomial time, whether it is the ic-representation for some $k \in \mathbb{R}_{>0}$: One has to verify whether A is a reduced principal ideal and whether A is the nearest ideal to k. One can verify whether a is minimal by computing the neighbors of A and check whether the absolute value of the sum of a and the difference between neighbor ideal and A is less than a or not. On the other side if k is not known then it is a difficult problem to compute k as we will show.

Now, we can define the *Distance-problem* which has the following form: Given an ic-representation $\tilde{A} = (A, a)$ find $k \in \mathbb{R}_{\geq 0}$ such that $\tilde{A}$ is an ic-representation for k. Then k is called *distance value for $\tilde{A}$*. If k is a distance value for $\tilde{A}$ then each nonnegative element of $k + R\mathbb{Z}$ is a distance value for $\tilde{A}$ too.

Theorem 1. *There is a probabilistic polynomial time reduction from calculating the regulator R to solving the Distance-problem.*

Proof. Sketch: Randomly take some $k \in \mathbb{R}_{>0}$, compute the ic-representation $\tilde{A} = (A, a)$ for k. Then solve the Distance-problem for $\tilde{A}$. With high probability one gets $k' \neq k$ and $k' - k$ is a multiple of R. In the same way calculate several multiples of R. Take the gcd of them. With high probability one gets R. □

Let m be a positive real. Let A be a reduced principal ideal and $a \in \mathbb{R}$ such that A is the nearest ideal to $\delta(A) + a$. Let $\delta \in \delta(A)$. The mth power of (A, a) is a pair (B, d) where B is the reduced principal ideal which is nearest to $x = m(\delta + a)$ and d is the distance from x to B. This power is independent of the choice of δ and is denoted by $\exp((A, a), m)$. It is easy to see that if $A \in \mathcal{R}$, $a \in \mathbb{R}$, $t, m \in \mathbb{R}_{>0}$ then we have $\exp(\exp((A, a), t), m) = \exp(\exp((A, a), m), t)$. This statement is important for the construction of cryptographic protocols as the Diffie-Hellman protocol.

The *Discrete-Logarithm problem (DL-problem)* in the set of reduced principal ideals has the following form: Given (A, a) and (B, b). Let $m \in \mathbb{R}_{>0}$ such that $\exp((A, a), m) = (B, b)$. Compute the *discrete logarithm* $t = \lfloor m \rfloor$ of (B, b) with respect to (A, a). Thus $\exp((A, a), t)$ is that ic-representation which is an integer power of (A, a) and is the nearest one to (B, b) *less* than (B, b) according to the ordering given by the distance definition. Note that the discrete logarithm is not uniquely defined.

Theorem 2. *There is a probabilistic polynomial time reduction from the Distance-problem to solving the DL-problem.*

Proof. Sketch: Compute the right neighbor ideal A of $\mathcal{O}$ and a distance value d of $(A, 0)$. In order to solve the distance problem for (B, b) we compute the discrete logarithm $t \in \mathbb{N}$ of (B, b) with respect to $(A, 0)$. Then the ic-representation $(C, c) = \exp((A, 0), t)$ has the distance value $d * t$ and the distance between C and B is less than $c + d + b$. Since d is small by the choice of A (in fact it is less that $\deg(D)$) and c and b are small by the definition of ic-representation, one can compute the distance between C and B by following the sequence of neighbors starting in C until one finds B.

In parallel one computes the distance. (Of course c and b have to be put into the calculations too.) The sequence one has to consider is short by the same reasons and because the distance betweeen an ideal and the right neighbor of the right neighbor of that ideal is at least 1. □

Let A be a reduced principal ideal and $a \in \mathbb{R}$. Let $\delta \in \delta(A)$. The *square of* (A, a) is the second power of (A, a). We write $(A, a)^2$ for this. We call the problem of inverting the square function the *Square-Root problem (SR-problem)*. Note that the square root of an ic-representation is not necessarily unique. In the general case given an ic-representation there are two square roots with distance about $R/2$.

Theorem 3. *If K is a real-quadratic number field then there is a probabilistic polynomial time reduction from factoring rational integers to solving the SR-problem.*

Proof. Sketch: One randomly chooses $k \in \mathbb{R}_{>0}$ and computes an ic-representation (A, a) for k. Then one computes $(A, a)^2$ and uses the algorithm for computing the square root. With probability $1/2$ one gets a root (B, b) which is different from (A, a). The ideal $C = \text{REDUCE}(A * \text{INVERT}(B))$ is near to a so-called ambiguous ideal (i.e. $C^2 = \mathcal{O}$) which we can find by searching in a set of polynomially many neighbors of C. According to [18] one can factorize. □

In the case of real-quadratic congruence function fields no such reduction is known. But since for special real-quadratic congruence function fields we know that the SR-problem is equivalent to compute square roots in the group of points of an elliptic curve (see [19]) we assume that the SR-problem is intractable, and maybe more difficult than in number fields.

At last we introduce the *Diffie-Hellman problem (DH-problem)* in the cycle of reduced principal ideals of a real-quadratic A-field: Given some ic-representations $(A, a), (B, b), (C, c)$, such that $\exp((A, a), m) = (B, b)$ and $\exp((A, a), n) = (C, c)$ for some unknown $m, n \in \mathbb{N}$ compute $\exp((A, a), m * n)$.

It is not known how difficult the Diffie-Hellman problem is. Nevertheless it is supposed to be infeasible. The only known attack is the straightforward one, i.e. to compute the appropriate discrete logarithms.

Finally we have the following results:

Theorem 4. *There is a polynomial time reduction from solving the DL-problem to solving the Distance-problem.*

There is a polynomial time reduction from solving the SR-problem to solving the Distance-problem.

There is a polynomial time reduction from solving the DH-problem to solving the Distance-problem.

Proof. Sketch: Given two ic-representations (A, a) and (B, b). In order to compute m with $\exp((A, a), m) = (B, b)$ we compute a distance value k_1 for (A, a) and a distance value k_2 for (B, b) and solve the equation $k_1 * m = k_2$ with $m \in \mathbb{R}_{>0}$. If $m \notin \mathbb{N}$ there exists no solution to the DL-problem otherwise $\lfloor m \rfloor$ is a solution.

In order to solve the SR-problem for some ic-representation (A, a) one has to compute a distance value k for it and to compute an ic-representation for $k/2$.

In order to solve the DH-problem one has to compute the appropriate discrete logarithms and combine them. □

We summarize: The Distance problem and the DL-problem are equivalent with respect to probabilistic polynomial time reductions. The DH-problem and the SR-problem may be not as difficult as the Distance problem but there is strong evidence that they are infeasible too.

In real-quadratic number fields the Distance problem and the SR-problem can be shown to be at least as difficult as the integer factorization problem. As stated in [14] the DL-problem (and then the Distance problem too) in real-quadratic congruence function fields may even be worse than in real-quadratic number fields, since for the latter algorithms with subexponential complexity are known while the best algorithms known for congruence function fields take exponential running time. In [19] evidence is given that the SR-problem is difficult even in the case of some "simple" real-quadratic congruence function fields. Thus one may assume the Distance problem and the SR-problem in real-quadratic congruence function fields to be infeasible too.

Finally we have to explain that our definitions of the Distance problem, the DL- and the SR-problem may be different from others given in the literature. Often one meets definitions for these problems in which the minimal distance, the minimal discrete logarithm or the ic-representation which is root and has the minimal distance value, is the solution one has to find. But in a lot of cryptographic applications the system can be broken if the attacker is able to find one but not necessarily the minimal distance value.

4 Arithmetic in the Cycle of Reduced Principal Ideals

A detailed description of the arithmetic in real-quadratic number fields can be found in [3]. In [14] the arithmetic in real-quadratic congruence function fields is precisely described. These techniques easily can be extended in an appropriate manner to the manipulation of pairs (A, a), where A is a reduced principal ideal and $a \in \mathbb{R}$. Thus we do not describe the technical details of the following algorithms but only explain their specification. Note that we have to deal with approximations $\tilde{a} \in \mathbb{Q}$ whenever some real number a has to be used. All the mentioned algorithms take polynomial running time.

Given an ideal B the algorithm REDUCE returns a reduced ideal C equivalent to B and a generator γ of B relative to C. Given ic-representations (A, a) und (B, b) the procedure MULT computes an ic-representation (C, c) for $\delta^*(A) + a + \delta^*(B) + b$. We write $(A, a) * (B, b)$ in short. The algorithm EXP computes $\exp((A, a), x)$ given $A \in \mathcal{R}$, $a \in \mathbb{Q}$, $x \in \mathbb{N}$. EXP determined its result by means of binary exponentiation. (In [14] EXP is called POWER.) The procedure SQUARE can be implemented by starting EXP with third parameter 2. But one can achieve more efficient implementations. See the procedure DOUBLE in [3] and [14]. Given an ic-representation (A, a) the procedure INVERT computes an ic-representation (C, c) such that $\delta(C) + c = -(\delta(A) + a) \bmod R$.

5 Cryptographic Protocols

In this section we present a secure bit commitment scheme based on the difficulty of the SR-problem and a secure oblivious transfer protocol based on the DH-problem in the cycle of reduced principal ideals in a real-quadratic A-field.

5.1 The Bit Commitment Scheme

We start with the bit commitment scheme. Alice and Bob agree in some pre-protocol on the A-field they want to use.

The commitment phase
Alice wants to commit herself secretly to a bit $b \in \{0, 1\}$ to Bob.

1. Bob randomly chooses $k \in \mathbb{R}_{>0}$, computes its ic-representation $\tilde{B} = (B, c)$ and sends $\tilde{B}$ to Alice.
2. Alice randomly chooses $k' \in \mathbb{R}_{>0}$, computes its ic-representation $\tilde{A} = (A, a)$, sets $\tilde{C} = \tilde{A}^2$, if $b = 0$, $\tilde{C} = \tilde{A}^2 * \tilde{B}$, if $b = 1$ and sends $\tilde{C}$ to Bob.

Opening the commitment
Alice has to show b to Bob and prove that she commited to b in the commitment phase.

1. Alice sends k' and b to Bob.
2. Bob accepts this if and only if the ic-representation of $2 * k' + b * k$ is $\tilde{C}$. (To avoid problems which may arise by the use of approximations both Alice and Bob use the same precision, the same algorithms and the same sequence of operations to compute $\tilde{C}$.) Otherwise he rejects.

Obviously Bob will accept if Alice correctly follows the protocol. We have to show that Bob can not find out which bit Alice commited to until she opens her commitment and that Alice can not change her mind and open $\tilde{C}$ as commitment to $1 \oplus b$.

Since $\tilde{C}$ is a random ic-representation Bob can not find out how it was constructed.

Without loss of generality suppose Alice commited to $b = 1$ and then wants to convince Bob she commited to 0. Then she has to compute d such that $2 * d = 2 * k' + k \bmod R$ in order to send $d, 0$ to Bob. But she does not know k. To be more precise: If Alice is able to find d she is able to compute the square root of $\tilde{B}$ since $2 * |d - k'|$ is a distance value of $\tilde{B}$. Thus Alice is not able to cheat if the SR-problem is infeasible.

The above protocol can be modified if Alice wants to commit to a bit to a large group of people: A trusted center has to publish $\tilde{B}$. Then Alice performs the same operations as in the above protocol and all persons in the group can verify the opening of her commitment in the same way we explained it above for Bob.

5.2 An Oblivious Transfer Protocol

We use ideas presented in [1]. We describe how an interactive oblivious transfer of a pair of strings (s_0, s_1) is accomplished.

Again Alice and Bob agree on an A-field and some ic-representation $\tilde{G}$.

1. Bob chooses randomly an ic-representation $\tilde{B}$ and sends this to Alice.
2. Analoguously Alice chooses randomly an ic-representation $\tilde{A}$ and sends this to Bob.
3. Both compute $\tilde{C} = \tilde{A} * \tilde{B}$.
4. Bob randomly chooses a bit $b \in \{0, 1\}$ and a rational integer x and computes $\tilde{D} = \exp(\tilde{G}, x)$. If $b = 0$ then he sets $\tilde{D}_0 = \tilde{D}$ and $\tilde{D}_1 = \tilde{C} * \text{INVERT}(\tilde{D})$. If $b = 1$ then he sets $\tilde{D}_1 = \tilde{D}$ and $\tilde{D}_0 = \tilde{C} * \text{INVERT}(\tilde{D})$. Then he sends $(\tilde{D}_0, \tilde{D}_1)$ to Alice.
5. Alice tests whether the product of both ic-representations is $\tilde{C}$. If not she rejects. Otherwise Alice randomly chooses two rational integers y_0, y_1, computes $A_0 = \exp(\tilde{G}, y_0)$, $A_1 = \exp(\tilde{G}, y_1)$ and sends (A_0, A_1) to Bob.
6. In case of a real-quadratic number field Bob and Alice have to exchange some control information as in the protocol described in [7] to cope with problems caused by the used approximations. Otherwise this step is not necessary. In all cases then Alice can compute $\gamma_0 = \exp(\tilde{D}_0, y_0)$ and $\gamma_1 = \exp(\tilde{D}_1, y_1)$ and Bob only knows γ_b, since he does not know the discrete logarithm of $\tilde{D}_{1-b}$. (To be more precise: he can not solve the DH-problem for $\tilde{D}_{1-b}$ and $\tilde{A}_{1-b}$.)
7. Alice sends $r_0 = s_0 \oplus \gamma_0$ and $r_1 = s_1 \oplus \gamma_1$ to Bob.
8. Bob computes $s_b = \gamma_b \oplus r_b$.

For details of this protocol one has to use techniques of [7] and [14].

Bob is not able to compute both secrets s_0 and s_1 since he is not able to compute γ_{1-b} if the Diffie-Hellman problem is infeasible.

Even more efficient and secure variants of the above protocol can be constructed by adapting the protocols in [1].

5.3 Higher Protocols

Since one can easily construct some self-reducible problems from the Distance-problem, the DL-problem and the SR-problem, one can easily implement some *zero-knowledge protocols* based on these problems.

Moreover, the SR-problem can be used for the construction of a variant of the square root identification scheme by Goldwasser, Micali and Rackoff (see [11]).

Bit commitment and oblivious transfer protocols form the basis of a lot of *higher* protocols. By these and some zero-knowledge protocols one can construct more complex protocols as for example variants of the protocols presented in [9].

Acknowledgements
The authors would like to thank Andreas Stein for very helpful discussions.

References

1. Mihir Bellare, Silvio Micali, *Non-Interactive Oblivious Transfer and Applications*, Proceedings of CRYPTO'89, 1989.
2. D.J. Bernstein, A.K. Lenstra, *A general number field sieve implementation*, In: A.K. Lenstra, H.W. Lenstra Jr.(Eds.) The Development of the Number Field Sieve (LNM 1554), Springer Verlag, 1993, pp. 103–126.
3. Ingrid Biehl, Johannes Buchmann, *Algorithms for Quadratic Orders*, Proceedings of Symposia in Applied Mathematics, vol. 48, American Mathematical Society, 1994, pp. 425–451.
4. Ingrid Biehl, Johannes Buchmann, Christoph Thiel, *Cryptographic Protocols Based on Discrete Logarithms in Real-quadratic Orders*, Proceedings of CRYPTO'94, Springer, 1995.
5. Johannes Buchmann, Jürgen Loho, Jörg Zayer, *An Implementation of the General Number Field Sieve*, Proceedings of CRYPTO'93 (LNCS 773), Springer Verlag, pp. 159–165, 1993.
6. Johannes Buchmann, Christoph Thiel, Hugh C. Williams, *Short Representation of Quadratic Integers*, Proceedings of CANT, Springer, 1992.
7. Johannes Buchmann, Hugh C. Williams, *A Key Exchange System Based on Real-quadratic Fields*, Proceedings of CRYPTO'89, Springer, 1989, pp. 335–343.
8. J.P. Buhler, H.W. Lenstra, C. Pomerance, *Factoring integers with the number field sieve*, LNCS 1554, pp. 50-94, 1993, Springer-Verlag.
9. Claude Crepeau, Jeroen van de Graaf, Alain Tapp, *Committed Oblivious Transfer and Private Multi-Party Computation*, Proceedings of CRYPTO'95, pp. 110-123, 1995.
10. W. Diffie, M. Hellman, *New Directions in Cryptography*, IEEE Trans. Inform. Theory 22, pp. 472–492, 1976.
11. S. Goldwasser, S. Micali, C. Rackoff, *The knowledge complexity of interactive proof systems*, SIAM Journal on Computing, 18:186–208, 1989.
12. D. Gordon, *Discrete Logarithms in GF(p) Using the Number Field Sieve*, SIAM Journal on Discrete Mathematics, 1993, pp. 124–138.

13. Renate Scheidler, *Compact Representation in Real Quadratic Congruence Function Fields*, to appear in the Proceedings of ANTS II.

14. Renate Scheidler, Andreas Stein, Hugh C. Williams, *Key Exchange in Real Quadratic Congruence Function Fields*, Designs, Codes and Cryptography, vol.7, no.1/2, pp. 153-174, 1996.

15. Oliver Schirokauer, Damian Weber, Thomas Denny, *Discrete Logarithms and the Effectiveness of the Index Calculus Method*, to appear in the Proceedings of ANTS II, 1996.

16. Bruce Schneier, *Applied Cryptography, Second Edition*, John Wiley and Sons, Inc., 1996.

17. D. Shanks, *The Infrastructure of a Real Quadratic Field and its Applications*, Proceedings of the 1972 Number Theory Conference, Boulder, pp. 217–224, 1972.

18. R.J. Schoof, *Quadratic fields and factorization*, In: H.W. Lenstra, R. Tijdemans (Eds.), Computational methods in number theory, Part II, Math. Centrum Tracts 155, pp. 235–286, 1982.

19. Andreas Stein, *Equivalences Between Elliptic Curves and Real Quadratic Congruence Function Fields*, to appear in the Proceedings of PRAGOCRYPT'96.

20. Douglas R. Stinson, *Cryptography, Theory and Practice*, CRC Press, 1995.

21. Christoph Thiel, *On the Complexity of Some Problems in Algorithmic Algebraic Number Theory*, PhD Thesis, Universität des Saarlandes, 1995.

22. Andre Weil, *Basic Number Theory*, Springer, 1973.

Minding your p's and q's

Ross Anderson[1], Serge Vaudenay[2]

[1] Computer Laboratory, Pembroke Street, Cambridge, CB2 3QG, England
[2] Ecole Normal Supérieure — DMI***, 45 rue d'Ulm, 75230 Paris, France

Abstract. Over the last year or two, a large number of attacks have been found by the authors and others on protocols based on the discrete logarithm problem, such as ElGamal signature and Diffie Hellman key exchange. These attacks depend on causing variables to assume values whose discrete logarithms can be calculated, whether by forcing a protocol exchange into a smooth subgroup or by choosing degenerate values directly. We survey these attacks and discuss how to build systems that are robust against them. In the process we elucidate a number of the design decisions behind the US Digital Signature Standard.

1 Introduction

The large majority of actual attacks on conventional cryptosystems are due to blunders in design, implementation and operation, which are typically discovered by chance and exploited in an opportunistic way [2, 3]. We have not yet accumulated comparable experience of the failure modes of public key cryptosystems, but the early indications are that nothing much has changed: an implementation of the Fiat-Shamir identification scheme [14] is reported to have failed because the application always used the same random challenge [22, 23].

Any system can be compromised by a gross blunder of this kind; but public key systems present a large number of subtle failure modes [5]. Some are variants on the middleperson attack or exploit the semantics of public key systems in general, while others depend on the mathematical features of particular systems.

In this paper, we investigate protocols based on the discrete logarithm problem such as ElGamal signature, Diffie-Hellman key exchange and the Chor-Rivest system. We describe a family of simple attacks, some of them new, which have been found by the authors and others over the last year or two. These attacks enable us to explain the design of the US digital signature standard [24].

2 ElGamal and related protocols

The original ElGamal signature uses a large prime p as its modulus and a generator g of the group Z_p^* as its base. These values are common, and may be issued by authority; each user has a secret key x and a corresponding public key

---

*** *Laboratoire d'Informatique*, research group affiliated with the CNRS.

$y = g^x \bmod p$. To sign a message M, the signer first picks a random k which is coprime to $p - 1$ and issues the signature (r, s) where

$$r = g^k \bmod p \tag{1}$$

$$s = \frac{M - xr}{k} \bmod p - 1 \tag{2}$$

Writing the second equation as $sk + xr \equiv M \bmod p - 1$, we see that a valid signature is checked by verifying

$$r^s y^r \equiv g^M \pmod{p}$$

We shall show that this system is quite insecure, unless considerable care is taken in the choice of parameters.

2.1   The effect of the choice of p

Suppose that $p - 1 = qw$, where w is smooth (i.e., all its prime factors are small). This was the case with the primes p and q originally proposed with the US digital signature standard (DSS):

$$\frac{p - 1}{q} = 2^{70} 3^{46} 5^{30} 7^{25} 11^{20}$$

(see [1]). Then the group Z_p^* in which we are operating has a subgroup of order q, in which discrete log is hard, and a subgroup of order w in which it is easy.

The effect is that keys can be recovered modulo w. An attacker can solve the equation $(g^q)^z \equiv y^q \pmod{p}$ in the group of order w, giving x modulo w, and then derive every message key k modulo w from equation (2). This was originally pointed out by van Oorschot and Wiener [32]; and also by Anderson, Vaudenay, Preneel and Nyberg in the context of subliminal channels, where the effect is to create one or more broadband covert channels [6]. However, there are serious practical security implications as well.

In order to generate the message keys k for successive signatures, a random number generator is required, and the use of ElGamal signatures with the above prime p has the effect of disclosing 352 out of every 512 bits of the generator's output. The typical generator has resonances and other features that can be exploited (see for example [20]), with the result that further bits of message keys k might be inferred by an adversary. Once a single key k modulo q is compromised, the signing key x can easily be calculated.

The amount of information leaked will depend on the choice of p, and in particular on the factors of $p - 1$. The above choice of p may be the worst possible, but even the best possible — say $p = 2qr + 1$ where both q and r are prime — will still leak one bit of message key per signature. So the choice of p is not enough to completely prevent the leakage of key material. A better approach is to use a base element g that generates a prime order subgroup of Z_p^*; then we are doing our cryptographic operations in a single group, rather than in two groups at a time. This is exactly the approach taken by the designers of DSS, which has

$$r = (g^k \bmod p) \bmod q$$
$$s = \frac{h(M) + xr}{k} \bmod q$$

This blocks the above attack, and also (contrary to the popular misconception) reduces the bandwidth available for use as a subliminal channel.

2.2 Attacks based on interaction between k and g

After the DSS was introduced, there was some controversy about whether a trapdoor could be hidden in the primes p and q by, for example, choosing them to be numbers which could be respresented compactly by a polynomial of degree four or five, so that the authority could calculate discrete logarithms using the number field sieve [11].

But no-one seems to have stopped to think about the choice of base g.

A simple forgery attack on ElGamal consists of chosing $k = (p-1)/2$. Then $r = p - 1$, so the secret key x is hidden by r in the product xr modulo $p - 1$. Unfortunately, this cannot work unless $M = (p-1)/2$ or $M = p-1$ since k is not invertible modulo $p-1$. But the authority can use this idea to provide valid parameters with a hidden trapdoor.

If the authority chooses the base g such that he knows the discrete logarithm k of $r = (p-1)/2$ (for instance by chosing $g = r^{1/k} \bmod p$ for random invertible k until it is a generator), then he is able to choose this k which enables to compute s (he needs to know $x \bmod 2$ but this can easily be obtained by checking whether y is a quadratic residue or not.)

More generally, the authority can isolate a smooth factor w of $p-1$ and choose g such that he knows the discrete logarithm k of some $j(p-1)/w$ between 0 and $p - 1$. The ability to compute s from k is then equivalent to the knowledge of $x \bmod w$ which, as we have seen, is easy when w is smooth.

A similar forgery attack was recently found by Bleichenbacher. Suppose that $p - 1 = qw$ as before with w smooth, and that the authority can choose a g which divides w. Then a valid signature can be forged on any message M as

$$r = (p-1)/g \pmod{p}$$
$$s = (M - ry_q)(p-3)/2 \pmod{p-1}$$

where y_q is the smooth part of the public key y (i.e. a solution of $(g^q)^z \equiv y^q \bmod p$). This attack will also work in the more general case that the authority knows a small multiple cq of q with $0 < c < w$; see [7, 8] for details.

Bleichenbacher's attack is particularly pernicious as it means that if an implementer chooses $g = 2$ for performance reasons, as we understand has happened, then signatures can be forged independently of the choice of p.

To thwart attacks of this kind, we can check that $(p-1)/\gcd(r, p-1)$ is not too smooth, or, once again, work in a subgroup of prime order. Another approach is to replace M by $h(r, M)$ as in the Schnorr signature [27, 28] (see [26]).

However, even using the DSS does not completely give complete protection, as we shall see below.

2.3 The design of the digital signature standard

During World War 2, a slogan prominently displayed in a number of the cryptanalysts' huts at Bletchley Park was 'If it's not checked, it's wrong' [15]. This prudent approach to cryptology is just as valid in the world of discrete logarithm based systems as it was in the days of rotor machines.

Consider what happens if the verifier's software does not systematically check whether $0 \leq r < p$ (this is not explicitly demanded in ElGamal's original paper [13]). A valid signature can easily be forged for any message as follows. Choose values for both s and r_{p-1} and compute

$$r_p = g^{\frac{M}{s}} y^{-\frac{r_{p-1}}{s}} \pmod{p}$$

Then it is straightforward to find a value r which fits the values of both r_{p-1} mod $p-1$ and r_p mod p by using the Chinese Remainder Theorem. Of course, the typical length of the r we obtain will be twice that of p. This attack has independently been discovered by Bleichenbacher [7, 8].

We conclude that DSS is simply ElGamal with many of the bugs fixed, and with a rather simple optimization (the reduction of r modulo q) that reduces the length of the signature and the amount of arithmetic needed to verify it.

However, DSS is not entirely bug-free. Firstly, the reduction mod q introduces a new bug: the authority can choose q to be the difference between $h(M)$ and $h(M')$ for two known messages M and M'. These two messages will then have the same signature [31]. Note that this kind of bug is avoided if M is hashed together with r, as in the Schnorr signature [27, 28].

Secondly, the authority might issue a base g with small order instead of order q. Honest signers would be unable to produce a valid signature, but it will be easy for anyone to forge one (by picking random signatures until one is valid with this g). So if the application may use a large number of different moduli and bases some of which come from non-trusted parties (as is the case with the UK government's new Euroclipper proposal [9]), then the cautious implementer will check that order of any base he uses for the first time. Other attacks based on the fact that g is not certified are also possible (see [31]).

The above two weaknesses probably do not matter in most digital signature applications, but it seems prudent practice to require a proof of origin of the p and q (for example, that they are generated using known seed values via a one-way hash function) and to check the order of g.

However, careless designs that permit degenerate values such as in these two examples can be deadly for Diffie Hellman key agreement protocols.

3 Diffie Hellman-like protocols

In the original Diffie Hellman Protocol, everything works modulo a fixed prime p. Two participants Alice and Bob first agree on this prime and a generator g of Z_p^*; then Alice picks a random a and sends $g^a \bmod p$ to Bob, who picks a random b and sends $g^b \bmod p$ to Alice. They then compute a shared private key as $g^{ab} \bmod p$.

3.1 The middleperson attack

In the traditional middleperson attack, Charlie sits between Alice and Bob. He sets up one key with Alice (pretending to be Bob), and another key with Bob (pretending to be Alice). He then acts as a message relay between them, and can intercept all their traffic. Attacks of this kind are a serious pitfall for designers of public key protocols, and can manifest themselves in various ways.

The traditional countermeasure is a key confirmation protocol in which Alice and Bob authenticate either the key they think they have just agreed, or the components they think they exchanged in order to agree it. We shall now show that these two countermeasures are not in fact equivalent; there are attacks in which Charlie forces Alice and Bob to share a key that he can calculate.

If a careless implementation does not check the received values, then Charlie can simply intercept both g^a and g^b and replace them with 0 or 1. Alice and Bob end up sharing a 'secret' that Charlie knows too.

Assuming as before that $p - 1 = qw$ with w smooth, a more sophisticated attack is for Charlie to replace the numbers g^a with g^{aq} and g^b with g^{bq}. In this way, the exchange is forced into the smooth subgroup of Z_p^*; he can then compute the discrete logarithm of $g^{aq} \bmod p$ to the base g^q and apply it to $g^{bq} \bmod p$, getting the shared key g^{abq}. This attack was discovered by van Oorschot and Wiener [32]; for more discussion on key agreement protocols, see Just and Vaudenay [18].

3.2 Attacks on elliptic curve systems

Other variants on Diffie Hellman use elliptic curves. A typical system uses curves of order $4p$, where p is prime [30]; in this case, an attacker can use the above techniques to force the key exchange into a subgroup of order 4, in which discrete logarithms may be extracted by inspection.

But regardless of whether we are operating in a rational or elliptic curve group, so long as its order is composite we have to be careful how we fortify the Diffie Hellman protocol against middleperson attacks (in which Charlie simultaneously masquerades as Bob to Alice and as Alice to Bob). We shall now discuss a few of the protocols that are vulnerable in this way.

3.3 Other Diffie-Hellman-like protocols

There are many variants of the Diffie-Hellman Protocol (see [12, 17, 21] for instance), which fail to specify that prime order bases should be used. We leave finding attacks to the reader as a exercise.

We also understand that in some secure telephone products, the two participants authenticate the key by reading out a hash of the agreed key. This is not sufficient against attacks of the kind described above, as the participants would end up authenticating $g^{abq} \bmod p$. Even if the base g were the generator of a prime order subgroup, then the telephone equipment should check that the received protocol variables were elements of order q, in case degenerate values had been inserted instead.

When trying to prevent such attacks, designers would be well advised to follow the principle that robust protocols are explicit ones [5]. As well as choosing a prime order base and checking received variables, we should also authenticate not just g^{ab} but also g^a, g^b, and all relevant environmental information such as Alice's and Bob's names and the date.

Mea culpa: one of us disregarded this principle in [4]. There, an authentication mechanism (of which the details are irrelevant here) was devised that enabled Alice and Bob to check whether they shared the same session key. This gives no protection against the above attacks.

4 Chor-Rivest-like Cryptosystems

At the beginning of public key cryptography, knapsack ciphers seemed very attractive, but almost all of them have been broken by latice reduction techniques (the Chor-Rivest system [10] remained unbroken until recently [29]).

We have noticed two recent attempts to make cryptosystems based on multiplicative knapsack problems.

4.1 The Lenstra Cryptosystem

The Lenstra Cryptosystem [19] is inspired by Chor-Rivest. It also works in a finite field $GF(q^h)$, where q is a prime power. Chor-Rivest has the surprising property of being efficient when computing discrete logarithms in $GF(q^h)$ is easy [10]. Lenstra's variant is a little less efficient but does not require this property. It is moreover provably at least as secure as Chor-Rivest.

Basically, given public parameters q, h and s (as well as the representation of the fields), the Lenstra Cryptosystem uses public keys $v_1, \ldots, v_s$ in $GF(q^h)$. A message is first encoded (by using a public encoding rule) into a sequence $m_1, \ldots, m_s$ of positive integers such that $m_1 + \ldots + m_s = h$. Encrypting the message consists in computing $v_1^{m_1} \ldots v_s^{m_s}$ in $GF(q^h)$. A complicated forgery algorithm (which involves secret keys for the v_i) lets us decrypt.

Here we notice that the order $q^h - 1$ of the multiplicative group may well be smooth (for instance, for each factor n of h, $q^n - 1$ is a factor of $q^h - 1$). Thus it may be possible to compute discrete logarithms in $GF(q^h)^*$. But computing $w_i = \log v_i$ reduces the cipher to a knapsack equation $m_1 w_1 + \ldots + m_s w_s$ (actually, a Chor-Rivest problem). Therefore (as mentioned by Lenstra) the ability to compute discrete logarithms reduces the security to exactly that of Chor-Rivest.

4.2 The Naccache-Stern Cryptosystem

A more complex example is given by a new public-key cryptosystem recently proposed by Naccache and Stern and based on multiplicative knapsacks [23, 25]. In this protocol, the public parameters are a set of prime numbers $p_1, \ldots, p_n$ and a prime p such that $p > p_1 \times \ldots \times p_n$. The secret key is an exponent s, and the public key is a set of integers $v_1, \ldots, v_n$ such that $v_i{}^s \equiv p_i \pmod{p}$. To encrypt an n-bit message $m_1 \ldots m_n$, we compute $c = v_1{}^{m_1} \times \ldots \times v_n{}^{m_n} \bmod p$. To decrypt the message, we raise c to the power s and solve $c^s = p_1{}^{m_1} \times \ldots \times p_n{}^{m_n} \bmod p$.

The authors already mentioned an information leakage in the cryptosystem. Namely, with the use of the Legendre symbol, the encryption leaks the bit

$$\left(\frac{c}{p}\right) = \left(\frac{v_1}{p}\right)^{m_1} \times \ldots \times \left(\frac{v_n}{p}\right)^{m_n} \tag{3}$$

This corresponds to the factor two in $p - 1$. More generally, for any smooth factor w of $p - 1$, one can compute the mod w part of the discrete logarithms of all the v_i and c: if g is a primitive w-th root of 1 modulo p, let $v_i^{\frac{p-1}{w}} \equiv g^{a_i}$ $\pmod{p}$ and $c^{\frac{p-1}{w}} \equiv g^b \pmod{p}$. By computing all a_is and b, we obtain the equation

$$b \equiv m_1 a_1 + \ldots + m_n a_n \pmod{w} \tag{4}$$

This is a standard knapsack problem which can be solved by usual latice reduction tricks [16] provided that w is large enough (typically, larger than 2^n).

In [25], the authors propose using quadratic residues p_is to fix the problem of information leakage and to use only a strong prime p $(p = 2q + 1)$ to avoid this kind of attack.

5 Conclusions

When designing systems based on the discrete logarithm problem, we must be careful to avoid degenerate cases. If we use a group with smooth subgroups, then there may be many such cases. In particular, naïve Diffie Hellman — whether modulo a rational prime or over an elliptic curve — can be attacked by forcing it into a subgroup in which the discrete log problem is easy. Some of the conventional ways of preventing middleperson attacks prevent such forcing attacks, but many do not.

Even without smooth subgroups, there are many things that can go wrong if we do not carefully specify the limit values and check them punctiliously at runtime. The system parameters, the secret keys and the message keys can often be chosen to be weak, and these weaknesses can interact in ways that are not at all obvious.

In any case, with all systems based on discrete logarithm problems, it seems prudent practice to use a group of prime order, unless there are good reasons not to; such reasons can include using keys for multiple different purposes. However, such advanced applications are dangerous, and designers should take extra care.

Our results have also explained the design of the US digital signature standard. It is really just ElGamal with most of the bugs fixed.

Finally, what 'good reasons' might there be to use a group of composite order? Well, different sets of people may know a secret key in different subgroups. We have already shown in [6] that this can be used to create broadband narrowcast subliminal channels in signature schemes — by means of which messages may be sent undetectably to precisely those parties who know a signing key modulo a specific factor of $p-1$. Composite groups might also be used in applications such as key escrow protocols, where we might wish the same key to be used for escrowed encryption and unescrowed signature. However, this will be the subject of a different paper.

References

1. RJ Anderson, "Practical RSA Trapdoor", in *Electronics Letters* v 29 no 11 (27/5/93) p 995
2. RJ Anderson, "Why Cryptosystems Fail", in *Communications of the ACM* v 37 no 11 (Nov 94) pp 32–40
3. RJ Anderson, SJ Bezuidenhoudt, "On the Reliability of Electronic Payment Systems", in *IEEE Transactions on Software Engineering* v 22 no 5 (May 1996) pp 294–301
4. RJ Anderson, TMA Lomas, "On fortifying key negotiation schemes with poorly chosen passwords", in *Electronics letters* v **30** no 12 (23rd July 1994) pp 1040–1041
5. RJ Anderson, RM Needham, "Robustness principles for public key protocols" in *Advances in Cryptology — CRYPTO '95*, Springer LNCS v 963 pp 236–247
6. R Anderson, S Vaudenay, B Preneel, K Nyberg, "The Newton Channel", in *Preproceedings of the First International Workshop on Information Hiding* (30/5-1/6/96, Cambridge, UK) pp 143–148; proceedings to be published in Springer LNCS series
7. D. Bleichenbacher, "Generating ElGamal Signatures Without Knowing the Secret Key", in *Advances in Cryptology — Eurocrypt 96*, Springer LNCS v 1070 pp 10–18
8. D. Bleichenbacher, *'Efficiency and Security of Cryptosystems based on Number Theory'* Dissertation ETH No. 11404, Swiss Federal Institute of Technology, Zürich (1996)
9. "Securing Electronic Mail within HMG — part 1: Infrastructure and Protocol" 21 March 1996, CESG document T/3113TL/2776/11
10. B Chor, RL Rivest, "A knapsack-type public key cryptosystem based on arithmetic in finite fields", in *IEEE Transactions on Information Theory, v 34 (1988) pp 901–909*

11. Y Desmedt, P Landrock, A Lenstra, K McCurley, A Odlyzko, R Rueppel, M Smid, "The Eurocrypt 92 Controversial Issue — Trapdoor Primes and Moduli", in *Advances in Cryptology — Eurocrypt 92*, Springer LNCS v 658 pp 194–199

12. W Diffie, PC van Oorschot, MJ Wiener, "Authentication and authenticated key exchanges", in *Designs, Codes and Cryptography* v 2 (1992) pp 107–125

13. T ElGamal, "A Public Key Cryptosystem and a Signature Scheme based on Discrete Logarithms", *IEEE Transactions on Information Theory* v 31 no 4 (1985) pp 469–472

14. A Fiat, A Shamir, "How to prove yourself: practical solutions to identification and signature problems", in *Advances in Cryptology — CRYPTO 86*, Springer LNCS v 263 pp 186–194

15. FH Hinsley, A Stripp, *'Codebreakers'*, OUP 1993

16. A Joux, J Stern, "Lattice Reduction: a Toolbox for the Cryptanalyst", to appear in *Journal of Cryptology*

17. N Jefferies, C Mitchell, M Walker, "A Proposed Architecture for Trusted Third Party Services", in *Cryptography: Policy and Algorithms*, Springer LNCS v 1029 pp 98–104

18. M Just, S Vaudenay. "Authenticated multi-party key agreement", *in these proceedings*

19. HW Lenstra, Jr., "On the Chor-Rivest Knapsack Cryptosystem", in *Journal of Cryptology* v 3 (1991) pp 149–155

20. L Letham, D Hoff and A Folmsbee, "A 128K EPROM Using Encryption of Pseudorandom Numbers to Enable Read Access", in *IEEE Journal of Solid State Circuits* v SC-21 (Oct 1986) pp 881 - 888

21. T Matsumoto, Y Takashima, H Imai. "On Seeking Smart Public-Key-Distribution Systems". in *Transactions of the IECE of Japan* (1986) pp 99–106

22. D Naccache, "Unless modified Fiat-Shamir is insecure", in *Proceedings of the 3rd Symposium on State and Progress of Research in Cryptography: SPRC 93*, Rome, Italy 15–16 Feb 1993 pp 172–180, *published by Fondazione Ugo Bordoni*

23. D Naccache, *'Signature Numérique et Preuves à Divulgation Nulle, Cryptanalyse, Défense et Outils Algorithmiques'*, Thèse de Doctorat de l'Ecole Nationale Supérieure des Télécommunications ENST 95 E 019 (1995)

24. National Institute of Standards and Technology, *'Digital Signature Standard'*, FIPS Publication 186 (19 May 1994)

25. D Naccache, J Stern, "A new public-key encryption scheme", *presented at Luminy, September 1995*

26. D Pointcheval, J Stern. "Security proofs for signature schemes", in *Advances in Cryptology — Eurocrypt 96*, Springer LNCS v 1070 pp 387–398

27. CP Schnorr, "Efficient identification and signature for smart cards", in *Advances in Cryptology — CRYPTO 89*, Springer LNCS v 435 pp 239–252

28. CP Schnorr, "Efficient signature generation by smart cards", in *Journal of Cryptology* v 4 (1991) pp 161–174

29. CP Schnorr, HH Hörner, "Attacking the Chor-Rivest Cryptosystem by improved lattice reduction", in *Advances in Cryptology — Eurocrypt 95*, Springer LNCS v 921 pp 1–12

30. R Schroeppel, H Orman, S O'Malley, O Spatschek, "Fast Key Exchange with Elliptic Curve Systems", in *Advances in Cryptology — Crypto 95*, Springer LNCS v 963 pp 43–56

31. S Vaudenay, "Hidden collisions on DSS", in *Advances in Cryptology — CRYPTO '96*, Springer LNCS v 1109 pp 83–88

32. P. van Oorschot, M. J. Wiener, "On Diffie-Hellman key agreement with short exponents", in *Advances in Cryptology — Eurocrypt 96*, Springer LNCS v 1070 pp 332–343

Authenticated Multi-Party Key Agreement

Mike Just[1] and Serge Vaudenay[2]

[1] School of Computer Science, Carleton University, Ottawa, ON, Canada, K1S 5B6,
e-mail: just@scs.carleton.ca
[2] Ecole Normale Supérieure–DMI, 45, rue d'Ulm, 75230 Paris Cedex 05, France,
e-mail: Serge.Vaudenay@ens.fr

Abstract. We examine key agreement protocols providing (i) key authentication (ii) key confirmation and (iii) forward secrecy. Attacks are presented against previous two-party key agreement schemes and we subsequently present a protocol providing the properties listed above.
A generalization of the Burmester-Desmedt (BD) model (Eurocrypt '94) for multi-party key agreement is given, allowing a transformation of any two-party key agreement protocol into a multi-party protocol. A multi-party scheme (based on the general model and a specific 2-party scheme) is presented that reduces the number of rounds required for key computation compared to the specific BD scheme. It is also shown how the specific BD scheme fails to provide key authentication.
Key Words: key agreement, authentication, confirmation, forward secrecy.

1 Introduction

Private-key cryptography is widely used in security networks. Though it assumes that parties who share the same secret key are both secure, and do not reveal their key, it is still more efficient than public-key cryptography for most applications. To allow several parties willing to communicate using private-key cryptography while avoiding any long-term common private keys, the parties need to first agree on the same *session key* following a *key establishment protocol.*

Key establishment protocols can be divided into two categories. A *key transfer* protocol is a key establishment protocol in which one party securely transfers a key to the other parties participating in the protocol. A *key agreement protocol* is a key establishment protocol in which the parties contribute information that jointly establishes a shared secret key. (See [16] for an overview.)

In the early origins of public-key cryptography, a two-party key agreement protocol due to Diffie and Hellman (DH) was proposed [6]. There have been many attempts to provide authentic key agreement based on DH [7, 11, 12, 13, 20] In a separate direction, several attempts have been made to extend DH to a multi-party protocol [10, 17, 18], the most efficient being the result of Burmester and Desmedt [5].

This paper deals with key agreement protocols based on DH that use public-key techniques. We do not require the aid of an on-line or trusted third party[3].

---

[3] We require a trusted center for creating public-key certificates for each user. However,

Users interact via an exchange of messages to obtain a common key.

Section 2 presents several definitions and building blocks that are used in the construction of our key agreement protocols. Section 3 demonstrates attacks to previous two-party protocols and presents the new key agreement protocol. Section 4 discusses the multi-party model, the specific Burmester/Desmedt protocol, as well as our own, and examines attacks against each.

1.1 Definitions and Notations

Let m be a prime and $\alpha \in \mathbb{Z}_m^*$ an element with order q, where q is a prime such that $q|m-1$ and computing discrete logarithms in the group generated by α is difficult (see recommended parameters given in [19]). All operations in this paper will take place in $\mathbb{Z}_m$, unless otherwise noted. We will be working in a network of n users, t of which participate in the key agreement protocol. Each user U has a long-term public key $p_U = \alpha^{s_U}$ for a random secret-key $s_U \in_R^4 \mathbb{Z}_q^*$. We use I_U to refer to information identifying user U, i.e. name. We assume that each user has a copy of every other public key a priori, or equivalently that certification is used so that each public-key is identity-based. If this is not the case then I_U will also contain a certified copy of U's public key. We denote by h_K a Message Authentication Code (MAC), i.e. [15]. Furthermore, we assume that this MAC (of a hash function) behaves as a random oracle in the sense that its output reveals no meaningful information about its input. See [14] for details.

1.2 Summary of Results

We begin by examining a Diffie-Hellman based 2-pass key agreement protocol that has appeared in several variations in the literature. Two minor (repairable) attacks against this scheme are presented as well as two more serious attacks given that the attacker has some extra information available to him. It is also shown how the property of (perfect) *forward secrecy* as defined in [7] (as well as Section 2) has been mistakenly attributed to this protocol.

Subsequently we present a Diffie-Hellman based 3-pass protocol (Protocol IIA) which provides for (i) key authentication, (ii) key confirmation and (iii) forward secrecy (see Section 2 for definitions). The protocol is based on a general framework that is evident in several other key agreement schemes found in the literature. We examine the security of our protocol against some passive and active attacks.

We extend our two-party results by generalizing the specific multi-party protocol of Burmester and Desmedt [5] to obtain a multi-party key agreement model. Using our specific two-party protocol and this model, we are able to obtain a multi-party protocol (Protocol MIIA) which reduces the amount of communication required between participants (as compared to the scheme of [5]). It is

---

this can be completed off-line, and the center is not required to maintain the secrecy of any information for any users.

[4] We denote an element x chosen randomly and independently from a set S by $x \in_R S$.

also shown how the scheme of Burmester and Desmedt [5] fails to provide key authentication. Attacks against Protocol MIIA are also examined.

2 Fundamentals

In this paper, we build from 1-pass key transfer (KT) protocols to multiple pass key agreement (KA) protocols. Where a KT protocol involves contributions from only 1 user, KA protocols involve mutual contributions to the final key. When a KA protocol involves more than 2 users, we refer to it as a multi-party key agreement (MPKA) protocol. If referring to properties that apply to both two-party and multi-party protocols, we simply refer to KA protocols.

We say that a key agreement protocol is *successful* if each of the parties accepts the identity of the other party, and terminate with the same key. The protocol provides *key authentication* if the ability for computing the key implies knowledge of the secret corresponding to the identity of one expected participant. Key authentication implies key confidentiality. For if only intended parties can compute the key, then unintended parties cannot compute the key. *Key confirmation* (direct authentication in [7]) is provided if the protocol aborts unless participants demonstrate knowledge of the same shared session key. Note that in this context an encrypted exchange subsequent to the KA protocol "demonstrates knowledge" of the key. The distinction is that for key confirmation, knowledge of the key is demonstrated prior to the end of the KA protocol (and is usually achieved by encrypting or hashing a known quantity). A key agreement protocol provides *forward secrecy* (perfect forward secrecy in [7] and [9]) if the loss of any long-term secret keying material does not allow the compromise of keys from previously wire-tapped sessions. Since *perfect* usually makes reference to information theory, we avoid it here. We note the compromise of long-term secret keys does not necessarily mean that they were obtained via an inversion of the long-term public key. Since users must store their secret keys for use in key computation, the secret keys may also be obtained through lack of suitable physical security measures.

Our goal throughout is for a dynamic set of users to securely compute a *session key* K for the purpose of participating in a secure communication session. Long-term public keys for each user serve to authenticate while short-term per-session tokens serve to add freshness to the KA protocol and hence to the computation of K.

2.1 Key Transfer Protocols

The traditional DH problem (upon which our protocols are based) can be stated as follows. Given α as defined in Section 1.1 and inputs $y = \alpha^x$ and $y' = \alpha^{x'}$, compute (we omit reference to m for simplicity) $DH(\alpha; y, y') = \alpha^{xx'}$. Likewise, for long-term public parameters $p_A = \alpha^{s_A}$ and $p_B = \alpha^{s_B}$, we have $DH(\alpha; y, p_A) =$

A	B
$x \in_R \mathbb{Z}_q, y = \alpha^x$ $\quad\xrightarrow{\quad y, I = I_A \quad}\quad$ $K = y^{s_B} \left(= \alpha^{x s_B}\right)$	
$K = p_B{}^x$	
$x \in_R \mathbb{Z}_q, y = p_B{}^x$ $\quad\xrightarrow{\quad y, I = I_A \quad}\quad$ $K = y^{s_B{}^{-1}} \left(= \alpha^x\right)$	
$K = \alpha^x$	

Fig. 1. Protocol IA(top) and IB(bottom)

$\alpha^{s_A x}$ and $\mathrm{DH}(\alpha; p_A, p_B) = \alpha^{s_A s_B}$.[5] The DH problem is the basis for the two 1-pass KA (i.e. Key Transfer) protocols given in Figure 1. Protocol IA can be considered to be a DH protocol with one fixed parameter. Protocol IB is a simple variation on the first.

The key computation for Protocol IA is $\mathrm{DH}(\alpha; y, p_B)$ and $\mathrm{DH}(p_B; p_B{}^x, \alpha)$ for Protocol IB. Since each computation has one fixed parameter, these protocols are no harder than a DH computation (with two random parameters). Due to page limitations, protocols based on Protocol IB appear in Appendix A.

2.2 Framework for Key Authentication

The framework for our KA protocols follows similar work from [2, 7, 11, 12, 13, 20]. It consists of a 3-pass authentic key agreement protocol as shown in Figure 2. The values y and y' are random tokens generated by each user (that will be used in the key computation). The offsets "1:" and "2:" are included to prevent potential rebound attacks possible given the similarity of the inputs to the hash by both A and B. I and I' refer to the identities of the respective participants. The terms $<y>$ and $<y'>$ refer to pseudo-corroboration of the fact that the originating user actually constructed the term enclosed in the $<>$s. (By pseudo-corroboration we mean that it is not a true zero-knowledge proof of possession, nor is it as costly as one.) Particularly for our case, given that user A has constructed $y = \alpha^x$, A should also be able to produce $<y> = (y'p')^x$ for random y'. The difficulty of this task is considered in Theorem 2. (We note that such precautions have also been noted by Burmester [4].) As mentioned in Section 1.1, we assume that the output of h_K behaves as a random oracle in that it reveals no meaningful information about its input. The output of this hash serves to provide for key confirmation as well as the pseudo-corroboration described above.

This framework is by no means entirely new and is clearly evident in the works cited above. Whereas encryption and signatures are used in the respective

---

[5] This is an abuse of notation. Since p_A and p_B are fixed for each protocol run, their inclusion in the calculation should be distinguished from y and y' which are randomly chosen for each run. The result being that an ability to compute $\mathrm{DH}(\alpha; y, y')$ implies an ability to compute $\mathrm{DH}(\alpha; y, p_B)$ yet the reverse implication is still open.

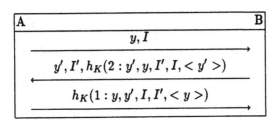

Fig. 2. Generic Authenticated Key Agreement

schemes of Krawczyk [11] and Diffie et al. [7] for authentication, we incorporate the public keys of each user directly into the key computation, as was done in [13, 12, 20]. Also, the use of a MAC for providing key confirmation replaces the use of an encryption function (which is unnecessary since there is no decryption taking place – and relaxes the possibility of export restrictions).

Though not as formalized as the work of [2] (which assumes only the existence of a pseudorandom function), the reliance on the DH problem by each of the remaining works cited above (including the current paper) allows for the provision of forward secrecy (a property not achieved in [2]). Such a property may be attractive for the robustness of the security in most commercial applications where customers does not always protect their secret long-term key sufficiently.

3   Authenticated Key Agreement

In this section, we extend Protocol IA to provide for authenticated key agreement. (Similarly, see Appendix A for extensions of Protocol IB.) The desirable properties being (i) key authentication, (ii) key confirmation and (iii) forward secrecy (see Section 2). (The provision of these properties are examined more closely in Section 3.2.) Throughout the section, $p = p_A$ is the public key extracted from I, while $p' = p_B$ is extracted from I' (though the same notation follows if the public keys are *a priori* available).

3.1   Protocols Based on IA

Consider the two party key agreement protocol between users A and B from [13] given in Figure 3. (Similar protocols for which there was no key confirmation are given in [12, 20] and were attacked by Burmester [4].) Two minor attacks against Protocol A0 in the absence of a proper implementation are

- E IMPERSONATES B TO A. In place of B, E sends $\{y' = 0, I' = I_B, z' = h_K(y', I, I')\}$ to A. A believes that B is the only party that is able to compute K. However, since $K = 0$, the key is easily obtained (by E or anyone else), hence a lack of key authentication.

$$\begin{array}{ll}
\textbf{A} & \textbf{B} \\
\end{array}$$

$$
\begin{array}{lcr}
x\in_R\mathbb{Z}_q, y=\alpha^x & \xrightarrow{\quad y, I=I_A \quad} & x'\in_R\mathbb{Z}_q, y'=\alpha^{x'} \\
 & & K=p^{x'}y'^{s_B} \\
 & & z'=h_K(y',I,I') \\
K=(y')^{s_A}(p')^x & \xleftarrow{\quad y', I'=I_B, z' \quad} & \\
z'\overset{?}{=}h_K(y',I,I') & &
\end{array}
$$

Fig. 3. Protocol A0: $K=\alpha^{s_A x'+s_B x}$

- E IMPERSONATES A TO A. This more subtle attack succeeds so long as A does not verify that he is communicating with "himself". Suppose A is an automated system providing access to an encrypted session with a computer database. Access is granted to those users who successfully complete the protocol. After an initiation of the protocol by A, E selects $\tilde{x}\in_R\mathbb{Z}_q$ and simulates the protocol as if $x'=\tilde{x}-x$. i.e. E computes $y'=\alpha^{\tilde{x}}/y$, as well as $K=p_A^{\tilde{x}}$ and sends $\{y', I'=I_A, z'=h_K(y',I,I')\}$ to A.

Obvious solutions to both attacks are to implement the protocol so that trivial messages such as y (or y') $=0$ or 1 are disallowed and that $I\neq I'$. The latter condition may be too restrictive. Possibly for maintenance purposes, some applications may want the option of having $I=I'$. However, the following more serious attacks motivate a solution that also appears to thwart the second attack described above.

- E IMPERSONATES B TO A. (GIVEN THAT E POSSESSES s_A.) It is obvious that s_A allows E to impersonate A to any user. However, suppose that A is an Automatic Teller Machine and the engineer E who initially performs the setup of A, is able to obtain s_A. After A initiates the protocol, E chooses $y'=\alpha^{\tilde{x}}/p_B$. Given s_A and $\tilde{x}$, E can easily compute K.
- E IMPERSONATES B TO A (OR A TO B). (GIVEN THAT E POSSESSES $\alpha^{s_A s_B}$.) Since s_A and s_B are long-term secrets this attack allows unlimited impersonations given only $\mathrm{DH}(\alpha;p_A,p_B)$. To impersonate A, E computes and sends $y=\alpha^{\tilde{x}}/p_A$ to B. Given $\tilde{x}$ and $\alpha^{s_A s_B}$, E can easily compute K. Similarly, E can impersonate B to A.

In each of these last two attacks, E does not know the discrete logarithm of its token, i.e. y or y', motivating the inclusion of a demonstration of knowledge of the construction of the token as discussed in Section 2 and included in Protocol IIA below. Also of note for Protocol A0 is the fact that it *does not provide* for forward secrecy (as claimed in [13]). Note that recovery of *both* long-term secret keys s_A and s_B allows the computation of $K=y^{s_B}(y')^{s_A}$ for all previous sessions involving A and B. In Figure 4 we present Protocol IIA which appears to prevent the aforementioned attacks and uses the framework from Figure 2.

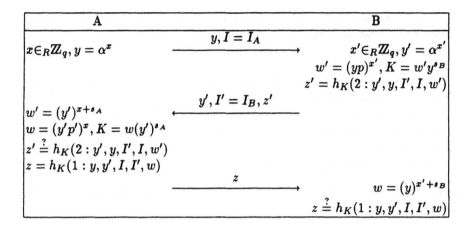

Fig. 4. Protocol IIA: $K = \alpha^{xx' + x's_A + xs_B}$

3.2 Passive and Active Attacks

In this section, we analyze the resistance of Protocol IIA to passive and active attacks by demonstrating equivalence to variations of the DH problem. (Similar arguements can be made for Protocol IIB from Appendix A.) Hence, throughout this section, we assume that DH computations (as described in Section 2) are infeasible without the proper, corresponding secret information. Also, we assume that the hash h_K behaves like a random oracle, in the sense that it's output cannot be distinguished from random output.

A *passive attack* whose aim is key recovery for a given session involves eavesdropping on messages passed between participants for that session. The attack is successful if the session key can be recovered with a probabilistic polynomial time algorithm given as input, the eavesdropped message passes as well as any other publicly available parameters.

Theorem 1. *Protocol IIA is secure against passive attack and provides forward secrecy unless the Diffie-Hellman problem can be solved.*

We note that given a DH oracle, one can easily solve for the session key in protocol IIA using only a passive attack. This is done by computing

$$K = \text{DH}(\alpha; y, y')\text{DH}(\alpha; y, p_B)\text{DH}(\alpha; y', p_A).$$

Proof. (sketch) Consider Protocol IIA. We need to show that recovery of all long-term secret keys does not allow recovery of previous session keys. Assume the opposite is true. Then given s_A and s_B corresponding to the respective long-term public keys p_A and p_B allows recovery of the key $K = \alpha^{xx' + xs_B + x's_A}$. From this, we are able to compute $\alpha^{xx'}$ for random y and y'; a contradiction to the assumption that DH computations are computationally infeasible.

Since computing the final key with the extra knowledge of s_A and s_B is hard, it must be at least as hard without it. Protocol IIA is therefore secure against passive attacks. □

An *impersonation attack* involves an attacker who is given access to all publicly available information and attempts to successfully complete a protocol with B (resp. A) by impersonating A (resp. B). Recall that a key agreement protocol is successful if each of the parties accept the identity of the other, and terminate with the same key. Note that since Protocol IIA provides key confirmation, this assumes knowledge of the session key K.

Theorem 2. *Protocol IIA is secure against impersonation attack given that Protocol IA is secure.*

Proof. (sketch) If z' is accepted by A, it has necessarily been produced by someone who is able to compute both the pair $(y', (yp)^{x'})$ and the key K by using the (supposed) random y. From K and $(yp)^{x'}$, is it easy to compute y'^{s_B}. Since y is fresh and s_B is supposed to be secret, z' has been forged by B unless IA is insecure.

Similarly, if z is accepted by B, it has been produced by someone able to compute y'^{s_A} from a fresh y'. □

Notice that for Theorem 2, there is an implicit assumption that Protocol IA does not reveal any partial information, i.e. each run of Protocol IA produces a key of the form $DH(\alpha; y, p_B)$ for some random y and fixed p_B. Also note that this does not preclude more imaginative attacks. It simply states that one participant cannot successfully complete Protocol IIA by impersonating another, given only the publicly available parameters.

4 Authenticated Multi-Party Key Agreement

We propose here a generic construction of a multi-party key agreement protocol MP from a two-party key agreement protocol P.[6] We assume that all users $u_1, u_2, \ldots, u_t$ are arranged on a ring and we will consider indices of u_i to be taken between 1 to t modulo t.

1. Each pair (u_i, u_{i+1}) processes protocol P to obtain a session key K_i.
2. Each u_i computes and broadcasts $W_i \equiv \frac{K_i}{K_{i-1}}$.
3. Upon receiving the broadcasts from other users, u_i computes the key

$$K \equiv K_{i-1}{}^t W_i{}^{t-1} W_{i+1}{}^{t-2} \cdots W_{i-2} \equiv K_1 K_2 \cdots K_t.$$

Equivalently, we can use $W_i = K_i - K_{i-1}$ and $K = K_1 + \ldots + K_t$ (or even $W_i = K_i \oplus K_{i-1}$ and $K = K_1 \oplus \ldots \oplus K_t$), for example. Since addition is much cheaper than multiplication, such computations have an obvious practical

---

[6] The construction is a generalization of the scheme from [5].

benefit. Verification that all the following discussions hold for this modification is left to the reader.

For a specific implementation of this model we use Protocol IIA from Section 3 to obtain the respective multi-party protocol MIIA (likewise for Protocol IIB from Appendix A). Notice that for Protocol MIIA, u_i sends the same token (i.e. $y_i = y_i'$) to both u_{i+1} and u_{i-1}.

4.1   Attack to Burmester/Desmedt Scheme

In this section we demonstrate how the scheme of Burmester and Desmedt (BD) [5] does not provide key authentication. BD is a specific case of the model describe above with DH as protocol P and makes use of zero-knowledge techniques for authenticating each user. We make use of an attack first put forth in [13].

The adversary E positions himself between any two users A and B and convinces B that he shares a key with E (though E will be unable to compute K), yet B actually shares K with A. A believes (and in fact does) share K with B. Hence, key authentication is not provided as the person with whom B believes he is sharing the key (namely E), is not able to actually compute the key (as only A and B can compute the key). Subsequent to this attack, messages that A sends to B will be interpreted by B as coming from E. One can imagine an attack where B is a bank and A and E are customers.

From [5], each user i has a public key pair (β_i, γ_i) where $\beta_i = \alpha^{v_i}$ and $\gamma_i = \alpha^{w_i}$. This version assumes that users' public keys are a priori available. The attack proceeds as follows. A selects $x \in_R \mathbb{Z}_q$ and sends $\{y := \alpha^x, I := I_A\}$ to B. E intercepts the communication so now A authenticates y to E with a zero-knowledge interactive proof of knowledge of the discrete log of $\beta_A{}^y \gamma_A$ (namely $v_A y + w_A$) using methods described in [5]. E sends y to B, and using his public key pair (β_E, γ_E), authenticates y to B. B sends $\{y', I := I_B\}$ to E. E simply forwards this message to A and allows B to authenticate y' to A. A and B complete the protocol by broadcasting W_A and W_B respectively.

The attack succeeds because of the lack of "binding" between the messages exchanged between A and B and lack of protection of the names of the intended recipients of the messages. These properties are identified in [1] as being important for obtaining a secure and authentic cryptographic protocol.

The authentication between pairs of users in [5] requires 1 round for the DH key token exchange, k rounds for the authentication of the tokens (for a security parameter k) and 1 round for the broadcast of the W_i's, giving a total of $k + 2$ rounds. Protocol MIIA requires 3 rounds for the processing of Protocol IIA (including authentication of tokens) and 1 round for the broadcast of the W_i's, giving a total of 4 rounds. If more than 2 rounds are used for the authentication of the tokens in the Burmester-Desmedt scheme, our schemes are more efficient in terms of the number of rounds.

4.2 Passive Attacks

In this section, we show that the multi-party model specifically implemented with Protocol IIA (to produce MIIA) is provably secure against a passive attacker. (Similar arguements can be made for an implementation with Protocol IIB from Appendix A.) This is done by illustrating their equivalence to the respective schemes from Section 3 (using the same techniques as given in [5]).

Theorem 3. *Given an even, polynomial number t of randomly chosen users with long-term keys that are uniformly distributed, Protocol MIIA is as secure against passive attacks as Protocols IIA.*

Proof. We first note that breaking Protocol IIA obviously enables one to break Protocol MIIA (solve for each K_i followed by computation of their product).

Now, given $p_1 = p_B = \alpha^{s_B}$, $y_1 = y' = \alpha^{x'}$, $p_t = p_A = \alpha^{s_A}$ and $y_t = y = \alpha^{x}$, we want to solve for the key $\alpha^{x_t x_1 + x_t s_1 + x_1 s_t}$ (i.e. $\alpha^{xx' + x s_B + x' s_A}$ from Protocol IIA) by using an oracle that solves for the MIIA key. We must first prepare the remaining input to the MIIA oracle. We first compute for $i = 2, \ldots, t - 1$, $p_i = p_{i-2}\alpha^{b_i}$ and $y_i = y_{i-2}\alpha^{c_i}$ using random b_i and c_i. This "randomizes" the virtual users as if we had $s_i = s_{i-2} + b_i$ and $x_i = x_{i-2} + c_i$ providing a good distribution. For $i = 1, \ldots, t - 2$, we can now compute

$$W_i = \left(\frac{p_{i+1}y_{i+1}}{p_{i-1}y_{i-1}}\right)^{x_i} \left(\frac{y_{i+1}}{y_{i-1}}\right)^{s_i} = (\alpha^{b_{i+1}}\alpha^{c_{i+1}})^{x_i}(\alpha^{c_{i+1}})^{x_i} = y_i^{b_{i+1}}(y_i p_i)^{c_{i+1}}$$

Since t is even, we also have that

$$p_t \equiv p_2 g^{-b_2} \equiv p_4 g^{-b_2 - b_4} \equiv \cdots \equiv p_{t-2} g^{-b_2 - b_4 - \cdots - b_{t-2}}$$
$$p_1 \equiv p_3 g^{-b_3} \equiv p_5 g^{-b_3 - b_5} \equiv \cdots \equiv p_{t-1} g^{-b_3 - b_5 - \cdots - b_{t-1}},$$

(and similarly for y_t and y_1) allowing us to compute

$$W_{t-1} \equiv \left(\frac{p_t y_t}{p_{t-2}y_{t-2}}\right)^{x_{t-1}} \left(\frac{y_t}{y_{t-2}}\right)^{s_{t-1}}$$
$$\equiv (y_{t-1})^{-b_3 - b_5 - \cdots - b_{t-1}}(y_{t-1}p_{t-1})^{-c_3 - c_5 - \cdots - c_{t-1}}$$
$$W_t \equiv \left(\frac{p_1 y_1}{p_{t-1}y_{t-1}}\right)^{x_t} \left(\frac{y_1}{y_{t-1}}\right)^{s_t}$$
$$\equiv (y_t)^{-b_3 - b_5 - \cdots - b_{t-1}}(y_t p_t)^{-c_3 - c_5 - \cdots - c_{t-1}}.$$

Inputting all the y_i, p_i and W_i to the MIIA oracle, produces the output K. We have $K_i = \alpha^{x_{i-1}x_i + x_i s_{i-1} + x_{i-1}s_i}y_i^{b_{i+1}}(y_i p_i)^{c_i+1}$. From K and the W_i, we can obtain any K_i. More specifically, for u_1 we solve for K_1, from which we obtain $\alpha^{x_t x_1 + x_t s_1 + x_1 s_t}$. $\qquad\square$

4.3   Information Revealed by the Protocol

We need to verify whether the W_i's broadcast by each user reveal any information about the secret key s_i. Given the public key p_i of user u_i, we assign p_{i-1}, p_{i+1} to dishonest users u_{i-1} and u_{i+1} and allow them to simultaneously execute a multi-party protocol to obtain y_i and W_i from u_i. We present an attack on protocol MIA to illustrate this issue, and show the security of Protocol MIIA.

In MIA, using the real public keys of the dishonest users, we get $W_i = \frac{p_{i+1}^{x_i}}{y_{i-1}^{s_i}}$ and $y_i = \alpha^{x_i}$. Colluding users can compute $p_{i+1}^{x_i} = y_i^{s_{i+1}}$ obtaining $y_{i-1}^{s_i}$. Hence, this protocol (no matter if it aborts) can be followed to use u_i as an oracle to raise any chosen y_{i-1} to the secret key s_i. We can easily imagine how this allows recovery of a previous session key: in a previous session, $\tilde{K}_{i-1}$ is $\tilde{y}_{i-1}^{s_i}$, and since $\tilde{y}_{i-1}$ can be eavesdropped on the channel, one can ask u_i to raise it to s_i to obtain $\tilde{K}_{i-1}$, followed easily by computation of the previous session key $\tilde{K}$.

If they complete Protocol MIIA (hence succeeded Protocol IIA), colluding users u_{i-1} and u_{i+1} obtain from u_i, $W_i = \frac{K_i}{K_{i-1}}$ as well as y_i' and y_i. Since u_{i-1} (u_{i+1}) has been able to produce z_{i-1} (z_{i+1}') and complete IIA before W_i is broadcast, he knew how to compute K_{i-1} (K_i).[7] Thus, active attacks do not recover more information than passive ones from the W_i.

4.4   Active Attacks

For Protocol MIIA, a traditional impersonation attack where user E successfully completes a protocol (including key computation in our case) with B (resp. A) by impersonating A (resp. B) would occur in step 1 from Section 4. (Recall from the previous section, the W_i released during step 2 provide no extra information.) According to Theorem 2, this is unlikely.

In all of the MP schemes we have investigated thus far, there has been an implicit assumption that if you were able to successfully complete a protocol with several users, then each of these users is honest. Relaxing this assumption introduces the following possible attacks (which are applicable to our schemes as well as the Burmester-Desmedt scheme).

Consider a multi-party protocol between users A, B, C and D who are oriented on a ring. If C's left and right partners are B and D (i.e. the users with whom C will perform protocol P) then B, C and D can collude by *shielding* C. By this we mean that B and D can construct their messages such that C can impersonate some Z. This is possible since no direct authentication is performed between users A and C. At the end of the protocol, A could be made believe that the protocol consists of users A, B, Z and D. Of course, this would not allow C (impersonating Z) to compute the key on his own (see Section 3.2) but the key can be given to C by one of B or D (C's colluding partners).

A solution to this attack is to include an additional step at the end of the protocol whereby each user i broadcasts the quantity $s_i(h_K(W_1, W_2, \ldots, W_t))$,

---

[7] This is necessary under the assumption that knowledge of K_{i-1} (or K_i) is necessary for computation of the keyed hash in Protocol IIA.

which is i's signature on the keyed hash of the W_i's broadcast in step 2 of the multi-party protocol described in Section 4. Since our protocols are public-key based, the signature scheme can be easily implemented using ElGamal signatures [8] for example.

Note that the solution above works assuming that C is not able to falsify Z's signature. A possible attack to this assumption occurs in [3]. Here, the authors present a so-called *Middleperson Attack*. Suppose we have Protocol 1, consisting of users A, B and C and Protocol 2 consisting of users B, C and Z. The attack involves C sitting in the middle of the two simultaneous protocols. C would impersonate Z in Protocol 1 and impersonate A in Protocol 2. Any challenges that C would be required to compute (as if they came from Z), including possible signatures, in Protocol 1 would be obtained directly from Z in Protocol 2 (and vice-versa for impersonating A in Protocol 2). At this point, users see Protocol I as consisting of users A, B and Z and Protocol II of users B, A and Z. Similar to the attack above, C would be unable to compute the key on his own as he is really only acting as a 'wire' between the two protocols, and passing along messages. Once again, he would require a collusion with B to obtain K (for the attack to be of any real use).

The solution presented to the attack in [3] was a hardware one rather than a crytographic one. Also note that the property of key authentication was never really violated since that principal attacker C was never able to compute the key on his own. Depending upon the application, the practicality of such attacks must be individually examined.

5 Conclusion

In this paper, we presented two new key agreement protocols, the two-party Protocol IIA and its multi-party counterpart, Protocol MIIA. Protocol IIA appears to improve upon several others for which long-term public keys are used in the key computation (and for which several attacks were given here). Their use in key computation is an alternative to the use of digital signatures.

Protocol MIIA is derived from our generalization of the multi-party protocol of Burmester and Desmedt (BD) [5]. A nice feature of the protocol is that it allows for authentication of participating users without requiring that each user authenticate every other user. Though one must be careful with such methods as evidenced by the shielding attack from Section 4.4.

Protocol MIIA differs from the scheme of BD in how participants are authenticated. Rather than using zero-knowledge techniques (which are susceptible to the attack from Section 4.1), we essentially use Diffie-Hellman computations in key confirmation. It seems likely that many of the other two-party key agreement protocols mentioned here can also provide for a multi-party protocol using the generalization from Section 4.

Acknowledgements. Thanks to Paul Van Oorschot for suggesting the current topic for research. Using a different group structure for the computation of the

W_i and K_i in Section 4 was suggested by Kazue Sako. Thanks to an anonymous referee for the fourth attack (where E possess $\alpha^{s_A s_B}$) given in Section 3.1. Thanks to Yvo Desmedt for pointing out the existence of [4].

Note. The first author is supported by an NSERC graduate fellowship. The second author is employed by the CNRS. This work was partially completed while the second author was visiting the School of Computer Science at Carleton University and supported by an NSERC grant.

References

1. M. Abadi, R. Needham, "Prudent Engineering Practice for Cryptographic Protocols", *DEC SRC Research Report* **125**, June 1, 1994.
2. M. Bellare, P. Rogaway, "Entity Authentication and Key Distribution", *Advances in Cryptology: Proceedings of CRYPTO '93*, Springer-Verlag, 1993, pp.232-249.
3. S. Bengio, G. Brassard, Y. Desmedt, C. Goutier, J. Quisquater, "Secure Implementation of Identification Systems", *Journal of Cryptology*, Vol. 4, 1991, pp. 175-183.
4. M. Burmester, "On the Risk of Opening Distributed Keys", *Advances in Cryptology: Proceedings of Crypto '94*, Springer-Verlag, 1994, pp.308-317.
5. M. Burmester, Y. Desmedt, "A Secure and Efficient Conference Key Distribution System", *Advances in Cryptology: Proceedings of Eurocrypt '94*, Springer-Verlag, 1995, pp.275-286.
6. W. Diffie, M. Hellman, "New Directions in Cryptography", *IEEE Transactions on Information Theory*, IT-22(6), November 1976, pp.644-654.
7. W. Diffie, P.C. van Oorschot, M.J. Wiener, "Authentication and Authenticated Key Exchanges", *Designs, Codes and Cryptography*, Vol. 2, 1992, pp. 107-125.
8. T. ElGamal, "A Public Key Cryptosystem and a Signature Scheme Based on Discrete Logarithms", *IEEE Transactions on Information Theory*, Vol. 31, pp. 469-472, 1985.
9. C. Günther, "An Identity-Based Key Exchange Protocol", *Advances in Cryptology: Proceedings of Eurocrypt '89*, Springer-Verlag, 1989, pp.29-37.
10. I. Ingemarsson, D. Tang, C. Wong, "A Conference Key Distribution System", *IEEE Transactions on Information Theory*, Vol. IT-28, No.5, Sept. 1982, pp.714-720.
11. H. Krawczyk, "SKEME: A Versatile Secure Key Exchange Mechanism for Internet", *Proceedings of the Internet Society Symposium on Network and Distributed System Security*, Feb. 1996 (also presented at the *Crypto '95* rump session).
12. T. Matsumoto, Y. Takashima, H. Imai, "On Seeking Smart Public-Key Distribution Systems", *The Transactions of the IECE of Japan*, Vol. E. 69, No. 2, February 1986, pp. 99-106.
13. A. Menezes, M. Qu, S. Vanstone, "Some New Key Agreement Protocols Providing Implicit Authentication", presented at the *Workshop on Selected Areas in Cryptography (SAC '95)*, Carleton University, Ottawa, ON., pp. 22-32.
14. D. Pointcheval, J. Stern, "Security Proofs for Signature Schemes", *Advances in Cryptology: Proceedings of Eurocrypt '96*, Springer-Verlag, 1996, pp.387-398.
15. B. Preneel, *Cryptographic Hash Functions*, Kluwer Academic Publishers (to appear, 1996).
16. R. Rueppel, P. van Oorschot, "Modern Key Agreement Techniques", *Computer Communications Journal*, Vol. 17, July 1994, pp. 458-465.

17. D. Steer, L. Strawczynski, W. Diffie, M. Wiener, "A Secure Audio Teleconference System", *Advances in Cryptology: Proceedings of CRYPTO '88*, Springer-Verlag, 1988, pp.520-528.
18. M. Steiner, G. Tsudik, M. Waidner, "Diffie-Hellman Key Distribution Extended to Group Communication", *3rd ACM Conference on Computer and Communications Security*, New Dehli, India, March 14-16, 1996.
19. P. van Oorschot, M. Wiener, "On Diffie-Hellman Key Agreement with Short Exponents", *Advances in Cryptology: Proceedings of Eurocrypt '96*, Springer-Verlag, 1996, pp.332-343.
20. Y. Yacobi, "A Key Distribution 'Paradox' ", *Advances in Cryptology: Proceedings of CRYPTO '90*, Springer-Verlag, 1990, pp.268-273.

A Protocols Based on IB

The protocols in Figure 5 require *a priori* knowledge of public keys (or an extra message pass). Protocol B0 was given in [13] (an adaptation of a scheme from [12]). Similar attacks to those presented in Section 3.1 can be mounted against Protocol B0. Protocol IIB prevents the attacks and provides forward secrecy. The key computation is identical to the two-pass protocols from [13, 12].

A		B
$x \in_R \mathbb{Z}_q, y = p_B{}^x$	$\xrightarrow{\quad y, I = I_A \quad}$	$x' \in_R \mathbb{Z}_q, y' = p^{x'}$
		$K = \alpha^{x'} y^{s_B{}^{-1}}$
		$z' = h_K(y', I, I')$
$K = (y')^{s_A{}^{-1}} \alpha^x$	$\xleftarrow{\quad y', I' = I_B, z' \quad}$	
$z' \stackrel{?}{=} h_K(y', I, I')$		
$x \in_R \mathbb{Z}_q, y = p_B{}^x$	$\xrightarrow{\quad y, I = I_A \quad}$	$x' \in_R \mathbb{Z}_q, y' = p^{x'}$
		$w' = \alpha^{x'}, K = y^{s_B{}^{-1} x'}$
		$z' = h_K(2 : y', y, I', I, w')$
$w' = (y')^{s_A{}^{-1}}$	$\xleftarrow{\quad y', I' = I_B, z' \quad}$	
$w = \alpha^x, K = (y')^{s_A{}^{-1} x}$		
$z' \stackrel{?}{=} h_K(2 : y', y, I', I, w')$		
$z = h_K(1 : y, y', I, I', w)$		
	$\xrightarrow{\quad\quad z \quad\quad}$	$w = (y)^{s_B{}^{-1}}$
		$z \stackrel{?}{=} h_K(1 : y, y', I, I', w)$

Fig. 5. Protocol B0(top): $K = \alpha^{x+x'}$; Protocol IIB(bottom): $K = \alpha^{xx'}$

Cryptography and the Internet: Lessons and Challenges

Kevin S. McCurley

Sandia National Laboratories*

Abstract. The popularization of the Internet has brought fundamental changes to the world, because it allows a universal method of communication between computers. This carries enormous benefits with it, but also raises many security considerations. Cryptography is a fundamental technology used to provide security of computer networks, and there is currently a widespread engineering effort to incorporate cryptography into various aspects of the Internet. The system-level engineering required to provide security services for the Internet carries some important lessons for researchers whose study is focused on narrowly defined problems. It also offers challenges to the cryptographic research community by raising new questions not adequately addressed by the existing body of knowledge. This paper attempts to summarize some of these lessons and challenges for the cryptographic research community.

1 Introduction

The Internet has been around for a long time, but the last year we have witnessed an explosion of interest and growth of the Internet. At the time of this writing, most of the interest surrounds the development of electronic commerce at the consumer level, but as a universal method of communication between computers we can expect many other interesting applications in the future, including such things as electronic stock markets and worldwide systems for retrieving computerized medical information.

Most of the current and future uses of the Internet have security considerations associated with them. Unfortunately, much of the Internet was designed without much attention to security. A large-scale engineering effort is currently underway to "bolt on some security" to many pieces of the existing Internet infrastructure, including the Domain Name Service (DNS), routing protocols (e.g., OSPF), and the hypertext transport protocol (HTTP). Moreover, as new capabilities are being developed, they are incorporating a variety of security mechanisms into them. For the most part they are using relatively unsophisticated cryptography (e.g., shared key MACS based on MD5).

The purpose of my lecture is to describe some lessons that this engineering effort provides to the research community, and describe some future challenges

* Author's address is Organization 9224, MS 1109, Sandia National Laboratories, Albuquerque, NM 87185, USA.

that can be expected to arise in securing the future global information infrastructure. Because of the short-term nature of this engineering work, the paper here will describe some of the lessons and challenges only in broad terms. It can be expected that after ten years, the value of some of the individual mechanisms that are developed by this engineering effort will be forgotten. At the same time, we are undergoing fundamental changes in the way we use and think about information, and the Internet drives this home.

At Crypto '96, Whitfield Diffie delivered a presentation in which he observed that widespread use of radio communication has been one of the biggest historical changes on the development of cryptography. Looking forward in time and predicting the next trend in cryptography is a risky business, but I believe that the Internet will also mark a sea change in the development and use of cryptography. The development of radio marked a tremendous change in the frequency and nature of communication, bringing with it new problems in securing communication due to the fundamental fact that radio is easily subject to eavesdropping. My reasons for believing that the Internet will bring a similar revolution in cryptography can be traced to three fundamental trends:

- The Internet is global. Communication across the Internet does not respect national boundaries and must conform to many different local cultures and standards of how information is handled. This has the potential to improve the level of understanding between different nations, but it also has the potential to highlight our differences and thereby spark conflicts. As computer networks become increasingly interlocked, parties communicating across the Internet will be increasingly distrustful, which makes cryptography all the more important.
- Communication between computers across the Internet involves some initiated directly by humans (current examples include email and web browsing), but will increasingly involve communication that follows automatic procedures for gathering and processing information. Cryptography has traditionally been a manual process between trusting parties, and new key management strategies will be required to address the increasing amount of automated communication.
- Communication across the Internet is not limited in scale by the size of the radio spectrum or physical limitations of distance, and can therefore scale to to an enormous volume of communication. This growth will not be easy, and serious problems of addressing and routing have yet to be experienced. This rapid growth will also strain our ability to devise effective key management mechanisms and cryptographic primitives.

For the most part, the most interesting problems in cryptography arise from how we *use* information, and not how we communicate it. The focus on the Internet is primarily justified by the fact that it marks a turning point in expanding the way we process information. New applications such as electronic commerce, data harvesting, and remote control of experiments bring with them a complicated set of requirements, and new cryptographic mechanisms will need be required to ensure their efficacy.

Because of the rapid chaotic development of the Internet, it would be inappropriate to concentrate too closely on details in this archival publication. Instead, this paper will flesh out some broad challenges and lessons that the Internet will force on cryptography, and leave the details of their current form to the oral presentation.

2 Lessons from the Current Engineering Effort

Much of the current work on cryptography and Internet security is engineering rather than science, and from a first glance would seem to be pretty routine deployment of existing techniques. Examples include various public key certification hierarchies and the IPSEC security enhancements to the underlying packet transmission protocol. From these engineering exercises there are valuable lessons to be learned for guiding future research directions, and in this section I will try to highlight just a few.

Lesson 1: What's in a name?

In designing cryptographic protocols that use public-key cryptography, theoreticians often ignore the difficulty of identifying public keys with the various parties of the protocol. Early engineering attempts to design a public-key certification hierarchy centered around the X509 standard, and was originally planned to have a single name space for all certificates. Unfortunately, for various reasons this has proved to be slow in coming, and there are now multiple emerging proposals for directory services and an associated public key certification hierarchy (e.g., [3]). Naming conventions are important not only to cryptographic key management, but are also important for authorizations within a larger context. It is common practice today to use address-based authorization because we are unskilled in recognizing the names of entities at a finer level of detail. In the future we should expect that associations of names for entities will be much more important, particularly in an environment where untrusting parties are introduced to each other and wish to carry out a mutually beneficial communication and/or computation. For example, a consumer who wishes to order food from a fast food restaurant might logically expect the domain kfc.com domain to be associated with the restaurant chain of the same name. Within a different context however, kfc.com might refer to another company, and kfc might refer to the initials of an individual. Such complications can be difficult to engineer around, but highlight the need to maintain a well-defined name space for entities in a cryptographic protocol.

Lesson 2: Firewalls are here to stay

The original design of the Internet was for a research environment in which little more was at stake than people's reputations, and it was assumed that nobody would take serious advantage of existing weaknesses. The commercialization of the Internet infrastructure has evolved along roughly the same lines, where organizations whose members more or less trust each other will place themselves inside a "universal trust domain". When connecting these domains to the Internet as a whole, they concentrate their security at a single point of connection, known as a firewall. This eliminates the need to protect every machine and individual within the organization, and allows more freedom of sharing within the organizational boundary.

Firewall technology has proved to be very cost effective in minimizing human resources required to secure an organization, but are becoming unwieldy as the Internet embraces more and more protocols for carrying out communication and distributed protocols (e.g., video conferencing, active content in electronic mail, etc). Still, firewalls are likely to become more important in the future as organizations develop develop stronger internal information bonds.

The use of firewalls can greatly complicate cryptographic protocols however, since they are natural candidates for mounting "man in the middle" attacks. Cryptographic protocols will need to be developed to address the situation where an intermediary takes some of the responsibility for protecting parties against attacks, because the economic case for such engineering systems with firewalls is too strong to ignore.

Lesson 3: Implement security at the appropriate layer

Computer networks are traditionally described in terms of the seven-layer ISO model. In such a model, the highest level is where users interact with the network through applications, and the lowest level is a physical hardware level. The Internet protocol is more naturally thought of in terms of four layers, consisting of application (e.g., HTTP and SMTP mail), transport (e.g., UDP and TCP), network (e.g, IP, ICMP), and a physical link layer. The separation of a network design into layers allows for modular design, and separates the responsibility of the different layers. From a security perspective, it creates some confusion because the overall design of a network carries with it assumptions about how the different layers will interoperate. In order to build security into applications using this layered approach, we will need to choose the appropriate layer at which to apply cryptography.

In general it is axiomatic that the lower the layer, the higher the performance that can be achieved with cryptographic primitives. For example, at the physical link layer, encryption can easily be handled by hardware devices designed to handle data in appropriately sized chunks. Unfortunately the lower layers do not expose the security requirements of the underlying information, and for example the key management at the physical hardware layer might be problematic if there is a requirement to protect the confidentiality of information from multiple sources that share the physical layer. This is an example of the fact that the higher the layer, the easier it is to match cryptographic services with security requirements of the ultimate application.

The requirements of different applications are quite diverse, and cryptographic mechanisms need to match these requirements. For example, mail messages need only be checked after the entire message is received and read by the recipient, but TCP stream based applications like telnet need to be encrypted and authenticated in real time as bytes are received, before they are acted upon. It is unnatural to expect that the same algorithms and key management techniques would be used for each of these. Sometimes there is enough commonality between applications that a single mechanism can be applied to several. An example is the Secure Socket Layer (SSL), which provides security services for a range of applications that require a connection-oriented transmission service.

At a lower level, work is proceeding on providing basic security for the network layer, using independent IP packets. The IP security options (IPSEC) for the next generation of the IP protocol are intended to provide independent services of authentication and encryption, using a choice of several different algorithms. IPSEC includes provision for both authentication and confidentiality. There is currently no support for non-repudiation, which effectively limits the services that intermediaries such as firewalls can provide.

In addition, the IP layer relies upon various routing protocols to deliver packets. These routing protocols are of varying kinds, including both link-state and distance-vector approaches. Of the two, distance-vector is somewhat harder to protect with cryptography, since the information that is passed between routers is *derived* from information from other routers, but does not represent the original information supplied by those routers [1]. Hence digital signatures are of limited utility, since routers must still rely on their neighbors to validate information received from other routers before computing routes.

3 Challenges for the future

Challenge 1: The Definition of Alice

Most of the difficulty in engineering cryptographic systems has to do with understanding the trust relationships between different entities involved in a protocol. In theoretical work, we often speak of simple entities such as "Bob" and "Alice" as if they were themselves infinitely capable universal trust domains. In real systems, it is more natural to think of parties involved in the protocol as distributed systems in themselves. For example, when a person is using a web browser to investigate and purchase goods over the Internet, they are in fact acting as part of a system consisting of the person, their computer, their display system, their input/output devices, the operating system, the network, and possibly a cryptographic token. Exactly where Alice stops and the rest of the world begins is unclear for the purposes of analyzing cryptographic algorithms. In all likelihood, the infrastructure that she uses will also be used for other purposes, including possibly her employment and her personal life. In order for Alice to engage in a cryptographic protocol, she will need to store secret information, produce cryptographically secure random numbers, perform computations and communications, as well as deal with the goals of the protocol. In pre-electronic days, these were tasks that she was able to carry out with little more than paper and pencil. The new electronic infrastructure offers to make her life "easier" by handling very complex data presentation and management tasks on her behalf. In order for Alice to have any trust in the system to act on her behalf, she may wish to understand these actions, but the complexity of modern information systems precludes this. This raises an (admittedly ill-defined) point regarding the analysis of cryptographic protocols: we should do as much as possible reduce the complexity of actions and information that Alice must place her trust in. As the complexity of information systems increases with time, it becomes increasingly important to narrowly define the complexity of the systems that Alice must trust.

Challenge 2: Flexible International Key Escrow

There is no doubt that there are instances when some parties will wish to have the encryption keys of other escrowed, whether for national security interests, political interests, or simply in an organization that wishes to protect it's information assets against the eventuality of an information custodian becoming unavailable. Putting aside the political issue of whether key escrow is desirable in a given situation, the problem of key escrow raises several interesting problems in the design of cryptographic protocols. First among these is the requirement to design a key management framework that will reflect the various access requirements that entities will place upon a key escrow service. Second is the need to minimize the overhead of such a system.

Challenge 3: Scalable cryptographic primitives

For many applications, our current state of knowledge concerning the amount of computation required to carry out various cryptographic primitives will severely limit the application of cryptography in the future. While computers continue to get faster at an astounding rate, there is still a continuing need to explore the boundaries on what the minimal amount of computation and communication required to perform specific cryptographic tasks. Examples include cryptographic hashing, key exchange, digital signature construction and verification, batch processing, and basic encryption. For example, IPv6 offers the option for all data across the Internet to be encrypted and authenticated on a packet-by-packet basis. While it is possible to encrypt and authenticate data streams at a very rapid rate already, there is continued pressure to use the computational capability at the endpoints to process the data stream content for the application rather than consuming resources for cryptographic protection.

Challenge 4: Electronic Commerce Issues

The primary reason for a rising interest by society in the Internet is directly derived from the perception that the Internet offers a promise of new ways to conduct commerce. A ubiquitous communication infrastructure provides a convenient way to offer information products and contact customers for electronic commerce. Ideas for electronic cash that have originated in the cryptographic research community are now being seriously considered as a mechanism for supporting these new forms of electronic commerce. Delivery of information services begs for a lightweight payment protocol that supports a very low transaction cost. This in turn gave birth to the investigation of micropayment protocols such as Millicent [2], Payword, and Micromint [4]. As people figure out new ways to make money through a global communication and computing infrastructure, we can expect new requirements to come forth for electronic payment protocols.

Challenge 5: Denial of Service attacks

The ability to freely communicate with a vast number of parties leads to the need for parties to protect themselves against denial of service attacks. I have recently started receiving a tremendous amount of email whose purpose is to advertise a product. If such communication is not regulated in the future, then it will become an individual's responsibility to flexibly filter such nonsense. Cryptography offers a mechanism to address such concerns, in part based on the emergence of a cryptographically based electronic commerce system. Future attacks can be limited through the use of protocols that require payment in order to consume some resource. The scalability of payment systems is likely to be the deciding factor in their effectiveness.

In such a short paper, I cannot begin to describe the total range of problems and lessons that the Internet brings to cryptography. We should however expect major changes in direction to occur in years to come.

References

1. S. L. Murphy and M. R. Badger, "Digital Signature Protection of the OSPF Routing Protocol", Proceedings of the 1996 Symposium on Network and Distributed Systems Security, IEEE, 1996.
2. Mark S. Manasse, "The Millicent Protocols for Electronic Commerce, Procceedings of the 1st USENIX Workshop on Electronic Commerce, July, 1995.
3. Ronald L. Rivest, "SDSI - A Simple Distributed Security Infrastructure", preprint, 1996.
4. Ronald L. Rivest and Adi Shamir, Payword and MicroMint - Two Simple Micropayment Schemes, preprint, 1996. Available at
http://theory.lcs.mit.edu/~rivest/RivestShamir-mpay.ps.

Generating Standard DSA Signatures Without Long Inversion

Arjen K. Lenstra

Citibank, N.A., 4 Sylvan Way, Parsippany, NJ 07054, U.S.A.
E-mail: arjen.lenstra@citicorp.com

Abstract. We show how the generation of a random integer k modulo q and the subsequent computation of $k^{-1} \bmod q$ during the signature phase of the NIST digital signature algorithm (DSA) can be replaced by the simultaneous generation of a pair $(k, k^{-1} \bmod q)$. The k generated by our method behaves as an unpredictable integer modulo q that cannot, as far as we know, be efficiently distinguished from a truly randomly generated one. Our approach is useful for memory-bound implementations of DSA, because it avoids modular inversion of large integers. It is different from the inversion-free but non-standard method from [10], thus avoiding possible patent issues and incompatibility with standard DSA signature verification implementations. Another application of our method is in the 'blinding' operation that was proposed by Ron Rivest to foil Paul Kocher's timing attack on RSA, or in any other situation where one needs a random number and its modular inverse.

1 Introduction

Each user of the NIST digital signature algorithm (DSA) has a public key (p, q, g, y) and a corresponding secret key x. Here p is a $(512 + i \cdot 64)$-bit prime for some $i \in \{0, 1, \ldots, 8\}$, $g \in (\mathbf{Z}/p\mathbf{Z})^*$ is an element of order q for a 160-bit prime divisor q of $p - 1$, and $y \in (\mathbf{Z}/p\mathbf{Z})^*$ and $x \in \{1, 2, \ldots, q-1\}$ are such that $y = g^x$ (cf. [11]). Powers of g are represented in the usual way by integers in $\{1, 2, \ldots, p-1\}$.

The signature of a message m consists of a pair (r, s) such that $r \equiv t \bmod q$ with $t = g^k \in (\mathbf{Z}/p\mathbf{Z})^*$ and $s \equiv (H(m) + xr)/k \bmod q$ for a randomly chosen $k \in \{1, 2, \ldots, q-1\}$ and a 160-bit hash $H(m) \in \mathbf{Z}$ of the message m. It is required that k be chosen such that $s \not\equiv 0 \bmod q$. Both r and s must be represented by integers in $\{1, 2, \ldots, q-1\}$. To verify a signature (r, s) for a message m, the verifier computes $u \equiv H(m)/s \bmod q$, $v \equiv r/s \bmod q$, and $w = g^u y^v \in (\mathbf{Z}/p\mathbf{Z})^*$, and accepts the signature if $r \equiv w \bmod q$.

The computationally most intensive part of the signature and verification phases of DSA are the 'modular exponentiations' modulo the fixed modulus p: one modular exponentiation during the signature generation to compute t, and two during the verification [1] to compute w. Furthermore, there are a few modular multiplications modulo the fixed modulus q, and one inversion modulo q in the signature and verification phase each.

In this note we restrict ourselves to the computation that has to be carried out by the signer. We assume that the signer is computationally weak. Our purpose is to implement the signature phase of DSA in a time and memory efficient fashion. In particular we consider the computation of $k^{-1} \bmod q$ for a randomly selected k. Notice that the secret key x can be computed if k is exposed for any signature, or if the same k is used more than once by the same signer.

In a DSA implementation where modular arithmetic is implemented using standard arithmetic (i.e., first the product is computed and next its remainder modulo the modulus), it should be possible to implement the extended Euclidean algorithm with little extra overhead—either in software or on-chip, and possibly with inclusion of 'Lehmer's trick' (cf. [5: 4.5.2]—throughout this note we refer to this method as 'Lehmer's inversion'). This would make it possible to compute $k^{-1} \bmod q$ at a very small fraction of the cost of a modular exponentiation with modulus p, using only a few divisions on integers of at most 160 bits.

Many implementations of cryptographic protocols, however, do not use standard arithmetic but *Montgomery arithmetic*. If the modulus is fixed, this allows division-free modular multiplication and exponentiation [9]. Compared to regular modular arithmetic it is often faster and implementations require less code. Montgomery arithmetic does, however, not offer a convenient way to directly implement Lehmer's inversion. Nevertheless, since

$$(1.1) \qquad\qquad k^{-1} \equiv k^{q-2} \bmod q,$$

Montgomery arithmetic can, in principle, also be used for the computation of $k^{-1} \bmod q$ in cases where, as in DSA, the modulus q is prime. Thus, if only Montgomery arithmetic is available, $k^{-1} \bmod q$ can be computed at about 1/40th to 1/10th (depending on the relative sizes of p and q) of the cost of a modular exponentiation with modulus p and with hardly any memory overhead. Although this is reasonably fast, it is considerably slower than Lehmer's inversion.

A faster solution was proposed in [10]: replace the signature (r, s) by the triple (r, a, b) with $a = (H(m) + xr) \cdot d \bmod q$ and $b = k \cdot d \bmod q$ for some randomly chosen $d \in \{1, 2, \ldots, q-1\}$, thus avoiding computation of any modular inverses by the signer. The verifier can then compute $1/s \bmod q$ as $b/a \bmod q$. So, both in the original DSA and in this variation the verifier has to carry out one inversion modulo q. Despite its simplicity and elegance this method has three disadvantages. In the first place, the protocol is slightly different from the standard DSA protocol, which might cause incompatibilities with verifiers that follow the standard. In the second place, this method requires twice the number of random bits required by standard DSA. Whether or not these two

---

[1] The two modular exponentiations during the verification can be performed simultaneously at the cost of about 5/4th of a single modular exponentiation (cf. [16]).

disadvantages create a problem in practice depends on the intended application of the implementation. Finally, usage of this method might require a license because it is, to the best of our knowledge, patented.

The purpose of this note is to provide an alternative method to generate k and k^{-1} mod q. Except for the way k and k^{-1} mod q are generated, our method follows the standard DSA protocol, does not require division of 'random' integers of about 160 bits, and is suitable for memory-bound-chip implementations. With the proper parameter selection its speed is competitive with Lehmer's inversion. Our method is thus substantially faster than the method based on (1.1), but it uses slightly more memory. It uses modular multiplication with a fixed modulus q, for which Montgomery arithmetic can be used.

Although our method was developed specifically for application in DSA, it can be used in any application where a random number and its modular inverse are needed. As an alternative example we mention the 'blinding' operation for RSA encryption or signature generation. As shown by Paul Kocher (cf. [7]), timing information of the 'secret computation' $y = x^d$ mod n for several known x's (where n is the composite public modulus and d is the secret exponent corresponding to the public exponent e, i.e., $e \cdot d \equiv 1$ mod $\varphi(n)$) might reveal d.

To foil this so-called 'timing attack', Ron Rivest suggested first to blind x as $x' = xk^e$ mod n for a random integer k, next to replace the secret computation by $y' = x'^d$ mod n, and finally to compute y as $y'k^{-1}$ mod n (cf. [4]). The pair $(k, k^{-1}$ mod $n)$ necessary for the blinding can be obtained using straightforward application of Lehmer's inversion, using the proper variation of (1.1) (namely $k^{-1} \equiv k^{ed-1}$ mod n), or by means of the method presented in this note.

We assume that integer arithmetic modulo some radix $R = 2^B$, for some reasonably large B, can be carried out efficiently. The value $R = 2^{32}$ would certainly suffice, and $B = 16$ might also be enough; $B = 8$ is probably too small. Our method requires division of integers of at most $160 + B$ bits by integers of at most B bits, multiplication of integers of at most 160 bits by integers of at most B bits, and the extended Euclidean algorithm on integers of at most B bits. The additional memory required for these three functions should be small compared to what is needed for Lehmer's inversion of 160-bit numbers.

In Section 2 we describe our method for the simultaneous computation of k and k^{-1} mod q, in Section 3 we discuss the unpredictability of the resulting k and k^{-1} mod q, and in Section 4 we compare the run times and code sizes of software implementations of our method and of the methods discussed above.

2 Simultaneous generation of k and k^{-1} mod q

Our method to simultaneously generate k and k^{-1} mod q is based on the following three simple observations:

1. the inverse modulo q of a random number t of at most B bits can easily be computed;

2. a product modulo q of sufficiently many such t^z's, with each z randomly selected from $\{-1, 1\}$, and the inverse modulo q of this product can both easily be computed; and

3. neither such a product nor its inverse can efficiently be distinguished from a random number modulo q (cf. Section 3).

This leads to the following algorithm for the simultaneous computation of k and $k^{-1} \bmod q$.

2.1 Algorithm. Initialize k and $\bar{k}$ both as 1 (cf. Remark 2.2). Let $m > 2b$, for appropriately chosen positive integers b and m (cf. Section 3). For $i = 1, 2, \ldots, m$ in succession perform steps (1) through (4):

1. Select a random integer $t \in \{2, 3, \ldots, R - 1\}$ and compute $q_t \equiv -q \bmod t$ with $q_t \in \{1, 2, \ldots, t - 1\}$, using one 160-bit by B-bit division.

2. Attempt to compute $q_t^{-1} \bmod t$ using the extended Euclidean algorithm on integers of at most B bits (cf. Remark 2.4); return to Step (1) upon failure (i.e., if t and q_t are not co-prime), proceed to Step (3) otherwise.

3. Compute $t^{-1} \bmod q$ as $(q \cdot q_t^{-1} + 1)/t$, using one 160-bit by B-bit multiplication, and one $(160 + B)$-bit by B-bit division.

4. Let $s = 0$ if $i \leq b$, let $s = 1$ if $b < i \leq 2b$, and let s be randomly selected from $\{0, 1\}$ if $2b < i \leq m$. Replace k by $k \cdot t^{1-2s} \bmod q$ and $\bar{k}$ by $\bar{k} \cdot t^{2s-1} \bmod q$; this takes two modular multiplications modulo q.

Return k and $\bar{k} = (k^{-1} \bmod q)$.

Correctness. Because $q_t \equiv -q \bmod t$ we have that t divides $q \cdot q_t^{-1} + 1$, i.e., that $(q \cdot q_t^{-1} + 1)/t$ is an integer. This implies that $t \cdot ((q \cdot q_t^{-1} + 1)/t)$ equals 1 modulo q, so that $t^{-1} \bmod q$ is computed correctly. The correctness of the remainder of the algorithm follows immediately from that fact that $1 - 2s$ equals either 1 or -1.

2.2. Remark. In Montgomery arithmetic modulo q an integer x is represented by $\hat{x} = x \cdot R_q \bmod q$, for some appropriate power R_q of R. Consequently, the Montgomery product $\hat{z}$ of the Montgomery numbers $\hat{x} = x \cdot R_q \bmod q$ and $\hat{y} = y \cdot R_q \bmod q$ equals $z \cdot R_q \bmod q$ with $z \equiv x \cdot y \bmod q$. To find $\hat{z}$ given $\hat{x}$ and $\hat{y}$, it suffices to compute the ordinary product of $\hat{x}$ and $\hat{y}$, followed by a division by R_q modulo q. The latter division can be done using shifts, which is one of the reasons that Montgomery arithmetic may be preferable to regular modular arithmetic modulo q.

If the regular modular multiplication modulo q in the computation of k and $\bar{k}$ is replaced by Montgomery multiplication, the results will be $k \cdot R_q^{-m} \bmod q$ and $k^{-1} \cdot R_q^{-m} \bmod q$ instead of k and $k^{-1} \bmod q$. At least one of these results will have to be (Montgomery) multiplied by an appropriate power of R_q to get a correct result. This can easily be achieved by initializing k and $\bar{k}$ as appropriate powers of R_q. Which power depends on the rest on the implementation. For on-chip implementation the powers of $R_q \bmod q$ can be 'hard-wired' during the personalization of the chip, at the time the other fixed DSA-related values, like q and p, are initialized as well.

Because one of the multipliers (t) in Step (4) is at most B bits long, one of the two modular multiplications in Step (4) can be replaced by a 'partial' Montgomery multiplication: compute the ordinary product, and next divide by R (instead of R_q) modulo q. This is about $160/B$ times faster than a 'full' Montgomery multiplication.

2.3. Remark. In practice the bits s in Step (4) can be randomly selected for all i, as long as s is at least b times equal to 0 and at least b times equal to 1. See also Section 3.

2.4. Remark. If t is odd, Step (2) can be carried out using the fast division-free binary version of the extended Euclidean algorithm (cf. Appendix). Because for B-bit integers the binary method is considerably faster than the standard method, we only use odd t's in our implementation.

3 Security Considerations

Obviously, the k's as generated by Algorithm (2.1) are not ordinary random numbers in $\{1, 2, \ldots, q-1\}$ as is required in DSA. The danger of replacing truly random values by values that have more 'structure' or otherwise certain known arithmetic properties is well known. This is for instance illustrated by a series of four papers, alternatingly by Schnorr and de Rooij—with both Schnorr's original method to efficiently generate x^k's modulo q for random looking k's (cf. [13]) and his fix (cf. [14]) broken by de Rooij's subsequent attacks (cf. [1, 2]).

If b and m are relatively small, it is in principle possible to distinguish k's generated by our method from truly randomly generated ones. For instance, with $B = 32$, $b = 2$, and $m = 5$, one may try and divide k and its inverse by the product of two B-bit integers, and check if the inverse modulo q of any of the results is a small (i.e., $3B$-bit) number that is the product of three smaller ones. The efficiency of this 'attack' is questionable, however, and even if it were efficient it would be of limited use because the value for k is not revealed in DSA. The obvious next question is whether a signature (r, s) computed with a truly randomly generated k can be distinguished from a signature computed with a k generated by Algorithm (2.1), and whether this would undermine the security of the signature. We are not aware of a method to do this in a feasible amount of time, even for $B = 32$, $b = 2$, and $m = 5$. Nevertheless, we encourage (and look forward to) cryptanalysis of our method, strongly advise against its application before it has extensively been scrutinized, and encourage prospective users to consult future cryptology proceedings.

With $B = 32$ we found that, as long as the total number of random bits used to generate the t's is at least [2] 160 and $b \geq 2$, the k as generated by Algorithm (2.1), using the random number generator provided in LIP, the author's package

---

[2] Here we only count the bits for the t's for which t and q_t are co-prime. With properly selected t's the survival rate of the t's can be made very high, so that only a small number of random bits is wasted.

for long integer arithmetic (cf. [6]), cannot efficiently be distinguished from 160-bit values directly generated by that same generator, using several standard statistical tests: Marsaglia's diehard test (cf. [8]), and an efficient fixed size subset sum test developed by S. Rajagopalan and R. Venkatesan (cf. [12]) based on Goldreich-Levin hard core bits (cf. [3]) and U. Vazirani's subset sum test (cf. [15]).

The selection of the t's can be done in many ways. Some care should be taken that they do not have too many factors in common. To increase the probability that this happens they could for instance be chosen congruent to 1 modulo 30. This choice also increases the survival rate of the t's in Step (2) of Algorithm (2.1).

Even though the executions of Step (4) of Algorithm (2.1) require $m - 2b$ additional random bits, the approach sketched there is probably better than assigning half of the t's to k and the other half to $\bar{k}$ because it makes it harder to predict how many 'small factors' contributed to k and how many to $k^{-1} \bmod q$. Also the powers of R_q might be distributed in some random fashion over k and $k^{-1} \bmod q$ (cf. Remark 2.2).

4   Comparison with other Methods

Run times. We implemented Algorithm (2.1) using the method from the Appendix and the long integer package LIP (cf. [6]). Averaging over 100 different 160-bit primes q and 100 k's per q, we found that Algorithm (2.1) with $B = 32$, $b = 2$, and $m = 5$ took 0.8 milliseconds on a Sparc 10/51 workstation. Note that this choice allows about 160 random bits for the choice of the t's and thus satisfies the requirements mentioned in Section 3. For each of the resulting k's we also computed $k^{-1} \bmod q$ using two other methods: Lehmer's inversion [3] took 1 millisecond per k, and the exponentiation method based on (1.1) took 11.7 milliseconds per k. The 0.8 and 11.7 millisecond timings can be improved slightly using Montgomery arithmetic. Obviously, the run time of Algorithm (2.1) is linear in m; for the more 'secure' choice $b = 5$, $m = 15$, for example, we found that Algorithm (2.1) takes on average 2.3 milliseconds.

From these run times we conclude that for DSA Algorithm (2.1) can be made competitive with Lehmer's inversion, but that, if the latter is available, it hardly makes sense to use Algorithm (2.1). In an environment where this is not the case and where Montgomery arithmetic is used, however, Algorithm (2.1) is substantially faster than the 'standard' solution based on the use of (1.1). Because the run time of the latter method is proportional to $(\log q)^3$ and the other two are only quadratic in $\log q$ (because b and m are proportional to $\log q$), the advantage of Algorithm (2.1) compared to (1.1) becomes more apparent for larger q. For instance, for 512-bit primes q, Algorithm (2.1) with

---

[3] Lehmer's inversion applied to sufficiently large integers is more efficient than the method from the Appendix applied to large integers.

$b = 6$ and $m = 16$ takes on average 7 milliseconds, Lehmer's inversion needs 4 milliseconds, and the method based on (1.1) takes 210 milliseconds.

Code sizes. In a scenario as in DSA where regular modular multiplication and exponentiation or Montgomery multiplication and exponentiation are available, computing the inverse using the exponentiation method based on (1.1) requires no additional code. Algorithm (2.1) requires, as mentioned in Section 1, code for division of $(160+B)$-bit integers by B-bit integers (this is most likely already available if regular modular arithmetic is used for the remainder of DSA), multiplication of 160-bit integers by B-bit integers (already available either in regular or Montgomery arithmetic), and the extended Euclidean algorithm on integers of at most B bits. In LIP this would lead to an overhead of 100 lines of code for the division and 60 lines for the inversion (or only 60 if regular modular arithmetic is used). For Lehmer's inversion one needs full-blown long integer division, and the inversion code. In LIP this would lead to an overhead of 150 lines for the division and 200 lines for Lehmer's inversion (or only 200 lines if regular arithmetic is used). All these figures are *very* rough upper bounds as they include formatting, defines, and many statements to make the code generally applicable but that are not all needed in any specific application.

Which of the three alternatives is preferable depends on the actual implementation and other system characteristics, requirements, and specifications. We have not been able to carry out any comparisons using smartcards.

Acknowledgments. Acknowledgments are due to S. Haber, R. Venkatesan, and S. Rajagopalan for their assistance. The work presented in this paper was done at Bellcore.

References

1. P. de Rooij, *On the security of the Schnorr scheme using preprocessing*, Advances in Cryptology, Eurocrypt'91, Lecture Notes in Comput. Sci. **547** (1991) 71–80.
2. P. de Rooij, *On Schnorr's preprocessing for digital signature schemes*, Advances in Cryptology, Eurocrypt'93, Lecture Notes in Comput. Sci. **765** (1994) 435–439.
3. O. Goldreich, L. A. Levin, *Hard core bits for any one way function*, 22nd Annual ACM symposium on theory of computing (1990); J. Symbolic Logic **58** (1993) 1102–1103.
4. B. Kaliski, *Timing attacks on Cryptosystems*, RSA Laboratories' Bulletin, Number 2, January 1996.
5. D. E. Knuth, *The art of computer programming*, volume 2, *Seminumerical algorithms*, second edition, Addison-Wesley, Reading, Massachusetts, 1981.
6. A. K. Lenstra, *LIP, Long integer package*, available by anonymous ftp from `ftp.ox.ac.uk:/pub/math/freelip/freelip_1.0.tar.gz`.
7. J. Markoff, *Secure digital transactions just got a little less secure*, New York Times, December 11, 1995.
8. G. Marsaglia, *Diehard randomness tests package*, available by e-mail from the author (`geo@stat.fsu.edu`).
9. P. L. Montgomery, *Modular multiplication without trial division*, Math. Comp. **44** (1985) 519–521.

10. D. Naccache, D. M'Raïhi, D. Raphaeli, S. Vaudenay, *Can D.S.A. be improved — complexity trade-offs with the digital signature standard*, Preproceedings Eurocrypt'94 (1994) 85–101.
11. NIST, *A proposed federal information processing standard for digital signature standard (DSS)*, Federal Register **56** (1991) 42980–42982.
12. S. Rajagopalan, R. Venkatesan, work in progress.
13. C. P. Schnorr, *Efficient identification and signatures for smart cards*, Advances in Cryptology, Crypto'89, Lecture Notes in Comput. Sci. **435** (1990) 239–251.
14. C. P. Schnorr, *Efficient signature generation by smart cards*, Journal of Cryptology **4** (1991) 161–174.
15. U. Vazirani, Randomness, adversaries and computations, Ph.D. thesis, UC Berkeley, 1986.
16. S.-M. Yen, C. Laih, A. K. Lenstra, *A note on multi-exponentiation*, IEE Proceedings, Computers and digital techniques **141** (1994).

Appendix

Because this method does not seem to be generally known, we review an efficient and division-free method to compute $n^{-1} \bmod p$ for odd p and n with $0 < n < p$ and p and n co-prime:

Binary extended Euclidean algorithm. Let $n_1 = n$, $m_1 = 1$, $n_2 = p$, and $m_2 = 0$. Throughout the algorithm we have that $m_i \cdot n \equiv n_i \bmod p$, for $i = 1, 2$. First, as long as n_1 is even, replace n_1 by $n_1/2$ and m_1 by $m_1/2 \bmod p$ (because p is odd, dividing m_1 by 2 modulo p can be done either by right-shifting m_1 if m_1 is even, or by right-shifting $m_1 + p$ if m_1 is odd). Next, perform steps (1) through (6), until the algorithm terminates:

1. If n_1 equals 1, return $m_1 = n^{-1} \bmod p$ and terminate;
2. If n_1 equals n_2 then n and p are not co-prime: report failure and terminate;
3. If $n_1 < n_2$ swap n_1 and n_2 and swap m_1 and m_2;
4. Replace n_1 by $n_1 - n_2$ and replace m_1 by $m_1 - m_2$ (note that the resulting n_1 is even);
5. Replace n_1 by $n_1/2$ and m_1 by $m_1/2 \bmod p$;
6. If n_1 is even return to Step (5), otherwise return to Step (1).

This binary extended Euclidean algorithm is much more efficient than the standard extended Euclidean algorithm when applied to B-bit integers. As mentioned in the footnote in Section 4, however, it is less efficient than Lehmer's inversion when applied to 160-bit or larger integers. Note that for B-bit integers Lehmer's inversion is identical to the standard extended Euclidean algorithm.

A Fast Software Implementation for Arithmetic Operations in $GF(2^n)$

Erik De Win*, Antoon Bosselaers, Servaas Vandenberghe,
Peter De Gersem*, Joos Vandewalle

Katholieke Universiteit Leuven, ESAT-COSIC
K. Mercierlaan 94, B-3001 Heverlee, Belgium
tel. +32-16-32.10.50, fax. +32-16-32.19.86
{erik.dewin,antoon.bosselaers,servaas.vandenberghe,
peter.degersem,joos.vandewalle}@esat.kuleuven.ac.be

Abstract. We present a software implementation of arithmetic operations in a finite field $GF(2^n)$, based on an alternative representation of the field elements. An important application is in elliptic curve cryptosystems. Whereas previously reported implementations of elliptic curve cryptosystems use a standard basis or an optimal normal basis to perform field operations, we represent the field elements as polynomials with coefficients in the smaller field $GF(2^{16})$. Calculations in this smaller field are carried out using pre-calculated lookup tables. This results in rather simple routines matching the structure of computer memory very well. The use of an irreducible trinomial as the field polynomial, as was proposed at Crypto'95 by R. Schroeppel et al., can be extended to this representation. In our implementation, the resulting routines are slightly faster than standard basis routines.

1 Introduction

Elliptic curve public key cryptosystems are rapidly gaining popularity [M93]. The use of the group of points of an elliptic curve in cryptography was first suggested by Victor Miller [M85] and Neal Koblitz [K87]. The main advantage of using this particular group is that its discrete logarithm problem seems to be much harder than in other candidate groups (e.g., the multiplicative group of a finite field). The reason is that the various subexponential algorithms that exist for these groups up to now cannot be applied to elliptic curves. The best known algorithm for computing logarithms on a non-supersingular (see [M93]) elliptic curve is the Pohlig-Hellman attack [PH78]. Because of the difficulty of the discrete logarithm problem, the length of blocks and keys can be considerably smaller, typically about 200 bits.

Although the group of points of an elliptic curve can be defined over any field, the finite fields $GF(2^n)$ of characteristic 2 are of particular interest for cryptosystems, because they give rise to very efficient implementations in both hardware

---

* N.F.W.O. research assistant, sponsored by the National Fund for Scientific Research (Belgium).

(e.g., [AMV93]) and software (e.g., [HMV92] and [SOOS95]). The group operation consists of a number of elementary arithmetic operations in the underlying field: addition/subtraction, squaring, multiplication, and inverse calculation. The speed with which these elementary operations can be executed is a crucial factor in the throughput of encryption/decryption and signature generation/verification.

To do calculations in a finite field $GF(2^n)$, the field elements are represented in a basis. Most implementations use either a standard basis or an optimal normal basis. In a *standard basis*, field elements are represented as polynomials of the form $a_0 + a_1 x + \cdots + a_{n-1} x^{n-1}$, where all a_i are elements of $GF(2)$, i.e., they are 0 or 1, and addition is done modulo 2. Field operations on these elements consist of operations on polynomials, e.g., a field multiplication can be calculated as a multiplication of polynomials followed by a reduction of the result modulo a fixed irreducible polynomial of degree n. In a *normal basis* an element is represented as $b_0 \beta + b_1 \beta^2 + b_2 \beta^{2^2} + \cdots + b_{n-1} \beta^{2^{n-1}}$, where β is a fixed element of the field and all b_i are elements of $GF(2)$. A normal base allows for a very fast squaring; multiplication is more complex than in standard basis, but this does not deteriorate efficiency if an *optimal* normal basis [MOVW88] is used. The optimal normal basis representation seems to be more appropriate for hardware, but the fastest software implementations that have been reported (e.g., [SOOS95]) use a standard basis.

The implementation presented in this paper uses a third representation of field elements that has some advantages in software. Before introducing this representation in Sect. 3, we describe elliptic curve operations in a little more detail in Sect. 2. In Sect. 4 we discuss field operations in the new representation and we compare them to standard basis in Sect. 5. We conclude the paper with some timing results.

Part of the results in this paper are based on [DD95] and [V96].

2 The Elliptic Curve Group Operation

An elliptic curve is the set of solutions (x, y) of a bivariate cubic equation over a field. In the context of public key cryptosystems, the field is often $GF(2^n)$ and the equation is of the form $y^2 + xy = x^3 + ax^2 + b$, where a and b are elements of the field and $b \neq 0$. An "addition"-operation can be defined on the set of solutions if the *point at infinity* O is added to this set. Let $P = (x_1, y_1)$ be an element with $P \neq O$, then the inverse of P is $-P = (x_1, x_1 + y_1)$. Let $Q = (x_2, y_2)$ be a second element with $Q \neq O$ and $Q \neq -P$ then the sum $P + Q = (x_3, y_3)$ can be calculated as (see e.g., [SOOS95]):

$$x_3 = \lambda^2 + \lambda + x_1 + x_2 + a$$
$$y_3 = \lambda(x_1 + x_3) + x_3 + y_1$$
$$\lambda = \frac{y_1 + y_2}{x_1 + x_2} .$$

These formulas are valid only if $P \neq Q$; for $P = Q$ they are a little different:

$$x_3 = \lambda^2 + \lambda + a$$
$$y_3 = x_1^2 + (\lambda + 1)x_3$$
$$\lambda = x_1 + \frac{y_1}{x_1} \ .$$

The point at infinity O serves as the identity element. A multiple of P, i.e., P multiplied by a natural number k, can be calculated by repeated doubling and adding. The inverse operation of this, i.e., deriving k when P and kP are given, is the elliptic curve discrete log problem, which is considered to be a very hard operation, since its running time is approximately $\mathcal{O}(2^{n/2})$.

The equations show that an elliptic curve addition can be calculated with a number of additions, multiplications, squarings, and inversions in the underlying field $GF(2^n)$. We will see that the addition and squaring of elements of $GF(2^n)$ are simple operations and that they require negligible time relative to the multiplication and inversion. Thus, doubling a point or adding two points on an elliptic curve takes approximately two field multiplications and one field inversion.

In an actual implementation of an elliptic curve cryptosystem, other operations are needed as well. E.g., a quadratic equation has to be solved when *point compression* [MV96] is applied. Some cryptographic algorithms require the order of the group to be known, which can be calculated by Schoof's algorithm [S85] or one of its improved versions [LM95]. However, we will concentrate in this paper on basic arithmetic operations in $GF(2^n)$: addition, squaring, multiplication, and inversion.

3   An Alternative Representation for the Field Elements

It is well known that a field can be considered as a vector space over one of its subfields. The proper subfields of $GF(2^n)$ are the fields $GF(2^r)$, with $r|n$ and $0 < r < n$. Most implementations take $r = 1$, i.e., they choose a basis $\{\gamma_0, \gamma_1, \ldots, \gamma_{n-1}\} \subset GF(2^n)$ and the field elements are represented as $a_0\gamma_0 + a_1\gamma_1 + \cdots + a_{n-1}\gamma_{n-1}$, where all $a_i \in GF(2)$. The software implementations in this kind of bases are characterized by a large number of bitwise operations, e.g., testing a single bit and shifting a word over a number of bits. Although these operations are available, standard microprocessors are more suited for word operations.

Generally, r can be chosen to be any divisor of n. In [HMV92] a polynomial basis over $GF(2^8)$ is suggested. We examined the slightly more general case where r is a multiple of 8. This limits the possible values of n to multiples of r, but if r is not too large, this causes no practical limitation.

In principle there are no restrictions on the kind of basis that is used (polynomial, normal ...). Although more work has to be done on this, we believe that a polynomial basis is most suited because a number of the advantages of (optimal) normal bases disappear when $r > 1$.

If we define $m = n/r$, then an element of $GF(2^n)$ can be represented as a polynomial $\alpha_0 + \alpha_1 x + \cdots + \alpha_{m-1} x^{m-1}$, where the α_i are elements of $GF(2^r)$. An important benefit of this basis is that each coefficient is represented by r bits and fits nicely in a computer word if $r = 8$, 16, or 32 (or even 64 on 64-bit processors). Arithmetic with these polynomials is identical to that with ordinary polynomials, except that operations on the coefficients are carried out in $GF(2^r)$.

To calculate in $GF(2^r)$, a basis has to be chosen too, but this can be simplified by the use of lookup tables. After choosing a particular basis for $GF(2^r)$, we look for a generator γ and calculate all pairs (α, i) such that $\alpha = \gamma^i$ ($\alpha \in GF(2^r) \setminus \{0\}$; $0 \le i < 2^r - 1$). These pairs are stored in two tables: a log-table sorted on α and an alog-table sorted on i. Each of them takes about 2^r words of r bits, resulting in a total memory requirement of about 512 bytes for $r = 8$ and 256 Kbytes for $r = 16$. The option $r = 32$ (and a fortiori $r = 64$) is excluded because of excessive memory needs. These tables can be used to efficiently calculate in $GF(2^r)$, e.g., the product of two elements $\alpha, \beta \in GF(2^r) \setminus \{0\}$ is

$$\alpha\beta = \texttt{alog}[(\texttt{log}[\alpha] + \texttt{log}[\beta]) \bmod (2^r - 1)] \ ,$$

and also an inversion operation can be calculated with only two table lookups:

$$\alpha^{-1} = \texttt{alog}[-\texttt{log}[\alpha] \bmod (2^r - 1)] \ .$$

If we want polynomials to represent finite field elements, all operations have to be done modulo a fixed irreducible polynomial of degree m. In principle this polynomial can also have coefficients in $GF(2^r)$, but if we can find an irreducible polynomial with coefficients in $GF(2) \subset GF(2^r)$, many table lookups can be saved in the reduction operation. The search for such an irreducible polynomial can be simplified by using the fact that an m-th degree polynomial that is irreducible over $GF(2)$, is also irreducible over $GF(2^r)$ if $\gcd(m, r) = 1$ [LN83, p. 107]. This limits m to odd numbers because r is a power of 2. We will show that the reduction operation can be speeded up even further if an irreducible *trinomial* is used [SOOS95], where the requirements for the middle term are a little different than in [SOOS95]. These special irreducible polynomials are easy to find, Table 1 lists all irreducible trinomials $1 + x^t + x^m$ with $7 \le m \le 15$ and $t \le \lfloor m/2 \rfloor$.[3]

4   Field Operations

In a polynomial basis, field operations are reduced to operations on polynomials. E.g., a field multiplication consists of a multiplication of the two polynomials representing the multiplicands, followed by a reduction of the result modulo the irreducible polynomial. Therefore, we will consider mainly operations on polynomials.

---

[3] It is easy to show that $1 + x^t + x^m$ is irreducible iff $1 + x^{m-t} + x^m$ is irreducible.

Table 1. List of all irreducible trinomials $1 + x^t + x^m$ with $7 \leq m \leq 15$ and $t \leq \lfloor m/2 \rfloor$. The corresponding field size is given for $r = 16$.

degree	field size	trinomial
7	112	$1 + x + x^7$ $1 + x^3 + x^7$
9	144	$1 + x + x^9$ $1 + x^4 + x^9$
11	176	$1 + x^2 + x^{11}$
15	240	$1 + x + x^{15}$ $1 + x^4 + x^{15}$ $1 + x^7 + x^{15}$
17	272	$1 + x^3 + x^{17}$ $1 + x^5 + x^{17}$ $1 + x^6 + x^{17}$

4.1 Representation of Polynomials in Memory

It is natural to store the coefficients of a polynomial in consecutive r-bit words of computer memory. To keep the routines as general as possible, we also used one word to store the length of the polynomial. In summary, a k-th degree polynomial A is stored in an array of length $k + 2$, where the first array-element A_0 contains the number of coefficients $k + 1$ (rather than the degree k), A_1 contains the constant coefficient, ... and $A_{k+1} = A_{A_0}$ contains the coefficient of the highest power of x. A zero polynomial is represented by $A_0 = 0$.

4.2 Addition

Addition in a finite field with characteristic 2 is easy: just add the corresponding bits modulo 2. Note that addition and subtraction modulo 2 are the same operations; they both correspond to a binary exclusive or (exor, $\oplus$) operation.

4.3 Multiplication

Multiplication of polynomials can be done using the shift-and-add method, where the addition is replaced by an exor. Below is an algorithm that computes the product of A and B and stores it in C (the notation of Sect. 4.1 is used).

```
1  if A_0 = 0 or B_0 = 0 then
2     C_0 = 0
3  else {
```

```
4      initialize C to zero
5      for i = 1 to A₀ do
6        if Aᵢ ≠ 0 then
7          for j = 1 to B₀ do
8            if Bⱼ ≠ 0 then
9              C_{i+j-1} = C_{i+j-1} ⊕ alog[(log[Aᵢ] + log[Bⱼ]) mod (2ʳ - 1)]
10     C₀ = A₀ + B₀ - 1
11  }
```

This is a very simple algorithm, although it might look a little complicated with the tests $A_i \neq 0$ and $B_j \neq 0$, which are necessary because the log of zero is undefined. No bit manipulations are needed. The complexity is linear in the product of the lengths of the multiplicands.

A number of optimizations are possible in an actual implementation. E.g., when the test in line 6 is successful, $\log[A_i]$ can be stored in a register during the execution of the inner loop. Also, the log's of the words of B can be stored in a temporary array at the beginning of the algorithm to reduce the number of table lookups in the inner loop.

4.4 Squaring

The square of a polynomial with coefficients in $GF(2^r)$ can be calculated in a more efficient way than multiplying it by itself. The reason is that the square of a sum equals the sum of the squares because the cross-term vanishes modulo 2. The square of a polynomial is then given by

$$\left(\sum_{i=0}^{m-1} \alpha_i x^i\right)^2 = \sum_{i=0}^{m-1} \alpha_i^2 x^{2i} \ .$$

This results in the following algorithm to compute $B = A^2$.

```
if A₀ = 0 then
    B₀ = 0
else {
    for i = 1 to A₀ - 1 do {
        if Aᵢ ≠ 0 then
            B_{2i-1} = alog[2 log[Aᵢ] mod (2ʳ - 1)]
        else
            B_{2i-1} = 0
        B_{2i} = 0
    }
    B_{2A₀-1} = alog[2 log[A_{A₀}] mod (2ʳ - 1)]
    B₀ = 2A₀ - 1
}
```

The complexity of this algorithm is linear in the length of the argument. For practical lengths it is much faster than multiplication.

4.5 Modular Reduction

In most cases, the result of a polynomial multiplication or squaring has to be reduced modulo an irreducible polynomial. In general, a reduction of a polynomial A modulo a polynomial B will cancel the highest power of A, say A_i, by adding (or subtracting) a multiple of B of the form $\alpha B x^{i-B_0}$ to A, where $\alpha = A_i B_{B_0}^{-1}$. This operation is repeated for decreasing values of i, until the degree of A is smaller than the degree of B.

A much simpler algorithm is obtained when B is a trinomial with coefficients in $GF(2)$, because the calculation of α and αB is considerably simplified. The resulting algorithm is given below. A is the polynomial to be reduced, m is the degree, and t is the middle term of the irreducible trinomial, i.e., all B_i are zero, except for B_1, B_{t+1} and B_{m+1}, which are 1.

```
for i = A_0 downto m' do {
    A_{i-m} = A_{i-m} ⊕ A_i
    A_{i+t-m} = A_{i+t-m} ⊕ A_i
    A_i = 0
}
update A_0
```

Each time the loop is executed, r bits of A are cancelled. If the word length of the processor, denoted by w, is larger than r, then it is more efficient to eliminate w bits at the same time, but this induces some restrictions on the trinomial. E.g., if $r = 16$ and $w = 32$, A_i and A_{i-1} can be eliminated in one loop-operation if there is no overlap between A_{i-1} and A_{i+t-m}. This condition is satisfied if $m - t \geq w/r$.

4.6 Inversion

In general $B = A^{-1} \bmod M$ iff there exists an X such that $BA + XM = 1$, where A, B, X and M are polynomials in our case. B (and also X) can be computed with an extension of Euclid's algorithm for finding the greatest common divisor, a high level description of which is given below (deg() denotes the degree of a polynomial).

initialize polynomials $B = 1$, $C = 0$, $F = A$ and $G = M$

```
1   if deg(F) = 0 then return B/F₁
2   if deg(F) < deg(G) then exchange F,G and exchange B,C
3   j = deg(F) - deg(G),  α = F_{F₀}/G_{G₀}
4   F = F + αx^j G,  B = B + αx^j C
5   goto 1
```

This algorithm maintains the invariant relationships $F = BA + XM$ and $G = CA + YM$ (there is no need to store X and Y). In each iteration the degree of the longer of F and G is decreased by adding an appropriate multiple of the shorter.

The invariant relationships are preserved by performing the same operation on B and C. These operations are repeated until F or G is a constant polynomial.

In step 4 of this algorithm, the degree of F is decreased by at least one unit, but there is also a chance that the second-highest power of x is cancelled in F, etc. If all F_i can be considered as random, it can be shown that the degree of F is lowered by $q/(q-1)$ on average, where $q = 2^r$ is the size of the subfield. This number equals 2 for a standard basis, but quickly approximates 1 for larger subfields. On the other hand, for fixed n, convergence is faster for larger r, because in each step the length of A is decreased by about r bits. Therefore this algorithm is faster in a polynomial basis over $GF(2^r)$ than in a standard basis.

In [SOOS95] the *almost inverse* algorithm is proposed to calculate inverses in standard basis. It finds a polynomial B and an integer k satisfying $BA + XM = x^k$. The inverse can be found by dividing x^k into B modulo M. The algorithm can be generalized to polynomials over larger subfields. A high level description is given below.

initialize integer $k = 0$, and polynomials $B = 1$, $C = 0$, $F = A$, $G = M$

```
0   while F contains factor x do F = F/x, C = Cx, k = k+1
1   if deg(F) = 0 then return B/F₁, k
2   if deg(F) < deg(G) then exchange F,G and exchange B,C
3   α = F₀/G₀
4   F = F + αG, B = B + αC
5   goto 0
```

The algorithm maintains the invariant relationships $x^k F = BA + XM$ and $x^k G = CA + YM$ (again, there is no need to store X and Y). Line 0 removes any factor x from F while preserving the invariant relationships. Note that after line 0 neither F nor G have a factor x. Line 2 makes sure that $\deg(F) \geq \deg(G)$. Line 4 is crucial: it adds a multiple of G to F (and the same multiple of C to B and implicitly the same multiple of Y to X to preserve the invariant relationships), such that F has a factor x again, which will be extracted in the next loop.

When analyzing the almost inverse algorithm, we observe that its behaviour is very similar to the Euclidean algorithm given above. The main difference is that it cancels powers of x from lower degree to higher degree, whereas the Euclidean algorithm moves from higher degree to lower degree. In standard basis, the former has two important benefits. Firstly, many bitwise shift operations are saved in line 4 because there is no multiplication by x^j. Secondly, if $\deg(F) = \deg(G)$ before line 4, which happens in roughly 20 % of the cases, the addition of G will decrease the degree of F. This reduces the number of iterations and hence the execution time.

These two advantages of the almost inverse algorithm are irrelevant for polynomials over larger subfields: there are no bitwise shift operations and, if $\deg(F) = \deg(G)$, the probability that the degree of F is decreased in line 4 is very small (approximately $1/q$). The somewhat surprising conclusion is that the Euclidean algorithm and the almost inverse algorithm have a comparable speed for polynomials over $GF(2^r)$, the former is even slightly more efficient because there is no division by x^k.

5 Comparison with Standard Basis

An important advantage of working with coefficients in $GF(2^r)$ is that no bit operations are needed. A disadvantage is that the word size is limited because of the memory requirements for the lookup tables. This limitation can be bypassed in the modular reduction and in the final division step after the almost inverse algorithm, but for the multiplication and the almost inverse algorithm, which represent the majority of the total execution time of an elliptic curve addition, we see no obvious way to handle w bits in one step. Therefore, an increase in processor word size is likely to result in a larger speed gain for standard basis implementations than for implementations based on polynomials over $GF(2^r)$.

We compare our multiplication algorithm in a little more detail to the basic multiplication algorithm in standard basis given below. We use $<<$ and $>>$ to denote a bitwise shift-operation to the left and to the right respectively, and we let the line numbers start from 21 to avoid confusion with the multiplication algorithm of Sect. 4.3.

```
21 if A₀ = 0 or B₀ = 0 then
22    C₀ = 0
23 else {
24    for i = 1 to A₀ do
25       for j = 0 to w − 1 do
26          if j-th bit of Aᵢ is 1 then {
27             lower = B₁ << j
28             higher = B₁ >> (w − j)
29             Cᵢ = Cᵢ ⊕ lower
30             for k = 2 to B₀ do {
31                C_{k+i−1} = C_{k+i−1} ⊕ higher
32                lower = B_k << j
33                higher = B_k >> (w − j)
34                C_{k+i−1} = C_{k+i−1} ⊕ lower
35             }
36             C_{B₀+i} = C_{B₀+i} ⊕ lower
37          }
38    update C₀
39 }
```

The loop formed by lines 24 and 25 is iterated n times. The test on line 26 is successful in 50 % of the cases on average, such that the loop on lines 30 to 35 is executed $n/2$ times. This loop runs over n/w values, such that lines 31 to 34 are executed $n^2/(2w)$ times. In the multiplication algorithm of Sect. 4.3, the loop on line 5 is iterated n/r times and the test on line 6 is almost always true (i.e., with probability $(2^r − 1)/2^r$). The same reasoning can be repeated for lines 7 and 8, such that the inner loop on line 9 is executed about $(n/r)^2$ times. So we can state approximately that the algorithm in Sect. 4.3 will be faster if executing line 9 once takes less time than executing lines 31 to 34 $r^2/(2w)$ times (for $r = 16$ and $w = 32$ this factor equals 4). Which one is faster depends heavily on the programming language, compiler, microprocessor, and cache size. Similar comparisons can be made for the inversion (the other field operations constitute only a negligible part of the execution time of an elliptic curve operation).

Note that the standard basis algorithm given above can be optimized further. One important optimization, which we used for our timings, is to precalculate a table of shifted versions of B to avoid the shift operations in the inner loop.

6 Timings

We timed our routines for $r = 8$ and $r = 16$. For $r = 8$ the lookup tables take only 512 bytes and will fit in the first-level cache memory of any present day microprocessor; for $r = 16$ this is not the case, but the number of words is smaller for fixed n. The latter was considerably faster in our tests, therefore we will only give timings for this case.

The routines were written in ANSI-C. We used the WATCOM C 10.6 compiler and executed the tests in protected mode on a Pentium/133 based PC. Table 2 gives detailed timing results for $GF(2^{177})$ in standard basis and $GF(2^{176})$ in a polynomial basis over $GF(2^{16})$. We used an irreducible trinomial for the modular reduction and inversion. For standard basis, the word size w equals 32 bits. The listed figures are for the fastest routines, e.g., the almost inverse algorithm for standard basis and the extended Euclidean algorithm for polynomials over $GF(2^{16})$. All routines have a comparable optimization level, although we put a little less effort in the reduction, squaring and addition routines, since they have a minor impact on the overall elliptic curve operations.

Table 2 also contains timing estimates for some elliptic curve operations. These estimates were calculated by adding the times needed for the various suboperations. For the exponentiation (i.e., the repeated elliptic curve group operation), a simple double-and-add/subtract algorithm was assumed. With this algorithm, 176 doublings and on average 59 additions/subtractions are needed for one exponentiation.

The figures in table 2 show a small but significant advantage for the representation of the field elements as polynomials over $GF(2^{16})$. However, the proportions might change and even be reversed depending on the implementation, computer platform, field size, optimization level, etc. In addition to the possible speed gain, the routines for this alternative representation tend to be more readable and less error prone than for standard basis.

7 Conclusion

We have presented a software implementation of basic arithmetic operations in finite fields of characteristic 2. We have shown that other representations than

Table 2. Times for basic operations on polynomials over GF(2) and over GF(2^{16}). The lengths of the polynomials are suited for field operations in GF(2^{177}) and GF(2^{176}) respectively. The tests were run on a Pentium/133 based PC using the WATCOM 10.6 ANSI-C compiler.

	standard basis	pol. over GF(2^{16})
mult. 177/176 bits × 177/176 bits	71.8 μs	62.7 μs
inversion 177/176 bits	225 μs	160 μs
mod. red. 353/351 bits to 177/176 bits	8.1 μs	1.8 μs
squaring 177/176 bits	2.7 μs	5.9 μs
addition 177/176 bits	1.1 μs	1.2 μs
EC addition (est.)	404 μs	306 μs
EC doubling (est.)	411 μs	309 μs
EC exponentiation 177 bit exponent (est.)	96 ms	72 ms

standard basis and (optimal) normal basis can be used and can have some important benefits. An interesting result is that the almost inverse algorithm offers no advantages for calculating inverses of polynomials over a subfield larger than GF(2).

Acknowledgment

We would like to thank R. Schroeppel for helpful comments on his Crypto'95 paper.

References

[AMV93]   G.B. Agnew, R.C. Mullin and S.A. Vanstone, "An implementation of elliptic curve cryptosystems over $F_{2^{155}}$," *IEEE Journal on Selected Areas in Communications*, Vol. 11, no. 5 (June 1993), pp. 804–813.

[BCH93]   H. Brunner, A. Curiger and M. Hofstetter, "On computing multiplicative inverses in GF(2^n)," *IEEE Transactions on Computers*, Vol. 42, no. 8 (1993), pp. 1010–1015.

[DD95]   E. De Win and P. De Gersem, *Studie en implementatie van arithmetische bewerkingen in GF(2^n)*, Master Thesis K.U.Leuven, 1995. (in Dutch)

[HMV92]   G. Harper, A. Menezes and S. Vanstone, "Public-key cryptosystems with very small key lengths," *Advances in Cryptology, Proc. Eurocrypt'92, LNCS 658*, R.A. Rueppel, Ed., Springer-Verlag, 1993, pp. 163–173.

[K87]   N. Koblitz, "Elliptic curve cryptosystems," *Mathematics of Computation*, Vol. 48, no. 177 (1987), pp. 203–209.

[LM95]   R. Lercier and F. Morain, "Counting the number of points on el-
           liptic curves over finite fields: strategies and performances," *Ad-
           vances in Cryptology, Proc. Eurocrypt'95, LNCS 921*, L.C. Guillou and
           J.J. Quisquater, Eds., Springer-Verlag, 1995, pp. 79–94.

[LN83]   R. Lidl and H. Niederreiter, *Finite fields*, Addison-Wesley, Reading,
           Mass., 1983.

[M93]   A. Menezes, *Elliptic curve public key cryptosystems*, Kluwer Academic
           Publishers, 1993.

[M85]   V.S. Miller, "Use of elliptic curves in cryptography," *Advances in Crypto-
           logy, Proc. Crypto'85, LNCS 218*, H.C. Williams, Ed., Springer-Verlag,
           1985, pp. 417–426.

[MOVW88]   R. Mullin, I. Onyszchuk, S. Vanstone and R. Wilson, "Optimal normal
           bases in $GF(p^n)$," *Discrete Applied Mathematics*, Vol. 22 (1988/89),
           pp. 149–161.

[MV96]   A. Menezes and S. Vanstone, "Standard for RSA, Diffie-Hellman and re-
           lated public key cryptography," Working draft of IEEE P1363 Standard,
           Elliptic Curve Systems, February 15, 1996.

[PH78]   S. Pohlig and M. Hellman, "An improved algorithm for computing logar-
           ithms over $GF(p)$ and its cryptographic significance," *IEEE Transactions
           on Information Theory*, Vol. 24 (1978), pp. 106–110.

[S85]   R. Schoof, "Elliptic curves over finite fields and the computation of square
           roots mod p," *Mathematics of Computation*, Vol. 44 (1985), pp. 483–494.

[SOOS95]   R. Schroeppel, H. Orman, S. O'Malley and O. Spatscheck, "Fast key ex-
           change with elliptic curve systems," *Advances in Cryptology, Proc.
           Crypto'95, LNCS 963*, D. Coppersmith, Ed., Springer-Verlag, 1995,
           pp. 43–56.

[V96]   S. Vandenberghe, *Snelle basisbewerkingen voor publieke sleutelsystemen
           gebaseerd op elliptische curven over* $GF(2^n)$, Master Thesis K.U.Leuven,
           1996. (in Dutch)

Hash Functions Based on Block Ciphers and Quaternary Codes*

Lars Knudsen and Bart Preneel**

Katholieke Universiteit Leuven, Dept. Electrical Engineering-ESAT,
Kardinaal Mercierlaan 94, B–3001 Heverlee, Belgium
{lars.knudsen,bart.preneel}@esat.kuleuven.ac.be

Abstract. We consider constructions for cryptographic hash functions based on m-bit block ciphers. First we present a new attack on the LOKI-DBH mode: the attack finds collisions in $2^{3m/4}$ encryptions, which should be compared to 2^m encryptions for a brute force attack. This attack breaks the last remaining subclass in a wide class of efficient hash functions which have been proposed in the literature. We then analyze hash functions based on a collision resistant compression function for which finding a collision requires at least 2^m encryptions, providing a lower bound of the complexity of collisions of the hash function. A new class of constructions is proposed, based on error correcting codes over $GF(2^2)$ and a proof of security is given, which relates their security to that of single block hash functions. For example, a compression function is presented which requires about 4 encryptions to hash an m-bit block, and for which finding a collision requires at least 2^m encryptions. This scheme has the same hash rate as MDC-4, but better security against collision attacks. Our method can be used to construct compression functions with even higher levels of security at the cost of more internal memory.

1 Introduction

Hash functions are functions which map a string of arbitrary size to a short string of fixed length (typically 128...160 bits). Hash functions which satisfy security properties (collision resistance, second preimage resistance, and preimage resistance) are widely used in cryptographic applications such as digital signatures, password protection schemes, and conventional message authentication.

We consider hash functions based on block ciphers with block length and key length both equal to m bits. Such a block cipher defines, for each m-bit key, a permutation on m-bit strings. The main argument to construct hash functions based on block ciphers is the minimization of the design and implementation effort. Additionally, the trust in existing block ciphers can be transferred to hash functions. These arguments are historically very important (DES [10] was

---

* The work in this paper was initiated while the authors were visiting the Isaac Newton Institute, Cambridge, U.K., February 1996

** N.F.W.O. postdoctoral researcher, sponsored by the National Fund for Scientific Research (Belgium).

seen as a main building block for practical cryptography), and have gained more importance due to the recent cryptanalytical successes achieved by H. Dobbertin [7, 8] on custom designed hash functions such as MD4 [26] and MD5 [27].

The main disadvantage of this approach is that specific hash functions are likely to be more efficient. One also has to take into account that legal restrictions on the use and import or export of hash functions might be weaker than those applying to encryption algorithms. Finally, block ciphers may exhibit some weaknesses that are only important if they are used in a hashing mode. The (semi)-weak keys of DES and the corresponding fixed points [20], and the key schedule weakness of SAFER [13] are good illustrations of this fact.

We define the *hash rate* of a hash function based on an m-bit block cipher as the number of m-bit message blocks processed per encryption or decryption.

After the publication of several weak proposals in the late 1970s, the first secure constructions for a hash function based on a block cipher were the scheme by Matyas, Meyer, and Oseas [18] and its dual, which is widely known as the Davies-Meyer scheme[1]. Both schemes have rate 1, and give a hash result of only m bits (which explains the name *single block length hash functions*). Finding a collision for such a scheme using the birthday paradox [30] requires about $2^{m/2}$ encryptions, while finding a (second) preimage requires about 2^m encryptions. Later it was shown that there exist essentially two secure single block length hash functions in this model, and that 12 different schemes can be obtained by applying a linear transformation to the inputs [24]. One of these schemes has been specified in ISO/IEC 10118 [12].

Since most block ciphers have a block length of $m = 64$ bits, the need for *double block length* hash functions became apparent. The goal of these constructions is to achieve a security level against brute force collision attacks of at least 2^m encryptions. Three main classes of hash functions have been proposed:

- Hash functions with rate 1 and with an internal memory of $2m$ bits; most of these constructions have been broken (see for example [14]), a notable exception being the LOKI-DBH mode proposed at Auscrypt'90 [4]. In this paper it will be shown that a collision attack for this hash function requires only $2^{3m/4}$ encryptions; the attack is more general and shows that there are no hash functions in this class for which finding a collision requires more than $2^{3m/4}$ operations.
- MDC-2 (rate 1/2) and MDC-4 (rate 1/4) [2]; their security to brute force collision attacks is about 2^m encryptions, and to preimage attacks about $2^{3m/2}$ respectively 2^{2m} encryptions. For the important practical case of DES, $m = 64$, but the key is only 56 bits long; a collision search requires then only 2^{55} encryptions for both schemes, and a preimage can be obtained after 2^{83} respectively 2^{109} encryptions [22]. A further generalization of MDC-2 has been included in ISO/IEC 10118 [12].
- Merkle's schemes, the best of which has rate 0.276 (for a 64-bit block cipher with a 56-bit key) [19]. A security proof is given which assumes that the

---

[1] This scheme was apparently known to Meyer and Matyas ca 1979.

underlying single block length hash function is secure. If DES is used, the rate becomes about 0.266, and finding a collision requires at least 2^{56} operations [19, 22]. A practical disadvantage are the inconvenient block sizes.

In summary, the known constructions do not provide an acceptable security level against parallel brute force collision attacks: it follows from [25, 28] that a security level of at least $2^{75} \ldots 2^{80}$ encryptions is required, which is not offered by any of the current proposals. Moreover, a similar or higher security level for preimage attacks would be desirable as well.

In this paper we try to resolve this problem by proposing a new efficient construction for a hash function based on a block cipher for which finding a collision requires at least $2^{qm/2}$ encryptions (with $q \geq 2$), and finding a preimage requires at least 2^{qm} encryptions. For $q = 2$, the constructions are more efficient than existing proposals with the same security level. The new constructions result in a parallelizable hash function, the security of which can be related to that of the well known single block length hash functions. The basic ingredients of the scheme will be the use of a larger internal memory and a quaternary error correcting code.

The remainder of this paper is organized as follows. In §2 we review a general model and some properties of hash functions. §3 gives the new attack on the LOKI-DBH mode. In §4 it is shown that extending the existing schemes to triple and quadruple solutions does not result in an improved security level. Our new construction for a hash function based on block ciphers is presented in §5, and §6 contains the conclusions.

2 Hash Functions

A *hash function* is an easily implementable mapping from the set of all binary sequences to the set of binary sequences of some fixed length. Almost all hash functions described in the literature are *iterated hash functions*, i.e., they are based on an easily computable function $h(\cdot, \cdot)$ from two binary sequences of respective lengths m and l to a binary sequence of length m. The message M is split into blocks M_i of l bits or $M = (M_1, M_2, \ldots, M_n)$. If the length of M is not a multiple of l, M is padded using an unambiguous padding rule. The value H_n of length m is obtained by computing iteratively

$$H_i = h(H_{i-1}, M_i) \qquad i = 1, 2, \ldots, t, \tag{1}$$

where H_0 is a specified *initial value* denoted with IV. The function h is called the *compression function* or the hash round function. The *hash result* is then obtained by applying an output transformation g to H_n, or $\text{Hash}(IV, M) = H = g(H_t)$. Note that the output transformation is often the identity function.

The theoretical work on the security of hash functions has concentrated on the reduction of the security of $\text{Hash}(\cdot)$ to that of $h(\cdot, \cdot)$ [5, 16, 19, 21]. For these reductions to work in practice, we need to append an additional block at the end of the input string which contains its length. This operation, proposed independently by R. Merkle [19] and I. Damgård [5] is known as MD-strengthening. If MD-strengthening is used, one can prove the following connection between the security of a hash function and of its compression function.

Theorem 1. *Let* Hash($\cdot$) *be an iterated hash function with MD-strengthening. Then preimage and collision attacks on* Hash($\cdot, \cdot$) *(where an attacker can choose IV freely) have about the same complexity as the corresponding attacks on* $h(\cdot, \cdot)$.

Note that in practical applications, the *IV* of a hash function is fixed in the specifications. This might lead to a higher security level; Theorem 1 gives a lower bound on the security of Hash($IV, \cdot$).

The use of a secure compression function $h(\cdot, \cdot)$ allows for the replacement of the iterative construction by a parallelizable tree construction [5].

In view of the above, it is remarkable that most practical hash functions do not have a collision resistant compression function (the most important exceptions are the DES based hash functions of R. Merkle [19]). For the first class of hash functions (as discussed in §1) it was shown that collisions for the compression function require at most $2^{m/2}$ encryptions [11]; the same result was proved for a large class of related hash functions of rate 1/2. Collisions for the compression function of MDC-2 and MDC-4 can be found in time respectively 2^{28} and 2^{41} [22]. Collisions for the compression function of MD5 have been presented in [6, 8].

In the following $E_Z(X)$ denotes the encryption of the m-bit plaintext X under the m-bit key Z, and $D_Z(Y)$ denotes the decryption of the m-bit ciphertext Y under the m-bit key Z. It will be assumed that the block cipher has no weaknesses, i.e., for every key it can be modeled as a random permutation (see for example [19]).

3   Attacks on LOKI-DBH

Consider the following general form of a double block length hash function:

$$\begin{cases} H_i^1 = E_A(B) \oplus C \\ H_i^2 = E_R(S) \oplus T \end{cases} \tag{2}$$

For a scheme of hash rate 1, A, B, and C are binary linear combinations of the m-bit vectors H_{i-1}^1, H_{i-1}^2, M_i^1, and M_i^2, and R, S, and T are binary linear combinations of the vectors H_{i-1}^1, H_{i-1}^2, M_i^1, M_i^2, and H_i^1. If H_i^1 and H_i^2 can be computed independently, the hash function is called *parallel*; if H_i^2 depends on H_i^1, the hash function is called *serial*.

In [14] L. Knudsen and X. Lai present attacks on a large number of double block length hash functions of hash rate 1 for fixed IV. However, for one class of functions their (second) preimage attacks required a huge table of 2^m $2m$-bit values; no collision attacks were reported for these hash functions. In the following we provide the last piece of the puzzle by presenting attacks on all hash functions of hash rate 1 defined by (2) which are much faster than brute force attacks and which require only small memory. In particular these attacks break the LOKI-DBH hash function [4].

We consider double block length hash functions for which H_i^1 (or H_i^2) can be written as

$$H_i^1 = E_A(B) \oplus C \qquad \text{with} \qquad \begin{bmatrix} A \\ B \\ C \end{bmatrix} = L \cdot \begin{bmatrix} H_{i-1}^1 \\ H_{i-1}^2 \\ M_i^1 \\ M_i^2 \end{bmatrix} \qquad (3)$$

where L is a binary 3×4 matrix. This includes all double block length hash functions of hash rate 1 (serial or parallel), as defined in (2), but also more complex schemes. Also, we will rewrite A and B of (3) as follows

$$\begin{bmatrix} A \\ B \end{bmatrix} = N_1 \cdot \begin{bmatrix} H_{i-1}^1 \\ H_{i-1}^2 \end{bmatrix} \oplus N_2 \cdot \begin{bmatrix} M_i^1 \\ M_i^2 \end{bmatrix} \qquad (4)$$

where N_1 and N_2 are 2×2 binary submatrices of L.

Theorem 2. *For the double block length hash functions of hash rate 1, whose compression functions have the form of (2), the complexities of second preimage and preimage attacks are upper bounded by about 4×2^m. The complexity of a collision attack is upper bounded by about $3 \times 2^{3m/4}$. For all but two classes of hash functions, the complexity of the collision attack is at most $4 \times 2^{m/2}$.*

Proof: Consider the general form (2). In the following we will attack the compression function H_i^1 and use the notation of (3). The proofs for $Rank(L) < 3$ and for $Rank(L) = 3, Rank(N_2) = 1$ were given in [14]. In the following let $\text{Rank}(L) = 3$ and $\text{Rank}(N_2) = 2$.

Since $\text{Rank}(L) = 3$, A, B, and C are linearly independent, and H_i^1 can be written as

$$\begin{aligned} H_i^1 &= E_A(B) \oplus C^0 \\ &= E_A(B) \oplus A \oplus C^1 \\ &= E_A(B) \oplus B \oplus C^2 \\ &= E_A(B) \oplus A \oplus B \oplus C^3 \end{aligned}$$

with C_0, C_1, C_2, and C_3 different from zero. $\text{Rank}(N_2) = 2$ implies that one of the four variables C^0, C^1, C^2 or C^3 does not contain any of the message variables M_i^1, M_i^2 or $M_i^1 \oplus M_i^2$. Let C^j denote that variable.

The cases $C^j = C^0$ and $C^j = C^1$ were discussed in [14]. If $C^j = C^2$, we assume without loss of generality that $C^2 = H_{t-1}^1$. We present meet-in-the-middle attacks which are faster than brute-force attacks and distinguish between the (second) preimage attack and the collision attack.

The (second) preimage attack:

1. Backward step: choose 2^m values for (A, B) and compute

$$H'^1_{t-1} = C^2 = E_A(B) \oplus B \oplus H_t^1 \qquad \text{for the given value of } H_t^1.$$

2. Forward step: choose 2^m values for $(M''^1_{t-1}, M''^2_{t-1})$ and compute $(H''^1_{t-1}, H''^2_{t-1})$ from (H^1_{t-2}, H^2_{t-2}).

Find matches $H''^1_{t-1} = H'^1_{t-1}$. For every match use equation (4) to find the values of (M^1_t, M^2_t) from (A, B) and $(H''^1_{t-1}, H''^2_{t-1})$ (note Rank(N_2) = 2). Finally compute the corresponding value of H^2_t. The quantities in the meet-in-middle attack are m bits long, so this gives us about $(2^m \times 2^m)/2^m = 2^m$ values of $(H^1_{t-1}, H^2_{t-1}, M^1_t, M^2_t)$ all hitting the same value of H^1_t. Thus, we will find messages hitting H^2_t as well with probability about 63%; the total number of operations is about 4×2^m.

The collision attack:

1. Backward step: choose $2^{3m/4}$ values for A and B and compute

$$H'^1_{t-1} = C^2 = E_A(B) \oplus B \oplus H^1_t \qquad \text{for the given value of } H^1_t.$$

2. Forward step: choose $2^{3m/4}$ values for $(M''^1_{t-1}, M''^2_{t-1})$ and compute $(H''^1_{t-1}, H''^2_{t-1})$ from (H^1_{t-2}, H^2_{t-2}).

Find matches $H''^1_{t-1} = H'^1_{t-1}$. For every match compute the values of (M^1_t, M^2_t) from (A, B) and $(H''^1_{t-1}, H''^2_{t-1})$ using equation (4) and the corresponding value of H^2_t. Since the quantities in the meet-in-middle attack are m bits long, this gives us about $(2^{3m/4} \times 2^{3m/4})/2^m = 2^{m/2}$ values of $(H^1_{t-1}, H^2_{t-1}, M^1_t, M^2_t)$ all hitting the same value of H^1_t. Thus, by the birthday paradox we will find among these a match for H^2_t with probability $1 - \exp\left((2^{m/2})^2)/2^{m+1}\right) \approx 39\%$ [9]. The total number of operations is equal to $3 \times 2^{3m/4}$.

If $C^j = C^3$, we choose random values for A and B and compute

$$C^3 = E_A(B) \oplus A \oplus B \oplus H^1_t.$$

Then we proceed similarly as in the previous case. The LOKI-DBH hash function [4] is an instance of this class of hash functions. ∎

4 Triple and Quadruple Constructions

When the compression function consists of several subfunctions $(H^1_i, \ldots, H^n_i$ as above) care has to be taken. As illustrated by the attacks presented in the previous section, compression functions for which it is possible to invert (parts of) the outputs are vulnerable to a meet-in-the-middle attack. Therefore we will require that each of the subfunctions H^j_i have the form of a secure single block length hash function [24].

Moreover, since most block ciphers have a block length of 64 bits, a bruteforce collision attack on a double block length hash function, as defined by (2), will never take more than 2^{64} operations. Recent work by van Oorschot and Wiener [28] shows how parallelization techniques can be used to find collisions for such hash functions in reasonable time and at a reasonable cost (less than a month with 10 mio. US$).

This leads us to specify the requirements for a hash function based on an m-bit block cipher with compression function consisting of subfunctions $H_i^1, \ldots, H_i^n$ as follows.

1. Each function H_i^j is preimage resistant, i.e., given $y = H_i^j(X)$ about 2^m encryptions are required to find an X' such that $H_i^j(X') = Y$.
2. A collision attack on the compression function takes at least 2^m operations.

The first requirement above implies that the subfunctions have the form of a secure single block length hash function [24]. It may help the reader at this point to think of the subfunction h_i as the compression function of the Davies-Meyer hash function:

$$h_i(M_i, H_{i-1}) = E_{M_i}(H_{i-1}) \oplus H_{i-1} . \tag{5}$$

The second requirement above implies that the number of subfunctions must be at least three, i.e., $n \geq 3$.

The compression function of a triple block length hash function based on a block cipher involves three functions H_i^1, H_i^2, H_i^3. One iteration will involve three chaining variables $H_{i-1}^1, H_{i-1}^2, H_{i-1}^3$ and at least one message variable M_i. It is clear that we cannot meet both our requirements above. Indeed, it will be possible to make the inputs to one of the subfunctions (e.g., H_i^1) constant by an appropriate choice of the input variables; subsequently the remaining freedom in the variables can be used for a brute force collision search on H_i^2 and H_i^3. This freedom corresponds to two variables.

A similar result holds for quadruple block length hash functions. One iteration will involve at least five variables. One can make the inputs to two of the subfunctions constant by an appropriate choice of the input variables; the remaining freedom, corresponding to one variable, can be used for a brute force collision search on the other two subfunctions.

In the next section we show that hash functions exist meeting our two requirements for schemes with $n > 4$.

5 A New General Construction

In this section we present a new general construction for a collision resistant hash function based on an m-bit block cipher, that is, where collisions will take more than 2^m operations. The construction extends a simple hash mode which is believed to be secure to a multiple hash mode. The security of the new construction can be proved based on the following two assumptions:

- the simple hash mode is secure;
- no shortcuts can be found to break independent instances of the simple hash mode.

First we make the assumptions more precise, and subsequently we present a new construction and prove that its security can be derived from the assumptions. Then extensions of the construction are discussed and a complete example is provided.

5.1 Security assumptions

We now state the two assumptions required to prove the security of the new construction.

Assumption 1 (Davies-Meyer) *Let $E_K(.)$ be an m-bit block cipher with an m-bit key K. Define the compression function h to be the Davies-Meyer function (5). Then finding collisions for h requires about $2^{m/2}$ encryptions (of an m-bit block), and finding a (second) preimage for h requires about 2^m encryptions.*

This assumption is motivated by fact that the Davies-Meyer scheme (and 11 variants of this scheme, see [24]) seems to be secure; a similar assumption has been used and heuristically motivated by R. Merkle in [19].

Assumption 2 (Multiple Davies-Meyer) *Let $f_1, f_2, \ldots f_n$, be different instantiations of the Davies-Meyer function, that is, $f_i(X_i, Y_i) = E_{X_i}(Y_i) \oplus Y_i$ (these can be obtained by fixing $\lceil \log_2 n \rceil$ key bits to different values). Consider a compression function with $2k$ m-bit input blocks, Z_i, which are expanded by an affine mapping to the n pairs $(X_i, Y_i)^2$. Assume that the output of the compression function depends on all $2k$ blocks, and, more precisely, the matrix of the affine expansion mapping has rank $2k$.*

Assume a simultaneous collision for $f_1, f_2, \ldots f_n$, has been found, i.e., two different sets of input values $\{z_i\}$ and $\{z_i'\}$ yielding equal outputs for all n functions. Let $\{f_j\}$ be the set of N functions, $N \leq n$, which depend on the input blocks Z_i and Z_i' for which $z_i \neq z_i'$. Let the rank of the submatrix of the functions $\{f_j\}$ be $N - v$. Then it is assumed that finding simultaneous collisions for these N functions f_i requires at least $2^{vm/2}$ encryptions, and finding a simultaneous (second) preimage for the N functions requires at least 2^{vm} encryptions.

This assumption can be justified with an appropriate assumption about the underlying block cipher of a multiple Davies-Meyer compression function. More precisely, consider 2 different subfunctions f_i and f_j and assume that the inputs to one subfunction f_i are dependent on the inputs to another subfunction f_j. Then if the block cipher is secure, we assume that two inputs colliding for f_i will collide also for f_j with probability 2^{-m}. In other words, our assumption is that, if the block cipher is secure, finding collisions simultaneously for f_i and f_j for dependent inputs will not be easier than a brute-force attack.

Consider a multiple Davies-Meyer compression function with n subfunctions and assume that a simultaneous collision have been found as discussed in Assumption 2. Since the rank of the submatrix of the N functions $\{f_j\}$ is $N - v$,

---

[2] The choice of an even number of input blocks is not mandatory, but this choice will become clear later.

it will be possible to find collisions for $N - v$ of these functions independently of each other. Our assumption then says that finding simultaneous collisions also for the remaining v functions requires at least $2^{vm/2}$ encryptions, and finding a simultaneous (second) preimage requires at least 2^{vm} encryptions. Thus, the best an attacker can hope for is a brute force attack on the v remaining functions.

5.2   The new construction

The following theorem describes the new construction and gives a proof for its security.

Theorem 3. *If there exists a quaternary $[n, k, d]$ code of length n, dimension k, and minimum distance d, with $2k > n$, and $n = O(m)$, then there exists a parallel hash function based on an m-bit block cipher for whose compression function finding a collision requires at least $2^{(d-1)m/2}$ encryptions and finding a second preimage requires at least $2^{(d-1)m}$ encryptions provided that Assumption 2 holds. The hash function has an internal memory of $n \cdot m$ bits, and a rate of $(2k/n) - 1$.*

Proof: The proof is constructive. The compression function consists of n functions f_i with $1 \leq i \leq n$ (see Assumption 2) which have been made different by fixing $\lceil \log_2 n \rceil$ key bits to different values. The input to the compression function consists of $2k$ m-bit blocks: the n chaining variables H^1 through H^n (the output of the n functions of the previous iteration) and r message blocks M^1 through M^r, with $r = 2k - n > 0$. In the following, every individual bit of these m-bit blocks is treated in the same way. The bits of two consecutive input blocks are pairwise combined yielding k elements of $GF(2^2)$. These elements are encoded using a quaternary $[n, k, d]$ code, resulting in n elements of $GF(2^2)$. Each of these elements represents the 2-bit inputs to one of the n functions. The individual input bits are obtained by representing the elements of $GF(2^2)$ as a vector space over $GF(2)$. This construction guarantees that the conditions for Assumption 2 are satisfied for the value $v = d - 1$. By a linear transformation of the $2k$ inputs it is possible to obtain a compression function, where the inputs to the first k subfunctions are independent of each other. The inputs to the last $n - k$ subfunctions will depend on the inputs to the first k subfunctions. The minimum distance of the quaternary code ensures that the inputs to at least $d-1$ of the last $n - k$ functions will depend on the inputs to the first k functions. Since $n - k \geq d - 1$ [17] the result follows immediately.   ∎

The security bound will be slightly smaller than indicated, since a number of key bits have to be fixed. However, $n = O(m)$, and thus the resulting reduction of the security level will be negligible. The above bound is a lower bound and the existence of attacks meeting this bound is not guaranteed. Later we give a concrete proposal of a compression function constructed as above, for which the complexity of the best known attacks are even higher than the proven lower bound.

The existence of efficient constructions for $d = 3$ follows from the existence of perfect Hamming codes over $GF(2^2)$ (see for example [17, 179–180] or [3]).

Theorem 4. *Let q be a prime power. The (perfect) Hamming codes over GF(q) have the following parameters:*

$$\left[n = \frac{q^s - 1}{q - 1}, k = n - s, d = 3\right].$$

The resulting codes can be shortened without decreasing the minimum distance, which implies the following result:

Corollary 5. *There are parallel hash functions based on an m-bit block cipher for which for the compression function finding a collision requires at least 2^m encryptions and finding a second preimage requires at least 2^{2m} encryptions provided that Assumption 2 holds. The following rates can be obtained in function of the internal memory: $n = 5$, rate 1/5, $n = 8$, rate 1/4, $n = 10$, rate 2/5, $n = 12$, rate 1/2, and $n = 21$, rate 5/7 ($s = 3$). For large values of n, the rate is about*

$$1 - \frac{\log_2(3n + 1)}{n}$$

which is very close to 1.

To obtain an even higher level of security, one can use other codes to construct schemes for $d = 4$, e.g. using the codes $[9, 5, 4], [12, 8, 4], [16, 12, 4]$, see [3].

Corollary 6. *There are parallel hash functions based on an m-bit block cipher for which for the compression function finding a collision requires at least $2^{3m/2}$ encryptions and finding a second preimage requires at least 2^{3m} encryptions provided that Assumption 2 holds. The following rates can be obtained in function of the internal memory: $n = 9$, rate 1/9, $n = 12$, rate 1/3, $n = 16$, rate 1/2.*

Notes:

1. Apart from the simple security proof and the relatively high rates, the schemes have the advantage that n encryptions can be carried out in parallel. The disadvantage of the schemes is the increased amount of internal memory.

2. For the (second) preimage attack, the security bounds assume that the entropy of the unknown part of the input is at least $(d - 1)m$ bits.

3. Theorem 3 only considers the strength against attacks on the compression function. The strength of the hash function itself could be improved by dividing the output of a single f_i function over all the other functions. However, proving a stronger security bound is probably quite difficult.

5.3 Extensions

The construction has the property that the size of the hash result is larger than the security level of the hash function would suggest. This could be a problem in applications where 'near collisions' are not acceptable [1] (e.g., it is feasible to find two hash values which have $n-d+1$ colliding blocks). In that case, an output transformation can be defined which compresses the result of the final iteration.

We present here two approaches, which do not affect the provable security (both techniques can be combined; an example is given in § 5.4 below).

Denote with $n_{\min}$ the smallest possible value of n for a given value of d, such that Theorem 3 holds (e.g., for $d = 3$, $n_{\min} = 5$, and $d = 4$, $n_{\min} = 9$). If $n_{\min} < n$, compress the n blocks to $n_{\min}$ blocks using the new construction with $n_{\min}$ parallel blocks (since $n_{\min} < n$, this hash function will have a lower rate than the original one).

If a reduction is required to less than $n_{\min}$ blocks, one can use a number of parallel and independent instances of Merkle's hash function based on a block cipher [19]. This will be rather slow compared to the new construction, but this is not so important since Merkle's function is only required for the output transformation.

5.4 A practical example

We present the details of a concrete proposal based on an $[8, 5, 3]$ quaternary code, which is obtained by shortening the $[21, 18, 3]$ Hamming code. The hash function uses $n = 8$ parallel encryptions, and hashes $2 \cdot 5 - 8 = 2$ 64-bit message blocks, resulting in a rate of $1/4$. Using a 64-bit block cipher with a 64-bit key, finding a collision for the compression function requires at least 2^{64} encryptions, and finding a (second) preimage requires at least 2^{128} encryptions. Later we describe the best attacks we have found, which requires even more encryptions.

The generator matrix of the $[8, 5, 3]$ Hamming code over $\mathrm{GF}(2^2)$ has the following form:

$$
\begin{bmatrix}
1 & 0 & 0 & 0 & 0 & 0 & 1 & 1 \\
0 & 1 & 0 & 0 & 0 & 1 & 0 & \alpha \\
0 & 0 & 1 & 0 & 0 & 1 & 0 & \beta \\
0 & 0 & 0 & 1 & 0 & 1 & 0 & 1 \\
0 & 0 & 0 & 0 & 1 & 1 & 1 & 0
\end{bmatrix}
\tag{6}
$$

here $0 = [00]$, $1 = [01]$, $\alpha = [10]$, and $\beta = [11]$. The order of the chaining variables is chosen to be $H_{i-1}^1, M_i^1, H_{i-1}^3, H_{i-1}^4, H_{i-1}^5, H_{i-1}^6, H_{i-1}^7, H_{i-1}^8, H_{i-1}^2, M_i^2$, but can be chosen arbitrarily (the motivation for this particular choice is indicated below). This results in the following compression function, where $h(X, Y)$ denotes $E_X(Y) \oplus Y$:

$$H_i^1 = f_1(H_{i-1}^1, M_i^1)$$
$$H_i^2 = f_2(H_{i-1}^3, H_{i-1}^4)$$
$$H_i^3 = f_3(H_{i-1}^5, H_{i-1}^6)$$
$$H_i^4 = f_4(H_{i-1}^7, H_{i-1}^8)$$
$$H_i^5 = f_5(H_{i-1}^2, M_i^2)$$
$$H_i^6 = f_6(H_{i-1}^3 \oplus H_{i-1}^5 \oplus H_{i-1}^7 \oplus H_{i-1}^2, H_{i-1}^4 \oplus H_{i-1}^6 \oplus H_{i-1}^8 \oplus M_i^2)$$
$$H_i^7 = f_7(H_{i-1}^1 \oplus H_{i-1}^2, M_i^1 \oplus M_i^2)$$
$$H_i^8 = f_8(H_{i-1}^1 \oplus H_{i-1}^3 \oplus H_{i-1}^4 \oplus H_{i-1}^6 \oplus H_{i-1}^7, M_i^1 \oplus H_{i-1}^3 \oplus H_{i-1}^5 \oplus H_{i-1}^6 \oplus H_{i-1}^8)$$

In addition, the 8 functions are made different by fixing the values of 3 key bits to the block cipher.

Although we have proved a lower bound on the complexity of attacks on the above compression function we have not succeeded in finding such attacks. Indeed the best collision attack we know is the following. Fix the inputs to H_i^1 and H_i^5. This yields constant values also for H_i^7. Find independently $2^{m/3}$-fold collisions for each of H_i^2, H_i^3, and H_i^4. This will require about $3 \times 2^{4m/3}$ encryptions of the block cipher [23]. These three sets are combined to a set of 2^m simultaneous collisions for H_i^2, H_i^3, and H_i^4. With a high probability one of these collisions yield a collision also for H_i^6 and H_i^8. Therefore the best known collision attack requires about $3 \times 2^{4m/3}$ encryptions of the block cipher. We need to fix three bits of the key, which gives a security level for collision attacks of about 2^{81} for $m = 64$.

In the case of DES [10], one needs to fix an additional 2 key bits in order to avoid the complementation property, and the (semi-)weak keys and the associated (anti-)fixed points (bits 2 and 3 of the key are fixed to 01 [2]). Since DES has a 56-bit key, the effective key size will be reduced to 51 bits, resulting in a security level of $2^{4 \cdot 51/3} = 2^{68}$. By fixing two key bits and three plaintext bits, this could be improved to 2^{72}, which seems to be sufficient to preclude brute force collision search at the cost of a more complex implementation. The order of the chaining variables above was chosen to ensure that the message variables do not occur as key input to the block cipher. The most important reason for this is to obtain a hash rate of 1/4 since the key size is less than the block size in DES; moreover, this avoids giving an attacker the advantage in 'real' attacks on the hash function with a fixed value of IV (compared to attacks on the compression function) of being able to choose the keys.

A reduction of the eight 64-bit blocks to three 64-bit blocks using two parallel instantiations of Merkle's construction (resulting in a rate of about $0.25 \times 0.5 = 1/8$) requires about 64 DES encryptions.

Note that the 2^m complexity of MDC-2 is the best known attack against the hash function, while against Merkle's scheme and our schemes the 2^m complexity is against the compression functions and is a lower bound for the complexity of an attack on the hash function. The complexity of the best known attack against the compression function of MDC-2 is only $2^{m/2}$.

6 Conclusion

We have demonstrated that designing efficient hash functions with minimal internal memory based on an m-bit block cipher is a difficult problem. Moreover, none of the previous proposals provides a protection better than 2^m against brute force collision search. By changing the model slightly (i.e., by increasing the size of the internal memory, and by introducing an output transformation), it is possible to obtain a compression function and thus a hash function for which the security can be proved based on a plausible assumption. The proposed construction achieve the same efficiency as the best current proposals (namely rate

1/4, or 4 encryptions to hash a single block) but a higher security level, or a higher efficiency for the same security level. For large value of the internal memory, rates close to one can be obtained. Also, the constructions allows for a high degree of parallelism, which will yield even more efficient implementations.

Acknowledgments

The authors wish to thank Tor Helleseth and Torleiv Kløve for helpful discussions of useful codes.

References

1. R. Anderson, "The classification of hash functions," *Codes and Cyphers: Cryptography and Coding IV*, P.G. Farrell, Ed., Institute of Mathematics & Its Applications (IMA), 1995, pp. 83–93.
2. B.O. Brachtl, D. Coppersmith, M.M. Hyden, S.M. Matyas, C.H. Meyer, J. Oseas, S. Pilpel, M. Schilling, *"Data Authentication Using Modification Detection Codes Based on a Public One Way Encryption Function,"* U.S. Patent Number 4,908,861, March 13, 1990.
3. A.E. Brouwer, "Linear code bound," http://www.win.tue.nl/win/math/dw/voorlincod.html.
4. L. Brown, J. Pieprzyk, J. Seberry, "LOKI – a cryptographic primitive for authentication and secrecy applications," *Advances in Cryptology, Proc. Auscrypt'90, LNCS 453*, J. Seberry, J. Pieprzyk, Eds., Springer-Verlag, 1990, pp. 229–236.
5. I.B. Damgård, "A design principle for hash functions," *Advances in Cryptology, Proc. Crypto'89, LNCS 435*, G. Brassard, Ed., Springer-Verlag, 1990, pp. 416–427.
6. B. den Boer, A. Bosselaers, "Collisions for the compression function of MD5," *Advances in Cryptology, Proc. Eurocrypt'93, LNCS 765*, T. Helleseth, Ed., Springer-Verlag, 1994, pp. 293–304.
7. H. Dobbertin, "Cryptanalysis of MD4," *Fast Software Encryption, LNCS 1039*, D. Gollmann, Ed., Springer-Verlag, 1996, pp. 53–69.
8. H. Dobbertin, "Cryptanalysis of MD5 compress," Presented at the rump session of Eurocrypt'96, May 1996.
9. W. Feller, *"An Introduction to Probability Theory and Its Applications, Vol. 1,"* Wiley & Sons, 1968.
10. FIPS 46, *"Data Encryption Standard,"* Federal Information Processing Standard (FIPS), Publication 46, National Bureau of Standards, U.S. Department of Commerce, Washington D.C., January 1977.
11. W. Hohl, X. Lai, T. Meier, C. Waldvogel, "Security of iterated hash functions based on block ciphers," *Advances in Cryptology, Proc. Crypto'93, LNCS 773*, D. Stinson, Ed., Springer-Verlag, 1994, pp. 379–390.
12. ISO/IEC 10118, *"Information technology – Security techniques – Hash-functions, Part 1: General and Part 2: Hash-functions using an n-bit block cipher algorithm,"* IS 10118, 1994.
13. L.R. Knudsen, "A Key-schedule Weakness in SAFER K-64," *Advances in Cryptology, Proc. Crypto'94, LNCS 839*, Y. Desmedt, Ed., Springer-Verlag, 1994, pp. 274–286.

14. L.R. Knudsen, X. Lai, "New attacks on all double block length hash functions of hash rate 1, including the parallel-DM," *Advances in Cryptology, Proc. Eurocrypt'94, LNCS 959*, A. De Santis, Ed., Springer-Verlag, 1995, pp. 410–418.

15. L.R. Knudsen, X. Lai, B. Preneel, "Attacks on Fast Double Block Length Hash Functions". Submitted to the Journal of Cryptology.

16. X. Lai, *"On the Design and Security of Block Ciphers,"* ETH Series in Information Processing, Vol. 1, J.L. Massey, Ed., Hartung-Gorre Verlag, Konstanz, 1992.

17. F.J. MacWilliams, N.J.A. Sloane, *"The Theory of Error-Correcting Codes,"* North-Holland Publishing Company, Amsterdam, 1978.

18. S.M. Matyas, C.H. Meyer, J. Oseas, "Generating strong one-way functions with cryptographic algorithm," *IBM Techn. Disclosure Bull.*, Vol. 27, No. 10A, 1985, pp. 5658–5659.

19. R. Merkle, "One way hash functions and DES," *Advances in Cryptology, Proc. Crypto'89, LNCS 435*, G. Brassard, Ed., Springer-Verlag, 1990, pp. 428–446.

20. J.H. Moore, G.J. Simmons, "Cycle structure of the DES for keys having palindromic (or antipalindromic) sequences of round keys," *IEEE Trans. on Software Engineering*, Vol. SE–13, No. 2, 1987, pp. 262–273.

21. M. Naor, M. Yung, "Universal one-way hash functions and their cryptographic applications," *Proc. 21st ACM Symposium on the Theory of Computing*, ACM, 1989, pp. 387–394.

22. B. Preneel, "Analysis and design of cryptographic hash functions," *Doctoral Dissertation*, Katholieke Universiteit Leuven, 1993.

23. B. Preneel, R. Govaerts, J. Vandewalle, "On the power of memory in the design of collision resistant hash functions," *Advances in Cryptology, Proc. Auscrypt'92, LNCS 718*, J. Seberry, Y. Zheng, Eds., Springer-Verlag, 1993, pp. 105–121.

24. B. Preneel, R. Govaerts, J. Vandewalle, "Hash functions based on block ciphers: a synthetic approach," *Advances in Cryptology, Proc. Crypto'93, LNCS 773*, D. Stinson, Ed., Springer-Verlag, 1994, pp. 368–378.

25. J.-J. Quisquater, J.-P. Delescaille, "How easy is collision search? Application to DES," *Advances in Cryptology, Proc. Eurocrypt'89, LNCS 434*, J.-J. Quisquater, J. Vandewalle, Eds., Springer-Verlag, 1990, pp. 429–434.

26. R.L. Rivest, "The MD4 message digest algorithm," *Advances in Cryptology, Proc. Crypto'90, LNCS 537*, S. Vanstone, Ed., Springer-Verlag, 1991, pp. 303–311.

27. R.L. Rivest, "The MD5 message-digest algorithm," *Request for Comments (RFC) 1321*, Internet Activities Board, Internet Privacy Task Force, April 1992.

28. P.C. van Oorschot, M.J. Wiener, "Parallel collision search with application to hash functions and discrete logarithms," *Proc. 2nd ACM Conference on Computer and Communications Security*, ACM, 1994, pp. 210–218.

29. M.J. Wiener, "Efficient DES key search," *Technical Report TR-244*, School of Computer Science, Carleton University, Ottawa, Canada, May 1994. Presented at the rump session of Crypto'93.

30. G. Yuval, "How to swindle Rabin," *Cryptologia*, Vol. 3, No. 3, 1979, pp. 187–189.

Generalized Feistel Networks

Kaisa Nyberg

Finnish Defence Forces, CIS Division, Helsinki, Finland
Email: viesti@pp.kolumbus.fi

Abstract. A simple network of small s-boxes can be proven secure against differential and linear cryptanalysis. Upperbounds of the differential probabilities and the linear correlations are derived for a generalized Feistel network having 1, 2, 3 or 4 s-boxes in parallel per round. It is conjectured that the results hold in general.

1 Introduction

The Feistel network is one of the most commonly used structures in iterated block ciphers. One round of a Feistel network is defined as follows.

$$Y_1 = X_1 \oplus F(X_2, K)$$
$$Y_2 = X_2$$
$$Y_1' = Y_2$$
$$Y_2' = Y_1$$

where (X_1, X_2) is the data input to the round, K is the round key and (Y_1', Y_2') is the data output of the round taken as input to the next round. The Feistel structure provides invertible transformations independently of whether the round function F is invertible or not, and can be used to generate random permutations from random functions.

One of the useful features of the classical Feistel network is that it provides diffusion of the input blocks. After two rounds of the network the diffusion is complete, that is, both output blocks depend on both input blocks. However, for a strong cipher, this is not sufficient. In addition, it must be required that the round function has good diffusion and confusion properties. The Feistel network is used to spread these properites over the whole cipher block. Three approaches to the design of the round function can be identified.

The first approach, the one used in the DES, is to construct the round function from a set of parallel substitution transformations, s-boxes, and to "glue" the s-boxes together by expanding the input data so that two neighbouring s-boxes share some input, and by permuting the output bits of the s-box set. This permutation has a major impact to the cryptographical properties of the network and represents a hard design challenge in the lack of theoretical support.

The second approach is to use just one large strong s-box. As shown in [3] and [2] (see also [1]) such a Feistel network is unconditionally proven resistant against certain differential and linear cryptanalytical attacks. In theoretical examples of this type of networks the round functions have been simple algebraic functions, which may cause other weaknesses. Recently, M. Matsui proposed a new cipher structure of a Feistel network, where the round function is itself a Feistel network [4]. This network is proven secure against differential and linear cryptanalysis, which can be shown by iterating the existing security results for Feistel structures. This way, starting from small s-boxes one can at each iteration double the size of the s-box to produce sufficiently large and strong s-boxes.

Thirdly, it was proposed in [6] to use the network itself to produce sufficient diffusion. This approach has been used in the design of the hash-functions MD4, MD5 and HAVAL, which are examples of what in [5] are called generally *unbalanced Feistel networks*. In most cases the data input blocks X_1 and X_2 are of different sizes and, consequently, the inputs and outputs of the round function are of different length.

The purpose of this contribution is to show that proven security against differential and linear cryptanalysis can be achieved with a network of small s-boxes. The major advantages of small s-boxes are that they can be implemented as tables, and if generated randomly, they can be efficiently tested for required properties.

We follow the third approach and investigate an iterated structure, which we call *generalized Feistel network*. The round function of this network is weak compared to previous proposals. It consists only of a set of parallel s-boxes with equal input and output sizes. The network is balanced, that is, the input blocks X_1 and X_2 are of equal length, but instead of swapping the two output blocks, we devide the output blocks into subblocks which then are permuted. In this way, the s-boxes are gradually diffused by means of the network, without auxiliary permutations in the round function.

2 Generalized Feistel Network

The general idea sketched in the introduction has many possible realizations, all of which are not good (see below Section 5). Let us consider one typical example defined as follows.

Let $X_1, X_2, \ldots, X_{2n}$ be the input block to the ith round of the network, where the length of each subblock X_j is d. Given n $d \times d$ s-boxes $F_1, F_2, \ldots, F_n$ and n round keys $K_{i1}, K_{i2}, \ldots, K_{in}$, the output $Y_1', Y_2', \ldots, Y_{2n}'$ is computed using the following formulas.

$$Y_{n+1-j} = X_{n+1-j} \oplus F_j(X_{j+n} \oplus K_{ij}), \ j = 1, 2, \ldots, n$$
$$Y_j = X_j, \ j = n+1, \ldots, 2n$$
$$Y_1' = Y_{2n},$$
$$Y_j' = Y_{j-1}, \ j = 2, \ldots, 2n$$

This generalized Feistel network with $n = 4$ is depicted in Figure 1. In the next sections the resistance against differential and linear cryptanalysis is demonstrated for this network.

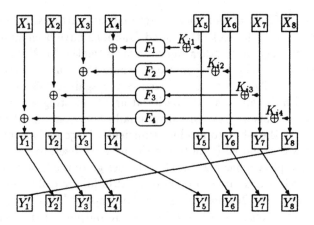

Fig. 1. The ith round of the generalized Feistel network for $n = 4$.

3 Resistance Against Differential Cryptanalysis

3.1 General Case

We assume that the round keys, which are xored to the input data at each round are independent and uniformly random. Let us consider the probability of a differential, i.e., the probability that a given input difference gives a certain given output difference after executing some number of rounds of the network. In practise, this probability depends on the key that is actually used, and on the chosen plaintext pair, and is hard to determine. However, it is reasonable to assume that for each fixed plaintext pair, these probabilities do not vary significantly. Therefore, and because the key is secret and chosen uniformly at random, we restrict ourselves to show that in average, taken over all possible values of the key, the probability of a differential is sufficiently small. Moreover, since the key is xored to the data at each round, this average probability is independent of the chosen plaintext pair. In what follows we refer to this average probability by calling it simply the probability of the differential.

We make the following notation

$$P_i(\delta, \epsilon) = P_X\{F_i(X + \delta) + F_i(X) = \epsilon\}, \tag{1}$$

for $i = 1, 2, \ldots, n$, where X is a uniformly distributed random variable in $GF(2^d)$. Let us denote by p the maximum value of $P_i(\delta, \epsilon)$, taken over all $\delta \neq 0$, all ϵ and $i = 1, 2, \ldots, n$. Further, we denote by p_0 the maximum value of $P_i(\delta, 0)$ over all $\delta \neq 0$ and $i = 1, 2, \ldots, n$.

The purpose of this work is to demonstrate that the generalized Feistel networks give proven security against differential cryptanalysis in the sense, that the average probability of each differential over sufficiently many rounds is bounded from above by a constant, which depends on the qualities of the s-boxes and the dimension of the network.

In the following subsection we show in detail that for $n = 4$, the probability of each differential over sixteen rounds is less than or equal to $p^8 + p_0^8$. For $n = 1$, that is, for the classical Feistel network, an upperbound of $2p^2$ was proved in [3] for differentials over at least four rounds. The upperbound can be easily refined to $p^2 + p_0^2$. For $n = 2$ and $n = 3$ it can be shown that the upperbounds are $p^4 + p_0^4$ and $p^6 + p_0^6$, respectively. For $n = 2$, it takes eight rounds to get the differential probability below this bound, for $n = 3$, it takes twelve rounds. Based on these results we state the following conjecture.

Conjecture 1 *If a generalized Feistel network has n parallel s-boxes per round, the average probability of each differential over at least $4n$ rounds is less than or equal to $p^{2n} + p_0^{2n}$.*

The "iterative characteristic" takes $4n$ rounds to make its probability below p_0^{2n}. We conjecture that the sum of the probabilities of all other characteristics of a differential over at least $4n$ rounds is upperbounded by p^{2n}. Let us sketch the beginning of the proof. Assume that the differential involves N possibly non-zero input differences to s-boxes. The corresponding output differences from the s-boxes can be considered as variables in $GF(2^d)$. Since the output difference of the differential is fixed, we have $2n$ linear relations between these variables. Consequently, the number of free variables is $N - 2n$. Each characteristic in the differential correspond to an assignment of values to these variables. The probability of a characteristic is a product of N s-box probabilities of the form $P_i(\delta, \epsilon)$, see (1). By summing up over all values of the $N - 2n$ output difference variables we obtain the probability of the differential. When estimating its probability, one starts by estimating $2n$ s-box probabilities in the product by the upperbound p and then the $N - 2n$ s-box probabilities sum up to one. Unfortunately, the differentials that admit such a simple treatment are rare, as can be seen in the next subsection where a detailed treatment of the case $n = 4$ is given.

3.2   Differentials for $n = 4$

In Table 1 a differential over 16 rounds is depicted. This is the most powerful differential, since it contains the "iterative charactristic" which we get by taking all t-variables and s-variables equal to zero. The probability of the iterative characteristic is less than or equal to p_0^8.

The first row between two lines is the input difference vector to the round and the second vector is the output difference before the permutation. The horizontal line represents the network permutation. As the t- and s-variables vary we get all differential characteristics leading from the input difference $(a, 0, 0, 0, 0, 0, 0, 0)$ to the output difference $(b, 0, 0, 0, 0, 0, 0, 0)$. The notation has been chosen to make a distinction between the s-variables s_{ij}, which occur only in input differences, and the t-variables t_j which occur both in input and output differences.

Let us now consider the multitude of characteristics in this differential excluding the iterative characteristic. Hence at least one of the t-variables is non-zero.

a	0	0	0	0	0	0	0
a	0	0	0	0	0	0	0
0	a	0	0	0	0	0	0
0	a	0	0	0	0	0	0
0	0	a	0	0	0	0	0
0	0	a	0	0	0	0	0
0	0	0	a	0	0	0	0
0	0	0	a	0	0	0	0
0	0	0	0	a	0	0	0
0	0	0	t_1	a	0	0	0
0	0	0	0	t_1	a	0	0
0	0	s_{2a}	t_2	t_1	a	0	0
0	0	0	s_{2a}	t_2	t_1	a	0
0	s_{3a}	s_{21}	t_3	t_2	t_1	a	0
0	0	s_{3a}	s_{21}	t_3	t_2	t_1	a
s_{4a}	s_{31}	s_{22}	t_4	t_3	t_2	t_1	a
a	s_{4a}	s_{31}	s_{22}	t_4	t_3	t_2	t_1
s_{41}	s_{32}	s_{23}	t_5	t_4	t_3	t_2	t_1
t_1	s_{41}	s_{32}	s_{23}	t_5	t_4	t_3	t_2
s_{42}	s_{33}	s_{24}	t_6	t_5	t_4	t_3	t_2
t_2	s_{42}	s_{33}	s_{24}	t_6	t_5	t_4	t_3
s_{43}	s_{34}	s_{25}	t_7	t_6	t_5	t_4	t_3
t_3	s_{43}	s_{34}	s_{25}	t_7	t_6	t_5	t_4
s_{44}	s_{35}	s_{26}	b	t_7	t_6	t_5	t_4
t_4	s_{44}	s_{35}	s_{26}	b	t_7	t_6	t_5
s_{45}	s_{36}	0	0	b	t_7	t_6	t_5
t_5	s_{45}	s_{36}	0	0	b	t_7	t_6
s_{46}	0	0	0	0	b	t_7	t_6
t_6	s_{46}	0	0	0	0	b	t_7
0	0	0	0	0	0	b	t_7
t_7	0	0	0	0	0	0	b
0	0	0	0	0	0	0	b
b	0	0	0	0	0	0	0

Table 1. The most powerful differential for $n = 4$.

Clearly, if in (1) $\delta = 0$ then $\epsilon = 0$ and $P_i(0,0) = 1$. This must be taken into attention when estimating the probability of the differential. Therefore we split into four cases: 1. $t_1 \neq 0$ and $t_7 \neq 0$; 2. $t_1 = 0$ and $t_7 \neq 0$; 3. $t_1 \neq 0$ and $t_7 = 0$; 4. $t_1 = t_7 = 0$.

Case 1: $t_1 \neq 0$ **and** $t_7 \neq 0$. The probability of each characteristic belonging to this case is a product of the probabilities, which we have listed in the first column of Table 2. We show that the sum of the probabilities of these characteristics is upperbounded by $P_1(a, t_1)P_4(b, t_7)p^8$. The estimation is made at 6 steps, which are shown in columns 2-7 of Table 2.

probability	Step 1 estimate	Step 2 sum over	Step 3 sum over	Step 4 sum over	Step 5 sum over	Step 6 sum over
$P_1(a, t_1)$						
$P_2(a, s_{2a})$					s_{2a}	
$P_3(a, s_{3a})$	$\leq p$					
$P_4(a, s_{4a})$	$\leq p$					
$P_1(t_1, t_2)$					t_2	
$P_2(t_1, s_{21})$	$\leq p$					
$P_3(t_1, s_{31})$	$\leq p$					
$P_4(t_1, s_{41})$	$\leq p$					
$P_1(t_2, s_{2a} + t_3)$				t_3		
$P_2(t_2, s_{3a} + s_{22})$		s_{3a}				
$P_3(t_2, s_{4a} + s_{32})$		s_{4a}				
$P_4(t_2, t_1 + s_{42})$				s_{42}		
$P_1(t_3, s_{21} + t_4)$		s_{21}				
$P_2(t_3, s_{31} + s_{23})$		s_{31}				
$P_3(t_3, s_{41} + s_{33})$		s_{41}				
$P_4(t_3, t_2 + s_{43})$			s_{43}			
$P_1(t_4, s_{22} + t_5)$			s_{22}			
$P_2(t_4, s_{32} + s_{24})$			s_{32}			
$P_3(t_4, s_{42} + s_{34})$			s_{34}			
$P_4(t_4, t_3 + s_{44})$			s_{44}			
$P_1(t_5, s_{23} + t_6)$			s_{23}			
$P_2(t_5, s_{33} + s_{25})$			s_{33}			
$P_3(t_5, s_{43} + s_{35})$		s_{35}				
$P_4(t_5, t_4 + s_{45})$				t_4		
$P_1(t_6, s_{24} + t_7)$				s_{24}		
$P_2(t_6, s_{34} + s_{26})$		s_{26}				
$P_3(t_6, s_{44} + s_{36})$		s_{36}				
$P_4(t_6, t_5 + s_{46})$					t_5	
$P_1(t_7, s_{25} + b)$				s_{25}		
$P_2(t_7, s_{35})$	$\leq p$					
$P_3(t_7, s_{45})$					s_{45}	
$P_4(t_7, t_6)$						t_6
$P_1(b, s_{26})$	$\leq p$					
$P_2(b, s_{36})$	$\leq p$					
$P_3(b, s_{46})$						s_{46}
$P_4(b, t_7)$						

Table 2. Probabilities of characteristics for $t_1 \neq 0$ and $t_7 \neq 0$.

At Step 1 we choose eight probabilities with nonzero input difference which are upperbounded by p. At Step 2 we choose eight probabilities to be summed up over the eight s-variables that were the output differences in the probabilities estimated at Step 1. After this it is possible to sum up seven more probabilities over s-variables. At Step 4 we sum up over t_3, t_4 and three more s-variables.

Then it is possible to sum up over t_2, t_5 and two s-variables. Finally, at Step 6, we sum up over t_6 and the remaining one s-variable.

Case 2: $t_1 = 0$ and $t_7 \neq 0$. If $t_1 = 0$ it follows that $t_2 = s_{21} = s_{31} = s_{41} = 0$ and $s_{2a} = t_3$, $s_{22} = s_{3a}$, $s_{32} = s_{4a}$ and $s_{42} = 0$. Consequently, the differential characteristics in this category involve at most 28 non-trivial s-box differentials, Similarily, as in Case 1 we list their probabilities in Table 3 and show how to proceed in showing that the sum of the probabilities of these characteristics is less than or equal to $P_1(a,0)P_4(b,t_7)p^8$.

probability	Step 1 estimate	Step 2 sum over	Step 3 sum over	Step 4 sum over	Step 5 sum over	Step 6 sum over
$P_1(a,0)$						
$P_2(a,t_3)$						t_3
$P_3(a,s_{3a})$						s_{3a}
$P_4(a,s_{4a})$	$\leq p$					
$P_1(t_3,t_4)$			t_4			
$P_2(t_3,s_{23})$					s_{23}	
$P_3(t_3,s_{33})$			s_{33}			
$P_4(t_3,s_{43})$			s_{43}			
$P_1(t_4,s_{3a}+t_5)$					t_5	
$P_2(t_4,s_{4a}+s_{24})$		s_{4a}				
$P_3(t_4,s_{34})$			s_{34}			
$P_4(t_4,t_3+s_{44})$			s_{44}			
$P_1(t_5,s_{23}+t_6)$				s_{23}		
$P_2(t_5,s_{33}+s_{25})$		s_{25}				
$P_3(t_5,s_{43}+s_{35})$		s_{35}				
$P_4(t_5,t_4+s_{45})$		s_{45}				
$P_1(t_6,s_{24}+t_7)$				s_{24}		
$P_2(t_6,s_{34}+s_{26})$		s_{26}				
$P_3(t_6,s_{44}+s_{36})$		s_{36}				
$P_4(t_6,t_5+s_{46})$		s_{46}				
$P_1(t_7,s_{25}+b)$	$\leq p$					
$P_2(t_7,s_{35})$	$\leq p$					
$P_3(t_7,s_{45})$	$\leq p$					
$P_4(t_7,t_6)$	$\leq p$					
$P_1(b,s_{26})$	$\leq p$					
$P_2(b,s_{36})$	$\leq p$					
$P_3(b,s_{46})$	$\leq p$					
$P_4(b,t_7)$						

Table 3. Probabilities of characteristics for $t_1 = 0$ and $t_7 \neq 0$.

Case 3: $t_1 \neq 0$ and $t_7 = 0$. By turning the preceding case upside down we get that the sum of the probabilities of these characteristics is less than or equal to $P_1(a, t_1)P_4(a, 0)p^8$.

Case 4: $t_1 = t_7 = 0$. Now

$$t_2 = t_6 = s_{2a} = s_{21} = s_{31} = s_{41} + a = s_{45} = s_{35} = s_{25} + b = 0$$

and further,

$$s_{2a} + t_3 = s_{3a} + s_{22} = s_{4a} + s_{32} = s_{42} = s_{24} = s_{34} + s_{26} = s_{44} + s_{36} = t_5 + s_{46} = 0.$$

Hence these characteristics involve at most 20 non-zero input differences. The corresponding probabilities are listed in Table 4.

probability	Step 1 estimate	Step 2 sum over	Step 3 sum over	Step 4 sum over
$P_1(a, 0)$				
$P_2(a, t_3)$				
$P_3(a, s_{3a})$	$\leq p$			
$P_4(a, s_{4a})$	$\leq p$			
$P_1(t_3, t_4)$	$\leq p$			
$P_2(t_3, s_{23})$	$\leq p$			
$P_3(t_3, a + s_{33})$	$\leq p$			
$P_4(t_3, s_{43})$	$\leq p$			
$P_1(t_4, s_{3a} + t_5)$		s_{3a}		
$P_2(t_4, s_{4a})$		s_{4a}		
$P_3(t_4, s_{34})$		s_{34}		
$P_4(t_4, t_3 + s_{44})$		s_{44}		
$P_1(t_5, s_{23})$		s_{23}		
$P_2(t_5, s_{33} + b)$		s_{33}		
$P_3(t_5, s_{43})$		s_{43}		
$P_4(t_5, t_4)$			t_4	
$P_1(b, s_{34})$	$\leq p$			
$P_2(b, s_{44})$	$\leq p$			
$P_3(b, t_5)$				t_5
$P_4(b, 0)$				

Table 4. Probabilities of characteristics for $t_1 = t_7 = 0$ and $t_3 \neq 0$.

Assume first that $t_3 \neq 0$. As shown in Table 4, it takes only four steps to show that the sum of the probabilities of such characteristics is less than or equal to

$$P_1(a, 0)P_4(b, 0)p^8 \sum_{t_3 \neq 0} P_2(a, t_3).$$

If $t_3 = 0$ then also $t_4 = 0$. Since the iterative characteristic has been considered separately and is excluded here, it follows that if $t_3 = 0$ then $t_5 \neq 0$. The sum of the probabilities of these characteristics is equal to

$$P_1(a,0)P_4(b,0)P_2(a,0) \times$$
$$\sum_{t_5 \neq 0} P_3(a,t_5)P_4(a,0)P_1(t_5,0)P_2(t_5,a+b)P_3(t_5,0)P_4(t_5,0)P_1(b,0)P_2(b,0)P_3(b,t_5)$$

and is upperbounded by $P_1(a,0)P_4(b,0)P_2(a,0)p^8$.

Hence the sum of the probabilities of all characteristics in Case 4 is upperbounded by $P_1(a,0)P_4(b,0)p^8$.

By combining the four cases and including the iterative characteristic we get that the probability of the differential depicted in Table 1 is upperbounded by $p_0^8 + p^8$. The other differentials can be considered similarily. For differentials which do not include the iterative characteristic the upperbound is p^8 and can often be achieved with much less than 16 rounds. We state the following result.

Theorem 1. *If a generalized Feistel network has four parallel S-boxes per round, the average probability of each differential over at least sixteen rounds is less than or equal to $p^8 + p_0^8$.*

3.3 Network with Bijective S-boxes for $n = 4$

If all S-boxes of the generalized Feistel network are bijective, it follows that $p_0 = 0$. Then it follows from Theorem 1 that all differentials over sixteen rounds have probabilities smaller than or equal to p^8. But as it turns out in the bijective case, it suffices to extend the differential over twelve rounds to take its probability below this upperbound.

In Table 5 we give a typical example of a differential of a Feistel network with bijective S-boxes.

Since $a \neq 0$, it follows that both t_1 and t_2 are nonzero. This facilitates the estimation of the probability of the differential which is performed in Table 6.

Other differentials of this network can be considered similarly. Hence we claim the following result.

Theorem 2. *If a generalized Feistel network has four parallel bijective S-boxes per round, the average probability of each differential over at least twelve rounds is less than or equal to p^8.*

a	0	0	0	0	0	0	0
a	0	0	0	0	0	0	0
0	a	0	0	0	0	0	0
0	a	0	0	0	0	0	0
0	0	a	0	0	0	0	0
0	0	a	0	0	0	0	0
0	0	0	a	0	0	0	0
0	0	0	a	0	0	0	0
0	0	0	0	a	0	0	0
0	0	0	t_1	a	0	0	0
0	0	0	0	t_1	a	0	0
0	0	s_{2a}	t_2	t_1	a	0	0
0	0	0	s_{2a}	t_2	t_1	a	0
0	s_{3a}	s_{21}	t_3	t_2	t_1	a	0
0	0	s_{3a}	s_{21}	t_3	t_2	t_1	a
s_{4a}	s_{31}	s_{22}	b	t_3	t_2	t_1	a
a	s_{4a}	s_{31}	s_{22}	b	t_3	t_2	t_1
s_{41}	s_{32}	0	0	b	t_3	t_2	t_1
t_1	s_{41}	s_{32}	0	0	b	t_3	t_2
s_{42}	0	0	0	0	b	t_3	t_2
t_2	s_{42}	0	0	0	0	b	t_3
0	0	0	0	0	0	b	t_3
t_3	0	0	0	0	0	0	b
0	0	0	0	0	0	0	b
b	0	0	0	0	0	0	0

Table 5. A differential for $n = 4$ and bijective S-boxes.

probability	Step 1 estimate	Step 2 sum over	Step 3 sum over
$P_1(a, t_1)$		t_1	
$P_2(a, s_{2a})$		s_{2a}	
$P_3(a, s_{3a})$		s_{3a}	
$P_4(a, s_{4a})$		s_{4a}	
$P_1(t_1, t_2)$	$\leq p$		
$P_2(t_1, s_{21})$	$\leq p$		
$P_3(t_1, s_{31})$	$\leq p$		
$P_4(t_1, a + s_{41})$	$\leq p$		
$P_1(t_2, s_{2a} + t_3)$	$\leq p$		
$P_2(t_2, s_{3a} + s_{22})$	$\leq p$		
$P_3(t_2, s_{4a} + s_{32})$	$\leq p$		
$P_4(t_2, t_1 + s_{42})$	$\leq p$		
$P_1(t_3, s_{21} + b)$		s_{21}	
$P_2(t_3, s_{31})$		s_{31}	
$P_3(t_3, s_{41})$		s_{41}	
$P_4(t_3, t_2)$		t_2	
$P_1(b, s_{22})$		s_{22}	
$P_2(b, s_{32})$		s_{32}	
$P_3(b, s_{42})$		s_{42}	
$P_4(b, t_3)$			t_3

Table 6. Estimation of the differential probability for bijective S-boxes.

In [3], Nyberg and Knudsen proved that for $n = 1$ an upperbound of $2p^2$ holds for differentials over three rounds. It was pointed out by Aoki and Ohta in [1] that the factor 2 can be removed from this upperbound.

For similar grounds, as in the general case, we belive that the following conjecture holds.

Conjecture 2 *If a generalized Feistel network has n parallel bijective s-boxes per round, the average probability of each differential over at least 3n rounds is less than or equal to p^{2n}.*

4   Resistance Against Linear Cryptanalysis

Linear cryptanalysis exploits large expected correlations between linear combinations of the input bits and the output bits over some number of rounds of the network. Clearly, these correlations depend on the actual key used. But since the key is secret to the cryptanalyst we consider the average correlations taken over uniformly distributed and independent round keys. For simplicity, we consider only the known plaintext attack and assume that the plaintext is uniformly random data. Then, by [2], Theorems 1 and 2, the average squared correlation between an input linear combination and an output linear combination can be computed as the sum of the products of the squared correlations of all possible subsequent round approximations. We make the following notation

$$C_i(\alpha, \beta) = |2P_X\{\alpha \cdot X = \beta \cdot F_i(X)\} - 1|,$$

for $i = 1, 2, \ldots, n$, where X is a random variable which is uniformly distributed in $GF(2^d)$. Let us denote by c the maximum of the correlations $C_i(\alpha, \beta)$ over all $\beta \neq 0$, α and $i = 1, 2, \ldots, n$ and by c_0, the maximum of $C_i(0, \beta)$ over all $\beta \neq 0$ and $i = 1, 2, \ldots, n$.

0	0	0	0	a	0	0	0
0	0	0	0	a	0	0	0
0	0	0	0	0	a	0	0
0	0	0	0	0	a	0	0
			$\vdots$ (six rounds)				
t_4	t_3	t_2	t_1	a	s_{4a}	s_{31}	s_{22}
t_4	t_3	t_2	t_1	s_{41}	s_{32}	s_{23}	t_5
t_5	t_4	t_3	t_2	t_1	s_{41}	s_{32}	s_{23}
t_5	t_4	t_3	t_2	s_{42}	s_{33}	s_{24}	t_6
t_6	t_5	t_4	t_3	t_2	s_{42}	s_{33}	s_{24}
t_6	t_5	t_4	t_3	s_{43}	s_{34}	s_{25}	t_7
t_7	t_6	t_5	t_4	t_3	s_{43}	s_{34}	s_{25}
t_7	t_6	t_5	t_4	s_{44}	s_{35}	s_{26}	b
			$\vdots$ (two rounds)				
0	0	b	t_7	t_6	s_{46}	0	0
0	0	b	t_7	0	0	0	0
0	0	0	b	t_7	0	0	0
0	0	0	b	0	0	0	0
0	0	0	0	b	0	0	0

Table 7. The most powerful overall linear approximation for $n = 4$.

It has been observed by many authors that, for the Feistel network, the linear approximation trails and differential characteristics are mirror images of each other. For generalized Feistel networks, we obtain the linear approximations if we interchange the n leftmost columns of differentials and the n rightmost columns. For example, the differential of Table 1 can be transformed to a linear approximation system depicted in Table 7. It shows all linear approximation trails which constitute the overall approximation of the linear combination $(0, 0, 0, 0, b, 0, 0, 0) \cdot Y$ of the output bits by the linear combination $(0, 0, 0, 0, a, 0, 0, 0) \cdot X$ of the input bits. Similarily, Table 5 can be modified to represent an overall linear approximation over twelve rounds with bijective s-boxes. Tables 2-4 and 6 can be used for the estimation of the squared correlation if $P_i(x, y)$ is replaced by $C_i^2(y, x)$. Consequently, we have the following result.

Theorem 3. *If a generalized Feistel network has four s-boxes in parallel per round, the average squared correlation between a linear combination of input bits and a non-zero linear combination of output bits from sixteen, or more rounds of the network is less than or equal to $(c^2)^8 + (c_0^2)^8$. If, moreover, the s-boxes are bijective, then the average squared correlation is less than or equal to $(c^2)^8$ for twelve or more rounds.*

Equivalently to Conjectures 1 and 2 it seems that Theorem 3 holds in general for an arbitrary number n of s-boxes so that $4n$ rounds suffices to satisfy the upperbound $(c^2)^{2n} + (c_0^2)^{2n}$, and if the s-boxes are bijective, $3n$ rounds suffices for the upperbound $(c^2)^{2n}$.

5 Conclusions

5.1 Strong S-boxes

For $d \times d$ s-boxes F, the smallest possible value for both p and c^2 is 2^{1-d}, which can be obtained simultaneously only if d is odd. Such s-boxes are provided by bijective functions $F(x) = x^{2^k+1}$, $\gcd(k, d)=1$, which are of algebraic degree two, and their inverses, which are of algebraic degree $(d + 1)/2$.

Examples of s-boxes with p and c^2 less than or equal to 2^{2-d} are numerous and include also bijective functions in all even dimensions d. Using Theorems 2 and 3, taking $n = 4$, $d = 8$ and selecting four bijective s-boxes with p and c^2 less than or equal to 2^{-6} one gets a network of twelve rounds that gives proven resistance of order 2^{-48} against linear and differential attacks. For comparison, it is interesting to note that the strongest characteristic of the DES over twelve rounds has probability approximately 2^{-48} and the best squared linear correlation over twelve rounds of the DES is approximately 2^{-32}.

5.2 Other Tappings Between Rounds

Naturally, similar results can be derived for generalized Feistel networks with a different permutation of blocks between the rounds. However, not all permutations are strong. In the worst case, it is possible that a network of $2n$ blocks can be split into n parallel independent Feistel networks. This would be the case if for example, with $n = 4$ the tapping is chosen such that $Y_k' = Y_{9-k}$, $k = 1, 2, \ldots, 8$ (see Figure 1). Clearly, such splitting cannot occur if, after the functions F_i have been arranged, the block permutation is chosen in such a way that the network reaches complete diffusion (on the block level) after $2n$ rounds. This seems also to be sufficient to prove the same strength against differential and linear cryptanalysis as in the above theorems.

Our network permutation which is the cyclic shift by one block has another useful feature. It is easy to see, that if in decryption, the functions $F_1, F_2, \ldots, F_n$ are addressed in the reverse order, then the same cyclic shift permutation is applied between the rounds. In particular, if we choose $F_j = F_{n+1-j}$, for $j = 1, 2, \ldots, \lfloor n/2 \rfloor$, then the encryption and the decryption networks are the same.

Also in this sense the proposed network is a generalization of the classical Feistel network.

Acknowledgement

The author thanks Bruce Schneier for useful discussions on unbalanced Feistel networks while staying at the Isaac Newton Institute.

References

1. K. Aoki, K. Ohta, Strict evaluation of the maximum average of differential probability and the maximum average of linear probability, preprint, February 1996.
2. K. Nyberg, Linear approximation of block ciphers, in Advances in Cryptology - EUROCRYPT '94 (Ed. A. De Santis), LNCS 950, Springer-Verlag, 1995, 439-444.
3. K. Nyberg, L. Knudsen, Provable security against a differential attack, J. Crypt. 8, Number 1, 1995, 27-38.
4. M. Matsui, New structure of block ciphers with provable security against differential and linear cryptanalysis, in Fast Software Encryption (Ed. D. Gollmann), LNCS 1039, Springer-Verlag, 1996, 205-218.
5. B. Schneier, J. Kelsey, Unbalanced Feistel networks and block cipher design, in Fast Software Encryption (Ed. D. Gollmann), LNCS 1039, Springer-Verlag, 1996, 121-144.
6. Y. Zheng, T. Matsumoto and H. Imai, On the construction of block ciphers provably secure and not relying on any unproven hypotheses, in Advances in Cryptology – CRYPTO'89, LNCS 435, Springer-Verlag, 1990, 461-480.

On Applying Linear Cryptanalysis to IDEA

Philip Hawkes[1] and Luke O'Connor[*,2]

[1] Department of Mathematics, University of Queensland, Brisbane, Australia.
pmh@maths.uq.oz.au
[2] Distributed Systems Technology Centre (DSTC), Brisbane, Australia.
oconnor@dstc.edu.au

Abstract. Linear cryptanalysis is a well-known attack based on linear approximations, and is said to be *feasible* for an n-bit block cipher if the data complexity is at most 2^n. In this paper we consider IDEA with independent and uniformly distributed subkeys, referred to as IDEA with extended subkeys. We prove that any linear approximation of IDEA with extended subkeys, generalized to R rounds, requires at least $R + \lfloor \frac{R}{3} \rfloor$ approximations to the multiply operation. We argue that the best approximations are based on approximating least significant bits in the round operations and show that the probability of selecting a key for which such a linear cryptanalysis is feasible on IDEA is approximately 2^{-100}.

1 Introduction

The security of International Data Encryption Algorithm (IDEA) [5] is based on mixing operations from distinct algebraic groups. The operations used by IDEA are $\oplus$, bitwise exclusive-OR; $\boxplus$, addition modulo 2^m; and $\odot$, multiplication modulo $2^m + 1$, where $2^m + 1$ is a prime and $0 \cdots 0 \stackrel{\text{def}}{=} 2^m$. Since $2^m + 1$ is prime for $m \in \{4, 8, 16\}$, we let $n = 4m$ and observe that IDEA can be scaled to a block size of 16 and 32 bits, referred to as IDEA(16) and IDEA(32), respectively (we will also refer to IDEA as IDEA(64) when appropriate). Linear cryptanalysis (LC) [6] is an attack that replaces the nonlinear components of a cipher, typically S-boxes, with linear approximations which allow information about the secret key to be determined when a sufficient number of plaintext/ciphertext pairs are available. Applying LC to IDEA is complicated by several factors including (a) the nonlinear operations being approximated are key-dependent and operate on large block sizes, (b) the subkeys are combined using nonlinear operations, and (c) the output of an approximated operation may form the input to another operation to be approximated in the same round.

The significance of the last complication is that the independence of the approximations cannot always be hypothesized by assuming the subkeys are independent, as is possible for DES. Thus it has to be argued carefully how the

---

* The work reported in this paper has been funded in part by the Cooperative Research Centres program through the Department of the Prime Minister and Cabinet of Australia.

Piling-Up lemma [6] is to be applied, if at all. However, there is seemingly no other practical method for deriving linear approximations between the plaintext and ciphertext other than combining approximations across rounds [2].

The success of LC depends on the nonlinearity of the operations being approximated, often S-boxes. Since modular addition is highly linear, we will concentrate on approximating linearities in the multiply operation. Our analysis begins by proving that if R rounds of IDEA have to be approximated then at least $R + \lfloor \frac{R}{3} \rfloor$ approximations to the multiply operation must be made. For an operation $\ominus$ we will say that the least significant bit (LSB) approximation to $\ominus$ is given as $1 \cdot X + 1 \cdot (X \ominus Z) = 0$. We will argue that the best linear approximation between the plaintext and ciphertext of IDEA is given by using an LSB approximation at each operation that needs to be approximated. Such approximations are 'plausibly best' since they approximate the multiply operation with high probability, and approximate the addition operation with probability one. We note that the differential cryptanalysis (DC) of IDEA [4] is also based on 'plausibly best' arguments, as is the recent LC and DC analysis of RC5 [3]. LSB approximations have been used to find weak keys in IDEA [1].

We will refer to subkeys that are uniformly and independently distributed as extended subkeys, and most results on differential and linear cryptanalysis assume extended subkeys. Using LSB approximations we construct a linear approximation between the plaintext and ciphertext that is *optimal* in that it uses the minimum number of approximations to the multiply operation. Further, the probability of this approximation can be determined using the Piling-Up lemma assuming extended subkeys. In particular, we prove that for IDEA(n), $n \in \{16, 32, 64\}$, the fraction of extended keys for which a LC based on LSB approximations is feasible is $2^{-15.3}$, $2^{-45.9}$ and $2^{-100.8}$, respectively. Under the plausible assumption that the LSB approximations are the best approximations, IDEA is secure against linear cryptanalysis in the extended subkey model.

The paper is organized as follows. In §2 we examine round approximations and derive a lower bound on the number of approximations needed at each round. In §3 we show how the Piling-Up lemma can be used to determine the probability of certain approximations. And finally in §4 we argue that LSB approximations yield the best probabilities for a LC of IDEA and determine the fraction of extended keys for which the data complexity of such a LC is feasible.

2 Linearities in the Round Function

IDEA consists of eight full rounds and one 'half round', referred to as the output transformation. The ciphertext at the beginning of round r will be denoted $C^{(r)} = C_1^{(r)} C_2^{(r)} C_3^{(r)} C_4^{(r)}$, where the plaintext is denoted as $P = C^{(1)}$, and the encryption of P is denoted as $C = C^{(10)}$. We will use R to denote the number of full rounds, and assume that the operation at the $(R + 1)$st round is the output transformation. For IDEA the number of rounds is $R = 8$ but we will express our results in terms of general R. The main result of this section is to show that any LC of IDEA will require at least $R + \lfloor \frac{R}{3} \rfloor$ approximations to the multiply operation. This can be proved essentially using algebra as the linear approximation must guarantee that cancellation of intermediate ciphertext values, which restricts the set of possible approximations considerably. In the next section will we discuss how to use the Piling-Up Lemma to determine the probability of certain classes of linear approximations.

The first step in LC is to determine a linear approximation between $C^{(r)}$ and $C^{(r+1)}$ of the form

$$\alpha^{(r)} \cdot C^{(r)} + \alpha^{(r+1)} \cdot C^{(r+1)} = 0 \tag{1}$$

where $\alpha^{(r)} = \alpha_1^{(r)} \alpha_2^{(r)} \alpha_3^{(r)} \alpha_4^{(r)}$ for r, $1 \leq r \leq R+1$. Note that (1) does not involve the round key, and this peculiarity will be discussed in the next section.

Proposition 1 A round approximation at round r can be represented by a *round association* $RA_{u,v}^{(r)}$ defined as

$$RA_{u,v}^{(r)} = (a_1^{(r)}, a_2^{(r)}, a_3^{(r)}, a_4^{(r)}) \xrightarrow{M_r, A_r} (b_1^{(r)}, b_2^{(r)}, b_3^{(r)}, b_4^{(r)}) \tag{2}$$

where $a_i^{(r)}, b_i^{(r)} \in \{0, 1\}$, and $u = \sum_{i=1}^{4} a_i^{(r)} \cdot 2^{4-i}$, $v = \sum_{i=1}^{4} b_i^{(r)} \cdot 2^{4-i}$. The $a_i^{(r)}(b_i^{(r)})$ indicate if the i-th block of the input (output) is involved in the round approximation. The round association involves M_r approximations to the $\odot$ operation and A_r approximations to the $\boxplus$ operation. □

For example, the round association $RA_{10,12}^{(r)} = (1, 0, 1, 0) \xrightarrow{1,1} (1, 1, 0, 0)$ denotes a linear approximation between the first and third blocks of the round input and the first and second blocks of the round output, involving one approximation to the $\odot$ and $\boxplus$ operations. Round associations are a convenient way of representing similar round approximations that require the same number of group approximations.

Lemma 1. The only round associations which require one approximation to $\odot$ are those given in Table 1. □

As the round function is the same for each (full) round, the possible round associations are the same for each round, however the round associations for the output transformation will be different. These round associations, called *transform associations*, are denoted by $TA_{u,v}^{(R+1)}$ and are all of the form $(\alpha_1, \alpha_2, \alpha_3, \alpha_4) \xrightarrow{M_{R+1}, A_{R+1}} (\alpha_1, \alpha_3, \alpha_2, \alpha_4)$.

A sequence of round associations followed by a transform association can also be joined together to form a linear association between the plaintext and ciphertext of a cipher. Round associations can be joined to form associations across several rounds. We will say that RA_{u_1,v_1} and RA_{u_2,v_2} are *compatible* if $v_1 = u_2$, and write this fact as $RA_{u_1,v_1} \longrightarrow RA_{u_2,v_2}$.

Definition 1 A linear association $LA_{u,v} = (a_1, a_2, a_3, a_4) \xrightarrow{M, A} (b_1, b_2, b_3, b_4)$ for R-round IDEA is a set of R round associations $\{RA_{u_r,v_r}^{(r)} \mid 1 \leq r \leq R\}$ and a transform association $TA_{u_{R+1},v_{R+1}}^{(R+1)}$ that can be ordered as

$$RA_{u,v_1}^{(1)} \longrightarrow RA_{v_1,v_2}^{(2)} \longrightarrow \cdots \longrightarrow RA_{v_{R-1},v_R}^{(R)} \longrightarrow TA_{v_R,v}^{(R+1)} \tag{3}$$

All RAs requiring 1 approximation to $\odot$ per round		
$RA_{4,1}$	$(0,1,0,0) \xrightarrow{1,3} (0,0,0,1)$	
$RA_{4,3}$	$(0,1,0,0) \xrightarrow{1,3} (0,0,1,1)$	$\alpha_3^{(r+1)} \neq \alpha_4^{(r+1)}$
$RA_{5,3}$	$(0,1,0,1) \xrightarrow{1,1} (0,0,1,1)$	$\alpha_3^{(r+1)} = \alpha_4^{(r+1)}$
$RA_{6,5}$	$(0,1,1,0) \xrightarrow{1,4} (0,1,0,1)$	
$RA_{6,7}$	$(0,1,1,0) \xrightarrow{1,4} (0,1,1,1)$	$\alpha_3^{(r+1)} \neq \alpha_4^{(r+1)}$
$RA_{6,10}$	$(0,1,1,0) \xrightarrow{1,3} (1,0,1,0)$	
$RA_{6,14}$	$(0,1,1,0) \xrightarrow{1,3} (1,1,1,0)$	$\alpha_1^{(r+1)} \neq \alpha_2^{(r+1)}$
$RA_{10,12}$	$(1,0,1,0) \xrightarrow{1,1} (1,1,0,0)$	$\alpha_1^{(r+1)} = \alpha_2^{(r+1)}$
Compatible RAs requiring 2 approximations to $\odot$ per round		
$RA_{3,6}$	$(0,0,1,1) \xrightarrow{2,3} (0,1,1,0)$	
$RA_{7,5}$	$(0,1,1,1) \xrightarrow{2,4} (0,1,0,1)$	
$RA_{7,6}$	$(0,1,1,1) \xrightarrow{2,4} (0,1,1,0)$	no conditions
$RA_{12,6}$	$(1,1,0,0) \xrightarrow{2,2} (0,1,1,0)$	
$RA_{14,6}$	$(1,1,1,0) \xrightarrow{2,3} (0,1,1,0)$	
$RA_{14,10}$	$(1,1,1,0) \xrightarrow{2,3} (1,0,1,0)$	

Table 1. The first group of RAs in the table are all RAs requiring one approximation to the multiply operation per round. The second group of RAs are all RAs that are compatible with the first group of RAs in the sense that $RA_{u_1,v_1} \longrightarrow RA_{u_2,v_2} \longrightarrow RA_{u_3,v_3}$ where $RA_{u_1,v_1}, RA_{u_3,v_3}$ belong to the first group of RAs, and RA_{u_2,v_2} belongs to the second group.

where $u = u_1, v = v_{R+1}$ and $M = \sum_{r=1}^{R} M_r$, $A = \sum_{r=1}^{R} A_r$. A linear association is *optimal* for R-round IDEA if M is minimal. $\square$

The linear association $LA_{6,10} = (0,1,1,0) \xmapsto{11,17} (1,0,1,0)$ indicates that there is a linear approximation between the second and third subblocks of the plaintext and the first and third subblocks of the ciphertext, which requires eleven approximations of the $\odot$ operation and seventeen approximations of the $\boxplus$ operation.

It can be verified from Table 1 that there does not exist three compatible round associations each requiring one approximation to the multiply operation. When R is a multiple of three the number of approximations to the multiply operation is then at least $R + R/3$, but slightly more when $R \not\equiv 0 \mod 3$.

Corollary 1 For IDEA with R rounds, every linear approximation of the form $\alpha \cdot P + \beta \cdot C + \gamma \cdot Z = 0$ that is derived from linear approximations to the round function and output transformation requires at least $R + \lfloor \frac{R}{3} \rfloor + [R \not\equiv 0 \mod 3]$ linear approximations to the multiply operation, where $[\cdot]$ is a boolean predicate evaluating to 0 or 1. $\square$

Proof. (Sketch) Every three rounds requires at least four approximations to the multiply operation. If R is a multiple of three then no approximation to the multiply operation need be made in the output transformation. □

For 8-round IDEA, Corollary 1 states that at least eleven approximations to

$LA_{5,6}$	$(0,1,0,1)$	$\xrightarrow{11,18}$ $(0,1,1,0)$	$(5,3,6,10,12,6,10,12,6,6)$
$LA_{6,4}$	$(0,1,1,0)$	$\xrightarrow{11,20}$ $(0,1,0,1)$	$(6,10,12,6,10,12,6,5,2,4)$
$LA_{6,5}$	$(0,1,1,0)$	$\xrightarrow{11,18}$ $(0,1,0,1)$	$(6,10,12,6,10,12,6,5,3,5)$
$LA_{6,6}$	$(0,1,1,0)$	$\xrightarrow{11,20}$ $(0,1,1,0)$	$(6,14,6,10,12,6,10,12,6,6)$
$LA_{6,10}$	$(0,1,1,0)$	$\xrightarrow{11,17}$ $(1,0,1,0)$	$(6,10,12,6,10,12,6,10,12,10)$
$LA_{10,6}$	$(1,0,1,0)$	$\xrightarrow{11,17}$ $(0,1,1,0)$	$(10,12,6,10,12,6,10,12,6,6)$

Table 2. Selective optimal linear associations of 8-round IDEA. The linear association $LA_{6,4}$ makes use of the round association $RA_{5,2} = (0,1,0,1) \xrightarrow{2,3} (0,0,1,0)$, which is not listed in Table 1.

the multiply operation are required, and any optimal linear association will require exactly this number of approximations. There are many optimal linear associations which can be derived from the round associations given in Table 1.

Lemma 2. The number of optimal linear associations for R-round IDEA, denoted $\lambda(R)$, is given as

$$\lambda(R) = \begin{cases} 2^{\lfloor \frac{R}{3} \rfloor} & \text{when } R \equiv 0 \bmod 3, \\ 8 \cdot 2^{\lfloor \frac{R}{3} \rfloor} & \text{when } R \equiv 1 \bmod 3, \\ 9 \cdot 2^{\lfloor \frac{R}{3} \rfloor} & \text{when } R \equiv 2 \bmod 3. \end{cases}$$

□

Table 2 shows examples of optimal linear associations $LA_{u,v}$ for 8-round IDEA, where one optimal linear association for each possible value of the pair u,v has been given. A linear association of the form in (3) is denoted in Table 2 by the $(R+2)$-tuple $(u, v_1, v_2, \ldots, v_{R-1}, v_R, v)$.

The basic LC attack can be modified to derive approximations of the form

$$\alpha \cdot P + \beta \cdot C + \delta_1 \cdot F_1(Z_1) + \delta_R \cdot F_R(Z_R) + \gamma \cdot Z = 0 \tag{4}$$

where $F_1(Z_1)$ is the output of the first round and $F_R(Z_R)$ the output of the last round before the output transformation. If δ_1 or δ_R are nonzero then this modification is referred to as the $1R$-method, and if both δ_1 and δ_R are nonzero then the modification is referred to as the $2R$-method. The $1R$- and $2R$-methods proceed by guessing the relevant keys bits of Z_1 and/or Z_R to the approximation and taking the correct key to be the one which maximizes the probability of (4) deviating from one half. LC can be extended to kR-attacks, but the trade-off in complexity is that each additional term of the form $\delta_i \cdot F_i(Z_i)$ requires partial exhaustive testing of the subkey Z_i.

Corollary 1 is derived assuming that no rounds of IDEA avoid approximation through using kR-methods for some $k > 0$. However, we observe that kR-methods remove a number of rounds at the beginning and end of an iterated mapping, leaving a 'core' of internal rounds to be approximated. For example, in IDEA if the first two rounds and the output transformation are removed using a $3R$-method then there still remains a core of six rounds to be approximated.

Corollary 2 For IDEA with R rounds, every linear approximation that uses a kR-method requires at least $(R - k) + \lfloor \frac{R-k}{3} \rfloor$ approximations to the multiply operation.

$\square$

In any case, the size of k is expected to be small since at least 2^{16k} additional key counters will be required to perform a kR-method LC on IDEA. In the next section we show how to use the Piling-Up lemma to determine lower bounds on the probabilities of optimal linear associations.

3   Applying the Piling-Up Lemma

The round associations defined in the previous section denote classes of round approximations by suppressing the actual details of how and which operations are approximated. Note that each round of IDEA has fourteen possible operations to be approximated: the four group operations in the key combining phase, the four group operations in the MA-structure, and six XOR operations. Any round approximation of the form

$$\alpha^{(r)} \cdot C^{(r)} + \alpha^{(r+1)} \cdot C^{(r+1)} = 0 \tag{5}$$

will necessarily be comprised of approximations to some subset of the fourteen possible group operations. The main obstacle to applying the Piling-Up lemma directly is the fact that the lemma assumes the approximations are independent. For ciphers such as DES the independence of the approximations can be guaranteed by assuming extended subkeys, which generally follows for any cipher that feeds key-dependent input into static key-independent mappings (for example, S-boxes). However, IDEA is designed to feed key-independent input into dynamic key-dependent mappings.

Our proposal is to look at a class of optimal linear associations for which the set of approximations to the multiply operation are independent for extended subkeys, and hence permit the Piling-Up lemma to be applied. In fact, we shall be considering optimal linear associations which are plausibly the best associations as they require the fewest number of approximations to the multiply operation.

To obtain the independence of the multiply approximations we will require some restriction on the form of approximations for the addition operation. We will say that an approximation to one of the operations in IDEA is *trivial* if it is correct with probability one (that is, true for all keys). For example, $0 \cdot X + 0 \cdot (X \boxplus Z) = 0$ is a trivial approximation.

Theorem 3. Assuming extended subkeys in IDEA, and that all approximations to the addition operation are trivial, each approximation to the multiply operation in an optimal linear association is independent. □

Corollary 3 Assuming optimal linear associations give linear associations of the highest probability, then the data complexity of a LC of R-round IDEA with extended subkeys where no kR-methods are used is at least

$$\left| 2^{T-1} \cdot \prod_{i=1}^{T} \left(p_i - \frac{1}{2} \right) \right|^{-2} \tag{6}$$

where p_i is the probability of the i-th approximation to the multiply operation, $1 \le i \le T$ and $T = R + \lfloor \frac{R}{3} \rfloor + [R \not\equiv 0 \bmod 3]$. □

Remark 1: The probabilities p_i are key-dependent and their calculation is addressed in the next section.

Remark 2: If a kR-method is used then the data complexity of LC is bounded from below by (6) when $T = (R - k) + \lfloor \frac{R-k}{3} \rfloor$.

Remark 3: In a LC not using kR-methods the purpose is to find a linear approximation of the form

$$\alpha \cdot P + \beta \cdot C + \gamma \cdot Z = 0, \tag{7}$$

followed by a maximum likelihood procedure to determine the one bit of information encoded in the sum $\gamma \cdot Z$. Note that linear associations constructed from round associations of the form (1) imply that $\gamma = 0$. While this prevents information of the form $\gamma \cdot Z$ to be determined about the key, we plausibly maintain that any approximation of the form (7) for which $\gamma \ne 0$ occurs with probability less than the optimal linear associations given above, thus bounding the data complexity of LC from below.

Further an approximation of the form in (1) with $\gamma = 0$ still permits kR-methods to be applied, which is how LC is used to obtain significant information about the key in addition to the one bit afforded by $\gamma \cdot Z$ for nonzero γ. □

Even though Theorem 3 means that the Piling-Up lemma can be applied to determine the data complexity of a given instance of an optimal linear association, there is still the issue of coping with the key-dependent nature of the multiply operation. In the next section we will argue that $1 \cdot X + 1 \cdot (X \odot Z) = 0$, or the LSB (least significant bit) approximation, applied to each occurrence of the multiply operation that must be approximated, yields the plausibly best (highest) probability for a LC.

4 LSB Approximations

Our analysis in this section focuses on determining the effectiveness of linear approximations to IDEA(n), $n \in \{16, 32, 64\}$, when the same approximation $\alpha \cdot X + \beta \cdot (X \odot Z) = 0$ is applied to each multiply operation being approximated. One advantage of this approach is that a generating function can be used to obtain the fraction of keys for which LC is feasible, as pursued in §4.1.

We conjecture that using repeated LSB approximations gives the best success for a LC of IDEA. Intuitively, LSB approximations are the best since they approximate the multiply operation with high probability, approximate the addition operation with probability one. So while other approximations may yield higher probabilities when only considering approximations to the multiply operation, these probabilities are almost certain to drop to below the probability of repeated LSB approximations when approximations to the addition operation are accounted for. Also, it can be argued that for many round approximations the addition operations in the MA-structure do not receive inputs that are uniformly distributed, and thus if they are to be approximated non-trivially then the approximation must hold for all keys and all inputs. The LSB approximation is the only such approximation for the addition operation ($0 \cdot X + 0 \cdot (X \boxplus Z) = 0$ is also trivial but does not lead to useful approximations).

We first consider the probability of a LC based on LSB approximations averaged over all possible subkeys, assuming each is equally likely.

Lemma 4. For IDEA(n), $n \in \{16, 32, 64\}$, the average deviation p_n^* of the probability of an LSB approximation to $\odot$ from one half, assuming random inputs and random key is

$$p_n^* \stackrel{\text{def}}{=} 2^{-m} \cdot \sum_{Z \in Z_2^m} \left| \left(2^{-m} \cdot \sum_{X \in Z_2^m} [1 \cdot X + 1 \cdot (X \odot Z) = 0] \right) - \frac{1}{2} \right|$$

and $p_{16}^* = 2^{-3}$, $p_{32}^* = 2^{-5.73}$ and $p_{64}^* = 2^{-11.48}$ where $n = 4m$.

Corollary 4 Assume that optimal linear associations using the LSB approximation to the multiply operation give linear associations of the highest probability. Then for 8-round IDEA(n), $n \in \{16, 32, 64\}$, with extended subkeys, the deviation $|p - \frac{1}{2}|$ of a linear approximation $\alpha \cdot P + \beta \cdot C + \gamma \cdot Z = 0$ requiring eleven approximations to the multiply operation is at most 2^{-23}, $2^{-53.1}$ and $2^{-116.3}$ respectively.

Proof. Use Corollary 3 with $T = 11$. $\qquad\square$

Recall that LC is said to be *feasible* for an n-bit block cipher if the data complexity is at most 2^n. If $|p - \frac{1}{2}|$ is the deviation of a given approximation then the associated data complexity is roughly $|p - \frac{1}{2}|^{-2}$. Then denoting the deviations from Corollary 4 as $p_n, n \in \{16, 32, 64\}$, it follows that the expected data complexity exceeds 2^n when the key is random since $p_n > 2^n$, let alone $(p_n)^2$.

However, this approach suggests that the average bias in a linear approximation is small only for a *random key* and does not indicate if *particular keys* give a much higher probability of success. In the next section we continue our analysis of the LSB approximation and enumerate the fraction of extended keys for which LC is feasible.

4.1 A Generating Function Approach

The *linear success* of a particular linear approximation between the plaintext and ciphertext will be defined as the fraction of extended keys for which a LC using the approximation is feasible. In this section we will examine the linear success of 8-round IDEA(n), $n \in \{16, 32, 64\}$, with extended subkeys assuming eleven LSB approximations to the multiply operation are made, which is the number required for an optimal linear association of 8-round IDEA. The analysis can be easily altered if the number of approximations is increased or decreased.

The fraction of extended keys for which a LC is feasible using exactly eleven approximations of the form $\alpha \cdot X + \beta \cdot (X \odot Z) = 0$ can be determined by the following generating function

$$F_{\alpha,\beta,n}(x) = \left(\sum_{Z \in Z_2^m} \frac{1}{2^m} x^{\log_2(p(\alpha,\beta,Z))} \right)^{11} = \left(\sum_{0 < q \le \frac{1}{2}} a_q x^{\log_2(q)} \right)^{11}, \quad (8)$$

where $p(\alpha, \beta, Z) = \left| \Pr(\alpha \cdot X + \beta \cdot (X \odot Z) = 0) - \frac{1}{2} \right|$ and a_q is the fraction of subkeys Z for which $p(\alpha, \beta, Z) = q$. Expanding the polynomial yields terms of the form $f x^q$, indicating the fraction f of extended keys for which

$$\sum_{i=1}^{11} \log_2 p(\alpha, \beta, Z_i) = q \quad (9)$$

where Z_i is the subkey used in the i-th approximation. Then using the Piling-Up lemma (as we can from Theorem 3), a LC is infeasible if

$$\left| p - \frac{1}{2} \right|^{-2} = \left| 2^{10} \cdot \prod_{i=1}^{11} p(\alpha, \beta, Z_i) \right|^{-2} \ge 2^n \iff \sum_{i=1}^{11} \log_2 p(\alpha, \beta, Z_i) \le -\frac{n}{2} - 10.$$

It follows that the fraction of subkeys that permit a feasible LC based on repeated LSB approximations is given by summing all coefficients f of $f x^q$ in $F_{1,1,n}$ for which $q \ge -\frac{n}{2} - 10$. Deleting terms for which the exponent of x was less than this bound yields a reduced polynomial, denoted $F_{1,1,n}^*(x)$, and $F_{1,1,n}^*(1)$ gives the linear success when all eleven multiply operations are approximated as $1 \cdot X + 1 \cdot (X \odot Z) = 0$.

For IDEA(16) all relevant exponents x^q of $F_{\alpha,\beta,16}^*(x)$ must satisfy $q \ge -18$. $F_{1,1,16}(x)$ and $F_{1,1,16}^*(x)$ can be calculated as

$$F_{1,1,16}(x) = \left(\frac{1}{2} x^{-3} + \frac{1}{8} x^{-1} \right)^{11},$$

$$F_{1,1,16}^*(x) = \frac{1.164}{10^{10}} x^{-12} + \frac{5.122}{10^9} x^{-14} + \frac{1.024}{10^7} x^{-16} + \frac{1.229}{10^6} x^{-18}.$$

The linear success of this linear approximation is $F^*_{1,1,16}(1) = 1.337 \times 10^{-6} = 2^{-19.5}$, meaning that there is about one chance in a million that repeated LSB approximations could be successfully used in a LC against IDEA(16). Deriving similar polynomials $F_{1,1,32}$ and $F_{1,1,64}$ allows us to prove

Lemma 5. A LC of 8-round IDEA(n), $n \in \{16, 32, 64\}$, with extended subkeys, based on repeated LSB approximations of the multiply operation is feasible for at most $2^{-19.5}$, $2^{-45.9}$ and $2^{-100.8}$ of the possible extended keys respectively. $\square$

To test our conjecture that repeated LSB approximations are the best, we examined approximations in IDEA(16) more closely. By considering all α, β, the approximation with the highest linear success was $F^*_{14,14,16}(1) = 2^{-15.3}$, with $F^*_{11,11,16}(1) = 2^{-19.2}$ being the next best, which is only a slight improvement over repeated LSB approximations. However, when the probabilities of approximating the addition operation were determined, and accounted for, repeated LSB approximations gave the best linear success.

5 Conclusion

LC is well-suited to ciphers, such as DES, where the subkeys are combined using the XOR operation and the nonlinear operations consist of relatively small fixed tables (S-boxes). Ciphers such as IDEA and RC5 that combine the key nonlinearly, and use key and/or data-dependent nonlinear operations, are more difficult to analyze. Our results show how the Piling-Up lemma can be applied to an LC of IDEA, and thus derive linear associations from round approximations. By using repeated LSB approximations we have avoided the need to approximate (with probability less than one) the addition operations of IDEA, which almost certainly makes the resulting approximations the most probable. Further, by using generating functions we have been able to bound the fraction of keys for which LC is feasible on IDEA when LSB approximations are used.

References

1. J. Daemen, R. Govaerts, and J. Vandewalle. Weak keys for IDEA. *Advances in Cryptology, CRYPTO'93, Lecture Notes in Computer Science, vol. 773, D. Stinson ed., Springer-Verlag*, pages 224–231, 1994.
2. C. Harpes and J.L. Kramer, G. G.and Massey. Generalisation of linear cryptanalysis and the applicability of Matsui's piling-up lemma. *Advances in Cryptology, EUROCRYPT'95, Lecture Notes in Computer Science, vol. 921, L. C. Guillou, J. Quiquater ed., Springer-Verlag*, pages 24–38, 1995.
3. B. S. Kaliski Jr. and Y. L. Yin. On differential and linear cryptanalysis of the RC5 encryption algorithm. *Advances in Cryptology, CRYPTO'95, Lecture Notes in Computer Science, vol. 963, D. Coppersmith ed., Springer-Verlag*, pages 171–184, 1995.
4. X. Lai. *On the design and security of block ciphers.* ETH Series in Information Processing, editor J. Massey, Hartung-Gorre Verlag Konstanz, 1992.

5. X. Lai, J. Massey, and S. Murphy. Markov ciphers and differential cryptanalysis. In *Advances in Cryptology, EUROCRYPT'91, Lecture Notes in Computer Science, vol. 547, D. W. Davies ed., Springer-Verlag*, pages 17–38, 1991.
6. M. Matsui. Linear cryptanalysis method for DES cipher. *Advances in Cryptology, EUROCRYPT'93, Lecture Notes in Computer Science, vol. 765, T. Helleseth ed., Springer-Verlag*, pages 386–397, 1994.

A Multi-Recastable Ticket Scheme for Electronic Elections *

Chun-I Fan and Chin-Laung Lei

Department of Electrical Engineering
National Taiwan University
Taipei, Taiwan, R.O.C.

Abstract. In this paper, we propose a multi-recastable ticket scheme for electronic elections based on blind signatures. In our election scheme, every voter of a group can obtain an m-castable ticket (m-ticket). Through the m-ticket, the voter can participate in m different designated elections held in this group. In each of the m elections, the voter can cast his vote by making appropriate modifications to the m-ticket. To obtain an m-ticket from the authority, only one round of registration is required for the voter. It turns out that our scheme greatly reduces the network traffic between the voters and the authority. The security of our scheme relies on the difficulty of solving the square roots of an integer in Z_n^*. In the proposed scheme, the identities of voters are protected against the authority by means of the blind signature techniques, and it is infeasible for an intruder to forge any legal vote in this scheme due to the properties of quadratic residues.

1   Introduction

Due to the fast progress of networking technologies, many advanced network services have been proposed. Among these services, electronic election is a popular one, since the electronic election makes it possible for a voter in a remote site to cast his vote through the communication networks. Over the past years, many important achievements related to this topic have been presented in the literature, such as secure election schemes [1, 2, 6, 9, 10, 11, 12, 19, 20] , blind signature schemes [4, 7, 8] and untraceable e-mails [3, 5, 15]. The techniques of blind signatures and untraceable e-mails make it possible to protect the privacy of the voters in an open network environment. Both practical and theoretical researches on secure electronic elections have been studied extensively. The theoretical research often focuses on the proof protocols embedded in the election schemes [2, 6, 19] , while the practical research pays attention to the efficiency of the election schemes [1, 9, 11, 15].

Generally, a practical electronic election scheme consists of two types of participants, an authority and voters. The voters cast the votes with their own

---

* This research was supported in part by the National Science Council of the Republic of China under grant NSC-86-2221-E-002-014.

individual intentions, and the authority verifies and tallies all the votes cast. In a typical electronic election scheme, every registered voter can obtain a vote in an encrypted form from the authority, and then the voter casts his vote by sending it to the authority at a proper time.

In this paper, a multi-recastable ticket scheme for electronic elections based on blind signatures is proposed. In our scheme, every voter of a group can obtain an m-castable ticket (m-ticket), which is an $(m+2)^{th}$-square root of an integer in an encrypted form, from the authority. The m-ticket can be re-used m times by modifying it in each election; that is, by modifying the m-ticket, the voter can participate in m different designated elections held in the group. In the kth election $1 \leq k \leq m$, the voter makes appropriate modifications to the m-ticket, and then cast the result of the modifications as the legal vote of the kth election. The vote can be verified by using the related information published in the kth election.

In our scheme, it requires only one round of registration for the voter to obtain such an m-ticket from the authority, so the network traffic can be greatly reduced. It is infeasible for an intruder to forge a legal vote in any of the m elections since computing the square roots of an element in Z_n^* is difficult where n is an integer with large prime factors [17]. Every voter can examine if his vote is tallied by the authority, and verify whether all the votes published by the authority are correct or not. Since all the voters have to cast their votes, the correctness of tally is guaranteed in our election scheme. By the techniques of blind signatures and sender untraceable e-mails, the privacy of the voters is protected against the authority in the proposed scheme.

The rest of the paper is organized as follows. In section 2, we review the blind signature scheme used in our election scheme. The proposed election scheme is described in section 3. The correctness and security of the proposed scheme are examined in section 4. Finally, a concluding remark is given in section 5.

2 Blind Signatures

Blind signature techniques make it possible to protect the privacy of the voters against the authority when the voters request their votes from the authority. Generally, a blind signature scheme consists of two kinds of participants, a signer and requesters. A requester requests signatures from the signer, and the signer issues blind signatures to the requester. There are two sets of messages known to the signer, one contains the signatures actually performed by him; the other contains the signatures submitted by the requesters for verification later. The key point is that the actual correspondence between these two sets of signatures is unknown to the signer. This property is usually referred to as the unlinkability property.

We have proposed an efficient blind signature scheme based on quadratic residues in [7], and a space-reduced version of [7] is presented in [8]. Under a modulus n, x is a quadratic residue (QR) in Z_n^* if and only if there exists an integer y in Z_n^* such that $y^2 \equiv_n x$. Given x, it is infeasible to compute the square root y if n contains large prime factors and the factorization of n is unknown [17]. The protocol in [8] consists of four phases: (1) initialization, (2) requesting, (3) signing, and (4) extraction. In the initialization phase, the signer publishes all the necessary information. To obtain the signature of a message, a requester submits an encrypted version of the message to the signer in the requesting phase. In the signing phase, the signer computes the blind signature of the encrypted message, and then sends the result back to the requester. At last, the requester extracts the signature from the result he receives in the extraction phase. The details of the blind signature scheme are described as follows.

1. **Initialization:** The signer randomly selects $n = p_1 p_2$ where p_1, p_2 are distinct large primes and $p_1 \equiv p_2 \equiv 3 \pmod 4$. Then, the signer publishes n.

2. **Requesting:** To request the signature of a plaintext w in Z_n^*, a requester randomly chooses r and $(u^2 + v^2)$ in Z_n^*, and then submits $(r^4 w(u^2 + v^2) \bmod n)$ to the signer. If w has no redundancy, a suitable one-way hashing function should be applied to w in order to avoid the multiplicative attacks. After receiving $(r^4 w(u^2 + v^2) \bmod n)$, the signer randomly selects x and y such that $r^4 w(u^2 + v^2)(x^2 + y^2)$ is a QR in Z_n^*, and then sends x and y to the requester.

   After receiving x and y, the requester sends $(b^2(uy - vx) \bmod n)$ to the signer where b is an integer randomly chosen by the requester in Z_n^*.

3. **Signing:** After receiving $(b^2(uy - vx) \bmod n)$, the signer computes,

   $$r^4 w(u^2 + v^2)(x^2 + y^2)(b^2(uy - vx))^{-2}$$
   $$\equiv_n r^4 b^{-4} w(u^2 + v^2)(x^2 + y^2)(uy - vx)^{-2}$$
   $$\equiv_n r^4 b^{-4} w((ux + vy)^2 + (uy - vx)^2)(uy - vx)^{-2}$$
   $$\equiv_n r^4 b^{-4} w((ux + vy)^2 (uy - vx)^{-2} + 1).$$

   Since the signer knows the primes p_1 and p_2, the signer can derive an integer t in Z_n^* [13, 17] such that,

   $$t^4 \equiv_n r^4 b^{-4} w((ux + vy)^2 (uy - vx)^{-2} + 1).$$

   Then, the signer sends t to the requester.

4. **Extraction:** After receiving t, the requester computes $s = r^{-1} bt \bmod n$ and $c = (ux + vy)(uy - vx)^{-1} \bmod n$. The signature of w is (s, w, c). To verify the signature (s, w, c), one can examine if $s^4 \equiv_n w(c^2 + 1)$.

In [8], we have shown that every signature (s, w, c) produced by the above protocol satisfies that $s^4 \equiv_n w(c^2 + 1)$, and it is infeasible for an intruder to forge any legal signature.

3   The Proposed Scheme

In this section, we introduce a multi-recastable ticket scheme for electronic elections. The proposed election scheme is especially suitable for the following cases of elections. In a group with a fixed number of members, it is estimated that a sequence of d designated elections will be held during a period of time, and the exact subject of each election may be not yet ascertained until the election is to be held. It is an example of such cases that the senators exercise their affirmative or oppositive opinions on a sequence of d designated proposals of the Senate where d is an estimated possible maximum number of proposals which will be proposed during the senators' term. By performing our election scheme, initially, every senator can obtain an m-ticket, $m \geq d$. Through the m-ticket, the senator can participate in the d elections in accordance with the d proposals of the Senate. In the kth election, $1 \leq k \leq m$, the senator extracts the kth vote from the m-ticket, and then cast it as the legal vote of the kth election for the kth proposal. The d elections can be successfully finished by performing the proposed scheme.

In our scheme, there are two kinds of participants, an authority and a group of voters. The voters cast the votes with their intentions, and the authority verifies and tallies all the votes cast. Our protocol consists of six stages: (1) initialization, (2) requesting, (3) registration, (4) extraction, (5) the kth election, $1 \leq k \leq m$, and (6) the kth tally, $1 \leq k \leq m$, where m is a positive integer. The authority publishes the necessary information in the initialization stage. To obtain an m-ticket, a voter submits an encrypted version of a message to the authority in the requesting stage. In the registration stage, the authority computes the blind signature of the message, and then sends the result back to the voter. The voter extracts the m-ticket from the result he receives in the extraction stage. In the kth election, $1 \leq k \leq m$, the voter cast the kth vote extracted from the m-ticket. In the kth tally, $1 \leq k \leq m$, the authority verifies all the kth votes cast by the voters, and computes the tally of the kth election. The details of our scheme are presented as follows.

1. **Initialization:** The authority randomly chooses 4 distinct large primes p_1, p_2, p_3, and p_4 where $p_i \equiv_4 3$ for every i, $1 \leq i \leq 4$, and computes $n_{aff} = p_1 p_2$, $n_{opp} = p_3 p_4$, and $n = p_1 p_2 p_3 p_4$. The authority publishes n, n_{aff}, and n_{opp}. If a sequence of at most m designated elections will be held, $m \geq 1$, the authority publishes a set of redundancy strings $\{RE_0, RE_1, ... , RE_m\}$.

2. **Requesting:** Let H and R_0 be two strings randomly chosen by a voter, and $||$ be the concatenation operator. The voter forms $w_0 = (H||RE_0||R_0)$ in Z_n^*. For every i with $1 \leq i \leq m$, w_i is computed in Z_n^* by the voter such that $(w_i \bmod n_{aff}) = (H||RE_i||R_{i,aff})$ and $(w_i \bmod n_{opp}) = (H||RE_i||R_{i,opp})$ where $R_{i,aff}$ and $R_{i,opp}$ are two strings randomly selected by the voter. Since n_{aff} and n_{opp} are relatively prime, and $n = n_{aff} n_{opp}$, w_i can be derived by the Chinese remainder theorem. To request an m-ticket, the voter randomly chooses r and $(u^2 + v^2)$ in Z_n^*, and then the voter submits,

$$((u^2 + v^2) r^{2^{m+2}} \prod_{i=0}^{m} w_i^{2^{i+1}} \bmod n)$$

to the authority. In addition, set a dummy value $w_{m+1} = 1$.

After receiving $((u^2 + v^2)r^{2^{m+2}} \prod_{i=0}^{m} w_i^{2^{i+1}} \bmod n)$, the authority randomly selects x and y such that,

$$a = ((x^2 + y^2)(u^2 + v^2)r^{2^{m+2}} \prod_{i=0}^{m} w_i^{2^{i+1}} \bmod n)$$

is a QR in Z_n^*, and then sends x and y to the voter.

After receiving x and y, the voter sends $((uy - vx)b^{2^{m+1}} \bmod n)$ to the authority where b is an integer randomly chosen by the voter in Z_n^*.

3. **Registration:** After receiving $(uy - vx)b^{2^{m+1}}$, the authority computes,

$$a((uy - vx)b^{2^{m+1}})^{-2}$$

$$\equiv_n ((x^2 + y^2)(u^2 + v^2)r^{2^{m+2}} \prod_{i=0}^{m} w_i^{2^{i+1}})((uy - vx)b^{2^{m+1}})^{-2}$$

$$\equiv_n r^{2^{m+2}} b^{-2^{m+2}} ((ux + vy)^2 + (uy - vx)^2)(uy - vx)^{-2} \prod_{i=0}^{m} w_i^{2^{i+1}}$$

$$\equiv_n r^{2^{m+2}} b^{-2^{m+2}} ((ux + vy)^2 (uy - vx)^{-2} + 1) \prod_{i=0}^{m} w_i^{2^{i+1}} .$$

Since the authority knows the primes p_1, p_2, p_3, and p_4, the authority can derive an integer t in Z_n^* [13, 17] such that,

$$t^{2^{m+2}} \equiv_n r^{2^{m+2}} b^{-2^{m+2}} ((ux + vy)^2 (uy - vx)^{-2} + 1) \prod_{i=0}^{m} w_i^{2^{i+1}}$$

Then, the authority sends t to the voter.

4. **Extraction:** After receiving t, the voter computes $s = r^{-1}bt \bmod n$ and $c = (ux + vy)(uy - vx)^{-1} \bmod n$. The m-ticket is $(s, \prod_{i=0}^{m} w_i^{2^{i+1}} \bmod n, c)$. To verify the m-ticket, the voter can examine if,

$$s^{2^{m+2}} \equiv_n (c^2 + 1) \prod_{i=0}^{m} w_i^{2^{i+1}} .$$

In addition, the voter computes $\beta_0 = (s^{2^m} \prod_{i=1}^{m+1} w_i^{-2^{i-1}} \bmod n)$, and the voter submits (β_0, w_0, c) to the authority by a sender untraceable e-mail [3, 5] before the beginning of the 1st election.

After receiving (β_0, w_0, c), the authority verifies if $\beta_0^{2^2} \equiv_n (c^2 + 1)w_0^2$ and RE_0 is a proper sub-string of w_0. If true, the authority publishes (β_0, w_0, c).

Through the m-ticket $(s, \prod_{i=0}^{m} w_i^{2^{i+1}} \bmod n, c)$, the voter can participate in each election among the m elections held in the group.

5. **The kth election, $1 \le k \le m$:** In the kth election, $1 \le k \le m$, the voter computes,

$$\beta_k = (s^{2^{m-k}} \prod_{i=k+1}^{m+1} w_i^{-2^{i-k-1}} \bmod n).$$

If the voter would like to cast an affirmative vote (or an oppositive vote, respectively) in the kth election, then through a sender untraceable e-mail [3, 5], he submits, w_{k-1}, and $(\beta_{k,aff}, w_{k,aff}, c)$ (or $(\beta_{k,opp}, w_{k,opp}, c)$, respectively) to the authority where $(\beta_{k,aff} = \beta_k \bmod n_{aff})$, $(w_{k,aff} = w_k \bmod n_{aff})$, $(\beta_{k,opp} = \beta_k \bmod n_{opp})$, and $(w_{k,opp} = w_k \bmod n_{opp})$. It is not necessary to send c to the authority in every election since they can only be submitted to the authority once in the extraction stage.

6. **The kth tally, $1 \leq k \leq m$:** After receiving w_{k-1}, and $(\beta_{k,aff}, w_{k,aff}, c)$ (or $(\beta_{k,opp}, w_{k,opp}, c)$), the authority verifies whether $w_{k,aff}$ (or $w_{k,opp}$) has the header $(H\|RE_k)$, and if $k > 1$, the authority verifies whether both $(w_{k-1} \bmod n_{aff})$ and $(w_{k-1} \bmod n_{opp})$ are with the same header $(H\|RE_{k-1})$ or not, where H can be obtained from w_0 in the extraction stage. The authority computes $\delta_{0,H} = 1$ and,

$$\delta_{k,H} = (w_{k-1}^{2^k} \delta_{k-1,H} \bmod n).$$

The authority verifies if,

$$\beta_{k,aff}^{2^{k+2}} \equiv_{n_{aff}} (c^2 + 1) w_{k,aff}^{2^{k+1}} \delta_{k,H}$$

or

$$\beta_{k,opp}^{2^{k+2}} \equiv_{n_{opp}} (c^2 + 1) w_{k,opp}^{2^{k+1}} \delta_{k,H}.$$

If true, the vote is legal. It publishes, w_{k-1}, $\delta_{k,H}$, and $(\beta_{k,aff}, w_{k,aff}, c)$ (or $(\beta_{k,opp}, w_{k,opp}, c)$). Similarly, c can only be published once in the extraction stage. In addition, the authority publishes all the other legal votes it receives, and computes the tally of the kth election.

4 Security Analysis

We examine the correctness and the security of our proposed election scheme in this section. Theorem 1 ensures the correctness of the proposed scheme.

Theorem 1. *If $(\beta_{k,aff}, w_{k,aff}, c)$ or $(\beta_{k,opp}, w_{k,opp}, c)$, $1 \leq k \leq m$, is an affirmative vote or an oppositive vote produced in the kth election by our proposed scheme, then,*

$$\beta_{k,aff}^{2^{k+2}} \equiv_{n_{aff}} (c^2 + 1) w_{k,aff}^{2^{k+1}} \delta_{k,H}$$

or

$$\beta_{k,opp}^{2^{k+2}} \equiv_{n_{opp}} (c^2 + 1) w_{k,opp}^{2^{k+1}} \delta_{k,H}.$$

Proof. As $\beta_k \equiv_n (s^{2^{m-k}} \prod_{i=k+1}^{m+1} w_i^{-2^{i-k-1}})$, $\beta_k^{2^{k+2}} \equiv_n (s^{2^{m-k}} \prod_{i=k+1}^{m+1} w_i^{-2^{i-k-1}})^{2^{k+2}}$

$\equiv_n ((r^{-1}bt)^{2^{m-k}} \prod_{i=k+1}^{m+1} w_i^{-2^{i-k-1}})^{2^{k+2}}$

$\equiv_n ((r^{-2^{m+2}} b^{2^{m+2}} t^{2^{m+2}})^{2^{-k-2}} \prod_{i=k+1}^{m+1} w_i^{-2^{i-k-1}})^{2^{k+2}}$

$$\equiv_n (((ux + vy)^2(uy - vx)^{-2} + 1) \prod_{i=0}^{m} w_i^{2^{i+1}})(\prod_{i=k+1}^{m+1} w_i^{-2^{i-k-1}})^{2^{k+2}}$$

$$\equiv_n ((c^2 + 1) \prod_{i=0}^{m} w_i^{2^{i+1}})(\prod_{i=k+1}^{m+1} w_i^{-2^{i-k-1}})^{2^{k+2}}$$

$$\equiv_n ((c^2 + 1) \prod_{i=0}^{m} w_i^{2^{i+1}})(\prod_{i=k+1}^{m+1} w_i^{-2^{i+1}}) \equiv_n (c^2 + 1) \prod_{i=0}^{k} w_i^{2^{i+1}}.$$

Since $\beta_k^{2^{k+2}} \equiv_n (c^2 + 1) \prod_{i=0}^{k} w_i^{2^{i+1}}$, and both n_{aff} and n_{opp} can divide n, we have the following two congruences,

$$\beta_k^{2^{k+2}} \equiv_{n_{aff}} (c^2 + 1) \prod_{i=0}^{k} w_i^{2^{i+1}}$$

and

$$\beta_k^{2^{k+2}} \equiv_{n_{opp}} (c^2 + 1) \prod_{i=0}^{k} w_i^{2^{i+1}}.$$

From the proposed scheme, we can derive $\delta_{k,H} = \prod_{i=0}^{k-1} w_i^{2^{i+1}} \bmod n$. It follows that,

$$\beta_{k,aff}^{2^{k+2}} \equiv_{n_{aff}} (c^2 + 1)w_{k,aff}^{2^{k+1}}\delta_{k,H}$$

and

$$\beta_{k,opp}^{2^{k+2}} \equiv_{n_{opp}} (c^2 + 1)w_{k,opp}^{2^{k+1}}\delta_{k,H}.$$

$\square$

Given an integer, it is computationally infeasible to derive any square root of the integer in $Z_{n_{aff}}^*$ or $Z_{n_{opp}}^*$ without the trapdoors p_1, p_2, p_3, and p_4 [17]. Since every plaintext w_i, $0 \le i \le m$, contains some appropriate redundancy, the construction of an unauthorized vote by multiplicative attacks is infeasible. In our scheme, p_1, p_2, p_3, and p_4 are kept secret by the authority, so it is infeasible for others to produce any legal m-ticket.

Let g be a one-way permutation function [14, 18]. To guarantee that every voter can choose a unique header H, he can select $H = g(id\|R)$ where id is the identity of the voter and R is a string randomly chosen by the voter.

In the kth election for every k, $1 \le k \le m$, if a voter submits both his affirmative vote $(\beta_{k,aff}, w_{k,aff}, c)$ and his oppositive vote $(\beta_{k,opp}, w_{k,opp}, c)$, the authority can detect it by checking whether $w_{k,aff}$ and $w_{k,opp}$ are with the same header $(H\|RE_k)$ or not. If the voter does so, then his votes are considered to be invalid.

Given $w_{k,aff}$, the authority cannot derive $w_{k,opp}$ since it does not have $R_{k,opp}$. Similarly, the authority cannot derive $w_{k,aff}$ even if he knows $w_{k,opp}$. In addition, given $(\beta_{i,aff}, w_{i,aff}, c)$ or $(\beta_{i,opp}, w_{i,opp}, c)$ for all i, $1 \le i \le k$, it is infeasible for the authority to produce $(\beta_{k+1,aff}, w_{k+1,aff}, c)$ or $(\beta_{k+1,opp}, w_{k+1,opp}, c)$ since he does not know w_{k+1}.

If x, y are selected by the authority during a certain run of registration, then for every m-ticket $(s, \prod_{i=0}^{m} w_i^{2^{i+1}} \bmod n, c)$, there exists a great amount of $(u',$ $v')$'s such that $c = (u'x + v'y)(u'y - v'x)^{-1} \bmod n$. In addition, since all $(r,$ u, $v)$'s are kept secret by the voters, all the m-tickets are equally likely from the authority's point of view. Therefore, it is computationally infeasible for the authority to derive the exact correspondence between the messages he actually sign and the votes cast by the voters. Although the intentions of voters are public in the tally stage of the scheme, by the techniques of blind signatures and sender untraceable e-mails, their identities are still protected against the authority.

5 Discussions and Conclusions

In this paper, we have proposed a multi-recastable ticket scheme for electronic elections. The computation time of the proposed scheme can be greatly reduced by storing some intermediate computation results for later usage. In addition, the initialization, the requesting, the registration and the extraction stages of the proposed scheme can be pre-processed before the beginning of the 1st election. In the proposed election scheme, sender untraceable e-mails or anonymous channels are used when the voters submit their votes to the authority. The computation and communication cost of the untraceable e-mails presented in the literature are often considered to be expensive. Instead of the untraceable e-mails, we can distribute the power of the single authority to multiple independent authorities in order to reduce the cost.

Acknowledgment

We would like to thank the unknown referees of this paper for their valuable comments.

References

1. Boyd, C. A., 'A new multiple key ciphers and an improved voting scheme,' Advances in Cryptology-EUROCRYPT'89, LNCS 434, Springer-Verlag, 1990, pp. 617-625.
2. Benaloh, J. C. and Tuinstra, D., 'Receipt-free secret-ballot elections,' Proc. 26th ACM Symp. on the Theory of Computing, 1994, pp. 544-553.
3. Chaum, D., 'Untraceable electronic mail, return addresses, and digital pseudonyms,' Communications of the ACM, vol. 24, no. 2, 1981, pp. 84-88.
4. Chaum, D., Fiat, A., and Naor, M., 'Untraceable electronic cash,' Advances in Cryptology-CRYPTO'88, LNCS 403, Springer-Verlag, 1982, pp. 319-327.
5. Chaum, D., 'The dining cryptographers problem: unconditional sender and recipient untraceability,' Journal of Cryptology, vol. 1, 1988, pp. 65-75.
6. Cohen, J. D. and Fisher, M. J., 'A robust and verifiable cryptographically secure election scheme,' Proc. 26th IEEE Symp. on Foundations of Computer Science, 1985, pp. 372-382.

7. Fan, C. I. and Lei, C. L., 'Efficient blind signature scheme based on quadratic residues,' Electronics Letters, vol. 32, no. 9, 1996, pp. 811-813.

8. Fan, C. I. and Lei, C. L., 'Low-computation blind signature schemes based on quadratic residues,' Technical Reports, Department of Electrical Engineering, National Taiwan University, R.O.C., 1996.

9. Fujioka, A., Okamoto, T. and Ohta, K., 'A practical secret voting scheme for large scale elections,' Advances in Cryptology-AUSCRYPT'92, LNCS 718, Springer-Verlag, 1992, pp. 244-251.

10. Iversen, K. R., 'A cryptographic scheme for computerized general elections,' Advances in Cryptology-CRYPTO'91, LNCS 576, Springer-Verlag, 1991, pp. 405-419.

11. Juang, W. S., Lei, C. L. and Fan, C. I., 'A collision free secret ballot protocol for computerized general elections,' International Computer Symposium, Taiwan, R.O.C., 1994. (A revised version will appear in Computers & Security.)

12. Nurmi, H., Salomaa, A. and Santean, L., 'Secret ballot elections in computer networks,' Computers & Security, vol. 10, 1991, pp. 553-560.

13. Peralta, R. C., 'A simple and fast probabilistic algorithm for computing square roots modulo a prime number,' IEEE Trans. Inform. Theory, vol. 32, no. 6, 1986, pp. 846-847.

14. Pohlig, S. and Hellman, M. E., 'An improved algorithm for computing logarithms over GF(p) and its cryptographic significance,' IEEE Trans. on Inform. Theory, vol. 24, 1978, pp. 106-110.

15. Park, C., Itoh, K. and Kurosawa, K., 'All/nothing election scheme and anonymous channel,' Advances in Cryptology-EUROCRYPT'93, LNCS 765, Springer-Verlag, 1993, pp. 248-259.

16. Pollard, J. M. and Schnorr, C. P., 'An efficient solution of the congruence $x^2 + ky^2 = m \pmod{n}$,' IEEE Trans. Inform. Theory, vol. 33, no. 5, 1987, pp. 702-709.

17. Rabin, M. O., 'Digitalized signatures and public-key functions as intractable as factorization,' Techhhhnical Report, MIT/LCS/TR212, MIT Lab., Computer Science, Cambridge, Mass. Jan. 1979.

18. Rivest, R. L., Shamir, A. and Adleman, L., 'A method for obtaining digital signatures and public key cryptosystems,' Communications of the ACM, vol. 21, no. 2, 1978, pp. 120-126.

19. Sako, K. and Kilian, J., 'Secure voting using partially compatible homomorphisms,' Advances in Cryptology-CRYPTO'94, LNCS 839, Springer-Verlag, 1994, pp. 411-424.

20. Slessenger, P. H., 'Socially secure cryptographic election scheme,' Electronics Letters, vol. 27, no. 11, 1991, pp. 955-957.

Some Remarks on a Receipt-Free and Universally Verifiable Mix-Type Voting Scheme

Markus Michels · Patrick Horster

Theoretical Computer Science and Information Security
University of Technology Chemnitz-Zwickau,
Straße der Nationen 62, D-09111 Chemnitz, Germany
E-mail: {mmi,pho}@informatik.tu-chemnitz.de

Abstract. At Eurocrypt'95 Sako and Kilian presented the first Mix-type voting scheme which is receipt-free and universally verifiable.
In this contribution we analyze this scheme and show that the coercer must not collude with any center. Otherwise its robustness is lost. As a result, the assumed coercer model is clarified. More seriously, it is further pointed out that the privacy of votes can't be guaranteed, if only one Mix-center is honest. Hence, under the commonly used assumption that only one Mix-center must be honest, the voting scheme is insecure unless modified.

1   Introduction

Electronic voting is an interesting application of public key cryptography. Voting schemes have to satisfy several requirements, in particular (e.g. [FuOO92, BeTu94])

- *Completeness:* All valid votes are counted correctly, if all participants are honest.
- *Robustness:* Dishonest voters, other participants or outsiders can't disturb or disrupt an election.
- *Privacy:* The votes are casted anonymously.
- *Unreusability:* Every voter can vote only once.
- *Eligibility:* Only legitimate voters can vote.
- *Fairness:* A voter casts his vote independently and is not influenced (e.g. by publishing intermediate results of the election, copying and casting of the encrypted voting slip of another voter as his own vote).
- *Verifiability:* The tally can not be forged, as it can be verified by every voter. The verifiability is *local*, if a voter can only check if his own vote is counted correctly. If it is possible to verify whether all votes are counted correctly, then the verifiability is *universal*.
- *Receipt-freeness:* A voter can't prove to a coercer, how he has voted. As a result, verifiable vote buying is impossible.

Several schemes have been proposed, they can be divided in the class of schemes *without administrators* (e.g. [HuTe90, PfWa92]), schemes *with administrators*, which use *special encryption functions* to guarantee the anonymity of the votes (e.g. [BeYu86, Iver91, BeTu94, SaKi94, CFSY96]) and schemes with administrators which use *anonymous channels* to guarantee the anonymity of the votes. Within the latter class there are schemes based either on a *general* anonymous channel (e.g. [FuOO92, HoMP95]), a *special type* of an anonymous channel [Chau81, OkFO93]) or an anonymous channel based on *concrete* cryptographic mechanisms. The first voting based on such a channel was suggested by Park, Itoh and Kurusawa [PaIK93]. In particular, they used a Mix-net protocol with ElGamal encryption. A Mix-net [Chau81] consists out of n single Mix-centers and its goal is the realization of an anonymous channel. The input of the Mix-net is a number of messages. They will be transformed by the Mix-centers successively. The output of a Mix-net consists of the same messages but in a distinct order, in such a way that the link between a message and the sender of this message is unknown. It is usually assumed that only one of the Mix-centers must be honest. However, the Mix-net protocol proposed in [PaIK93] was shown to be vulnerable to some attacks [Pfit94] and there are further problems with the voting scheme as well [MiHo96]. At Eurocrypt'95, Sako and Kilian [SaKi95] suggested a voting scheme that is based on an improved Mix-net with ElGamal encryption. Receipt-freeness and universal verifiability are claimed to be gained.

The main contribution of this paper is the analysis of the used Mix-net protocol and the used coercer model in the scheme given in [SaKi95]. In particular, we point out that the mix-net is vulnerable to some known active and a new passive attack. While the active attacks can't be applied in the voting scheme environment, the new passive attack can. As a result, under the commonly used assumption that only one Mix-center must be honest, the privacy of the votes can't be guaranteed. Additionally, we discuss some coercer models and show that the coercer must not collude with *any* Mix-center. Otherwise the correctness of the tally can't be guaranteed.

In the next section we give a brief review of the used Mix-net protocol in [SaKi95], discuss some known attacks in section 3 and present a new attack in section 4. After that, we review the voting scheme due to Sako and Kilian. Finally, in section 6, we examine some attacks.

2 A Mix-net protocol

As already mentioned, the voting scheme presented in [SaKi95] is based on a modification of the Mix-net protocol presented by Park, Itoh and Kurosawa [PaIK93]. Although their original protocol was shown to be insecure [Pfit94], the modifications of the protocol should dwarf this attack. We give a short description of this Mix-net protocol here.

The primes p and q with $q|(p-1)$ and the generator g of order q are the public system parameters. Furthermore, $x_i \in \mathbf{Z}_q^*$ is the secret and $y_i := g^{x_i} \pmod{p}$ is the public key of Mix-center i. For simplicity, let $w_i := \prod_{j=i+1}^{n} y_j \pmod{p}$.

To shuffle a message m, any sender picks a random $r_0 \in \mathbf{Z}_q^*$ and transmits

$$Z_1 := (G_1, M_1) = (g^{r_0} \pmod{p}, w_0^{r_0} \cdot m \pmod{p})$$

to the Mix-center 1. If Mix-center i $(1 \leq i \leq n-1)$ gets a list of values $Z_i := (G_i, M_i)$ (one value from each sender), then (for each value) he picks r_i at random, computes

$$G_{i+1} := G_i \cdot g^{r_i} \pmod{p}, M_{i+1} := M_i \cdot w_i^{r_i}/G_i^{x_i} \pmod{p}$$

and sends all values $Z_{i+1} = (G_i, M_i)$ in a shuffled order to Mix-center $i+1$. Mix-center n can recover all messages m by computing

$$m := M_n/G_n^{x_n} \pmod{p}.$$

To guarantee that he followed the protocol, each Mix-center i proves that he constructed $H_i := G_i^{x_i} \pmod{p}$ and Z_i correctly. The first is done by releasing H_i and a zero-knowlegde protocol given in [SaKi95] (called DECRYPT) and the latter by another zero-knowledge protocol given in [SaKi95] (called SHUFFLE). These proofs are not essential to understand our attacks later.

3 Discussion of known attacks

Clearly, the attack proposed by Pfitzmann [Pfit94] can still be applied, if only the Mix-net protocol is considered: If a dishonest sender Bob wants to find out what Alice sends and knows Alice's ciphertext (G_1, M_1) related to her message m, then he sends $(G_1^s \pmod{p}, M_1^s \pmod{p})$ as his own ciphertext. If all messages are published on a public board, he computes $M^s \pmod{p}$ for every plaintext M in the public board and compares it with every plaintext. If there is a match, then $m = M$ with a high probability. As a result, in general the Mix-net protocol is not secure, although all Mix-centers might be honest. If the messages should satisfy a redundancy scheme (or are restricted to a few valid messages) the Mix-center n can refuse to publish Bob's message. But how should he prove to a third party, that his behavior is correct without leaking Bob's message? Furthermore, without loss of generality, we have to assume that the last Mix-center is dishonest. If he colludes with Bob, they can see together what Alice has sent, although Mix-center n might refuse to publish Bob's message.

Similar attacks were discussed in [SaKi95] concerning the problem of copying of votes. All these attacks have in common that Bob chooses his ciphertext in relation to Alice's ciphertext. However, as we will see later, the (encrypted) votes are not chosen arbitrarily by the voter, but are chosen out of two different possibilities given by the first Mix-center. If all communication is taped on a public board, then the attacks described above can't be applied in the voting scheme.

4 A new attack

We now investigate a new attack. More precisely, we assume that all Mix-centers except the jth's collude, but a colluding participant is not needed. Furthermore, the colluders need not to derivate from the protocol. Thus the attack is *passive* in contrary to the attacks mentioned in the last section. Alice sends

$$(G_1, M_1) := (g^{r_0} \pmod{p}, m \cdot \prod_{t=1}^{n} y_i^{r_0} \pmod{p}))$$

to Mix-center 1, together with her identity. Then the message is sent through the Mix-net as described above. Mix-center $j - 1$ sends

$$(G_j, M_j) := (g^{r_0+R} \pmod{p}, m \cdot \prod_{t=j}^{n} y_t^{r_0+R} \pmod{p}))$$

to the honest Mix-center j, where $R \equiv \sum_{t=1}^{j-1} r_t \pmod{q}$. Note that Mix-center j reveals $H_j := G_j^{x_j} \pmod{p}$. Then all colluding Mix-centers can compute

$$M := M_j / \left(H_j \cdot \prod_{t=j+1}^{n} G_j^{x_t} \right) \equiv m \cdot \left(\prod_{t=j}^{n} y_t^{r_0+R} \right) \cdot G_j^{-x_j} \cdot \prod_{t=j+1}^{n} G_j^{-x_t}$$

$$\equiv m \cdot \left(\prod_{t=j}^{n} y_t^{r_0+R} \right) \cdot y_j^{-r_0-R} \cdot \prod_{t=j+1}^{n} y_t^{-r_0-R} \equiv m \pmod{p}$$

together. Note that the first $j-1$ Mix-centers are necessary to know that (G_j, M_j) is related to Alice ciphertext and the last $n - j$ Mix-centers are important for the computation above, as their secret key is used. We will see later that this attack can be applied in the voting scheme.

5 The voting scheme

We describe the voting scheme given in [SaKi95] now: The initialization of the scheme is based on the initialization of the Mix-net protocol described above. Additionally, each voter i possesses a key pair $(a_i, \alpha_i := g^{a_i} \pmod{p})$ for a chameleon bit commitment scheme [BrCC88] that is used for committing random strings. This is needed here for proving the order of the votes to the voter and gives the voter the opportunity to "prove" to the coercer whatever he wants. Furthermore, the election is restricted to a "yes/no" vote. The votes which can be casted are fixed, m_1 for the "yes", m_0 for the "no"-vote.

1. First, the last Mix-center n commits a random string $\pi^{(i,n)}$ of length $l + 1$ bit to voter i using the public key α_i. He picks random $r_{2n-1}, r_{2n} \in \mathbf{Z}_q^*$, computes with $w_0 := \prod_{i=1}^{n} y_i \pmod{p}$

$$v_0 := (\bar{G}_n, \bar{M}_n) = (g^{r_{2n}} \pmod{p}, m_0 \cdot w_0^{r_{2n}} \pmod{p})$$

$$v_1 := (\bar{G}_n', \bar{M}_n') = (g^{r_{2n-1}} \pmod{p}, m_1 \cdot w_0^{r_{2n-1}} \pmod{p})$$

and places (v_0, v_1) if the first bit of $\pi^{(i,n)} = 0$ and (v_1, v_0) otherwise. He proves in zero-knowledge (using the protocol **prove 1-0 vote** in [SaKi95]) that v_0, v_1 are constructed properly. The random string $\pi^{(i,n)}$ (except the first bit) is used in this zero-knowledge protocol.

2. The Mix-center n decommits $\pi^{(i,n)}$ through an untappable channel to the voter. Then, only the voter knows the order of v_0, v_1.

3. The next Mix-center j ($j = n - 1, \ldots, 1$) gets $((\bar{G}_{j+1}, \bar{M}_{j+1}), (\bar{G}'_{j+1}, \bar{M}'_{j+1}))$ or $((\bar{G}'_{j+1}, \bar{M}'_{j+1}), (\bar{G}_{j+1}, \bar{M}_{j+1}))$ from Mix-center $j+1$ for each voter i, commits a $l + 1$ bit string $\pi^{(i,j)}$ to the voter and picks random $r_{2j-1}, r_{2j} \in \mathbf{Z}_q^*$. In the first case, he computes

$$(\bar{G}_j, \bar{M}_j) := (\bar{G}_{j+1} \cdot g^{r_{2j}} \pmod{p}, \bar{M}_{j+1} \cdot w_0^{r_{2j}} \pmod{p})$$

$$(\bar{G}'_j, \bar{M}'_j) := (\bar{G}'_{j+1} \cdot g^{r_{2j-1}} \pmod{p}, \bar{M}'_{j+1} \cdot w_0^{r_{2j-1}} \pmod{p})$$

and in the second case he computes

$$(\bar{G}_j, \bar{M}_j) := (\bar{G}'_{j+1} \cdot g^{r_{2j}} \pmod{p}, \bar{M}'_{j+1} \cdot w_0^{r_{2j}} \pmod{p})$$

$$(\bar{G}'_j, \bar{M}'_j) := (\bar{G}_{j+1} \cdot g^{r_{2j-1}} \pmod{p}, \bar{M}_{j+1} \cdot w_0^{r_{2j-1}} \pmod{p}).$$

Then he places the pairs as $((\bar{G}_j, \bar{M}_j), (\bar{G}'_j, \bar{M}'_j))$ if the first bit of the bitstring is one and otherwise in reverse order. Using **prove SHUFFLE** he can prove that he followed the protocol correctly by choosing λ in each round depending on the first unused bit of the bitstring. Note that there are only two choices for λ, because only two orders are possible. Therefore λ is completely determined by the random bit of the bitstring.

4. By decommitting the bitstring, the order of the Mix-centers' output is revealed only to the voter.

5. The steps 2 and 3 are repeated for every Mix-center. Then there are $(z_1, \ldots, z_t) \in \{0, 1\}^t$, such that the voter gets the pairs

$$(\bar{G}_1, \bar{M}_1) = (g^{\sum_{t=1}^{n} r_{2 \cdot t - z_t}} \pmod{p}, m_0 \cdot w_0^{\sum_{t=1}^{n} r_{2 \cdot t - z_t}} \pmod{p})$$

$$(\bar{G}'_1, \bar{M}'_1) = (g^{\sum_{t=1}^{n} r_{2 \cdot t + z_t - 1}} \pmod{p}, m_1 \cdot w_0^{\sum_{t=1}^{n} r_{2 \cdot t + z_t - 1}} \pmod{p}).$$

6. The voter knows which pair is which vote and posts his choice to the Mix-center 1. Now this pair is sent through the Mix-net to the Mix-center n, who is able to recover the voter's vote. Note that the form of one pair can be interpreted as the encrypted vote by the voter with "random" $\sum_{t=1}^{n} r_{2 \cdot t - z_t} \pmod{q}$ or $\sum_{t=1}^{n} r_{2 \cdot t + z_t - 1} \pmod{q}$. Therefore, it can be easily sent through the Mix-net protocol described above.

7. The last center reveals the votes and everybody can compute the tally.

6 Examining some attacks

6.1 Coercer model

The model of a coercer depends on the number of administrators in the voting scheme. Here we focus on a scheme with several administrators, each Mix-center can be regarded as an administrator. We can distinguish several abilities the coercer might have to control the voter. It might be called level of *voter-control*.

1. The coercer knows all public values only. He is not able to see physically what the voter sends as his vote.
2. The coercer knows all public values. Furthermore he sees what the voter sends as his vote, but there are possibilities during the election for the voter to communicate with the administrators privately.
3. The coercer knows all public values. Furthermore he sees what the voter sends as his vote, but there are possibilities during the election for the administrators to send private information to the voter.
4. The coercer knows all public values and he controls all communications of the voter during the election. Only in the initialization of the system the voter can communicate with the administrators privately.
5. The coercer knows all public values and controls all communications between the voter and the administrators.

Furthermore it can be distinguished with whom the coercer might collude and form a coalition. This might be called *level of coalition*. Possible colluders are

1. other voters,
2. at least one administrator
3. all administrators

In the protocol given in [SaKi95] the coercer has voter-control level 3 and coalition level 1 abilities: Assume that the one center and the coercer colludes. The coercer forces the voter i to reveal his secret key a_i, which he then posts to the dishonest Mix-center. This Mix-center can forge the decommitment of the random string and therefore the way, how he has shuffled. As a result, it's possible that the voter's vote is counted wrongly. Although the cheaters can't determine the result according to their wishes, this influences the output of the election and violates the robustness of the voting scheme. Therefore, it must be assumed that the coercer does not collude with *any* Mix-center.

6.2 Unsuccessful attack on the privacy of casted votes

Assume that the voter Bob, the first and the last center collude. Their goal is to find out how Alice has voted. If Bob knows Alice's ciphertext, he can transform this as described in section 3 (exponent by a random s) and sends it through the Mix-net instead of his vote. Clearly, the first center will notice that, as he still knows the two pairs he has posted to Bob (which are different from the ciphertext he gets) and the last center can see that Bob's vote is neither a "yes" nor a "no" vote. By computing the s-root of Bob's vote, it is easily computable how Alice has voted. However, if the first center is forced to accept just one of the two votes he has sent to the voters (e.g. everything is written on a public board), then this attack fails.

6.3 Successful attack on the privacy of casted votes

Assume that only Mix-center j is honest, while the other Mix-centers are dishonest and collude. Again, the goal is to find out how Alice has voted. All Mix-centers prepare two votes for Alice,

$$(g^{r_0} \pmod p), m_0 \cdot w_0^{r_0} \pmod p)), (g^{\bar{r}_0} \pmod p), m_1 \cdot w_0^{\bar{r}_0} \pmod p))$$

and r_0 and $\bar{r}_0$ is the sum of the used r's of all Mix-centers. Now Alice sends one of the votes back to Mix-center 1, say (G_1, M_1), which is published together with Alice's identity on the public board. This is necessary to avoid the forgery mentioned above. Then the attack described in section four can be applied. Thus the colluding Mix-centers can find out how Alice has voted. As a result, the privacy property is violated, if only one Mix-center is honest and the scheme is insecure under the commonly used assumption that only one Mix-center must be honest.

7 Conclusion

We reviewed the Mix-net protocol given in [SaKi95] and showed its vulnerability to some known and a new attack. Then we described the voting scheme given in [SaKi95] briefly. We have presented several coercer models and pointed out that the coercer must not collude with any Mix-center. This fact was independently observed by Gennaro, Jakobsson and Schoenmakers. Furthermore, we showed that the privacy of votes isn't guaranteed in the voting scheme described in [SaKi95], if only one Mix-center is honest. This results in the insecurity of the voting scheme under the commonly used assumption, that only one Mix-center must be honest. It seems that the attack can be prevented if at least two Mix-centers are assumed to be honest and therefore – under this assumption – the scheme might remain secure. After being informed by the authors, Sako suggested a modification of the used Mix-net protocol that seems to avoid this weakness, even if only one Mix-center is honest [Sako95].

8 Acknowledgments

The authors would like to thank Rossario Gennaro, Markus Jakobsson, Berry Schoenmakers and Tobias Zimmer for helpful comments.

References

[BeTu94]   J.C.Benaloh and D.Tuinstra, "Receipt-Free Secret-Ballot Elections", Symposium on the Theory of Computing'94, (1994), pp. 544–53.

[BeYu86]   J.C.Benaloh, M.Yung, "Distributing the Power of a Government to Enhance the Privacy of Voters", Proc. of Symposium of Principles of Distributed Computing, (1986), pp. 52–62.

[BrCC88]   G.Brassad, D.Chaum, C.Crepéau, "Minimum disclosure proofs of knowledge", Journal of Computer and System Science, Vol. 37, (1988),
pp. 156–189.

[Chau81]   D.Chaum, "Untraceable electronic mail return addresses and digital
pseudonyms", Communcations of the ACM, Vol. 24, No. 2, Feb., (1981),
pp. 84–88.

[CFSY96]   R.J.F.Cramer, M.Franklin, L.A.M.Schoenmakers, M.Yung, "Multi-au-
thority secret-ballot elections with linear work", Lecture Notes in Computer Science 1070, Advances in Cryptology: Proc. Eurocrypt'96, Springer
Verlag, (1996), pp. 72–83.

[FuOO92]   A.Fujioka, T.Okamoto, K.Ohta, "A practical secret voting scheme for
large scale elections", Lecture Notes in Computer Science 718, Advances
in Cryptology: Proc. Auscrypt'92, Springer Verlag, (1992), pp. 244–51.

[HoMP95]   P.Horster, M.Michels, H.Petersen, "Blind Multisignatures and their relevance for electronic voting", Proc. 11th Annual Computer Security Applications Conference, IEEE–Press, (1995), pp. 149–156.

[HuTe90]   M.Huang, S.Teng, "Security, Verifiability, and Universality in Distributed
Computing", Journal of Algorithm, Vol. 11, (1990), pp. 492–521.

[Iver91]   K.R.Iversen, "A Cryptographic Scheme for Computerized General Elections", Lecture Notes in Computer Science 576, Advances in Cryptology:
Proc. Crypto'91, Springer Verlag, (1992), pp. 405–419.

[MiHo96]   M.Michels, P.Horster, "Cryptanalysis of a voting scheme", Proc. Communications and Multimedia Security II, Chapman & Hall, (1996).

[OkFO93]   T.Okamoto, A.Fujioka, K.Ohta, "A practical secret voting scheme without anonymous channels", Symposium on Cryptography and Information
Security, SCIS 93-1C, (1993), 12 pages.

[PaIK93]   C.Park, K.Itoh, K.Kurosawa, "All/Nothing Election Scheme and Anonymous Channel", Lecture Notes in Computer Science 765, Advances in
Cryptology: Proc. Eurocrypt'93, Springer Verlag, (1994), pp. 248–259.

[Pfit94]   B.Pfitzmann, "Breaking an efficient anonymous channel", Lecture Notes
in Computer Science 950, Advances in Cryptology: Proc. Eurocrypt'94,
Springer Verlag, (1995), pp. 332–340.

[PfWa92]   B.Pfitzmann, M.Waidner, "Unconditionally Untraceable and Fault-
tolerant Broadcast and Secret Ballot Election", Hildesheimer Informatik-
Berichte, Department of Computer Science, University of Hildesheim,
Germany, May, (1992).

[Sako95]   K.Sako, "An improved universally verifiable mix-type voting scheme",
manuscript, October, (1995), 6 pages.

[SaKi94]   K.Sako, J.Kilian, "Secure Voting Using Partially Compatible Homomorphisms", Lecture Notes in Computer Science 839, Advances in Cryptology: Proc. Crypto'94, Springer Verlag, (1994), pp. 411–424.

[SaKi95]   K.Sako, J.Kilian, "Receipt-Free Mix-Type voting scheme", Lecture Notes
in Computer Science 921, Advances in Cryptology: Proc. Eurocrypt'95,
Springer Verlag, (1995), pp. 393–403.

Observations on Non-repudiation

Jianying Zhou and Dieter Gollmann

Department of Computer Science
Royal Holloway, University of London
Egham, Surrey TW20 0EX, United Kingdom
email: {zhou,dieter}@dcs.rhbnc.ac.uk

Abstract. This paper discusses non-repudiation services regarding the transfer of a message and classifies the roles of trusted third parties involved in non-repudiation services. We examine the selective receipt problem and the generation of time evidence, analyse the current state of the ISO/IEC 13888 drafts on non-repudiation mechanisms, and present a fair non-repudiation protocol including time evidence to promote the development of these drafts.

Keywords: non-repudiation, communications security, ISO standards

1 Motivation

Repudiation is one of the possible security threats existing in social and electronic environments. Consider first some of the problems that can arise in the world of paper-based business transactions. Paper documents, such as contracts, quotations, bids, orders, invoices, and cheques play a critical role in the conduct of business between organizations. However, many problems can occur in their handling, such as

- forged documents;
- disputed filing time of a document;
- documents accidentally corrupted or fraudulently modified within an organization or while in transit between organizations; and
- documents lost or delayed during mail delivery.

There are two possibilities regarding each of these events. A document could be genuine or a forgery; it could have been sent to the recipient or never been mailed at all; it could reach the destination or get lost in delivery; it could be delivered intact or corrupted in delivery; it could be delivered in time or delayed. If two possibilities of an event cannot be distinguished, a party related to the event could make one of the following 'denials':

- denial of authorship of a document;
- denial of sending a document;
- denial of receiving a document; and
- denial of sending or receiving a document at a given time.

To aid in systematically dealing with these problems, various mechanisms are employed, such as signatures, notarisation, receipts, postmarks, and certified mail. If good business practices are followed, there will usually be an adequate paper trail to make dispute resolution straightforward.

With electronic business transactions, the problems that can arise are analogous to those for paper-based transactions. In some aspects they are more difficult to resolve than those with paper-based transactions, mainly because entities are distributed and transactions cannot be done face to face, and there is less physical evidence available. In other aspects, however, problems with electronic transactions are easier to solve because of the availability of sophisticated technologies such as digital signatures.

In general, disagreements relate to whether a particular event occurred, when it occurred, what parties were involved in the event and what information was associated with the event. The key point is that parties potentially involved in a dispute should be able to obtain sufficient evidence to establish what had actually happened. With the help of such evidence, parties may be able to resolve their differences themselves, or if necessary, settle their disputes under arbitration. Non-repudiation services are intended to provide evidence to make the parties involved in a particular event accountable for their actions.

Non-repudiation services can be supplied by protocols based on security mechanisms such as digital signatures, notarisation and data integrity mechanisms, with support from other security services. The frameworks and mechanisms of non-repudiation are being standardized by ISO/IEC in a number of documents, all still at DIS or CD stage [3, 4, 5, 6]. The mechanisms in ISO/IEC 13888 [5, 6] "ignore" the problem of *selective receipt* in a non-repudiation service, where the recipient can decide whether or not to acknowledge the receipt of a message after seeing the message.

The paper is organized as follows. Non-repudiation services regarding message transfer are discussed in Section 2. Section 3 classifies the roles of trusted third parties involved in non-repudiation services. In Section 4, ISO/IEC 13888 non-repudiation mechanisms are analysed and some problems are pointed out. A fair non-repudiation protocol with time information is presented in Section 5.

2   Model of Non-repudiation

Repudiation is defined as "denial by one of the entities involved in a communication of having participated in all or part of the communication" [1]. In a communications session, there are two possible ways of transferring a message.

- The originator sends the message to the recipient directly; or
- The originator submits the message to a trusted third party called the *delivery authority* which then delivers the message to the recipient.

The originator's action is then sending a message, the recipient's action is receiving a message, the delivery authority's actions are accepting a message and delivering the message. To establish each participant's accountability for its actions, the following non-repudiation services are required.

- *Non-repudiation of origin (NRO)* is intended to protect against the originator's false denial of having sent the message.
- *Non-repudiation of receipt (NRR)* is intended to protect against the recipient's false denial of having received the message.
- *Non-repudiation of submission (NRS)* is intended to provide evidence that the originator submitted the message for delivery.
- *Non-repudiation of delivery (NRD)* is intended to provide evidence that the message has been delivered to the recipient.

In *direct* communication, as the originator and the recipient potentially do not trust each other, the originator is not sure that the recipient will acknowledge a message it has received. On the other hand, the recipient will only acknowledge messages it has received. In order to put two parties in an equal position, a trusted third party will usually be involved. Of course, the extent of its involvement varies between different protocols. In our fair non-repudiation protocol proposed in [9], only a 'low weight notary' is required.

In *indirect* communication, a delivery authority is involved and the message will be transferred between one-way trusted pairs. The originator believes that the delivery authority will not repudiate receiving the submitted message and will collect a receipt when the message is delivered to the recipient. The recipient also believes that the delivery authority will work properly.

Disputes may not only relate to the occurrence, but also to the time of the occurrence of a particular action. For example, there was a submission deadline for Asiacrypt'96. The evidence about the time of sending or receiving a paper would have been critical to resolve a dispute over a late submission. We first consider this problem in direct communication. The originator and the recipient could add a time stamp in non-repudiation evidence NRO and NRR respectively. Unfortunately, this does not solve our problem. The originator can add an arbitrary time stamp in NRO. How can the recipient and the judge believe that the message was sent at that time? Of course, the originator cannot believe the time stamp in NRR either. In another scenario, the originator may ask a time stamping authority to append a trusted time stamp to NRO and digitally sign the result. However, it can only prove that the message was sent *after* that time. The originator can falsely claim it sent the message before the specific date by obtaining a trusted time stamp on NRO in advance. Similarly, the trusted time stamp on NRR can only prove that the message was received *before* that time. The recipient can falsely claim it received the message after the specific date by applying for a trusted time stamp on NRR late. Therefore, the originator and the recipient cannot provide evidence about the time of sending and receiving a message in direct communication.

This problem could be solved in indirect communication. The delivery authority can provide trusted time stamps in non-repudiation evidence *NRS* and *NRD* to identify when the message was submitted and delivered.

3 Roles of Trusted Third Parties

A *trusted third party* is a security authority or its agent, trusted by other entities with respect to security-related activities [2]. Trusted third parties play important roles in non-repudiation services. Depending on the non-repudiation mechanisms used and the non-repudiation policy in force, trusted third parties may be involved in different ways to assist participants to generate, verify, or transfer non-repudiation evidence, and resolve disputes. There are trivial lists of trusted third party involvement in [3, 4], which do not help understanding the real role of a trusted third party in non-repudiation services. We classify the following types of trusted third parties that may be involved in a non-repudiation service.

Certification Authority

A *certification authority* generates key certificates which guarantee the authenticity of verification keys to be used for non-repudiation purposes. It also provides the revocation list of certificates in order to determine the validity of old verification keys. Certification authorities are always required when digital signatures are used for evidence generation. They will usually be off-line in a non-repudiation service.

Notary

A *notary* is trusted by the communicating entities to provide correct evidence on their behalf or verify evidence correctly. Properties about the message exchanged between entities, such as its origin and integrity, can be assured by the provision of a notarisation mechanism.

A notary is often required by a non-repudiation service and is usually on-line. When symmetric cryptography is used for evidence generation, the evidence should be generated by a notary on behalf of the originator and the recipient. When digital signatures are used for evidence generation, trusted time stamps regarding the time of evidence generation should be provided by a notary to settle a possible dispute over the validity of the signature keys used by the originator and the recipient for evidence generation.

There is an application of an on-line notary in mechanisms **M1** and **M2** of ISO/IEC 13888-2 [5], where the trusted third party generates and verifies non-repudiation evidence *NRO* and *NRR* on behalf of the originator and the recipient.

There is another application of an on-line notary in a fair non-repudiation protocol [9], where the message key is notarized by the trusted third party on the request of the originator, and serves as part of non-repudiation evidence for both the originator and the recipient.

Delivery Authority

As mentioned in the last section, a *delivery authority* is trusted to deliver a message from one entity to another and provide them with corresponding evidence. There is an application of an in-line delivery authority in mechanism **M3** of ISO/IEC 13888-2 [5]. But the trusted third party also acts as a notary and provides the originator and the recipient with NRR and NRO rather than NRD and NRS. We will propose a non-repudiation protocol using a delivery authority in Section 5, where the delivery authority provides evidence about the time of submission and delivery of a message.

Adjudicator

The ultimate purpose of a non-repudiation service is to resolve disputes about the occurrence or non-occurrence of a claimed event or action. An *adjudicator* is a judge capable of resolving disputes by evaluating the evidence against a non-repudiation policy. It will not be involved in a non-repudiation service unless there is a dispute and a request for arbitration. The judgement will be based on the evidence provided by disputing parties involved in a non-repudiation service. For example, with NRO/NRR, the adjudicator can settle the dispute over the origin/receipt of a message; with NRS/NRD, the adjudicator can settle the disputes over the submission/delivery of a message and the time of submission/delivery if a trusted time stamp is included in NRS/NRD.

4   ISO's Non-repudiation Mechanisms

ISO/IEC 13888 provides a set of non-repudiation mechanisms based on symmetric and asymmetric cryptographic techniques [5, 6]. Flaws and limitations exist as we discuss here. The following notation is employed in the analysis of these mechanisms.

- X, Y: concatenation of two messages X and Y.
- $[X]$: message X is optional.
- $H(X)$: a one-way hash function of message X.
- $R(X)$: a redundancy function of message X.
- $gK(X)$: an integrity mechanism for message X with key K.
- $eK(X)$: encryption of message X with key K.
- $sK(X)$: digital signature of message X with the private key K.
- S_A: the private signature key of principal A.

- $SENV_K(X)$: a secure envelope which is generated by using symmetric cryptographic techniques and allows the holder of secret key K to authenticate the integrity and origin of message X.
- TTP: the trusted third party.
- A: the originator of a non-repudiation service; we let A also denote a secret key held only by A and the TTP.
- B: the recipient of a non-repudiation service; we let B also denote a secret key held only by B and the TTP.
- N: a secret notarisation key held only by the TTP.
- M: the message to be sent from A to B.
- f: a flag indicating that the secure envelope or digital signature is attached to the appropriate data.
- $key\ id$: a distinguishing identifier of the secret key N used by the TTP.
- $msg\ id$: a data string which can uniquely identify the message protected by a secure envelope.
- NRO: non-repudiation of origin of M.
  $NRO = [key\ id], [msg\ id], SENV_N(z)$ where $z = f_{NRO}, A, B, H(M)$;
  or $NRO = sS_A(f_{NRO}, B, M)$.
- NRR: non-repudiation of receipt of M.
  $NRR = [key\ id], [msg\ id], SENV_N(z')$ where $z' = f_{NRR}, A, B, H(M)$;
  or $NRR = sS_B(f_{NRR}, A, M)$.
- PON: the verification result (positive or negative) of a NRO or NRR presented to the TTP.

4.1 Mechanisms Using Symmetric Techniques

ISO/IEC CD 13888-2 [5] contains three mechanisms providing *non-repudiation of origin* and *non-repudiation of receipt* [1] services (**M1,M2,M3**). **M1** only provides non-repudiation of origin and optionally non-repudiation of receipt at the recipient's prerogative. It is suitable for the situation where the originator does not care whether the recipient will acknowledge its message. For example, a merchant may send its catalogue over networks and wants to protect against forgery of its catalogue, so customers can be sure what is provided at which price by the merchant.

M2 and **M3** try to provide a *mandatory* non-repudiation of receipt service. But the *selective receipt* problem may arise if communicating parties do not play fair or if the communication channel is unreliable. In the following, we make a detailed analysis of **M2** and **M3**, where NRO and NRR are generated by secure envelopes.

---

[1] ISO/IEC 13888 uses *non-repudiation of delivery*. We prefer the term "receipt" since we feel that the term "delivery" is more appropriate to describe the function performed by message transfer systems.

M2(13888-2): mandatory NRO and NRR

1. $A \to TTP : SENV_A(z)$
2. $TTP \to A : SENV_A(NRO)$
3. $A \to B : \quad M, z, NRO$
4. $B \to TTP : SENV_B(NRO)$
5. $TTP \to B : SENV_B(PON, NRO, NRR)$
6. $TTP \to A : SENV_A(NRR)$

In **M2**, A first asks TTP to generate NRO and then sends M, z, NRO to B at Step 3. This leaves B in an advantageous position. After receiving the message M, B may examine its contents. If B then aborts the protocol run at Step 4, no one will get evidence that B has received the message. It is naive to count upon the recipient always to acknowledge the receipt of a message in a non-repudiation service. Therefore, this mechanism achieves no more than **M1** and cannot be applied in the situation where the originator always needs a receipt of the message it wants to send. For example, a merchant delivering electronic goods over computer networks to a customer may want to receive payment from the customer at the same time. Obviously, **M2** cannot be applied in such a situation.

M3(13888-2): mandatory NRO and NRR with intermediary TTP

1. $A \to TTP : M, SENV_A(z)$
2. $TTP \to A : SENV_A(NRO)$
3. $TTP \to B : M, z, NRO$
4. $B \to TTP : SENV_B(NRO)$
5. $TTP \to B : SENV_B(PON, NRO, NRR)$
6. $TTP \to A : SENV_A(NRR)$

In **M3**, TTP acts as a delivery authority to transfer the message M from A to B as well as a notary to generate and verify non-repudiation evidence NRO and NRR. However, there is no difference between **M3** and **M2** in the establishment of mandatory non-repudiation of receipt. Although TTP can witness having sent M to B, B can still deny receipt of the message with claims of communication channel failure. Actually, B may receive M with a corrupted NRO at Step 3 and send the corrupted NRO to TTP for verification at Step 4. Then the verification will fail and non-repudiation of origin and receipt are not established. B may also receive M with a correct NRO but send a corrupted NRO to TTP deliberately. Even more, B may abort the protocol run at Step 4 without acknowledging TTP's message. Only after receiving a request for verification of NRO from B and obtaining a positive result, will TTP provide NRR to A to establish non-repudiation of receipt. The *selective receipt* problem cannot be avoided unless there exists an assumption that the communication channel is *completely* reliable so that TTP is entitled to provide NRR to A after delivering the message to B without waiting for B's acknowledgement. However, this is a strong and frequently unwarranted assumption.

Technical Flaws

M1, M2 and **M3** in [5] use secure envelopes to protect the integrity and origin of a message as well as to generate non-repudiation evidence. All of them would have a serious flaw if they are implemented improperly. Two methods are proposed for the construction of a secure envelope in [5]:

1. Secure envelope construction via an integrity mechanism:

$$SENV_K(X) = X, gK(X).$$

2. Secure envelope construction via encipherment:

$$SENV_K(X) = eK(X, R(X)).$$

If the secure envelopes are generated by encipherment, and *msg id* in *NRO* and *NRR* is omitted[2] or not a collision-free hash function of the message, then attacks may occur in those mechanisms even if the communicating parties play fair. More specifically, if

$$NRO = SENV_N(z) = eN(z, R(z)),$$

an intruder could modify message 3 to

$$3. \ A/TTP \rightarrow B : \quad M'', z'', eN(z, R(z))$$

where $z'' = f_{NRO}, A, B, H(M'')$ and $M'' \neq M$. As z in *NRO* is encrypted by *TTP*'s own secret key N, B is unable to check whether z'' matches z in *NRO*. *TTP* cannot detect the attack either because B only sends $SENV_B(NRO)$ to *TTP* at Step 4. At the end of the protocol run, B is convinced by *TTP*'s positive verification result that A sent M'', but actually possesses evidence that A sent M.

To avoid such an attack, Step 4 in those mechanisms should be changed to

$$4. \ B \rightarrow TTP : \quad SENV_B(z, NRO)$$

so that *TTP* can check that z contained within the encrypted *NRO* is the same as z supplied by B. *TTP* then only returns a positive reply if the two copies of z match; thereby B has a guarantee that *NRO* applies to the message M and not some other message. A similar modification of Step 6 in **M2** and **M3** is necessary for A to know which message the *NRR* it received from *TTP* refers to.

Alternatively, the definition of secure envelope using encipherment could be modified as to [4]

$$SENV_K(X) = X, eK(H(X)).$$

If this change is made, neither method of creating a secure envelope will provide data confidentiality. Actually, confidentiality is not required in non-repudiation services and unnecessary use of encryption may cause export barriers.

---

[2] It is a reasonable assumption because *msg id* is defined as optional in *NRO* and *NRR*.

4.2 Mechanisms Using Asymmetric Techniques

ISO/IEC CD 13888-3 [6] specifies the following two separate mechanisms for non-repudiation of origin and non-repudiation of receipt, where NRO and NRR are generated by digital signatures.

1. Mechanism for non-repudiation of origin

$$A \to B: \quad f_{NRO}, B, M, NRO$$

2. Mechanism for non-repudiation of receipt

$$B \to A: \quad f_{NRR}, A, NRR$$

where B must have received the message M from A before constructing NRR.

The second mechanism is open to the threat of *selective receipt* and has limited application. In the history of ISO/IEC 13888-3, the problem of *selective receipt* in a non-repudiation service was noticed. There were two non-repudiation mechanisms (**M2,M3**) dealing with this problem without the involvement of on-line and in-line trusted third parties in [7]. They are described as follows:

M2(13888-3): mandatory NRO and NRR using a hash function

A *promise of exchange* $POE = sS_A(f_{POE}, B, H(M))$ and an acknowledgment $ACP = sS_B(f_{ACP}, A, H(M))$ are constructed using an integrity check function.

1. $A \to B : f_{POE}, B, H(M), POE$
2. $B \to A : f_{ACP}, A, ACP$
3. $A \to B : f_{NRO}, B, M, NRO$
4. $B \to A : f_{NRR}, A, NRR$

M3(13888-3): mandatory NRO and NRR using encryption

This mechanism uses encryption to construct the *promise of exchange* $POE = sS_A(f_{POE}, B, eK(M))$ and the acknowledgment $ACP = sS_B(f_{ACP}, A, eK(M))$.

1. $A \to B : f_{POE}, B, eK(M), POE$
2. $B \to A : f_{ACP}, A, ACP$
3. $A \to B : f_{NRO}, B, K, NRO$
4. $B \to A : f_{NRR}, A, NRR$

M2 and **M3** employ a similar idea. To prevent B from acknowledging only convenient messages, A first sends a promise of exchange POE which does not reveal the contents of the message. **M2** uses $H(M)$ in its POE while **M3** uses $eK(M)$ in its POE. After receiving an acknowledgement ACP from B, A then sends M (**M2**) or K (**M3**) with NRO and waits for NRR from B. However, this does not solve the problem as B can still refuse to send the last message, leaving A without a proof of receipt. The mechanisms had to declare that Step 3 and Step 4 are *mandatory* and to rely on arguments like the following *consecutiveness* property to justify why such mechanisms would meet their purpose.

If B obtains NRO after a preliminary promise, then B must send NRR back to A. Otherwise, B is proved to be wrong by the adjudicator.

It is not clear how the adjudicator can establish that B did obtain NRO other than by accepting A's word that NRO was sent and assuming that the network will deliver the message. As pointed out in [9], relying on properties external to the protocol is unsatisfactory from a theoretical viewpoint and dangerous from a practical viewpoint. As a result, **M2** and **M3** have been superseded, and the problem of *selective receipt* in a non-repudiation service has to be "ignored" for lack of satisfactory solutions.

5 Fair Non-repudiation with Time Information

We have proposed a fair non-repudiation protocol in [9], where the originator and the recipient communicate directly with minimized involvement of a TTP acting as a 'low weight notary'. In some applications, the originator and the recipient may need evidence about the time of sending and receiving a message besides the evidence of NRO and NRR. In our protocol, the evidence about the time that the message key and thus the message is available can be provided by the TTP. However, the originator can only submit the message key to the TTP after obtaining the reply to its commitment from the recipient. The originator would not like to take the responsibility of late submission caused by the recipient's late reply. The protocol presented in this section (see Figure 1) mainly protects against such a dispute.

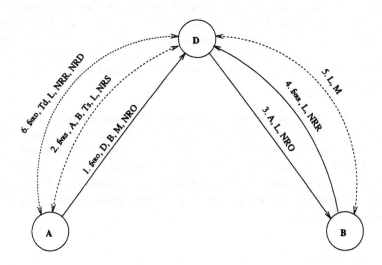

Fig. 1. A Fair Non-repudiation Protocol Including Time Information

Suppose the originator A wants to send the message M to the recipient B by employing a delivery authority D. We assume that A, B, and D are each equipped with their own private signature key and the relevant public verification keys. Flags indicate the intended purpose of a (signed) message. The notation in the protocol description is as follows.

- L: a unique label chosen by D to identify the message M.
- T_s: the time that D received A's submission.
- T_d: the time that M is delivered and available to B.
- $NRO = sS_A(f_{NRO}, D, B, M)$: non-repudiation of origin of M.
- $NRS = sS_D(f_{NRS}, A, B, T_s, L, NRO)$: non-repudiation of submission of M.
- $NRR = sS_B(f_{NRR}, D, A, L, NRO)$: non-repudiation of receiving a message labeled L.
- $NRD = sS_D(f_{NRD}, A, B, T_d, L, NRR)$: non-repudiation of delivery of M.

The protocol works under the assumption that the communication channel is not permanently broken. Steps 2, 5 and 6 are *"ftp get"* operations [8], where A and B fetch messages from D.

$$1.\ A \to D : f_{NRO}, D, B, M, NRO$$
$$2.\ A \leftrightarrow D : f_{NRS}, A, B, T_s, L, NRS$$
$$3.\ D \to B : A, L, NRO$$
$$4.\ B \to D : f_{NRR}, L, NRR$$
$$5.\ B \leftrightarrow D : L, M$$
$$6.\ A \leftrightarrow D : f_{NRD}, T_d, L, NRR, NRD$$

To prevent B from selectively acknowledging receipt, D first informs B that a message labeled L is awaiting collection. B can decide whether or not to collect the message. Only after B has committed itself to collecting the labeled message, will D store M and NRD (including B's commitment NRR) in a publicly readable directory. They should be retrieved by B and A respectively. Here, we further assume that B is not in a position to make a *selective receipt* by eavesdropping.

With NRS, A can prove that D received its submission of M at the time of T_s. With NRR, A can prove that B is committed to collect the message labeled L. The consistency between the label L and the message M is guaranteed by D. With NRD, A can prove that D has made M publicly available at the time of T_d and B can always retrieve it (according to our assumption). B can use NRO to verify the message M obtained at Step 5. With NRO, B can also prove that M originated from A.

6 Conclusion

Non-repudiation services provide evidence about the occurrence of a particular action and always require a trusted third party to be involved in some capacity, acting as certification authority, notary, delivery authority or adjudicator. We have considered two special features of non-repudiation services. Some applications require evidence about the time of an event. Such evidence is not available when parties communicate directly and can only be provided by a delivery authority in indirect communication. Secondly, we have considered solutions to the selective receipt problem. There are no satisfactory mechanisms in the current version of ISO/IEC 13888 [5, 6] which also contain technical flaws so that significant improvements of these drafts are required. We propose a protocol that addresses both issues by modifying the fair non-repudiation protocol given in [9]. In particular, we have to change the role of the trusted third party which now also has to act as a delivery authority.

Acknowledgements

Thanks to Chris Mitchell for making available his collection of ISO documents. We are grateful to the anonymous referees for useful comments on this paper. The first author would also like to thank the British Government and the K C Wong Education Foundation for their support through an ORS Award and a K C Wong Scholarship.

References

1. ISO 7498-2. *Information processing system - Open systems interconnection - Basic reference model, Part 2: Security architecture.* International Organization for Standardization, 1989.
2. ISO/IEC CD 10181-1. *Information technology - Open systems interconnection - Security frameworks in open systems, Part 1: Overview of open systems security framework.* ISO/IEC JTC1/SC21 N8509, April 1994.
3. ISO/IEC DIS 10181-4. *Information technology - Open systems interconnection - Security frameworks in open systems, Part 4: Non-repudiation.* ISO/IEC, 1995.
4. ISO/IEC 3rd CD 13888-1. *Information technology - Security techniques - Non-repudiation, Part 1: General model.* ISO/IEC JTC1/SC27 N1274, March 1996.
5. ISO/IEC 3rd CD 13888-2. *Information technology - Security techniques - Non-repudiation, Part 2: Using symmetric encipherment algorithms.* ISO/IEC JTC1/SC27 N1276, January 1996.
6. ISO/IEC 2nd CD 13888-3. *Information technology - Security techniques - Non-repudiation, Part 3: Using asymmetric techniques.* ISO/IEC JTC1/SC27 N1379, June 1996.
7. ISO/IEC 3rd WD 13888-3. *3rd working draft on Non-repudiation, Part 3: Mechanisms using asymmetric techniques.* ISO/IEC JTC1/SC27/WG2 N224, July 1993.
8. J. B. Postel and J. K. Reynolds. *File transfer protocol.* RFC 959, October 1985.
9. J. Zhou and D. Gollmann. *A fair non-repudiation protocol.* Proceedings of 1996 IEEE Symposium on Security and Privacy, pages 55-61, Oakland, CA, May 1996.

On the Efficiency of One-Time Digital Signatures

Daniel Bleichenbacher[1] and Ueli Maurer[2]

[1] Bell Laboratories
600 Mountain Avenue
Murray Hill, NJ 07974

[2] Department of Computer Science
Swiss Federal Institute of Technology (ETH Zurich)
CH-8092 Zürich, Switzerland

Abstract. Digital signature schemes based on a general one-way function without trapdoor offer two potential advantages over digital signature schemes based on trapdoor one-way functions such as the RSA system: higher efficiency and much more freedom in choosing a cryptographic function to base the security on. Such a scheme is characterized by a directed acyclic computation graph and an antichain in a certain partially ordered set defined by the graph. Several results on the achievable efficiency of such schemes are proved, where the efficiency of a scheme is defined as the ratio of the size of messages that can be signed and the number of one-way function evaluations needed for setting up the system. For instance, the maximal achievable efficiency for trees is shown to be equal to a constant $\gamma \approx 0.4161426$ and a family of general graphs with substantially greater efficiency 0.476 is demonstrated. This construction appears to be close to optimal.

Key words. Cryptography, Digital signature, One-way function, Directed acyclic graph, Partially ordered set.

1 Introduction

One can distinguish between three types of digital signature schemes. The first type of scheme was proposed by Lamport [7] and generalized in [8], [9], [5], [14] and [1]. Once it is set up, it can only be used for signing a predetermined number (e.g. one) of messages from a certain message space. The second type of schemes, the first realization of which was the RSA system [11], can be used an unlimited number of times. In contrast to the first type of scheme, the second requires strong mathematical structure in the underlying one-way function. A third type of scheme was proposed by Rompel [12] based on work by Naor and Yung [10]. The security of these schemes can provably be based on an arbitrary one-way function, but they are inefficient. The purpose of this paper is to discuss the design and analysis of schemes of the first type, where the emphasis is on efficiency and freedom in the choice of the cryptographic function on which the system is based. In contrast to Rompel's work, our goal is not to prove rigorously that the security is equivalent to the security of the one-way function(s).

There are two different motivations for investigating and possibly using the first type of schemes despite their limited number of uses. First, they can be based on virtually every cryptographic one-way function[3] (OWF), a very general cryptographic primitive, whereas the few schemes of the second type proposed so far are based on OWFs with a very strong mathematical structure. The diversity of conjectured difficult problems (such as the integer factoring problem [11] or the discrete logarithm problem in certain finite groups [13]) on which their security can be based is thus severely limited. While such mathematical structure is appealing to the designer and the users of a system, it could for an adversary just as well be the key to breaking the system if he is able to exploit the structure in a way not foreseen by the designer. Second, the first type of scheme is potentially more efficient because a general OWF, which for this purpose not even needs to be collision-free, can be realized much more efficiently than OWFs with appropriate structure. Moreover, these schemes have applications in efficiency-critical smartcard applications [6], in on-line/off-line signatures [5] and in the signature schemes of [3].

The general concept of a digital signature schemes of the first type was formalized in [1]. The purpose of this paper is to discuss constructions for such schemes and to prove several results on the achievable efficiency, in particular for computation graphs that are trees. The outline of the paper is as follows. To make the paper reasonably self-contained, the basic ideas underlying [1] are briefly discussed in Section 2, and the definitions are summarized in Section 3. In Section 4 several types of graphs and constructions are analyzed and lower and upper bound results on their efficiency are derived. The special case of trees is discussed in Section 5 and the best known general graph construction is presented in Section 6.

2 One-time Digital Signature Schemes

The general idea of a one-time signature scheme is that the secret key is used as the input to a sequence of OWF evaluations which results in a sequence of intermediate results and finally in the public key. The one-wayness of the functions implies that it is infeasible to compute the secret key, or any intermediate result of the computation, from the public key.

A signature for a given message consists of a subset of the intermediate results of this computation, where the message to be signed determines which particular subset is revealed as the corresponding signature. There exist two important

---

[3] A one-way function f is a function that is easy to compute but computationally infeasible to invert, for suitable definitions of "easy" and "infeasible". It is not difficult to define a function that appears to be one-way. However, not even the existence of one-way functions, for a suitable definition, has been proved. To be secure in the context of this paper, one-way functions with certain very special properties should be avoided. For instance, a one-way function $f(x,y)$ with two arguments should satisfy $f(x,y) = f(y,x)$ for $x \neq y$ only with negligible probability. It is an open problem to characterize when a function is secure in our context.

requirements on these signatures. First, every signature must be verifiable, i.e., the public key must be computable from it. Second, in order to prevent forgery of signatures, the set of signatures (for the messages in the message space) must be compatible in the sense that no signature can be computed from the signature for a different message, without inverting a one-way function.

Let B be a suitable large set (e.g., the set of 64, 96 or 128-bit strings) which is the range of the OWFs. The input to each OWF evaluation consists of one or several elements of B. The secret key consists of one or a list of elements of B. Without loss of essential generality only schemes are considered for which the public key consists of only one element of B.

The structure of the computation leading from the secret key components to the public key can be represented as a directed acyclic graph $G = (V, E)$ with vertex set V and edge set E, where the vertices correspond to the secret key, the intermediate results, and the public key and where a directed edge (v_i, v_j) in E indicates that v_i is an input to the OWF computation resulting in v_j (see Figure 1, left side).

The graph G characterizing a one-time signature scheme is assumed to be known publicly, as is the mapping from messages to subsets of vertices (signature patterns), and can be used by all users. A user's signature for a given message consists of the values (for that user's secret key) corresponding to the vertices in the signature pattern for that message, when the computation according to G is performed for that user's secret key. A toy example of a signature scheme is shown in Figure 1.

In this paper we are interested in the design of efficient signature schemes based on graphs, where the size of the message space should be maximized while the size of the graph should be minimized. Because messages to be signed can first be hashed by a collision-free hash function to a short string (e.g., of 128 bits), it is sufficient that the message space of our schemes corresponds to the range of such a hash function (e.g., has size 2^{128}).

3 Definitions and Preliminaries

This section summarizes the relevant definitions from [1] and introduces the concept of efficiency. Throughout the paper, vertices and sets of vertices of a graph are denoted by small and capital letters, respectively, and graphs, posets as well as sets of sets of vertices are denoted by calligraphic letters.

Let C_m denote the DAG consisting of a single path connecting m vertices, i.e., a chain of length m. For k DAGs $G_1, \ldots, G_k$, let $G_1 \cdots G_k$ denote the graph consisting of unconnected copies of $G_1, \ldots, G_k$. If each of the graphs $G_1, \ldots, G_k$ has only one vertex of out-degree 0 (corresponding to the public key in our context), let $G = [G_1 \cdots G_k]$ be the DAG obtained from $G_1 \cdots G_k$ by introducing a new vertex v and directed edges from these k distinguished vertices to v.

We now define a one-time signature scheme based on a DAG $G = (V, E)$. The secret key pattern $S(G) \subset V$ and the public key pattern $P(G) \subset V$ are defined as the sets of vertices with in-degree 0 and out-degree 0, respectively. Let X be a

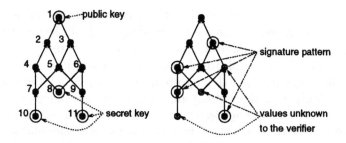

Fig. 1. A toy example of a one-time signature scheme. The secret key consists of the 3 vertices: 8, 10 and 11. One signature pattern (the set $\{3, 4, 7, 11\}$) is indicated on the right-hand side. The associated poset of this graph contains 29 signature patterns, but the maximal number of compatible signature patterns is 9. One maximal antichain consists of the sets $\{2, 5, 8, 11\}$, $\{2, 6, 7, 11\}$, $\{2, 6, 9, 10\}$, $\{3, 4, 7, 11\}$, $\{3, 4, 9, 10\}$, $\{3, 5, 8, 10\}$, $\{4, 5, 8, 9\}$, $\{4, 6, 7, 9\}$, and $\{5, 6, 7, 8\}$. All these signature patterns have size 4, but in general they have different sizes. The efficiency of this scheme is $(\log_2 9)/12 = 0.264$, which is better than Lamport's scheme with efficiency $1/6$.

subset of V. A vertex v is defined recursively to be *computable* from X if either $v \in X$ or if v has at least one predecessor and all predecessors are computable from X. A set Y is computable from X if every element of Y is computable from X. Note that V and hence every subset of V is computable from the secret key $S(\mathcal{G})$.

A set of vertices $X \subseteq V$ is called *verifiable* (with respect to the public key) if $P(\mathcal{G})$ is computable from X. Note that a set X is verifiable if and only if every maximal path (in the sense that it cannot be extended to a longer path or, equivalently, a path from a vertex in $S(\mathcal{G})$ to a vertex in $P(\mathcal{G})$) contains at least one element in X. A verifiable set X is *minimal* if no subset of X is verifiable. Two minimal verifiable sets X and Y are *compatible* if neither X is computable from Y nor Y is computable from X. A set of minimal verifiable sets is compatible if they are pairwise compatible.

The computability relation on the set of minimal verifiable sets of a graph is transitive, antisymmetric and reflexive, and hence the set of minimal verifiable sets of a graph $\mathcal{G}$, denoted $\mathcal{G}^*$, forms a partially ordered set $(\mathcal{G}^*, \leq)$ with computability as the order relation, i.e., we have $X \leq Y$ for $X, Y \in \mathcal{G}^*$ if and only if X is computable from Y. Note that two minimal verifiable sets of $\mathcal{G}$ are compatible if and only if they are incomparable in $(\mathcal{G}^*, \leq)$.

Definition 1. Minimal verifiable sets will in the following be called *signature patterns*. The *associated poset* of DAG $\mathcal{G}$, denoted $\mathcal{G}^*$, is the poset $(\mathcal{G}^*, \leq)$ of signature patterns of $\mathcal{G}$. A *one-time signature scheme* Γ for $\mathcal{G}$ is an antichain of the associated poset $\mathcal{G}^*$, and the maximal size of an anti-chain in $\mathcal{G}$ is denoted by $w(\mathcal{G})$.

A small example of a signature scheme is shown in Figure 1 and is discussed in the figure caption.

The important parameters of a one-time signature scheme Γ for a graph

$\mathcal{G} = (V, E)$ are the number $|V|$ of vertices which is equal to the number of function evaluations required for computing the public key from the secret key[4], the number $|\Gamma|$ of signatures (which is at least equal to the size of the message space), and the maximal size of signatures, $\max_{U \in \Gamma} |U|$.

This motivates the following problems. First, for a given graph $\mathcal{G}$ to find a large (ideally a maximal-sized) antichain in the associated poset. Second, for a given size of the message space to find a graph with few (ideally the minimal number of) vertices allowing the construction of a one-time signature scheme. Third, both problems should be treated with an additional constraint on the maximal size of signatures.

For a poset $\mathcal{Z} = (Z, \leq)$, a function $r : Z \to \mathbf{N}$ is called a *representation function* of $\mathcal{Z}$ if for all distinct $x, y \in Z$, $x \leq y$ implies $r(x) < r(y)$. Therefore $r(x) = r(y)$ implies that x and y are incomparable and hence for any representation function r of the associated poset $(\mathcal{G}^*, \leq)$ of a given DAG $\mathcal{G}$ and for any integer k, the set

$$\{U \in \mathcal{G}^* : r(U) = k\}$$

is a one-time signature scheme.

In order to find good signature schemes for a given graph, we need to find a good representation function. For $U \in \mathcal{G}^*$ for a given DAG $\mathcal{G}$, let $C_{\mathcal{G}}(U)$ be the set of vertices of $\mathcal{G}$ that are computable from U but are not contained in U:

$$C_{\mathcal{G}}(U) = \{v : v \notin U \text{ and } v \text{ is computable from } U\}.$$

Let $c_{\mathcal{G}} : \mathcal{G}^* \to \mathbf{N}$ be the function defined by

$$c_{\mathcal{G}}(U) = |C_{\mathcal{G}}(U)|.$$

The following theorem was stated in [1] without proof.

Theorem 1. *For any DAG $\mathcal{G}$ the function $c_{\mathcal{G}}$ is a representation function of the associated poset $\mathcal{G}^*$.*

Proof. Let U_1 and U_2 be distinct signature patterns with $U_1 \leq U_2$. We must prove that $|C_{\mathcal{G}}(U_1)| < |C_{\mathcal{G}}(U_2)|$. Let v be any element in $C_{\mathcal{G}}(U_1)$. All predecessors of v are computable from U_1 by definition. Since U_1 is computable from U_2 any vertex that is computable from U_1 is computable from U_2. Therefore all predecessors of v are computable from U_2. If v were in U_2 then U_2 would not be minimal. Thus $v \in C_{\mathcal{G}}(U_2)$ and we have $C_{\mathcal{G}}(U_1) \subseteq C_{\mathcal{G}}(U_2)$. Moreover, U_1 is not a subset of U_2 because U_2 is minimal. Hence there exists a vertex $s \in U_1$ with $s \notin U_2$ which is computable from U_2 because U_1 is computable from U_2. Therefore $s \in C_{\mathcal{G}}(U_2)$ and $s \notin C_{\mathcal{G}}(U_1)$ and thus we have $C_{\mathcal{G}}(U_1) \neq C_{\mathcal{G}}(U_2)$. Hence $C_{\mathcal{G}}(U_1)$ is a proper subset of $C_{\mathcal{G}}(U_2)$ which implies that $|C_{\mathcal{G}}(U_1)| < |C_{\mathcal{G}}(U_2)|$. □

A natural implementation of a one-way function with i arguments is to apply a one-way function with two arguments repeatedly $i - 1$ times, each time

---

[4] Here we have assumed that a secret key consisting of several components is generated from a single component by applying, for each component, a different one-way function to the secret key.

combining the previous result with a new argument. This computation can be represented as a binary tree. Without much loss of generality we therefore restrict the discussion in this paper to graphs with a maximal in-degree of 2, counting OWF evaluations with 1 or 2 arguments equaly. Furthermore, because a public key consisting of several components can be hashed to a single value, we restrict the discussion to graphs with a single vertex of out-degree 0 (whose value corresponds to the public key).

The efficiency of a signature scheme Γ for a graph $\mathcal{G}$ can be defined as the number of message bits, $\log_2 |\Gamma|$, that can be signed per vertex of the graph. However, the results on efficiency can be stated more nicely when the number of vertices is increased by one in the following definition.

Definition 2. The *efficiency* of a one-time signature scheme Γ for a graph $\mathcal{G}$ with n vertices, denoted $\eta(\Gamma)$, is defined by

$$\eta(\Gamma) = \frac{\log_2 |\Gamma|}{n+1}.$$

For example, the graph corresponding to Lamport's scheme for signing a k-bit message contains $6k - 1$ vertices when all the public-key components are hashed in a binary tree to result in a single public-key component. Hence the efficiency of the Lamport scheme is $1/6$.

In the sequel we discuss the problem of maximizing the number of signature patterns for a given number n of vertices under the restriction of maximal in-degree 2. Let $\nu(n)$ be the maximal number of signature patterns for graphs with n vertices and let $\mu(n)$ be the maximal number of compatible signature patterns for graphs with n vertices, i.e., let

$$\nu(n) = \max\{|\mathcal{G}^*| : \mathcal{G} = (V, E) \text{ with } |V| = n\}$$
$$\text{and} \quad \mu(n) = \max\{w(\mathcal{G}^*) : \mathcal{G} = (V, E) \text{ with } |V| = n\},$$

where vertices in $\mathcal{G}$ have fan-in at most 2 and $\mathcal{G}$ has a public key of size 1. The size of signatures is also an important efficiency parameter and schemes requiring only short signatures will be discussed in Section 4.3.

A simple relation between $\nu(n)$ and $\mu(n)$ is that for all $n \geq 1$,

$$\nu(n) \geq \mu(n) \geq \frac{\nu(n)}{n}. \tag{1}$$

The left inequality follows directly from the definition. To prove the right inequality, let $\mathcal{G}$ be a DAG with n vertices satisfying $|\mathcal{G}^*| = \nu(n)$. Since the range of $c_\mathcal{G}$ is a subset of $\{0, \ldots, n-1\}$ there exists an $i \in \{0, \ldots, n-1\}$ such that $|\{U \in \mathcal{G}^* : c_\mathcal{G}(U) = i\}| \geq \nu(n)/n$. According to Theorem 1, this set is a one-time signature scheme.

4 Efficient Constructions and Bounds on the Efficiency

In this section we investigate several constructions of one-time signature schemes, each of which leads to relations between the functions μ and ν.

4.1 Repetition of Graphs

The signature patterns of an unconnected collection $\mathcal{G}_1 \cdots \mathcal{G}_k$ of DAGs are the lists $[S_1, \ldots, S_k]$, where each S_i ranges over the signature patterns of $\mathcal{G}_i$. In other words $(\mathcal{G}_1 \cdots \mathcal{G}_k)^* = \mathcal{G}_1^* \times \cdots \times \mathcal{G}_k^*$ and hence $|(\mathcal{G}_1 \cdots \mathcal{G}_k)^*| = \prod_{i=1}^{k} |\mathcal{G}_i^*|$. When the $\mathcal{G}_i$ are graphs with $|\mathcal{G}_i| = n_i$ and $|\mathcal{G}_i^*| = \nu(n_i)$ for $1 \leq i \leq k$, the total number of signature patterns is $\prod_{i=1}^{k} \nu(n_i)$. Thus we have proved the following theorem, where the term $k-1$ is needed because according to our convention that graphs have only one vertex with out-degree 0, the k public key vertices of $\mathcal{G}_1, \ldots, \mathcal{G}_k$ must be combined by a binary tree with $k-1$ vertices.

Theorem 2. *For every list $n_1, \ldots, n_k$ of k positive integers,*

$$\nu(\sum_{i=1}^{k} n_i + k - 1) \geq \prod_{i=1}^{k} \nu(n_i). \tag{2}$$

In particular, $\nu((n+1)k - 1) \geq \nu(n)^k$.

4.2 Separate Representation Function Encoding

Generally it can be considerably easier to design a mapping from the message space to an arbitrary subset of the signature patterns of a graph $\mathcal{G}_1$ rather than to a subset of compatible signature patterns. The compatibility can be guaranteed by introducing a small additional graph $\mathcal{G}_2$. The graph $\mathcal{G}_2$ is used to compensate for the fact that the values of $c_{\mathcal{G}_1}$ vary over a wide range for all signature patterns of $\mathcal{G}_1$. (See the proof for a precise definition of the construction, a special case of which is actually used in smartcard applications [6].)

Theorem 3. *Let $\mathcal{G}_1$ and $\mathcal{G}_2$ be graphs with n_1 and n_2 vertices, respectively, such that $|\mathcal{G}_2^*| \geq n_1$. Then the graph $[\mathcal{G}_1 \mathcal{G}_2]$ has at least $|\mathcal{G}_1^*|$ compatible signature patterns, i.e., $w([\mathcal{G}_1 \mathcal{G}_2]^*) \geq |\mathcal{G}_1^*|$. In particular, for all s and n satisfying $\nu(s) \geq n$ we have*

$$\mu(s + n + 1) \geq \nu(n).$$

Proof. Let $\mathcal{G}_1$ and $\mathcal{G}_2$ be DAGs with s and n vertices, respectively, satisfying $|\mathcal{G}_1^*| = \nu(s) \geq n$ and $|\mathcal{G}_2^*| = \nu(n)$. For every partially ordered set with t elements one can number these elements from 0 to $t-1$ such that their order is preserved. Hence there exists a representation function r_1 for $\mathcal{G}_1$ assigning the integers $0, \ldots, \nu(s) - 1$ to the signature patterns of $\mathcal{G}_1$. (Note that for instance the public key is assigned the value 0.) Let r be a representation function for the graph $\mathcal{G} = [\mathcal{G}_1 \mathcal{G}_2]$ defined by $r(U) = c_{\mathcal{G}_2}(U_2) + r_1(U_1) + 1$ if the signature pattern S of $\mathcal{G}$ is defined by $U = U_1 \cup U_2$ where $U_1 \subset \mathcal{G}_1$ and $U_2 \subset \mathcal{G}_2$ are signature patterns of $\mathcal{G}_1$ and $\mathcal{G}_2$, respectively. Note that r is indeed a representation function because $r(U_1 \cup U_2) \leq r(U_1' \cup U_2')$ implies that either U_1' is not computable from U_1 or U_2' is not computable from U_2. $\square$

4.3 Schemes with Short Signatures

The size of a graph corresponding to a one-time signature scheme determines the computational effort for computing the public key from the secret key and is an important efficiency parameter. There are two additional requirements for making a scheme practical. First, as mentioned above, the mapping from the message space to the signature patterns must be simple and efficiently computable and second, signatures should be short. In this section we therefore discuss schemes with signature patterns consisting of at most l vertices. Let $\mu(n, l)$ and $\nu(n, l)$ be the maximal number of signature patterns of size at most l for a graph with n vertices, when the signature patterns are compatible, or not necessarily compatible, respectively.

Let $\mathcal{R}_{k,l} = \overbrace{C_k \cdots C_k}^{l \text{ times}}$ be the forest consisting of l chains of length k whose vertices will be denoted by $v_{i1}, \ldots, v_{ik}$ for the ith chain. In a practical implementation of such a scheme, the public key consisting of the l top elements of the chains would of course be hashed cryptographically to a single public-key component, i.e., the chains would be connected to a rake-shaped tree.

The poset $\mathcal{R}_{k,l}^{*}$ of signature patterns of $\mathcal{R}_{k,l}$ consists of all l-tuples $(v_{1,a_1}, \ldots, v_{l,a_l})$ with $1 \leq a_i \leq k$. In the poset (not the graph) terminology, it is equal to the product of l chains of length k and has $|\mathcal{R}_{k,l}^{*}| = k^l$ elements. Interestingly, it has been shown [4] that a poset consisting of a product of chains has the Sperner property. This implies that the maximal number of signature patterns can be obtained by using the representation function $c_{\mathcal{R}_{k,l}}$ defined in Section 3. The proof of the following theorem is omitted because of space limitations. It shows that for a fixed l, $w(\mathcal{R}_{k,l}^{*})$ can be written as a polynomial in k of degree $l - 1$ which is by a factor k smaller than the total number of signature patterns.

Theorem 4. *The number* $w(\mathcal{R}_{k,l}^{*})$ *of compatible signature patterns for the graph* $\mathcal{R}_{k,l}$ *satisfies*

$$w(\mathcal{R}_{k,l}^{*}) = \alpha_l k^{l-1} + O(k^{l-2}),$$

where $\alpha_l = \frac{1}{(l-1)!} \sum_{j=0}^{\lfloor (l-1)/2 \rfloor} (-1)^j \binom{l}{j} (l/2 - j)^{l-1}$ *and where* $\lim_{l \to \infty} \alpha_l \sqrt{l} = \sqrt{6/\pi}$.

We conjecture that the graph $\mathcal{R}_{k,l}$ is asymptotically optimal in the sense that

$$\lim_{l \to \infty} \mu(n, l) \sqrt{l} / (n/l)^{l-1} = \alpha_l. \tag{3}$$

However, there do exist graphs that are better than $\mathcal{R}_{k,l}$ in the coefficient of the second term k^{l-2}.

Rather than using a signature scheme for the graph $\mathcal{R}_{k,l}$, for which the mapping from the message space to the compatible signature patterns is not trivial, it is simpler to combine two rake graphs $\mathcal{G}_1 = \mathcal{R}_{k_1,l_1}$ and $\mathcal{G}_2 = \mathcal{R}_{k_2,l_2}$ by the construction of Section 3.2. The number $k_2^{l_2}$ of signature patterns of the second graph must be at least as large as the number $k_1 l_1$ of vertices of the first graphs. We therefore have

$$k_1 l_1 \leq k_2^{l_2} \implies \mu(k_1 + k_2 + 1, l_1 + l_2) \geq k_1^{l_1}.$$

Example. For instance, one can use $k_1 = 2^{10} = 1024$, $l_1 = 13$, $k_2 = 116$ and $l_2 = 2$. This scheme with signatures of size 15 allows to sign 130-bit messages which is compatible with the use of a cryptographically-secure hash function for hashing arbitrary messages to 128 bits prior to signing.

More generally, if in the construction of Section 3.2 the maximal size of signature patterns in $\mathcal{G}_1$ and $\mathcal{G}_2$ are l_1 and l_2, respectively, then the maximal size of signatures in the combined scheme is $l_1 + l_2$. The following corollary follows immediately.

Corollary 5. *For any l_1, k_1, l_2 and k_2 satisfying $\nu(n_2, l_2) \geq n_1$ we have*

$$\mu(n_1 + n_2 + 1, l_1 + l_2) \geq \nu(n_1, l_1).$$

5 Optimal Trees

In this section we only consider trees. The single node with out-degree 0 is called the root. Note that in contrast to most scenarios in computer science, our directed trees are directed from the leaves to the root. Let $\hat{\nu}(n)$ be the maximal number of signature patterns obtainable for a tree with n vertices and $\hat{\mu}(n)$ the maximal number of compatible signature patterns for a tree with n vertices. In analogy to the proof of (1) one can show that

$$\hat{\nu}(n) \geq \hat{\mu}(n) \geq \frac{\hat{\nu}(n)}{n} \tag{4}$$

Let A and B be two trees. Recall that $[AB]$ denotes the tree obtained from two A and B by introducing a new vertex v and connecting the roots of A and B to v. The following theorem from [2] characterizes the form of optimal trees.

Theorem 6. *For $n \leq 5$ the chain C_n of length n is an optimal tree in the sense that $\hat{\nu}(n) = |C_n^*| = n$. For $n > 5$ all optimal trees are of the form $[AB]$, where A and B are optimal trees. Hence no optimal tree can contain an edge from a vertex with in-degree 2 to a vertex with in-degree 1. For $n > 5$ we have*

$$\hat{\nu}(n) = 1 + \max_{1 \leq i \leq n-2} \{\hat{\nu}(i)\hat{\nu}(n - 1 - i)\}.$$

We now consider a tree construction which connects the roots of 2^n identical trees with a full binary tree of depth n.

Definition 3. Let $\tau_n(\mathcal{T})$ for $n \geq 0$ be defined recursively by $\tau_0(\mathcal{T}) := \mathcal{T}$ and $\tau_{n+1}(\mathcal{T}) := [\tau_n(\mathcal{T})\tau_n(\mathcal{T})]$. Let further the function $\rho : \mathbf{Z}^2 \to \mathbf{Z}$ be defined by $\rho(0, m) := m$ and $\rho(n+1, m) := \rho(n, m)^2 + 1$, and let the tree efficiency constant γ be defined by

$$\gamma = \lim_{n \to \infty} \frac{\log_2 \rho(n, 3)}{2^{n+2}} \approx 0.41614263726.$$

Finally, let the function g be defined by $g(\mathcal{T}) := \log_2 |\mathcal{T}^*|/(|\mathcal{T}| + 1)$.

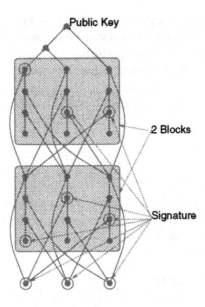

Fig. 2. The graph construction with the best known efficiency which converges asymptotically to 0.476 when the number of 12-vertex blocks (indicated by shaded areas) is increased. One particular signature pattern of size 9 is indicated.

Theorem 7. *The efficiency of every tree-based one-time signature scheme Γ is at most γ, i.e. $\eta(\Gamma) \leq \gamma$. Moreover,*

$$\hat{\mu}(n) \geq \frac{2^{\gamma n}}{2n}$$

and thus for every $\delta < \gamma$ there exists a tree-based one-time signature scheme Γ with $\eta(\Gamma) \geq \delta$.

The proof of Theorem 7 is given in the Appendix. Several results on the construction of optimal trees are proved in [2].

6 The Best Known Graph Construction

Figure 2 shows the one-time signature scheme with the currently best known efficiency. We consider graphs $\mathcal{H}_n$ consisting of n blocks of 12 vertices. Each block consists of 3 chains of length 4 and is connected to the next block in a periodic manner as illustrated in Figure 2, where $\mathcal{H}_2$ is shown as an example. The graphs $\mathcal{H}_3, \mathcal{H}_4, \ldots$ are similar to $\mathcal{H}_2$ but contain more blocks. The bottom layer of 3 vertices could be omitted and is shown only for reasons of symmetry.

A large (though not maximal) set of signature patterns for $\mathcal{H}_n$ can be described as follows. The bottom three vertices belong to each signature pattern. Each signature pattern contains one vertex of each of the three chains of each block. This would result in 64 combinations, but 13 of these must be excluded because the resulting signature pattern would not be minimal. The reason is that in these cases, not all vertices at lower layers would be needed for the verification. Thus $\mathcal{H}_n$ has at least 51^n signature patterns.

The efficiency of the corresponding signature scheme Γ_n is lower bounded by

$$\eta(\Gamma_n) \geq \frac{\log_2(51^n/(12n+5))}{12n+6}$$

and, asymptotically, by

$$\lim_{n \to \infty} \eta(\Gamma_n) \geq \frac{\log_2 51}{12} \approx 0.473.$$

A more careful analysis involving Markov chains shows that the achievable efficiency for $\mathcal{H}_n$ converges to $\log_2(\omega)/12$ where ω is the maximal root of $x^3 - 56x^2 + 173x - 54$. This value is 0.476.

7 Concluding Remarks

We suggest as a challenging open problem to find one-time signature schemes with higher efficiency than that of Section 6, or to prove an upper bound on the efficiency of all such schemes. We conjecture that no scheme has efficiency greater than $1/2$. Another open problem is to prove or disprove equation (3). Using Merkle's authentication tree [8] one can extend every one-time signature scheme to one that can be used a predetermined number of times rather than only once. However, this construction is known to be not optimal, and a further interesting problem is to design such schemes that are better than Merkle's construction applied to an optimal one-time signature scheme.

Appendix

The proof of Theorem 7 is divided into several steps, summarized in the following three lemmas. Recall that the functions ρ and g are defined in Definition 3.

Lemma 8. *For all $n \geq 0$,*

$$\rho(n, ab+1)^2 \leq \rho(n+1, a)\rho(n+1, b). \tag{5}$$

Moreover, for every fixed $m \in \mathbf{N}$, the function $\mathbf{N} \to \mathbf{N}: n \mapsto 2^{-n} \log_2 \rho(n, m)$ is monotonically increasing, and the function $\mathbf{N} \to \mathbf{N}: n \mapsto 2^{-n} \log_2(\rho(n, m) + 1)$ is monotonically decreasing.
Proof. For $n = 0$ equation (5) follows from $\rho(1, a)\rho(1, b) - \rho(0, ab+1)^2 = (a^2 + 1)(b^2 + 1) - (ab+1)^2 = (a - b)^2 \geq 0$. The lemma follows by induction on n; assuming (5) is satisfied for $n - 1$ implies that the difference of the right and the left side of (5) is positive:

$$\rho(n+1, a)\rho(n+1, b) - \rho(n, ab+1)^2 = (\rho(n, a)^2 + 1)(\rho(n, b)^2 + 1)$$
$$- (\rho(n-1, ab+1)^2 + 1)^2$$

$$\geq (\rho(n,a)^2 + 1)(\rho(n,b)^2 + 1)$$
$$-(\rho(n,a)\rho(n,b) + 1)^2$$
$$= (\rho(n,a) - \rho(n,b))^2 \geq 0.$$

To prove the second part of the lemma we note that

$$2^{-n-1} \log_2(\rho(n+1,m)) > 2^{-n-1} \log_2(\rho(n,m)^2) = 2^{-n} \log_2(\rho(n,m)).$$

This implies that the first function is monotonically increasing. On the other hand,

$$2^{-n} \log_2(\rho(n,m) + 1) = 2^{-n-1} \log_2((\rho(n,m) + 1)^2)$$
$$\geq 2^{-n-1} \log_2(\rho(n+1,m) + 1)$$

implies that the second function is monotonically decreasing. $\square$

Lemma 9. *Let A and B be trees with $|A^*| = a$ and $|B^*| = b$. Then*

(i) $|\tau_n(A)| = 2^n(|A| + 1) - 1.$
(ii) $|\tau_n(A)^*| = \rho(n,a).$
(iii) *For all trees $\tau_n([AB])$ we have $g(\tau_n([AB])) \leq \max(g(\tau_{n+1}(A)), g(\tau_{n+1}(B))).$*
(iv) *For every tree $\mathcal{T}$ there exist m and n such that $g(\tau_n(C_m)) \geq g(\mathcal{T}).$*

Proof.

(i) This follows by induction on n from $|\tau_0(A)| = |A|$ and $|\tau_{n+1}(A)| = 2|\tau_n(A)|+1.$

(ii) This follows by induction on n from $|\tau_0(A)^*| = a$ and
$|\tau_{n+1}(A)^*| = |[\tau_n(A)\tau_n(A)]^*| = |\tau_n(A)^*|^2 + 1.$

(iii) Assuming the contrary and using (i) and (ii) would imply that

$$\frac{\log_2 \rho(n, ab + 1)}{(|A| + |B| + 2)2^n} > \frac{\log_2 \rho(n + 1, a)}{(|A| + 1)2^{n+1}}$$

$$\frac{\log_2 \rho(n, ab + 1)}{(|A| + |B| + 2)2^n} > \frac{\log_2 \rho(n + 1, b)}{(|B| + 1)2^{n+1}}$$

Multiplying these equations by $(|A|+1)2^{n+1}$ and $(|B|+1)2^{n+1}$, respectively, and adding them gives $2\log_2 \rho(n, ab + 1) > \log_2 \rho(n + 1, a) + \log_2 \rho(n + 1, b)$, which is equivalent to $\rho(n, ab + 1)^2 > \rho(n + 1, a)\rho(n + 1, b)$. This contradicts Lemma 8.

(iv) It suffices to consider only a tree $\mathcal{T}$ with a maximal number $|\mathcal{T}^*|$ of signature patterns. By Theorem 6 no such tree can contain an edge from a vertex with in-degree 2 to a vertex with in-degree 1. Therefore $\mathcal{T}$ is either fully symmetric in the sense that every subtree is a chain or has two identical subtrees, i.e., it is of the form $\tau_n(C_m)$ for some m and n, or it is symmetric down to a certain level l and is asymmetric below. In the latter case, $\mathcal{T}$ is of the form $\tau_l([AB])$ for some $l > 0$ where A and B are different trees.

In the first case we are done. In the second case we can find a tree $\mathcal{T}_2$, by using (iii), such that $g(\mathcal{T}) \leq g(\mathcal{T}_2)$. By applying (iii) repeatedly we find a sequence of trees $\mathcal{T} = \tau_l([AB]), \mathcal{T}_2 = \tau_{l_2}([A_2 B_2]), \mathcal{T}_3 = \tau_{l_3}([A_3 B_3]), \ldots$ such that $g(\mathcal{T}) \leq g(\mathcal{T}_2) \leq g(\mathcal{T}_3) \leq \ldots$, where the sequence l, l_2, l_3 is strictly increasing and therefore this process must stop. Note that the depth of $\mathcal{T}_i$ cannot be greater than the depth of $\mathcal{T}$. Thus we can find some tree $\tau_n(\mathcal{C}_m)$ such that $g(\mathcal{T}) \leq g(\tau_n(\mathcal{C}_m))$. $\square$

Lemma 10. *For all $n \geq 2$*

$$\hat{\nu}(n) \geq 2^{\gamma n - 1} \tag{6}$$

Proof. Let $r = (n-2) \bmod 4$ and let $I = \{i_1, i_2, \ldots, i_k\} \subset \mathbf{Z}$ be the set of positions in the binary representation of $(n-2-r)/4$ that are 1. i.e., $(n-2-r)/4 = \sum_{i \in I} 2^i$. A tree $\mathcal{T}$ with $w(\mathcal{T}^*) \geq 2^{\gamma n - 1}$ can be obtained by connecting the trees $\mathcal{C}_{r+2}$ and $\tau_{i_1}(\mathcal{C}_3), \tau_{i_2}(\mathcal{C}_3), \ldots$ in a binary tree, i.e.,

$$\mathcal{T} = [\mathcal{C}_{(r+2)}[\tau_{i_1}(\mathcal{C}_3)[\tau_{i_2}(\mathcal{C}_3) \ldots [\tau_{i_{k-1}}(\mathcal{C}_3)\tau_{i_k}(\mathcal{C}_3)]]]].$$

We have $|\mathcal{T}| = r + 2 + \sum_{i \in I}(1 + |\tau_i(\mathcal{C}_3)|) = n$. It follows from Lemma 8 and from Lemma 9 (ii) that $|\tau_n(\mathcal{C}_3)| \geq 2^{\gamma 2^{n+2}} - 1$. Moreover we have

$$|\mathcal{T}^*| \geq (r+2) \prod_{i \in I} |\tau_i(\mathcal{C}_3)| = (r+2) \prod_{i \in I} (2^{\gamma 2^{i+2}} - 1)$$

$$\geq 2^{\gamma(r+2)} \prod_{i \in I} 2^{\gamma 2^{i+2}} \prod_{i \in I} \left(1 - \frac{1}{2^{\gamma 2^{i+2}}}\right) \geq 2^{\gamma n} \prod_{i \in I} \left(1 - \frac{1}{2^{\gamma 2^{i+2}}}\right),$$

where we have used the fact that $r + 2 > 2^{\gamma(r+2)}$ for $0 \leq r \leq 3$. Let $\beta = 2^{-4\gamma}$. Then

$$\prod_{i \in I} \left(1 - \frac{1}{2^{\gamma 2^{i+2}}}\right) = \prod_{i \in I} \left(1 - \beta^{2^i}\right) \geq 1 - \sum_{j \geq 1} \beta^j = 1 - \frac{\beta}{1 - \beta} > 0.5 \quad \square$$

We can now prove Theorem 7. It follows from Lemma 9 (iv) that it is sufficient to prove $g(\mathcal{T}) < \gamma$ for trees of the form $\tau_n(\mathcal{C}_m)$. According to Lemma 8 we have to find $m \in \mathbf{N}$ which maximizes $\lim_{n \to \infty} \log_2(\rho(n,m))/2^n(m+1)$. This is the case for $m = 3$ as will be shown below. By Lemma 8 it is sufficient to show that for each $m \neq 3$ there exists some n such that $\log_2(\rho(n,m)+1)/((m+1)2^n) < \gamma$. For $m \geq 6$ we have $\log_2(\rho(1,m)+1)/(2(m+1)) < \log_2((m+1)^2)/2(m+1) = \log_2(m+1)/(m+1) < 0.41 < \gamma$ and for the remaining m it can be checked that $\log_2(\rho(2,m)+1)/4(m+1) < 0.41 < \gamma$. This shows that for every tree $\mathcal{T}$ we have

$$|\mathcal{T}^*| \leq 2^{\gamma(|\mathcal{T}|+1)}$$

and therefore $\eta(\Gamma) \leq \gamma$ for the one-time signature scheme Γ given by a maximal antichain of $\mathcal{T}^*$.

From equation (4) and Lemma 10 it follows that $\hat{\mu}(n) \geq \frac{2^{\gamma n}}{2n}$. Thus for all n satisfying $n \geq 2 + \log_2(n)/(\gamma - \delta)$ we have $\hat{\mu}(n) \geq 2^{\delta(n+1)}$. Hence for all $\delta < \gamma$ there exists a one-time signature scheme with efficiency δ. $\square$

References

1. D. Bleichenbacher and U.M. Maurer, Directed acyclic graphs, one-way functions and digital signatures, *Advances in Cryptology - CRYPTO '94*, Y. Desmedt(ed.), Lecture Notes in Computer Science, Berlin: Springer-Verlag, vol. 839, pp. 75–82, 1994.

2. D. Bleichenbacher and U.M. Maurer, Optimal tree-based one-time digital signature schemes, *Proc. 13th Symp. on Theoretical Aspects of Computer Science (STACS'96)*, C. Puech and R. Reischuk (eds.), Lecture Notes in Computer Science, Berlin: Springer-Verlag, vol. 1046, pp. 363–374, 1996.

3. J.N.E. Bos and D. Chaum, Provably unforgeable signatures, *Advances in Cryptology - CRYPTO '92*, E. Brickell (ed.), Lecture Notes in Computer Science, Berlin: Springer Verlag, vol. 740, pp. 1–14, 1993.

4. N. de Brujin, C.A. van Ebbenhorst Tengebergen, and D.R. Kruyswijk, "On the set of divisors of a number," *Nieuw Arch. Wisk*, vol. 23, pp. 191–193, 1952.

5. S. Even, O. Goldreich and S. Micali, On-line/off-line digital signatures, *Advances in Cryptology - CRYPTO '89*, Lecture Notes in Computer Science, G. Brassard (ed.), Berlin: Springer Verlag, vol. 435, pp. 263–275, 1990.

6. N. Ferguson, personal communication, 1994.

7. L. Lamport, Constructing digital signatures from a one-way function, Technical Report SRI Intl. CSL 98, 1979.

8. R. Merkle, A certified digital signature, *Advances in Cryptology - CRYPTO '89*, Lecture Notes in Computer Science, G. Brassard (ed.), Berlin: Springer Verlag, vol. 435, pp. 218–238, 1990.

9. C. Meyer and S. Matyas, *Cryptography - a new dimension in computer data security*, John Wiley & Sons, Inc., 1982.

10. M. Naor and M. Yung, Universal one-way hash functions and their cryptographic significance, *Proc. 21st ACM Symp. on Theory of Computing (STOC)*, pp. 33–43, 1989.

11. R.L. Rivest, A. Shamir, and L. Adleman, A method for obtaining digital signatures and public-key cryptosystems, *Communications of the ACM*, vol. 21, no. 2, pp. 120–126, 1978.

12. J. Rompel, One-way functions are necessary and sufficient for secure signatures, *Proc. 22nd ACM Symp. on Theory of Computing (STOC)*, pp. 387–394, 1990.

13. C.P. Schnorr, Efficient identification and signatures for smart cards, Advances in Cryptology - Crypto '89, Lecture Notes in Computer Science, G. Brassard (ed.), Berlin: Springer-Verlag, vol. 435, pp. 239–252, 1990.

14. S. Vaudenay, One-time identification with low memory, *Proc. of EUROCODE '92*, Lecture Notes in Computer Science, Springer Verlag. CISM Courses and Lectures, no. 339, International Centre for Mechanical Sciences, P. Camion, P. Charpin and S. Harari (eds.), Berlin: Springer-Verlag, pp. 217–228, 1992.

A Hidden Cryptographic Assumption in No-Transferable Indentification Schemes

(Extended Abstract of ASIACRYPT'96)

Kouichi SAKURAI

Department of Computer Science and Communication Engineering,
Kyushu University, Hakozaki, Higashi-ku, Fukuoka 812-81, Japan
Email: sakurai@csce.kyushu-u.ac.jp

Abstract. A 4-move perfect zero-knowledge argument for quadratic residuosity is discussed and the identification scheme based on this protocol is shown to be no-transferable. Note that the soundness of all known previous no-transferable protocols require no computational assumption, while our proposed protocol assumes a restriction of the power of cheating provers. Furthermore, a new notion of practical soundness is introduced and the relationship between practical soundness and no-transferable is investigated. An important consequence is that perfect zero-knowledge arguments does not always satisfy no-transferable nor practical soundness.

1 Introduction

This paper discusses security of identification schemes based on the technique of zero-knowledge interactive protocols, especially soundness of the prover, while the previous works mainly focus on security against the verifier.

Weaker notions of ZK: The Fiat-Shamir scheme (also more general zero-knowledge protocols) is a serial iteration of an atomic 3-move protocol, then a simple way to decrease the round complexity is a direct parallelization of the serial version. However, a problem on the straightforward parallelization of Fiat-Shamir scheme is the failure of the technique of the proof of the zero-knowledgeness. Instead Feige, Fiat, and Shamir introduced the notion of no-transferable to characterize the security of the 3-move direct parallelization of FS-scheme. A weaken notion of zero-knowledge is proposed as witness hiding [FS90], and a connection to the notion, no-transferable is explored [CD92].

Argument model: A weak notion of soundness, the other condition of interactive proofs, which requires a computational assumption, introduced by Brassard et al. [BCC88] as the model of (interactive) arguments. In interactive arguments, the prover cannot break some cryptographic assumption (e.g. the hardness of factoring) while the communication with the verifier. An advantage of the weaker model of arguments over proof systems is that any NP-complete problems have perfect zero-knowledge arguments as proposed in [BCC88], while there are an evidence that NP-complete problems have no perfect zero-knowledge interactive proofs [For87]. The state of knowledge of provers in arguments were discussed in [BLP93, BCLL91], however, these are still theoretical and no previous works give any practical definition of security related with computational soundness.

Our proposed protocol and introduced practical soundness: This paper first consider a protocol for the Quadratic Residuosity (QR) Problem, which was originally proposed by Saito and Kurosawa [SK90], and shows that this prototocol is zero-knowledge argument under assuming the hardness of factoring. Furthermore, we shows that the protocol is no-transferable when we apply the protocol into an identification scheme such as the Fiat-Shamir setting.

Thus, the property of the protocol, which is not only argument but also no-transferable, suggests us to introduce a new notion of practical soundness and discuss the relationship between practical soundness and no-transferable.

Among these works on how to weaken security of zero-knowledge, our formulation on practical soundness is the first attempt to weak the soundness of cryptographic protocol. In fact, our protocol gives an evidence that the notion of no-transferable weakens not only the security (e.g. zero-knowledge) but also the soundness (e.g. language soundness).

Round-optimal ZK identification scheme: The proposed protocol for QR requires only 4-move communication between the prover and the verifier.

Designing optimal-round zero-knowledge interactive proofs without any unproven assumption is an interesting problem from theoretical points of view. On the other hand, constructing optimal-round secure identification scheme with possibly weak assumptions is an important topic from practical points of view.

We should note that if QR has a 4-move perfect ZKIP with no assumption still remains open. De Santis et al. [DDP94, DP94] showed a way of obtaining a 4-move perfect ZK interactive proof system for special languages associated with the quadratic residuosity. However, provers in their protocol [DDP94, DP94] requires not only the exact witness of the problem (e.g. a square root of I module N) but also the factorization of the modulus N as an additional knowledge in order to convince the verifier. Then, the protocol by [DDP94, DP94] cannot be applied to the Fiat-Shamir like ID-based identification schemes.

Previous known protocols require 5-move interaction [BMO90] or an additional unproven assumption [FS89]. Nevertheless, our proposed protocol supplies an optimal-round zero-knowledge identification scheme based on QR. In our protocol, if we assume the hardness of the factoring, no (polynomial-time powerful) prover convinces the verifier for the inputs $x \notin QR_N$, except the trusted center which generates the modulus N. The soundness of our protocol is as same as one of the original Fiat-Shamir scheme[FiS86] in such a practical setting.

Thus, this paper gives a positive answers to the open question that constructing an optimal-round zero-knowledge identification scheme based on QR.

Zero-knowledge vs. No-transferable: Readers may claim that the direct parallelization of the original Fiat-Shamir scheme needs only 3-move, and is also no-transferable, so such a 3-move protocol is enough to apply practical identification scheme. We clarify the gap between the 3-move no-transferable protocols and our 4-move one, then discuss the advantage/disadvantage among these protocols.

The main difference is that the 3-move protocols are no longer zero-knowledge, while our 4-move one is zero-knowledge. Indeed no-transferability is enough security to apply the protocol only into ordinary identification scheme, however, there are some practical situation, in which zero-knowledge property is indispensable. One of such applications is a public-key based message authentication scheme discussed by Okamoto and Ohta [OO90]. The ordinary message authentication scheme is based on a secret-key cipher algorithm like as DES. However, Okamoto and Ohta formulated a public-key based message authentication scheme as non-transitive digital signature scheme, and proposed a practical non-transitive digital signature scheme based on the Fiat-Shamir scheme. Their original paper [OO90] applies not only the serial-version of the Fiat-Shamir scheme but also the the parallel-version for constructing non-transitive digital signature schemes. However, the scheme based on the parallel-version is shown not to be no-transitive, i.e. an active receiver can transfer the evidence of the prover's authority on the message into any third party [SI93]. This is caused by a practical consequence from a theoretical result that no 3-move protocol is zero-knowledge [GK90]. Thus, to obtain an efficient non-transitive digital signature scheme, we have to find a sophisticated way of parallelizing the Fiat-Shamir scheme with preserving zero-knowledgeness. Our 4-move protocol answers to this request.

2 Notation and Definitions

Our model of computation is the interactive probabilistic Turing machines (both for the prover P and for the verifier V) with an auxiliary input. The common input is denoted by x and, and its length is denoted by $|x| = n$. We use $\nu(n)$ to denote any function vanishing faster than the inverse of any polynomial in n. More formally,

$$\forall k \in \mathbf{N} \ \exists n_0 \ s.t. \ \forall n > n_0 \ \ 0 \leq \nu(n) < \frac{1}{n^k}.$$

We define *negligible* probability to be the probability behaving as $\nu(n)$, and *overwhelming* probability to be the probability behaving as $1 - \nu(n)$.

Let $A(x)$ denote the output of a probabilistic algorithm A on input x. This is a random variable. When we want to make the coin tosses of A explicit, for any $\rho \in \{0,1\}^*$ we write $A[\rho]$ for the algorithm A with ρ as its random tape. Let $V_P(x)$ denote V's output after interaction with P on common input x, and let $M(x;A)$ (where A may be either P or V) denote the output of the algorithm M on input x, where M may use the algorithm A as a (blackbox) subroutine. Each call M makes to A is counted as a single computation step for M.

Definition 1. Let R be a relation $\{(x, w)\}$ testable in $\mathcal{P}$. Namely, given x and w, checking whether $(x, w) \in R$ is computed in polynomial time. The language associated with the relation R is defined to be $L_R = \{x : \exists y \text{ such that } (x, y) \in R\}$, and belongs to $\mathcal{NP}$. Conversely, every $\mathcal{NP}$ language L naturally induces a relation R_L, of which checking is done in polynomial time. For any x, its *witness set* $w(x)$ is the set of w such that $(x, w) \in R$.

3 Identification scheme and its security

3.1 Complexity assumptions in cryptographic setting

Fiat-Shamir identification scheme [FiS86] is based on the difficulty of computing modular square roots when the factorization of N is unknown. If the factoring assumption becomes not to hold, the identification system is no longer secure because everybody can convince users. Thus, such intractability assumptions are indispensable to construct identification schemes like as [FiS86].

3.2 A general definition of Identification scheme

We first give a definition of identification scheme of Fiat-Shamir like setting. As observed in subsection 3.1, an identification is constructed based on certain NP-relation R, of which hard instances are generated in probabilistic polynomial time [AABFH88].

Definition 2. An identification scheme based on a NP-relation R consists of two stages:

1. Initialization between a center and each user:
   The unique trusted center generates system parameters commonly used among all users as a part of the public key. Furthermore, the center generates user A's secret key SK_A and public key PK_A which satisfy the relation $R(SK_A, PK_A)$, and PK_A is published to other users.
2. Operation between any user A and a verifier B:
   User A demonstrates her identity to the verifier B by proving the fact that "she knows the secret key SK_A for the public key PK_A" via some protocol. At the end of the protocol, B decides if B accepts A or not.

3.3 No-transferable protocols

As mentioned in subsection 3.1, practical identification schemes needs some intractability problem. We denote the cryptographic assumption used in the identification scheme by $\mathcal{CA}$. Namely, practical user (in general, probabilistic poly-time power) cannot break the assumption $\mathcal{CA}$. The previous definitions[FFS87, Oka92] does not include the cryptographic assumptions, however, the following definition is given based on the cryptographic assumption $\mathcal{CA}$.

Definition 3. A prover A (resp. verifier B) who honestly acts is denoted by $\overline{A}$ (resp. $\overline{B}$). Let $\widetilde{A}$ be a dishonest prover who does not complete the Initial stage of Definition 2 and may deviate from the protocols. $\widetilde{B}$ is not a dishonest verifier.
   An identification scheme (A, B) is no-transferable if

1. $(\overline{A}, \overline{B})$ succeeds with overwhelming probability.
2. If there exists a coalition of $\widetilde{A}, \widetilde{B}$ with the property that, after a polynomial number of executions of $(\overline{A}, \widetilde{B})$ and relaying a transcript of the communication to $\widetilde{A}$, it is possible to execute $(\widetilde{A}, \overline{B})$ with nonnegligible probability of success, then there exists a probabilistic polynomial time algorithm M which breaks the assumption $\mathcal{CA}$.

Remark. Ohta and Okamoto [OhOk88] introduced a notion of security level over no-transferable protocols by refining the probability of the success of the prover's cheating. A no-transferable protocol is called to have security bound $\rho(|n|)$ if in the definition 3 the (non-negligible) probability of the success of the prover's cheating is not larger than or equal to $\rho(|n|)$.

3.4 Proofs of knowledge and Witness Hiding

Previous definitions of proofs of knowledge (Interactive) Proofs of knowledge was formulated by Feige-Fiat-Shamir [FFS87] and Tompa and Woll [TW87] from practical points of view. The original interactive proof systems [GMR85] is defined to prove membership of the given inputs of the language. In GMR-model, then, the prover's power is assumed to be unbounded. Feige, Fiat, and Shamir [FFS87] observed that, in the proposed protocol for QR [GMR85] (GI [GMW86]), if the polynomial time prover has a knowledge associated with the inputs, then he can convince the verifier that the input belongs the given language. They also gave a precise definition on the state that the prover possesses the knowledge by introducing the extractor.

Definition 4 [FFS87]. An interactive proof of knowledge for the relation R is a pair of interactive probabilistic Turing machines (P, V) satisfying:

Knowledge Completeness: For any $(x, w) \in R$, V accepts P's proof with overwhelming probability. Formally:

$$\forall (x, w) \in R \ \ Prob(V_{P(x,w)}(x) \, accepts) > 1 - \nu(|x|),$$

where the probability is taken over all of the possible coin tosses of P and V.

Knowledge Soundness: For any x, for any P^*, P^* can convince V to accept only if he actually "knows" a witness for $x \in$ dom R. A probabilistic polynomial time knowledge extractor M is used in order to demonstrate P^*'s ability to compute a witness. Formally:

$$\forall a \ \exists M \ \forall P^* \ \forall x \ \forall w' \ \forall \rho$$

$$Prob\left(V_{P^*[\rho](x,w')}(x) \, accepts\right) > 1/|x|^a \Rightarrow$$

$$Prob\left(M\left(x; P^*[\rho](x, w')\right) \in w(x)\right) > 1 - \nu(|x|),$$

where the probability is taken over all of the possible coin tosses of M and V.

Note that both P's and V's resource are bounded by probabilistic polynomial time in $|x|$.

Witness Hiding

Definition 5 [FS90]. An algorithm G is called a generator for relation R if on input 1^n it produces instances $(x, w) \in R$ of length n. A generator G is called invulnerable if for any polynomial time nonuniform cracking algorithm C,

$$Prob((x, C(x)) \in R) < \nu(|x|),$$

where $x = G(1^n)$. The probability is taken over the coin tosses of G and C.

Definition 6 [FS90]. Let (P, V) be a proof of knowledge system for relation R, and let G be a generator for this relation. (P, V) is witness hiding (WH) on (R, G) if there exists a witness extractor M which runs in expected polynomial time, such that for any nonuniform polynomial time V'

$$Prob(V'_{P(x,w)}(x) \in w(x)) < Prob(M(x; V', G) \in w(x)) + \nu(|x|),$$

where $x = G(1^n)$. The probability is taken over the distribution of the inputs and witness, as well as the the coin tosses of P and M. The witness extractor is allowed to use V' and G as blackboxes.

3.5 No-transferable vs. Witness-hiding

We discuss the relation between no-transferable and witness-hiding. Okamoto [Oka92] informally stated that the identification scheme based on a witness-hiding proof of knowledge is no-transferable. The next question is if the converse of this proposition. holds or not. Chen and Damgård [CD92] give a condition on (security bound of) no-transfrability, which required for a proof of knowledge to be witness-hiding.

Proposition 7. *Suppose that* (A, B) *is a proof of knowledge. If for any positive constant* c, *the identification scheme based on* (A, B) *releases no transferable information with security bound* $1/|n|^c$, *then* (A, B) *is witness hiding.*

The previous works [Oka92, CD92] discussed the relation between no-transferable and witness-hiding under the assumption that the protocol is a proof of knowledge, which holds without any computational assumption.

The next section shows that the converse of the proposition above does not hold by exhibiting a protocol, of which soundness requires certain computational assumption.

4 A 4-move protocol for quadratic residuosity

This section presents a 4-move protocol for quadratic residuosity and discusses the properties of the protocol. The discussed protocol is originally proposed by Saito and Kurosawa [SK90] as a zero-knowledge proof of membership of QR. Though the protocol does not satisfy soundness of proofs of membership on QR, Saito, Kurosawa, and Sakurai [SKS91] applyied the idea into a 4-move perfect ZK proof of knowledge on the certified logarithm problem.

4.1 The protocol

In the proposed protocol, at the first stage the verifier constructs the basis of the bit commitment and send the basis to the prover. Next the prover commits his random coins using the basis, and send the verifier to these committed values. Then, after receiving the verifier's challenges, the prover uses the EX-OR of the verifier's challenge bits and the prover's previous random bits as the coins which used by the prover in typical 3-move interactive protocols. A precise description is as follows.

The common inputs of the prover and the verifier is (I, N), where $I = s^2 \pmod{N}$ for some $s \in Z_N^*$. The prover P proves to the verifier V the fact that P knows the witness s. Let $k = |N|$. The proposed protocol consists of the following 3 subprotocols.

Subprotocol A (Construction of the basis of the bit commitment)

A1: V chooses $r \in_R Z_N^*$ and sends $y = r^2 \pmod{N}$ to P.

A2: V proves via a 3-move witness hiding protocol the facts that V knows a square root of y. The following steps is executed k independent times in *parallel*.

Subsubprotocol Aa

Aa1 V chooses independently $u \in_R Z_N^*$ and sends $w = u^2 \pmod{N}$ to P.

Aa2 P independently picks $b \in_R \{0, 1\}$, and sends b to V.

Aa3 V sends $z = r^b \times u \pmod{N}$ to P, where r is generated in the previous step A1.

Aa4 P verifies the V's answer by checking if $z^2 = y^b \times w \pmod{N}$.

Subprotocol B (Random bits generation by coin flipping)

B1: P chooses $t_i \in_R Z_N^*$ and $e_{Pi} \in_R \{0, 1\}$ for $i = 1, \ldots, k$, then sends $q_i = y^{e_{P_i}} \times t_i^2 \pmod{N}$ to V $(i = 1, \ldots, k)$.

B2: V chooses $e_{V_i} \in_R \{0, 1\}(i = 1, \ldots, k)$ and sends $e_{V_1} \ldots, e_{V_k}$ to P.

B3: P sets $E_i = e_{P_i} \oplus e_{V_i} (i = 1, \ldots, k)$. Each E_i is used in the next protocol as the V's challenge bits. Then P sends e_{P_i} and t_i for $i = 1, \ldots, k$.

B4: V verifies the P^*'s answer, i.e. checks if $q_i = y^{e_{P_i}} \times t_i^2 \pmod{N}$ for $i = 1, \ldots, k$.

Subprotocol C (Basic parallelized protocol for QR)

C1: P chooses $R_i \in_R Z_N^*$ and sends $X_i = R_i^2 \pmod{N}(i = 1, \ldots, k)$ to V.

C2: P computes $Y_i = s^{E_i} \times R_i \pmod{N}$ for $i = 1, \ldots, k$, where E_i is obtained in the protocol B, and sends $Y_i(i = 1, \ldots, k)$ to V.

C3: V verifies if $Y_i^2 = I^{E_i} \times X_i \pmod{N}$ for $i = 1, \ldots, k$.

We obtain the full protocol Λ by composing these sub(sub)protocols in the following manner;

Full protocol Λ
V1(A1,Aa1), **P1**(Aa2,B1,C1), **V2**(Aa3,B2), **P2**(Aa4,B3,C2), **V3**(B4,C3),

which is 4-move.

4.2 Properties of the protocol

Proposition 8. *If a (probabilistic polynomial time) prover with a $\sqrt{I} \pmod{N}$ causes the verifier to accept with probability 1.*

Next we consider the soundness of the protocol. However, a powerful cheating prover P^* can convince the verifier even when the input is not in QR.

Proposition 9. *Even if an input $I \notin QR_N$, a (powerful) prover P^* causes the verifier to accept with probability 1 (unless $QR \in BPP$).*

Proof: The cheating prover P^* convinces the verifier when the input I is not in QR_N as follows. Suppose that the cheating prover P^*'s power is not restricted. Then P^* can compute $\sqrt{y} \pmod{N}$. As the prover P^* knows $\sqrt{y} \pmod{N}$, the commitments q_i is *chameleon* in the sense of [BCY89] for the prover P^*. Namely, P^* can disclose freely both bit 0 and 1 as e_{Pi} after he commit at the stage B1. Then, at the subprotocol C, P^* can choose the value E_i at the stage C1 in advance as his will. This implies the following prover's cheating.

P^*'s cheating in subprotocol C

$C1^*$: P chooses $Y_i \in_R Z_N^*$ and $E_i \in_R \{0,1\}$ $(i = 1, \ldots, k)$ and sends $X_i = I^{E_i}/Y_i^2$ $(i = 1, \ldots, k)$ to V.

$C2^*$: P sends Y_i $(i = 1, \ldots, k)$ to V.

Clearly, the verifier V accepts the prover P^* above. ∎

Corollary 10. *The protocol protocol is not proofs of membership of the language QR unless QR ∈ BPP.*

However, this protocol releases nothing when $I \in QR_N$.

Proposition 11. *For (P, V') in the protocol Λ, there exists a simulator S which runs in expected polynomial time, for every V' and for $\forall I \in QR_N$, $S(I; V'(I)) = VIEW_{(P,V')}(I)$.*

Proof: We construct a simulator S for any (possibly dishonest) verifier V'. After running V' as the stage V1, the simulator first performs prover P's part of the stage P1 and gets the verifier V''s messages of the stage V2. If V' does not complete this stage successfully, S stops. Otherwise, S repeats the stage P1, each time with different randomly chosen challenges in A2a, until V' again successfully meets S's challenges. From the two successful executions S can find a $\sqrt{y}$ (mod N). Once S obtain such a information, S can disclose freely both bit 0 and 1 as e_{P_i} after he committed e_{P_i} at B1. This allows S to carry out P's part P2 without knowing a $\sqrt{I}$ (mod N). ∎

Therefor, this protocol is regarded as a perfect zero-knowledge argument under the assumption that the prover cannot cause the verifier to accept for $I \notin QR_N$. However, if a (cheating) prover with only polynomial-time power can easily cause the verifier to accept for $I \notin QR_N$, we cannot apply this protocol into Fiat-Shamir like ID-based identification scheme.

The following proposition guarantees security of the protocol in the application of identification scheme.

Proposition 12. *For any $I \in QR_N$, if P^* can convince V to accept, then he actually "knows" a witness $\sqrt{I}$ (mod N). Or, for any $I \notin QR_N$, if P^* can convince V to accept, then he actually "knows" the complete factorization of the integer N. A probabilistic polynomial time knowledge extractor M is used in order to demonstrate P^*'s ability to compute a witness (or the factorization). Formally:*

$$\forall a \,\exists M \,\forall P^* \,\forall I \in Z_N^* \,\forall w'$$

$$Prob\Big(V_{P^*(I,w')}(I) \, accepts\Big) > 1/|I|^a \Rightarrow$$

$$Prob\left(M\big(I; P^*(I, w')\big) = \left\{ \begin{array}{l} one\ of\ \sqrt{I}\ (mod\ N) \quad if\ I \in QR_N \\ the\ complete\ fact.\ of\ N\ otherwise \end{array} \right.\right) > 1 - \nu(|I|),$$

where the probability is taken over all of the possible coin tosses of M and V.

The proof of this proposition is given in [Sak95]. This proposition implies the following.

Theorem 13. *The identification scheme based on the proposed protocol is no-transferable under the assumption that factoring is hard.*

5 Round optimality

The proposed protocol in the previous section is 4-move, and we show that the protocol is optimal with respect to the round complexity. The lower bound of the round which zero-knowledge protocols needs is shown by Goldreich and Krawczyk [GK90]. Namely, Goldreich and Krawczyk [GK90] showed that the zero-knowledge interactive proof for a language needs at least 4-move unless the language is $\mathcal{BPP}$. Although our protocol is not proof of language, a further analysis of the argument of the proof in [GK90] induces the similar result.

First we introduce a weaker notion of proofs of knowledge. Bellare and Goldreich [BG92] gave rigorous definitions of proofs of knowledge. This paper refers to one idea of their definitions, which is weaker than the previous one [FFS87, TW87]: "proofs of knowledge should be defined in the case of only the correct inputs". It is should be noted that the knowledge extractor in the previous definition [FFS87, TW87] works for any input.

Definition 14. An interactive proof of *positive-side* knowledge for the relation R is a pair of interactive probabilistic Turing machines (P, V) satisfying the condition of **knowledge completeness** and

> **Positive-Side Knowledge Validity:**   For any $x \in L_R$, for any P^*, P^* can convince V to accept only if he actually "knows" a witness for $x \in L_R$.

The similar argument of the triviality theorem by Goldreich and Krawczyk [GK90] can be applied into the case of proofs of positive-side knowledge.

Theorem 15. *If an $\mathcal{NP}$-relation R has 3-move zero-knowledge protocol which satisfies positive-side knowledge soundness, then there exists a probabilistic polynomial time algorithm A*

$$A(x) = \begin{cases} y \ such \ that \ (x, y) \in R \ if \ x \in L_R \\ \qquad\qquad \perp \qquad\qquad if \ x \notin L_R \end{cases}$$

with overwhelming probability.

This is obtained by the same argument as [IS91], and the outline of the proof is given in Appendix A.

Corollary 16. *Protocol Λ is optimal with respect to the round complexity among perfect zero-knowledge proofs of positive-side knowledge on R_{QR} unless $QR \in \mathcal{BPP}$.*

6 Proposed new formulation of practical soundness

What is soundness Soundness is the condition on the object which the verifier accepts. In the proofs of language, soundness implies that the verifier accepts only the inputs that belongs to the language. In the proofs of knowledge, soundness implies that the verifier accepts only the provers who knows the good knowledge associated with the input.

6.1 A new soundness

We define a new soundness fitted to FSIS-setting by extending the observation on the proposed protocol. Our basic idea is that: we accept the cheating prover for $x \notin L_R$ if such a cheating requires much power than (the honest prover's) proving possession of a witness w for any input $x \in L_R$.

Definition 17. An identification scheme based on a relation R is called *practically sound* if it satisfying the condition that (1) for any $x \in L_R$, if P^* can convince V to accept, then he actually "knows" a witness of $w(x)$, or (2) for any $x \notin L_R$, if P^* can convince V to accept, then he actually "knows" a witness of $w(x)$ for any $x \in L_R$, A probabilistic polynomial time knowledge extractor M is used in order to demonstrate P^*'s ability to compute such these witnesses. Formally:

$$\forall a \, \exists M \, \forall P^* \, \forall x \in \{0,1\}^* \, \forall w'$$

$$Prob\left(V_{P^*(x,w')}(x) \, accepts \right) > 1/|x|^a \Rightarrow$$

$$Prob\left(M\left(x; P^*(x, w')\right) = \left\{ \begin{array}{ll} \text{a witness of } w(x) & \text{if } x \in L_R \\ \kappa \text{ s.t. } \exists D \text{ satisfying} & \\ \forall y \in L_R \quad D(y; \kappa) \in w(y) \text{ otherwise} \end{array} \right. \right) > 1 - \nu(|x|).$$

Thus, the identification scheme based on the relation R_{QR} of which operating stage is the proposed 4-move protocol is practically sound.

Remark. For a given composite number N and integer g $(0 < g < N)$, consider the following relation $R_{(N,g)}$

$$R_{(N,g)} \, (x, y) \iff y = g^x \pmod{N}.$$

Our 4-move protocol is also described based on this relation $R_{(N,g)}$. We discuss the identification scheme based on the relation $R_{(N,g)}$ of which operating stage is the 4-move protocol. The following property is obtained by the similar argument in proposition 12.

$$\forall a \, \exists M \, \forall P^* \, \forall y \in Z_N^* \, \forall w'$$

$$Prob\left(V_{P^*(y,w')}(y) \, accepts \right) > 1/|y|^a \Rightarrow$$

$$Prob\left(M\left(y; P^*(y, w')\right) = \left\{ \begin{array}{l} \text{one of } w(y) \\ \text{the complete factorization of } N \end{array} \right. \right) > 1 - \nu(|y|).$$

It should be noted that there are no known probabilistic polynomial-time algorithm to compute discrete logarithms over the modulus of the composite integer N even using the complete factorization of N. Then, in the case above, we *cannot* conclude that the identification is practically sound in our sense.

6.2 Comparison to the previous soundness

The following proposition gives a new sufficient condition on no-transferable identification.

Proposition 18. *Suppose that the operating protocol (A,B) of an identification scheme based on R satisfies three conditions that*

> 1. *knowledge completeness,*
> 2. *practical soundness,*
> 3. *zero-knowledgeness,*

then (A,B) is no-transferable under the assumption that the relation R is hard, i.e. there are no probabilistic polynomial time algorithm that compute a witness w(x) for an instance x.

Remark that this proposition holds even if we replace the third condition, zero-knowledgenes by a weaker one, witness hiding.

References

[AABFH88] Abadi,A., Allender,E., Broder,A, Feigenbaum,J., and Hemachandra,L.A., "On generating solved instances of computational problems," in Advances in Cryptology – Crypto'88, LNCS 403, *Springer-Verlag*, Berlin (1987).

[BCC88] Brassard, G., Chaum, D., and Crépeau, C., "Minimum Disclosure Proofs of Knowledge," *JCSS*, Vol.37, No.2, pp.156-189 (1988).

[BCLL91] Brassard,G., Crepeau, C., Laplante, S., and Leger, C., "Computationally convincing proofs of knowledge," *Proc. of the 8th STACS*, (1991).

[BCY89] Brassard, G., Crépeau, C., and Yung, M., "Everything in $\mathcal{NP}$ Can Be Argued in Perfect Zero-Knowledge in a Bounded Number of Rounds," Proc. of 16th ICALP'89, LNCS 372, *Springer-Verlag*, pp.123-136, Berlin (1989).

[BFL89] Boyar, J., Friedl, K., and Lund, C., "Practical zero-knowledge proofs:/ Giving hints and using deficiencies," *J. of Cryptology*, Vol.4, pp.185-206 (1991).

[BG92] Bellare, M., and Goldreich,O., "On defining Proofs of Knowledge," in Advances in Cryptology – Crypto'92, LNCS 740, *Springer-Verlag*, Berlin (1993).

[BLP93] Boyar, J., Lund,C., and Peralta,R., "On the communication complexity of zero-knowledge proofs," *J. Cryptology*, Vol.6, pp.65-85 (1993).

[BM92] Brickell, E. F. and McCurley, K.S "An Interactive Identification Scheme Based on Discrete Logarithms and Factoring," *J. of Cryptology*, Vol.5, pp.29-40 (1992).

[BMO90] Bellare, M., Micali, S., and Ostrovsky, R., "Perfect Zero-Knowledge in Constant Rounds," *ACM STOC*, pp.482-493 (May 1990).

[CD92] Chen,L., and Damgård, Y., "Security bounds for parallel versions of identification protocols," in Advances in Cryptology – Eurocrypt'92, LNCS 658, pp.461-466, *Springer-Verlag*, Berlin (1993).

[DDP94] De Santis, A., Di Crescenzo,G. and Persioano G., "The knowledge complexity of quadratic residuosity languages," *TCS*, 132, pp. 291-317 (1991).

[DP94] Di Crescenzo,G. and Persioano G., "Round-optimal perfect zero-knowledge proofs," IPL 50, pp.93-99 (1994).

[FFS87] Feige, U., Fiat, A., and Shamir, A., "Zero-Knowledge Proofs of Identity," *Journal of Cryptology*, Vol.1, pp.77-94 (1988); preliminary version in *Proc. of 19th STOC*, pp.210-217 (1987).

[FiS86] Fiat, A. and Shamir, A., "How to Prove Yourself," Advances in Cryptology – Crypto'86, LNCS 263, *Springer-Verlag*, Berlin, pp.186-199 (1987).

[For87] Fortnow, L., "The Complexity of Perfect Zero-Knowledge," *Proc. of 19th STOC*,pp.204-209 (1987).

[FS89] Feige, U. and Shamir, A., "Zero-Knowledge Proofs of Knowledge in Two Rounds," in Advances in Cryptology – Crypto'89, LNCS 435, pp.526-544, *Springer-Verlag*, Berlin (1990).

[FS90] Feige, U. and Shamir, A., "Witness Indistinguishable and Witness Hiding Protocols," *ACM STOC*, pp.416-426 (May 1990).

[GHY86] Galil, Z., Haber, S., and Yung, M., "Minimum-knowledge interactive proofs for decision problems," *SIAM Journal of Comp.*, Vol.18, No.4, pp.711-739, (1989).

[GK90] Goldreich, O. and Krawczyk, H., "On the Composition of Zero-Knowledge Proof Systems," in the Proceedings of ICALP'90, LNCS 443, pp.268-282, *Springer-Verlag*, Berlin (1990).

[GMR85] Goldwasser, S., Micali, S., and Rackoff, C., "The Knowledge Complexity of Interactive Proof Systems," *SIAM Journal of Comp.*, Vol.18, No.1, pp.186-208, (1989); preliminary version in *Proc. of 17th STOC*, pp. 291-304 (1985).

[GMW86] Goldreich, O., Micali, S., and Wigderson, A., "Proofs that Yield Nothing But Their Validity or All Languages in NP Have Zero-Knowledge Proofs," *Proc. of 27th FOCS*, pp.174-187, (1986).

[IS91] Itoh, T. and Sakurai, K., "On the Complexity of Constant Round ZKIP of Possession of Knowledge," Advances in Cryptology – Asiacrypt'91, LNCS 739, *Springer-Verlag*, Berlin, (1993).

[OhOk88] Ohta, K. and T.Okamoto, "A modification of the Fiat-Shamir scheme," in Advances in Cryptology – Crypto'88, LNCS 403, pp.31-53, *Springer-Verlag*, Berlin (1990).

[Oka92] Okamoto,T., "Provably Secure and Practical Identification Schemes and Corresponding Signature Schemes," in Advances in Cryptology – Crypto'92, LNCS 740, pp.31-53, *Springer-Verlag*, Berlin (1993).

[OO90] Okamoto,T. and Ohta, K., "How to utilize the randomness of zero-knowledge proofs," in Advances in Cryptology – Crypto'90, LNCS 537, pp.456-475, *Springer-Verlag*, Berlin (1991).

[Sak95] Sakurai,K. "On separating proofs of knowledge from proofs of membership of languages and its application to secure identification scheme," Proc. of COCOON'95, LNCS 959, pp.496-509, *Springer-Verlag*, Berlin (1995).

[SI93] Sakurai,K. and Itoh, T., "On the discrepancy between the serial and the parallel of zero-knowledge protocols" Advances in Cryptology – Crypto'92, LNCS 740, *Springer-Verlag*, Berlin, (1993).

[SK90] Saitoh, T. and Kurosawa, K., "4-Move Perfect ZKIP of Knowledge with No Assumption," *IEICE Tech. Rept.*, ISEC90-21 (1990).

[SKS91] Saitoh, T., Kurosawa, K., and Sakurai, K., "4-Move Perfect ZKIP of Knowledge with No Assumption," Advances in Cryptology – Asiacrypt'91, LNCS 739, *Springer-Verlag*, Berlin, (1993).

[TW87] Tompa, M. and Woll, H., "Random Self-Reducibility and Zero-Knowledge Interactive Proofs of Possession of Information," *Proc. of 28th FOCS*, pp.472-482 (1987).

A Sketch-proof of Triviality

In any three move interactive proof system (P, V) of positive-side knowledge on common input x, P first sends to V a message α, V responds to P with a message β, and P sends to V a message γ. Note that V's message β is constructed from the P's message α and V's (private) random coin tosses r. After the interactions above, V checks whether or not $\rho_V(x, r, \alpha, \gamma) =$ "accept," where ρ_V is a polynomial (in $|x|$) time computable predicate for the verifier V.

Without loss of generality, we assume that there exists a polynomial ℓ such that $|\alpha| = |r| = \ell(|x|)$.

We use the simulator S as a subroutine for constructing the algorithm A. Recall the whole simulation process is completely determined by the input x to the protocol the contexts of S's random tape R_S, and the responses by the verifier. Define the following procedure F_S that uses S as a subprocedure. For an input $x \in \{0,1\}^*$, the procedure F_S chooses $R_S \in_R \{0,1\}^{q(|x|)}$ and $r^{(i)} \in_R \{0,1\}^{\ell(|x|)}$ $(1 \leq i \leq t)$, then runs

S on input x and R_S. If S first generates $\alpha^{(1)}$, then the procedure F_S responds with $\beta^{(1)} = \beta_V(x, r^{(1)}, \alpha^{(1)})$. For the i-th different string $\alpha^{(i)}$ generated by S, F_S responds with $\beta^{(i)} = V(x, r^{(i)}, \alpha^{(i)})$, and if the same string $\alpha^{(j)}$ $(1 \leq j \leq i)$ is generated by S, then F_S responds with $\beta^{(j)}$ as before. Define a vector $(x, R_S, r^{(1)}, r^{(2)}, \ldots, r^{(t)})$ to be *successful* for S if $F_S(x, R_S, r^{(1)}, r^{(2)}, \ldots, r^{(t)}) = (x, r, \alpha, \gamma)$ is an accepting conversation for a verifier V, i.e., $\rho_V(x, r, \alpha, \gamma) = $ "accept," and a vector $(x, R_S, r^{(1)}, r^{(2)}, \ldots, r^{(t)})$ to be *successful* at i if it is successful for S and $\alpha = \alpha^{(i)}$, $r = r^{(i)}$.

In the proof of the result by Goldreich and Krawczyk[GK90] on proofs of languages, it is enough to show the existence of a string α (for each $x \in L_R$) such that for a nonnegligible fraction of all possible strings $r \in \{0, 1\}^{\ell(|x|)}$, there exists a string γ satisfying $\rho_V(x, r, \alpha, \gamma) = $ "accept." In the proof the theorem below, however, we have to present an efficient algorithm to generate a string α (for each $x \in L_R$) such that for a nonnegligible fraction of all possible strings $r \in \{0, 1\}^{\ell(|x|)}$, there exists a string γ satisfying $\rho_V(x, r, \alpha, \gamma) = $ "accept."

Goldreich-Krawczyk's result implies that there exists an index i $(1 \leq i \leq t)$ such that a nonnegligible fraction of all possible vectors $(x, R_S, r^{(1)}, r^{(2)}, \ldots, r^{(t)})$ are successful at i, because t is a polynomial in $|x|$. Thus there exists a nonnegligible fraction of all possible prefixes $(x, R_S, r^{(1)}, r^{(2)}, \ldots, r^{(i-1)})$, each of which has a nonnegligible fraction of all possible continuations $(r^{(i)}, r^{(i+1)}, \ldots, r^{(t)})$ being successful at the index i, i.e., the vector $(x, R_S, r^{(1)}, \ldots, r^{(i-1)}, r^{(i)}, \ldots, r^{(t)})$ is successful at the index i. For such an index i $(1 \leq i \leq t)$, define a set $\Upsilon(x, \alpha^{(i)})$ to be

$$\Upsilon(x, \alpha^{(i)}) = \left\{ r \in \{0, 1\}^{\ell(|x|)} \mid \exists \gamma \; \rho_V(x, r, \alpha^{(i)}, \gamma) = \text{"accept."} \right\}.$$

It follows from the observation above that the set $\Upsilon(x, \alpha^{(i)})$ is a nonnegligible fraction of all possible $r \in \{0, 1\}^{\ell(|x|)}$, i.e., there exists a polynomial p such that $\| \Upsilon(x, \alpha^{(i)}) \| / 2^{\ell(|x|)} \geq 1/p(|x|)$, where $p(|x|) < 2t(|x|)$. Here we call such a set $\Upsilon(x, \alpha^{(i)})$ to be *prolific*.

For any successful vector $(x, R_S, r^{(1)}, r^{(2)}, \ldots, r^{(t)})$ at an index i $(1 \leq i \leq t)$, it is easy to check whether or not the set $\Upsilon(x, \alpha^{(i)})$ is prolific. This can be done as follows:

(1) choose $s = |x| \cdot 2t(|x|)$ pairs $\langle u_k^{(i)}, u_k^{(i+1)}, \ldots, u_k^{(t)} \rangle \in_R \{0, 1\}^{(t-i+1) \cdot \ell(|x|)}$ $(1 \leq k \leq s)$.

(2) for each k $(1 \leq k \leq s)$, compute

$$(x, r_k, \alpha, \gamma_k) = F_M(x, R_S, r^{(1)}, \ldots, r^{(i-1)}, u_k^{(i)}, \ldots, u_k^{(t)}),$$

and check whether or not $(x, R_S, r^{(1)}, \ldots, r^{(i-1)}, u_k^{(i)}, \ldots, u_k^{(t)})$ is successful at i.

If $\Upsilon(x, \alpha^{(i)})$ is prolific, then there exists at least a single pair $\langle u_k^{(i)}, u_k^{(i+1)}, \ldots, u_k^{(t)} \rangle$ of $(t - i + 1)$ strings such that the vector $(x, R_S, r^{(1)}, \ldots, r^{(i-1)}, u_k^{(i)}, \ldots, u_k^{(t)})$ is successful at the index i with overwhelming probability; otherwise there does not exist any successful pair of strings with overwhelming probability. Consider the following interactive proof system (P^*, V):

Input: $x \in \{0, 1\}^*$.

    P1-1: P^* chooses $R_S \in_R \{0, 1\}^{q(|x|)}$ and $r^{(j)} \in_R \{0, 1\}^{\ell(|x|)}$ $(1 \leq j \leq t)$.

    P1-2: P^* computes $(x, r, \alpha, \gamma) = F_S(x, R_M, r^{(1)}, r^{(2)}, \ldots, r^{(t)})$.

    P1-3: If $\rho_V(x, r, \alpha, \gamma) = $ "reject," then P^* halts; otherwise P^* continues.

    P1-4: P^* determines with F_S an index i $(1 \leq i \leq t)$ such that $\alpha = \alpha^{(i)}$ and $r = r^{(i)}$.

    P1-5: P^* checks whether or not the set $\Upsilon(x, \alpha^{(i)})$ is prolific.

P1-6: If $\Upsilon(x, \alpha^{(i)})$ is not prolific, then P^* halts; otherwise P^* continues.

$P \to V$: $\alpha = \alpha^{(i)}$.

V1: V chooses $r \in_R \{0,1\}^{\ell(|x|)}$, and computes $\beta = \beta_V(x, r, \alpha^{(i)})$.

$V \to P$: β

P2-1: P^* checks whether or not $r \in \Upsilon(x, \alpha)$.

P2-2: If $r \notin \Upsilon(x, \alpha)$, then P^* halts (or gives up); otherwise P^* continues.

P2-3: P^* chooses $(t - i)$ strings $\delta^{(j)} \in_R \{0,1\}^{\ell(|x|)}$ $(i + 1 \le j \le t)$ and computes

$$(x, r, \alpha, \gamma) = F_M(x, R_M, r^{(1)}, \ldots, r^{(i-1)}, r, \delta^{(i+1)}, \ldots, \delta^{(t)}).$$

$P \to V$: γ.

V2: V checks whether or not $\rho_V(x, r, \alpha, \beta) =$ "accept."

Note that in step P2-1, P^* can check whether or not $r \in \Upsilon(x, \alpha)$ in (probabilistic) polynomial (in $|x|$) time. When receiving $r \in \Upsilon(x, \alpha)$, P^* chooses $(t - i)$ strings $u^{(j)} \in_R \{0,1\}^{\ell(|x|)}$ $(i + 1 \le j \le t)$, and computes

$$(x, r, \alpha, \gamma) = F_S(x, R_S, r^{(1)}, \ldots, r^{(i-1)}, r, u^{(i+1)}, \ldots, u^{(t)}).$$

It is easy to see that $r \in \Upsilon(x, \alpha)$ iff $\rho_V(x, r, \alpha, \gamma) =$ "accept."

It follows from the definition of positive-side validity that there exists a probabilistic polynomial (in $|x|$) time algorithm E with blackbox access to P^* (see the protocol above.) that on input $x \in L_R$, outputs y such that $(x, y) \in R$ with overwhelming probability.

Let T be the polynomial time when E terminates for input $x \in L_R$ with overwhelming probability. The construction of the algorithm A is as follows:

Input: $x \in \{0, 1\}^*$.

1. A runs E (with blackbox access to P^*) on input x.
2. If E outputs y, then A_R checks whether or not $(x, y) \in R$. If $(x, y) \in R$, then A halts and outputs y; otherwise A halts and outputs "$\perp$."
3. If E does not terminate until the time T, then A halts and outputs "$\perp$."

It is easy to see that the algorithm A runs in probabilistic polynomial time. Thus there exists a probabilistic polynomial (in $|x|$) time algorithm that on input $x \in \{0, 1\}^*$, outputs y such that $(x, y) \in R$ if L_R, and outputs "$\perp$" otherwise, with overwhelming probability. $\square$

Electronic Money and Key Management from Global and Regional Points of View

Shigeo Tsujii

Department of Information and System Engineering
Faculty of Science and Engineering
Chuo University
Kasuga 1-13-27, Bunkyo-ku, Tokyo, 112 Japan

Abstract. This paper discusses Electronic Commerce and Encryption Policy from global and regional view points as well as from technical, institutional, and cultural view points. After considering the revolution of structures of civilization and concepts of culture due to penetration of Global Information Infrastructure, this paper explains recent development of electronic money and introduces discussions held in the Organization for Economic Cooperation and Development (OECD) meeting of the ad hoc Group of Experts on Cryptography Policy.

1 Introduction

Electronic Commerce and Encryption Policy will be considered from both global (international) and regional (national) points of view, and not only from technical but also institutional and cultural points of view.

Firstly, the revolution of structures of civilization and concepts of culture due to penetration of Global Information Infrastructure (GII) will be considered. Secondly, recent development of electronic money will be explained, referring to the report of the "Study Group on Electric Commerce and Electronic Money" (chaired by the author) issued by the Ministry of Post and Telecommunications of Japan. Next, discussions held in the OECD meeting of the ad hoc Group of Experts on Cryptography Policy, of which the author is a member, will be introduced.

2 Revolutions by Information Networks in Civilization Structures and Concepts of Culture

Though it is not always academically convincing, the memory of the social and political impact created by the 1993 paper of Professor Huntington of Harvard University is still fresh in the minds of many. In his paper, Professor Huntington represents the post-cold war world as a confrontation between the Western and Islamic - Confucian civilizations. Personally, I believe that such confrontations will gradually dissolve under the borderless trends that information networks are now being undergone.

Also in the work "Collision or Co-existence of Civilization?" published in 1994 by some social scientist, there is good deal of discussion devoted to the theories of Huntington, but there is disconcertingly little, thought not completely none, concern of the impact that information networks will have on culture and society.

In considering culture and civilization of the 21st century, it is impossible to leave out the standpoint from information networks, and in this stage where information technology is spreading with great speed, it is not altogether meaningless to have theories on culture and civilization from many fields, even which may be naive and unsophisticated. Though this may seem presumptuous for an engineer with no knowledge on the methods of sociology, I would like to propose my own (rather extreme) theory, to emphasize the importance of information security.

The increasing interest taken in the issues on the multimedia and the rapid popularization of the Internet are not only signs of the trends in personalization and borderlessness in information networks; they have also served to diffuse knowledge and technology on information security, hitherto monopolized by a handful of researchers.

The global permeation of information networks, of which the most obvious is the Internet, can be foreseen to cause drastic changes in the structure of civilizations and concepts of culture. Although it is extremely difficult to state what culture is in a single definition — indeed it is often said that there are as many definitions of culture as there are anthropologists — here, when we say *civilization* we will mean infrastructures universal to mankind, and we will use *culture* as a generic term for the thoughts and ideas, values, ideas of beauty and patterns of living and behavior characteristic of some particular group of people. Among the internationally universal infrastructures, the usual information-related are printing, postal services, telephones and broadcasting, and we hardly need to say that they have been of enormous importance in cultural exchanges between different regions and races. For example, the global dominance of western culture happened not because the modern ideas of liberty, equality, and philanthropy are irrefutable truths, but rather because the printing technology enabled rapid transmission of information.

However, the influence which future development of information networks will exert on civilization and culture will probably be of quite another kind. Free access to the so-called multimedia, including documents and images, as well as the receiving and dispatching of information on the individual level is becoming possible all around the world. And with the international development of such information networks, we must cope with the problems arising from inter-country differences in legal institutions and customs.

Also, such economical infrastructures as electronic acquisition, symbolized by CALS (Continuous Acquisition and Lifecycle Support), are steadily being constructed internationally. It is impossible to create a physical custom house in an information network. In an information network society, not only will such electronic networks become a major infrastructure, but we may expect that their speed and widespread distribution will cause the creation of an infrastructure that is both internationally rational and clear in concordance with legal institutions and economical systems.

As CALS is sometimes said to be an abbreviation of "Commerce At Light Speed", information networks are a place where business transactions are conducted at the speed of light, and things are accomplished under international law, instead of laws unique to each particular country. Also, the circumstances, historical and otherwise, suggest that English will probably become the official language to be used in electronic business transactions.

In order to ensure smoothness of such economic activities, it is necessary to internationalize the legal institutions to keep up with the borderless trend. Such internationalization is also necessary for security, to control any crimes committed on international networks. Since the legal institutions of each country reflect the ethical values of its people, it will not be an easy job to alter them. However I believe that both the ethical values and legal institutions will gradually assimilate internationally, to a certain level.

Let me take up the protection of privacy as one of the grounds of my belief in the standardization of ethical values. In EU (European Union), a plan which will prevent the transfer of personal information from EU countries to another country of inadequate. The pressure from the spread of an international network may raise the awareness of privacy, as well as strengthening the legal protection.

In such a way, the borderless trend of information networks will cause not only the networks themselves, but also legal institutions, economical systems, and even languages to dilate as a global civilization infrastructure.

This means that the various activities of humankind, and the culture that is their result, will be underlaid by a hitherto unthinkably rich foundation of civilization. This will have profound consequences on the concept and structure of culture itself. Let us make a few statements on this subject.

In his work "Minjo Isshin" (Revolutions in Conditions of the People) published in 1879, Yukichi Fukuzawa uses the word *information* for the first time as a Japanese, and argues the large influence that telegraphy and mail should have on Japan. Needless to say, the introduction of Western civilization has had a great impact on Japanese culture. Nevertheless, the Japanese people still have an emotional solidarity, and the culture is different from that of the western world, in particular America. However, it is difficult to have collusion in the CALS. Taking the risk of being over-schematic, the outcome of the encounter of the integral-type eastern culture based on duty and humanity, and the differential-type western culture based on contracts, is quite obvious. The future economical activities on information network may completely change our ethical viewpoints.

Of course, it must be admitted that human nature does not change so easily, and the counter-argument that the nature and values of a people, nurtured over many years by the particular climate of a specific region, do not alter simply because of the spread of information networks, certainly has a point. Let us discuss this a little in detail. Aside from the issue of whether human nature will change fundamentally or not, recently, the author made a small discovery. Until about thirty or forty years ago, there were frequent ads to "overcome erythrophobia". However these have now become quite rare. And there is also the following phrase from a certain book: "As another type of neurosis frequent among Japanese youths before the second world war, there is a symptom called erythrophobia. However, this has gradually disappeared since the 1960's. This is thought to be due to the rapid weakening of the tension experienced by a Japanese youth before his elders." This seems to be in general agreement with the facts. Had the weakening trend already begun in 1967, when Chie Nakae's "Human Relationships in a Vertical Society" published ?

The spread of information networks causes weakening in the rank dominations, often called flattening of organization. This flattening occurs not only in organizations, but the lessening of vertical ranking is also happening in emotional and ethical values. At a symposium held in Fukuoka in March 1993, which had a general meeting, the author made a lecture based on the present subject, and the chairman of the session related one of his personal experiences: "A long time ago when I was studying in Germany, I received an invitation from the senior professor who was the chair. To this I replied by telephone, and was later admonished as having been very rude". However, in this age where we greatly rely on e-mail for correspondence, there is not such thing as rudeness. Plus, the international property of e-mail is serving to decrease the cultural differences, such as notions of rank. Everywhere, such notions are approaching those of America, who probably possesses the weakest connection of such vertical rankings. This cannot be classified as either good or bad: the qualities of information networks makes it inevitable.

Also, from a different viewpoint, we may say that personal differences between individuals of a certain race, are greater than those between the average types of each race. When the individual is liberated from the small group through information networks, and leans to live as an individual, there should be a structural change in culture. The twenty-first century may see a decline in the nationalistic and racial differences in beliefs, values, and ethics, and the rise of a global culture bonded by individual hobbies, specialties and ideas of beauty.

To sum it up, we have predicted the arrival of an information network society in which the foundations of civilization, including the economical system and law institutions will diversify and expand on a global scale, and with an equally widespread culture. And for the existence and welfare of such a society, information security is indispensable. Hence, in considering information security, the axis of the national state and people is just as important as the international axis. We must resign ourselves to our destiny of improving informational security amid worries in this rectangular coordinate system.

As another background of information security, we must also consider the effect on society of the enormous increase in capacity of information networks due to optical fibers. The progress of the technology of communication in optical fibers is quite breathtaking, however the present transmission capacity does not utilize even a hundredth of the latent potential. In the 21st century, when Fiber to the Home is accomplished, we may anticipate a society where the individual is directly liked with the source of information (let us call such a society a directly-liked society or a direct-type society), on all sides. On the political side, there can be direct democracy with elections by electronic balloting (may or may not be a good idea), on the industrial side there can be order-production based on direct connection between the designing-production factories, and on the entertainment side, we may imagine camera manipulated from the receiving side, producing scenes constructed to personal taste (camera on demand). We must improve information security, keeping such high densifying of information networks in mind.

By information security, we mean more than such defensive techniques as cryptography for the maintenance of secrecy of information. We mean technology for a society in which information networks play a central role, (as opposed to paper-based and interview-based), technology to assure reliability of, and give value to information, for example, authentication and signature, technology to promote the distribution of information property.

However, relationships of trust in a new society cannot be built solely by technology. It is needless to point out the importance of legal institutions and ethics. Next we pick up issues of Electronic money and encryption policy as typical examples to consider the discussions stated above.

3   Issues Concerning Electronic Money

Money is a medium of exchange in the from of notes and coins that express numerical values. Electronic money does away with the need for a physical medium; the numerical values are stored on an integrated circuit card or personal computer. In a transaction, value is debited from one party and credited to the other. A transaction becomes an exchange of information.

In a strict sense, electronic money is not an all purpose pre-paid card, though, in a broader sense, such a card can also be called Electronic money.

It is cut out for the need that a physical exchange means has more flexibility in transactions. People do not need to carry cash. Transactions can be carried out between parties separated by long distances. They need not see each other.

An experiment with electronic money in the form of an IC card is being conducted in Swindon, England, a city with about 200-thousand residents. But the system is having problems catching on. People are tied to thinking in terms of conventional money. The benefits of electronic money cannot be seen when it is used in a local area. Electronic money really comes into its own in transactions between people in different countries or where one or both parties are in a remote area.

Another advantage with electronic money is that it can be used for small transactions involving minor sums like 10 or 20 cents, for example, if the user wants to purchase a copy of a single page or video frame on a computer network. Banks are unwilling to handle such small transfers.

Electronic money still has a number of problems to be solved before full-scale penetration. For the time being, it may be wise to use Electronic money for transactions in minor sums, or so-called 'micro-payments', rather than for large transactions.

A number of areas have to be addressed if electronic money is to be used in a big way. Safety, economy, direct transaction and anonymity need to be maintained. In the case of cash, the issuing authorities have developed intricate printing and watermarking.

Costs have to be kept down and the transactions have to be made as direct and simple as possible. The user's anonymity has to be protected. Banks and authorities should be kept from knowing what the user has purchased, as being implemented in e-cash system using blind signatures proposed by D. Chaum. This is necessary to protect privacy.

These issues can be addressed by technology. Aside from technology, we need legislation. Electronic money could catch on as an international currency and come into collision with separate national currencies, disrupting economic systems. Until now currencies have been protected by national barrier. Currencies have been an important means of maintaining separate national identities. However, electronic money can by-pass national borders.

Too much emphasis on anonymity could invite a flow of bad, underground money. It could also see funds being transferred to countries where there are cheaper tax rates (tax haven), thereby depriving other countries of tax income. The development of a money market on the internet could generate turmoil.

A full-scale introduction of electronic money will require careful analysis of the results of various experiments, international discussions, and adequate evaluation of credit worthiness and insurance systems among currency issuing authorities.

In the following, the summary of the report issued by the "Study Group of Electronic Commerce and Electronic Money", which the present author chairs, will be described.

The Summary of the Report [3]

A Impact of Electronic Money on Businesses and Fiscal Policy

The introduction of electronic money is expected to have the following effects on businesses and fiscal policy:

- More business opportunities for small companies.
  It will be easy for small companies to reach consumers in remote locations.
- Increased demand for software products.
  The price of software products is expected to decrease due to lower distribution and billing costs. Lower prices will likely fuel the demand for this kind of products.
- Creation of new information services.
  As it becomes easier to levy changes, new information services are likely to be established in the areas of electronic newspapers, books and publications.

- Demand for electronic money-related Goods and Services. Demand is anticipated in areas such as: a) devices to handle electronic money (IC cards, electronic purses, card readers), b) electronic money management systems, and c) authentication services.
- Difficulties in levying taxes and carrying out criminal investigations.
  It becomes very difficult for tax officials to know the contents of transactions in which electronic money flows across national borders. Transactions of this kind can be carried out by criminal organizations for money-laundering purposes.
- Effect on financial policy.
  The issuing of electronic money as well as the way it is used may have undesirable effects on financial policy. A thorough research of the possible consequences of the use of electronic money is necessary.
- Risk of counterfeit electronic money.
  Electronic money is based on cryptography technology. If the cryptographic algorithms used in electronic money are broken, there exists the possibility of counterfeiting in large scale.

A.1 The Necessity for International Cooperation

Networks will remove all barriers to the transfer of electronic money across national borders. Nations should therefore cooperate and promote test projects that involve electronic commerce and electronic money.

A.2 Institutional Issues on Electronic Money

Legal Aspects of Electronic Money

Currently, Japan has no laws for regulating electronic money. The application of existing laws to electronic money may not be appropriate; inconsistencies in both the interpretation and application of laws may be a consequence of not having laws created specifically for electronic money. Creation of such laws should be thoroughfully considered.

Sharing the Burden of Operating the Infrastructure for Electronic Money

The following are suggestions as to who should bear the development and operating costs of the infrastructure needed for using electronic money:

- Each party involved in a transaction should bear the cost of the transaction in proportion to the benefits it receives;
- To promote the use of electronic money, particularly in the period immediately after it becomes available, we recommend that the cost of transactions be as inexpensive as possible, preferably free.

Actually, as consumers and retailers realize that none of the costs associated with traditional billing procedures apply to electronic billing, it will be difficult to impose new charges (handling fee, etc) to them.

A.3 Determination of Responsibilities and Losses in Anomalous Transactions

In the event of any accident or improper handling of data during a transaction, it seems obvious to expect that the parties involved in the transaction share responsibility and losses equally. However, in order to promote the use of electronic money, it is important that consumers and retailers will be affected by anomalous transactions as little as possible. Also, it is recommended that consumers that use electronic money for businesses transactions negotiate with retailers contracts that specify how responsibilities and eventual losses will be shared in case an accident happens.

B International Flow of Electronic Money

Monetary systems are currently implemented on the basis of monetary sovereignty. When electronic money flows across national borders, there exists the possibility that the party to which the money was transferred exchanges it for hard currency. In this case, the question of what currency was used in the transaction arises.

There are three possibilities respect to the currency used in international electronic money transfers:

– A single currency is used;
– Several currencies are used;
– No currency is used (electronic money is genuinely electronic).

The electronic flow of currency belonging to a particular country may threaten the monetary sovereignty of other countries. Therefore, international electronic money transfers require that countries cooperate on this matter.

B.1 Laws for Protection of the Consumer

– Validity period of contracts
– Validity of data sent with typographical errors
– Validity of transactions carried out with impersonators
– Validity of data that was altered while on transit to its destination
– Procedure used in case of fraudulent commercial practices or products with defects
– Procedure used in case of loss or misappropriation of electronic money

B.2 Creation of an Agency for Validating Electronic Data

When a transaction is carried out between two people that live far away from each other, there are several documents that show that the transaction took place. Examples of such documents are postal orders, time-stamped postal receipts, etc.

In transactions that involve exchange of data in electronic form, cryptographic technology is used to guarantee the integrity of messages, to certificate the identity of the parties that participate in the exchange, and to make it impossible for any of them to afterwards negate that the transaction has taken place. The importance of technological advances in this area, require the development of a system that matches these advances. To this respect, the creation of an independent certification agency seems to be the most suitable choice.

B.3 Protection of Personal Information and Privacy

In some electronic commerce testbed projects currently undergone in Japan, information about the consumers, such as gender, age and occupation, is registered and made available to retailers, which, in turn, use this information for consumer behavior analysis and strategic marketing planning.

Since this information is gathered from many different sources, there exists the danger that errors may corrupt it as it flows through the different processing stages; erroneous consumer information may result in large losses for retailers.

In addition to cryptography as the technological means for ensuring the privacy of customer data, the establishment of regulations for protecting the privacy of customer data in electronic transactions must be considered.

C The Role of Certification Authority

C.1 Services Provided by Certification Authorities

Basic Services

- User identification
- Public key registration, management, and disposal
- Public key certification
- Public key notification and delivery

Added Services

- Public key generation and renewal
- Certification of message dispatch and receipt
- Interconnectivity and interoperatibility with other certification authorities
- User support

C.2 Requirements upon a Certification Authority

The case in which only basic services are provided and the case in which added services are also provided must be considered separately.

Only Basic Services Provided

- Ability to verify the identity of applicants for public key, so as to avoid impersonation
- Expertise in cryptography technology
- Equity and neutrality in dealing with applicants for public key

- Secure management of public keys. Measures must be taken for preventing modification of the data base in which keys are stored as well as loss of keys due to physical damage of the devices in which the data is stored.
- Fast delivery, renewal, and disposal of keys; immediate issuing of public key certificates
- Easy access to services
- Prevention of internal malfunctions
- Protection of applicants' personal information and privacy. Any information that the certification authority may have obtained in the process of verifying the identity of applicants, or information concerning when a public key was granted, or information related to when and from whom there was an inquiry about the public key used by a certain person must be kept secret.
- Solid financial base. The certification authority may have to compensate an applicant for any accident or damage that was specified in the contract negotiated between it and the applicant.

Added Services Also Provided

- Protection of secrecy of communications. The certification authority can obtain information about the content, delivery time, and intended recipient of messages. This information must be kept secret.
- Interconnectivity and interoperability with other certification authorities. If several certification authority exist, measures must be taken to ensure that their services can be accessed by users safely and effortlessly.

C.3 Bearer Certification Authority

A certification authority links people with public keys and provides certification of validity of public keys. In this sense, it offers a service comparable to public services such as certification of personal seal. Consequently, if a private institution is to undertake the role of certification authority, it is necessary that it fulfills the requirements mentioned in the previous section.

Moreover, in the case of electronic commerce, users are able to carry out transactions with any other user connected to the network. Some of these users will have registered their key in a different certification authority, some others in the same. It is necessary therefore that the interconnection and interoperation of certification authorities be guaranteed, for which it is desirable that the certification authority be the owner of a wide area network.

C.4 Institutional Issues Concerning Certification Authority

Reliability Issues

The reliability of the certification authority can be preserved by means of the following methods:

- Reliability is preserved by other certification authorities

- Hierarchical method
- Flat method
- Disclosure of all relevant technical and management information
- Institutional warranties
- Policy for establishing uniform guidelines
- Policy that legislates the necessary requisites for establishing certification authorities

If the certification authority also provides added services, it is preferable that the security of communications be preserved legally and not by means of guidelines.

With respect to this point, it has been lectured that in the case in which the certification authority is a telecommunication carrier, the legal instruments for preserving the secrecy of communications are the "Telecommunication Business Law", "Standards for Commercial Telecommunication Equipment" and "Standards for Telecommunication Network Security and Reliability". In any other case, appropriate legal instruments for preserving the secrecy of communications must be taken into account when the legal duties of the certification authority are considered.

Effectiveness of the Service Provided by the Certification Authority

The requirements upon the services to be provided by the certification authority as well as the measures to be taken in case of accidents or improper handling of information must be specified in a contract to be negotiated between users and the certification authority. It is also necessary to investigate what legal framework would be appropriate for the services provided by the certification authority.

Key Escrow System

In the Key Escrow System, proposed in the U.S.A., the government entrusts the cryptographic key to an authorized certification authority. By following the corresponding legal procedures, the government can get this key in cases in which national security is in danger.

Although any government investigation always attracts criticism, this topic, in particular, is drawing much interest from the international community. It is therefore necessary for Japan to cooperate closely with other nations in order to investigate these opinions on the basis of the "freedom of expression" and "secrecy of communications" guaranteed by the Japanese constitution.

International Cooperation of National Certification Authorities

It is in the best interest of users that international standards for regulating the creation and operation of certification authorities and the services they provide be developed.

(End of the summary of the report)

4 Discussions on Global Encryption Policy in OECD

With the development of the GII, especially of electronic commerce and key managements, OECD held an ad hoc meeting on global cryptography policy at the end of December, 1995. In the succeeding meeting in February 1996, OECD decided to draw up guidelines of cryptography policy and established the ad hoc group of experts on cryptography (the author is serving as a member of the ad hoc group).

In the ad hoc group, discussion is going on as follows; Based on the general recognition that cryptography is an important component for security of information in the development and promotion of GII, general principles is now being discussed on the following items.

(1) Providing Security with Confidence
(2) Voluntary Choice of Encryption
(3) Development
(4) Standards for Cryptographic Method
(5) Government Responsibilities and Regulation
(6) Key Management
(7) Liability
(8) Government Access

The guidelines will be drawn up at the end of 1996.

5 Conclusion

Electronic commerce and key management including key escrow systems should be simultaneously considered from international (global) and national (or regional) points of view. It goes without saying that there may be some contradictions between international and national policies. Each country has its own constitution, legal institution, customs, national sentiments and so on.

In particular Asian countries have different cultures from Western ones. Having a regard for the culture of each country, we have to make international coordination for the construction of GII. It is not an easy task. However we have to continue to make an effort for global information society.

References

[1] S. Tsujii, "Multi-media and information security — Revolutions in Civilization Structures and Cultural Concepts —," *Workshop on Multi-Media and Information Security*, Hokuriku JAIST, Nov. 1995.

[2] S. Tsujii, "Electronic Money," NHK (Japan Broadcasting Cooperation), broadcasted in April 1996.

[3] The Ministry of Post and Telecommunications of Japan, *The Report of the Study Group on Electronic Commerce and Electronic Money in the Ministry of Post and Telecommunications of Japan*, April 1996.

Limiting the Visible Space Visual Secret Sharing Schemes and Their Application to Human Identification

Kazukuni Kobara and Hideki Imai

Institute of Industrial Science, The University of Tokyo
Roppongi, Minato-ku, Tokyo 106, Japan
E-mail: kobara@imailab.iis.u-tokyo.ac.jp

Abstract. In this paper, we propose new uses of visual secret sharing schemes. That is, we use visual secret sharing schemes to limit the space from which one can see the decoded image. (We call this scheme limiting the visible space visual secret sharing schemes (LVSVSS).) We investigate the visibility of the decoded image when the viewpoint is changed, and categorize the space where the viewpoint belongs according to the visibility. Finally, we consider the application of LVSVSS to human identification, and propose a secure human identification scheme. The proposed human identification scheme is secure against peeping, and can detect simple fake terminals. Moreover, it can be actualized easily at a small cost.

1 Introduction

It is very dangerous to trust only one person or only one organization to manage very important information. To deal with these kinds of situations, a scheme to share a secret with some members, called a secret sharing scheme or a (k, n) threshold scheme, was proposed by A. Shamir [1]. In a (k, n) threshold scheme, a secret is divided into n pieces. Each single piece looks like random data by itself. In order to decode the secret, members have to gather k pieces. That is, k persons' permission is required to decode the secret. Since then, various studies on secret sharing schemes have been carried out. In particular, visual secret sharing schemes (VSS), originally proposed by M. Naor and A. Shamir [2], are very interesting. In these schemes, members who have shared a secret can decode it without help of computers in the decoding process. Shared secret (image) are printed on transparencies as patterns. Members can decode the secret (image) by stacking some of them, and see it.

However, even if one uses these secret sharing schemes, once an attacker peeps at the decoded image, it might be leaked out easily. To deal with this, some people may decode it after confirming that no attacker is around. However, even though that can be confirmed, preoccupation about peeping still exists. A video camera may be set on somewhere secretly. Some people may decode it after covering it by a piece of cloth, or a corrugated carton, or by hands. However, it is troublesome to cover it with worrying about others' eyes and cameras every

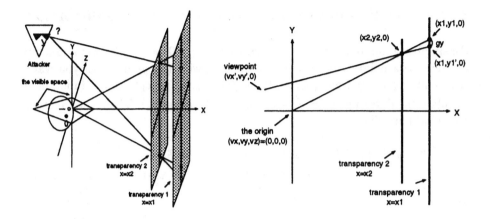

Fig. 1. The principle of limiting the visible space.

Fig. 2. The relation between the viewpoint and the distortion.

time a secret is decoded. Moreover, watching something secretly is enough to arise suspicious of immoral behavior.

In this paper, we propose new usage of visual secret sharing schemes. We call this scheme limiting the visible space visual secret sharing schemes (LVSVSS). That is, we use the VSS to limit the space from which one can see a decoded image. We investigate the visibility of the decoded image when the viewpoint is changed, and categorized the space where the viewpoint belongs according to the visibility. Finally, we consider the application of LVSVSS to human identification, and propose a secure human identification scheme. The proposed human identification scheme is secure against peeping, and can detect simple fake terminals. Moreover, it can be actualized easily at a small cost.

2 The principle of limiting the visible space

The principle of limiting the visible space is very simple (see Fig.1). The patterns are printed on transparencies so that an image can be decoded when a space is left between the transparencies. The separation of the transparencies make the space from which the decoded image can be seen smaller. We call this space "the visible space". Attackers out of the visible space can not see it.

Let the point from which the decoded image can be seen correctly be the origin of the coordinate axes, and the x, y, z axes are set. Transparency 1 is located on $x = x_1$ and transparency 2 on $x = x_2$. Let the points overlapping each other be (x_1, y_1, z_1) (transparency 1) and (x_2, y_2, z_2) (transparency 2), when the viewpoint is on the origin. Then the following equations are held:

$$y_1 = \frac{x_1}{x_2} y_2 \ , \qquad z_1 = \frac{x_1}{x_2} z_2. \qquad (1)$$

3   The relation between the viewpoint and the distortion

For simplicity, we consider the $x-y$ plane where $z = 0$ (see Fig.2). Let a function to calculate a point y_1' on $x = x_1$ overlapping with $(x_2, y_2, 0)$ when you watch the point $(x_2, y_2, 0)$ from $(v_x', v_y', 0)$ be $f(v_x', v_y', x_2, y_2, x_1)$, and a function to calculate the difference $g_y = y_1' - y_1$ be $g(v_x', v_y', x_2, y_2, x_1)$. Then, the functions are defined as follows:

$$f(v_x', v_y', x_2, y_2, x_1) = a(v_x', x_2, x_1)y_1 + b(v_x', x_2, x_1, v_y')$$
$$= a(v_x', x_2, x_1)(y_1 - b'(v_x', x_1, v_y')) + b'(v_x', x_1, v_y'), \quad (2)$$

$$g(v_x', v_y', x_2, y_2, x_1) = (a(v_x', x_2, x_1) - 1)y_1 + b(v_x', x_2, x_1, v_y')$$
$$= a'(v_x', x_2, x_1)(y_1 - b'(v_x', x_1, v_y')), \quad (3)$$

where

$$a(v_x', x_2, x_1) = \frac{(x_1 - v_x')x_2}{(x_2 - v_x')x_1} \quad (4)$$

$$a'(v_x', x_2, x_1) = \frac{(x_1 - x_2)v_x'}{(x_2 - v_x')x_1} \quad (5)$$

$$b(v_x', x_2, x_1, v_y') = \frac{(x_2 - x_1)v_y'}{(x_2 - v_x')} \quad (6)$$

$$b'(v_x', x_1, v_y') = \frac{x_1 v_y'}{v_x'}. \quad (7)$$

As a matter of course:

$$y_1' = f(v_x', v_y', x_2, y_2, x_1) \quad (8)$$
$$g_y = g(v_x', v_y', x_2, y_2, x_1). \quad (9)$$

In the same way as the $x - y$ plane on $z = 0$, z_1' and g_z on the $x - z$ plane where $y = 0$ can be calculated.

$$z_1' = f(v_x', v_z', x_2, z_2, x_1) \quad (10)$$
$$g_z = g(v_x', v_z', x_2, z_2, x_1) \quad (11)$$

Therefore, a point on $x = x_1$ overlapping with a point (x_2, y_2, z_2) is (x_1, y_1', z_1'), and the vector $\mathbf{g}$ from (x_1, y_1, z_1) to (x_1, y_1', z_1') is $(0, g_y, g_z)$.

3.1 When the viewpoint is on the $y - z$ plane where $x = 0$.

When the viewpoint is on the $y - z$ plane where $x = 0$, $a(v'_x, x_2, x_1)$ in the equation (2) and (3) becomes 1. Therefore,

$$\mathbf{g} = (0, b(0, x_2, x_1, v'_y), b(0, x_2, x_1, v'_z))$$
$$= (0, \frac{x_1 - x_2}{x_2}(-v'_y), \frac{x_1 - x_2}{x_2}(-v'_z)). \tag{12}$$

It can be seen that the distortion vector $\mathbf{g}$ is independent from the points on the transparencies. So it looks as if all the points on the transparency 2 drifted from the corresponding points on the transparency 1 for the same length.

3.2 When the viewpoint is in the space $x < x_2$ but $x \neq 0$.

When the viewpoint is in the space $x < x_2$ but $x \neq 0$, the distortion vector $\mathbf{g}$ is as follows:

$$\mathbf{g} = (0, a'(v'_x, x_2, x_1)(y_1 - b'(v_x, x_1, v'_y)), a'(v'_x, x_2, x_1)(z_1 - b'(v_x, x_1, v'_z)))$$
$$= (0, \frac{(x_1 - x_2)v'_x}{(x_2 - v'_x)x_1}(y_1 - \frac{x_1 v'_y}{v'_x}), \frac{(x_1 - x_2)v'_x}{(x_2 - v'_x)x_1}(z_1 - \frac{x_1 v'_z}{v'_x})) \tag{13}$$

where $v'_x \neq 0$. Therefore, it looks as if all the points on the transparency 2 radially drifted from the corresponding points on the transparency 1. The center is $(x_1, x_1 v'_y/v'_x, x_1 v'_z/v'_x)$ and the length of the drift is $((x_1 - x_2)v'_x)/((x_2 - v'_x)x_1)$ times longer than the distance between the center and the point on the transparency 1.

4 The relation between the shift of two corresponding cells and its density (visibility).

We consider $(2, 2)$ threshold schemes. Transparencies consist of square cells with sides c. Each of cell has 2×2 square pixels with sides d. A pixel is black or transparent. Therefore, when the two transparencies are stacked each other, it looks like black if 4 pixels are black in the cell, and white if 2 pixels are black. Let me call the types of black cells and white cells B_i and W_i $(1 \leq i \leq 6)$ respectively. We show all kinds of the cells in Fig.3 with the situation of the shift. In order to measure the visibility, we define the density as the rate of black area in a cell first. Then let the length of the shift be g_z and g_y respectively, and the expected value of the density where the shift is (g_y, g_z) be $EG_{B_i}(g_y, g_z)$ and $EG_{W_i}(g_y, g_z)$ respectively. $EG_{B_i}(g_y, g_z)$ and $EG_{W_i}(g_y, g_z)$ $(0 \leq g_y, g_z < 2d)$ can be expressed as follows:

$$EG_{B_1}(g_y, g_z)$$
$$= \begin{cases} 1 - \frac{1}{4d}g_z - \frac{1}{8d}g_y + \frac{1}{8d^2}g_z g_y & (0 \leq g_z < d, 0 \leq g_y < 2d) \\ \frac{3}{4} & (d \leq g_z, 0 \leq g_y) \end{cases} \tag{14}$$

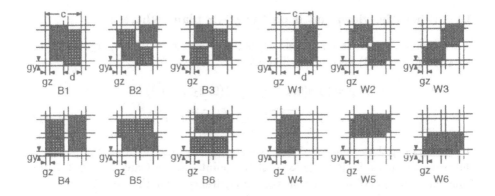

Fig. 3. All kinds of the cells with the shift.

$EG_{B_2}(g_y, g_z)$

$$= \begin{cases} 1 - \frac{3}{8d}(g_y + g_z) + \frac{5}{8d^2}g_z g_y & (0 \le g_z < d, 0 \le g_y < d) \\ \frac{1}{2} + \frac{1}{8d}g_z + \frac{1}{2d}g_y - \frac{1}{4d^2}g_z g_y & (d \le g_z < 2d, 0 \le g_y < d) \\ \frac{1}{2} + \frac{1}{2d}g_z + \frac{1}{8d}g_y - \frac{1}{4d^2}g_z g_y & (0 \le g_z < d, d \le g_y < 2d) \\ \frac{5}{4} - \frac{1}{4d}(g_z + g_y) + \frac{1}{8d^2}g_z g_y & (d \le g_z < 2d, d \le g_y < 2d) \end{cases} \quad (15)$$

$EG_{B_3}(g_y, g_z)$

$$= \begin{cases} 1 - \frac{3}{8d}(g_y + g_z) + \frac{1}{2d^2}g_z g_y & (0 \le g_z < d, 0 \le g_y < d) \\ \frac{1}{2} + \frac{1}{8d}g_z + \frac{1}{4d}g_y - \frac{1}{8d^2}g_z g_y & (d \le g_z < 2d, 0 \le g_y < d) \\ \frac{1}{2} + \frac{1}{4d}g_z + \frac{1}{8d}g_y - \frac{1}{8d^2}g_z g_y & (0 \le g_z < d, d \le g_y < 2d) \\ \frac{3}{4} & (d \le g_z < 2d, d \le g_y < 2d) \end{cases} \quad (16)$$

$EG_{B_4}(g_y, g_z)$

$$= \begin{cases} 1 - \frac{1}{8d}g_y - \frac{1}{2d}g_z + \frac{1}{4d^2}g_z g_y & (0 \le g_z < d, 0 \le g_y < 2d) \\ \frac{1}{4} + \frac{1}{4d}(g_y + g_z) - \frac{1}{8d^2}g_z g_y & (d \le g_z, 0 \le g_y < 2d) \end{cases} \quad (17)$$

$$EG_{B_5}(g_y, g_z) = EG_{B_1}(g_z, g_y) \quad (18)$$

$$EG_{B_6}(g_y, g_z) = EG_{B_4}(g_z, g_y) \quad (19)$$

$$EG_{W_i}(g_y, g_z) = \frac{3}{2} - EG_{B_i}(g_y, g_z). \quad (20)$$

$EG_{B_i}(g_y, g_z)$ is shown in Fig.4. If $(2d \le g_z)$ or $(2d \le g_y)$, EG_{B_i} and EG_{W_i} take the same value $3/4$. Let the density in a black part and in a white part of a

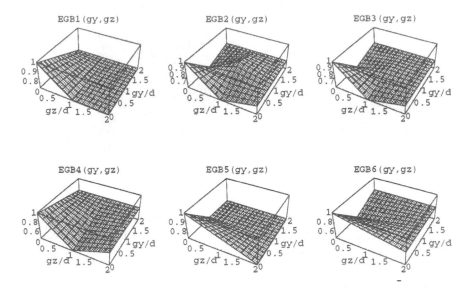

Fig. 4. The expected value of the density of the black cells versus the length of the shift $EG_{B_i}(g_y, g_z)$.

decoded image be $EG_B(g_y, g_z)$ and $EG_W(g_y, g_z)$ respectively. If all kinds of cells are used uniformly, $EG_B(g_y, g_z)$ and $EG_W(g_y, g_z)$ can be expressed as follows:

$$EG_B(g_y, g_z) = \frac{1}{6} \sum_{i=1}^{6} EG_{B_i}(g_y, g_z) \tag{21}$$

$$EG_W(g_y, g_z) = \frac{1}{6} \sum_{i=1}^{6} EG_{W_i}(g_y, g_z)$$
$$= \frac{3}{2} - EG_B(g_y, g_z). \tag{22}$$

The visibility of a part of a decoded image depends on the difference of the density between black cells and white cells of which the part of the image consists. Therefore, we use the normalized value $2|EG_B(g_y, g_z) - EG_W(g_y, g_z)|$ as a measure of the visibility $EG(g_y, g_z)$.

$$EG(g_y, g_z) = 2|EG_B(g_y, g_z) - EG_W(g_y, g_z)| \tag{23}$$

$EG(g_y, g_z)$ is shown in Fig.5. You should pay attention to the region around $(g_y, g_z) = (\pm d, 0)$ or $(g_y, g_z) = (0, \pm d)$. In these regions, the visibility is a little bit higher than the neighborhood and the black and white are reversed.

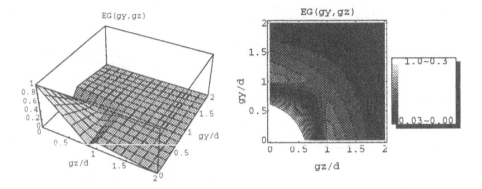

Fig. 5. The visibility of a part of a decoded image where the shift of the cells are (g_y, g_z), $EG(g_y, g_z)$. (The right side shows the contour map of $EG(g_y, g_z)$)

5 Categorization of the space

In this section, we categorize the space where the viewpoint belongs according to the visibility of the decoded image. For simplicity, we consider a $x - y$ plane where $z = 0$, and suppose the visibility of a cell is categorized as follows:

$$0 \leq |g_y| < g_0 : \text{clearly visible}$$
$$g_0 \leq |g_y| < c : \text{slightly visible}$$
$$c \leq |g_y| \qquad : \text{invisible}$$

where g_y, g_0 and c denotes the length measured on the transparency 1. c is a length of a side of the cell, and g_0 depends on the sensitivity of a person. When $v_x' \neq 0$, we should consider the difference of the size of the corresponding two cells. However, if $a(v_x', x_2, x_1) \simeq 1$, or the corresponding two cells do not overlap at all, the effect is very small or not at all. Therefore we can ignore the difference of the size under those conditions.

The visibility of the whole image can be guessed from the visibility of the image on the boundary $(x_1, \pm r_1, 0)$ and the size of the clearly visible region or slightly visible region on the image. The size of the region can be derived from the length from the most visible point to the point where the corresponding two points are shifted as g_y on $x = x_1$ and $z = 0$. Let the length be s_y. s_y is given by the following equation:

$$s_y = \begin{cases} g_y \frac{(x_2 - v_x')x_1}{(x_1 - x_2)v_x'} & (x_2 > v_x' > 0) \\ \infty & v_x' = 0 \\ -g_y \frac{(x_2 - v_x')x_1}{(x_1 - x_2)v_x'} & (v_x' < 0) \end{cases} \tag{24}$$

By substituting g_y for g_0 or c, the size of the slightly visible region and the clearly visible region on the image can be derived. We show s_y versus v_x' in Fig.6.

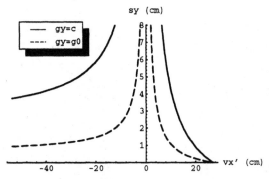

Fig. 6. s_y versus v_x' ($x_1 = 30cm, x_2 = 27cm$, $c = 0.25cm$, $g_0 = c/4$).

Then the viewpoints where the difference between y_1' and y_1 is g_y can be derived by the following equation:

$$v_y' = \left(\frac{g_y}{x_1 - x_2} + \frac{y_1}{x_1} \right) v_x' - \frac{x_2 g_y}{x_1 - x_2}. \tag{25}$$

Therefore, by substituting g_y for $\pm g_0$ or $\pm c$, and y_1 for $\pm r_1$ respectively, the space where the viewpoint belongs can be categorized as follows (see Fig.7):

visible space One (or an attacker) can see the whole decoded image clearly.

partly visible space One (or an attacker) can not see the whole decoded image clearly, but can see a part of it.

> **space 1** One (or an attacker) may see the region around the center of the decoded image clearly, but can not see the region around the boundary at all.
>
> **space 2** One (or an attacker) may see a region somewhere between the center and one boundary of the decoded image clearly, but can not see the region around the opposite boundary at all.
>
> **space 3** One (or an attacker) may see a region around one boundary of the decoded image clearly, but can not see the region around the opposite boundary at all.
>
> **space 4** One (or an attacker) may see the region around the center of the decoded image clearly, and may also see the region around boundary slightly.
>
> **space 5** One (or an attacker) may see a region somewhere between the center and one boundary of the decoded image clearly, and may also see the region around the opposite boundary slightly.

slightly visible space One (or an attacker) can not see the decoded image clearly, but may see the whole decoded image or a part of the decoded image slightly.

> **space 6** One (or an attacker) may see a region around one boundary of the decoded image slightly, but can not see the opposite boundary at all.
>
> **space 7** One (or an attacker) may see the whole decoded image slightly, but can not see it clearly.

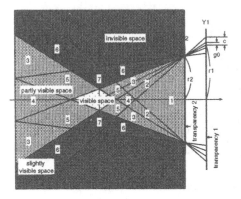
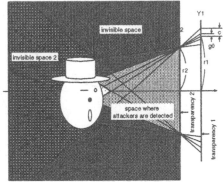

Fig. 7. Visible space properties.　**Fig. 8.** Visible space properties in practical.

invisible space One (or an attacker) can not see the decoded image at all.

If the size of the section of the slightly visible space and the visible space is designed to be smaller than the size of one's head or face, attackers can not see the decoded image at all from everywhere. Because when an attacker see it from behind the person, a part of the decoded image where the attacker can see is hidden behind the person's head, and when from before the person, the attacker can be detected before the image is decoded (see Fig.8). The size of the section of the slightly visible space and the visible space can be changed by controlling the length of the sides of the cells c. Let l be the length from the origin $(0, 0, 0)$ to the border between invisible space and slightly visible space on $x = 0$, $z = 0$. The relation between c and l is given by the following equation:

$$c = \frac{(x_1 - x_2)}{x_2} l. \tag{26}$$

6　Applications to Human Identification

Current human identification schemes using secret codes or passwords are not secure enough against peeping at the input process. To overcome this problem, some schemes have been proposed by several researchers.

One such schemes use the Zero-Knowledge Interactive Proof [3] [6] or One-Time password [7]. These schemes are robust against wire tapping. However, in these schemes, verifiers do not verify human provers themselves, although they verify whether the devices are identical. Therefore we call these schemes "indirect human identification schemes" to tell them apart from "direct human identification schemes" in which verifiers can verify the provers themselves. On the other hand, direct human identification schemes which are a little bit robust

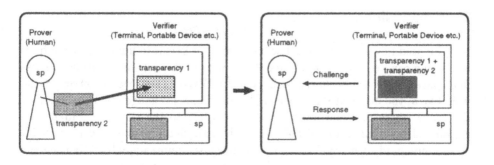

Fig. 9. Application of LVSVSS to challenge-response type direct human identification.

against peeping have been proposed [8] [9]. These schemes use simple challenge-response protocols so that human provers can make responses by themselves. (We call these schemes "challenge-response type direct human identification schemes " (CRDHI).) These schemes are certainly secure against peeping at either of challenges or accepted responses, but not so secure against both of them [10], because attackers can guess provers' secret from several pairs of challenges and their corresponding responses. This is a serious problem of these schemes.

However, if we can prevent attackers peeping at either the challenges or the accepted responses, we can make these schemes extremely secure against peeping. That is the reason why we propose to apply LVSVSS to CRDHI. In the proposed scheme, verifiers display challenges by using LVSVSS. The detail is as follows (see Fig.9). First, a verifier makes a transparency 2 and give it to a prover secretly. The prover selects a secret as his/her secret s_p and inform it to the verifier secretly. In the identification process, the verifier makes a pattern so that a challenge is decoded when the transparency 2 is stacked on it, and displays it. The prover stacks his/her transparency (transparency 2) on the display and see the decoded challenge. Then, he/she makes the response from s_p and the decoded challenge, and returns it. Finally the verifier verify the response. The prover can see the decoded challenges, but attackers can not peep at them. Therefore, the security against peeping becomes exceedingly higher. Moreover, by using the proposed scheme, it is possible to detect simple fake terminals before they input a response. Because simple fake terminals can not display proper patterns which proper challenges are decoded by stacking the prover's transparency on, although high-grade fake terminals may be able to do it.

Another advantage of the proposed identification scheme is that it can be actualized easily at a small cost.

7 Conclusions

We proposed new usage of visual secret sharing schemes to limit the space from which one can see the decoded image. We named this scheme limiting the visible space visual secret sharing schemes (LVSVSS). Then, we investigated the visibility of the decoded image when the viewpoint is changed, and categorized the space where the viewpoint belongs according to the visibility. Finally, we considered the application of LVSVSS to human identification, and proposed a secure human identification scheme. The proposed human identification scheme is secure against peeping, and can detect simple fake terminals.

References

1. A. Shamir. "How to share a secret". *Communications of the ACM*, 22(11):612–613, 1979.
2. M. Naor and A. Shamir. "Visual cryptograpy". In *Proc. of EUROCRYPTO '94, LNCS 950*, pages 1–12. Springer–Verlag, 1994.
3. A. Fiat and A. Shamir. "How to prove yourself". In *Proc. of CRYPTO '86, LNCS 263*, pages 186–194. Springer–Verlag, 1986.
4. A. Shamir. "An efficient identification scheme based on permuted kernels". In *Proc. of CRYPTO '89, LNCS 435*, pages 606–609. Springer–Verlag, 1990.
5. J. Stern. "A new identification scheme based on syndrome decoding". In *Proc. of CRYPTO '93, LNCS 773*, pages 13–21. Springer–Verlag, 1994.
6. J. Stern. "Designing identification scheme with keys of short size". In *Proc. of CRYPTO '94, LNCS 839*, pages 164–173. Springer–Verlag, 1994.
7. N. Haller. "The S/KEY(TM) one-time password system". In *Proc. of the Internet Society Symposium on Network and Distributed System Security*, pages 151–158, 1994.
8. T. Matsumoto and H. Imai. "Human identification through insecure channel". In *Proc. of EUROCRYPT '91, LNCS 547*, pages 409–421. Springer–Verlag, 1991.
9. H. Ijima and T. Matsumoto. "A simple scheme for challenge–response type human identification (in Japanese)". In *Proc. of Symposium on Cryptography and Information Security (SCIS94-13C)*, 1994.
10. K. Kobara and H. Imai. "On the properties of the security against peeping attacks on challenge-response type direct human identification scheme using uniform mapping (in Japanese)". *IEICE Trans.(A)*, J79-A(8), 8 1996.

Towards Characterizing When Information-Theoretic Secret Key Agreement Is Possible

Ueli Maurer   and   Stefan Wolf

Department of Computer Science
Swiss Federal Institute of Technology (ETH Zurich)
CH-8092 Zurich, Switzerland
E-mail addresses: {maurer,wolf}@inf.ethz.ch

Abstract. This paper is concerned with information-theoretically secure secret key agreement in the general scenario where three parties, Alice, Bob, and Eve, know random variables X, Y, and Z, respectively, with joint distribution P_{XYZ}, for instance resulting from receiving a sequence of random bits broadcast by a satellite. We consider the problem of determining for a given distribution P_{XYZ} whether Alice and Bob can in principle, by communicating over an insecure channel accessible to Eve, generate a secret key about which Eve's information is arbitrarily small. When X, Y, and Z are random variables that result from a binary random variable being sent through three arbitrary independent channels, it is shown that secret key agreement is possible if and only if $I(X;Y|Z) > 0$, i.e., under the sole condition that X and Y have some (arbitrarily weak) statistical dependence when given Z.

Keywords: Cryptography, Secret key agreement, Unconditional security, Information theory.

1   Introduction

Information-theoretically secure key agreement has recently attracted much attention in research in cryptography [9],[3],[7],[1],[5]. Two of the approaches that have been considered are based on quantum cryptography (e.g., see [1]) and on the exploitation of the noise in communication channels. In contrast to quantum cryptography, which is expensive to realize, noise is a natural property of every physical communication channel. This paper illustrates that noise in communication channels can be used for unconditionally secure secret key agreement and, furthermore, that it is advantageous to combine error control coding and cryptographic coding in a communication system.

We consider the classical cryptographic problem of transmitting a message M from a sender (referred to as Alice) to a receiver (Bob) over an insecure communication channel such that an enemy (Eve) with access to this channel is unable to obtain useful information about M. In the classical model of a cryptosystem (or cipher) introduced by Shannon [8], Eve has perfect access to the insecure channel; thus she is assumed to receive an identical copy of the ciphertext C received by the legitimate receiver Bob, where C is obtained by Alice as a function of the plaintext message M and a secret key K shared by Alice and Bob. Shannon defined a cipher system to be perfect if $I(M;C) = 0$, i.e., if the ciphertext gives no information about the plaintext or, equivalently, if M and C are statistically independent[1]. When a perfect cipher is used to encipher a message M, an enemy can do no better than guess M without even looking at the ciphertext C. Shannon proved the pessimistic result that perfect secrecy can be achieved only when the secret key is at least as long as the plaintext message or, more precisely, when $H(K) \geq H(M)$.

For this reason, perfect secrecy is often believed to be impractical. In [7] this pessimism has been relativized by pointing out that Shannon's apparently innocent assumption that, except for the secret key, the enemy has access to precisely the same information as the legitimate receiver, is very restrictive and that indeed in many practical scenarios, especially if one considers the fact that every transmission of data is ultimately based on the transmission of an analog signal subject to noise, the enemy has some minimal uncertainty about the signal received by the legitimate receiver(s).

Wyner [9] and subsequently Csiszár and Körner [3] considered a scenario in which the enemy Eve is assumed to receive messages transmitted by the sender Alice over a channel that is noisier than the legitimate receiver Bob's channel. The assumption that Eve's channel is worse than the main channel is unrealistic in general. It was shown in [7] that this assumption can be unnecessary if Alice and Bob can also communicate over a completely insecure (but authenticated) public channel.

For the case where Alice, Bob, and Eve know the random variables X, Y, and Z, respectively, with joint distribution P_{XYZ}, the rate at which Alice and Bob can generate a secret key by public discussion over an insecure channel is defined in [7] as follows.

Definition 1. The *secret key rate of X and Y with respect to Z*, denoted by $S(X;Y\|Z)$, is the maximum rate at which Alice and Bob can agree on a secret key S such that the rate at which Eve obtains information about S is arbitrarily small. In other words, it is the maximal R such that for every $\varepsilon > 0$ and for all sufficiently large N there exists a protocol, using public discussion over an insecure but authenticated channel, such that Alice and Bob have the same key S with probability at least $1 - \varepsilon$, satisfying

$$\frac{1}{N}I(S;UZ^N) \leq \varepsilon \quad \text{and} \quad \frac{1}{N}H(S) \geq R - \varepsilon ,$$

where U denotes the collection of messages sent over the insecure channel by Alice and Bob, and $Z^N = [Z_1, \ldots, Z_N]$.

---

[1] We assume that the reader is familiar with the basic information-theoretic concepts. For a good introduction we refer to [2].

The following lower and upper bounds for the secret key rate are proved in [7]:

$$\max\{I(X;Y) - I(X;Z), I(Y;X) - I(Y;Z)\} \leq S(X;Y\|Z)$$

and

$$S(X;Y\|Z) \leq \min\{I(X;Y), I(X;Y|Z)\} . \tag{1}$$

As already mentioned, it was shown by an example in [7] that the secret key rate $S(X;Y\|Z)$ can be strictly positive even when both $I(X;Z) > I(X;Y)$ and $I(Y;Z) > I(Y;X)$. In this example a satellite broadcasts (symmetrically distributed and independent) random bits to Alice, Bob, and Eve over independent binary symmetric channels with bit error probabilities 20%, 20%, and 15%, respectively.

In this paper we consider the general scenario of three arbitrary independent memoryless discrete binary-input channels and prove that the secret key rate $S(X;Y\|Z)$ is strictly positive unless Eve's channel is perfect or X and Y are independent. In other words, Alice and Bob can generate a secret key as long as they both receive an arbitrarily small but positive amount of information about the satellite signal and Eve has an arbitrarily small but positive amount of uncertainty about the satellite signal. For instance, even if Alice's and Bob's error probabilities are close to 50% and Eve's error probability is close to 0 in the case of binary symmetric channels, secret key agreement is possible. Similar to the general channel coding problem, where the existence of very good codes is known but no specific example has so far been constructed, the protocols for secret key agreement described here are not efficient in general. More efficient protocols for special cases are described in [6].

2 The Scenario and the Main Result

Let R be an arbitrary binary random variable, and let X, Y, and Z be arbitrary discrete random variables, generated from R by independent channels C_A, C_B, and C_E, respectively, i.e.,

$$P_{XYZ|R} = P_{X|R} \cdot P_{Y|R} \cdot P_{Z|R} , \tag{2}$$

where $P_{X|R}$, $P_{Y|R}$, and $P_{Z|R}$ are the specifications of the channels C_A, C_B, and C_E, respectively. In other words, X, Y, and Z are statistically independent when given R. This scenario is illustrated in Figure 1. The following is a different but equivalent characterization for our scenario. There exist $0 \leq \lambda \leq 1$ and probability distributions $P_X^{(1)}$, $P_X^{(2)}$, $P_Y^{(1)}$, $P_Y^{(2)}$, $P_Z^{(1)}$, and $P_Z^{(2)}$ such that

$$P_{XYZ} = \lambda \cdot P_X^{(1)} \cdot P_Y^{(1)} \cdot P_Z^{(1)} + (1 - \lambda) \cdot P_X^{(2)} \cdot P_Y^{(2)} \cdot P_Z^{(2)},$$

i.e., P_{XYZ} is the weighted sum of two "independent distributions" of XYZ. The results of this paper hold for all distributions with this property.

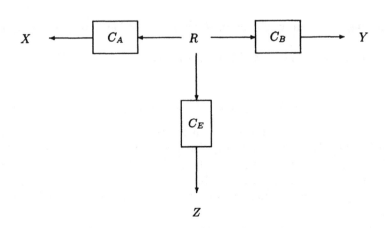

Fig. 1. The scenario of three independent channels.

We assume in the following that the distribution P_{XYZR} is publicly known. The main result of this paper is the following theorem which characterizes completely the cases for which $S(X;Y||Z) > 0$, i.e., for which secret key agreement is possible in principle.

Theorem 2. *Let R be a binary random variable, and let X, Y, and Z be discrete random variables (with ranges $\mathcal{X}$, $\mathcal{Y}$, and $\mathcal{Z}$, respectively), generated from R by independent channels, i.e., $P_{XYZ|R}(x,y,z,r) = P_{X|R}(x,r) \cdot P_{Y|R}(y,r) \cdot P_{Z|R}(z,r)$ for all $x \in \mathcal{X}$, $y \in \mathcal{Y}$, $z \in \mathcal{Z}$, and $r \in \{0,1\}$. Then the secret key rate is strictly positive, i.e., $S(X;Y||Z) > 0$, if and only if $I(X;Y|Z) > 0$.*

Up to now it has been completely open whether this condition was sufficient. The *necessity* of the condition follows immediately from the upper bound in (1). The proof of Theorem 2 is subdivided into several steps stated below as lemmas. We begin with the special case where R is a symmetric binary random variable and all three channels are binary symmetric channels.

3 The Binary Symmetric Scenario

Let $P_R(0) = P_R(1) = 1/2$ and consider three independent binary symmetric channels C_A, C_B, and C_E with bit error probabilities α, β, and ε, respectively, i.e., we have

$$P_{X|R}(0,0) = 1 - \alpha, \quad P_{Y|R}(0,0) = 1 - \beta, \quad \text{and} \quad P_{Z|R}(0,0) = 1 - \varepsilon,$$

where $0 \le \alpha < 1/2$, $0 \le \beta < 1/2$, and $0 < \varepsilon \le 1/2$.

Alice can send a randomly chosen bit C to Bob by the following protocol, which was already presented in [7]. Let N be fixed. Alice sends $[C \oplus X_1, C \oplus$

$X_2, \ldots, C \oplus X_N]$ over the public channel. Bob computes $[(C \oplus X_1) \oplus Y_1, \ldots, (C \oplus X_N) \oplus Y_N]$ and accepts if and only if this is equal to either $[0, 0, \ldots, 0]$ or $[1, 1, \ldots, 1]$. In other words, Alice and Bob make use of a repeat code of length N with the only codewords $[0, 0, \ldots, 0]$ and $[1, 1, \ldots, 1]$. Eve on the other hand can compute $[(C \oplus X_1) \oplus Z_1, \ldots, (C \oplus X_N) \oplus Z_N]$.

We show first that for all possible choices of α, β, and ε, in particular even if Eve's channel is superior to both Alice's and Bob's channel, Eve's error probability γ_N about the bit sent by Alice when using the optimal strategy for guessing this bit decreases asymptotically slower than Bob's error probability β_N for $N \longrightarrow \infty$, given that Bob accepts. (Note that γ_N is an *average* error probability, and that for a particular realization, Eve's error probability depends on the particular received string and on the message sent from Alice to Bob.)

Lemma 3. *For the above notation and assumptions, there exist b and c, $b < c$, such that $\beta_N \leq b^N$ and $\gamma_N \geq c^N$ for all sufficiently large N.*

Proof. We can assume that $\alpha = \beta$, i.e., that Alice's and Bob's channels are identical. If for example $\alpha < \beta$, Alice could (for the purpose of this proof) cascade her channel with another binary symmetric channel to obtain a situation corresponding to a binary symmetric channel with error probability β. This additional channel must be binary symmetric with error probability $(\beta - \alpha)/(1 - 2\alpha)$. (In a subsequent paper we will show that in this scenario, it is not necessary to assume $\alpha = \beta$.)

As in [7], let α_{rs} ($r, s \in \{0, 1\}$) be the probability that the single bit 0 sent by Alice is received by Bob as r and by Eve as s. Then

$$\alpha_{00} = (1 - \alpha)^2 (1 - \varepsilon) + \alpha^2 \varepsilon ,$$
$$\alpha_{01} = (1 - \alpha)^2 \varepsilon + \alpha^2 (1 - \varepsilon) ,$$
$$\alpha_{10} = \alpha_{11} = \alpha(1 - \alpha) .$$

Let $p_{a,N}$ be the probability that Bob accepts the message sent by Alice. Then

$$\beta_N = \frac{1}{p_{a,N}} \cdot (\alpha_{10} + \alpha_{11})^N = \frac{1}{p_{a,N}} \cdot (2\alpha - 2\alpha^2)^N$$

and

$$\gamma_N \geq \frac{1}{2} \cdot \frac{1}{p_{a,N}} \cdot \binom{N}{N/2} \alpha_{00}^{N/2} \alpha_{01}^{N/2} \tag{3}$$

(we have assumed without loss of generality that N is even). The expression $\binom{N}{N/2} \alpha_{00}^{N/2} \alpha_{01}^{N/2} / p_{a,N}$ is the conditional probability that Bob receives the correct codeword and Eve receives the same number of 0's and 1's, given that Bob accepts. This is one of $N/2$ positive terms in γ_N, and hence clearly a lower bound on γ_N. In the case where Eve receives the same number of 0's and 1's, her error probability about the bit sent by Alice is $1/2$, independent of the guessing strategy she uses. Thus (3) gives a lower bound for Eve's average error probability for all possible strategies.

Stirling's formula (see for example [4]) states that $n!/((n/e)^n \cdot \sqrt{2\pi n}) \to 1$ for $n \to \infty$, and thus for sufficiently large even N we have

$$\binom{N}{N/2} = \frac{N!}{((N/2)!)^2} \geq \frac{1}{2} \cdot \frac{N^N \cdot \sqrt{2\pi N} \cdot e^N}{e^N \cdot (N/2)^N \cdot \pi N} = \frac{1}{\sqrt{2\pi N}} \cdot 2^N . \tag{4}$$

Hence

$$\gamma_N \geq \frac{1}{2} \cdot \frac{1}{p_{a,N}} \cdot \frac{1}{\sqrt{2\pi N}} \cdot 2^N \cdot \sqrt{\alpha_{00}\alpha_{01}}^N = \frac{C}{\sqrt{N}} \cdot \frac{(2\sqrt{\alpha_{00}\alpha_{01}})^N}{p_{a,N}}$$

for some constant C, and for sufficiently large N. For $0 < \varepsilon \leq 1/2$ we have

$$\sqrt{\alpha_{00}\alpha_{01}} = \sqrt{(1 - 2\alpha + \alpha^2 - \varepsilon + 2\alpha\varepsilon)(\alpha^2 - 2\alpha\varepsilon + \varepsilon)} > \alpha - \alpha^2. \tag{5}$$

For $\varepsilon = 0$ equality holds in (5), and for $\varepsilon > 0$ the greater factor of the product is decreased by the same value by which the smaller factor is increased. Thus the product is greater. (For $\varepsilon = 1/2$ the factors are equal, and the left side of (5) is maximal, as expected.) From

$$(1-2\alpha+2\alpha^2)^N \leq p_{a,N} = (1-2\alpha+2\alpha^2)^N + (2\alpha-2\alpha^2)^N < 2 \cdot (1-2\alpha+2\alpha^2)^N \tag{6}$$

(we have used that $1 - 2\alpha + 2\alpha^2 > 2\alpha - 2\alpha^2$ for $\alpha < 1/2$) we conclude that $\beta_N \leq b^N$ and $\gamma_N \geq c^N$, for some $c > b$, and for all sufficiently large N. $\qquad\square$

The fact that Eve has a greater error probability than Bob when guessing C does not automatically imply that Eve has a greater uncertainty about this bit in an information theoretic sense, and that $S(X;Y\|Z) > 0$. The next lemma shows that the result of Lemma 3 is sufficient for a positive secret key rate. It will also be used in the proof of Theorem 2.

Lemma 4. *Let X, Y, and Z be arbitrary random variables, and let C be a bit, randomly chosen by Alice. Assume that for all N, Alice can generate a message M from X^N (where $X^N = [X_1, \ldots, X_N]$) and C (and possibly some random bits) such that with some probability $p_N > 0$, Bob (who knows M and Y^N) publicly accepts and can compute a bit C' such that $\text{Prob}[C \neq C'] \leq b^N$ for some $b \geq 0$. If in addition, given that Bob accepts, for every strategy for guessing C when given M and Z^N the average error probability γ_N is at least c^N for some $c > b$ and for sufficiently large N, then $S(X;Y\|Z) > 0$.*

Proof. According to the first inequality of (1) is suffices to show that Alice and Bob can, for some N, construct random variables $\hat{X}$ and $\hat{Y}$ from X^N and Y^N by exchanging messages over an insecure, but authenticated channel, such that

$$I(\hat{X};\hat{Y}) - I(\hat{X};\hat{Z}) > 0 \tag{7}$$

with $\hat{Z} = [Z^N, U]$, where U is the collection of all messages sent over the public channel.

Let $\hat{X}$ and $\hat{Y}$ be defined as follows. If Bob accepts, let $\hat{X} = C$ and $\hat{Y} = C'$, and if Bob (publicly) rejects, let $\hat{X} = \hat{Y} =$ "reject". We show that (7) holds for sufficiently large N. If Bob accepts then

$$H(C|C') \leq h(b^N) \leq 2b^N \cdot \log_2(1/b^N) = 2b^N \cdot N \cdot \log_2(1/b) < c^N$$

for sufficiently large N (where $h(p) = -p\log_2 p - (1-p)\log_2(1-p)$ is the binary entropy function, the first inequality follows from Jensen's inequality, and the reason for the second inequality is that $-p\log_2 p \geq -(1-p)\log_2(1-p)$ for $p \leq 1/2$). On the other hand

$$H(C|\hat{Z}) = \sum_{\hat{z} \in \mathcal{Z}^N \times \mathcal{M}} P_{\hat{Z}}(\hat{z}) \cdot H(C|\hat{Z} = \hat{z}) = E[h(q(\hat{Z}))] \geq E[q(\hat{Z})] = \gamma_N \geq c^N,$$

where $q(\hat{z})$ is the probability of guessing C incorrectly with the optimal strategy (i.e., $q(\hat{z}) \leq 1/2$), given that $\hat{Z} = \hat{z}$. Given that Bob publicly rejects, we have $H(\hat{X}|\hat{Y}) = H(\hat{X}|\hat{Z}) = H(\hat{X}|U) = 0$. From $p_N > 0$ we conclude that $I(\hat{X};\hat{Y}) - I(\hat{X};\hat{Z}) > 0$. □

4 Generalizing the Binary Symmetric Scenario

First we show that the above results hold even when Eve knows R precisely with a certain probability smaller than 1. This is the case if Z is generated from R by a binary erasure channel instead of a binary symmetric channel, i.e., if Z is either equal to a special erasure symbol Δ, or else $Z = R$.

Lemma 5. Consider the binary symmetric scenario of the previous section with $\alpha = \beta$ and where C_E is replaced by an erasure channel C_E^* (with erasure symbol Δ), independent of the pair (C_A, C_B), and with transition probabilities

$$P_{Z|R}(\Delta, 0) = \delta_0, \ P_{Z|R}(0, 0) = 1 - \delta_0, \ P_{Z|R}(\Delta, 1) = \delta_1, \ P_{Z|R}(1, 1) = 1 - \delta_1,$$

where $\delta_0, \delta_1 > 0$. Then the statement of Lemma 3 holds also.

Proof. We show first that we can assume without loss of generality that C_E^* is symmetric. Let $\delta_0 < \delta_1$, and let an oracle be given that tells Eve the correct bit R with probability $(\delta_1 - \delta_0)/\delta_1$ if $R = 1$ and $Z = \Delta$. The additional information provided by this oracle cannot increase Eve's error probability. The random variable Z, together with the oracle, is equivalent to a random variable generated from R by a symmetric binary erasure channel with erasure probability $\delta_0 =: \delta$, and which is independent of the pair (C_A, C_B).

Let $0 < \rho < \min\{\delta, 1 - \delta\}$. For sufficiently large N, the probability that the number of bits known to Eve is even and lies between $(1 - \delta - \rho)N$ and $(1 - \delta + \rho)N$ is at least $1/3$. Assume without loss of generality that N and $(1 - \delta - \rho)N$ are even integers. We give a lower bound for Eve's average error probability γ_N about the bit sent by Alice, given that Bob accepts. As in the proof of Lemma 3, we obtain a lower bound for γ_N by taking a (small) part of all positive terms in γ_N, and again, this is a lower bound for any strategy for guessing the bit sent by Alice. We have

$$\gamma_N \geq \frac{1}{2} \cdot \frac{(1 - 2\alpha + 2\alpha^2)^N}{p_{a,N}} \cdot \frac{1}{3} \cdot \binom{(1 - \delta - \rho)N}{(1 - \delta - \rho)N/2} \cdot \ \cdots$$

$$\cdots \ \cdot \left(\frac{(1-\alpha)^2}{(1-\alpha)^2 + \alpha^2} \right)^{(1-\delta+\rho)N/2} \left(\frac{\alpha^2}{(1-\alpha)^2 + \alpha^2} \right)^{(1-\delta+\rho)N/2}$$

$$\geq \frac{1}{6 \cdot p_{a,N} \cdot \sqrt{2\pi(1 - \delta - \rho)N}} \cdot \left[(1 - 2\alpha + 2\alpha^2)^{\delta-\rho} 2^{1-\delta-\rho} (\alpha - \alpha^2)^{1-\delta+\rho} \right]^N$$

for sufficiently large N. Here we have made use of (4). The first expression is $1/2$ times a lower bound for the conditional probability that Bob receives the correct codeword, that Eve knows an even number of bits which lies between $(1-\delta-\rho)N$ and $(1-\delta+\rho)N$, and that she receives the same number of 0's and 1's in her reliable bits, given that Bob accepts. The expressions $(1 - \alpha)^2/((1 - \alpha)^2 + \alpha^2)$ and $\alpha^2/((1-\alpha)^2 + \alpha^2)$ are the conditional probabilities that $R = X$ and $R \neq X$, respectively, given that $X = Y$. Bob's error probability, given that he accepts, is, like before, $\beta_N = (2\alpha - 2\alpha^2)^N/p_{a,N}$. For sufficiently small (positive) ρ we have

$$(1 - 2\alpha + 2\alpha^2)^{\delta-\rho} 2^{1-\delta-\rho} (\alpha - \alpha^2)^{1-\delta+\rho} > 2\alpha - 2\alpha^2$$

because $\delta > 0$ and $1 - 2\alpha + 2\alpha^2 > 2\alpha - 2\alpha^2$. Considering (6), the lemma is proved. $\qquad\square$

The next generalization step shows that it is unnecessary to assume that the random variables X, Y, and Z are symmetric. It is shown that an "appropriate" situation with *asymmetric* random variables can be transformed into a different "appropriate" situation with *symmetric* binary random variables $\tilde{X}$, $\tilde{Y}$, and $\tilde{R}$. The situation discussed in Lemma 6 is illustrated in Figure 2.

Lemma 6. *Let X, Y, and R be (possibly asymmetric) binary random variables with $0 < P_R(0) < 1$, and where X and Y are generated from R by independent channels C_A and C_B, where C_A satisfies*

$$P_{X|R}(0,0) > P_{X|R}(0,1) \tag{8}$$

$$P_{X|R}(1,1) > P_{X|R}(1,0)$$

and C_B satisfies the same conditions with X replaced by Y. Let further Z be generated from R by a binary erasure channel C_E^*, independent of the pair (C_A, C_B), with positive erasure probabilities. Then there exist binary random variables $\tilde{X}$, $\tilde{Y}$, $\tilde{Z}$, and $\tilde{R}$ such that $\tilde{X}$ and $\tilde{Y}$ can be obtained from X and Y, respectively, and such that the following statements hold:

1. $P_{\tilde{X}}(0) = P_{\tilde{Y}}(0) = P_{\tilde{R}}(0) = 1/2$.

2. $\tilde{X}$ and $\tilde{Y}$ can be interpreted as being generated from $\tilde{R}$ by independent identical binary symmetric channels $\tilde{C}_A$ and $\tilde{C}_B$ with error probability $\tilde{\alpha} < 1/2$.

3. The random variable $\tilde{Z}$ can be interpreted as being generated from $\tilde{R}$ by an erasure channel $\tilde{C}_E^*$, independent of the pair $(\tilde{C}_A, \tilde{C}_B)$, with erasure probabilities $\tilde{\delta}_0, \tilde{\delta}_1 > 0$ such that $\tilde{Z} = \Delta$ only if $Z = \Delta$, i.e., we have $\tilde{Z} = \tilde{R}$ unless Z provides no information about R and $\tilde{R}$. (Equivalently we could say that $\tilde{Z}$ gives exactly the same information about $\tilde{R}$ as Z together with some additional information that can be thought as being provided by an oracle.)

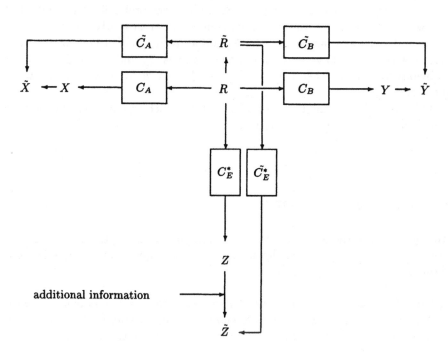

Fig. 2. The scenario described in Lemma 6.

Proof. Without loss of generality we can assume $P_R(0) \geq 1/2$. Let $\tilde{R}$ be generated from R by the following channel:

$$P_{\tilde{R}|R}(0,0) = \frac{1}{2 \cdot P_R(0)} \ , \quad P_{\tilde{R}|R}(1,0) = 1 - \frac{1}{2 \cdot P_R(0)} \ , \quad P_{\tilde{R}|R}(1,1) = 1 \ .$$

$\tilde{R}$ is obviously symmetric.

Assume first $P_X(0) \geq 1/2$. The symmetric random variable $\tilde{X}$ is generated from X as follows:

$$P_{\tilde{X}|X}(0,0) = \frac{1}{2 \cdot P_X(0)} \ , \quad P_{\tilde{X}|X}(1,0) = 1 - \frac{1}{2 \cdot P_X(0)} \ , \quad P_{\tilde{X}|X}(1,1) = 1 \ .$$

Then

$$P_{\tilde{X}|\tilde{R}}(0,0) = 2 \cdot P_{\tilde{X}\tilde{R}}(0,0) = 2 \cdot P_{\tilde{X}\tilde{R}XR}(0,0,0,0)$$

$$= 2 \cdot P_R(0) \cdot P_{X|R}(0,0) \cdot \frac{1}{2 \cdot P_R(0)} \cdot \frac{1}{2 \cdot P_X(0)}$$

$$= \frac{1}{2} \cdot \frac{P_{X|R}(0,0)}{P_{X|R}(0,0) \cdot P_R(0) + P_{X|R}(0,1) \cdot P_R(1)} > \frac{1}{2}$$

because $P_R(1) > 0$, and because of (8). Hence $\tilde{X}$ can be seen as generated from $\tilde{R}$ by a binary symmetric channel $\tilde{C}_A$ with crossover probability $\tilde{\alpha} < 1/2$. The case where $P_X(0) < 1/2$ can be treated completely analogously.

A similar cascade can be made for Y, and as in the proof of Lemma 3, we can assume without loss of generality that the channels $\tilde{C}_A$ and $\tilde{C}_B$ are identical. It is obvious that the independence of $\tilde{C}_A$ and $\tilde{C}_B$ follows from the same property of C_A and C_B.

Finally, let $\tilde{Z}$ be equal to $\tilde{R}$ unless $Z = \Delta$, in which case $\tilde{Z} = \Delta$. It is obvious that $\tilde{Z}$ has all the required properties. $\qquad\square$

5 The General Scenario

We now consider the general scenario of random variables R, X, Y, and Z as described in Theorem 2. The following lemma states equivalent characterizations of the condition $I(X;Y|Z) > 0$.

Lemma 7. *Under the assumptions of Theorem 2 (the discrete random variables X, Y, and Z result from a binary random variable R being sent through independent channels), the following three conditions are equivalent:*

(1) $I(X;Y|Z) > 0$.
(2) $I(X;R) > 0$, $I(Y;R) > 0$, and $H(R|Z) > 0$.
(3) The following three conditions are satisfied:
   (i) There exist $x, x' \in \mathcal{X}$ such that

$$P_{X|R}(x,0) > P_{X|R}(x,1) \quad and \quad P_{X|R}(x',0) < P_{X|R}(x',1) , \quad (9)$$

   (ii) there exist $y, y' \in \mathcal{Y}$ such that

$$P_{Y|R}(y,0) > P_{Y|R}(y,1) \quad and \quad P_{Y|R}(y',0) < P_{Y|R}(y',1) , \quad (10)$$

   (iii) and there exists $z \in \mathcal{Z}$ such that

$$P_Z(z) > 0 \quad and \quad 0 < P_{R|Z}(0,z) < 1 . \quad (11)$$

Proof. First we give an alternative characterization of the independence of the three channels, i.e., of $P_{XYZ|R} = P_{X|R} \cdot P_{Y|R} \cdot P_{Z|R}$. (We sometimes omit all the arguments of the probability distribution functions. In this case the statements hold for all possible choices of arguments. For example, $P_{X|Y} = P_X$ stands for $P_{X|Y}(x, y) = P_X(x)$ for all $x \in \mathcal{X}$ and $y \in \mathcal{Y}$.) From

$$P_{YZ|R} = \sum_{x \in \mathcal{X}} P_{XYZ|R} = \sum_{x \in \mathcal{X}} P_{X|R} \cdot P_{Y|R} \cdot P_{Z|R} = P_{Y|R} \cdot P_{Z|R}$$

and

$$P_R \cdot P_{YZ|R} \cdot P_{X|YZR} = P_{XYZR} = P_R \cdot P_{X|R} \cdot P_{Y|R} \cdot P_{Z|R}$$

we conclude that $P_{X|YZR} = P_{X|R}$ and, analogously, that $P_{Y|XZR} = P_{Y|R}$ and $P_{Z|XYR} = P_{Z|R}$.

(1) implies (2). Let $I(X; Y|Z) > 0$. Assume $I(X; R) = 0$. Then $P_{X|YZR} = P_{X|R} = P_X$, and X is also independent of YZ (and hence of Z). Thus

$$I(X; Y|Z) = H(X|Z) - H(X|YZ) = H(X) - H(X) = 0 ,$$

which is a contradiction. We conclude that $I(X; R) > 0$ and by a symmetric argument that $I(Y; R) > 0$. Finally assume $H(R|Z) = 0$. Then

$$I(X; Y|Z) = H(X|Z) + \underbrace{H(R|XZ)}_{0} - H(X|YZ) - \underbrace{H(R|XYZ)}_{0}$$

$$= H(XR|Z) - H(XR|YZ)$$

$$= \underbrace{H(R|Z)}_{0} + H(X|RZ) - \underbrace{H(R|YZ)}_{0} - H(X|RYZ)$$

$$= H(X|R) - H(X|R) = 0 ,$$

which is a contradiction. Hence $H(R|Z) > 0$.

(2) implies (3). Let $I(X; R) > 0$, that is X and R are not statistically independent, which implies that there exist $x, x' \in \mathcal{X}$ such that (9) holds. Similarly we conclude the existence of appropriate y and y' from $I(Y; R) > 0$. Finally, $P_{R|Z}(0, z) \in \{0, 1\}$ for all $z \in \mathcal{Z}$ with $P_Z(z) > 0$ would imply that $H(R|Z) = 0$. Hence (11) holds for some $z \in \mathcal{Z}$.

(3) implies (1). It suffices to prove that $I(X; Y|Z = z) > 0$ because $P_Z(z) > 0$. This is equivalent to the fact that X and Y are not statistically independent, given $Z = z$. We show that

$$P_{X|YZ}(x, y, z) > P_{X|YZ}(x, y', z) . \tag{12}$$

For both $\overline{y} = y$ and $\overline{y} = y'$, we have

$$P_{X|YZ}(x, \overline{y}, z) = P_{X|R=0}(x) \cdot P_{R|YZ}(0, \overline{y}, z) + P_{X|R=1}(x) \cdot P_{R|YZ}(1, \overline{y}, z) .$$

Because $P_{X|R=0}(x) > P_{X|R=1}(x)$, (12) holds if

$$P_{R|YZ}(0, y, z) > P_{R|YZ}(0, y', z) .\qquad(13)$$

Using $P_{R|YZ} = P_{Y|R} \cdot P_{RZ}/(P_{Y|Z} \cdot P_Z)$, (13) follows from

$$P_{Y|R=0}(y) \cdot [P_{Y|R=0}(y') \cdot P_{R|Z=z}(0) + P_{Y|R=1}(y') \cdot P_{R|Z=z}(1)] > \cdots$$

$$\cdots > P_{Y|R=0}(y) \cdot P_{Y|R=0}(y') > \cdots$$

$$\cdots > P_{Y|R=0}(y') \cdot [P_{Y|R=0}(y) \cdot P_{R|Z=z}(0) + P_{Y|R=1}(y) \cdot P_{R|Z=z}(1)] .\qquad(14)$$

Both inequalities in (14) follow from the fact that $0 < P_{R|Z=z}(0) < 1$, and because of (10). □

We are now ready to prove Theorem 2.

Proof of Theorem 2. According to Lemma 7, there exist $x, x' \in \mathcal{X}$ and $y, y' \in \mathcal{Y}$ such that (9) and (10) hold. We can assume that X and Y are *binary* random variables with $\mathcal{X} = \{x, x'\}$ and $\mathcal{Y} = \{y, y'\}$: Alice and Bob publicly reject a realization if $X \notin \{x, x'\}$ or if $Y \notin \{y, y'\}$. (More precisely, Alice and Bob both receive such binary random variables $\overline{X}$ and $\overline{Y}$ from X and Y, respectively, with positive probability.)

Furthermore, there exists $z \in \mathcal{Z}$ such that (11) holds. Suppose that Eve knows the bit R unless $Z = z$ (an oracle that tells Eve the bit R if $Z \neq z$ cannot increase her error probability). This situation is equivalent to the one where Eve receives a random variable $\overline{Z}$ that is generated by an erasure channel C_E^* with some (positive) erasure probabilities δ_0 and δ_1, and such that the channels of Alice, Bob, and Eve are independent, and is illustrated in Figure 3. The probability that Alice and Bob accept N consecutive realizations of X and Y is strictly positive for every N. Lemmas 6, 5, and 4 now imply that $S(X; Y \| Z) > 0$. Note that in this application of Lemma 4 the event that Bob accepts means that Alice and Bob both accept a sufficiently large number N of consecutive realizations of X and Y (if Alice does not accept, she sends $M = $"reject" over the public channel), and that Bob accepts the received message sent by Alice. □

6 Concluding Remarks

We have derived a simple characterization of whether information-theoretic secret key agreement is possible in the case of discrete random variables X, Y, and Z that are generated from a binary random variable sent over three independent noisy channels.

The condition that R is a *binary* random variable is crucial in Theorem 2. To see this, consider the following scenario: R is uniformly distributed in $\mathcal{R} := \{r_{00}, r_{01}, r_{10}, r_{11}\}$, and X, Y, and Z are binary random variables, generated from

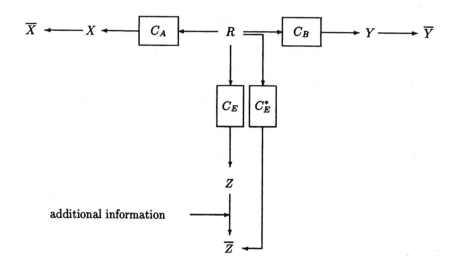

Fig. 3. The situation in the proof of Theorem 2.

R by the following independent channels (let δ be the Kronecker symbol, i.e., $\delta_{ij} = 1$ if $i = j$, and otherwise $\delta_{ij} = 0$):

$$P_{X|R}(x, r_{ij}) = \delta_{xi} , \quad P_{Y|R}(y, r_{ij}) = \delta_{yj} , \quad P_{Z|R}(z, r_{ij}) = \delta_{z, i \oplus j} .$$

Note that, for all $r_{ij} \in \mathcal{R}$, $Z = X \oplus Y$, that is $I(X; Y|Z) = 1$. On the other hand $I(X; Y) = 0$, and hence $S(X; Y\|Z) = 0$.

The general scenario of *arbitrary* random variables is more complicated. One can state conditions for both $S(X; Y\|Z) > 0$ and $S(X; Y\|Z) = 0$, but an exact characterization appears to be difficult. We only mention here that in general the conditions $I(X; Y) > 0$ and $I(X; Y|Z) > 0$ together are *not* sufficient for achieving a positive secret key rate.

The presented protocols are computationally efficient, but they are not efficient in terms of the size of the generated secret key. For special cases, e.g., for the scenario of three binary symmetric channels, there exist protocols that are much more efficient with respect to the effective key generation rate (see [6]).

References

1. C. H. Bennett, F. Bessette, G. Brassard, L. Salvail, and J. Smolin, Experimental quantum cryptography, *Journal of Cryptology*, Springer Verlag, Vol. 5, No. 1, pp. 3-28, 1992.
2. T. M. Cover and J. A. Thomas, Elements of information theory, Wiley Series in Telecommunications, 1992.
3. I. Csiszár and J. Körner, Broadcast channels with confidential messages, *IEEE Transactions on Information Theory*, vol. IT-24, pp. 339-348, 1978.

4. W. Feller, An introduction to probability theory and its applications, 3rd edition, Vol. 1, Wiley International, 1968.
5. M. J. Fischer and R. N. Wright, Bounds on secret key exchange using a random deal of cards, *Journal of Cryptology*, Springer Verlag, Vol. 9, No. 2, pp. 71-99, 1996.
6. U. M. Maurer, Protocols for secret key agreement based on common information, *Advances in Cryptology - CRYPTO '92*, Lecture Notes in Computer Science, Berlin: Springer-Verlag, Vol. 740, pp. 461-470, 1993.
7. U. M. Maurer, Secret key agreement by public discussion from common information, *IEEE Transactions on Information Theory*, Vol. 39, No. 3, pp. 733-742, 1993.
8. C. E. Shannon, Communication theory of secrecy systems, *Bell System Technical Journal*, Vol. 28, pp. 656-715, Oct. 1949.
9. A. D. Wyner, The wire-tap channel, *Bell System Technical Journal*, Vol. 54, No. 8, pp. 1355-1387, 1975.

Key Sharing Based
on the Wire-Tap Channel Type II Concept
with Noisy Main Channel

V. Korjik and D. Kushnir

St. Petersburg University of Telecommunications,
Department of Communication Theory,
Moika 61, 191186, St. Petersburg, Russia.
Email: bymey@iec.spb.su

Abstract. We give a solution to the following problem: how to upper bound an eavesdropper's information on the key shared by legal users when eavesdropper obtains at most s digits of her choice from each block of length $n > s$ transmitted between legal users on noisy channel. In particular an eavesdropper obtains no information on the key. We consider a regular coding without public discussion on channel required for privacy amplification. This approach can be used also for design of the ramp schemes extended on noisy channels.

1 Introduction

Ozarow and Wyner [1] have introduced the wire-tap channel type II concept, when eavesdropper obtains at most s digits of her choice from each block of the length $n > s$ transmitted between legal users. They proposed a randomized coset coding to upper bound the information leaking to eavesdropper. In case of *key sharing* by legal parties this encoding procedure is equivalent to a transmission of truly random binary string $\mathbf{x}$ of length n from one legal party (Alice) to other (Bob) and generation both Alice's and Bob's binary key string $\mathbf{z}$ of length k as the following linear transformation

$$\mathbf{z} = \mathbf{x}G^T, \tag{1}$$

where G is the generator matrix of some (n, k)-binary linear code V.

Ozarow and Wyner have proved, that the information gained by the eavesdropper with s "taps" can be found as follows

$$I_0 = k - \min_{|I|=n-s} rank(\langle G_i : i \in I \rangle), \tag{2}$$

where G_i, $1 \leq i \leq n$ are column vectors of the generator matrix G, $\langle G_i : i \in I \rangle$ denotes the space generated by those vectors inside the bracket and $|I|$ is cardinality of the set I.

In a particular $I_0 = 0$ if $s \leq d - 1$ where d is the minimum code distance of the code V. Then an eavesdropper has no information on the key $\mathbf{z}$.

Four years later Bennett *et al.* [2] have re-discovered this result using the notion of (N, J, K)-function. But the authors of the above mentioned papers [1] and [2] could not solve the problem of no eavesdropping when a channel for transmission **x** from Alice to Bob is a noisy one. Bennett *et al.* [2] have described a so called *bit twiddling* protocol which can be used to reconcile the final strings **z** and still leave the eavesdropper with no information. But such a protocol is impractical, however, when there are multiple errors in the initial string **x** received by Bob.

We give a solution to this open problem. Moreover, our approach can be extended to the case when an eavesdropper gains some information on the key that is the case $s > d - 1$. Then Wei has proved [3] that the information leaking to an eavesdropper can be computed as

$$I_0 = \Delta \text{ if and only if} \tag{3}$$

$$d_\Delta(V) \le s \le d_{\Delta+1}(V),$$

where $d_r(V)$, $1 \le r \le k$ is the weight hierarchy of the code V. (Further results on weight hierarchies of different codes can be found in the papers of Helleseth, Kløve and Ytrehus [4,5]). We will show in the next section that (3) keeps true after some reduction of key string **z** even though Alice transmits to Bob the check string **y** over a public channel to provide a correction of errors by Bob in his string **x** corrupted by noise. This opportunity does not follow immediately from the results of [2] because the elimination protocol based on (N, J, K) function can not be extended from eavesdropper's knowledge of s physical bits to knowledge of s bits of information in more general sense. We will consider also more general q-ary case in the sequel.

2 A Secure Key Sharing in the Presence of the Eavesdropper with s Taps and Multiple Transmission Errors

Let $\mathbf{x} \in GF(q)^N$ be a q-ary uniformly distributed n-string transmitted on a communication channel from Alice to Bob. We assume, as before, that the eavesdropper Eve obtains at most s digits of her choice from **x** and a transmission channel between Alice and Bob is noisy. Then Bob receives from Alice $\tilde{\mathbf{x}}$ as a corrupted by channel noise version of **x**. We propose a protocol between Alice and Bob to form some common randomness $\tilde{\mathbf{z}}$ without errors and to upper bound Eve's information about this randomness.

Let G be the generator matrix of some q-ary linear (n, k) code with the minimum code distance d. Then we determine the following matrix transformations of the initial string **x**, where all operations being performed over a field $GF(q)$:

$$\mathbf{z} = \mathbf{x}G^T, \tag{4}$$

$$\tilde{\mathbf{z}} = \mathbf{z}H_2 = \mathbf{x}G^T H_2, \tag{5}$$

where H_2 is $(0,1)$ $k \times (k-r)$ matrix containing exactly one 1 in each column and at most one 1 in each row. (In fact this transformation saves some $k-r$ digits of z and deletes the remaining ones.)

$$y = zH_1 = xG^T H_1, \qquad (6)$$

where H_1 is some q-ary $(k \times r)$ matrix. All matrices G, H_1 and H_2 are public. Alice transmits publicly to Bob the check string y to provide an error correction on $\tilde{x}$. Eve can learn the check string y received on a noiseless channel.

After correction of errors contained in $\tilde{x}$, Alice and Bob will take $\tilde{z}$ as a *common randomness (key)*.

Theorem. Let $x \in GF(q)^n$ be an uniformly distributed n-string, $\tilde{z}$ and y are given by (5) and (6), respectively. Then there exists such a matrix H_2 defined by (5), that the eavesdropper will obtain no information if she knows at most $s \le d-1$ digits of x and check string y, when the rank of H_1 is equal to r.

To prove this theorem we need to prove the following lemma:

Lemma. Let $Z, \tilde{Z}, Y$ be the probability spaces that describe the random strings, $z, \tilde{z}, y$, respectively, and E be the probability space that models the eavesdropper's information on z. Then the following inequality is true

$$I(\tilde{Z}; E, Y) \le I(Z; E), \qquad (7)$$

$$\text{whenever } det H \ne 0, \qquad (8)$$

$$\text{where } H = [H_1 | H_2].$$

(The condition (8) was found by Martin van Dijk for a binary case [1].)

Proof of lemma. By information-theoretic relations [6] we have

$$I(\tilde{Z}; E, Y) = I(\tilde{Z}; Y) + I(\tilde{Z}; E|Y). \qquad (9)$$

Let us prove at first that if (8) is true, then $I(\tilde{Z}; Y) = 0$. To do it we consider the joint probability $Prob[\tilde{z}, y] = Prob[zH]$. Condition (8) implies that H is a $r \times r$ nonsingular matrix and therefore $Prob[\tilde{z}, y] = Prob[z = (\tilde{z}, y)H^{-1}] = q^{-k}$ for any $\tilde{z}$, y because z is uniformly distributed on $GF(q)^k$. On the other hand for any y

$$Prob[y] = \sum_{z_1 \in GF(q)^{k-r}} Prob[z = (y, z_1)H^{-1}] = q^{k-r}q^{-k} = q^{-r}. \qquad (10)$$

In a similar manner we obtain that for any $\tilde{z}$

$$Prob[\tilde{z}] = \sum_{z_2 \in GF(q)^r} Prob[z = (z_2, \tilde{z})H^{-1}] = q^r q^{-k} = q^{-k+r}. \qquad (11)$$

---

[1] Marten van Dijk. Private communication.

Combining (10) and (11) we obtain that $Prob[\tilde{\mathbf{z}}, \mathbf{y}] = Prob[\mathbf{y}] \cdot Prob[\tilde{\mathbf{z}}]$ for any $\tilde{\mathbf{z}}, \mathbf{y}$ and hence $I(\tilde{Z}; Y) = 0$. Adding $I(E; Y) \geq 0$ on the right in (9) now gives

$$I(\tilde{Z}; E, Y) \leq I(\tilde{Z}; E|Y) + I(E; Y) = I(\tilde{Z}, Y; E).$$

But $\mathbf{z} = (\tilde{\mathbf{z}}, \mathbf{y})H^{-1}$ and hence $I(\tilde{Z}, Y; E) = I(Z; E)$. This completes proof of lemma.

Proof of theorem. If (8) is true, the theorem is an immediate consequence of lemma, because $I(Z; E) = 0$ for $s \leq d - 1$. (Although the last equality has been proved in [1] and [2] for binary case it can be easy extended to q-ary case.) On the other hand, if rank $H_1 = r$, there exists a set of r rows of this matrix, that are linear independent. If we choose these rows in the matrix H_2 to be zero rows and put a single 1 in the remaining rows of H_2, we obtain that $det[H_1|H_2] \neq 0$.

It follows from theorem that Alice can transmit to Bob the special chosen check string $\mathbf{y}$ to be used for correction of errors in $\bar{\mathbf{x}}$ (corrupted version of $\mathbf{x}$) and Eve has as before no information on the final string $\tilde{\mathbf{z}}$.

In the binary case ($q = 2$) Eve will obtain information given by (3) if she knows $s > d - 1$ digits of $\mathbf{x}$ and the check string $\mathbf{y}$ when the rank of (0,1) matrix H_1 is equal to r. It follows from lemma and the fact that $I(Z; E) = I_0$, where I_0 is determined by (3). (Similar result could be obtained for q-ary case if (3) be extended to nonbinary codes.)

Unfortunately, the linear transformation (4) changes the probability distribution of errors on $\mathbf{z}$. These errors are no longer described by the model of BSC without memory even though there is such a channel model between Alice and Bob. Therefore it is impossible to choose matrix H_1 corresponding to the known classes of the error correction codes with large minimum code distances and constructive algorithms of decoding.

To get over this difficulty we remark that matrix product $G^T H_1$ in (6) determines a code with the check string $\mathbf{y}$ to the initial string $\mathbf{x}$. It results in a problem to find a matrix H_1, which provides a "good" q-ary linear $(n + r, n)$ code with the information string $\mathbf{x}$ and the check string $\mathbf{y}$ given by (6). We can take, for example, RS codes, BCH or Goppa codes to provide a large minimum code distance and a constructive algorithm of decoding. Let $H_0 = [H_0|I_r]$ be the check matrix of such a "good" code presented in a reduced-echelon form. Then our problem is equivalent to the solution of the following matrix equation in H_1

$$G^T H_1 = \tilde{H}_0^T. \tag{12}$$

If the code V with generator matrix G is a *linear code* with a *complementary dual code* (or a LCD code), which is defined to be a linear code V whose dual code $V^\perp$ satisfies the condition $V \cap V^\perp = \{0\}$, then $det(G \cdot G^T) \neq 0$ [7] and the matrix equation (12) has the simple solution

$$H_1 = (G \cdot G^T)^{-1} \cdot G\tilde{H}_0^T. \tag{13}$$

A result of linear algebra [8] applies to conclude that $rank H_1 \geq rank \tilde{H}_0$. On the other hand, always $rank H_1 \leq r$. If we choose such a "good" code that $rank \tilde{H}_0 = r$ then $rank H_1 = r$ and the statement of theorem follows. In addition we have to choose some set of r linear independent rows of H_1 to form the matrix H_2.

It is easy to show that $rank \tilde{H}_0 = r$, i.e., that $\tilde{H}_0$ has a full rank for any binary Hamming code and any RS code. To check the condition $rank \tilde{H}_0 = r$ for some other linear code, for example, for BCH code one can compute the rank of $\tilde{H}_0$ directly because it is a polynomial time problem. Since each linear code has many information sets we can take any of them and compute the rank of the remaining part of the generator matrix. Taking the information set at random we can find a full rank matrix in several iterations. (Simulation on computer shows that the number of iterations is typically less than ten. We have checked that for many of binary BCH codes $\tilde{H}_0$ are full rank matrices).

Yang and Massey have found [9] that LCD code can be taken as q-ary cyclic codes if their lengths are relatively prime to the characteristic p of $GF(q)$ and they are reversible ones. So it is not difficult to choose q-ary or binary matrices G and H_1 satisfying the conditions of the theorem and to compute the matrix H_2.

Then Alice generates at random the string $\mathbf{x}$, computes $\tilde{\mathbf{z}}$ and $\mathbf{y}$ by (5) and (6), respectively, transmits to Bob $\mathbf{x}$ on a channel with s "taps" and $\mathbf{y}$ on a public channel. Having received $\tilde{\mathbf{x}}$ and $\tilde{\mathbf{y}}$ as the corrupted versions of $\mathbf{x}$ and $\mathbf{y}$ in transmission channels, respectively, Bob corrects errors in $\tilde{\mathbf{x}}$ using the code given by the check matrix H_0 and forms a key by (5) assuming that $\tilde{\mathbf{x}} = \mathbf{x}$ after correction of errors. This completes a perfect secure protocol for a key sharing, when $s \leq d - 1$.

If the weight hierarchy of the binary linear code V given by the generator matrix G is known, then this protocol corrects errors and permits the use of (3) to compute the information leaking to eavesdropper when $s > d - 1$.

3   A Comparison with Privacy Amplification

Our paper gives a solution to an open problem [1,2] how to eliminate eavesdropper's information and reconcile a common randomness in the presence of severe transmission errors. A complexity of our approach is equivalent to a complexity of a classic problem of algebraic coding theory - how to find the code with the largest possible minimum code distance among all (n, k) and $(n + r, n)$ linear q-ary codes and how to chose $(n + r, n)$ code with a constructive error correction algorithm. A problem of rank evaluation can be solved in polynomial time by testing randomly chosen check matrices on computer. RS codes provide very simple solutions to these problems but unfortunately q-ary codes are not always matched with the models of transmission errors and eavesdropping.

It is interesting to compare this approach with privacy amplification. Recall that for a binary case it is a mapping of $GF(2)^n$ into $GF(2)^{k'}$ by hash functions chosen randomly from universal$_2$ class [2]. Alice transmits to Bob: the random string $\mathbf{x}$ of the length n on channel with s "taps", the check string $\mathbf{y}$ of length r on public channel and randomly chosen hash function on public noiseless channel. Bob corrects errors on $\mathbf{x}$ using check string $\mathbf{y}$ and then both Alice and Bob compute a common key by hashing. Privacy amplification theorem [2] gives the upper bound for information I_0 leaking to the eavesdropper in the following manner

$$I_0 \leq 2^{-(n-k'-s-r)}/\ln 2. \tag{14}$$

It is very nice that there is an exponential decrease I_0 from the difference $[n - (k' + s + r)]$, because one can provide I_0 as small as desired given a fixed fraction $(k' + s + r)/n$. But what should be the numerical value of I_0: 10^{-3} or 10^{-100}, for example? It is remarkable above all that information criterion is unfavorable one for the key security. In fact, assuming that we share the key for some symmetric cryptosystem and an adversary has more symbols of ciphertext than unicity distance of cryptosystem said above, she (Eve) has full information on the key even before key eavesdropping. The benefit of her key eavesdropping is to reduce the number of operations required to compute the key.

If we use the method of key sharing described above by relations (4), (5), (6) and the conditions of theorem are hold, the eavesdropper has no information on the key. This makes no sense in eavesdropping at all. Moreover, the case $s > d-1$ is equivalent to a decrease in a key size at Δ bits, where Δ is determined by (3). But we cannot say that the privacy amplification is equivalent to a decrease in a key size at least I_0 bits in general, where I_0 is bounded by (14).

To upper bound the probability of correct decoding of a real key given I_0 we can apply Fano's inequality [6]. It will be the largest value P_{cd} satisfying inequality

$$k' + (1 - P_{cd})\log_2 \frac{(1 - P_{cd})}{2^{k'} - 1} + P_{cd}\log_2 P_{cd} \leq I_0. \tag{15}$$

It is easy to see from (15) that $P_{cd} \approx 2^{-k'}$ if $I_0 \approx 2^{-k'}$. Putting this value into (14) we obtain the following rough condition of no information after a key eavesdropping for privacy amplification

$$k' \approx \frac{n - s - r}{2}. \tag{16}$$

Let us compare two described above approaches for the example. There exists a shortened binary $(858, 258)$ BCH code with $d \geq 151$ and a shortened binary $(988, 858)$ BCH code with $d \geq 27$ and therefore if $(858, 258)$ can be chosen as a LCD code we can take $n = 858$, $k = 258$, $r = 130$. It provides no information about the final key string of length 128 after eavesdropping at most 150 arbitrary symbols from blocks of length 858 and simultaneously a correction of errors with multiplicity at least 13 on blocks of length 988. If we let the same parameters $n = 858, s = 150, r = 130$ in (16) we obtain the length k' of final key string equals 289 after privacy amplification approach. It is better than in the previous case. But we have to take into consideration that the privacy amplification method [2] requires a public transmission of hash functions over the channel.

One can find the similarity between described above a key distribution scheme and the so called ramp secret sharing scheme [10]. In fact, we can send the q-ary digits of x to n different users as the shadows of a common secret key $\tilde{z}$ given by (5). Then this secret key can easily be reconstructed from all these shadows. There is no information about the common key in any coalition of s shadows if $s \leq d - 1$ and there is a predetermined level of uncertainty (see (3)) if $s > d - 1$. Moreover, it is possible to correct errors contained in the shadows when the same level of security is maintained. So we obtain (k, n, n) scheme in terms of ramp schemes.

4 A Practical Implementation of the Wire-tap Channel Type II Concept with a Noisy main Channel

4.1 The Information Transmission on a Telecommunication Network with a Switching of Messages

Suppose that an eavesdropper is connected to some but not all nodes of the telecommunication network. Then she will be able to receive only the packets transmitted through the nodes of her presence. It results in the randomized model of the wire-tap channel type II concept. The main channel will be noisy in this case if the network is not a local one.

4.2 The Bunch of Optical Fiber Lines

It is not easy to provide the undetected eavesdropping of information from all optical fiber lines of the bunch. Then it results in the wire-tap channel type II concept if the legal parties use a parallel code for transmission of blocks and an eavesdropper is connected to a part of optical fiber lines only. The main channel, in this case, is a very slightly noisy one.

4.3 Quantum Cryptography

The quantum key distribution method is known described by Bennett *et al.* [11] in which two users exchange a random quantum transmission, consisting of very faint flashes of polarized light. Consider conservatively the following strategy, that is the best possible one from eavesdropper's point of view:

1. All photon pulses containing at least two photons give the complete information about corresponding bits to eavesdropper and not produce any error in the raw quantum transmission.

2. The pulses with single photons are processed by an eavesdropper with the help of the intercept/resent strategy. In this case Eve intercepts these pulses and reads them in bases of her choosing. Then Eve fabricates pulses of the same polarization as she detected, which she sends to Bob. If Eve uses the rectilinear and circular bases only she has the probability 1/2 to obtain one deterministic information bit of each pulse. It results in the randomized wire-tap channel type II concept. The main channel will be noisy because Eve's tampering gives the error probability 1/4 in corresponding pulses.

4.4 Key Sharing on Noisy Secrete Channel

Let us consider the key sharing on an ideal secrete channel without any eaves-dropping. This means that Alice and Bob will share the binary string z of the length k providing that in (7), $I(Z; E) = 0$. But if this channel is noisy Bob obtains a key string with errors. To correct these errors Alice can form a check string y by (6) and transmit it to Bob using a public channel. The reduction of the initial key string z to $\tilde{z}$ by (5) in the conditions of theorem, keeps the ideal key sharing even though an eavesdropper receives the check string y without errors.

Acknowledgments

We would like to thank J. Massey for his remark about a solution of the matrix equation (12) for LCD codes and M. Yung for his comment about the similarity between the wire-tap channel type II concept and ramp secret sharing schemes.

References

1. L.H. Ozarow and A.D. Wyner, "Wire-tap channel II," AT&T Bell Labs Tech. J., vol. 63, 1984.
2. C.H. Bennett, G. Brassard, J-M. Roberts., "Privacy amplification by public discussion." SIAM J. Comput., vol. 17, N.2, April 1988.
3. V.K. Wei, "Generalized Hamming weights for linear codes," IEEE Trans. on IT, vol. 37, N 5, September 1991.
4. T. Helleseth, T. Kløve, Ø. Ytrehus "Generalized Hamming weights for linear codes." IEEE Trans. on IT, vol. 38, 1992.
5. T. Helleseth, T. Kløve, Ø. Ytrehus "On generalizations of the Griesmer bound." Referts in informatics, no. 87, Department of Informatics, University of Bergen, Sept. 1993.
6. R.B. Ash, "Information Theory." (Dover, New York), 1990.
7. J. L. Massey. "Linear codes with complementary duals." Discrete Mathematics 106/107, 1992.
8. B. Noble, J.W. Daniel. "Applied Linear Algebra." 2nd ed. Prentice-Hall, England Clifts, NJ,1977.
9. X. Yang, J. L. Massey. "The condition for a cyclic code to have a complementary dual." Discrete Mathematics, 108/109, 1993.
10. G. R. Blakley and C. Meadows. "Security of ramp schemes." Crypto'84.
11. C. H. Bennett, F. Bessette, G. Brassard, L. Salvail, J. Smolin. "Experimental Quantum Cryptography." Journal of Cryptology, vol. 5, no. 1, 1992.

Generalization of Higher Order SAC to Vector Output Boolean Functions

Kaoru KUROSAWA and Takashi SATOH

kurosawa@ss.titech.ac.jp, tsato@ss.titech.ac.jp

Tokyo Institute of Technology
2–12–1 O-okayama, Meguro-ku, Tokyo 152, Japan

Abstract. S-boxes (vector output Boolean functions) should satisfy cryptographic criteria even if some input bits (say, k bits) are kept constant. However, this kind of security has been studied only for scalar output Boolean functions. SAC(k) is a criterion for scalar output Boolean functions of this type. This paper studies a generalization of SAC(k) to vector output Boolean functions as the first step toward the security of block ciphers against attacks which keep some input bits constant. We show the existence, bounds and enumeration of vector Boolean functions which satisfy the generalized SAC(k). A design method and examples are also presented.

1 Introduction

An $n \times m$ S-box (i.e. with n input bits and m output bits) of DES-like block ciphers can be described as a vector output mapping $F : \{0,1\}^n \to \{0,1\}^m$, or a collection of scalar output Boolean functions $F = (f_1, \ldots, f_m)$. Then, not only each component function f_i but also their linear combinations should satisfy cryptographic criteria. From this point of view, extensions of some cryptographic criteria of scalar output Boolean functions to vector output Boolean functions have been studied recently [3, 4, 13, 18]. For example, it is known that F is uniformly distributed if and only if all nonzero linear combinations of component functions f_i are balanced [4, 11, 20]. f satisfies perfect nonlinear if $f(x) \oplus f(x \oplus \alpha)$ is balanced for any $\alpha \neq 0$. $F = (f_1, \ldots, f_m)$ satisfies perfect nonlinear if all nonzero linear combinations of $\{f_i\}$ satisfy perfect nonlinear. Nyberg showed an upper bound on m such that $m \leq n/2$ for F which satisfies perfect nonlinear [13]. Chabaud and Vaudenay introduced the notion of almost bent functions and almost perfect nonlinear functions [3].

On the other hand, a Boolean function should satisfy cryptographic criteria even if some input bits (say, any k bits) are kept constant. (There may be a differential/linear cryptanalysis of this type.) However, this kind of security has been studied only for scalar output Boolean functions.

SAC(k) is a criterion for scalar output Boolean functions of this type [6]. A scalar output Boolean function $f : \{0,1\}^n \to \{0,1\}$ satisfies SAC if $f(x) \oplus f(x \oplus \alpha)$ is balanced for any α such that $W(\alpha) = 1$, where $W(\alpha)$ denotes the Hamming weight of α [21]. f satisfies SAC(k) if every function obtained from

$f(x_1, \cdots, x_n)$ by keeping any k input bits constant satisfies SAC [6]. Several researchers studied the properties of SAC(k) [5, 6, 8–10, 15–17, 19]. Especially, Preneel showed that f satisfies SAC(k) if f is quadratic and every variable x_i occurs in at least $k + 1$ second order terms of the algebraic normal form [16]. Preneel, Govaerts and Vandewalle [15] showed the number of quadratic functions which satisfy SAC(k) for $3 \leq n \leq 7$.

This paper studies a generalization of SAC(k) to vector output Boolean functions as the first step toward the security of block ciphers against attacks which keep some input bits constant. We say that $F(x_1, \cdots, x_n) = (f_1, \ldots, f_m)$ is an (n, m, k)-SAC function if all nonzero linear combinations of $f_1, \ldots, f_m$ satisfy SAC(k). Then we show the existence, bounds and enumeration of (n, m, k)-SAC functions. A design method and examples are also given. Our results are as follows.

1. Existence:
   There exists an (n, m, k)-SAC function if there exists a linear $[N, m, k + 1]$ code such that
   $$N = \begin{cases} n - 1 & \text{if } n \text{ is even} \\ n - 2 & \text{if } n \text{ is odd .} \end{cases} \tag{1}$$

   The proof is constructive. That is, a design method is given in the proof.
2. Bounds:
   We present an upper bound on k such that
   $$k \leq \min(\lfloor \frac{2^{m-1}(n-1)}{2^m - 1} \rfloor - 1, 2\lfloor \frac{2^{m-2}n}{2^m - 1} \rfloor - 1) .$$

   We also present a Singleton-type bound such that
   $$m \leq n - k - 1 .$$

   This bound is tight if $k = 0$. It is also tight if $k = 1$ and n is even.
3. Enumeration:
   The number of (n, m, k)-SAC functions is also important. Denoting such number by $|B(n, m, k)|$, we show that
   $$|B(n, m, k)| \geq C(n, m)2^{(n+1)m} ,$$

   where
   $$C(n, m) \stackrel{\triangle}{=} (2^N - 1) \cdots (2^N - 2^i) \cdots (2^N - 2^{m-1}) .$$

   N is given by (1).

2   Preliminaries

$x = (x_1, \cdots, x_n)$, where $x_i = 0$ or 1. f or f_i denote a mapping from $\{0,1\}^n$ to $\{0,1\}$. f is balanced if $|\{x \mid f(x) = 0\}| = |\{x \mid f(x) = 1\}| = 2^{n-1}$. F denotes a mapping from $\{0,1\}^n$ to $\{0,1\}^m$. F is uniformly distributed if $|\{x \mid F(x) = \beta\}| = 2^{n-m}$ for any $\beta \in \{0,1\}^m$. For an n-bit vector α, $W(\alpha)$ denotes the Hamming weight of α.

Definition 1. [6, 21]

1. f satisfies the *strict avalanche criterion* (SAC) if $f(x) \oplus f(x \oplus \alpha)$ is balanced for any $\alpha \in \{0, 1\}^n$ such that $W(\alpha) = 1$.
2. f satisfies SAC(k) if any function obtained from f by keeping any k input bits constant satisfies SAC. SAC(0) is the same as SAC.

The following form is called the *algebraic normal form* of f.

$$f(x_1, \ldots, x_n) = a_0 \oplus \bigoplus_{i=1}^{n} a_i x_i \oplus \bigoplus_{1 \le i < j \le n} a_{ij} x_i x_j \oplus \cdots \oplus a_{12\ldots n} x_1 x_2 \ldots x_n .$$

ord(f) denotes the degree of the highest order term in the algebraic normal form.

Proposition 2. *[6] There exists no f which satisfies SAC($n - 1$).*

Proposition 3. *[16] If f satisfies SAC($n - 2$) or SAC($n - 3$), then ord(f)=2. If f satisfies SAC(k) for $0 \le k \le n - 3$, then ord(f) $\le n - k - 1$.*

Proposition 4. *[16] Suppose that ord(f) $= 2$ and $n > 2$. Then, f satisfies SAC(k) if and only if every variable x_i occurs in at least $k + 1$ second order terms of the algebraic normal form, where $0 \le k \le n - 2$.*

Proposition 5. *[11] For $n \ge m$, $F(x_1, \ldots, x_n) = (f_1, \ldots, f_m)$ is uniformly distributed if and only if all nonzero linear combinations of $f_1, \ldots, f_m$ are balanced.*

3   Tool from Graph Theory

We use graph theory in this paper. The vertices of a graph will be identified with variables of a Boolean function. A graph G is a pair of (V, E), where $V = \{x_1, \ldots, x_n\}$ is a set of vertices and $E = \{(x_i, x_j)\}$ is a set of edges, where (x_i, x_j) denotes an edge between x_i and x_j. K_n denotes a complete graph with n vertices. The chromatic index $q(G)$ of a graph G is the smallest number of colors needed to color the edges of G so that no two adjacent edges have the same color.

Proposition 6. *[1](p.248)*

$$q(K_n) = \begin{cases} n - 1 & \text{if } n \text{ is even} \\ n & \text{if } n \text{ is odd} . \end{cases}$$

Proof. See Appendix.   □

A graph $H = (V', E')$ is a subgraph of G if $V' \subseteq V$, $E' \subseteq E$ and all the relationships of G are preserved.

Definition 7. A subgraph $H = (V', E')$ of $G = (V, E)$ is called a 1-factor of G if $V = V'$ and the degree of every vertex of H is exactly 1.

Corollary 8. *[7] K_{2p} can be decomposed into $(2p-1)$ edge-disjoint 1-factors $H_1 = (V, E_1), \cdots, H_{2p-1} = (V, E_{2p-1})$.*

The proof of Proposition 6 provides an algorithm which decomposes K_{2p} into $(2p-1)$ edge-disjoint 1-factors. For example, K_8 is decomposed into seven edge-disjoint 1-factors as follows.

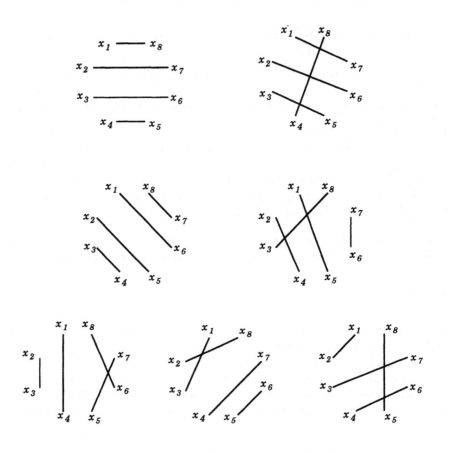

Fig. 1. edge-disjoint 1-factors of K_8

4 (n, m, k)-SAC function

Definition 9. We say that $F(x_1, \cdots, x_n) = (f_1, \cdots, f_m)$ is an (n, m, k)-SAC function if any nonzero linear combination of $f_1, \cdots, f_m$ satisfies SAC(k).

In this section, we show the existence of (n, m, k)-SAC functions by using graph theory and linear error correcting codes. It is also presented how to design (n, m, k)-SAC functions.

4.1 Existence

A binary linear code of length N, dimension m and the minimum distance d is denoted by a linear $[N, m, d]$ code.

Theorem 10. *There exists an (n, m, k)-SAC function if there exists a linear $[N, m, k+1]$ code such that*

$$N = \begin{cases} n-1 & \text{if } n \text{ is even} \\ n-2 & \text{if } n \text{ is odd} \end{cases}. \tag{2}$$

The proof will be given in the next subsection. How to construct such F is also illustrated in the proof.

Proposition 11 (Gilbert-Varshamov bound)[12]. *There exists a linear $[n, m, d]$ code if*

$$2^{n-m} > \sum_{j=0}^{d-2} \binom{n-1}{j}.$$

Corollary 12. *There exists an (n, m, k)-SAC function if*

$$m < n - 1 - \log_2 \sum_{j=0}^{k-1} \binom{n-2}{j} \quad \text{and } n \text{ is even} \tag{3}$$

or

$$m < n - 2 - \log_2 \sum_{j=0}^{k-1} \binom{n-3}{j} \quad \text{and } n \text{ is odd}. \tag{4}$$

Proof. From Theorem 10 and Proposition 11. ☐

Corollary 13. *There exists an (n, m, k)-SAC function such that*

(1) $k = 2, n = 2^u$ and $m = n - u - 1$.
(2) $k = 3, n = 2^u$ and $m = n - u - 2$.

Proof.

(1) Apply Theorem 10 to the Hamming code which is a linear $[2^u - 1, 2^u - u - 1, 3]$ code.
(2) Apply Theorem 10 to the extended Hamming code which is a linear $[2^u - 1, 2^u - u - 2, 4]$ code.

☐

4.2   Proof of Theorem 10: (Construction)

Definition 14. Let $V = \{x_1, \cdots, x_{2p}\}$ be the set of vertices of K_{2p}. From Corollary 8, K_{2p} is decomposed into $(2p - 1)$ edge-disjoint 1-factors $H_1 = (V, E_1), \cdots, H_{2p-1} = (V, E_{2p-1})$. For each H_l, define a quadratic Boolean function g_l as follows.

$$g_l(x_1, \ldots, x_{2p}) \triangleq \bigoplus_{(x_i, x_j) \in E_l} x_i x_j \ .$$

We say that $g_1, \cdots, g_{2p-1}$ are *associated functions* of K_{2p}.

Claim 15. *Let $g_1, \cdots, g_{2p-1}$ be associated functions of K_{2p}. Then,*

(1) In each g_l, each variable x_i appears in exactly one second order term.
(2) Any two different g_i and g_j have no terms in common.

Proof. (1) Because H_l is a 1-factor of K_{2p}. (2) Because H_i and H_j $(i \neq j)$ are edge-disjoint. $\qquad\square$

Definition 16. For n, let p be an integer such that $n = 2p$ or $n = 2p + 1$. Let $g_1, \cdots, g_{2p-1}$ be associated functions of K_{2p}. Define

$$\hat{f}_i \triangleq \begin{cases} g_i & \text{if } n = 2p \\ g_i \oplus x_i x_{2p+1} & \text{if } n = 2p + 1 \end{cases}$$

for $1 \leq i \leq 2p - 1$. We say that $\hat{f}_1, \cdots, \hat{f}_{2p-1}$ are *basic functions* of n.

Claim 17. *Let $\hat{f}_1, \cdots, \hat{f}_{2p-1}$ be basic functions of n, where $n = 2p$ or $2p + 1$. Then,*

(1) In each $\hat{f}_l$, each variable x_i appears in at least one second order term.
(2) Any two different $\hat{f}_i$ and $\hat{f}_j$ have no terms in common.

Proof. Note that $x_i x_{2p+1}$ does not appear in $g_l(x_1, \ldots, x_{2p})$. Then, from Claim 15, this claim is obtained. $\qquad\square$

Lemma 18. *Let $\hat{f}_1, \cdots, \hat{f}_{2p-1}$ be basic functions of n, where $n = 2p$ or $2p + 1$. Let $(b_1, \cdots, b_{2p-1})$ be any binary vector with Hamming weight at least $k + 1$. Let*

$$f \triangleq (b_1, \cdots, b_{2p-1})(\hat{f}_1, \cdots, \hat{f}_{2p-1})^T \ .$$

Then f satisfies SAC(k).

Proof. From Claim 17, we see that each variable appears in at least $k + 1$ second order terms of f. Then from Proposition 4, f satisfies SAC(k). $\qquad\square$

(Proof of Theorem 10)

From (2), we see that $N = 2p-1$ for either $n = 2p$ or $2p+1$. Let $\hat{f}_1, \cdots, \hat{f}_{2p-1} (= \hat{f}_N)$ be basic functions of n. Let Q be a generator matrix of a linear $[N, m, k+1]$ code. Define $F = (f_1, \cdots, f_m)$ as

$$(f_1, \cdots, f_m)^T \triangleq Q(\hat{f}_1, \cdots, \hat{f}_N)^T.$$

We show that F is an (n, m, k)-SAC function. Let a nonzero linear combination of $f_1, \cdots, f_m$ be $h = c_1 f_1 + \cdots c_m f_m$. Then,

$$h = (c_1, \cdots, c_m)(f_1, \cdots, f_m)^T = (c_1, \cdots, c_m)Q(\hat{f}_1, \cdots, \hat{f}_N)^T .$$

Let

$$(b_1, \cdots, b_N) \triangleq (c_1, \cdots, c_m)Q .$$

Then, the Hamming weight of $(b_1, \cdots, b_N)$ is at least $k+1$ because $(b_1, \cdots, b_N)$ is a codeword of the linear $[N, m, k+1]$ code. Now, h is written as

$$h = (b_1, \cdots, b_N)(\hat{f}_1, \cdots, \hat{f}_N)^T.$$

Then from Lemma 18, h satisfies SAC(k). Therefore, F is an (n, m, k)-SAC function. □

5 Upper bounds on (n, m, k)-SAC functions

In (n, m, k)-SAC functions, k should be as large as possible. Equivalently, m should be as large as possible. In this section, we present two upper bounds. One is an upper bound on k which is derived from the bound on k-resilient functions. The other bound has a similar form to Singleton bound for error correcting codes.

5.1 Bound derived from k-resilient functions

Definition 19. $F(x_1, \cdots, x_n) = (f_1, \cdots, f_m)$ is an (n, m, k)-resilient function if a function obtained from F by keeping any k input bits constant is uniformly distributed.

Proposition 20. [2] If there exists an (n, m, k)-resilient function, then

$$k \le \lfloor \frac{2^{m-1} n}{2^m - 1} \rfloor - 1$$

and

$$k \le 2\lfloor \frac{2^{m-2}(n + 1)}{2^m - 1} \rfloor - 1 .$$

Define

$$A(x_1, \cdots, x_n) \triangleq F(x_1, \cdots, x_n) \oplus F(x_1 \oplus 1, x_2, \cdots, x_n) .$$

Theorem 21. *If $F(x_1, \cdots, x_n)$ is an (n, m, k)-SAC function, then $A(0, x_2, \cdots, x_n)$ is an $(n-1, m, k)$-resilient function.*

Proof. Suppose that $A(0, x_2, \cdots, x_n)$ is not an $(n-1, m, k)$-resilient function. Without loss of generality, we can assume that $A(0, \cdots, 0, x_{k+2}, \cdots, x_n)$ is not uniformly distributed. That is, $(x_2, \cdots, x_{k+1})$ are fixed to $(0, \cdots, 0)$. Note that

$$A(0, \cdots, 0, x_{k+2}, \cdots, x_n) = A(1, 0, \cdots, 0, x_{k+2}, \cdots, x_n)$$

from the definition of A. Therefore, we see that $A(x_1, 0, \cdots, 0, x_{k+2}, \cdots, x_n)$ is not uniformly distributed because $A(0, \cdots, 0, x_{k+2}, \cdots, x_n)$ is not uniformly distributed. On the other hand, since F satisfies SAC(k). $A(x_1, 0, \cdots, 0, x_{k+2}, \cdots, x_n)$ must be uniformly distributed. This is a contradiction. □

Corollary 22. *If there exists an (n, m, k)-SAC function, then there exists an $(n-1, m, k)$-resilient function.*

Corollary 23. *If there exists an (n, m, k)-SAC function, then*

$$k \leq \min(\lfloor \frac{2^{m-1}(n-1)}{2^m - 1} \rfloor - 1, 2\lfloor \frac{2^{m-2}n}{2^m - 1} \rfloor - 1) . \tag{5}$$

Proof. From Proposition 20 and Corollary 22. □

5.2 Singleton-type bound

Theorem 24. *In an (n, m, k)-SAC function,*

$$m \leq n - k - 1 . \tag{6}$$

Proof. First, we show that $m \leq n-1$ for $(n, m, 0)$-SAC functions. For an $(n, m, 0)$-SAC function F, choose α such that $W(\alpha) = 1$ arbitrarily and let $A(x) \triangleq F(x) \oplus F(x \oplus \alpha)$. Then A is uniformly distributed from Proposition 5. On the other hand, it is clear that $A(x) = A(x \oplus \alpha)$. However, if $m = n$, it is impossible that A satisfies both of these two conditions. Therefore, $m \leq n - 1$ for $(n, m, 0)$-SAC functions.

Next, for an (n, m, k)-SAC function $F(x_1, \cdots, x_n)$, consider $F(0, \cdots, 0, x_{k+1}, \cdots, x_n)$. Then, we obtain an $(n-k, m, 0)$-SAC function. That is, if there exists an (n, m, k)-SAC function, then there exists an $(n-k, m, 0)$-SAC function. Therefore, it must hold that $m \leq (n-k) - 1$ for (n, m, k)-SAC functions. □

We show that the above bound is tight if $k = 0$. We also show that it is tight if $k = 1$ and n is even.

Theorem 25. *There exists an $(n, n-1, 0)$-SAC function.*

Proof. First, suppose that n is even. Consider a linear code such that a generator matrix Q is the $(n-1) \times (n-1)$ identity matrix. This is a linear $[n-1, n-1, 1]$ code. Then, there exists an $(n, n-1, 0)$-SAC function from Theorem 10.

Next, suppose that $n = 2p+1$. Let $\hat{f}_1, \cdots, \hat{f}_{2p-1}$ be basic functions of n. Define $F = (f_1, \cdots, f_{2p})$ as follows.

$$f_i \triangleq \begin{cases} \hat{f}_i & \text{for } 1 \leq i \leq 2p-1 \\ (x_1 \oplus \cdots \oplus x_{2p})x_{2p+1} & \text{for } i = 2p \ . \end{cases}$$

We will show that F is an $(n, n-1, 0)$-SAC function. Let h be a nonzero linear combination of $f_1, \cdots, f_{2p}$. For some $S \subseteq \{1, \cdots, 2p-1\}$ such that $S \neq \emptyset$, h is written as

$$h = \bigoplus_{i \in S} f_i = \bigoplus_{i \in S} \hat{f}_i$$

or

$$h = \bigoplus_{i \in S} f_i \oplus f_{2p} = \bigoplus_{i \in S} \hat{f}_i \oplus f_{2p} \ .$$

If $h = \bigoplus_{i \in S} \hat{f}_i$, then h satisfies SAC(0) from Lemma 18. Next, suppose that $h = (\bigoplus_{i \in S} \hat{f}_i) \oplus f_{2p}$. Then, h is written as

$$h = (\bigoplus_{i \in S} g_i) \oplus (\bigoplus_{i \in S} x_i)x_{2p+1} \oplus x_{2p}x_{2p+1}$$
$$= \bigoplus_{i \in S} g_i \oplus (\bigoplus_{j \in \bar{S}} x_j)x_{2p+1} \oplus x_{2p}x_{2p+1} \ , \tag{7}$$

where $\bar{S} = \{1, 2, \ldots, 2p-1\} \setminus S$.

We show that each variable appears in at least one second order term of h. Remember that g_i is a function of $x_1, \cdots, x_{2p}$. Therefore, x_{2p+1} does not appear in g_i. Then from Claim 15 (2), no second order term of (7) is cancelled. Now, it is clear that x_{2p+1} appears in at least one second order term of h. Next, each x_i such that $1 \leq i \leq 2p$ appears in exactly one second order term of g_j such that $j \in S$ from Claim 15 (1). Hence, each x_i such that $1 \leq i \leq 2p$ appears in at least one second order term of h. Then, from Proposition 4, h satisfies SAC(0). Therefore, F is an $(n, n-1, 0)$-SAC function. □

Corollary 26. *There exists an $(n, n-2, 1)$-SAC function if n is even.*

Proof. From Corollary 12. □

6 Enumeration of (n, m, k)-SAC functions

In this section, we show a lower bound on the number of (n, m, k)-SAC functions. Let

$$B(n, m, k) \triangleq \{F \mid F \text{ is an } (n, m, k)\text{-SAC function}\}$$
$$C(n, m) \triangleq (2^N - 1)(2^N - 2) \cdots (2^N - 2^i) \cdots (2^N - 2^{m-1}),$$

where N is given by (2).

Theorem 27. $|B(n, m, k)| \geq C(n, m)2^{(n+1)m}$.

Proof. From the proof of Theorem 10, we see that there exists a distinct F for each generator matrix of a linear $[N, m, k + 1]$ code. The number of such matrices is equal to the number of bases of an m-dimensional subspace of an $(n - 1)$-dimensional space over $GF(2)$. An i-dimensional space over $GF(2)$ has 2^i vectors. Therefore, the number of bases of an m-dimensional space is given by $C(n, m)$. Further, it is known that linear and constant terms have no influence on SAC(k) [5, 16]. Therefore, this theorem holds. □

7 Example

In this section, we show an $(8, 7, 0)$-SAC function, an $(8, 6, 1)$-SAC function and an $(8, 4, 2)$-SAC function by using the method of Sect. 4.2.

Basic functions of $n = 8$ are as follows (see Fig. 1) :

$$\hat{f}_1 = x_1 x_8 \oplus x_2 x_7 \oplus x_3 x_6 \oplus x_4 x_5 ,$$
$$\hat{f}_2 = x_1 x_7 \oplus x_2 x_6 \oplus x_3 x_5 \oplus x_4 x_8 ,$$
$$\hat{f}_3 = x_1 x_6 \oplus x_2 x_5 \oplus x_3 x_4 \oplus x_7 x_8 ,$$
$$\hat{f}_4 = x_1 x_5 \oplus x_2 x_4 \oplus x_3 x_8 \oplus x_6 x_7 ,$$
$$\hat{f}_5 = x_1 x_4 \oplus x_2 x_3 \oplus x_5 x_7 \oplus x_6 x_8 ,$$
$$\hat{f}_6 = x_1 x_3 \oplus x_2 x_8 \oplus x_4 x_7 \oplus x_5 x_6 ,$$
$$\hat{f}_7 = x_1 x_2 \oplus x_3 x_7 \oplus x_4 x_6 \oplus x_5 x_8 .$$

- $(8, 7, 0)$-SAC function

  $F(x_1, \ldots, x_8) = (\hat{f}_1, \ldots, \hat{f}_7)$ is an $(8, 7, 0)$-SAC function.
- $(8, 6, 1)$-SAC function

  A generator matrix of a linear $[7,6,2]$ code is given by $Q = (I_6, J)$, where I_6 is the 6×6 identity matrix and $J = (1, \cdots, 1)^T$. Let

$$(f_1, \cdots, f_6)^T = Q(\hat{f}_1, \cdots, \hat{f}_7)^T .$$

Then

$$f_1 = \hat{f}_1 \oplus \hat{f}_7 , \quad f_2 = \hat{f}_2 \oplus \hat{f}_7 ,$$
$$f_3 = \hat{f}_3 \oplus \hat{f}_7 , \quad f_4 = \hat{f}_4 \oplus \hat{f}_7 ,$$
$$f_5 = \hat{f}_5 \oplus \hat{f}_7 , \quad f_6 = \hat{f}_6 \oplus \hat{f}_7 .$$

  Now, $F(x_1, \ldots, x_8) = (f_1, \ldots, f_6)$ is an $(8, 6, 1)$-SAC function.
- $(8, 4, 2)$-SAC function

  A generator matrix of $[7,4,3]$ Hamming code is given by

$$Q = \begin{pmatrix} 1 & 0 & 0 & 0 & 1 & 1 & 0 \\ 0 & 1 & 0 & 0 & 0 & 1 & 1 \\ 0 & 0 & 1 & 0 & 1 & 0 & 1 \\ 0 & 0 & 0 & 1 & 1 & 1 & 1 \end{pmatrix} .$$

Let

$$(f_1', \cdots, f_4')^T = Q(\hat{f}_1, \cdots, \hat{f}_7)^T \ .$$

That is,

$$f_1' = \hat{f}_1 \oplus \hat{f}_5 \oplus \hat{f}_6 \ , \quad f_2' = \hat{f}_2 \oplus \hat{f}_6 \oplus \hat{f}_7 \ ,$$
$$f_3' = \hat{f}_3 \oplus \hat{f}_5 \oplus \hat{f}_7 \ , \quad f_4' = \hat{f}_4 \oplus \hat{f}_5 \oplus \hat{f}_6 \oplus \hat{f}_7 \ .$$

Then, $F(x_1, \ldots, x_8) = (f_1', \ldots, f_4')$ is an $(8, 4, 2)$-SAC function.

8 Concluding Remarks

We have presented a generalization of higher order SAC to vector output Boolean functions which are defined as (n, m, k)-SAC functions. Corollary 23 and Theorem 24 give upper bounds on k and m of (n, m, k)-SAC functions. Corollary 12 and Corollary 13 give lower bounds on k and m. Thus, our principal results are upper bounds and lower bounds on k and m of (n, m, k)-SAC functions. They imply fundamental bounds on the structure of effective S-boxes. We have also shown a lower bound on the number of (n, m, k)-SAC functions.

A design method has been presented in Sect. 4.2. Note that associate functions (see Def. 14) are Maiorana-type bent functions. Therefore, if n is even, each component function of our (n, m, k)-SAC functions is a bent function as well. However, our design method has several weaknesses; F has low algebraic degree, it is not very uniform, and the difference distribution table is not very uniform.

It will be future work to study the compatibility between (n, m, k)-SAC functions and fixing their potential weakness, and to improve the upper bound and lower bounds on k and m.

References

1. C. Berge. *Graphs and Hypergraphs*. North-Holland Publishing Company, 1973.
2. J. Bierbrauer, K. Gopalakrishnan and D.R. Stinson, Orthogonal arrays, resilient functions, error correcting codes and linear programming bounds. http://bibd.unl.edu/~stinson/. To appear in *SIAM Journal on Discrete Mathematics*. Also, In *Advances in Cryptology — CRYPTO '94 Proceedings, Lecture Notes in Computer Science* 839, pages 247–256. Springer-Verlag, 1994.
3. F.Chabaud and S.Vaudenay. Links between differential and linear cryptanalysis. In *Advances in Cryptology — EUROCRYPT '94 Proceedings, Lecture Notes in Computer Science* 950, pages 356–365. Springer-Verlag, 1995.
4. B. Chor, O. Goldreich, J. Hastad, J. Freidmann, S. Rudich, and R. Smolensky. The bit extraction problem or t-resilient functions. In *Proceedings of the 26th IEEE Annual Symposium on Foundations of Computer Science*, pages 396–407, 1985.
5. T.W. Cusick. Boolean functions satisfying a higher order strict avalanche criterion. In *Advances in Cryptology — EUROCRYPT '93 Proceedings, Lecture Notes in Computer Science* 765, pages 102–117. Springer-Verlag, 1994.

6. R. Forré. The strict avalanche criterion : spectral properties of Boolean functions and an extend definition. In *Advances in Cryptology — CRYPTO '88 Proceedings*, *Lecture Notes in Computer Science* 403, pages 450–468. Springer-Verlag, 1990.

7. N. Hartsfield and G. Ringel. *Pearls in Graph Theory*. Academic Press.

8. S. Lloyd. Counting functions ratifying a higher order strict avalanche criterion. In *Advances in Cryptology — EUROCRYPT '89 Proceedings*, volume 434 of *Lecture Notes in Computer Science*, pages 63–74. Springer-Verlag, 1990.

9. S. Lloyd. Counting binary functions with certain cryptographic properties. *Journal of Cryptology*, **5**:107–131, 1992.

10. S. Lloyd. Balance, uncorrelatedness and the strict avalanche criterion. *Discrete Applied Mathematics*, **41**:223–233, 1993.

11. S. Lidl and Niederreiter. Finite Fields, Encyclopedia of Mathematics and Its Applications 20, Corollary 7.39. *Cambridge University Press*, 1983.

12. F. J. MacWilliams and N. J. A. Sloane. The theory of error-correcting codes. *North-Holland Publishing Company*, 1977.

13. K. Nyberg. Perfect nonlinear S-boxes. In *Advances in Cryptology — EUROCRYPT '91 Proceedings*, *Lecture Notes in Computer Science* 547, pages 378–386. Springer-Verlag, 1991.

14. L. O'Cornnor. An upper bound on the number of functions satisfying the strict avalanche criterion. *Information Processing Letters*, **52**:325–327, 1994.

15. B. Preneel, R. Govaerts, and J. Vandewalle. Boolean functions satisfying higher order propagation criteria. In *Advances in Cryptology — EUROCRYPT '91 Proceedings*, *Lecture Notes in Computer Science* 547, pages 141–152. Springer-Verlag, 1991.

16. B. Preneel, W. Van Leekwijck, L. Van Linden, R. Govaerts, and J. Vandewalle. Propagation characteristics of Boolean functions. In *Advances in Cryptology — EUROCRYPT '90 Proceedings*, *Lecture Notes in Computer Science* 473, pages 161–173. Springer-Verlag, 1991.

17. J. Seberry, X. M. Zhang, and Y. Zheng. Highly nonlinear balanced Boolean functions satisfying high degree propagation criterion. Technical Report No. 93-1, Department of Computer Science, The University of Wollongong, Australia, 1993.

18. J. Seberry, X. M. Zhang, and Y. Zheng. Systematic generation of cryptographically robust S-boxes. In *Proceedings of the First ACM Conference on Computer and Communications Security*, pages 171–182. The Association for Computing Machinery, November 1993.

19. J. Seberry, X. M. Zhang, and Y. Zheng. Improving the strict avalanche characteristics of cryptographic functions. *Information Processing Letters*, **50**:37–41, 1994.

20. J. Seberry, X. M. Zhang, and Y. Zheng. Relationships among nonlinearity criteria. In *Advances in Cryptology — EUROCRYPT '94 Proceedings*, *Lecture Notes in Computer Science* 950, pages 376–388. Springer-Verlag, 1995.

21. A. F. Webster and S. E. Tavares. On the design of S-boxes. In *Advances in Cryptology — CRYPTO '85 Proceedings*, *Lecture Notes in Computer Science* 218, pages 523–534. Springer-Verlag, 1986.

A   Proof of Proposition 6 [1]

A.1   CASE 1: n is even

Number the vertices $0, 1, 2, \ldots, n-1$ and place the vertices as shown in Fig. 2.

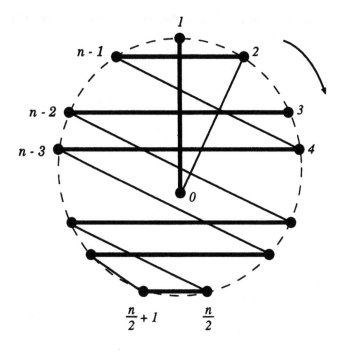

Fig. 2. perfect matchings of K_n

Let the first perfect matching (i.e., the edges of the first color) be

$$[0, 1], [2, n - 1], [3, n - 2], \ldots, [\frac{n}{2}, \frac{n}{2} + 1] .$$

These edges are the dark edges in Fig. 2.

By adding 1 modulo n to the index of each vertex except vertex 0 in the above matching, we obtain another perfect matching. This operation can be performed $n - 1$ times, and each time a new color is assigned to the resulting matching. No edge is colored twice, because each time the color edges form a different angle with the horizontal. However, each edge of K_n has been colored, and therefore $q(K_n) = n - 1$.

A.2   CASE2: n is odd

Consider the graph G' formed from K_n by adding a vertex x_0 that is joined to each vertex of K_n. From Case 1 above, we have

$$q(G') = (n + 1) - 1 = n .$$

Thus the edges of K_n can be colored with n colors. The edges of K_n cannot be colored with $n - 1$ colors, because then each color would correspond to a perfect matching, and a graph with odd order has no perfect matching. Thus

$$q(K_n) = n \ .$$

On the Correlation Immune Functions and Their Nonlinearity

Seongtaek Chee†, Sangjin Lee†, Daiki Lee†, Soo Hak Sung‡

† Section 0710, Yusong P.O. Box 106
Electronics and Telecommunications Research Institute
Taejon, 305-600, KOREA
E-mail : chee@dingo.etri.re.kr

‡ Dept. of Applied Math., Paichai Univ.
Doma 2 Dong, Seo Gu
Taejon, 302-735, KOREA

Abstract. In this paper, we consider the relationship between the nonlinearity and correlation immunity of functions suggested by P. Camion *et al.* For the analysis of such functions, we present a simple method of generating the same set of functions, which makes us possible to construct correlation immune functions with controllable correlation immunity and nonlinearity.

1 Introduction

Cryptographic Boolean functions paly an important role in the design of a nonlinear filter function or a nonlinear combiner in stream cipher as well as a primitive logic in block cipher.

In particular, the function whose output leaks no information about its input values is of great importance. Such functions called correlation immune functions were firstly introduced by T. Siegenthaler[4]. Since then the topic has been an active research area[1, 2, 3, 5, 6] and many stream ciphers have employed the correlation immune functions. P. Camion *et al.* [1] presented a method for constructing balanced correlation immune functions. J. Seberry *et al.* [3] discussed the nonlinearity and propagation characteristics of such functions.

The objective of this paper is to discuss the realtionship between the correlation immunity and nonlinearity of functions generated by P. Camion *et al.*'s method. In order to achieve such a goal, we present a simple method of generating the same set of functions, which makes us possible to construct correlation immune functions with controllable correlation immunity and nonlinearity.

The rest of this paper is organized as follows. Section 2 introduces notations and definitions that are needed in this paper. In Section 3, we describe our method for constructing correlation immune functions and discuss some properties for the generated functions that were already analyzed in [3], but rather complicated than ours. In the same section, we suggest a condition for obtaining maximal nonlinearity of the function. In Section 4, we present a systematic method to obtain the correlation immune functions described in Section 3 and give an example. Section 5 describes the relationship between the correlation immunity and nonlinearity of functions discussed in Section 4. In particular, we discuss the range of the correlation immunity with maximal nonlinearity. The conclusions are addressed in Section 6.

2 Basic Definitions

Let $\mathbb{Z}_2^n$ be the n-dimensional vector space with the binary n-tuples of elements $x = (x_1, \cdots, x_n)$. For $a = (a_1, \cdots, a_n)$, $b = (b_1, \cdots, b_n)$ in $\mathbb{Z}_2^n$, $a \cdot b = a_1 b_1 \oplus \cdots \oplus a_n b_n$ is the inner product of two vectors.

A function is said to be balanced if $\#\{x|f(x) = 0\} = \#\{x|f(x) = 1\}$. A function on $\mathbb{Z}_2^n$ is k-th order correlation immune($1 \leq k \leq n$) if $f(x)$ is statistically independent of any subset of k input variables $x_{i_1}, \cdots, x_{i_k} (1 \leq i_1 < \cdots < i_k \leq n)$ and k is called the correlation immunity of f. The algebraic normal form of f is as follows:

$$f(x_1, \cdots, x_n) = a_0 \oplus a_1 x_1 \oplus \cdots \oplus a_n x_n$$
$$\oplus a_{12} x_1 x_2 \oplus \cdots \oplus a_{n-1,n} x_{n-1} x_n$$
$$\oplus a_{123} x_1 x_2 x_3 \oplus \cdots \oplus a_{n-2,n-1,n} x_{n-2} x_{n-1} x_n$$
$$\vdots$$
$$\oplus a_{12 \cdots n} x_1 x_2 \cdots x_n.$$

The algebraic degree of a Boolean function, denoted by $deg(f)$, is defined as the maximum of the order of its product terms that have a nonzero coefficient in the algebraic normal form. A Boolean function with $deg(f) \leq 1$ i.e., $f(x) = a_0 \oplus a_1 x_1 \oplus \cdots \oplus a_n x_n$ is said to be affine. In particular, if $a_0 = 0$, it is said to be linear.

For two Boolean functions f and g, we define the distance between f and g by $d(f, g) = \#\{x|f(x) \neq g(x)\}$. The minimum distance between f and the set of all affine functions Λ, i.e., $min_{\lambda \in \Lambda} d(f, \lambda)$ is called the nonlinearity of f and denoted by N_f. In most cases, it will be more convenient to deal with $\hat{f}(x) = (-1)^{f(x)}$ that takes values in $\{-1, 1\}$.

The definitions of balancedness, correlation immunity and nonlinearity are derived from the Walsh-Hadamard transforms.

Definition 1. Let f be a Boolean function with domain the vector space $\mathbb{Z}_2^n$. The Walsh-Hadamard transform of $\hat{f}$ is the real-valued function $\hat{F}$ over the vector space $\mathbb{Z}_2^n$ defined as

$$\hat{F}(w) = \sum_x \hat{f}(x)(-1)^{w \cdot x}.$$

Lemma 2. *The Boolean function f is balanced iff $\hat{F}(0) = 0$.*

Lemma 3. [6] *For a Boolean function* f, f *is k-th order correlation immune iff* $\hat{F}(a) = 0$ *holds for any a with $1 \leq wt(a) \leq k$.*

Lemma 4. *Let f be a Boolean function of n variables. The nonlinearity of f is*

$$N_f = 2^{n-1} - \frac{1}{2} \max_w |\hat{F}(w)|.$$

3 Design of Correlation Immune functions

In this section, we present a method of construction correlation immune functions.

Theorem 5. *Let n, k and m be three positive integers with $n \geq 4$, $1 \leq k \leq n-3$, $1 \leq m < n-k$ and $S_{n,k,m} = \{A_y \in \mathbb{Z}_2^{n-m} \mid wt(A_y) \geq k+1,\ y \in \mathbb{Z}_2^m\}$. And, for any $a \in S_{n,k,m}$, let $t_a = \#\{y \in \mathbb{Z}_2^m \mid A_y = a\}$ and $t = \max_a t_a$. We now define a Boolean function $f : \mathbb{Z}_2^n \to \mathbb{Z}_2$ by*

$$f(y, x) = A_y \cdot x, \tag{1}$$

where $y = (y_1, \cdots, y_m) \in \mathbb{Z}_2^m$, $x = (x_1, \cdots, x_{n-m}) \in \mathbb{Z}_2^{n-m}$. Then the followings are hold:
  (i) *f is balanced.*
  (ii) *f is k-th order correlation immune.*
  (iii) *$N_f = 2^{n-1} - t2^{n-m-1}$.*
  (iv) *Let $A_y(i)$ be the i-th component of A_y.*
    If $\bigoplus_y A_y(i) = 1$ for some i $(1 \leq i \leq n - m)$, then $\deg(f) = m + 1$.

Proof. (i) Since $wt(A_y) \geq k + 1$, we have $A_y \neq 0$. Thus $\sum_x (-1)^{A_y \cdot x} = 0$. Therefore, we have

$$\hat{F}(0) = \sum_{y,x} (-1)^{f(y,x)} = \sum_{y,x} (-1)^{A_y \cdot x} = \sum_y \sum_x (-1)^{A_y \cdot x} = 0.$$

By Lemma 2, f is balanced.

(ii) For any $(b, a) \in \mathbb{Z}_2^n$ with $1 \leq wt(b, a) \leq k$, we note that

$$\begin{aligned}
\hat{F}(b, a) &= \sum_{y,x} (-1)^{f(y,x)} (-1)^{(b,a) \cdot (y,x)} \\
&= \sum_{y,x} (-1)^{A_y \cdot x} (-1)^{b \cdot y \oplus a \cdot x} \\
&= \sum_y (-1)^{b \cdot y} \sum_x (-1)^{(A_y \oplus a) \cdot x}.
\end{aligned} \tag{2}$$

Since $0 \leq wt(a) \leq k$ and $wt(A_y) \geq k+1$, we have $a \oplus A_y \neq 0$. Thus $\sum_x (-1)^{(A_y \oplus a) \cdot x} = 0$. Therefore, by eq. (2), we have $\hat{F}(b, a) = 0$. By Lemma 3, f is k-th order correlation immune.

(iii) By eq. (2), then

$$\hat{F}(b,a) = \sum_y (-1)^{b \cdot y} \sum_x (-1)^{(A_y \oplus a) \cdot x}$$

$$= 2^{n-m} \sum_{\{y \mid A_y = a\}} (-1)^{b \cdot y}. \tag{3}$$

Hence $\max_{b,a} |\hat{F}(b,a)| \leq 2^{n-m} \max_a t_a = t 2^{n-m}$. If we let $b = 0$ in eq. (3), we have

$$\hat{F}(0,a) = 2^{n-m} \#\{y \mid A_y = a\} = 2^{n-m} t_a.$$

It follows that

$$\max_{b,a} |\hat{F}(b,a)| \geq \max_a |\hat{F}(0,a)| = 2^{n-m} \max_a t_a = t 2^{n-m}.$$

Therefore, $\max |\hat{F}(b,a)| = t 2^{n-m}$. By Lemma 4, $N_f = 2^{n-1} - t 2^{n-m-1}$.

(iv) We note that

$$f(y,x) = (y_1 \oplus 1)(y_2 \oplus 1) \cdots (y_m \oplus 1) A_0 \cdot x$$
$$\oplus (y_1 \oplus 1)(y_2 \oplus 1) \cdots y_m A_1 \cdot x$$
$$\vdots$$
$$\oplus y_1 y_2 \cdots y_m A_{2^m - 1} \cdot x.$$

If $\oplus_y A_y(i) = 1$, then in the above expression, the term $y_1 y_2 \cdots y_m x_i$ is not cancelled. Hence $deg(f) = m + 1$. $\quad\square$

For convenience, we denote $C_n^m(k)$ by the set of Boolean functions generated by Theorem 5.

Clearly, for any $r : \mathbb{Z}_2^m \to \mathbb{Z}$, if we define $f(y,x) = A_y \cdot x \oplus r(y)$, then we can obtain the same results except (iii). The similar results are studied by in [3]. The main advantage of our method is that it is simple enough to analyze the relationship between correlation immunity and nonlinearity. Especially, our method presents the exact nonlinearity, on the other hand the lower bound of it was presented in [3]. This fact causes us to study which conditions make the nonlinearity maximal.

The following theorem is useful to find conditions for maximal nonlinearity of function in $C_n^m(k)$.

Theorem 6. *For given positive integers $n, k(n \geq 4, 1 \leq k \leq n - 3)$, and any positive integer t, let l_t be the smallest l such that*

$$t\left\{\binom{l}{k+1} + \binom{l}{k+2} + \cdots + \binom{l}{l}\right\} \geq 2^{n-l},$$

then we have $2^{l_1} \leq t 2^{l_t}$. i.e., $\min\{t 2^{l_t} \mid t = 1, 2, \cdots\} = 2^{l_1}$.

To prove Theorem 6, we need some lemmas. The following lemma is well-known, and we omit its proof.

Lemma 7. *For positive integers n, k, the following holds.*

$$\binom{n}{k} = \binom{n-1}{k} + \binom{n-1}{k-1}.$$

Lemma 8. *For positive integers n, k, the following holds.*

$$2\left\{\binom{n}{k+1} + \binom{n}{k+2} + \cdots + \binom{n}{n}\right\} \le \binom{n+1}{k+1} + \binom{n+1}{k+2} + \cdots + \binom{n+1}{n+1}.$$

Proof. By Lemma 7, we have

$$\binom{n+1}{k+1} + \binom{n+1}{k+2} + \cdots + \binom{n+1}{n+1}$$

$$= \left\{\binom{n}{k+1} + \binom{n}{k}\right\} + \left\{\binom{n}{k+2} + \binom{n}{k+1}\right\} + \cdots + \left\{\binom{n}{n} + \binom{n}{n-1}\right\} + 1$$

$$= \left\{\binom{n}{k+1} + \binom{n}{k+2} + \cdots + \binom{n}{n}\right\} + \left\{\binom{n}{k} + \binom{n}{k+1} + \cdots + \binom{n}{n-1}\right\} + 1$$

$$= 2\left\{\binom{n}{k+1} + \binom{n}{k+2} + \cdots + \binom{n}{n}\right\} + \binom{n}{k}.$$

$\square$

Lemma 9. *If $l \ge l_t$, then*

$$t\left\{\binom{l}{k+1} + \binom{l}{k+2} + \cdots + \binom{l}{l}\right\} \ge 2^{n-l}$$

where l_t is the value defined in Theorem 6.

Proof. By the definition of l_t,

$$t\left\{\binom{l_t}{k+1} + \binom{l_t}{k+2} + \cdots + \binom{l_t}{l_t}\right\} \ge 2^{n-l_t}.$$

Since $l \ge l_t$, we have

$$t\left\{\binom{l}{k+1} + \binom{l}{k+2} + \cdots + \binom{l}{l_t} + \cdots + \binom{l}{l}\right\}$$

$$\ge t\left\{\binom{l_t}{k+1} + \binom{l_t}{k+2} + \cdots + \binom{l_t}{l_t}\right\}$$

$$\ge 2^{n-l_t} \ge 2^{n-l}.$$

$\square$

Now, we can prove Theorem 6.

Proof of Theorem 6. If $t = 1$, then $t2^{l_t} = 2^{l_1}$. So lets show that $t2^{l_t} \geq 2^{l_1}$ when $t \geq 2$. If $t \geq 2$, then there is $p(p \geq 1)$ such that $2^p \leq t < 2^{p+1}$. If $l_1 - p \leq l_t$, then

$$t2^{l_t} \geq t2^{l_1-p} \geq 2^p 2^{l_1-p} = 2^{l_1}.$$

Hence if $l_1 - p \leq l_t$, the proof is completed. It remains to show that the case $l_t < l_1 - p$ is not happen. Suppose $l_t < l_1 - p$, i.e., $l_t \leq l_1 - p - 1$. Then, by Lemma 9,

$$t\left\{ \binom{l_1-p-1}{k+1} + \binom{l_1-p-1}{k+2} + \cdots + \binom{l_1-p-1}{l_1-p-1} \right\} \geq 2^{n-(l_1-p-1)}. \quad (4)$$

And, by Lemma 8,

$$t\left\{ \binom{l_1-p-1}{k+1} + \binom{l_1-p-1}{k+2} + \cdots + \binom{l_1-p-1}{l_1-p-1} \right\}$$
$$\leq 2^{p+1}\left\{ \binom{l_1-p-1}{k+1} + \binom{l_1-p-1}{k+2} + \cdots + \binom{l_1-p-1}{l_1-p-1} \right\}$$
$$\leq 2^p\left\{ \binom{l_1-p}{k+1} + \binom{l_1-p}{k+2} + \cdots + \binom{l_1-p}{l_1-p} \right\}. \quad (5)$$

By applying Lemma 8 to the eq. (5), we obtain

$$t\left\{ \binom{l_1-p-1}{k+1} + \binom{l_1-p-1}{k+2} + \cdots + \binom{l_1-p-1}{l_1-p-1} \right\}$$
$$\leq 2\left\{ \binom{l_1-1}{k+1} + \binom{l_1-1}{k+2} + \cdots + \binom{l_1-1}{l_1-1} \right\}.$$

Hence by eq. (4),

$$2\left\{ \binom{l_1-1}{k+1} + \binom{l_1-1}{k+2} + \cdots + \binom{l_1-1}{l_1-1} \right\} \geq 2^{n-(l_1-p-1)}.$$

Since $p \geq 1$, we have

$$\binom{l_1-1}{k+1} + \binom{l_1-1}{k+2} + \cdots + \binom{l_1-1}{l_1-1} \geq 2^{n-l_1+p} \geq 2^{n-(l_1-1)}.$$

By the definition of l_1, $l_1 \leq l_1 - 1$. But this is a contradiction. $\square$

The following theorem is one of major results of this paper.

Theorem 10. *For $f \in C_n^m(k)$, the maximal nonlinearity of f is $N_f = 2^{n-1} - 2^{l_1-1}$ and it can be obtained if $m = n - l_1$, $t = 1$, where l_1 is a value defined in Theorem 6.*

Proof. By the definition of A_y, t and m satisfy the following inequality:

$$t\left\{\binom{n-m}{k+1} + \binom{n-m}{k+2} + \cdots + \binom{n-m}{n-m}\right\} \geq 2^m. \tag{6}$$

In eq. (6), if we substitute $n - m$ with l, then

$$t\left\{\binom{l}{k+1} + \binom{l}{k+2} + \cdots + \binom{l}{l}\right\} \geq 2^{n-l} \tag{7}$$

and $N_f = 2^{n-1} - t2^{l-1}$ by Theorem 5-(iii). Hence for each $t(t = 1, 2, \cdots)$, the maximum nonlinearity is obtained if l is the smallest value satisfying eq. (7). That is, $\max_m N_f = \max_l N_f = 2^{n-1} - t2^{l_t-1}$. Therefore, by Theorem 6,

$$\max_{m,t} N_f = \max_{l,t} N_f = 2^{n-1} - \min_t t2^{l_t-1} = 2^{n-1} - 2^{l_1-1}.$$

$\square$

4 Method for constructing correlation immune function with controllable nonlinearity

In this section, using Theorem 10, we suggest a method for constructing correlation immune function with controllable nonlinearity .

Method for constructing k-th order correlation immune function with nonlinearity $N_f = 2^{n-1} - 2^{l_1-1}$

Input. $n(n \geq 4$; the number of input variables of Boolean function),
   $k(1 \leq k \leq n - 3$; correlation immunity)
Step 1. For $k + 1 \leq l \leq n$, find the smallest l satisfying

$$\binom{l}{k+1} + \binom{l}{k+2} + \cdots + \binom{l}{l} \geq 2^{n-l} \tag{8}$$

and let such a value l_1.
Step 2. Choose 2^{n-l_1} vectors $A_0, A_1, \cdots, A_{2^{n-l_1}-1}$ in $\mathbb{Z}_2^{l_1}$ with weight greater than or equal to $k + 1$.
Step 3. Define $f : \mathbb{Z}_2^n \to \mathbb{Z}_2$ by

$$f(y_1, \cdots, y_{n-l_1}, x_1, \cdots, x_{l_1}) = f(y, x) = A_y \cdot x.$$

We now discuss the above method step by step. First, for the input, since a function with algebraic degree 0 is constant, it is not balanced. And a function with algebraic degree 1, i.e., an affine function is of nonlinearity 0. Moreover, the sum of correlation immunity k and algebraic degree d of a function f is less than or equal to the number of input variables n and in particular if f is balanced, $k + d \leq n - 1$ [4]. Hence, for a balanced, nonlinear and correlation immune function, we have

$$k + d \leq n - 1, k \geq 1, d \geq 2.$$

To satisfy above requirement, $1 \leq k \leq n - 1 - d \leq n - 3$ and the smallest n is 4. The second, in **Step 1**, by the above, $k + 2 \leq n - 1$. Hence

$$\binom{n-1}{k+1} + \binom{n-1}{k+2} + \cdots + \binom{n-1}{n-1} \geq \binom{n-1}{k+1} + \binom{n-1}{k+2} \geq 2.$$

Hence we can find l_1 ($l_1 \leq n - 1$) satisfying eq. (8) in **Step 1**.
The third, in **Step 2**, the number of vectors in $\mathbb{Z}_2^{l_1}$ with weight greater than or equal to $k + 1$ is

$$\binom{l_1}{k+1} + \binom{l_1}{k+2} + \cdots + \binom{l_1}{l_1}$$

and it is greater than or equal to 2^{n-l_1} by **Step 1**. Hence we can choose 2^{n-l_1} vectors with weight greater than or equal to $k + 1$.
The function defined in **Step 3** fulfills the requirements of Theorem 10, so the balanced k-th order correlation immune function in **Step 3** has of nonlinearity $N_f = 2^{n-1} - 2^{l_1-1}$.

Example 1. We construct a balanced and nonlinear 1st order correlation immune function $f : \mathbb{Z}_2^7 \rightarrow \mathbb{Z}_2$.

Input : $n = 7, k = 1$
Step 1 : Since $\binom{3}{2} + \binom{3}{3} \not\geq 2^{7-3}$ and $\binom{4}{2} + \binom{4}{3} + \binom{4}{4} \geq 2^{7-4}$, we have $l_1 = 4$.
Step 2 : Choose 8 vectors in $A_i \in \mathbb{Z}_2^4$ with $wt(A_i) \geq 2$, say

$$\begin{aligned}
A_0 &= (1,1,0,0) \quad A_1 = (1,0,1,0) \\
A_2 &= (1,0,0,1) \quad A_3 = (0,1,1,0) \\
A_4 &= (0,1,0,1) \quad A_5 = (0,0,1,1) \\
A_6 &= (1,1,1,0) \quad A_7 = (1,1,0,1).
\end{aligned}$$

Step 3 : Define $f : \mathbb{Z}_2^7 \rightarrow \mathbb{Z}_2$ as follows.

$$\begin{aligned}
f(y,x) = A_y \cdot x =\ & (y_1 \oplus 1)(y_2 \oplus 1)(y_3 \oplus 1)(x_1 \oplus x_2) \\
& \oplus (y_1 \oplus 1)(y_2 \oplus 1)y_3(x_1 \oplus x_3) \oplus (y_1 \oplus 1)y_2(y_3 \oplus 1)(x_1 \oplus x_4) \\
& \oplus (y_1 \oplus 1)y_2 y_3(x_2 \oplus x_3) \oplus y_1(y_2 \oplus 1)(y_3 \oplus 1)(x_2 \oplus x_4) \\
& \oplus y_1(y_2 \oplus 1)y_3(x_3 \oplus x_4) \oplus y_1 y_2(y_3 \oplus 1)(x_1 \oplus x_2 \oplus x_3) \\
& \oplus y_1 y_2 y_3(x_1 \oplus x_2 \oplus x_4).
\end{aligned}$$

Then f is balanced, 1st order correlation immune with $N_f = 2^6 - 2^3 = 56$. And, since $\bigoplus_y A_y(1) = 1, \bigoplus_y A_y(2) = 1, \bigoplus_y A_y(3) = 0, \bigoplus_y A_y(4) = 0$, by Theorem 5-(iv), $deg(f) = n - l_1 + 1 = 4$.

5 Nonlinearity and Correlation Immunity

In this section, we discuss the relationship between correlation immunity and nonlinearity of function in $C_n^m(k)$.

Lemma 11. *Let n, k, l_1 be given as Theorem 6. Then $l_1 \geq [\frac{n}{2}] + 1$.*

Proof. By the definition of l_1,

$$\binom{l_1}{k+1} + \binom{l_1}{k+2} + \cdots + \binom{l_1}{l_1} \geq 2^{n-l_1}.$$

Thus

$$2^{l_1} - 2^{n-l_1} \geq \binom{l_1}{0} + \binom{l_1}{1} + \cdots + \binom{l_1}{k}. \tag{9}$$

Since the right hand side of eq. (9) is positive, $l_1 > n - l_1$. In all, $l_1 \geq [\frac{n}{2}] + 1$. $\square$

Lemma 12. *The necessary and sufficient condition for two integers n and x satisfy the following equation is $x \leq [\frac{n+1}{2}]$.*

$$\binom{n}{x+1} + \binom{n}{x+1} + \cdots + \binom{n}{n} \geq 2^{n-1}. \tag{10}$$

Proof. If n is even, then

$$\binom{n}{\frac{n}{2}} + \binom{n}{\frac{n}{2}+1} + \cdots + \binom{n}{n} > 2^{n-1},$$

$$\binom{n}{\frac{n}{2}+1} + \binom{n}{\frac{n}{2}+2} + \cdots + \binom{n}{n} < 2^{n-1}.$$

So, eq. (10) holds if $x \leq [\frac{n+1}{2}]$. And, if n is odd, then

$$\binom{n}{\frac{n+1}{2}} + \binom{n}{\frac{n+1}{2}+1} + \cdots + \binom{n}{n} = 2^{n-1}.$$

So, eq. (10) holds if $x \leq [\frac{n+1}{2}]$. $\square$

Theorem 13. *For a Boolean function f in $C_n^m(k)$, we have $N_f \leq 2^{n-1} - 2^{[\frac{n}{2}]}$, and the equality holds if and only if k satisfies the following*

$$\begin{cases} \binom{\frac{n}{2}+1}{k+1} + \binom{\frac{n}{2}+1}{k+2} + \cdots + \binom{\frac{n}{2}+1}{\frac{n}{2}+1} \geq 2^{\frac{n}{2}-1} & \text{if } n \text{ is even,} \\ \\ k \leq [\frac{n}{4}] & \text{if } n \text{ is odd.} \end{cases}$$

Proof. By Lemma 11, since $l_1 \geq [\frac{n}{2}] + 1$, we have

$$N_f = 2^{n-1} - 2^{l_1-1} \leq 2^{n-1} - 2^{[\frac{n}{2}]}$$

and the equality holds if $l_1 = [\frac{n}{2}] + 1$. Hence by definition of l_1, equality holds if the followings are satisfied:

$$\binom{[\frac{n}{2}]+1}{k+1} + \binom{[\frac{n}{2}]+1}{k+2} + \cdots + \binom{[\frac{n}{2}]+1}{[\frac{n}{2}]+1} \geq 2^{n-([\frac{n}{2}]+1)}, \tag{11}$$

$$\binom{[\frac{n}{2}]}{k+1} + \binom{[\frac{n}{2}]}{k+2} + \cdots + \binom{[\frac{n}{2}]}{[\frac{n}{2}]} < 2^{n-[\frac{n}{2}]}. \tag{12}$$

Since eq. (12) holds for any k, equality holds if and only if eq. (11) holds. If n is odd, since the right hand side of eq. (11) is $2^{[\frac{n}{2}]}$, by Lemma 12, eq. (11) holds if and only if

$$k+1 \leq \left[\frac{[\frac{n}{2}+1+1]}{2} \right] = \left[\frac{n-1}{4} \right] + 1 = \left[\frac{n}{4} \right] + 1$$

holds, *i.e.*, $k \leq [\frac{n}{4}]$. $\qquad\square$

By Theorem 13, we can construct $[\frac{n}{4}]$-th order correlation immune functions with nonlinearity $2^{n-1} - 2^{[\frac{n}{2}]}$ if n is odd. For the case of n even, we have the following

Corollary 14. *If n is even and $N_f = 2^{n-1} - 2^{[\frac{n}{2}]}$, the approximative upper bound of the correlation immunity k in Theorem 13 is*

$$k \leq \left[\frac{n}{4} + 0.335\sqrt{\frac{n}{2} + 1} \right]. \tag{13}$$

The proof of Corollary 14 is left to appendix.

In fact, for $n = 4 \sim 100$, even, if a function has nonlinearity $N_f = 2^{n-1} - 2^{\frac{n}{2}}$, which is the maximum among functions in $C_n^m(k)$, the range of correlation immunity given in Corollary 14 is actually correct except only for the case $n = 38$. In that case, eq. (13) gives $k \leq 10$, which is, in fact, $k \leq 11$.

It is natural to have a question what is the range of k if the nonlinearity of function in $C_n^m(k)$ is fixed. The following corollary, the proof of it is similar to that of Corollary 14, solves the problem.

Corollary 15. *If the function in $C_n^m(k)$ has nonlinearity $N_f = 2^{n-1} - 2^{l_1-1}$, then the approximative range of the correlation immunity k is as follows:*

$$\left[\frac{l_1 - 1}{2} + \frac{1}{2} + \frac{\sqrt{l_1 - 1}}{2} z_{2^{n-2(l_1-1)}} \right] \leq k \leq \left[\frac{l_1 - 1}{2} + \frac{1}{2}\sqrt{l_1} z_{2^{n-2l_1}} \right],$$

where $P(Z \geq z_\alpha) = \alpha$ and $Z \sim N(0,1)$.

For the case that if a function in $C_n^m(k)$ has maximum correlation immunity, we have the following

Corollary 16. *Let $k = n - 3$. Then the maximum nonlinearity of Boolean function $f \in C_n^m(k)$ is $N_f = 2^{n-1} - 2^{n-2} = 2^{n-2}$.*

The Fig. 1. represents the relationhip between correlation immunity and nonlinearity of functions in $C_n^m(k)$ for $n = 22$. Since the nonlinearity is too big to investigate its behavior precisely as k increases, we present the relationship between the correlation immunity and l_1, which determines the nonlinearity in Fig. 2.

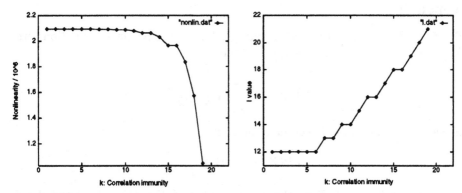

Fig. 1. Relationship between nonlinearity and correlation immunity

Fig. 2. Relationship between l_1 and correlation immunity

From the above two corollaries, we can construct Boolean functions with controllable nonlinearity and correlation immunity. Even though the range in the Corollaries 14 and 15 are approximative, the error range was verified small enough by our simulations.

6 Conclusions

The main results of this paper are associated with studying the relationship between correlation immunity and nonlinearity of functions in [1, 3]. Such results were possible by making the generating method simple and clear enough to discuss several properties. This paper may provide us with a new avenue towards studying between correlation immunity and nonlinearity in general correlation immune functions.

References

1. P. Camion, C. Carlet, P. Charpin and N. Sendrier, "On correlation-immune functions", *Advances in Cryptology - CRYPTO'91*, Springer-Verlag, pp. 86–100, 1992.

2. W. Meier and O. Staffelbach, "Nonlinearity criteria for cryptographic functions", *Advances in Cryptology - EUROCRYPT'89*, Springer-Verlag, pp. 549–562, 1990.
3. J. Seberry, X. M. Zhang and Y. Zheng, "On constructions and nonlinearity of correlation immune functions", *Advances in Cryptology - EUROCRYPT'93*, Springer-Verlag, pp. 181–199, 1994.
4. T. Siegenthaler, "Correlation immunity of non-linear combining functions for cryptographic applications", *IEEE Trans. on Inf. Th.*, **IT-30**, pp. 776–780, 1984.
5. Y. Xian, "Correlation-immunity of Boolean functions", *Electronics Letters*, **23**, pp. 1335–1336, 1987.
6. G. Xiao and J. Massey, "A spectral characterization of correlation-immune combining functions", *IEEE Trans. on Inf. Th.*, **IT-34**, pp. 569–571, 1988.

Appendix

Proof of Corollary 14. If a random variable X has the binomial distribution with parameters n and $\frac{1}{2}$, i.e., $X \sim b(n, \frac{1}{2})$, then

$$P(X \geq x) = \sum_{k=x}^{n} \binom{n}{k} (\frac{1}{2})^n.$$

Hence the condition for Theorem 13 holds if

$$P(X \geq k+1) \geq \frac{1}{4},$$

where $X \sim b(\frac{n}{2} + 1, \frac{1}{2})$. Then the following holds if $X \sim b(\frac{n}{2} + 1, \frac{1}{2})$ and $\frac{n}{2} + 1$ is large enough[1].

$$P(X \leq k) \simeq P(Z \leq \frac{k - \frac{\frac{n}{2}+1}{2} + \frac{1}{2}}{\frac{1}{2}\sqrt{\frac{n}{2}+1}}),$$

where $Z \sim N(0,1)$. Since $P(Z \leq 0.67) = 0.7486 \simeq \frac{3}{4}$, we have

$$\frac{k - \frac{\frac{n}{2}+1}{2} + \frac{1}{2}}{\frac{1}{2}\sqrt{\frac{n}{2}+1}} \leq 0.67.$$

Since $k \leq \frac{n}{4} + 0.335\sqrt{\frac{n}{2}+1}$, we have

$$k \leq \left[\frac{n}{4} + 0.335\sqrt{\frac{n}{2}+1}\right].$$

$\square$

---

[1] In usual case, we assume that $(\frac{n}{2}+1)\frac{1}{2} > 5$, i.e., $\frac{n}{2}+1 > 10$.

How to Date Blind Signatures

Masayuki Abe
abe@isl.ntt.jp

Eiichiro Fujisaki
fujisaki@sucaba.isl.ntt.jp

Tel: +81 468 59 2570 Fax: +81 468 59 3858
NTT Information and Communication Systems Laboratories
Nippon Telegraph and Telephone Corporation
1-2356 Take, Yokosuka-shi, Kanagawa, 238-03 Japan

Abstract. A blind signature provides perfect confidentiality to a message and signature pair. Due to this feature, the blind signature has one downside; the signer can not assure himself that the blinded message accurately contains the information he desires. In a practical sense, it is essential for the signer to include some term of validity in the signing message to prevent abusing. Of course the term must not violate the confidentiality of the message. This paper discusses partial blinding of a signed message. We consider RSA and it is proved that forging the proposed scheme by multiple signing is as difficult as breaking RSA. The strategy can be also applied to those blind signature schemes that use a trapdoor function. An electronic cash system is shown as an application of the proposed scheme. Unlike most privacy-protected electronic cash system, it successfully minimizes the growth of the bank's database.

1 Introduction

The blind signature, first introduced by D.Chaum in [1], is a scheme that yields a signature and message pair whose information does not leak to the signer. The scheme was implemented using RSA. Several blind signature schemes [2] have been developed since then and it has been proven that blind signatures could be realized by using any commutative random self-reducible problem [3].

Due to its confidentiality, blind signatures have been mainly used for electronic cash protocols [4,5,6,7,8] as a tool to protect customer's privacy.

In these protocols, the *personal information* which distinguishes messages or message holders must be kept from the signer's view. However, the signer must assure himself that the message contains accurate information without seeing it. The well known Cut and Choose mythology [4] introduced by D.Chaum can solve this problem. However, the vast amount of data needed to obtain sufficient security spoils its efficiency. S.Brands proposed a restrictive blind signature in [6] as a part of an electronic cash protocol. In his scheme, the signer signs a message which contains message holder's public key as a message holder can blind it only to a restricted form. A verifier checks the signer's signature, and then requests the message holder to endorse the transaction by signing with the secret key behind the public key in the message. If the message does not contain the correct public key, the endorsement fails. This scheme is believed to provide one solution for including personal information in an application where the customer must prove possession of the authorized secret to the verifier without showing the secret.

Another kind of check is the information that must be clearly indicated to the signer to check its validity. It is the *common information* among the players, of which the proof of possession is insufficient. One example is the term of signature validity. If a signature is not dated, it lasts as long as the signer's key lasts. This might be a problem in some applications. So, in practice, a way of dating the blind signature is needed. The other example, from an electronic cash scheme, is the amount of the payment (or a coin). It must be clearly checked between a bank, a customer, and a shop. Since the perfect confidentiality makes it difficult to include common information in the message, it is applied to the signer's key so that a key represents a piece of common information. Unfortunately, this approach narrows the variation of the common information because key management becomes too complex.

This paper proposes a partially blinded signature scheme where a part of the message is kept in the clear while the rest is kept in secret. Section 2 discusses the basic idea. An RSA-based scheme is developed in section 3. Security of the scheme and the possibility of applying it to other signature schemes are also discussed in section 3. In section 4, an electronic cash system that minimizes the size of the bank's database is shown as an application of the scheme.

2 Basic Idea

In order to make our goal clear, the blind signature scheme should be described.

Let x and $f(x)$ be the signer's private key and public key, respectively. $S(x, m)$ is the signer's signature to message m with private key x. The set $\{f(x), m, S(x, m)\}$ satisfies the verification equation $V(f(x), m, S(x, m))$.

Let $B(m, r)$ be a blinded message which is statistically or perfectly indistinguishable from m as long as blinding factor r is not revealed. Similarly, let $U(S, r')$ be an unblinded signature which is statistically or perfectly indistinguishable from S as long as blinding factor r' is not revealed.

The blind signature protocol is described as below.

(1) The sender sends a blinded message $B(m, r)$ to the signer.

(2) The signer signs the message with his secret key, and then sends the signature $S(x, B(m, r))$ to the sender.

(3) The sender checks if the signature satisfies the verifying function. Then unblinds the signature by calculating $U(S(x, B(m, r)), r')$ which is equal to $S(x, m)$. She then sends the unblinded signature and the message to the verifier.

(4) The verifier checks that the unblinded signature pair satisfies the verifying function.

Our goal is to add a constant c as common information to both the blinded signature triple and the unblinded one. Accordingly, the partially blinded signature set is $\{f(x), c, B(m,r), S(x,c,B(m,r))\}$ and the unblinded signature set is $\{f(x), c, m, S(x,c,m)\}$.

Moreover, there are two conditions:

(1) no one can forge c.

(2) no information except c can be transmitted from the signer to the verifier.

To follow the first condition, c must not work with $B(m,r)$ in the signing function. If not, the effect of c to the signature can be cancelled by unblinding. Thus the constant must work outside the scope of blinding or unblinding. However, if there exists an inverse signing function involving c, it is still easy for the sender to cancel c's effect and pretend c' instead.

Using a trapdoor function can solve this problem easily. Accordingly, instead of directly using c in the signing function, the signer uses the hidden constant $\bar{c}$ produced by the inverse function of the trapdoor. Since only the signer can calculate $\bar{c}$, it is hard for others to cancel $\bar{c}$'s effect from the signature. Using the trapdoor function, c works as if a part of the signer's public key. The signer opens the trapdoor backwards, and computes the corresponding secret key $x = f^{-1}(c)$.

A protocol based on RSA is developed in the next section.

3 Protocol

3.1 Description

Let c be common information whose length is $k-2$ bits. The function $\tau(c)$ calculates

$$\tau(c) = 2^{k-1} + 2h(c) + 1. \tag{1}$$

where $h(\cdot)$ is an one-way function. $\tau(c)$ is a formatting function designed to keep its domain in $2^{k-1} < \tau(c) < 2^k$ so that $\tau(c_i)$ does not divide $\tau(c_j)$ where $i \neq j$. Also, it is designed to produce odd numbers only so that it becomes relatively prime with λ. This prevents a kind of forgery by getting multiple signatures described latter. N is a product of two large primes p and q. N satisfies

$$s_i \mid \lambda \text{ for all prime } s_i \ (3 \leq s_i \leq 2^k - 1),$$

where λ is the LCM of $p-1$ and $q-1$. The prime e is an RSA public exponent which is larger than or equal to $2^k - 1$. The corresponding private key is d given by $ed = 1 \bmod \lambda$.

The partial blind signature protocol is as follows.

(1) The sender and the signer negotiate and agree on the constant c. Or it could be a common constant like the current date so that they can produce c independently.

(2) The sender randomly chooses a blind factor $R \in Z_N^*$ and blinds a message M by $Z = MR^{e\tau(c)}$, then sends Z to the signer. At this point, $e\tau(c)$ is a public key that contains common information.

(3) The signer calculates corresponding private key d_c by $d_c = 1/e\tau(c) \bmod \lambda$. His blinded signature is $\Phi = Z^{d_c} \bmod N$, and he sends it to the sender.

(4) Receiving the signature Φ, the sender recovers the signature to the bare message M by $S = \Phi/R \equiv M^{d_c} \bmod N$.

In the next subsection, we discuss the security of this protocol.

3.2 Security Considerations

Two types of cheating against the partial blind signature is considered here.

(1) The sender changes the negotiated constant c.

(2) The signer includes a hidden message to distinguish the transaction later.

First, type (1) is discussed. If an exponent $\tau(c_i)$ can be expressed by a polynomial P of any possible $\tau(c_j)$ as in

$$\tau(c_i) = P_i(\tau(c_j)), \tag{2}$$

the sender can forge the constant c. For example, let $\tau(c) = P_i(\tau(c-1)) = \tau(c-1) + 2$ as well as $\tau(\cdot)$ as is true in the previous subsection. Then the correct signature S to the message M with the constant c works as if it is also the correct signature to the message MS^2 with the constant $c-1$.

To prevent this kind of forgery, it is necessary to construct a signing message M from the intended message m through a one-way function $h(\cdot)$. The verifier then requests message m' that satisfies $MS^2 = h(m')$ that the sender can not show. As a result, the strength of the protocol against the forgery of this type depends on the strength of the specified one-way function.

Still, there is the possibility of forgery type (1) by getting multiple signatures to the same message M with different constants. Suppose the sender finds a combination of c_j which satisfies

$$S_i^{e\tau(c_i)} \equiv S_i^{\Pi e\tau(c_j)} \equiv M \bmod N \tag{3}$$

for some c_i.

The sender then gets the signature S_j to the message M with c_j. He then requests the signer to sign the previous signature S_j as the message with $c_{j'}$. By repeating this protocol for all j, the sender can obtain the signature S_j that passes verification for M with c_i.

However, once the forgery is successful, it means that the sender can cheat any constants. See the following lemma.

Lemma 1: If the sender can find a combination of c_j which satisfies equation (3) for some c_i, M and given N, he can then compute signatures for any constant c_k.

Proof 1: If the sender can find a combination of c_j which satisfies equation (3), the sender knows $\tau(c_i)$ and $\tau(c_j)$ that satisfies

$$e\tau(c_i) \equiv \prod e\tau(c_j) \bmod \lambda. \tag{4}$$

Then there exists a constant w that follows

$$e\tau(c_i) \equiv \prod e\tau(c_j) + w\lambda. \tag{5}$$

Since $\tau(\cdot)$ satisfies

$$\tau(c_i) \mid \tau(c_j) \text{ for all } i \text{ and } j \text{ where } i \neq j, \tag{6}$$

w can not be zero in equation (5).

Therefore, the sender obtains $w\lambda$ by subtracting $e\tau(c_i)$ from $\prod e\tau(c_j)$. Then by calculating $d = 1 / e\tau(c_k) \bmod w\lambda$, the sender can compute any equivalent secret exponent for any c_k.

(Q.E.D.)

The original RSA signature is to compute a signature S for some message M with a fixed secret exponent d and N. As described in lemma 1, the successful forger can compute any secret exponent including the one used for original RSA signature. So we conclude that this forgery is at least as hard as breaking the original RSA signature.

Considering the case if $\tau(c_i) = \Pi(c_j) / \Pi(c_k)$ holds, the one-way function prevents a forger to determine particular combination of c_j and c_k. Therefore as well as the former case, the strength against the forgery of this type depends on the strength of the specified one-way function. When implementing, the length of $\tau(c_i)$ should be kept long to some sort so that the possibility of collision becomes small.

There should be a discussion of the type (2) threat. Because constant c is clear to the sender and is negotiated at the beginning of or before the protocol, the signer can not include any information in c. Note that the sender must not agree to include any one-time elements in c which can distinguish the transaction.

Since the blindness holds to the message and signature sets as well as original RSA blind signature does, the signer and the verifier can not distinguish the blinded and unblinded signature sets.

The above forgery may not be inclusive for the common information. A similar discussion can be seen in [11,12]. Especially, [12] discusses some generalized RSA signature schemes which also apply the message to the exponent.

3.3 Application to other signature schemes

The reason why the RSA-based protocol uses the signer's public exponent is to ensure interoperability with the current public key certificate format based on X.509[13]. Therefore, for all theoretical intents, it is possible to omit the signer's public exponent e for simplicity. That is, the secret key is derived only from the agreed information by opening the trapdoor backward.

Once the agreed information takes over the portion of the signer's public key, it is similar to an ID-based public key system [9,10] where the key distribution center derives the signer's secret key from his well known identity while the proposed scheme derives it from the agreed information. So any ID based public key system which can construct a blind signature protocol can be used for yielding a partial blind signature protocol.

4 Application

In this section, one application of the partial blind signature to an efficient electronic cash system is discussed. Several privacy-protected electronic cash systems have been introduced, but the size of the database needed to store all the used coins must be basically infinite in order to detect double spending. This discourages bankers from putting this kind of system into practice. Against this problem, the proposed scheme is dramatically efficient as well as retaining its privacy protecting feature.

Figure 1 briefly depicts the withdrawal protocol of the limited database system. The bank's role is to issue a kind of ticket, which is exchangeable with corresponding electronic coins, receive the ticket and issue electronic coins. The other role of the bank, which is not depicted in Figure 1, is to verify paid coins.

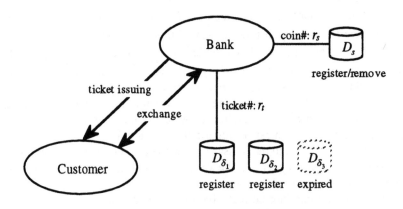

Fig. 1. Concept of Limited Database Electronic Cash System

The scenario is described below. Before the protocol starts, the bank distributes secure hash function $h(\cdot)$ and its public key modulus N used for tickets. For simplicity, the bank's public exponent is omitted from the protocol in subsection 3.1. Correspondingly, the public key $\{e_0, N_0\}$ used for coins is distributed.

(1) Customer sends a blinded message Z as
$$Z = h(r_t)R^{\tau(\alpha\|\delta_1)} \bmod N$$
where r_t is a unique random number, α is the amount to withdraw and δ_1 is today's date.

(2) The bank calculates corresponding secret key $d_{\alpha\delta_1}$ as

$$d_{\alpha\delta_1} = 1/\tau(\alpha\|\delta_1) \bmod \lambda(N).$$

Then signs Z and returns

$$\Phi = Z^{d_{\alpha\delta_1}} R \bmod N.$$

(3) The customer recovers signature S onto $h(r_t)$.

Within the specified period, the ticket S must be exchanged for electronic coins. The exchange procedure is as follows.

(4) The customer sends the ticket S and necessary data $\{\alpha, \delta_1, r_t\}$ to the bank.

(5) The bank verifies S with the corresponding verification function and check its validity with δ_1. If δ_1 has already expired, the ticket can not be accepted. Or, the bank searches database D_{δ_1} in order to make sure that r_t has not already been exchanged. If not, register r_t, issues a coin

$$C = h(\alpha, r_s, h(r_t))^{d_0} \bmod N_0,$$

and registers unique number r_s to database D_s.

When the customer uses the coin, the protocol runs as below.

(6) The customer sends C, α, r_s and r_t to a merchant.

(7) The merchant checks if they are correct as a coin, and passes them to the bank.

(8) The bank searches database D_s. If r_s is found, the bank returns OK and removes r_s from D_s. Otherwise returns NG to the merchant.

Thus the database D_s does not hold used coin entry. Moreover, after pre-determined relatively short period, for example a week, the unexchanged tickets issued on δ_i expire. The bank can then delete entire data in D_{δ_i}. These removal of the used coins and expired tickets limits the maximum size of the bank's database.

A on-line electronic cash system was discussed here, however, it is possible to make it an off-line type by replacing $h(r_t)$ with the customer's registered public key. In that case, the customer's privacy can be protected by pseudo individuality, i.e. his anonymous public key.

5 Conclusion

The concept of a new type of blind signature scheme has been introduced. The scheme allows the signer to add some information which the sender has approved beforehand into blinded signatures. It prevents the transfer of latent messages from the signer to the verifier without the sender. This new feature provides a way to stop the sender abusing the signature as well as assuring the sender that there is no hidden information which may infringe his privacy.

The scheme was successfully implemented on RSA. It has been proved that forging a signature by multiple signature attack is as hard as breaking RSA signature scheme. The possibility of applying the same strategy to ID based signature schemes has been shown.

An electronic cash system was described that uses the proposed scheme. The system prevents the unlimited growth of the bank's database, a well-known problem of previous electronic cash systems.

It remains as further work to construct a protocol that uses non-trapdoor signature schemes.

References

[1]   D.Chaum: Blind Signatures for Untraceable Payments, *Advances in Cryptology -Proceedings of Crypto'82*, Plenum Press, 1983, pp. 199-203.

[2]   D.Chaum, T.Pedersen: Wallet Databases with Observers, *Advances in Cryptology -CRYPTO'92*, LNCS 740, Springer Verlag, pp. 89-105.

[3]   T.Okamoto, K.Ohta: Divertible zero-knowledge interactive proofs and commutative random self-reducibility, *Advances in Cryptology - EUROCRYPT '89*, LNCS 434, Springer- Verlag, pp. 134-149.

[4]   D.Chaum, A.Fiat, M.Naor: Untraceable Electronic Cash, *Advances in Cryptology - CRYPTO '88*, LNCS 403, Springer Verlag, pp. 319-327.

[5]   D.Chaum: Online Cash Checks, *Advances in Cryptology - EUROCRYPT'89*, LNCS 434, Springer-Verlag, pp. 288-293.

[6]   S.Brands: Untraceable Off-line Cash in Wallets with Observers, *Advances in Cryptology - CRYPTO'93*, LNCS 773, Springer -Verlag, pp. 302-318.

[7]   T.Okamoto, K.Ohta: Universal Electronic Cash, *Advances in Cryptology - CRYPTO '91*, LNCS 576, Springer-Verlag, pp. 324-337.

[8]   T.Okamoto: An Efficient Divisible Electronic Cash Scheme, *Advances in Cryptology - CRYPTO'95*, LNCS 963, Springer, pp. 438-451.

[9]   A.Shamir: Identity-Based Cryptosystems and Signature Schemes, *Advances in Cryptology - Proceedings of CRYPTO'84*, Springer-Verlag, pp.47-53.

[10]   A.Fiat, A.Shamir: How to Prove Yourself: Practical solutions to identification and signature problems, *Advances in Cryptology- CRYPTO'86 Proceedings*, LNCS 263, Springer-Verlag, pp. 186-194.

[11]   Ganesan R., Y.Yacobi: A Secure Joint Signature and Key Exchange System, *Bellcore Technical Memorandum*, TM-ARH-1994.

[12]   W.Jonge, D.Chaum: Some Variations on RSA Signatures & Their Security, *Advances in Cryptology - Proceedings of CRYPTO'86*, Springer-Verlag, pp.49-59.

[13]   CCITT Recommendation X.509: The Directory-Authentication Framework, Consultation Committee, International Telephone and Telegraph, International Telecommunications Union, Geneva, 1989.

Provably Secure Blind Signature Schemes

David Pointcheval
David.Pointcheval@ens.fr

Jacques Stern
Jacques.Stern@ens.fr

Laboratoire d'Informatique
École Normale Supérieure
45, rue d'Ulm
F - 75230 PARIS Cedex 05

Abstract. In this paper, we give a provably secure design for blind signatures, the most important ingredient for anonymity in off-line electronic cash systems. Previous examples of blind signature schemes were constructed from traditional signature schemes with only the additional proof of blindness. The design of some of the underlying signature schemes can be validated by a proof in the so-called random oracle model, but the security of the original signature scheme does not, by itself, imply the security of the blind version. In this paper, we first propose a definition of security for blind signatures, with application to electronic cash. Next, we focus on a specific example which can be successfully transformed in a provably secure blind signature scheme.

1 Introduction

1.1 Electronic Cash

With the growing importance of the Internet and trade, electronic cash has become a very active research area. Basic cryptographic notions that lay a firm foundation for E-cash were introduced by David Chaum [6, 7, 8]. His aim was to produce an electronic version of money which retains the same properties as paper cash, primarily anonymity and control by the Bank. He claimed that the way to ensure anonymity went through the use of coins together with the notion of blind signatures. When a user withdraws money from the Bank, the Bank returns electronic coins which have been "blindly" signed. The user can then spend them at designated shops. Finally, the shops deposit the coins at the Bank (see figure 1). Blind signatures, on which this paper focus, will be defined below. They provide the tool by which the user gets a signature of a coin so that the Bank is unable to later recognize it. This technique is efficient in an one-line scenario. But if payment is off-line, there is no direct way to prevent a user to copy a coin and use it twice. This forgery is called "double spending". As a second step in the E-cash research, Chaum, Fiat and Naor [10] introduced the identity in the coin in such a way that the identity remains concealed, unless double spending happens, in which case it is revealed. This imposes a special

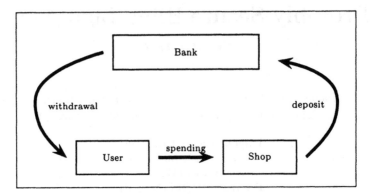

Fig. 1. Coin life

format for the coin. Since it is created by the user, the Bank has to verify whether this format has been respected. Chaum, Fiat and Naor applied the "cut-and-choose" technique. The Bank signs many more coins than useful and, by random choice, requests the user to disclose the structure of some of them. The drawback of this technique is that this increases the communication load between the Bank and the user and the space needed to store coins. There were several improvements [9, 21], and in 1993, appeared schemes without the "cut-and-choose" methodology [4, 3, 13, 12]. More recently, unconditional anonymity has been criticized because of money laundering or other possible crimes [19], and escrow-based schemes were put forward as a new direction of the research [18].

1.2 Blind Signatures

Since the beginning of E-cash, blind signature has been the most important tool. It is an interactive protocol which involves two entities, a Bank and a user. It allows a user to get a message signed by the Bank without revealing this message. The message–signature pair received by the user is statistically uncorrelated to the view obtained by the Bank during the execution of the protocol.

Several signature schemes have been turned into blind signature schemes. Here are the most well-known. In what follows, H is a hash function.

The Blind RSA Signature We first present a blind signature which is a transformation of the RSA signature scheme [24]. It was used by Chaum [6, 7, 8] for the withdrawal protocols of his first electronic cash system.

In the RSA context, we have a large composite number n, a public key e, and a secret key d. The signature of a message m is the eth root of $H(m)$, $\sigma = H(m)^{1/e} = H(m)^d \bmod n$.

Now, in order to obtain the signature of a secret message m, the user blinds it with a random value $r^e \bmod n$, and sends $m' = H(m)r^e \bmod n$ to the signer. The latter returns a signature σ' of m' such that $\sigma'^e = m' = r^e H(m) \bmod n$. Then, it is easy to remark that $\sigma = \sigma' r^{-1} \bmod n$ is a valid signature of m.

The Blind Schnorr Signature The Schnorr signature scheme [25] can also be turned into a blind signature scheme. The transformation was used in the first electronic cash systems without "cut-and-choose".

We have two large prime integers p and q, such that $q \mid p - 1$. They are published together with an element g of $(\mathbb{Z}/p\mathbb{Z})^*$ of order q. The signer creates a pair of keys, $x \in \mathbb{Z}/q\mathbb{Z}$ and $y = g^{-x} \bmod p$. He publishes y. A user wants a blind signature of a message m. In order to issue this signature, the signer chooses a random $k \in \mathbb{Z}/q\mathbb{Z}$, computes and sends the "commitment" $r = g^k \bmod p$. The user blinds it with two random elements $\alpha, \beta \in \mathbb{Z}/q\mathbb{Z}$, into $r' = rg^{-\alpha}y^{-\beta} \bmod p$, and computes the value $e' = H(m, r') \bmod q$. He sends the "challenge" $e = e' + \beta \bmod q$ to the signer who returns the value s such that $g^s y^e = r \bmod p$. One can easily verify that, with $s' = s - \alpha \bmod q$, (e', s') is a valid Schnorr signature of m since it satisfies $e' = H(m, g^{s'} y^{e'} \bmod p)$.

2 Security Proofs

2.1 The Random Oracle Model

In 1993, Bellare and Rogaway [1] formalized a model which allows proofs of security for various cryptographic schemes. Many of these algorithms use hash functions and cannot be proved secure from basic properties like one-wayness or collision freeness. Thus, hash functions are often an obstacle for proofs. In the random oracle model, hash functions are assumed to be really random functions and used as an oracle who answers a random value for each new query. Thus the obstacle disappears. The price to pay is the replacement of the hash function by some "ideal" object. Nevertheless, we feel that the resulting proof is a way to validate the design of a cryptographic scheme and to eliminate "poor" designs.

For example, in their paper [23], Pointcheval and Stern suggested that the original El Gamal's signature scheme [15] and DSS [20] did not follow a "good" design principle. This is in contrast with the Schnorr's signature scheme or, more generally, any transformation of a fair verifier zero-knowledge identification scheme, which are validated by a proof in the random oracle model. For the DSS design, Vaudenay [26] later showed a weakness which opens the way to a possible misuse of this scheme by the authority.

2.2 The Security of Signature Schemes

In recent years, general techniques for proving the security of signature schemes have been proposed. We refer the reader to [16] for the various definitions of security. The most general one is the "no-existential forgery under adaptively chosen-message attacks". It corresponds to a scenario where an attacker can ask the signature of new messages at any step of his computation and, still, is not be able to forge a new valid message–signature pair at the end. Both the RSA [24] and the Schnorr [25] signature schemes have been proved secure in the random oracle model. Proofs were given in the asymptotic framework of complexity theory. More recently, Bellare and Rogaway [2] modified the original RSA scheme in order to obtain an exact security result. At the same time, Pointcheval and Stern [23] obtained a proof of security for any signature scheme which comes from a fair verifier zero-knowledge identification scheme and also for a slight modification of El Gamal [15]. In these proofs, all entities are seen as probabilistic polynomial time Turing machines. Assuming that the attack exists, a collusion between the signer, the attacker and the random oracle, allows to construct a new Turing machine which solves a difficult problem (RSA or the discrete logarithm).

2.3 The Security of Blind Signatures

As far as we know, no formal notion of security has ever been studied, nor proved, in the context of blind signatures. However, it is a critical point in E-cash systems. In the context of blind signatures, the previous definitions of security are no longer significant. In fact, the existential forgery under an adaptively chosen-message is somehow the basis for blind signatures. Nevertheless, a fundamental property for E-cash systems is the guaranty that a user cannot forge more coins than the Bank gives him. In other words, after ℓ blind signatures of the Bank, the user must not be able to create more than ℓ coins. This form of security was more or less informally assumed in connection with several schemes, for example [5].

Definition 1 (The "one-more" forgery). For any integer ℓ, an $(\ell, \ell + 1)$-forgery comes from a probabilistic polynomial time Turing machine $\mathcal{A}$ that can compute, after ℓ interactions with the signer Σ, $\ell + 1$ signatures with non-negligible probability. The "one-more forgery" is an $(\ell, \ell + 1)$-forgery for some integer ℓ.

As usual, an attacker has several methods to achieve this forgery. We will focus on two kinds of attacks :

- the sequential attack: the attacker interacts sequentially with the signer.

- the parallel attack: the attacker interacts ℓ times in parallel with the signer. This attack is stronger. Indeed, the attacker can initiate new interactions with the signer before previous ones have been computed.

Previous methods of proofs used to establish the security of signature schemes no longer work since, during the collusion between the signer, the attacker and the random oracle, we loose control over the message that the signer receives since it comes from the attacker. As a consequence, the signer cannot be simulated without the secret key.

3 The Proposed Blind Signature Scheme

3.1 Witness Indistinguishability

In the following, we will focus on a specific three-pass "witness indistinguishable" identification scheme, and its transformation into a blind signature scheme. The notion of "witness indistinguishability" was defined by Feige and Shamir in [11] for the purpose of identification. In such a scheme, many secret keys are associated to a same public key. Furthermore, the views of two identifications using two distinct secret keys associated to a same public key are indistinguishable. For example, in the Fiat-Shamir protocol [14], the verifier cannot distinguish which square root the prover uses. Okamoto, in [22], proposed a witness indistinguishable adaptation of both the Schnorr [25] and the Guillou-Quisquater [17] identification schemes.

3.2 Provably Secure Blind Signature Schemes

As was already remarked, the technical difficulty to overcome comes from the fact that, in the colluding step, we no longer can simulate the signer without the secret key. We will use a scheme which admits more than one secret key for a given public key. This will make the collusion possible and we will constrain the attacker to output a different secret key.

Our candidate scheme is one of the schemes designed by Okamoto in [22]. For the reader's convenience, the adaptation of the Schnorr's scheme is on figure 2 and its blind version is on figure 3.

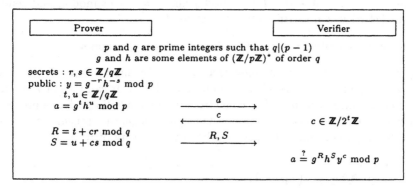

Fig. 2. Witness indistinguishable adaptation of the Schnorr's identification

3.3 Okamoto-Schnorr Blind Signature Scheme

The scheme uses two large primes p and q such that $q \mid (p - 1)$, and two elements $g, h \in (\mathbb{Z}/p\mathbb{Z})^*$ of order q. The Bank chooses a secret key $(r, s) \in ((\mathbb{Z}/q\mathbb{Z})^*)^2$ and publishes the public key, $y = g^{-r}h^{-s} \bmod p$. The protocol by which the user obtains a blind signature of the message m is as follows.

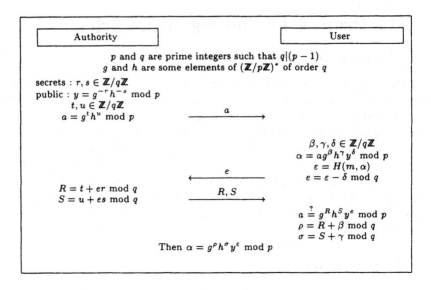

Fig. 3. Okamoto-Schnorr blind signature

- the Bank chooses $(t, u) \in ((\mathbb{Z}/t\mathbb{Z})^*)^2$, computes and sends $a = g^t h^u \bmod p$;

- the user chooses $\beta, \gamma, \delta \in \mathbb{Z}/q\mathbb{Z}$ to blind a into $\alpha = ag^\beta h^\gamma y^\delta \bmod p$. He computes the challenge $\varepsilon = H(m, \alpha)$ and sends $e = \varepsilon - \delta \bmod q$ to the Bank;

- the Bank computes $R = t + er \bmod q$ and $S = u + es \bmod q$, and sends a pair (R, S) which satisfies $a = g^R h^S y^e \bmod p$;

- the user computes $\rho = R + \beta \bmod q$ and $\sigma = S + \gamma \bmod q$.

Straightforward computations show that $\alpha = g^\rho h^\sigma y^\varepsilon \bmod p$, with $\varepsilon = H(m, \alpha)$.

A security proof for this scheme will be given below. It can be easily modified so as to cover other schemes that come from witness indistinguishable protocols. Especially, the blind Okamoto-Guillou-Quisquater signature scheme can be proposed (see figure 4) and proven relatively to the security of RSA.

4 The Main Result

Theorem 2. *Consider the Okamoto-Schnorr blind signature scheme in the random oracle model. If there exists a probabilistic polynomial time Turing machine which can perform a "one-more" forgery, with non-negligible probability, even under a parallel attack, then the discrete logarithm can be solved in polynomial time.*

Proof. Before we prove this result, we state a well-known probabilistic lemma:

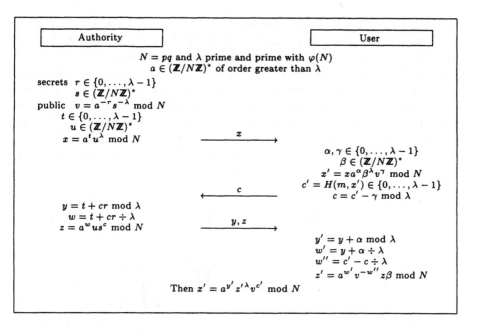

Fig. 4. Okamoto-Guillou-Quisquater blind Signature

Lemma 3 (The probabilistic lemma). *Let A be a subset of $X \times Y$ such that $\Pr[A(x,y)] \geq \varepsilon$, then there exists $\Omega \subset X$ such that*

i) $\Pr[x \in \Omega] \geq \varepsilon/2$

ii) *whenever $a \in \Omega$, $\Pr[A(a,y)] \geq \varepsilon/2$.*

With this lemma, we can split the set X in two subsets, a non-negligible subset Ω consisting of "good" x's which provide a non-negligible probability of success over y, and its complement, consisting of "bad" x's.

We will first outline the proof, then, since the technicalities are a bit intricate, we will simplify notations. Finally, we will complete the proof.

Outline of the Proof Let $\mathcal{A}$ be the "attacker". It is a probabilistic polynomial time Turing machine which succeeds, in its "one-more forgery", with non-negligible probability ε. Thus, there exists an integer ℓ such that after ℓ interactions with the authority, (a_i, e_i, R_i, S_i) for $i \in \{1, \ldots, \ell\}$, and a polynomial number Q of queries asked to the random oracle, $\mathcal{Q}_1, \ldots, \mathcal{Q}_Q$, $\mathcal{A}$ returns $\ell + 1$ valid signatures, $(m_i, \alpha_i, \varepsilon_i, \rho_i, \sigma_i)$ for $i = 1, \ldots, \ell + 1$. These signatures verify the required equations with $\varepsilon_i = H(m_i, \alpha_i)$.

The public data consist of two large primes p and q such that $q \mid (p-1)$ and two elements, g and h, of $(\mathbb{Z}/p\mathbb{Z})^*$ of order q. The authority (or the Bank) possesses a secret key (r, s) associated to public key $y = g^{-r}h^{-s}$, and a random tape Ω. Formally, the secret key (r, s) is stored in a specific part of the machine called the knowledge tape.

Through a collusion of the authority and the attacker, we want to compute the discrete logarithm of h relatively to g. We will use the technique of oracle replay formalized in [23]. We first run the attack with random keys, tapes and oracle f. We randomly choose an index j. We then replay with the same keys and random tapes, but a different oracle f' such that the $j - 1$ first answers are unchanged. We expect that, with non-negligible probability, both executions output a common α_i coming from the jth oracle query having two distinct representations relatively to g and h. In fact, $\alpha_i = g^r h^s = g^{r'} h^{s'}$, with $r' \neq r$, implies $\log_g h = (r - r')(s' - s)^{-1} \bmod q$. This collusion is represented on figure 5. Thus, the following lemma proves the theorem 2.

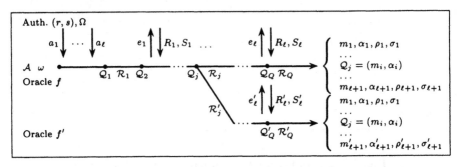

Fig. 5. Forking lemma

Lemma 4 (The forking lemma). *Randomly choose an index j, the keys and the random tapes. Run the attack twice with the same random tapes and two different random oracles, f and f', providing identical answers to the $j - 1$ first queries. With non-negligible probability, the different outputs reveal two different representations of some α_i, relatively to g and h.*

Cleaning up Notations We now clear up notational difficulties. Firstly, without loss of generality, we can assume that all the (m_i, α_i) are queries which have been asked during the attack. Otherwise, the probability of success would be negligible because of the randomness of the random oracle outputs. Secondly, we can assume that the indexes, $(Ind_1, \ldots, Ind_{\ell+1})$, of $(m_1, \alpha_1), \ldots, (m_{\ell+1}, \alpha_{\ell+1})$ in the list of queries are constant. As a result, the probability of success decreases from ε to $\rho \approx \varepsilon / Q^{\ell+1}$. The collusion is represented on figure 6, where the pair (r, s) is the secret key used by the authority, and where the random tape Ω of the authority determines the pairs (t_i, u_i) such that $a_i = g^{t_i} h^{u_i}$ for $i = 1, \ldots, \ell$. The distribution of (r, s, y) where r and s are random and $y = g^{-r} h^{-s}$ is the same as the distribution of (r, s, y) where r, y are random and s is the unique element in $(\mathbb{Z}/q\mathbb{Z})^\star$ such that $y = g^{-r} h^{-s}$. Accordingly, we will replace (r, s) by (r, y) and, similarly, each (t_i, u_i) by (t_i, a_i).

In the following, we will group $(\omega, y, a_1, \ldots, a_\ell)$ under variable ν, and τ will represent the ℓ-tuple $(t_1, \ldots, t_\ell)$. We will denote by $\mathcal{S}$ the set of all suc-

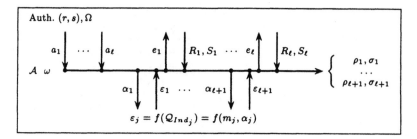

Fig. 6. General model

cessful data, *i.e.* quadruples (ν, r, τ, f) such that the attack succeeds. Then, $\Pr_{\nu,r,\tau,f}[(\nu, r, \tau, f) \in \mathcal{S}] \geq \rho$.

Proof of the Forking Lemma We want to prove that after a replay, we can obtain a common output α_i such that

$$\alpha_i = g^{\rho_i} h^{\sigma_i} y^{\varepsilon_i} = g^{\rho_i - r\varepsilon_i} h^{\sigma_i - s\varepsilon_i}$$
$$= g^{\rho'_i} h^{\sigma'_i} y^{\varepsilon'_i} = g^{\rho'_i - r\varepsilon'_i} h^{\sigma'_i - s\varepsilon'_i} \quad \text{with } \rho_i - r\varepsilon_i \neq \rho'_i - r\varepsilon'_i.$$

We can remark that, for each i, α_i only depends on ν, r, τ and the first $Ind_i - 1$ answers of f. The main question we have to study is whether or not the random variable $\chi_i = \rho_i - r\varepsilon_i$ is sensitive to queries asked at steps Ind_i, $Ind_i + 1$, etc. We expect that the answer is yes. A way to grasp the question is to consider the most likely value taken by this random variable when (ν, r, τ) and the $Ind_i - 1$ first answers of f are fixed. We are thus led to consider a function $c_i(\nu, r, \tau, f_i)$, where f_i ranges over the set of answers to the first $Ind_i - 1$ possible queries. Set

$$\lambda_i(\nu, r, \tau, f_i, c) = \Pr_f \left[\left(\chi_i(\nu, r, \tau, f) = c \right) \& \left((\nu, r, \tau, f) \in \mathcal{S} \right) \Big| f \text{ extends } f_i \right].$$

We define $c_i(\nu, r, \tau, f_i)$ as any value c such that $\lambda_i(\nu, r, \tau, f_i, c)$ is maximal. We then define the "good" subset $\mathcal{G}$ of $\mathcal{S}$ whose elements satisfy, for all i, $\chi_i(\nu, r, \tau, f) = c_i(\nu, r, \tau, f_i)$, where f_i denotes the restriction of f to queries of index strictly less than Ind_i, and the "bad" $\mathcal{B}$ its complement in $\mathcal{S}$.

Definition 5. We denote by Φ the transformation which maps any quadruple (ν, r, τ, f) to $(\nu, r+1, \tau - e, f)$, where $\tau - e = (t_1 - e_1, \ldots, t_\ell - e_\ell)$.

This transformation has useful properties (see figure 7).

Lemma 6. *Both executions corresponding to (ν, r, τ, f) and $\Phi(\nu, r, \tau, f)$ are totally identical w.r.t. the view of the attacker. Especially, outputs are the same.*

Proof. Let (ν, r, τ, f) be an input for the collusion. Replay with $r' = r + 1$ and $\tau' = \tau - e$, the same ν and the same oracle f. The answers of the oracle are unchanged and the interactions with the authority become

$$R'_i(r', t'_i, e_i) = t'_i + r'e_i = (t_i - e_i) + (r+1)e_i = t_i + re_i = R_i(r, t_i, e_i).$$

Thus, everything remains the same. □

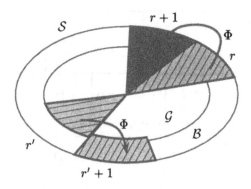

Fig. 7. Properties of Φ

Corollary 7. Φ *is a one-to-one mapping from* S *onto* S.

The following lemma shows that Φ sends the set G into B, except for a negligible part.

Lemma 8. *For fixed* (ν, r, τ), *the probability*

$$\Pr_f[((\nu, r, \tau, f) \in G) \,\&\, (\Phi(\nu, r, \tau, f) \in G)]$$

is bounded by $1/q$.

Proof. Assume that $\Pr_f[(\nu, r, \tau, f) \in \cup_{e_1,\ldots,e_\ell} Y(e_1, \ldots, e_\ell)] > 1/q$, where the set $Y(e_1, \ldots, e_\ell)$ is defined by the conditions $(\nu, r, \tau, f) \in G$, $\Phi(\nu, r, \tau, f) \in G$ and $(e_1, \ldots, e_\ell)$ are the successive questions asked to the authority. Then, there exists a ℓ-tuple $(e_1, \ldots, e_\ell)$ such that $\Pr_f[Y(e_1, \ldots, e_\ell)] > \frac{1}{q^{\ell+1}}$. Thus, there exist two oracles f and f' in $Y(e_1, \ldots, e_\ell)$ which provide distinct answers for some queries $Q_{Ind_j} = (m_j, \alpha_j)$ to the oracle, for some $j \in \{1, \ldots, \ell + 1\}$, and are such that answers to queries not of the form Q_{Ind_j} are similar. We will denote by i the smallest such index j. Then $f_i = f'_i$ and $\varepsilon_i \neq \varepsilon'_i$. Furthermore, we have $(\nu, r, \tau, f) \in G$, $\Phi(\nu, r, \tau, f) \in G$ and similarly $(\nu, r, \tau, f') \in G$, $\Phi(\nu, r, \tau, f') \in G$. Because of the property of Φ (see lemma 6), and by definition of G,

$$
\begin{aligned}
c_i(\nu, r, \tau, f_i) &= \rho_i(\nu, r, \tau, f) - r\varepsilon_i \\
&= \rho_i(\Phi(\nu, r, \tau, f)) - r\varepsilon_i = c_i(\nu, r{+}1, \tau{-}e, f_i) + ((r{+}1) - r)\varepsilon_i \\
c_i(\nu, r, \tau, f'_i) &= \rho_i(\nu, r, \tau, f') - r\varepsilon'_i \\
&= \rho_i(\Phi(\nu, r, \tau, f')) - r\varepsilon'_i = c_i(\nu, r{+}1, \tau{-}e', f'_i) + ((r{+}1) - r)\varepsilon'_i
\end{aligned}
$$

The equality $f_i = f'_i$ implies $c_i(\nu, r, \tau, f_i) = c_i(\nu, r, \tau, f'_i)$. Since we have assume $(e_1, \ldots, e_\ell) = (e'_1, \ldots, e'_\ell)$, then $c_i(\nu, r + 1, \tau - e, f_i) = c_i(\nu, r + 1, \tau - e', f'_i)$. Thus $\varepsilon_i = \varepsilon'_i$, which contradicts the hypothesis. $\qquad\Box$

Lemma 8 says that for any (ν, r, τ),

$$\Pr_f\left[\left((\nu, r, \tau, f) \in G\right) \,\&\, \left(\Phi(\nu, r, \tau, f) \in G\right)\right] \le 1/q.$$

By making the sum over all triplets (ν, r, τ), and using the bijectivity of Φ (corollary 7), we obtain

$$
\begin{aligned}
\Pr[\mathcal{G}] &= \Pr_{\nu,r,\tau,f}\left[\left((\nu,r,\tau,f) \in \mathcal{G}\right) \& \left(\Phi(\nu,r,\tau,f) \in \mathcal{G}\right)\right] \\
&\quad + \Pr_{\nu,r,\tau,f}\left[\left((\nu,r,\tau,f) \in \mathcal{G}\right) \& \left(\Phi(\nu,r,\tau,f) \in \mathcal{B}\right)\right] \\
&\leq \frac{1}{q} + \Pr_{\nu,r,\tau,f}[\Phi(\nu,r,\tau,f) \in \mathcal{B}] \leq \frac{1}{q} + \Pr[\mathcal{B}]
\end{aligned}
$$

Then, $\Pr[\mathcal{B}] \geq (\Pr[\mathcal{S}] - 1/q)/2$. Since $1/q$ is negligible w.r.t. $\Pr[\mathcal{S}]$, for enough large keys, we have, $\Pr[\mathcal{B}] \geq \Pr[\mathcal{S}]/3 \geq \rho/3$.

Conclusion We will use this probability to show the success of forking.

$$
\begin{aligned}
\frac{\rho}{3} \leq \Pr[\mathcal{B}] &= \Pr_{\nu,r,\tau,f}\left[\mathcal{S} \& \left((\exists i)\ \chi_i(\nu,r,\tau,f) \neq c_i(\nu,r,\tau,f_i)\right)\right] \\
&\leq \sum_{i=1}^{\ell+1} \Pr_{\nu,r,\tau,f}\left[\mathcal{S} \& \left(\chi_i(\nu,r,\tau,f) \neq c_i(\nu,r,\tau,f_i)\right)\right].
\end{aligned}
$$

There exists k such that $\Pr\left[\mathcal{S} \& \left(\chi_k(\nu,r,\tau,f) \neq c_k(\nu,r,\tau,f_k)\right)\right] \geq \rho/3(\ell+1)$.
Let us randomly choose the forking index i. With probability greater than $1/(\ell+1)$, we have guessed $i = k$. The probabilistic lemma 3 ensures that there exists a set X such that

i) $\Pr_{\nu,r,\tau,f}[(\nu,r,\tau,f_i) \in X] \geq \rho/6(\ell+1)$;

ii)   for all $(\nu,r,\tau,f_i) \in X$,
$$\Pr_f\left[(\nu,r,\tau,f) \in \mathcal{S} \& \left(\chi_i \neq c_i\right)\Big| f \text{ extends } f_i\right] \geq \rho/6(\ell+1).$$

Let us choose a random quadruple (ν,r,τ,f). With probability greater than $\left(\rho/6(\ell+1)\right)^2$, $(\nu,r,\tau,f) \in \mathcal{S}$, $(\nu,r,\tau,f_i) \in X$ and $\chi_i(\nu,r,\tau,f) \neq c_i(\nu,r,\tau,f_i)$.
We will denote by d the value $\chi_i(\nu,r,\tau,f)$ and by c the value $c_i(\nu,r,\tau,f_i)$.
Then, two cases appear relatively to $\lambda_i(\nu,r,\tau,f_i,d)$:

–   if $\lambda_i(\nu,r,\tau,f_i,d) \geq \rho/12(\ell+1)$, then, by definition of c_i, we know that
$\lambda_i(\nu,r,\tau,f_i,c) \geq \rho/12(\ell+1)$.

–   otherwise,
$$
\begin{aligned}
\lambda_i(\nu,r,\tau,f_i,d) &+ \Pr_{f'}\left[\mathcal{S} \& \left(\chi_i(\nu,r,\tau,f') \neq d\right)\Big| f' \text{ extends } f_i\right] \\
&= \Pr_{f'}\left[\mathcal{S} \,\middle|\, f' \text{ extends } f_i\right] \\
&\geq \Pr_{f'}\left[\mathcal{S} \& \left(\chi_i(\nu,r,\tau,f') \neq c\right)\Big| f' \text{ extends } f_i\right] \geq \rho/6(\ell+1).
\end{aligned}
$$

Both cases lead to $\Pr_{f'}\left[\mathcal{S} \& \left(\chi_i(\nu,r,\tau,f') \neq d\right)\Big| f' \text{ extends } f_i\right] \geq \rho/12(\ell+1)$.
Thus, if we replay with the same keys and random tapes but another random oracle f' such that $f'_i = f_i$, we obtain, with probability at least $\rho/12(\ell+1)$, a new success with $\chi_i(\nu,r,\tau,f') \neq d$. Then, both executions provide two different representations of α_i relatively to g and h.

Global Complexity of the Reduction By using a replay oracle technique with a random forking index, the probability of success is greater than

$$\frac{1}{\ell+1} \times \left(\frac{\rho}{6(\ell+1)}\right)^2 \times \frac{\rho}{12(\ell+1)} = \frac{1}{2(\ell+1)} \times \left(\frac{1}{6(\ell+1)} \times \frac{\varepsilon}{Q^{\ell+1}}\right)^3$$

where ε is the probability of success of an $(\ell, \ell+1)$-forgery and Q the number of queries asked to the random oracle. $\qquad\square$

5 Conclusion

Our result appears to be the first security result which opens a way towards provably secure E-cash systems by providing candidates for secure blind signatures. However, an open problem still remains: the complexity of the reduction is polynomial in the size of the keys but exponential in ℓ. We do not know whether it is possible to achieve polynomial time both in ℓ and the size of the keys.

Acknowledgements

The definition of "one-more" forgery came up during a discussion with Stefan Brands. We thank him for the time he spent explaining his scheme.

References

[1] M. Bellare and P. Rogaway. Random Oracles are Practical: a paradigm for designing efficient protocols. In *Proceedings of the 1st ACM Conference on Computer and Communications Security*, pages 62–73, 1993.

[2] M. Bellare and P. Rogaway. The Exact Security of Digital Signatures – How to Sign with RSA and Rabin. In U. Maurer, editor, *Advances in Cryptology – Proceedings of EUROCRYPT '96*, volume 1070 of *Lecture Notes in Computer Science*, pages 399–416. Springer-Verlag, 1996.

[3] S.A. Brands. An Efficient Off-line Electronic Cash System Based On The Representation Problem. Technical report, CWI (Centrum voor Wiskunde en Informatica), 1993. CS-R9323.

[4] S.A. Brands. Untraceable Off-line Cash in Wallets with Observers. In D. R. Stinson, editor, *Advances in Cryptology – proceedings of CRYPTO '93*, volume 773 of *Lecture Notes in Computer Science*, pages 302–318. Springer-Verlag, 1994.

[5] S.A. Brands. Off-Line Electronic Cash Based on Secret-Key Certificates. In *Proceedings of the 2nd International Symposium of Latin American Theoretical INformatics (LATIN' 95)*. Valparaíso, Chili, april 1995. Technical report, CWI (Centrum voor Wiskunde en Informatica), CS-R9506.

[6] D. Chaum. Blind Signatures for Untraceable Payments. In R. L. Rivest D. Chaum and A. T. Sherman, editors, *Advances in Cryptology - Proceedings of CRYPTO '82*, pages 199–203. Plenum, NY, 1983.

[7] D. Chaum. Security Without Identification: Transaction Systems to Make Big Brother Obsolete. *Communications of the ACM 28*, 10, october 1985.

[8] D. Chaum. Privacy Protected Payments: Unconditional Payer And/Or Payee Untraceability. In *Smartcard 2000*. North Holland, 1988.

[9] D. Chaum, B. den Boer, E. van Heyst, S. Mjølsnes, and A. Steenbeek. Efficient Off-line Electronic Checks. In J.-J. Quisquater and J. Vandewalle, editors, *Advances in Cryptology - Proceedings of EUROCRYPT '89*, volume 434 of *Lecture Notes in Computer Science*, pages 294–301. Springer-Verlag, 1990.

[10] D. Chaum, A. Fiat, and M. Naor. Untraceable Electronic Cash. In S. Goldwasser, editor, *Advances in Cryptology - Proceedings of CRYPTO '88*, volume 403 of *Lecture Notes in Computer Science*, pages 319–327. Springer-Verlag, 1989.

[11] U. Feige and A. Shamir. Witness Indistinguishable and Witness Hiding Protocols. In *Proceedings of the 22nd ACM Symposium on the Theory of Computing STOC*. ACM, 1990.

[12] N. Ferguson. Extensions of Single Term Coins. In D. R. Stinson, editor, *Advances in Cryptology - proceedings of CRYPTO '93*, volume 773 of *Lecture Notes in Computer Science*, pages 292–301. Springer-Verlag, 1994.

[13] N. Ferguson. Single Term Off-Line Coins. In T. Helleseth, editor, *Advances in Cryptology - Proceedings of EUROCRYPT '93*, volume 765 of *Lecture Notes in Computer Science*. Springer-Verlag, 1994.

[14] A. Fiat and A. Shamir. How to Prove Yourself: practical solutions of identification and signature problems. In A. M. Odlyzko, editor, *Advances in Cryptology - Proceedings of CRYPTO '86*, volume 263 of *Lecture Notes in Computer Science*, pages 186–194. Springer-Verlag, 1987.

[15] T. El Gamal. A Public Key Cryptosystem and a Signature Scheme Based on Discrete Logarithms. In *IEEE Transactions on Information Theory*, volume IT–31, no. 4, pages 469–472, july 1985.

[16] S. Goldwasser, S. Micali, and R. Rivest. A Digital Signature Scheme Secure Against Adaptative Chosen-Message Attacks. *SIAM journal of computing*, 17(2):281–308, april 1988.

[17] L.C. Guillou and J.-J. Quisquater. A Practical Zero-Knowledge Protocol Fitted to Security Microprocessor Minimizing Both Transmission and Memory. In C. G. Günter, editor, *Advances in Cryptology - Proceedings of EUROCRYPT '88*, volume 330 of *Lecture Notes in Computer Science*, pages 123–128. Springer-Verlag, 1988.

[18] M. Jakobsson and M. Yung. Revocable and Versatile Electronic Money. In *Proceedings of the 3rd ACM Conference on Computer and Communications Security*, 1996.

[19] D. Naccache and S. von Solms. On Blind Signatures and Perfect Crimes. *Computers and Security*, 11:581–583, 1992.

[20] NIST. Digital Signature Standard (DSS). Federal Information Processing Standards PUBlication 186, November 1994.

[21] K. Ohta and T. Okamoto. Universal Electronic Cash. In J. Feigenbaum, editor, *Advances in Cryptology – Proceedings of CRYPTO '91*, volume 576 of *Lecture Notes in Computer Science*, pages 324–337. Springer-Verlag, 1992.

[22] T. Okamoto. Provably Secure and Practical Identification Schemes and Corresponding Signature Schemes. In E. F. Brickell, editor, *Advances in Cryptology – Proceedings of CRYPTO '92*, volume 740 of *Lecture Notes in Computer Science*, pages 31–53. Springer-Verlag, 1992.

[23] D. Pointcheval and J. Stern. Security Proofs for Signature Schemes. In U. Maurer, editor, *Advances in Cryptology – Proceedings of EUROCRYPT '96*, volume 1070 of *Lecture Notes in Computer Science*, pages 387–398. Springer-Verlag, 1996.

[24] R. Rivest, A. Shamir, and L. Adleman. A Method for Obtaining Digital Signatures and Public Key Cryptosystems. *Communications of the ACM*, 21(2):120–126, february 1978.

[25] C.P. Schnorr. Efficient Identification and Signatures for Smart Cards. In G. Brassard, editor, *Advances in Cryptology – Proceedings of CRYPTO '89*, volume 435 of *Lecture Notes in Computer Science*, pages 235–251. Springer-Verlag, 1990.

[26] S. Vaudenay. Hidden Collisions on DSS. In N. Koblitz, editor, *Advances in Cryptology – proceedings of CRYPTO '96*, Lecture Notes in Computer Science. Springer-Verlag, 1996. to appear.

Cost-Effective Payment Schemes
with Privacy Regulation

David M'Raïhi

Gemplus - Cryptography Department
1 Place de la Méditerrannée
BP 636, F-95206 Sarcelles cedex- France
email : 100145.2261@compuserve.com

Abstract. In this paper, we introduce a new electronic money methodology : sub-contracting the blinding to a trustee and using an Identity-based piece of information to achieve provable privacy and security. This variation on the Brickel, Gemmel and Kravitz paradigm [2] offers protection against various attacks minimizing user's computational requirement. Furthermore, our scheme offers various complexity/privacy trade-offs without endangering the issuer's overall security.

1 Introduction

Blind signatures [4] allow a message to be signed without revealing to the signer any information on the message. Therefore, this cryptographic primitive offers interesting properties for designing anonymous electronic cash schemes. In [5], Chaum, Fiat and Naor proposed the first practical electronic cash system, using the blind signature paradigm to provide privacy and security for all involved parties. Then in [1], Brands exhibited constructions based on the representation problem to increase efficiency (avoiding cut-&-choose) without giving up the main aspect of a real cash system, i.e. the honest payer privacy. Ferguson [7] proposed a scheme based on the same concept, providing also tracability after the fact.

Nevertheless, perfect anonymity obtained through the usage of blind signature could open the way to a class of attacks pointed out by von Solm and Naccache [14]. A new concept involving a trustee during withdrawal was introduced by Brickell, Gemmell and Kravitz in an escrow-like e-cash scheme. Stadler, Camenish and Piveteau proposed *fair* blind signatures as a design primitive [15] that enables the bank to remove anonymity with the help of the trustee and put it into the context of e-cash [3]. However, these schemes assume the user's ability to fast computation and do not provide any protection against certain type of active attacks against the bank.

More recently [9], Jakobsson and Yung introduced the notion of Ombudsman (a government official in charge of the customers defense against abuses) yielding an efficient electronic money system where tracing does not only depend on the bank but requires the combined endeavors of the bank and the Ombudsman in the tracing process.

In this paper we propose an alternative model where blinding is sub-contracted to trustee(s), using Identity-linked *pseudonyms*, denoted $PIDs$. The core ideas are :

1. compel the user $\mathcal{U}$ to register at his bank acting as a Certification Authority $\mathcal{CA}$ to obtain n public values $PIDs$. These $PIDs$ are strongly linked to $\mathcal{U}$'s identity by a secret shared between $\mathcal{U}$ and $\mathcal{CA}$; without this certified information, $\mathcal{U}$ cannot initiate any communication with a trustee and therefore withdraw any electronic coin; this function is comparable to the registration at the Judge in [3] but with reduced communication and computation, simplifying also account management at the bank;

2. enable $\mathcal{U}$ to get a valid anonymous coin from the bank through a trusted party designed as Blinding Office $\mathcal{BO}$ for he performs a blinding signature protocol with $\mathcal{U}$'s bank after being convinced that $\mathcal{U}$ has previously registered at the bank; **Delegate Blinding** protocol enables therefore the user to get a certificate from $\mathcal{CA}$ on a value blinded by $\mathcal{BO}$; we may assume that there are different BOs, located in various places like currency exchange offices nowadays, where the users can withdraw anonymously e-cash from their accounts,

3. the privacy level is directly related to the amount of trust the user put in the $\mathcal{BO}$; furthermore, $\mathcal{BO}$ can link all payments performed with coins related to a given PID_i : privacy is regulated in n, i.e. $\mathcal{U}$'s privacy relies on his number of $PIDs$ and therefore on his storage and computational capacity.

The new model is somewhat different from the Ombudsman concept since $\mathcal{U}$ must trust both $\mathcal{CA}$ and $\mathcal{BO}$. However, $\mathcal{CA}$ and $\mathcal{BO}$ do not need to communicate to each other during withdrawal : separating $\mathcal{CA}$ and $\mathcal{BO}$ should avoid collusions to infer private information on users. Jakobsson and Yung considered also a very strong attack on the system, the so-called bank robbery where an attacker obtains the secret keys of the bank, and showed how to prevent against this attack. The previous trustee-based schemes do not protect the bankg against this kind of attack and in order to boost efficiency, neither do we in the scheme described in this paper. Nevertheless, we can observe that since $\mathcal{BO}$ delivers all the honestly withdrawn coins, it should be possible to introduce a double-verification of the coins by calling the $\mathcal{BO}$ during payment if a banks robbery has happened. $\mathcal{BO}$ must also stop immediately accepting withdrawal demand and protocols should be added in order to update securely $\mathcal{CA}$'s public keys at BOs and refund honest users who still have coins from previous withdrawal. We decide therefore to prevent only against the attacks also considered in Brickell et al. and Stadler et al. schemes to achieve high performance saving communication and computation time.

In section 3, the usage of a PID is described. A protocol designed for sub-contracting the blinding of public values is presented in section 4 and the delegation of the computation of any public information is developed in section 5. Finally, section 6 presents the implementation of an e-cash system providing privacy and security levels that depend on the user's motivation and section 7 sketches the proofs of the main security aspects of the scheme.

2 Notation

The following notation is used throughout this paper :

Symbol	Definition
α	primitive element of $\mathbb{Z}_p^*$, p prime
h	one-way hash function, in practice SHA can be used
f	one-way function such as exponentiation in a finite field
$\{E_{BO}, D_{BO}\}$	public-key encryption scheme of BO typically [12]
$\{S_{CA}, V_{CA}\}$	public-key signature scheme of CA
$\{S_U, V_U\}$	public-key signature scheme with pre-processing of U
$\{y, \hat{y}\}$	public information where $\hat{y}$ is obtained after blinding $y = f(x)$: $$\hat{y} = V_{CA}(r) \cdot y \Rightarrow S_{CA}(\hat{y}) = S_{CA}(V_{CA}(r) \cdot y) = r \cdot S_{CA}(y)$$ with x secret and r random number known by the receiver only

We propose to use RSA for CA's scheme and assume that inverting the signature (or deciphering) amounts to querying a random oracle. For the user's signature scheme, Schnorr [11] seems the most suitable and secure considering recent analysis [13].

3 Model of Trust

Trust is a key concept in the system and we define hereafter the assumptions :

1. U trusts BO and CA not to collude in order to trace payments without a court order (or a similar legal authorization)
2. U trusts BO not to disclose information closely related to his privacy
3. U trusts BO and CA not to impersonate him
4. CA trusts BO to deliver information required in a tracing process

4 Pseudo-ID

The **Delegate Blinding** protocol simply splits the blinding ability in order to transfer from CA to BO the capability to link y to ID. To achieve privacy, since BO has all the public values and can infer connections between a certain y and a user ID, we must introduce a new notion of pseudo-identity, denoted PID.

The basic idea consists in performing a Diffie-Hellman [6] key exchange between U and CA. CA will store U's ID and the pseudo-identities (or enough data to rebuild them upon request).

Definition 1. U is pseudo-identified by an authentication session using a secret embedded in PID and therefore linked to ID.

4.1 Pseudo-ID Generation

First, $\mathcal{U}$ presents a "physical" ID-proof to $\mathcal{CA}$; we may assume that $\mathcal{U}$ is physically present at $\mathcal{CA}$'s premises and provides a material proof such as a passport (when opening the account, for instance). $\mathcal{CA}$ delivers a certified token to enable $\mathcal{U}$ to perform pseudo identifications. $\mathcal{CA}$ generate PIDs by doing the following :

1. $\mathcal{CA}$ and $\mathcal{U}$ agree upon a Diffie-Hellman secret $s = \alpha^{ab} \bmod p$
2. $\mathcal{CA}$ sends $S_{\mathcal{CA}}(h(s))$ and stores $\{ID, s\}$
3. $\mathcal{U}$ builds $PID = E_{\mathcal{BO}}(s)|S_{\mathcal{CA}}(h(s))$ and stores $\{s, PID\}$

For a multi-pseudo generation, $\mathcal{CA}$ simply generates (in step 1) several b_is and computes the corresponding $\alpha^{b_i} \bmod p$. $\mathcal{CA}$ can expand all these secret values from a random seed $b_i = h(seed, i)$.

In this case, $\mathcal{CA}$ stores only $\{ID, \alpha^a \bmod p, seed, n\}$ where n is the number of PIDs generated. $\mathcal{U}$ will therefore perform $n + 1$ computations to get the n secrets $s_i = \alpha^{ab_i} \bmod p$. If $\mathcal{U}$ prefers to perform n different sessions, $\mathcal{CA}$ must store n tuples. $\mathcal{U}$ must then perform $2n$ computations.

We can observe that $\mathcal{U}$ may store s only and build the PIDs dynamically, depending on the $\mathcal{BO}$ where operations are performed.

4.2 Pseudo Identification

$\mathcal{U}$ sends a PID to $\mathcal{BO}$ who can decipher $E_{\mathcal{BO}}(s)$, verify the correctness of the signature on $h(s)$ and starts an authentication session involving the secret s shared by $\mathcal{U}$ and $\mathcal{BO}$.

5 Delegating the Blinding Phase

In this section, we describe how to delegate the tracing facility of a public information y from $\mathcal{CA}$ to a $\mathcal{BO}$. $\mathcal{U}$ gets a signature $\sigma = S_{\mathcal{CA}}(y)$ from $\mathcal{CA}$, without revealing his identity, by carrying-out the following protocol :

• Blinding

1. $\mathcal{U}$ pseudo-identifies himself and sends y to $\mathcal{BO}$
2. $\mathcal{BO}$ generates a random r, computes $\hat{y}$ and sends $\hat{y}$ to $\mathcal{U}$
3. $\mathcal{U}$ identifies himself to $\mathcal{CA}$ and sends $\hat{y}$ with the $\mathcal{BO}$ references (for correct encryption)
4. $\mathcal{CA}$ replies to $\mathcal{U}$ with $e = E_{\mathcal{BO}}(S_{\mathcal{CA}}(\hat{y}))$

• Unblinding

1. $\mathcal{U}$ sends e to $\mathcal{BO}$
2. $\mathcal{BO}$ decrypts e and (knowing y's blinding factor) unblinds $\sigma = S_{\mathcal{CA}}(y)$
3. $\mathcal{BO}$ sends σ to $\mathcal{U}$

6 Sub-contracting y Computation

In [10], Naccache et al. proposed a method to delegate the computation of rs required to generate DSA [8] signatures by sharing a common secret with a trusted Authority. From this secret, the trustee can pre-compute "coupons" which can be used to generate DSA signatures, saving time and effort.

In the following, we generalize this idea to the generation of any set of public pieces of information $y_i = f(x_i)$, where $x_i = h(x, i)$ and x is some random seed. The idea is to enable the pre-computation of a set of public values (coupons or public keys) to be further used for the generation of DLP-based signatures.

6.1 Protocol

1. $\mathcal{U}$ generates a random seed x and sends $e = E_{BO}(x)$ with the number of public values n to be generated
2. $\mathcal{BO}$ decrypts e and computes $x_i = h(x, i)$ and the corresponding public values $y_i = f(x_i)$
3. $\mathcal{BO}$ sends the set $\{y_i\}_{i \leq n}$ and a certificate $c = h(\{y_i\}, x)$ so that $\mathcal{U}$ can check the set's authenticity

6.2 Security Analysis

Clearly, an eavesdropper cannot use any y_i since he does not know the corresponding x_i. He must either :

1. Break E and extract x, which is infeasible given D's nature, or
2. Find collisions in h to generate $\tilde{x} \neq x_i$ such that $y_i = f(\tilde{x})$, (also assumed infeasible), or
3. Invert f, which is assumed one-way

$\mathcal{U}$ must of course trust $\mathcal{BO}$ not to impersonate him. This solution is well suited for smart-card applications where the device at one's hand has a relatively limited computation capacity. In this case, the user can entrust the person of his choice to sub-contract his privacy-related computations.

7 Electronic Money with Privacy Regulation

We will consider two settings, beginning with the usual one in which electronic money is implemented on low-cost smart-card. The central idea is that the computational effort required from the user depends on the privacy level he wants to achieve. We will assume hereafter that the user's signature scheme is a DLP-based scheme. $\mathcal{U}$'s public key is $y = g^x \bmod p$, where p is prime and $g \in \mathbb{Z}_p^*$ has order q, a prime divisor of $p - 1$.

7.1 Low Privacy

A coin is a tuple $\{y, data, \sigma\}$ where $\sigma = S_{\mathcal{CA}}(h(y|data))$ and data is any relevant information related to the coin (such as date of validity) added by $\mathcal{CA}$. $\mathcal{U}$ has a small set of public keys y certified through protocol 4.1. The idea is that payments are linkable by category (in other words $\mathcal{U}$ may be traced for some purchases related to a certain y_i but others made with y_j will not be related to $\mathcal{U}$). The maximal number of such categories is simply n. We will denote by c_i the category related to PID_i.

Definition 2. A user holds an n-privacy or regulated privacy (in n) when his purchases are only linkable inside a category and $\mathcal{CA}$ cannot trace alone transactions outside this category

Registration at the $\mathcal{CA}$: $\mathcal{U}$ visits $\mathcal{CA}$ and obtains n pseudonyms. This implies the computation of $n + 1$ exponentiations (or $2n$ if U prefers to perform several sessions rather than one multi-session); considering [13] size of parameters and [7] techniques, such an interaction will require about $50(n + 1)$ (respectively $100n$) multiplications, which is acceptable if performed once, for a reasonable value of n (say, 4 or 5).

Withdrawal : $\mathcal{U}$ interacts with a $\mathcal{BO}$ in this way :

1. $\mathcal{U}$ pseudo-identifies himself by presenting a PID of his choice
2. $\mathcal{BO}$ checks PID
3. $\mathcal{U}$ sends $\{E_{\mathcal{BO}}(x), v\}$, x random and v the number of values to be generated
4. $\mathcal{BO}$ generates a public key $y = f(h(x, 0))$ and a set of pre-computed values $\left\{r_i = g^{h(x,i)}\right\}_{1 \leq i \leq v}$ and sends them back to $\mathcal{U}$ with a certificate c
5. $\mathcal{U}$ sends c and, if correct, starts with $\mathcal{BO}$ a **Delegate Blinding**[1] of y and receive $\{\sigma, data\}$, where σ is $\mathcal{CA}$'s signature on $h(y|data)$
6. $\mathcal{U}$ checks σ and stores $\{x, y, data, \{r_i\}, \sigma\}$

We observe that $\{y, data, \sigma\}$ is multi-spendable and so, it could be suitable to offer the possibility to load only rs in case y is not completely spent after v transactions. Obviously, y and $\{r_i\}$ may be completely dissociated by sending two different encrypted randoms x_1 and x_2.

Payment : Payment is achieved in only one multiplication for [13] (two for DSA) and a hashing by $\mathcal{U}$. The shop $\mathcal{SH}$ computational effort is about 2 exponentiations which is acceptable considering that his calculation ressources are greater that user's ones. The protocol can also support the challenge semantics introduced by Jakobson and Yung and offer extensions of the system by letting part of the challenge indicates payment-related information.

---

[1] when $\mathcal{CA}$ sends e, he subtracts the value of the coin from $\mathcal{U}$'s account; a possible extension would be that $\mathcal{CA}$ uses different secrets corresponding to different coin values (which implies adding a tag to y).

1. $\mathcal{U}$ sends a coin $\{y, data, \sigma\}$
2. $\mathcal{SH}$ checks σ and sends a message m including the amount, a random challenge and (possibly) some other application data
3. $\mathcal{U}$ generates $a = S_U(y, m)$, using a pre-computed r_i
4. $\mathcal{SH}$ makes sure that the coin has not expired and $V_{\mathcal{U}}(a, y, m) = \mathtt{True}$

Deposit : $\mathcal{SH}$ sends the transactions corresponding to coins spent during a given. $\mathcal{CA}$ checks coin s correctness and performs double-deposit and overspending detections.

1. $\mathcal{SH}$ sends the transaction $\log t = \{y, \sigma, data, a, m\}$ to $\mathcal{CA}$
2. $\mathcal{CA}$ checks :
   - $V_{\mathcal{CA}}(\sigma, y) = V_{\mathcal{U}}(a, y, m) = \mathtt{True}$
   - the coin is still valid
   - t has not been deposited already
3. $\mathcal{CA}$ accepts the transaction and credits $\mathcal{SH}$'s account

Furthermore, $\mathcal{CA}$ will check in the already-deposited coin list if the coin was overspent. If a certain y_i was double-spent, $\mathcal{CA}$ will ask for a tracing procedure[2] which consists in $\mathcal{CA}$ and $\mathcal{BO}$ joining forces to build a link between y_i and the coin-spender's ID.

7.2 High Privacy

Privacy can be regulated according to the user's motivation by increasing the number of PIDs to an optimum which is one per payment. This implies in practice a high-storage device such as a PCMCIA card or an electronic wallet. In this case, the withdrawal will only consist in a pseudo-identification followed by the delegate blinding of y.

8 Security

We will sketch the proofs of some security aspects of the new system.

8.1 Pseudo-Identification

An observer cannot get any information on s unless he breaks the Diffie-Hellman protocol. We can state the following lemmas :

Lemma 3. *Only $\mathcal{U}$ and $\mathcal{CA}$ know s.*

Proof Sketch. Follows directly from the Diffie-Hellman assumption. □

---

[2] this should include Judge's control to avoid unauthorized privacy disclosure.

Lemma 4. *Assuming that CA follows honestly protocol 4.1, it is always possible to relate PID to ID.*

Proof Sketch. From Lemma 3, and assuming that CA will not try to impersonate U, only U will be able to present a PID_i corresponding to a single s_i. CA can retrieve U's ID from this *Pseudo-ID* by querying his database (or re-computing the different s_i in case of storage optimization). □

Theorem 5. *Only U can pseudo-identify himself to BO using one of his PID_i*

Proof Sketch. U sends a PID_i to BO who deciphers it to get a s_i. BO verifies $S_{CA}(h(s_i))$ to make sure that CA previously stored a tuple related to this PID_i. From Lemma 3 and 4, it follows that BO can authenticate U using the secret s_i and therefore build a link to his identity ID. □

8.2   Delegate Blinding

As stated by Theorem 6 the main feature of this protocol is the impossibility for the user to get a signature on y without the help of BO. We will sketch the proof hereafter :

Theorem 6. *U cannot obtain a valid signature on y without BO's help.*

Proof Sketch. U may try not to interact with BO and generate a couple $\{y, \hat{y}\}$ of his own by computing $\hat{y} = V_{CA}(r) \cdot y$, where r is a random generated by U. He must nevertheless send $\hat{y}$ to CA who replies with $e = E_{BO}(\hat{y})$; then prior to unblinding $S_{CA}(\hat{y})$, which is possible since U knows the blinding factor r, U must invert BO's encryption scheme (E) which is assumed infeasible. □

We can also observe that if U colludes with a BO, CA can infer the BO's identity since if the user sends bad BO's references, decryption of e is not possible anymore.

8.3   Payment Scheme

Lemma 7. *The proposed scheme achieves overspending detection.*

Proof Sketch. Would a set of transactions t_i, corresponding to a single y, exceed the coin-value, CA can assume overspending because of user's signature scheme property (only U can sign new messages). CA can ask BO to trace U (the control by a judge in the course of a legal procedure might be added). BO will double-check t_i and that the total amount exceeds the coin-value and if confirmed, will reveal PID. □

Theorem 8. *The proposed scheme achieved regulated privacy w. r. t. to BO's honesty in the tracing process.*

Proof Sketch. Assuming a transaction $t = \{y, \sigma, a, m\}$ deposited at $\mathcal{CA}$; $\mathcal{CA}$ saw only $\hat{y}$ during withdrawal. Consequently, he cannot link the transaction to the ID received at this time. $\mathcal{BO}$ can only link t to the PID_i used by $\mathcal{U}$ during withdrawal. In case of overspending, $\mathcal{BO}$ and $\mathcal{CA}$ can join forces and link t to the ID which corresponds to the faulty PID_i. They can also link all payments related to this PID_i (in other words, $\{t_j\} \in c_i$). But $\mathcal{CA}$ cannot get any information on other transactions related to the other $PIDs$ since $\mathcal{BO}$ helps to trace only the transaction in c_i. Furthermore, $\mathcal{CA}$ will only be able to link transactions related to a given y. From that, he cannot trace a honest user without the help of $\mathcal{BO}$ but only suspect that some user performed transactions in a certain category c_i. Eventually, it follows from Lemma 7 that $\mathcal{CA}$ cannot falsely engage $\mathcal{BO}$ in a tracing procedure. □

Finally, let us underline that $\mathcal{U}$ and/or $\mathcal{BO}$ cannot create electronic money without breaking $\mathcal{CA}$'s signature scheme.

9 Conclusion

This paper presented a new simple and efficient payment scheme which combines the usage of a pseudonym, strongly linked to user's identity, with the delegation of public-key blinding. The scheme enables a user to trade-off privacy against computational complexity.

Furthermore, by introducing a user-representative, which is fully trusted by the user, we can provide a possible direction for low-cost device oriented applications, such as simple smart-cards, where privacy-level relies on the user-only decision.

10 Acknowledgments

It is a pleasure to thank Jacques Stern for advice and helpful comments during this research work, Markus Jakobson for valuable comments and suggestions and an anonymous referee for useful remarks.

References

[1] S. Brands, "Untraceable Off-line Cash in Wallet with Observers", Advances in Cryptology - CRYPTO '93, LNCS **773**, pp. 302-318.

[2] E. Brickell, P. Gemmel and D. Kravitz, "Trustee-based Tracing Extensions to Anonymous Cash and the Making of Anonimous Change", Proceedings of 6th. annual Symposium on Discrete Algorithm (SODA), 1995, ACM Press, pp. 457-466.

[3] J. Cammenish, J-M. Piveteau and M. Stadler, "An Efficient Fair Payment System", Third ACM Conference on Computer and Communications Security, 1996, ACM Press, pp. 88-94.

[4] D. Chaum, "Blind Signatures for Untraceable Payments", Advances in Cryptology - Proceedings of Crypto 82, Plenum, NY, pp. 199-203.

[5] D. Chaum, A. Fiat and M. Naor, "Untraceable Electronic Cash", Advances in Cryptology - CRYPTO '88, LNCS **403**, pp. 318-327.

[6] W. Diffie and M. Hellman, "New Directions in Cryptography", IEEE Tans. Info. Theory IT-**22**, Nov. 1976, pp. 644-654.

[7] N. Ferguson, "Extensions of Single Term Coins", Advances in Cryptology - CRYPTO '93, LNCS **773**, pp. 292-301.

[8] FIPS PUB 186, February 1, 1993, Digital Signature Standard.

[9] M. Jakobsson and M. Yung, "Revokable and Versatile Electronic Money", Third ACM Conference on Computer and Communications Security, 1996, ACM Press, pp. 76-87.

[10] D. Naccache, D. M'Raïhi, S. Vaudenay and D. Raphaeli, "Can DSA be improved ? - Complexity trade-offs with the Digital Signature Standard", Advances in Cryptology - EUROCRYPT '94, LNCS **950**, pp. 77-85.

[11] D. Pointcheval, J. Stern, "Security Proofs for Signature Schemes", Advances in Cryptology - EUROCRYPT '96, LNCS **1070** pp. 387-398.

[12] R. Rivest, A. Shamir and L. Adleman, "A method for Obtaining Digital Signatures and Public-Key Cryptosystems", Communications of the ACM, v. **21**, n. 2, Feb 1978, pp. 120-126.

[13] C. Schnorr, "Efficient identification and signatures for smart-cards", Advances in Cryptology - EUROCRYPT '89, LNCS **765**, pp. 435-439.

[14] S. von Solms and D. Naccache, "On Blind Signatures and Perfect Crimes", Computers and Security, **11** (1992) pp. 581-583.

[15] M. Stadler, J-M. Piveteau and J. Cammenish, "Fair Blind Signatures", Advances in Cryptology - EUROCRYPT '95, LNCS **921**, pp. 209-219.

Mis-representation of Identities in E-cash Schemes and how to Prevent it

Agnes Chan[1], Yair Frankel[2] *, Philip MacKenzie[2,3] *, Yiannis Tsiounis[1] **

[1] Northeastern University
College of Computer Science
161 Cullinane Hall
Boston, Massachusetts 02115
ahchan@ccs.neu.edu, yiannis@ccs.neu.edu

[2] Sandia National Laboratories
1515 Eubank SE
Albquerque, New Mexico 87123
yair@cs.sandia.gov

[3] Department of Mathematics and Computer Science
Boise State University
Boise, Idaho 83725
philmac@cs.idbsu.edu

Abstract. In Crypto '93, S. Brands presented a very efficient off-line electronic cash scheme based on the representation problem in groups of prime order. In Crypto '95 a very efficient off-line divisible e-cash scheme based on factoring Williams integers was presented by T. Okamoto. We demonstrate one efficient attack on Okamoto's scheme and two on Brands' scheme which allow users to mis-represent their identities and double-spend in an undetectable manner, hence defeating the most essential security aspect of the schemes. The attack on Brands' scheme (which we suspect, given his previous related results, was an inadvertent omission) is also applicable to T. Eng and T. Okamoto's divisible e-cash scheme (presented in Eurocrypt '94) which uses Brands' protocols as a building block.

We present an efficient modular fix which is applicable to any use of the Brands' idea, and we discuss how to counteract the attack on Okamoto's scheme. Hence the original results remain significant contributions to electronic cash.

1 Introduction

In Crypto '95, Okamoto [Oka95] presented a very efficient off-line divisible e-cash system, whose security is based on factoring a Williams integer. We discover

---

* This work was performed under U.S. Department of Energy contract number DE-AC04-94AL85000.
** This author's research was partially funded by GTE Laboratories Incorporated, Waltham MA.

an attack on this scheme that allows a user to double-spend undetectably by falsifying his identity at account opening. We also discuss ways for the bank to counteract the attack, thus preserving the significance of the result.

In Crypto '93, Brands presented a very efficient off-line electronic cash scheme based on the representation problem in groups of prime order [Bra93b]. In Eurocrypt '94, Eng and Okamoto [EO94] used [Bra93b] as a building block to construct an off-line divisible e-cash scheme. We discover two flaws that are applicable in both schemes. These attacks allow a misbehaving user to deterministically construct an incorrect identity and spend his electronic coins multiple times without being identified. Though our attacks are severe, the fix is simple. Hence, we believe that the original contributions are strong and represent important electronic cash systems to be further studied and improved.

In Section 2 we review the protocol in [Oka95] and discuss an attack on the scheme and how to counteract it. In Section 3, we review the protocols in [Bra93b] and [EO94] and discuss how to break and repair them.

2   Okamoto's Divisible Scheme

We proceed with a short description of Okamoto's scheme; we refer the reader to [Oka95] for details.

In this scheme, each user U has a composite number $N = PQ$ such that N is a Williams integer[4] associated with U.

In **the account opening protocol** the user U selects random primes P, Q with $|P| = |Q|$ and shows $g^P, g^Q \pmod{\mathcal{P}}$ to the bank $\mathcal{B}$, where g is a generator of the subgroup of prime order $(\mathcal{P}-1)/2$, $\mathcal{P}$ is prime and $|\mathcal{P}| \geq 4|P| + 10$. The bank $\mathcal{B}$ provides the user with an "electronic license" on a number $N = PQ$ after the user proves that N is indeed the product of P, Q.

Withdrawal of the coin (performed over an authenticated channel between U and $\mathcal{B}$) is nothing more than an RSA blind signature [Cha83] on $H(N||b)$, where H is a one-way function, b is a random value, and the private RSA key used by $\mathcal{B}$ to sign is dependent on the value of the coin.

The payment protocol (performed over an anonymous channel between U and the shop $\mathcal{S}$) consists of the coin authentication and denomination revelation stages.

At coin authentication, $\mathcal{S}$ verifies the bank's RSA signature on $H(N||b)$, the correctness of the electronic license on N, and that the Jacobi symbols of -1 and 2 over N are 1 and -1 respectively: $(-1/N) = 1, (2/N) = -1$. This last step guarantees that N has an odd number of prime factors which are congruent to $3 \bmod 8$, and an odd number of factors congruent to $7 \bmod 8$.

At denomination revelation, U reveals the square root mod N of some random numbers. Also, $\mathcal{S}$ (indirectly) checks that N has only two prime factors.

---

[4] $N = PQ$ is a Williams integer iff P, Q are primes, and $P \equiv 3 \bmod 8, Q \equiv 7 \bmod 8$.

If $\mathcal{U}$ over-spends a coin, $\mathcal{B}$ obtains two square roots of the same number, and factors N to obtain P, Q, thus breaking the user's anonymity.

2.1 Attacking the Scheme

We show how the user can cheat at account opening so that he can later over-spend by an arbitrary amount without being identified. We exploit the weakness in the coin authentication and denomination revelation protocols. Instead of the tests checking that N is a product of two prime factors, the tests only prove that N is a product of odd powers of two primes.

At **account opening**, $\mathcal{U}$ chooses primes $P_1 \equiv 3 \bmod 8, Q_1 \equiv 7 \bmod 8$, two odd numbers i, j, and two integers $i' < i, j' < j$. $\mathcal{U}$ then uses $P = P_1^{i'} Q_1^{j'}, Q = P_1^{i-i'} Q_1^{j-j'}$. $\mathcal{B}$ gives $\mathcal{U}$ an electronic license on $N = PQ = P_1^{i} Q_1^{j}$.

At **withdrawal**, $\mathcal{U}$ uses $N = P_1^{i} Q_1^{j}$.

At **payment**, all the verifications would still succeed: $(-1/N) = 1, (2/N) = -1$ and N contains only odd powers of two prime factors. Upon factoring N, however, the bank would only obtain $P_2 = P_1^{i} \neq P$ and $Q_2 = Q_1^{j} \neq Q$.

2.2 Counteracting the Attack

If $\mathcal{B}$ knows the nature of the attack, it can still trace the user, albeit at a higher cost. Two counteractions are now presented.

Countermeasure After Deposit: The bank must first find i, j (and P_1, Q_1) from P_2, Q_2 and then try all possible combinations of i, j until it finds P, Q. To reduce the required computation, some of the values for i, j can be excluded by having $\mathcal{S}$ check, at payment time, whether N is divisible by some small primes (i.e. by putting a lower bound on the size of P_1, Q_1, and hence an upper bound on i, j).

Using the parameters of [Oka95] ($|P| = |Q| = 256$ bits), and if the shop, at payment, checks that N is not divisible by the primes less than 2^{13}, then $2^{13} < P_1 < P_2 = P_1^{i} < N < 2^{512}$ and so $i, j, i + j < 40$. This checking requires only the same amount of computation as one exponentiation.[5] Since i, j are odd integers, at most 20 integer root operations (which are as efficient as exponentiations) are needed for finding i, j, P_1, Q_1. To find P, we need to try all combinations of (i', j'), for $i' < i, j' < j$. Since the worst case occurs when $i = 21, j = 19$, there are at most $21 * 19 = 399$ such combinations. Each combination gives rise to one exponentiation[6] (g^P). Thus, in the worst case, at most 420 exponentiations are needed to trace $\mathcal{U}$. The bank would also have to perform around 400 searches

---

[5] There are approximately $2^{13}/13 \approx 630$ primes less than 2^{13}; 630 divisions are comparable to one exponentiation of the size used in [Oka95]—which needs 1,200 multiplications.

[6] Computing each new candidate value of P requires only 1 multiplication, and therefore can be ignored.

on its account database (one for each candidate value for (P, Q)). The efficiency costs are well within the limits of the system (e.g., compared to the account opening which takes 4,000 exponentiations).

It is very important to note that *this computation is only performed after it is known that a coin has been double-spent*, and the malicious user needs to be identified. This computation will be performed very rarely, and even then the associated costs can be charged to the malicious user.

Okamoto's fix During Withdrawal: After presenting our attack to Okamoto [Oka96], he was able to suggest other methods to prevent the attack with reasonable efficiency costs. His fix and other comments are provided in the appendix B.

3 Schemes Based on the Representation Problem

We give a short description of Brands' and Eng-Okamoto's original schemes. We encourage the reader to refer to the original descriptions [Bra93b, EO94] for further details. Readers familiar with [Bra93b, EO94] may skip Sections 3.1 and 3.2.

3.1 Brands' Scheme

In **the bank $\mathcal{B}$'s set up protocol** (performed once), primes p and q are chosen such that $q|(p-1)$. Afterwards, generators g, g_1, g_2 of G_q are defined, where G_q is the subgroup of prime order q of the multiplicative group Z_p^*. Secret key $x \in_R Z_q^*$ is created. Hash functions $\mathcal{H}, \mathcal{H}_0$, from a family of collision intractable (or, ideally, correlation-free one way) hash functions are also defined. $\mathcal{B}$ publishes $p, q, g, g_1, g_2, g^x, \mathcal{H}, \mathcal{H}_0$.

In the **user $\mathcal{U}$'s setup** (account establishment) protocol, $\mathcal{B}$ associates $\mathcal{U}$ with $I = g_1^{u_1}$, where $u_1 \in Z_q$ is generated (and only known) by $\mathcal{U}$, and $g_1^{u_1} g_2 \neq 1$. $\mathcal{B}$ transmits $z = (Ig_2)^x$ to $\mathcal{U}$ (alternatively, $\mathcal{B}$ publishes $h_1 = g_1^x, h_2 = g_2^x$ as part of its public key, and $\mathcal{U}$ calculates $z = h_1^{u_1} h_2$ instead).

The **withdrawal protocol** (performed over an authenticated channel between $\mathcal{B}$ and $\mathcal{U}$) creates a "restrictively blind" signature of I. $\mathcal{U}$ will end up with a Schnorr-type [Sch91] signature on $(Ig_2)^s$, where s is a random number chosen by $\mathcal{U}$ and kept secret. The exact form of the signature is $\text{sign}(A, B) = (z', a', b', r')$ with the following two equations being satisfied:[7]

$$g^{r'} = h^{\mathcal{H}(A,B,z',a',b')}a' \text{ and } A^{r'} = z'^{\mathcal{H}(A,B,z',a',b')}b', \text{ where } h = g^x \quad (1)$$

The withdrawal protocol, taken verbatim from [Bra93b]:

---

[7] Our notation here is slightly different from [Bra93b].

$\mathcal{U}$ $\mathcal{B}$

$$w \in_R Z_q$$
$$a \leftarrow g^w$$

$s \in_R Z_q^*$ $\xleftarrow{a,b}$ $b \leftarrow (Ig_2)^w$
$A \leftarrow (Ig_2)^s$
$z' \leftarrow z^s$
$x_1, x_2, u, v \in_R Z_q$
$B \leftarrow g_1^{x_1} g_2^{x_2}$
$a' \leftarrow a^u g^v$
$b' \leftarrow b^{su} A^v$
$c' \leftarrow H(A, B, z', a', b')$
$c \leftarrow c'/u \bmod q$ $\xrightarrow{c}$

$g^r \stackrel{?}{=} h^c a$ $\xleftarrow{r}$ $r \leftarrow cx + w \bmod q$
$(Ig_2)^r \stackrel{?}{=} z^c b$
$r' \leftarrow ru + v \bmod q$

At **payment** (performed between $\mathcal{U}$ and the shop S over an anonymous channel), $\mathcal{U}$ supplies a point on a "line" (terminology borrowed from secret-sharing schemes) to S that is uniquely determined by the shop's identity (I_S). Two such points determine $\mathcal{U}$'s identity. Hence, double-spenders are identified.

The payment protocol, taken verbatim from [Bra93b]:

$\mathcal{U}$ S

                                 $\xrightarrow{A,B,\text{sign}(A,B)}$ $A \stackrel{?}{\neq} 1$
                                                                              $d \leftarrow \mathcal{H}_0(A, B, I_S, \text{date/time})$
                                 $\xleftarrow{d}$

$r_1 \leftarrow d(u_1 s) + x_1 \bmod q$
$r_2 \leftarrow ds + x_2 \bmod q$ $\xrightarrow{(r_1, r_2)}$ Verify $\text{sign}(A, B)$
                                                                              $g_1^{r_1} g_2^{r_2} \stackrel{?}{=} A^d B$

Deposit: The shop deposits the coin by providing the bank with a transcript of the deposit. If the user $\mathcal{U}$ associated with $I = g_1^{u_1}$ spends the coin twice, the bank obtains two transcripts (d, r_1, r_2) and (d', r_1', r_2') and the relation

$$g_1^{(r_1 - r_1')/(r_2 - r_2')} = I$$

holds. See [Bra93b] for details.

3.2   Eng and Okamoto's Scheme

The setup and withdrawal protocols of [EO94] are the same as in [Bra93b], with the exception of the construction of $T = B = g_1^{x_1} g_2^{x_2}$ (B is denoted by T

in [EO94]), where (x_1, x_2) are of a special form, in order to help "divide" the coin later on. But this does not affect the way the withdrawal protocol works, since T is blindly signed by the bank, without any further verification.

In **the payment protocol**, at coin authentication, sign(A, T) is verified. At denomination revelation, $\mathcal{U}$ shows a number β to $\mathcal{S}$ and proves that β is correctly constructed.[8] Then the payment protocol of [Bra93b] is performed, with β substituting for B. The construction of β guarantees that if $\mathcal{U}$ over-spends, the bank ends up with two equations of the form:

$$r_1 \leftarrow d(u_1 s) + x_1 \quad \text{and} \quad r_2 \leftarrow ds + x_2,$$

exactly as in [Bra93b].

3.3 How to Misbehave

We show how a user may misbehave in the setup (account-opening) protocol in such a way as to be able to spend a coin arbitrarily many times without being identified.

Attack 1: Represent I in (g_1, g_2) At setup, $\mathcal{U}$, instead of using $I = g_1^{u_1}$, chooses $I = g_1^{u_1} g_2^{u_2}$, for random u_1, u_2. In the case where $\mathcal{B}$ does not compute z, $\mathcal{U}$ can still compute z by himself given $h_1 = g_1^x$ and $h_2 = g_2^x$: $z = (Ig_2)^x = (g_1^{u_1} g_2^{u_2} g_2)^x = h_1^{u_1} h_2^{(u_2+1)}$.

$\mathcal{U}$ conducts **the withdrawal protocol** (unmodified), to end up with a signature on $A = g_1^{u_1 s} g_2^{(u_2+1)s}$ and $B = g_1^{x_1} g_2^{x_2}$. $\mathcal{U}$ can do this since he knows z, and the representation of I with respect to *(w.r.t.)* (g_1, g_2). The signature for $(A = (g_1^{u_1} g_2^{u_2+1})^s, B = g_1^{x_1} g_2^{x_2})$ is $(z' = (g_1^{u_1} g_2^{u_2+1})^{xs}, a' = g^{wu+v}, b' = (g_1^{u_1} g_2^{u_2+1})^{wsu+sv}, r' = \mathcal{H}(A, B, z', a', b')x + wu + v \bmod q)$ for s, u, v randomly chosen by $\mathcal{U}$. The signature clearly satisfies (1).

At **payment** time, the two responses supplied by $\mathcal{U}$ to $\mathcal{S}$ (or, in the case of [EO94], obtained by $\mathcal{B}$ if $\mathcal{U}$ over-spends) will now be:

$$r_1 = de + x_1 \quad \text{and} \quad r_2 = df + x_2$$

Where (e, f) is the representation of A w.r.t. (g_1, g_2), i.e. $A = g_1^e g_2^f$, $e = u_1 s, f = (u_2+1)s$. After two payments, $\mathcal{B}$ can obtain $e = u_1 s, f = (u_2+1)s$. But this last system has two equations and three unknown (to $\mathcal{B}$) variables,[9] u_1, u_2, s. Hence, $\mathcal{B}$ will not be able to compute u_1, u_2, *even if it knew the nature of the attack*, and $\mathcal{U}$ will remain unidentified after double-spending.

Note that even after an arbitrary number of payments, $\mathcal{B}$ cannot obtain any more information than e and f. Therefore *the user can spend the coin arbitrarily many times without being identified*.

---

[8] The exact form of β and its proof of correctness are irrelevant to our attacks.

[9] Extracting s by using the gcd of (e, f) is impossible since we are working mod q.

Attack 2: Represent I in (g_1, g_2, g) In a generalization of the previous attack, $\mathcal{U}$ selects $I = g_1^{u_1} g_2^{u_2} g^{u_3}$ for some u_1, u_2, u_3. $\mathcal{U}$ obtains z from $\mathcal{B}$, or computes $z = h_1^{u_1} h_2^{u_2+1} h^{u_3}$. We now show that $\mathcal{U}$ is still able to obtain a signature for $A = (g_1^{u_1} g^{u_2+1})^s$, and to spend the coin multiple times without being identified.

All we need to note is that upon receipt of (a, b) from $\mathcal{B}$ at withdrawal time, $\mathcal{U}$ uses $b'' = b/a^{u_3} = (g_1^{u_1} g_2^{u_2+1})^w$ instead of b. The flaw explored here is the extra information $(a = g^w)$ given to $\mathcal{U}$ from the bank, which nevertheless is necessary for the protocol's completion.

3.4 How to Repair the Schemes

To counteract both attacks, $\mathcal{U}$ must provide $\mathcal{B}$ with a (minimal-knowledge) proof of knowledge of the representation of I w.r.t. g_1 during setup. An efficient proof of this form is the Schnorr-type identification scheme [Sch91].

We must note that a similar proof of knowledge is used in Brands [Bra93a] published before [Bra93b] (at withdrawal instead of setup time) for a different purpose *and in a different protocol* (for instance, I is generated differently): "When a user $\mathcal{U}$ wants to withdraw a coin from his account (...) he first convinces $\mathcal{B}$ that the money will indeed be withdrawn from his own account"[Bra93a, p. 38]. This proof of authenticity can be achieved in other ways and does not appear to be intended to prevent an attack similar to the one presented here (i.e., using $I = g_1^{u_1} g_2^{u_2} g_3^{u_3}$ instead of $I = g_1^{u_1} g_2^{u_2}$). However, we suspect that Brands had anticipated our attack even for [Bra93b], which is different than [Bra93a]. It is probably the lack of proof of the necessity of this verification (probably in conjunction with efficiency concerns) that led to its omission from [Bra93b]. We should note that those familiar with e-cash have missed this attack, as seen in [EO94]; our purpose in this paper is to bring forth and explain this problem, as the existing published literature left the point unclear resulting in such propagated errors.

In appendix A, Brands' response on our attack is given.

Also, a comment by Eng and Okamoto [EO94, p. 314, Section 3.5] stating that the scheme can be modified for $I = g_1^{u_1} g_2^{u_2}$, refers to making the scheme similar to [Bra93a] (i.e., using 3 instead of 2 generators); hence the similar attack (mentioned above) and a similar modular fix would be applicable to this modification as well.

Remark. (**On how "restrictive" is the withdrawal protocol**). We now comment on the fact that the withdrawal protocol is a "restrictive blind signature" (on $I = g_1^{u_1}$) as described in Assumption 1 in [Bra93b] *only if* it is combined with a payment protocol[10] which verifies that A is represented w.r.t. (g_1, g_2): observe that using the attacks of section 3.3, $\mathcal{U}$ can start the withdrawal protocol with $I = g_1^{u_1}$ and end up with a signature on $A = g_1^{u_1 s} g_2^s g^{u_3 s}$ (by using $z = h_1^{u_1} h_2 h^{u_3}$, and $b'' = b a^{u_3}$ instead of b). Although we do not know how to

---

[10] Assumption 1 is presented after the withdrawal protocol but before the payment protocol in [Bra93b].

guard against this variation, the schemes are not broken, since $\mathcal{U}$ does not end up with a spendable coin (because A is not represented w.r.t. (g_1, g_2)).

4 Conclusion

In Crypto '93 (S. Brands), Eurocrypt '94 (T. Eng and T. Okamoto) and Crypto '95 (T. Okamoto) three practical electronic cash protocols were presented. We have shown how the "mis-representation" of an ID can be used to break schemes based on the representation problem or on factoring a Williams integer. We also presented a modular fix to the first two schemes, thus enabling further usage of the representation problem for efficient e-cash. Counter-measures for Okamoto's scheme were also shown. Hence we believe that the original contributions are strong and are important electronic cash systems to be studied and improved.

Acknowledgements

We thank K. McCurley for his discussions on Williams integers. We also thank T. Okamoto for many interesting discussions on electronic cash and for providing us with the comments included in the appendix. We thank S. Brands for his comments.

References

[Bra93a] S. Brands. An efficient off-line electronic cash system based on the representation problem. Technical Report CS-R9323, CWI (Centre for Mathematics and Computer Science), Amsterdam, 1993. anonymous ftp: ftp.cwi.nl:/pub/CWIreports/AA/CS-R9323.ps.zip.

[Bra93b] S. Brands. Untraceable off-line cash in wallets with observers. In *Advances in Cryptology — Crypto '93, Proceedings (Lecture Notes in Computer Science 773)*, pages 302–318. Springer-Verlag, 1993.

[Cha83] D. Chaum. Blind signatures for untraceable payments. In D. Chaum, R.L. Rivest, and A. T. Sherman, editors, *Advances in Cryptology. Proc. Crypto '82*, pages 199–203, Santa Barbara, 1983. Plenum Press N. Y.

[EO94] T. Eng and T. Okamoto. Single-term divisible electronic coins. In *Advances in Cryptology — Eurocrypt '94, Proceedings*, pages 306 – 319, New York, 1994. Springer-Verlag.

[Oka95] T. Okamoto. An efficient divisible electronic cash scheme. In Don Coppersmith, editor, *Advances in Cryptology, Proc. of Crypto '95 (Lecture Notes in Computer Science 963)*, pages 438–451. Springer-Verlag, 1995. Santa Barbara, California, U.S.A., August 27–31.

[Oka96] T. Okamoto, 1996. Personal communication.

[Sch91] C. P. Schnorr. Efficient signature generation by smart cards. *Journal of Cryptology*, 4(3):161–174, 1991.

A Brands' Comments

Brands provided us with the following comment by e-mail on 8/22/96:[11]

> This paper states that it shows two efficient "attacks" on my cash system of Crypto 1993, and then shows how to "repair" the "break". Apart from the fact that the "two" attacks are actually the same, the attack does not pertain to a shortcoming of my system: it is the mere result of an inadvertent ommision from my side of a fact well known to me. Namely, the "attack" and "repair" are already present in my 1993 technical report (referenced by the authors), as is apparent from page 38 and in particular from the paragraph starting at the bottom of page 43 (pointing out the need to prove correct formation). The accidental omission of the fact in my Crypto 93 paper, which is a summary of the technical report, has been pointed out to me by several people already around two years ago (amongst others by Masayuki Abe of NTT, cryptographers from university of Leuven, and cryptographers of Hildesheim university). Nobody, including myself, bothered to write about it since it was clearly not a security flaw, and moreover obvious from the informal description of the workings of the system.

B Okamoto's Fix and Comments

Okamoto provided us with the following:

Here we will give a modification of our paper presented at Crypto'95 [Oka95] in order to fix the security flaw pointed out in this paper. All notations here follow [Oka95], especially Subsection 5.1 (The Opening Protocol).

In our modification, bank B additionally requires customer U to prove to B in a zero-knowledge manner that P and Q are coprime, in the opening protocol. That is, U proves to B that there exists a pair of positive integers, (c, d), such that $cP - dQ = 1$.

The additional subprotocol for this purpose is as follows: (This subprotocol should be placed in step 3 of the opening protocol [Oka95].)

1. First, U calculates (c_0, d_0), such that $c_0 P + d_0 Q = 1$. W.l.o.g., we assume that $Q > c_0 > 0$ and $-P < d_0 < 0$. Let $c = c_0 + iQ$, $d = -d_0 + iP$ (i: an appropriate integer, $0 < i < 5$) such that $(1/2)n_1^{1/2} < c, d < n_1^{1/2}$. Then, $cP - dQ = 1$.
   U then generates random numbers, R_c, R_d, R_c', $R_d' \in Z_{Prime}$.
   U calculates the following values: $\gamma_0 = BC_g(R_c, c)$, $\gamma_1 = BC_x(R_c', c) = BC_g(R_c', cP)$, $\delta_0 = BC_g(R_d, d)$, $\delta_1 = BC_y(R_d', d) = BC_g(R_d', dQ)$.
   U sends γ_0, γ_1, δ_0, and δ_1 to B.

---

[11] This is printed verbatim, and we are not responsible for its content. We decided not to comment on it since the reasons for publishing these attacks are clearly stated in the paper's main body.

2. U uses the COMPARE COMMITMENTS protocol with $[(1/2)n_1^{1/2}, n_1^{1/2}]$ to prove that U knows how to open $\gamma_0 = BC_g(R_c, c)$ and $\gamma_1 = BC_x(R'_c, c)$ in $[0, (3/2)n_1^{1/2}]$.

   U also uses the COMPARE COMMITMENTS protocol with $[(1/2)n_1^{1/2}, n_1^{1/2}]$ to prove that U knows how to open $\delta_0 = BC_g(R_d, d), \delta_1 = BC_y(R'_d, d)$ in $[0, (3/2)n_1^{1/2}]$.

3. U opens (as a base-g commitment) the product $\gamma_1 \delta^{-1} \bmod \mathcal{P}$ to reveal a 1 (i.e., reveals $R^* = R'_c - R'_d \bmod Prime$ such that $BC_g(R^*, 1) = \gamma_1 \delta^{-1} \bmod \mathcal{P}$.

As for the efficiency, the additional subprotocol requires just two executions of the COMPARE COMMITMENTS protocol. The total opening protocol requires many (more than 50) executions of the protocols which are comparable to the COMPARE COMMITMENTS protocol. Therefore, the additionally required execution amount is just a few percent of the total of the opening protocol.

Finally we describe the COMPARE COMMITMENTS protocol, since we found several typos in the description of [Oka95].

Protocol: COMPARE COMMITMENTS

Common input: x, x' and $(\mathcal{P}, G, g, h, I)$.

What to prove: U knows (R, R', s) such that $x = BC_g(R, s)$, $x' = BC_h(R', s)$ and $s \in I \pm e$.

Execute the following k times:

1. U chooses t_1 uniformly in $[0, e]$, and sets $t_2 = t_1 - e$. U sends to B the unordered pair of commitments $(T_1, T'_1), (T_2, T'_2)$, where each component of the pair is ordered and $(T_i, T'_i) = (BC_g(S_i, t_i), BC_h(S'_i, t_i))$.
2. B selects a bit $\beta \in \{0, 1\}$ and sends it to U.
3. U sends to B one of the following:
   (a) if β is 0, opening of both (T_1, T'_1) and (T_2, T'_2)
   (b) if β is 1, opening of $x \cdot T_i \bmod \mathcal{P}$ and $x' \cdot T'_i \bmod \mathcal{P}$ ($i \in \{1, 2\}$), such that $s + t_i \in I$.
4. B checks the correctness of U's messages.

Here, let the interval be $I = [a, b]$ ($= \{x | a \le x \le b\}$), $e = b - a$, and $I \pm e = [a - e, b + e]$.

$\mathcal{P}$ and $Prime$ are primes such that $\mathcal{P} - 1 = 2 \cdot Prime$.

G, $g \in Z_{\mathcal{P}}^*$, and $\mathrm{Ord}(G) = \mathrm{Ord}(g) = Prime$.

$BC_g(R, s) = G^R g^s \bmod \mathcal{P}$, where $s, R \in Z_{Prime}$. This is called a base-g commitment.

"Indirect Discourse Proofs": Achieving Efficient Fair Off-Line E-cash

Yair Frankel*, Yiannis Tsiounis**, Moti Yung***

Abstract. Cryptography has been instrumental in reducing the involvement of over-head third parties in protocols. For example; a *digital signature scheme* assures a recipient that a judge who is not present at message transmission will nevertheless approve the validity of the signature. Similarly, in *off-line electronic cash* the bank (which is off-line during a purchase) is assured that if a user double spends he will be traced.

Here we suggest the notion of *Indirect Discourse Proofs* with which one can prove indirectly yet efficiently that a third party has a certain future capability (i.e., assure Trustees can trace). The efficient proofs presented here employ algebraic properties of exponentiation (or functions of similar homomorphic nature).

Employing this idea we present the concept of "Fair Off-Line e-Cash" (FOLC) system which enables tracing protocols for identifying either the **coin** or its **owner**. Recently, the need to trace and identify coins with owners/withdrawals was identified (to avoid blackmailing and money laundering). Previous solutions that assured this traceability (called fair e-cash as they balance the need for anonymity and the prevention of criminal activities) involved third parties at money withdrawals. In contrast, FOLC keeps any third party uninvolved, thus it is "fully off-line e-cash" even when law enforcement is added (i.e., it is off-line w.r.t. law enforcement at withdrawals and off-line w.r.t. the bank at payments).

1 Introduction

Direct involvement of parties performing only administrative tasks (e.g., assuring that potential future actions are enabled) is undesirable in electronic transactions. Such excessive involvement increases the over-head and the required synchronization among protocol members. Examples of areas where involvement of a judge in the actual protocol was eliminated are digital signatures, contract signing and simultaneous exchange protocols. In this work we suggest a basic idea that avoids direct involvement of administrative third parties as a general tool and use it for a crucial task. Third party involvement is replaced by a tool

* Sandia National Laboratories, 1515 Eubank SE, Albquerque, New Mexico 87123, e-mail: yair@cs.sandia.gov. This work was performed under U.S. Department of Energy contract number DE-AC04-94AL85000.
** Northeastern University, College of Computer Science, 161 Cullinane Hall, Boston, Massachusetts 02115, e-mail: yiannis@ccs.neu.edu. This author's research was partially funded by GTE Laboratories Incorporated, Waltham MA.
*** Work done at IBM T.J. Watson Research Center, e-mail: moti@cs.columbia.edu.

in which an active participant proves that in case of future events like mishaps, attacks, and disputes, the administrative party (authority, judge, agents) will be able to take proper actions (if necessary). We call such proofs "indirect discourse proofs" — where the prover refers to the cryptographic capabilities of a third party rather than invoking the third party itself at the time of proof.

In the area of electronic-cash, third party involvement was reduced. Namely, off-line systems (first introduced in [CFN90] and then developed further, in e.g., [OO92, FY93, Fer93b, Bra93b, Oka95]), the bank's ($\mathcal{B}$) involvement in the payment transaction between a user ($\mathcal{U}$) and a receiver ($\mathcal{R}$) was eliminated. Users withdraw electronic "coins" from the bank and use them to pay a receiver (a shop). The receiver subsequently deposits the coins back to the bank. In the process users remain anonymous, unless they spend a single coin more than once (double-spend). This last property (whenever sufficient) allows the bank to be off-line during payment.

Unfortunately, it was pointed out that anonymous electronic cash can become a tool for criminal activities [vSN92, BGK95, SPC95]. The anonymity provided to the owner of a coin allows for money laundering and for perfect blackmailing. Hence any large scale application of e-cash may be thwarted by a government unless there is a mechanism to prevent such criminal activities. Two previous methods were suggested to solve the criminal activity in off-line e-cash systems. (These are escrowed cash by Brickell, Gemmell and Kravitz [BGK95] and signature-message linking via fair blind signatures by Stadler, Piveteau and Camenisch [SPC95].) However, in contrast with our solution, they both employ on-line fair withdrawals (i.e., the Trustees are involved in every withdrawal).

In this work we suggest employing indirect discourse proofs to implement an electronic cash scheme which is fair (i.e., identifiable by proper Trustees but anonymous otherwise). The user proves that the judge (Trustee), in the future, will be able to identify the owner (of the coin) or the coin (that originated from a withdrawal) when legally required. Yet the Trustee itself does not have to be present in the withdrawal (nor in payment or deposit), similar to a judge in a signature scheme. This is an analogous requirement to the bank not being present in the payment transaction. We, thus, call these "Fair Off-Line e-Cash" systems (FOLC). The resulting systems prevent both money laundering and black-mailing, and are efficient.

Structure of the paper: In Section 2 we model FOLC and present the various notions of traceability. Then, in Section 3 we show the necessity of conditional security and certain cryptographic tools in FOLC. We also present a generic modular extension which can turn existing e-cash schemes into FOLC systems. In Section 4, we discuss a variation of the e-cash protocol in [Bra93b] which we build upon. Then we add indirect discourse proofs to this scheme to provide the owner tracing protocol assuming a trusted receiver (Section 5.1) and then without a trusted receiver (Section 5.2). Finally, the coin tracing protocol is realized in Section 6.

Recent related work: Very recently and independently, [Sta96a], based on [Sta96b], have suggested an off-line solution to cash tracing. Our second, more efficient, indirect discourse proof schemes seem to achieve similar results to [Sta96b] but (based on initial comparisons) perhaps 30 times faster. We also note that [JY96] introduced the recent notion of revokable e-money against a direct strong attack on the bank. They propose a third party with a secret channel connection to the bank (an alarm channel) to cope with such strong direct attacks on the bank itself. We do not deal with such attacks in our model.

Assumptions: The security of our protocols are based on the security of the Brands [Bra93b] electronic cash scheme. (This scheme, in turn, assumes that the hash functions used are perfect (i.e., random oracles), and (as [Sch91]) that Schnorr identification schemes leak no useful information.[4]) For anonymity for some of our protocols, we introduce a *matching Diffie-Hellman* assumption, which is a new variant on the hardness of Discrete Logarithms.

Remark: We employ Discrete Log. methods; these methods have been suggested in many of the more recent efficient e-cash schemes to bind identities (an unavoidable issue in off-line e-cash). This has started in [FY93] and continued by others [Bra93b, Fer93b, Fer93a] as well as in [Yac95] – a work we have been specifically asked to relate our work to in [ref96]. A closer look at the above works will reveal that, the use of Discrete Log. put aside, none is related to us: None has attempted to solve our problems, neither has any of these works even suggested the problems, the primitives and the notions introduced herein.

2 Fair Off-Line electronic Cash (FOLC)

Fair off-line electronic cash (FOLC) extends anonymous off-line electronic cash and involves a bank (B), a collection of users (a single user is called U), a collection of receivers (a single receiver is denoted by R), and a collection of Trustees (judges/escrow agents) which act like one party[5] (and are denoted as T). FOLC includes five basic protocols, three of which are the same as in off-line electronic cash: a *withdrawal protocol* with which U withdraws electronic coins from B while his account is debited, a *payment protocol* with which U pays the coin to R, and a *deposit protocol* with which R deposits the coin to B and has his account credited. The two additional protocols:

- The *owner tracing* protocol traces the identity of the owner of a specific coin. In this protocol B gives to T the view of a deposit protocol. T returns a string that contains identifying information which B can use to identify the owner (via the account databases).
- The *coin tracing* protocol traces the coin(s) that originated from a withdrawal. In this protocol, T, given the view of a withdrawal protocol from B, returns some information that originated from this withdrawal. B can use the returned value to find the coin(s) (by accessing its views of the deposit protocols).

---

[4] Since hash functions are assumed to be random oracles, this guarantees that the self-challenging Schnorr identification scheme leaks no useful information either [PS96].

[5] It is outside the scope of this paper to show how the power of the Trustees can be equally distributed. T should be envisioned as being a single trusted entity.

Hence, the *owner tracing* protocol allows the authorities to prevent money laundering, since they can find the origin of dubious coins. It also allows the authorities to find the identity of a customer that uses a service which is typically anonymous but sometimes (when crime is suspected) requires identification, while still providing anonymity for legitimate users.

The *coin tracing* protocol allows the authorities to find the destination of suspicious withdrawals. This can solve, for example, the blackmailing problem [vSN92]: a customer is blackmailed and forced to anonymously withdraw electronic coins, so that the blackmailer can use these coins without ever being identified, in effect committing a "perfect crime" (of course the victim has to complain and point at withdrawals). The mechanism also enables tracing of activities of a suspect user that is on a criminal list at the time of his withdrawals.

Indirect-discourse proof techniques assure that T can perform its functions. Note that two facts are important, for efficiency reasons:

(1) B supplies only a single view (of a withdrawal or deposit protocol) to T during these protocols. Therefore T does not have to perform any searching, but can immediately "open" the requested identifying information.

(2) The identifying information returned from T is already included in the corresponding protocols (account opening/deposit). Hence B only has to perform a search on a (presumably indexed) database, rather than having to make a computation for each candidate view. Also, in the case of the coin tracing protocol, the identifying information can be broadcasted to all potential receivers, in effect "blacklisting" all suspicious coins.

3 Basic Results

Next we show fundamental requirements for FOLC schemes. We start by showing that perfect anonymity is impossible when tracing is required and that FOLC may require more than the existence of any one-way permutation when implemented based on black-box reductions (otherwise its implementation may serve as a proof separating P from NP). Later we show a basic scheme which achieves tracing (ignoring efficiency) based on any public key encryption (which is believed to require more than the usage of one-way permutation as a black box). The more theoretical investigation of this section gives us better understanding of what is required; in later sections we consider more efficient schemes.

Theorem 1 *(1) Unconditional unlink-ability is impossible in FOLC even if only owner tracing or coin tracing is supported. (2) Further, any implementation of FOLC based on black box reduction from an arbitrary one-way permutation will separate P and NP (thus, it seems unplausible since it will yield a breakthrough in complexity theoretic proof techniques).*

Proof. (1) Assume the opposite. The information revealed at payment time for a coin which is only spent once must (for owner tracing) allow for T (holding a finite length key), to trace U. Namely, it can be viewed as an encryption of a user's identity. Unconditional unlinkability implies that this encryption is unconditional, e.g., a one-time pad. Now by viewing $(\mathcal{U}, \mathcal{B}, \mathcal{R})$ as a single entity, this implies that $(\mathcal{U}, \mathcal{B}, \mathcal{R})$ can encrypt an arbitrary number of messages (one for each coin) to $\mathcal{T}$. As is well known from Shannon [Sha49], since the encryption is unconditional, $\mathcal{T}$ and $(\mathcal{U}, \mathcal{B}, \mathcal{R})$ must share information proportional (linear to) the size of all the plaintexts. This contradicts the fact that $\mathcal{T}$'s key is of fixed finite length, hence $\mathcal{T}$ can not be off-line during withdrawals.[6] Similar arguments prove the claim in case only coin tracing is supported.

(2) Viewing now the two parties $(\mathcal{U}, \mathcal{S})$ and $(\mathcal{B}, \mathcal{T})$, we can achieve "key exchange" between them, by letting $\mathcal{U}$ dynamically choose a name uniformly at random from the exponentially large user names. Then, run the withdrawal (between the two parties) and the payment (internal to the first party) and deposit protocol (between the parties), and finally the user tracing protocol (internal to the second party). At this point the name chosen by the first party is recognized by the second. Note that without the last internal interaction between $\mathcal{B}$ and $\mathcal{T}$, the identity (name) is strongly concealed from the participants (due to the anonymity requirement), thus from outsiders (based on information available in non-internal interactions) as well. This proves that the protocol is indeed a "key exchange". Hence, by [IR89], it is most plausible that we need more than a one-way permutation (used as a black-box) for constructing FOLC. □

We now demonstrate an optimal (polynomially) secure scheme; all we assume about the payment is that the information used by the user in the withdrawal and payment protocols can be extended with random strings. This is the case in all the existing methods (that can be employed). Typically, this extendible information is the one that is blinded and given to the bank to sign. We reduce such systems in the presence of public-key systems to FOLC with owner and/or coin tracing.

Theorem 2 *Given off-line e-cash and public-key encryption, there exists a FOLC system in which anonymity is cryptographically (polynomially) secure [GM84].*

Proof. We assume the existence of an off-line e-cash system in which (1) at withdrawal the user sends to the bank some (extendible) information to process and (2) this information is later presented as a string of bits.

To achieve tracing we perform the following. First, the bank "flips coins into the user's well"; these are $poly(k)$ random coins encrypted by the bank; we call this field the tag. Then, the bank and the user engage in the withdrawal of a coin. $\mathcal{T}$ has a public key published. The user extends the information he sends to the bank with a probabilistic encryption of his identity based on $\mathcal{T}$'s public key, and a second probabilistic encryption of the tag. Namely, the user concatenates to the coin information two (random) encryptions. The user proves in zero-knowledge

---

[6] In effect, $\mathcal{T}$ can precompute his "engagement" in each withdrawal as is done in [BGK95], but this does not alter the required amount of communication; it only allows a shift to a more convenient time.

the NP statement that the two encryptions sent represent its known name and the encrypted tag. (This is doable since we assume encryption functions).

After the verification, the bank is assured that the coin is tagged with the user's name under the trustee's encryption and a tag. If we require coin tracing, the coins into the well are opened and the tag value gets known.

Payment is done by opening the coin and the ciphertext value of the two encryptions. Deposit means forwarding the coin information as in the original deposit protocol along with the ciphertexts to the bank. For tracing the bank can forward the encryptions to T who can recover the identity of the user (owner tracing) or the tag (coin tracing). This implements FOLC. □

4 The Basic Off-Line Electronic Cash Scheme

We now concentrate on efficient schemes which we build based on a modification of [Bra93b]. This modification is as secure as [Bra93b] except that its untraceability is computationally secure rather than unconditionally secure.

Bank's setup protocol: (performed once by $\mathcal{B}$)
Primes p and q are chosen such that $|p-1| = \delta + k$ for a specified constant δ, and $p = \gamma q + 1$, for a specified small integer γ. Then a unique subgroup G_q of prime order q of the multiplicative group Z_p and generators g, g_1, g_2 of G_q are defined. Secret key $X_\mathcal{B} \in_R Z_q$ is created.[7] Hash functions $\mathcal{H}, \mathcal{H}_0, \mathcal{H}_1, \ldots$, from a family of collision intractable (or, ideally, according to [Bra93b], correlation-free one way) hash functions are also defined. $\mathcal{B}$ publishes $p, q, g, g_1, g_2, (\mathcal{H}, \mathcal{H}_0, \mathcal{H}_1, \ldots)$ and its public keys $h = g^{X_\mathcal{B}}, h_1 = g_1^{X_\mathcal{B}}, h_2 = g_2^{X_\mathcal{B}}$.

User's setup (account opening) protocol: (performed for each user $\mathcal{U}$)
The bank $\mathcal{B}$ associates user $\mathcal{U}$ with $I = g_1^{u_1}$ where $u_1 \in G_q$ is generated by $\mathcal{U}$ and $g_1^{u_1} g_2 \neq 1$. $\mathcal{U}$ also proves (using the Schnorr identification scheme [Sch91]) to $\mathcal{B}$ that he knows how to represent I w.r.t. g_1. $\mathcal{U}$ computes $z' = h_1^{u_1} h_2 = (Ig_2)^{X_\mathcal{B}}$.

Withdrawal: (over an authenticated channel between $\mathcal{B}$ and $\mathcal{U}$)
The withdrawal protocol creates a "restrictively blind" signature [Bra93b] of I. $\mathcal{U}$ will end up with a Schnorr-type [Sch91] signature on $(Ig_2)^s$, where s is a random number (chosen by $\mathcal{U}$ and kept secret). The exact form of the signature is $sig(A, B) = (z, a, b, r)$ satisfying:

$$g^r = h^{\mathcal{H}(A,B,z,a,b)}a \quad \text{and} \quad A^r = z^{\mathcal{H}(A,B,z,a,b)}b \tag{1}$$

The withdrawal protocol:

---

[7] We assume, for simplicity, that only one denomination is used. A different key for each denomination is necessary.

$\mathcal{U}$ $\qquad\qquad\qquad\qquad\qquad\qquad\qquad\qquad\qquad\qquad\qquad$ $\mathcal{B}$

$$w \in_R Z_q$$

$\begin{aligned} s &\in_R Z_q \\ A &= (Ig_2)^s \\ z &= z'^s \end{aligned}$ $\qquad\xleftarrow{a',b'}\qquad$ $a' = g^w, b' = (Ig_2)^w$

$\begin{aligned} x_1, x_2, u, v &\in_R Z_q \\ B_1 &= g_1^{x_1}, B_2 = g_2^{x_2} \\ B &= [B_1, B_2] \\ a &= (a')^u g^v \\ b &= (b')^{su} A^v \\ c &= \mathcal{H}(A, B, z, a, b) \end{aligned}$

$c' = c/u$ $\qquad\xrightarrow{c'}\qquad$

$r = r'u + v \bmod q$ $\qquad\xleftarrow{r'}\qquad$ $r' = c'X_B + w$

At the end of the protocol $\mathcal{U}$ verifies: $g^r \overset{?}{=} h^{c'}a', (Ig_2)^r \overset{?}{=} z'^{c'}b'$.

Observe the only modification here is that B is "split" into two halves: B_1, B_2.

Payment: (performed between $\mathcal{U}$ and $\mathcal{R}$ over an anonymous channel)

At payment time $\mathcal{U}$ supplies information to the receiver $\mathcal{R}$ (which is later forwarded to the bank) so that if a coin is double-spent the user $\mathcal{U}$ is identified. The payment protocol ($\mathcal{U}$ and $\mathcal{R}$ agree on date/time):

$\mathcal{U}$ $\qquad\qquad\qquad\qquad\qquad\qquad\qquad\qquad\qquad\qquad\qquad$ $\mathcal{R}$

$\begin{aligned} A_1 &= g_1^{u_1 s} \\ A_2 &= g_2^s \end{aligned}$ $\quad[1] \xrightarrow{A_1, A_2, A, B, (z,a,b,r)}$ $\qquad A \overset{?}{=} A_1 A_2, \; A \overset{?}{\neq} 1$

$\qquad\qquad\qquad\qquad\qquad\qquad\qquad\qquad sig(A, B) \overset{?}{=} (z, a, b, r)$

$r_1 = d(u_1 s) + x_1 \quad [2] \xleftarrow{\quad d \quad} d = \mathcal{H}_1(A_1, B_1, A_2, B_2, I_\mathcal{R}, \text{date/time})$

$r_2 = ds + x_2 \qquad\;\; [3] \xrightarrow{r_1, r_2} \qquad g_1^{r_1} \overset{?}{=} A_1^d B_1$

$\qquad\qquad\qquad\qquad\qquad\qquad\qquad\qquad\qquad\qquad g_2^{r_2} \overset{?}{=} A_2^d B_2$

We now discuss anonymity which, as we know by now, can only be computational. We prove that if $\mathcal{B}$ can trace $\mathcal{U}$, then it can solve the following problem: for security parameter k, for a_i, b_i random ($i = 0, 1$), p a prime (with $|p - 1| = \delta + k$ for a specified constant δ) and for $g \in Z_p$ a generator of prime order $q = (p - 1)/\gamma$ (for a specified small integer γ), given $[g^{a_0}, g^{a_0 b_0}], [g^{a_1}, g^{a_1 b_1}]$ and $g^{b_r}, g^{b_{1-r}}$, $r \in_R \{0, 1\}$, find r with probability better than $1/2 + 1/k^c$ for any constant c for large enough k. Untraceability thus assumes that this problem is intractable; we suggest to name this the *matching Diffie-Hellman* assumption. Its difficulty seems to be a weaker assumption than the "Factoring and Diffie-Hellman" used in [Oka95] for user anonymity, which states that it is difficult to find r, given $[g^{a_0}, g^{b_0}], [g^{a_1}, g^{b_1}]$ and $(a_r b_r), (a_{1-r} b_{1-r})$, $r \in_R \{0, 1\}$, where a_i, b_i ($i = 0, 1$) are primes.

Theorem 3 *Let $\mathcal{U}$ and $\mathcal{R}$ agree on date/time (i.e., their clocks are synchronized). Under the matching Diffie-Hellman assumption and assuming a hash-function behaving like a random oracle exists, the above protocols form a computationally untraceable off-line coin scheme, otherwise as secure as Brands'.*

Proof. (Sketch) We first prove that the bank's and receiver's security is not decreased. The only modification from [Bra93b] is that the responses regarding A are verified independently, using A_1, B_1 and A_2, B_2 respectively. The information conveyed to $\mathcal{R}$ and $\mathcal{B}$ is a superset of that shown in the original Brands' [Bra93b] protocol. Moreover, $\mathcal{R}$ and $\mathcal{B}$ do not transmit different information than in the original protocol and the verifications performed test for everything the original verifications do. Also, the additional information shown to the receiver does not allow him to forge coins or spend the same coin as a user different than the one participating in the payment protocol, or else the user would be able to do the same (since the same information is available to the user). Hence the bank's and receiver's security is maintained.

Next we prove that anonymity of the user is maintained. Assume that the bank can trace the user, i.e., given the views of two withdrawal protocols and their corresponding payment protocols, it can distinguish with non-negligible probability which withdrawal matches which payment. All we need to show is that there exists a (polynomial) converting algorithm available to the bank which given an instance of the matching Diffie-Hellman problem translates it into an instance of the tracing problem; hence if the bank can trace the user it will break the matching Diffie-Hellman assumption.

The converting algorithm takes as input $[g^{a_0}, g^{a_0 b_0}], [g^{a_1}, g^{a_1 b_1}]$ and $g^{b_r}, g^{b_{1-r}}$, $r \in_R \{0, 1\}$ and produces two withdrawal views W_r, W_{1-r} in which $I_j = g_1^{b_j}$, for $j = \{r, 1-r\}$, and two payment views P_0, P_1 in which $A_{1,i} = g_1^{a_i b_i}, A_{2,i} = g_2^{a_i}$, for $i = \{0, 1\}$. The conversion from base g to g_1, g_2 is possible since the bank knows their correspondence (recall that g, g_1, g_2 are chosen by the bank). To create a withdrawal view the algorithm uses the value w chosen by the bank (after the bank sees $g_1^{b_j}$) and a random c' to calculate a', b', r'.

For each payment view, r_1, r_2 and d are chosen at random. B_1, B_2 are then computed so that the verification holds: $B_1 = A_1^{-d} g_1^{r_1}, B_1 = A_2^{-d} g_2^{r_2}$. Hence, the output of $\mathcal{H}_1$ on $(A, B_1, B_2, I_{\mathcal{R}}, \text{Date/Time})$ is chosen to be the value d; thus in the simulation the function used is $\mathcal{H}_1'$, which is still a random oracle (since d is random) and is similar to $\mathcal{H}_1$ except for its value on some (polynomially many) points. Nevertheless, this part of the simulated view is indistinguishable from the real protocol, since any two random oracles are, by definition, indistinguishable. (We note that a typical argument involving a random oracle is similar to ours: If the function is assumed to be a random oracle then to derive a reduction we may afford in the construction to modify the oracle on a polynomial size domain. Then, assuming the original function is indeed a random oracle, the security of the design is validated via such reductions.) z is computed as A^{X_B}; a, b are created randomly (for a random exponent e, $a = g^e, b = A^e$); and r is computed as $cX_B + e$, where c is the appropriate hash value.

It is easy to verify the correctness of these views, and that a legitimate user could create the same payment view for each withdrawal by selecting u, v such that $u = c/c'$ and $e = wu + v$. Finally, since—from [Bra93a]—every coin, independent of w, occurs with the same probability for each user, the distribution of the simulated views is indistinguishable from that of valid views, hence the tracing algorithm has a non-negligible probability of success. □

5 Owner Tracing

We will now demonstrate the concept of indirect discourse proofs by directly applying it to owner tracing, first when the receiver is considered trusted by the Trustees[8] in Section 5.1, and then without this trust in Section 5.2.

5.1 Trustees Trust Receiver

An off-line coin by its nature has its owner's identity embedded in it. In our system we also encrypt the user's identity using a public key encryption system (El Gamal [ElG85]), in such a way that the encryption is linked to the coin. Hence, Trustees can open the ciphertext to obtain the identity. An indirect discourse proof during payment assures the receiver that the encrypted identity is the same as the one embedded in the coin. The additions to the basic protocol are limited to a preliminary stage, in which the Trustee entity T is created, and to the indirect discourse proof included in the payment protocol.

T's public information: Public key $f_2 = g_2^{X_T}$ associated with private key $X_T \in_R G_q$.

Additions to the payment protocol: (i.e., $[i] + [i']$ is new flow i in protocol.)

$\mathcal{U}$		$\mathcal{R}$
$m \in_R Z_q$		
$D_1 = I g_2^{X_T m}$		
$D_2 = g_2^m$	$[1'] \xrightarrow{D_1, D_2}$	$D_2 \overset{?}{\neq} 1$
		$s_0, s_1, s_2 \in_R Z_q$
		$D' = D_1^{s_0} g_2^{s_1} D_2^{s_2}$
	$[2'] \xleftarrow{D', f_2'}$	$f_2' = f_2^{s_0} g_2^{s_2}$
$V = \mathcal{H}_1((D')^s/(f_2')^{ms})$	$[3'] \xrightarrow{V}$	$V \overset{?}{=} \mathcal{H}_1(A_1^{s_0} A_2^{s_1})$

---

[8] Trusting the receiver is actually not so terrible. If a user $\mathcal{U}'$ is framed by $\mathcal{U}$ and $\mathcal{R}$, he proves to the bank where he spent all his coins (or he reveals his secret information for all his withdrawals). Such an audit will convince T that $\mathcal{U}$ and $\mathcal{R}$ colluded. However, anonymity is lost for $\mathcal{U}'$, and $\mathcal{U}$ escapes identification.

Security and Correctness (Sketch) First we prove correctness. Let $F_y(x) = x^y \bmod P$. Observe that $p_1 = F_s(D_1)/F_{ms}(f_2) = I^s g_2^{X_T ms}/g_2^{X_T ms} = A_1$, $p_2 = F_s(g_2) = g_2^s = A_2$, and $p_3 = F_s(D_2)/F_{ms}(g_2) = g_2^{ms-ms} = 1$. If $\mathcal{U}$ and $\mathcal{R}$ behave correctly (as specified in the protocol) then $\mathcal{R}$'s verification in flow [3'] passes with probability 1. Just note that $V = \mathcal{H}_1(p_1^{s_0} p_2^{s_1})$.

Next, we demonstrate that the system is secure in two parts: secure for $\mathcal{U}$ (the indirect discourse proof is zero-knowledge) and secure for $\mathcal{R}$ ($\mathcal{R}$ is convinced of the construction of (D_1, D_2)). For any $s_0' \in Z_q$ there exist unique $s_1', s_2' \in Z_q$ such that $f_2' = f_2^{s_0'} g_2^{s_2'}$ and $D' = D_1^{s_0'} g_2^{s_1'} D_2^{s_2'}$. W.l.o.g.[9], we assume that $D', f_2' \in G_q$. Hence, since $\mathcal{R}$ is trusted not to reveal (s_0, s_1, s_2), even if $\mathcal{U}$ has unlimited power he can still not guess s_0 with probability greater than $\frac{1}{q}$.

We first prove security of $\mathcal{R}$ by contradiction on finding s_0. For simplicity, we assume that $\mathcal{U}$ has access to an oracle that solves discrete logarithms. Let $D_2 = g_2^m$ and let $D_1 \neq g_1^{u_1} g_2^{mX_T}$, i.e., let D_1, D_2 be constructed incorrectly. In particular, let $D_1 = g_1^{u_1'} g_2^{mX_T}$, with $u_1' \neq u_1$ since q is a prime. $\mathcal{U}$ can clearly compute $Z = (D')^s/(f_2')^{ms} = (g_1^{u_1' s})^{s_0} A_2^{s_1}$ since he knows m and s (using discrete log oracle and since q is a prime). If $\mathcal{U}$ could compute V, w.l.o.g. we assume he could also compute any $\tilde{A}$ where $V = \mathcal{H}_1(\tilde{A})$. Hence he could also compute $Z' = \tilde{A}/Z = g_1^{(u'-u_1')s s_0}$ for some $\tilde{A} = g_1^{u' s s_0} A_2^{s_1}$ (for some u') where $V = \mathcal{H}_1(\tilde{A})$. Then for this $\tilde{A}$, $\mathcal{U}$ could compute the log of Z' base $Y = g_1^{(u'-u_1')s}$, and hence some unique s_0' for that Z' (using the oracle, and since q is a prime). Since with extremely small probability $V = \mathcal{H}_1(G_q)$ and q is a prime, $\mathcal{U}$ can guess s_0 with probability better than $\frac{1}{q}$; a contradiction. That is, one of the $\tilde{A}$ will be correct ($u' = u_1$) and that one will return the correct s_0; the rest will be wrong but $\mathcal{U}$ has strictly less than q choices to choose from.

We next show that the only information revealed to $\mathcal{R}$ is (D_1, D_2), hence user anonymity is preserved. We show that $\mathcal{R}$ can simulate the history if he is allowed to choose (D_1, D_2). The simulator encrypts a D_1, D_2 encoding some user $\mathcal{U}'$ for any coin C consisting of, say, A_1', A_2'. It chooses s_0, s_1, s_2 with a random distribution. It then simulates the three flows by responding in [3'] with $\mathcal{H}_1((A_1')^{s_0}(A_2')^{s_1})$. Since $\mathcal{H}_1$ is a random oracle, this distribution is indistinguishable from the real one. Hence, the indirect discourse proof does not leak anything more than the El-Gamal encryption (D_1, D_2) of the user's identity, I.

In terms of **efficiency,** this protocol poses indeed minimal additional requirements to $\mathcal{U}$ (4 exponentiations) and $\mathcal{R}$ (7 exponentiations). Most important, T is off-line during withdrawal, payment and deposit.

5.2 Receivers Are Not Trusted

The idea here is to prove via a minimal-knowledge proof that the encryption (from Section 5.1) is correctly related to an encryption that the bank can decrypt and check at deposit time. To this end we use Schnorr knowledge proofs

---

[9] If D' or f_2' is of the form $v_1 v_2$ where $v_1 \notin G_q$, $v_2 \in G_q$ then we treat it as v_2.

to show the equality of logarithms of the two encryptions, where the bases of
the logarithms are appropriately verified. Here, we prove relations between secret values w.r.t. discrete logarithms, by exploiting the homomorphisms of the
exponent part. These kinds of proofs are particularly efficient.
We remind the reader that $h_2 = g_2^{X_B}$ is the bank's and $f_2 = g_2^{X_T}$ the Trustees'
public keys.

Payment: (Setup and withdrawal are as in the basic system.)

- $\mathcal{U}$ **computes the encryptions:** $\mathcal{U}$ picks $m \in_R Z_q$, and computes $D_1 = If_2^m$, $D_2 = g_2^m$, as before, and also $E_1 = I^s h_2^{ms} = A_1 h_2^{ms}$ and $E_2 = g_2^{ms}$.
- **Conduct indirect discourse proof** of (D_1, D_2) from section 5.1.
- $\mathcal{U}$ **prepares to prove the relation of encryptions:** $\mathcal{U}$ picks $x_3 \in_R Z_q$, and computes: (x_2 is from $B_2 = g_2^{x_2}$ in the basic protocol)

$$D_T = D_1^s, \quad y_{hf} = (h_2/f_2)^{x_3}, \quad y_2 = g_2^{x_3}, \quad y_{D_1} = D_1^{x_2}, \quad y_{D_2} = D_2^{x_2}$$

- $\mathcal{U}$ **conducts proof:** Sends all the above plus $r_2 = ds + x_2$ and $r_3 = em + x_3$ to $\mathcal{R}$, with $d = \mathcal{H}_2(A_1, B_1, A_2, B_2, D_2, E_2, y_{D_2}, D_T, D_1, y_{D_1}, \text{date/time}, ID_\mathcal{R})$ (instead of d as in the basic system), $e = \mathcal{H}_3(E_2, y_2, E_1, D_T, y_{hf}, \text{date/time}, ID_\mathcal{R})$.
- $\mathcal{R}$ **verifies:** (together with $(g_1)^{r_1} \stackrel{?}{=} A_1^d B_1$)

$$(g_2)^{r_2} \stackrel{?}{=} (A_2)^d B_2, \quad (D_2)^{r_2} \stackrel{?}{=} (E_2)^d y_{D_2}, \quad (D_T)^{r_2} \stackrel{?}{=} (D_1)^d y_{D_1}, \text{ and,} \quad (2)$$
$$(g_2)^{r_3} \stackrel{?}{=} (E_2)^e y_2, \quad (h_2/f_2)^{r_3} \stackrel{?}{=} (E_1/D_T)^e y_{hf} \quad (3)$$

Deposit: $\mathcal{R}$ sends a payment transcript to $\mathcal{B}$ (the indirect discourse proof can be omitted), and $\mathcal{B}$ verifies the proofs and signatures.

Security We now briefly overview the security of the protocol, in the sense that the protocol is secure for $\mathcal{R}$ ($\mathcal{R}$ can accept the coin, knowing that it is valid for deposit), for $\mathcal{B}$ ($\mathcal{B}$ is convinced that the Trustees can obtain $\mathcal{U}$'s identity from the coin) and for $\mathcal{U}$ ($\mathcal{R}$ and $\mathcal{B}$ cannot trace $\mathcal{U}$, nor do they end up with a coin that they can spend).

(2), (3) are the self-challenging Schnorr identification schemes which prove that $\mathcal{U}$ knows how to compute the corresponding logarithms, and that the follow-ing relationships hold (similar to [CEvdGP87] for Simultaneous Discrete Log):

$$(2) \iff log_{g_2}(A_2) = log_{D_2}(E_2) = log_{D_1}(D_T) \iff$$

$$\exists s \in Z_q: A_2 = g_2^s \land E_2 = D_2^s \land D_T = D_1^s \quad (4)$$

$$(3) \iff log_{h_2/f_2}(E_1/D_T) = log_{g_2}(E_2) \iff$$

$$\exists M \in Z_q: E_2 = g_2^M \land E_1/D_T = (h_2/f_2)^M \quad (5)$$

First we show that $\mathcal{R}$ is convinced that (E_1, E_2) is an El-Gamal signature of $\mathcal{U}$'s identity: $\mathcal{R}$ verified that (D_1, D_2) correctly "encode" $\mathcal{U}$'s identity (via the indirect discourse proof), i.e., $\exists\ m \in Z_q : g_2^m = D_2 \overset{(4)}{=} (E_2)^{1/s} \overset{(5)}{=} g_2^{M/s}$, i.e., $M = ms$. Then $\mathcal{R}$ can infer that $D_T \overset{(4)}{=} D_1^s = I^s f_2^{ms}$ and that $E_1 \overset{(5)}{=} (h_2/f_2)^M D_T = (h_2/f_2)^{ms} D_T = (h_2/f_2)^{ms} I^s f_2^{ms} = I^s h_2^{ms}$, i.e. that $(E_1 = I^s h_2^{ms}, E_2 = g_2^{ms})$ is the correct encryption of $A_1 = I^s$. Thus, $\mathcal{R}$ can accept the coin, knowing that $\mathcal{B}$ will accept it for deposit.

Next we show security for $\mathcal{B}$. $\mathcal{B}$, at deposit time, verifies (by decrypting (E_1, E_2)) that (E_1, E_2) is a correct encryption of A_1, i.e., $E_1 = A_1 h_2^M = I^s h_2^M$ for $E_2 = g_2^M$. Then, it can infer that $(h_2/f_2)^M D_T \overset{(5)}{=} E_1 = I^s h_2^M \iff D_T = I^s f_2^M \overset{(4)}{=} D_1^s \iff D_1 = I f_2^{M/s} = I f_2^m$, for $m = M/s$. Then $\mathcal{B}$ can verify that $D_2 \overset{(4)}{=} E_2^{1/s} \overset{(5)}{=} g_2^{M/s} = g_2^m$, i.e., that $(D_1 = I f_2^m, D_2 = g_2^m)$ is an El Gamal encryption with f_2 on I, hence that the Trustees can obtain $\mathcal{U}$'s identity.

In terms of security for $\mathcal{U}$, the indirect discourse proof is minimal-knowledge (see proof in Section 5.1). Then, if we assume (as in [Bra93b, Sch91]) that Schnorr proofs of knowledge reveal no useful information, the only extra information provided by $\mathcal{U}$ are the numbers D_T, E_2. Both of these are already known numbers (D_1, D_2) raised to (the random) s. Hence they do not reveal anything more about s than e.g., $A_2 = g_2^s$.

Efficiency: The protocol poses minimal additional communication and computation requirements (on the order of 7 exponentiations for $\mathcal{U}$ and 5 for $\mathcal{R}$), while still keeping $\mathcal{T}$ off-line in all cases.

6 Coin Tracing

Coin tracing is based on the same basic protocol from Section 4, and is similarly efficient to the other tracing protocols. The idea is this: at withdrawal time, $\mathcal{U}$ encrypts some information that is going to appear at payment time (namely, $A_2 = g_2^s$) using an El-Gamal encryption based on $\mathcal{T}$'s key, as in Section 5.1. The coins will be traced via A_2. For the Bank $\mathcal{B}$ to verify this encryption, a number $A' = A_1' A_2'$ (where $A_1' = A_2^x$, for some x) is needed (to substitute for $A = A_1 A_2$ in the indirect discourse proof), which is provided by $\mathcal{U}$. Then, by running an indirect discourse proof, $\mathcal{B}$ can verify that $\mathcal{U}$ has encrypted a number that is "contained" in A_1'. Subsequently, $\mathcal{B}$ (blindly) signs A', via the use of Brands' restrictive blind signature [Bra93b]. This signature shows that $\mathcal{B}$ has checked that $\mathcal{U}$ encrypted some information related to A'.

Now $\mathcal{R}$, at payment time, verifies this signature, and also verifies that the information included in A' is in fact A_2. This check has to be done at payment, since A_2 is hidden during withdrawal. Although a minimal part of the verification is performed at payment time, $\mathcal{R}$ does not need to be trusted, since the same verification can be done by $\mathcal{B}$ at deposit.

The Protocol:

$\mathcal{T}$'s **public information:** Public key $f_1 = g_1^{X_T}$ associated with private key $X_T \in_R Z_q$.

Withdrawal: (over an authenticated channel between B and U)

In addition to the basic protocol's restrictive blind signature, the following steps are performed:

- U: (This step can be pre-processed) Pick $n_1, n_2 \in_R Z_q$. Compute $N = n_1 n_2$, and:

$$A'_1 = A_2^{n_1} = g_2^{sn_1}, \quad A'_2 = g_1^{n_1}, \quad A' = A'_1 A'_2 = g_2^{sn_1} g_1^{n_1}$$
$$\bar{A} = A'^{n_2} = A_2^{n_1 n_2} g_1^{n_1 n_2} = g_2^{sn_1 n_2} g_1^{n_1 n_2} = g_2^{sN} g_1^{N}$$

  n_1 serves in blinding $A_2 = g_2^s$ within A'_1, while n_2 blinds A' within $\bar{A}$.

- U proves to B (using the Schnorr identification scheme) that he knows the representation of A'_1 w.r.t. g_2 and of A'_2 w.r.t. g_1. This is needed to guarantee the correctness of $\bar{A}$.

- U **supplies B with an El-Gamal encryption of** A_2 and conducts an indirect discourse proof to prove that: 1) The encryption is based on T's public key, i.e., T can open the encrypted message, and 2) The encrypted string is embedded in A'_1. The proof for these facts is the same as in Section 5.1.

U $\hspace{10cm}$ B

$m' \in_R Z_q$

$D'_1 = A_2 g_1^{X_T m'}$

$D'_2 = g_1^{m'}$

$\xrightarrow{A', A'_1, A'_2, D'_1, D'_2}$

$\hspace{6cm}$ $A' \overset{?}{=} A'_1 A'_2, \quad D'_2 \overset{?}{\neq} 1$

$\hspace{6cm}$ $s'_0, s'_1, s'_2 \in_R Z_q$

$\hspace{6cm}$ $\bar{D} = D_1'^{s'_0} g_1^{s'_1} D_2'^{s'_2}$

$\xleftarrow{\bar{D}, f_1'}$

$\hspace{6cm}$ $f_1' = f_1^{s'_0} g_1^{s'_2}$

$\bar{V} = \mathcal{H}_4((\bar{D})^{n_1}/(f_1')^{n_1 m'})$ $\xrightarrow{\bar{V}}$ $\hspace{3cm}$ $\bar{V} \overset{?}{=} \mathcal{H}_4((A'_1)^{s'_0} (A'_2)^{s'_1})$

- B signs $(\bar{A}, N)$ using the Brands restrictive blind signature protocol, with A' substituting Ig_2 of the original protocol [Bra93b], and N being blindly signed (as B in the original protocol). To denote that this signature is different from the one that signs the regular coin, the Bank will use different secret (X'_B) and public $(h' = g^{X'_B}, h'_1 = g_1^{X'_B}, h'_2 = g_2^{X'_B})$ keys.

U $\hspace{10cm}$ B

$A' = A_2^{n_1} g_1^{n_1}$ $\xrightarrow{A'}$ $\hspace{4cm}$ $\omega \in_R Z_q$

$\bar{A} = A'^{n_2}$ $\xleftarrow{\alpha', \beta'}$ $\hspace{3cm}$ $\alpha' = g^{\omega}, \beta' = A'^{\omega}$

$v, \nu \in_R Z_q$

$\zeta = (A_2 g_1)^{X'_B n_1 n_2}$

$\alpha = \alpha'^{v} g^{\nu}$

$\beta = \beta'^{n_2 v} \bar{A}^{\nu}$

$N = n_1 n_2$

$\varsigma = H(\bar{A}, N, \zeta, \alpha, \beta)$

$\varsigma' = \varsigma/v$ $\xrightarrow{\varsigma'}$ $\hspace{3cm}$ $\rho' = \varsigma' X'_B + \omega$

$\rho = \rho' v + \nu$ $\xleftarrow{\rho'}$

$(\zeta, \alpha, \beta, \rho)$ clearly satisfies (1) (with $B = N$, $A = \bar{A}$) and is a signature on $(\bar{A}, N)$.

Payment: (performed between $\mathcal{U}$ and $\mathcal{R}$ over an anonymous channel)
In addition to the basic payment protocol, $\mathcal{R}$ also verifies that A_2 is embedded in $\bar{A}$:

- $\mathcal{U}$ shows $(\bar{A}, N)$ and the signature on $(\bar{A}, N)$, which $\mathcal{R}$ verifies.
- $\mathcal{U}$ shows $N = n_1 n_2$. $\mathcal{R}$ verifies that $\bar{A} = A_2^N g_1^N$.

The **security** of this protocol depends on Brands' e-cash scheme and on the *matching Diffie-Hellman* assumption. Specifically:[10]

Theorem 4 *Based on the Brands' scheme being secure, the availability of a random oracle-like hash function and the matching D-H assumption, the above system is a correct secure FOLC.*

Efficiency: We keep $\mathcal{T}$ off-line at all times, while only requiring the signing of one additional value $(\bar{A})$ together with a cryptographic check that A_2 can be opened by $\mathcal{T}$. Hence the additional burden to $\mathcal{U}$, $\mathcal{B}$ and $\mathcal{R}$ is minimal.

Conclusion

We introduced the concept of off-line fair electronic cash (FOLC) and constructed a very efficient FOLC system. Our system can be implemented in smart cards (as much as Brands'), and still provide high levels of security, directly comparable to previously suggested e-cash systems [Bra93b, Oka95].

References

[BGK95]   E. F. Brickell, P. Gemmell, and D. Kravitz. Trustee-based tracing extensions to anonymous cash and the making of anonymous change. In *Symposium on Distributed Algorithms (SODA)*, 1995.

[Bra93a]   S. Brands. An efficient off-line electronic cash system based on the representation problem. Technical Report CS–R9323, CWI (Centre for Mathematics and Computer Science), Amsterdam, 1993.

[Bra93b]   S. Brands. Untraceable off-line cash in wallets with observers. In *Advances in Cryptology — Crypto '93, Proceedings (Lecture Notes in Computer Science 773)*, pages 302–318. Springer-Verlag, 1993.

[CEvdGP87] D. Chaum, J.-H. Evertse, J. van de Graaf, and R. Peralta. Demonstrating possession of a discrete logarithm without revealing it. In *Advances in Cryptology. Proc. of Crypto '86 (Lecture Notes in Computer Science 263)*, pages 200–212. Springer-Verlag, 1987.

[CF85]   J. C. Benaloh (Cohen) and M.J. Fischer. A robust and verifiable cryptographically secure election scheme. *Symp. on Foundations of Computer Science (FOCS)*, 1985.

[CFN90]   D. Chaum, Amos Fiat, and Moni Naor. Untraceable electronic cash. In *Advances in Cryptology —Crypto '88 (Lecture Notes in Computer Science)*, pages 319–327. Springer-Verlag, 1990.

---

[10] Proof and formalization omitted due to space limitations.

[ElG85] T. ElGamal. A public key cryptosystem and a signature scheme based on discrete logarithms. *IEEE Trans. Inform. Theory*, 31:469–472, 1985.

[Fer93a] N. Ferguson. Extensions of single term off-line coins. In *Advances in Cryptology — CRYPTO '93, (Lecture Notes in Computer Science 773)*, pages 292–301. Springer-Verlag, 1993.

[Fer93b] N. Ferguson. Single term off-line coins. In *Advances in Cryptology — EUROCRYPT '93, (Lecture Notes in Computer Science 765)*, pages 318–328. Springer-Verlag, 1993.

[FY93] M. Franklin and M. Yung. Secure and efficient off-line digital money. In *Proceedings of the 20-th International Colloquium on Automata, Languages and Programming (ICALP 1993), (Lecture Notes in Computer Science 700)*, pages 265–276. Springer-Verlag, 1993. Lund, Sweden, July 1993.

[GM84] S. Goldwasser and S. Micali. Probabilistic encryption. *Journal of Computer and System Sciences*, 28(2):270–299, April 1984.

[IR89] R. Impagliazzo and S. Rudich. Limits on the provable consequences of one-way permutations. In *Proceedings of the 21-st ACM Symp. Theory of Computing, STOC*, pages 44–61, May 15–17 1989.

[JY96] M. Jakobson and M. Yung. Revokable and versatile e-money. In *Proceedings of the third ACM Symp. on Computer and Communication Security*, 1996.

[Oka95] T. Okamoto. An efficient divisible electronic cash scheme. In *Advances in Cryptology, Proc. of Crypto '95 (Lecture Notes in Computer Science 963)*, pages 438–451. Springer-Verlag, 1995.

[OO92] T. Okamoto and K. Ohta. Universal electronic cash. In *Advances in Cryptology — Crypto '91 (Lecture Notes in Computer Science)*, pages 324–337. Springer-Verlag, 1992.

[PS96] D. Pointcheval and J. Stern. Security proofs for signature schemes. In U. Maurer, editor, *Advances in Cryptology, Proc. of Eurocrypt '96*, pages 387–398. Springer-Verlag, 1996. Zaragoza, Spain, May 11–16.

[ref96] Annonymous referee, 1996. Asiacrypt '96 program committee comment.

[Sch91] C. P. Schnorr. Efficient signature generation by smart cards. *Journal of Cryptology*, 4(3):161–174, 1991.

[Sha49] C. E. Shannon. Communication theory of secrecy systems. *Bell System Techn. Jour.*, 28:656–715, October 1949.

[SPC95] M. Stadler, J. M. Piveteau, and J. Camenisch. Fair blind signatures. In *Advances in Cryptology, Proc. of Eurocrypt '95*, pages 209–219. Springer-Verlag, 1995.

[Sta96a] M. Stadler, 1996. Personal communication.

[Sta96b] M. Stadler. Publicly verifiable secret sharing. In *Advances in Cryptology, Proc. of Eurocrypt '96*, pages 190–199. Springer-Verlag, 1996.

[vSN92] B. von Solms and D. Naccache. On blind signatures and perfect crimes. *Computers and Security*, 11(6):581–583, October 1992.

[Yac95] Y. Yacobi. Efficient electronic money. In J. Pieprzyk and R. Safavi-Naini, editors, *Advances in Cryptology, Proc. of Asiacrypt '94 (Lecture Notes in Computer Science 917)*, pages 153–163. Springer-Verlag, 1995. Wollongong, Australia, Nov. 28–Dec. 1.

The Validation of Cryptographic Algorithms

Jacques Stern

Jacques.Stern@ens.fr

Ecole Normale Supérieure
Laboratoire d'informatique
45, rue d'Ulm
75230 Paris Cedex 05

Abstract. Since the appearance of public-key cryptography in the seminal Diffie-Hellman paper, many new schemes have been proposed and many have been broken. Thus, the simple fact that a cryptographic algorithm has withstood cryptanalytic attacks for several years is, by itself, a kind of validation procedure. A completely different paradigm is provided by the concept of provable security. Stated in a more accurate way, this approach proposes computational reductions to well established problems such as factoring or the discrete logarithm problem. Recently, the scope of this method has been considerably widened by using a model where concrete cryptographic tools are replaced by ideal objects: in this model, DES is viewed as a random permutation and SHA as a random function with the appropriate range. Basically, this is another technique for spotting error designs and validating cryptographic algorithms. When cryptanalysis and security proofs combine with each other so that there is virtually no gap between them, the resulting picture becomes quite convincing. The present paper gives several examples of such a situation taken from various areas of cryptography such as signature schemes, public-key identification or even symmetric-key techniques.

1   Introduction

Since the appearance of public-key cryptography in the seminal Diffie-Hellman paper [4], many new schemes have been proposed and many have been broken. Thus, the simple fact that a cryptographic algorithm has withstood cryptanalytic attacks for several years is, by itself, a kind of validation procedure. In this approach, cryptanalysis is viewed as a heuristic measure of the strength of a new proposal. A completely different paradigm is provided by the concept of provable security. This significant line of research has tried to provide proofs in the asymptotic framework of complexity theory. Stated in a more accurate way, this approach proposes computational reductions to well established problems such as factoring or the discrete logarithm problem. Of course, these are not absolute proofs since cryptography ultimately relies on the existence of one-way functions and the $\mathcal{P}$ vs. $\mathcal{NP}$ question. Recently, the scope of this method has been considerably widened by using a model where concrete cryptographic tools are replaced by ideal objects: in this model, DES is viewed as a random permutation and SHA as a random function with the appropriate range. The method was put in systematic form in [1] using the name "Random Oracle Model" and has been quite successful as another technique for spotting error designs and validating cryptographic algorithms. When cryptanalysis and security proofs combine with each other so that there is virtually no gap between them, the resulting picture becomes quite convincing and, accordingly, conveys a reasonably high degree of practical assurance. The aim of the present paper is to give several examples of such a situation taken from various areas of cryptography such as signature schemes, public-key identification or even symmetric-key techniques. The examples include

1. A precise security analysis of the El Gamal signature scheme and its variants
2. A discussion of the size of the hash functions used in zero knowledge identification protocols
3. An account of the work of of Bellare, Kilian and Rogaway [2] on the security of cipher block chaining and a comparison of the hypotheses they use with cryptanalytic results concerning MACs

The first two items are related with previous work of the author. This is merely a matter of practicality: much more work of a similar vein due to many different authors can be found in the bibliography.

2   El Gamal Signatures

At EUROCRYPT 96, by some sort of unexpected coincidence, two papers devoted to the security of the El Gamal signature scheme appeared, one by Bleichenbacher and the other by Pointcheval and the author (see [3, 13]). The first was in the Cryptanalysis section and reported a potential weakness of the scheme whereas the second, included in the signature section, was able to formally prove the security of a variant of the same scheme. A closer look at both papers was even more puzzling since it was explained that the Bleichenbacher attack was applicable to the variant we discussed in the other paper. It was only through a deeper examination that the apparent contradiction could vanish since the security proof was correct for "almost all" choices of the parameters whereas the attack was tracking very specific values. In this section, we will briefly review the ElGamal scheme and its variant as well as the content of the two EUROCRYPT papers. Then we will investigate their "touching point" and derive practical consequences.

2.1   Brief Review of the Signature Scheme

The original El Gamal signature scheme [5] was proposed in 1985 but its security was never proved equivalent to the discrete logarithm problem nor to the Diffie-Hellman problem.

Description of the Original Scheme Let us begin with a description of the original scheme [5]:

- the key generation algorithm: it chooses a random large prime p of size n and a generator g of $(\mathbb{Z}/p\mathbb{Z})^*$, both public. Then, for a random secret key $x \in \mathbb{Z}/(p-1)\mathbb{Z}$, it computes the public key $y = g^x \bmod p$.
- the signature algorithm: in order to sign a signature of a message m, one generates a pair (r, s) such that $g^m = y^r r^s \bmod p$. To achieve this aim, one has to choose a random $K \in (\mathbb{Z}/(p-1)\mathbb{Z})^*$, compute the exponentiation $r = g^K \bmod p$ and solve the linear equation $m = xr + Ks \bmod (p-1)$. The algorithm finally outputs (r, s).
- the verification algorithm checks the equation $g^m = y^r r^s \bmod p$.

As already seen in the original paper, one cannot show that the scheme is fully secure because it is subject to existential forgery. Following a design that appears in the work of Schnorr [16], we proposed to modify the scheme by using a hash function f.

Description of the modified El Gamal scheme In this variant, we replace m by the hash value of the part of the computation bound not to change, namely $f(m, r)$.

- the key generation algorithm: unchanged.
- the signature algorithm: in order to sign a message m, one generates a pair (r, s) such that $g^{f(m,r)} = y^r r^s \bmod p$. In order to achieve this aim, one generates K and r the same way as before and solves the linear equation $f(m, r) = xr + Ks \bmod (p-1)$. The algorithm outputs $(r, f(m, r), s)$.
- the verification algorithm checks the signature equation with the obvious changes due to the hash function.

2.2 The Security Result

Of course, the hash functions that we had in mind were practical proposals such as e.g. MD5 [14] or SHS [11]. Still, in order to prove a security result we used the "random oracle model". On other terms, we treated the hash function as an oracle which produces a random value for each new query. Of course, if the same query is asked twice, identical answers are obtained. Proofs in this model ensure security of the overall design of a signature scheme provided the hash function has no weakness. For the modified scheme, we were able to prove a security result in the so-called adaptively chosen message scenario where the attacker can dynamically ask the legitimate user to sign any message, using him as a kind of oracle before he attempts to issue a fake signature. Our result applied to a large variety of moduli p, those for which $p-1$ has a single large prime factor Q. Those prime moduli are precisely used for cryptographic applications of the discrete logarithm problem. In order to give a more precise mathematical definition, we let $|p|$ denote the length of an integer p.

Definition 1. Let α be a fixed real. An α-hard prime number p is such that the factorization of $p-1$ yields $p-1 = QR$ with Q prime and $R \leq |p|^\alpha$.

Theorem 2. *Consider an adaptively chosen message attack in the random oracle model against schemes using α-hard prime moduli. Probabilities are taken over random tapes, random oracles and public keys. If an existential forgery of this scheme has non-negligible probability of success, then the discrete logarithm problem with α-hard prime moduli can be solved in polynomial time.*

2.3 Spotting the Weakness

We will not give the proof of the theorem just stated in the previous section, for which we refer to [13]. We will only mention that it deals with probabilistic polynomial time Turing machines and that we turn any attack into a machine $\mathcal{M}$ which, on input (g, y), outputs, with non-negligible probability, $x \in \mathbb{Z}/(p-1)\mathbb{Z}$ such that $y = g^x \bmod p$ (case 1) or $b \in \mathbb{Z}/R\mathbb{Z}$ and $t \in \mathbb{Z}/(p-1)\mathbb{Z}$ such that t is prime to Q and $bQ = g^t \bmod p$ (case 2). Probabilities are taken over g, y, and the random tapes of $\mathcal{M}$. Case 1, the "good" case immediately yields the discrete logarithm of y. As for the "bad" case 2, it only discloses the discrete logarithm of some small multiple bQ of Q. We could overcome the resulting difficulty by using randomization over g so as to solve discrete logarithms in general.

What if g is not randomly chosen? Then our argument collapses and we have thus spotted a weakness. More precisely, we have the following

Theorem 3. *From the knowledge of b and t such that t is prime to Q and $bQ = g^t \bmod p$, it is possible to generate signatures without the secret key for a significant proportion of the possible messages.*

Proof. Set $r = g^t \bmod p$. The equation to solve in order to produce the required signature reads $f(m, r) = xr + ts \bmod (p-1)$. Reducing modulo Q, we get $f(m, r) = ts \bmod Q$, which we can solve for s. As for the R-part, which reads $f(m, r) = xr + ts \bmod R$, it can be found by exhaustive search, regardless of the information on x but provided that the solution exists: if t is prime to R, this is always the case. Otherwise, the (unknown) quantity $f(m, r) - xr$ has to be a multiple of the gcd of t and R, which happens with significant probability.

2.4 The Bleichenbacher Attack

First note that theorem 3 does not actually use the full strength of the hypotheses that were needed for the security result: Q need not be prime and it is enough that $R = \frac{p-1}{Q}$ is smooth in order to make the required exhaustive search possible. Bleichenbacher's attack stems from the following:

Theorem 4. *Whenever g is smooth, divides $p-1$ and is not a quadratic residue modulo p, it is possible to generate signatures without the secret key for a significant proportion of the possible messages.*

Note that the above applies to the El Gamal scheme as well as to the variant discussed above.

Proof. Set $Q = \frac{p-1}{g}$ and $t = \frac{p-3}{2}$. Since g is not a quadratic residue, we have $g^{\frac{p-1}{2}} = -1 = p - 1 \bmod p$, hence $g^t = \frac{p-1}{g} = Q \bmod p$. The hypotheses of theorem 3 are met and thus a significant proportion of the messages can be signed. There is a minor problem due to the fact that t is not necessarily prime to Q. Actually, since $p - 3$ is a multiple of t, the gcd of t and $p - 1$ is at worse 2. A closer examination of the proof of theorem 3, with this observation in mind, shows that the conclusion remains.

2.5 The Final Picture

The apparent contradiction between Bleichenbacher's attack and our security result has thus vanished. Moreover, the overall picture is now very clear: the modified El Gamal signature scheme is secure provided the generator g of $(\mathbb{Z}/p\mathbb{Z})^\star$ is chosen at random. If it is not, then, as reported in [3], there is some danger that a trapdoor has been added. Thus, a reasonable requirement would be that the authority issues some sort of proof that g has been fairly manufactured, as was suggested for the modulus p of the digital signature standard (see [11]).

3 Hash Functions in Identification Protocols

At CRYPTO 93, the author introduced a zero-knowledge identification scheme based on the syndrome decoding problem from the theory of error-correcting codes ([18]). This work followed a line of research trying to find appropriate alternative techniques to number theory. Previous research along the same line had been earlier performed by Shamir who had designed another scheme based on the Permuted Kernel problem (see [17]). Both schemes used hash function at the so-called commitment stage. In the security analysis that we gave in our CRYPTO paper (see also [20]), we noticed that any attack could be turned into a machine which could either output some substitute to the secret key or else find collisions for the hash function, with overwhelming probability. Still, we felt that it might as well be the case that one-wayness was enough. Thus, results of further investigations that we undertook with Marc Girault (see [10]) came as a surprise: collision-freeness is really needed. Again, the correct picture came from the joint effort of security proofs and cryptanalysis.

3.1 Brief Description of the Scheme

The scheme is base on a fixed randomly generated binary matrix H of large size, $m \times n$, say 256×512. Each user U receives a secret key s_U, chosen at random by the authority among all n-bit words with a prescribed number p of 1's, say $p = 56$. This prescribed number p is also part of the system. The public identification of the user is computed as

$$i_U = H(s_U)$$

This allows a registered participant to perform the basic interactive protocol that enables any user U (which we call the prover) to identify himself to another entity (which we call the verifier). The protocol includes r rounds, each of these being performed as follows:

1. The prover picks a random n-bit word y together with a random permutation σ of the integers $\{1 \cdots n\}$ and sends commitments c_1, c_2, c_3 respectively as

$$c_1 = \langle \sigma || H(y) \rangle$$
$$c_2 = \langle y.\sigma \rangle$$
$$c_3 = \langle (y \oplus s_U).\sigma \rangle$$

to the verifier. In the above $\langle \rangle$ simply denotes the hash function.

2. The verifier sends a random element b of $\{0, 1, 2\}$.

3. If b is 0, then, the prover returns y and σ. If b is 1 then, the prover reveals $y \oplus s$ and σ. Finally, if b equals 2, then the prover discloses both $y.\sigma$ and $s_U.\sigma$.

4. If b equals 0, the verifier checks that commitments c_1 and c_2, which were made in step 1, have been computed honestly. More accurately, let $\tilde{y}$ and $\tilde{\sigma}$ be the answers received from the prover at step 3, then the equations to check are as follows:

$$c_1 = \langle \tilde{\sigma} || H(\tilde{y}) \rangle$$
$$c_2 = \langle \tilde{y}.\tilde{\sigma} \rangle$$

If b equals 1, the verifier checks that

$$c_1 = \langle \tilde{\sigma} || H(\tilde{y}) \oplus i_U \rangle$$
$$c_3 = \langle \tilde{y}.\tilde{\sigma} \rangle$$

Finally, if b is 2, the verifier checks the weight property and commitments c_2 and c_3, i.e. with obvious notations,

$$c_2 = \langle \tilde{y} \rangle$$
$$c_3 = \langle \tilde{y} \oplus \tilde{s} \rangle$$

The security result whose proof we omit, reads as follows:

Theorem 5. *Assume that some probabilistic polynomial-time adversary $\tilde{P}$ is accepted with probability $\geq (2/3)^r + \epsilon$, $\epsilon > 0$, after playing a constant number r of rounds of the identification protocol. Then there exists a polynomial-time probabilistic machine which outputs an acceptable key s from the public data or else finds collisions for the hash function, with overwhelming probability.*

Here an acceptable key is any word s with the prescribed weight such that $H(s) = i_U$.

3.2 Attacks Based on Collisions

In order to give an abstract treatment of the work appearing in [10], we introduce the following definition:

Definition 6. A *sample* for a hash function is a subset of its possible inputs. Given two samples S_1, S_2 for a hash function, a collision between these samples consists of $x_1 \in S_1$ and $x_2 \in S_2$ such that $\langle x_1 \rangle = \langle x_2 \rangle$.

We always assume implicitly that samples and hash values are produced by polynomial-time machines and that samples have exponential size whereas hash values have small length. Hence collisions do exist. The main result in [10] reads as follows.

Theorem 7. *Any adversary that can produce collisions between samples can be accepted without knowledge of the secret key.*

Proof. As shown in [10], the attacker can choose to attack any of the three commitments. We focus on c_2. The impostor selects a permutation σ and a word y'. He next considers two samples

1. The sample consisting of inputs to the hash function of the form $y_1.\sigma$ such that y_1 is a solution of the equation $H(y_1) = H(y') \oplus i_U$. Note that there are exponentially many such solutions.
2. The sample consisting of inputs to the hash function of the form $y_2.\sigma$ such that $y_2 \oplus y'$ has weight p.

Let y_1, y_2 be a collision between the samples. At each execution of the basic protocol, the impostor sends

$$c_1 = \langle \sigma || H(y_1) \rangle$$
$$c_2 = \langle y_1.\sigma \rangle = \langle y_2.\sigma \rangle$$
$$c_3 = \langle y'.\sigma \rangle$$

If the verifier asks $b = 0$, the cheater replies with y_1 and σ; if $b = 1$, he returns y', σ; finally, if $b = 2$, he answers $y_2.\sigma$ and $(y_2 \oplus y').\sigma$. In all three cases, the verifier is satisfied with the answer.

3.3 Practical Consequences

If we identify hash functions with random functions, then by the birthday paradox, the running time of finding collisions for samples is $O(\sqrt{2^k})$, where k is the size of the hash values. As a consequence, the practical meaning of the previous results is that 64 bit hash values should be avoided. Our identification scheme really needs long hash values and 128 bits is a minimum.

4 Cipher Block Chaining

At CRYPTO 94, Bellare, Kilian and Rogaway gave a security proof for the classical design known as cipher block chaining (see [2]). More accurately, they considered authentication of a message $x = x_1, \cdots, x_m$ by tagging x with a prefix of

$$f^{(m)}(x) = f(f(\cdots (f(f(x_1) \oplus x_2)) \oplus \cdots \oplus x_{m-1}) \oplus x_m)$$

where f is a block cipher (e.g. DES). Their setting was quite similar to the one discussed above in section 2, in that the attacker was allowed to request the MAC values of adaptively chosen messages. They were able to prove that any attack which distinguishes $f^{(m)}$ from random functions with significant probability, can be turned into a test distinguishing f itself from random functions. They had a more precise quantitative version that appears below and involves the number of queries q made by the attacker. If one compares this version with the collision attacks stemming from the birthday paradox, we see that there is a small gap. The aim of the present section is to understand this gap.

4.1 Brief Review of the Security Result

Consider an attack that distinguishes the CBC function $f^{(m)}$ built from a function f whose inputs are ℓ bit long. Let q be the number of queries asked, t be the time taken and ϵ be the success probability. The result of Bellare, Kilian and Rogaway reads as follows:

Theorem 8. *Assume $qm \leq 2^{(\ell+1)/2}$, then there is another algorithm that distinguishes f itself from a random function, whose success probability is $\epsilon' = \epsilon - 3q^2m^2 2^{-\ell-1}$. This algorithm asks $q' = qm$ queries and takes time $t + O(qml)$.*

We refer to [2] for the proof.

4.2 The Gap with Cryptanalysis

It is know that MAC collisions can be found through the birthday paradox by querying $\sqrt{2}2^{\ell/2}$ MAC values, where ℓ is the number of bits of the inputs to f. It is not surprising therefore that the authors of [2] have a condition that relates q, m and $2^{\ell/2}$. It turns out that this condition cannot be simply $q \leq O(2^{\ell/2})$. This follows from a result by Preneel and van Oorschot [12] who observe that if the messages have s trailing blocks in common, the number of MACs needed for finding a collision w.r.t. $f^{(m)}$ goes down to approximately $\sqrt{2/(s+1)}2^{\ell/2}$. Thus, collision can be found with $O(\frac{2^{\ell/2}}{\sqrt{m}})$ queries by setting $s = m - 1$ and this distinguishes $f^{(m)}$ from random functions. However, the condition from [2] reads $qm \leq 2^{(\ell+1)/2}$, whereas cryptanalysis hints towards a weaker condition of the form $q \leq O(\frac{2^{\ell/2}}{\sqrt{m}})$. It is unclear whether the gap can be narrowed.

5 Conclusion

The content of the present paper is methodological in character. We have shown several examples where security proofs and cryptanalysis almost match up. If they do, the resulting picture is very convincing in terms of practical security. If the match is not tight, it is often an indication that further research is needed.

References

1. Bellare, M., Rogaway, P.: Random oracles are practical: a paradigm for designing efficient protocols. In Proceedings of the 1st ACM Conference on Computer and Communications Security (1993) pp. 62–73.
2. Bellare, M., Kilian, J., Rogaway, P.: The security of cipher block chaining. In Advances in Cryptology – Proceedings of CRYPTO '94 (1994) vol. Lecture Notes in Computer Science 839 Springer-Verlag pp. 341–358.
3. Bleichenbacher, D.: Generating ElGamal signatures wothout knowing the secret key. In Advances in Cryptology – Proceedings of EUROCRYPT '96 (1996) vol. Lecture Notes in Computer Science 1070 Springer-Verlag pp. 10–18.
4. Diffie, W., Hellman, M.: New directions in cryptography. In IEEE Transactions on Information Theory (november 1976) vol. IT–22, no. 6 pp. 644–654.
5. ElGamal, T.: A public key cryptosystem and a signature scheme based on discrete logarithms. In IEEE Transactions on Information Theory (july 1985) vol. IT–31, no. 4 pp. 469–472.
6. Fiat, A., Shamir, A.: How to prove yourself: practical solutions of identification and signature problems. In Advances in Cryptology – Proceedings of CRYPTO '86 (1986) vol. Lecture Notes in Computer Science 263 Springer-Verlag pp. 186–194.
7. Goldwasser, S., Micali, S., Rackoff, C.: Knowledge complexity of interactive proof systems. In Proceedings of the 17th ACM Symposium on the Theory of Computing STOC (1985) pp. 291–304.
8. Goldwasser, S., Micali, S., Rivest, R.: A digital signature scheme secure against adaptative chosen-message attacks. SIAM journal of computing 17 (1988) pp. 281–308.
9. Guillou, L., Quisquater, J.: A practical zero-knowledge protocol fitted to security microprocessor minimizing both transmission and memory. In Advances in Cryptology – Proceedings of EUROCRYPT '88 (1989) vol. Lecture Notes in Computer Science 330 Springer-Verlag pp. 123–128.
10. Girault, M., Stern, J.: On the length of the cryptographic hash values used in identification schemes. In Advances in Cryptology – proceedings of CRYPTO '94 (1994) vol. Lecture Notes in Computer Science 839 Springer-Verlag pp. 202–215.
11. NIST: Secure Hash Standard (SHS). Federal Information Processing Standards PUBlication 180–1 April 1995.
12. Preneel, B., van Oorschot P.C., MDx-MAC and building fast MAC's from hash functions. In Advances in Cryptology – proceedings of CRYPTO '95 (1995) vol. Lecture Notes in Computer Science 963, Springer-Verlag pp. 1–14.
13. Pointcheval, D., Stern, J.: Security proofs for signature schemes. In Advances in Cryptology – Proceedings of EUROCRYPT '96 (1996) vol. Lecture Notes in Computer Science 1070 Springer-Verlag pp. 387–398.
14. Rivest, R.: The MD5 message-digest algorithm. RFC 1321 april 1992.

15. Rivest, R., Shamir, A., Adleman, L.: A method for obtaining digital signatures and public key cryptosystems. Communications of the ACM **21** (1978) pp. 120–126.
16. Schnorr, C.: Efficient identification and signatures for smart cards. In Advances in Cryptology – Proceedings of CRYPTO '89 (1990) vol. Lecture Notes in Computer Science 435 Springer-Verlag pp. 235–251.
17. Shamir, A.: An efficient identification scheme based on permuted kernels. In Advances in Cryptology – Proceedings of CRYPTO '89 (1990) vol. Lecture Notes in Computer Science 435 Springer-Verlag pp. 606–609.
18. Stern, J.: A new identification scheme based on syndrome decoding. In Advances in Cryptology – proceedings of CRYPTO '93 (1994) vol. Lecture Notes in Computer Science 773 Springer-Verlag pp. 13–21.
19. Stern, J.: Designing identification schemes with keys of short size. In Advances in Cryptology – proceedings of CRYPTO '94 (1994) vol. Lecture Notes in Computer Science 839 Springer-Verlag pp. 164–173.
20. Stern, J.: A new paradigm for public key identification. In IEEE Transactions on Information Theory (1996), to appear.

Convertible Group Signatures

Seung Joo Kim†, Sung Jun Park‡, Dong Ho Won†

†Dept. of Inform. Engineering, Sung Kyun Kwan Univ.,
300 Chunchun-dong, Suwon, Kyunggi-do, 440-746, KOREA
E-mail : {sjkim,dhwon}@dosan.skku.ac.kr
‡KISA, Security & Cryptology Team,
2nd Fl, Sejongro Daewoo Bldg.,
167 Naesu-dong, Jongro-gu, Seoul, 110-070, KOREA
E-mail : sjpark@dosan.skku.ac.kr

Abstract. Group signatures, introduced by Chaum and van Heyst at Eurocrypt'91, allow individual members of a group to sign messages on behalf of the group while remaining anonymous. Furthermore, in case of disputes later a trusted authority, who is given some auxiliary information, can identify the signer. In this paper, we introduce a new kind of group signature scheme, called "convertible group signatures". In these schemes, in addition to the properties of group signatures, release of a single bit string by the signer turns all of his group signatures into ordinary digital signatures. Then, we present a non-interactive selectively convertible group signature scheme.

1 Introduction

At Eurocrypt'91, D. Chaum and E. Heyst introduced the notion of group signatures, which allow members of a group to make signatures on behalf of the group in such a way that

1) only members of the group can sign messages.
2) the recipient of the signature can verify that it is a valid signature of that group, but cannot discover which group member made it.
3) in case of dispute later, the signature can be "opened" by either the group members together or a trusted authority, so that the person who signed the message is revealed.

In this paper, we propose a new type of group signatures, called "convertible group signatures". In addition to the properties of group signatures described above, it could be useful if the signer could turn all of his group signatures into ordinary digital signatures by release some secret information at some point after signing. Thus these signatures could be verified without the cooperation of group members or a trusted authority, but they should still be difficult to forge. We will call such group signatures "convertible group signatures".

1.1 Related Work

At Eurocrypt'91 conference, by D. Chaum and E. Heyst, group signatures were presented for the first time and four implementations were described. one protects the anonymity of the signer unconditionally, whereas the other three only give computational anonymity[3]. The properties of these schemes are that (see Table 1.) Furthermore, D. Chaum and E. Heyst also state the followings as open problems :

Table 1. Comparison of Chaum's four group signature schemes. "Independent, linear" means that the number is independent respectively linear in the number of group members.

Properties	Scheme 1	Scheme 2	Scheme 3	Scheme 4
Based on assumption	Any	Factoring	Factoring	Discrete Logarithm
Anonymity	Unconditional	Computational	Computational	Computational
Identification of the signer	Authority	Cooperation of group mem.	Cooperation of group mem.	Cooperation of group mem.
Inclusion of new group members	No	No	Yes	Yes
Type of signature	Any type	Undeniable	Undeniable	Undeniable
Length of the group's Public key	Linear	Linear	Linear	Linear
Number of computations during conf. pr.	Independent	Linear	Linear	Linear
Number of bits transmitted during conf. pr.	Independent	Independent	Independent	Linear
framing	Computational	Computational	Computational	Computational

– is it possible to construct a scheme in which certain subsets of the group members (e.g., the majority) can identify the signer (in an efficient way) ?
– is it possible to make digital group signatures other than by using undeniable signatures ?

At Eurocrypt'94, L. Chen and T. P. Pedersen present new group signature scheme, which hides the anonymity of the signer unconditionally and allows new members to join the group[4]. The following Table 2. shows the properties of the scheme. Also, L. Chen and T. P. Pedersen solve Chaum's first open problem, "Shared Identification of the Signer". And at JW-ISC'95 conference, Sung Jun Park and Dong Ho Won proposed a practical group signature scheme based on the γth-residuosity problem. Since Chaum's computationally privacy

Table 2. Comparison of Chen's two group signature schemes. "Independent, linear" means that the number is independent respectively linear in the number of group members.

Properties	Scheme 1	Scheme 2
Based on assumption	Any	Discrete Logarithm
Anonymity	Unconditionally	Computationally
Identification of the signer	by the authority	by the authority
Inclusion of new group members	Yes	Yes
Type of signature	Undeniable	Undeniable
Length of the group's public key	Linear	Linear
Number of computations during conf. pr.	Linear	Linear
Number of bits transmitted during conf. pr.	Linear	Linear
framing	Unconditionally	Computationally

protecting schemes and Chen's schemes used the undeniable signatures, it may be impractical for some applications because of its inefficiency and many interactions between the signer and verifier. Sung Jun Park and Dong Ho Won solve this problem by using the γth-residuosity problem[6][7][10]. Table 3. shows the properties of these schemes.

Also, the basic idea of "convertible" has been borrowed from [1]. At Crypto'90, J. Boyar, D. Chaum, I. Damgard and T. Pedersen present the concept of "convertible undeniable signatures" in which, release of a some secret information by the signer turns all of his undeniable signatures into ordinary signatures.

Table 3. Park's group signature scheme. "Independent, linear" means that the number is independent respectively linear in the number of group members.

Properties	Park's Scheme
Based on assumption	γ^{th}-residuosity & Discrete Logarithm
Identification of the signer	by the authority
Inclusion of new group members	Yes
Type of signature	PW-scheme
Length of the group's public key	Fixed
Number of computations during conf. pr.	Independent
Number of bits transmitted during conf. pr.	Independent

1.2 Contents

The next section presents a new concept called "convertible group signature schemes". Section 3 then sketches Park et al's non-interactive group signature scheme. In section 4, using the Park et al's group signature scheme, we construct a convertible group signature scheme. And in section 5, we simplify our scheme described above.

2 Convertible Group Signatures

The new technique called "convertible group signatures" achieves these objectives : In addition to the properties of group signatures, the signer can turn all of his signatures, which are originally group signatures, into ordinary digital signatures by release a single bit strings. Thus these signatures could be verified without the aid of the group members together or a trusted authority. To construct a convertible group signature scheme, the following conditions must be satisfied ;

1) only members of the group can make signatures.
2) the recipient of the signature can verify that it is a valid group signature, but cannot discover which member of the group created it.
3) if necessary, either the group members together or a trusted authority can identify the signer.
4) release of some secret information by the signer turns all of his group signatures into ordinary digital signatures, but they should still be difficult to forge.

We can change any previous group signature scheme into a convertible group signature scheme. But, for its efficiency, we take example by Park et al's non-interactive group signature scheme.

3 Park et al's Non-interactive Group Signature Scheme

At JW-ISC'95 conference, Sung Jun Park and Dong Ho Won proposed a non-interactive group signature scheme based on the γth-residuosity problem. All previous schemes have been interactive ; the validity of a group signature is proven by an interactive protocol between signer and verifier. Sung Jun Park et al solve this problem by using the γth-residuosity problem. In this section we review Park et al's scheme[1] briefly.

---

[1] [11] points out some problems in Park et al's group signature scheme. To fix up this problems, Sung Jun Park modifies his schemes now.

3.1 Mathematical Background

We begin with a brief review of terminologies and results in [8][9][13][14].

Definition 1. For given positive integer γ and n, an integer z is a γth-residue if $\gcd(z, n) = 1$ and there is an integer x such that $z = x^\gamma \bmod n$, a γth-nonresidue otherwise.

The γth-Residuosity Problem (γ^{th}-RP) means the problem of determining γ^{th}-residuosity of the given element $z \in \mathbb{Z}_n^*$, where $\mathbb{Z}_n^*$ is the set of integers relatively prime to n between 0 and n. When n is a prime, the problem is already solvable. However, for a given composite integer whose factorization is unknown, this problem is known to be very difficult. If γ is 2, the problem is called *Quadratic Residuosity Problem*, which is applied to many cryptographic protocols.

Definition 2. We call a triple (n, γ, y) "acceptable" if n, γ, and y satisfy the following three conditions :

1) n is the product of powers of different primes, i.e., $n = n_1 \cdot n_2 \cdots n_t$, where each n_i is an odd prime power.
2) γ is an odd integer greater than 2 with $\gcd(\gamma, \phi(n_l)) = \gamma$ for just one $1 \leq l \leq t$, and $\gcd(\gamma, \phi(n_i)) = 1$ for all $i \neq l$, $1 \leq l \leq t$. For the sake of simplicity, we will assume that $l = 1$.
3) y is an element of $\mathbb{Z}_n^*$, written as $y = h_1^{b_1\gamma+e} \prod_{j=2}^t h_j^{b_j} \bmod n$, where $0 < e < \gamma$, $\gcd(e, \gamma) = 1$, $1 \leq b_j \leq \phi(n_j)$ for each $1 \leq j \leq t$, and $< h_1, h_2, \cdots, h_t >$ is a generator-vector for $\mathbb{Z}_n^*$.

We claim that if (n, γ, y) is an acceptable triple, then y is a γth-nonresidue mod n.

Lemma 3. *If a triple (n, γ, y) is acceptable, there exist a unique i such that $z = y^i \cdot u^\gamma \bmod n$ for every z in $\mathbb{Z}_n^*$.*

We call i the class-index of z with respect to the acceptable triple (n, γ, y). There are two other problems related intimately to the γth-RP.

Definition 4. We define the followings :

1) γ^{th}-RP : Given n, γ and an element z in $\mathbb{Z}_n^*$, decide whether or not z is a γth-residue mod n.
2) Class-index-comparing problem : Given an acceptable triple (n, γ, y) and two elements $z_1, z_2 \in \mathbb{Z}_n$, judge whether or not z_1 and z_2 have the same class-index with respect to (n, γ, y).
3) Class-index-finding problem : Given an acceptable triple (n, γ, y) and an element $z \in \mathbb{Z}_n^*$, find the class-index of z with respect to (n, γ, y).

Lemma 5. *[13] The following relations hold :*

1) γ^{th}-RP and Class-index-comparing problem are equivalent;

2) γ^{th}-RP and Class-index-comparing problem are reducible to the Class-index-finding problem;

3) γ^{th}-RP and Class-index-comparing problem are equivalent to the Class-index-finding problem when $\gamma = O(poly(k))$, where $poly(\cdot)$ denotes a polynomial;

Park et al proved that the above relation 3) can be extended to the below relation.

Lemma 6. γ^{th}-RP and Class-index-comparing problem are equivalent to the Class-index-finding problem when $\gamma = O(poly_1(k))^{O(poly_2(k))}$, where $poly_1(\cdot)$ and $poly_2(\cdot)$ denote a polynomial;

3.2 Non-interactive Group Signature Scheme

Let GC be a group center and ID_G be a group identity information. First, GC selects $n = p \cdot q = (2\gamma^d fp' + 1) \cdot (2fq' + 1)$, y and h, where f, p' and q' are distinct primes and $\gcd(\gamma, q') = 1$, $\gcd(\gamma, f) = 1$, (n, γ^d, y) is an acceptable triple, h is a secure hash function.

GC selects b, written as $b = h_1^{2p'\gamma^d} \cdot h_2^{2q'} \bmod n$, where $< h_1, h_2 >$ is a generator-vector for $\mathbb{Z}_n^*$. That is, b has an order of $f \bmod n$ and b is a $(\gamma^d)^{th}$-residue $\bmod n$. Thus the class-index of b is zero. Also the class-index of b^s is zero for any element s in $\mathbb{Z}_n^*$. And the class-index of any element z in $\mathbb{Z}_n^*$ is the same as the class-index of $z \cdot b^s$. GC computes the class-index, i of ID_G and publishes $(n, \gamma^d, y^i, b, f, h)$ as a public group key and keep (p', q') secret.

Group member A selects a random number, s_A (where, $0 < s_A < f$) as his secret key and gives his identity information, ID_A and $b^{s_A} \bmod n$ to GC(these need not be protected for confidentiality). Then GC can always compute the value, x_A such that $ID_G = b^{-s_A} \cdot y^{-i} \cdot x_A^{-\gamma^d} \bmod n$. GC gives x_A to the member A secretly. Here, GC doesn't know the secret key, s_A of member A.

PROTOCOL FOR SIGNATURE GENERATION

To sign message m with the private key (s_A, x_A) perform the followings :

1. A selects the two random numbers, r_1, r_2, where $0 < r_1 < f$ and $0 < r_2 < n$. A computes the value V such that

$$V = b^{r_1} \cdot r_2^{\gamma^d} \pmod{n}.$$

2. A computes the hash value, $e = h(V, m)$.

3. A computes the two values, z_1, z_2 such that

$$z_1 = r_1 + s_A \cdot e \pmod{f},$$
$$z_2 = r_2 \cdot x_A^e \pmod{n}.$$

4. The group signature on message m is

$$sign(m) = (e, z_1, z_2).$$

PROTOCOL FOR SIGNATURE VERIFICATION

Any one can check that (e, z_1, z_2) is a valid group signature on m by verifying that :

1. Any one can compute

$$\overline{V} = (ID_G \cdot y^i)^e \cdot b^{z_1} \cdot z_2^{\gamma^d} \pmod{n}.$$

2. He(She) checks that

$$e \stackrel{?}{=} h(\overline{V}, m)$$

IDENTIFYING THE SIGNER

From the signature (e, z_1, z_2) on message m, the signer can be identified by GC, who knows $b^{s_A} \bmod n$ and the secret key, x_A of group member A.

1. For each member ID_j (for each $1 \leq j \leq n$), GC computes x_j such that

$$ID_G = b^{-s_j} \cdot y^{-i} \cdot x_j^{-\gamma^d} \pmod{n}.$$

2. Then, GC computes r_2 from z_2 and x_j. That is,

$$r_2 = z_2 \cdot x_j^{-e} \pmod{n}.$$

3. GC checks whether or not the following condition holds for ID_j.

$$b^{z_1} \stackrel{?}{=} (((ID_G \cdot y^i)^e \cdot b^{z_1} \cdot z_2^{\gamma^d}) \cdot r_2^{-\gamma^d}) \cdot (b^{s_j})^e \pmod{n}.$$

4. So GC can find the signer from (e, z_1, z_2).

4 First Convertible Group Signature Scheme

In this section we show how Park et al's group signature scheme can be changed into a convertible group signature scheme which satisfies with the four conditions mentioned above.

4.1 The Scheme

Using the Park et al's scheme, we can construct a convertible group signature scheme as follows. As before let GC be a group center and ID_G be a group identity information. Then GC selects $n = p \cdot q = (2\gamma^d f p' + 1) \cdot (2fq' + 1), y, b$ and h, where (n, γ^d, y) is an acceptable triple, b is an element of $\mathbb{Z}_n$, written as $b = h_1^{2p'\gamma^d} \cdot h_2^{2q'} \bmod n$, where $< h_1, h_2 >$ is a generator-vector for $\mathbb{Z}_n^*$, and h is a secure hash function. GC publishes $(n, \gamma^d, y^i, b, f, h)$ as a public group key and keep (p', q') secret.

Group member A selects a random number, s_A $(0 < s_A < f)$ as his secret key and gives ID_A and $b^{s_A} \bmod n$ to GC. Then GC computes the value, x_A such that $ID_G = b^{-s_A} \cdot y^{-i} \cdot x_A^{-\gamma^d} \bmod n$. GC gives x_A to the member A secretly.

GC publishes the complete list of $(b^{s_1}, \cdots, b^{s_t})$ together with the identity of the member having b^{s_j} (where, $1 \le j \le n$) as public key in a Trusted Public Directory. That is, the secret key of a member A is a triple (s_A, x_A), the public key is b^{s_A}. Here GC doesn't know the secret key, s_A of member A.

PROTOCOL FOR SIGNATURE GENERATION

To sign message m with the private key (s_A, x_A) perform the followings :

1. A selects the two random numbers, r_1, r_2, where $0 < r_1 < f, 0 < r_2 < n$. A computes the value V such that

$$V = b^{r_1} \cdot r_2^{\gamma^d} \pmod n.$$

2. A picks a random number, R and computes the hash value,

$$e = h(V, m, blob(b^{r_1} \bmod n, R)).$$

Hash value, e contains a blob committing to the value of b^{r_1}, but hiding b^{r_1} until the randomly selected R is revealed.

3. A computes the two values, z_1, z_2 such that

$$z_1 = r_1 + s_A \cdot e \pmod f,$$
$$z_2 = r_2 \cdot x_A^e \pmod n$$

4. The signature on message m is

$$sign(m) = (e, z_1, z_2, blob(b^{r_1}, R)).$$

PROTOCOL FOR SIGNATURE VERIFICATION

Any one can check that $(e, z_1, z_2, blob(b^{r_1}, R))$ is a valid group signature on m by verifying that :

1. The verifier computes

$$\overline{V} = (ID_G \cdot y^i)^e \cdot b^{z_1} \cdot z_2^{\gamma^d} \pmod n.$$

2. He(She) checks that

$$e \stackrel{?}{=} h(\overline{V}, m, blob(b^{r_1}, R)).$$

A group signature generated according to the protocol is always accepted since we have

$$b^{r_1} \cdot r_2^{\gamma^d} = (b^{-s_A} y^{-i} x_A^{-\gamma^d})^e \cdot b^{(r_1 + s_A e)} \cdot y^i \cdot (r_2 \cdot x_a^e)^{\gamma^d} \pmod{n}.$$

Now we show that only GC can identify the signer.

IDENTIFYING THE SIGNER

From the signature $(e, z_1, z_2, blob(b^{r_1}, R))$ on message m, the signer can be identified by GC, who knows the secret key, x_j of each group member ID_j.

1. For each member ID_j (for each $1 \le j \le n$), GC, who knows x_j, computes r_2 from z_2 and x_j. That is

$$r_2 = z_2 \cdot x_j^{-e} \pmod{n}.$$

2. Then, GC checks whether or not the following condition holds for each member ID_j.

$$b^{z_1} \stackrel{?}{=} (V \cdot r_2^{-\gamma^d}) \cdot (b^{s_j})^e \pmod{n}.$$

3. So GC can find the signer from $(e, z_1, z_2, blob(b^{r_1}, R))$.

4.2 Conversion of Signatures

All previous group signatures can be converted to ordinary signatures by releasing secret key, x_A. Thus anyone knowing x_A can verify signatures. After x_A is revealed, this cannot help a forger.

CONVERSION OF ALL SIGNATURES

1. The signer publishes secret key, x_A.
2. Everybody knowing x_A can compute r_2 from z_2, x_A. Thus he(she) can check that $(e, z_1, z_2, blob(b^{r_1}, R))$ is a signature on m by verifying that

$$b_1^z \stackrel{?}{=} (b^{r_1}) \cdot (b^{s_A})^e \pmod{n}.$$

Knowing randomly selected R such that $blob(b^{r_1}, R)$, anyone can verify a signature $(e, z_1, z_2, blob(b^{r_1}, R))$ on the message m by computing $h(V, m, blob((b^{z_1}) \cdot (b^{s_A})^{-e}, R))$, and verifying that it equals e. Therefore, a single signature corresponding to R can be converted to an ordinary digital signature by releasing R.

SELECTIVE CONVERSION

1. The signer reveals randomly selected R.

2. Anyone can check the signature by computing that

$$\overline{b^{r_1}} = (b^{z_1}) \cdot (b^{s_A})^{-e} \pmod{n},$$
$$\overline{e} = h(V, m, blob(\overline{b^{r_1}}, R)),$$
$$e \overset{?}{=} \overline{e}.$$

Note that even the GC cannot create the false converted signatures, which were originally group signatures. That is, the trust center does not know member's secret key, s_j (for all $1 \le j \le n$), and cannot impersonate a user without being detected. Of course, GC can still compute "false" secret keys linked to Alice, by choosing random selected $\overline{s}$ and computing $\overline{x}$. But since only the GC is able to compute x, the existence of two different $x, \overline{x}$ for the same user, Alice, is in itself a proof that GC has cheated. In particular, our scheme is almost as efficient as the Schnorr's scheme[12].

5 Second Convertible Group Signature Scheme

In this section we simplify above convertible group signature scheme and show a functionally equivalent scheme based on a simpler construction.

GC selects $n = p \cdot q = (2fp' + 1) \cdot (2fq' + 1)$, where f, p' and q' are distinct primes. It is recommended that f be about 160 bits and p', q' be about 234 bits. GC selects g, where g has an order of f (that is, $g^f = 1 \bmod n$). GC then picks the integer (γ, d) such that,

$$\gcd(\gamma, \phi(n)) = 1, \ 2^{159} < \gamma < 2^{160}, \ \gamma \cdot d = 1 \pmod{\phi(n)}.$$

GC publishes (n, γ, g, f, h) as a public group key and keep (d, p', q') secret. GC can generate the secret key of member A, as follows.

1. Group member A selects his secret key, $0 < s_A < f$ and sends ID_A and $b^{s_A} \bmod n$ to GC.
2. GC computes x_A such that

$$x_A = (ID_G \cdot g^{s_A})^{-d} \pmod{n}.$$

3. GC gives x_A to the member A secretly.

As before, GC publishes the complete list of $(g^{s_1}, \cdots, g^{s_t})$ together with the identity of the member having g^{s_j} (where, $1 \le j \le t$) as public key in a Trusted Public Directory. That is, the secret key of a member A is a pair (s_A, x_A), the public key is g^{s_A}. Here GC doesn't know the secret key, s_A of member A. x_A enables the GC to identify the signer, but not to sign. Now, all of the protocols are the same as the above, except that we use (γ, g) instead of (γ^d, b) and y^i is omitted.

6   Conclusion

This paper has presented the concept of "convertible group signatures". In addition to the properties of group signatures, convertible group signatures allow the signer to turn all of his group signatures into ordinary digital signatures by releasing of a single bit string. Using Park's non-interactive group signature scheme, we have presented a very efficient selectively convertible group signature scheme. The security of our scheme is based on the difficulty of γth-residuosity problem and discrete logarithm problem simultaneously. Furthermore, we showed a functionally equivalent scheme to the above.

References

1. J. Boyar, D. Chaum, I. Damgard and T. Pedersen, "Convertible undeniable signature", *Proc. Crypto'90*, pp. 195-208.
2. G. Brassard, D. Chaum, and C. Crepeau, "Minimum disclosure proofs of knowledge", *Journal of Computer and System Sciences*, vol. 37, 1988, pp. 156-189.
3. D. Chaum and E. van Heyst, "Group Signatures", *Eurocrypt'91*, pp. 257-265, 1991.
4. L. Chen and T. P. Pedersen, "New Group Signature Schemes", *Proc. of Eurocrypt '94*, pp. 163-173.
5. W. Diffie and M. Hellman, "New Directions in Cryptography", *IEEE Transactions on Information Theory IT-22*, pp. 644-654, 1976.
6. S. J. Park, I. S. Lee, and D. H. Won, "A Practical Group Signature", *Proc. of JW-ISC'95*, Japan, pp. 127-133, 1995. 1.
7. S. J. Park and D. H. Won, "A Practical Identity-based Group Signature", *Proc. of ICEIC'95*, China, pp. II-64II-67, 1995. 8.
8. S. J. Park and D. H. Won, "A Generalization of Public Key Residue Cryptosystem", *Proc. of JW-ISC'93*, Korea, pp. 202-206, 1993.
9. S. J. Park and D. H. Won, "A Generalized Public Key Residue Cryptosystem and Its Applications", *IEEE GLOBECOM'95*, Singapore , pp. 1179-1182, 1995. 11.
10. S. J. Park, Chung Ryong Jang, Kyung Sin Kim and D. H. Won, "A "Paradoxical" Identity-based Scheme Based on the γth-Residuosity Problem and Discrete Logarithm Problem", *An International Conference on Numbers and Forms, Cryptography and Codes*, Khabarovsk, Russia, 1994. 8.
11. Sangjoon Park, private communication.
12. C. P. Schnorr, "Efficient Signature Generation by Smart Cards", *Journal of Cryptology*, 4(3) : pp. 161-174, 1991.
13. Y. Zheng, "A Study on Probabilistic Cryptosystems and Zero-knowledge Protocol", *Master thesis*, Yokohama National University, 1988.
14. Y. Zheng, T. Matsumoto, and H. Imai, "Residuosity Problem and its Applications to Cryptography", *Trans. IEICE*, vol. E71, No. 8, pp. 759-767, 1988.

How to Utilize the Transformability of Digital Signatures for Solving the Oracle Problem

Masahiro MAMBO[1], Kouichi SAKURAI[2] and Eiji OKAMOTO[1]

[1] School of Information Science, Japan Advanced Institute of Science and Technology
1-1 Asahidai Tatsunokuchi Nomi Ishikawa, 923-12 Japan
Email: {mambo,okamoto}@jaist.ac.jp
[2] Dept. of Computer and Communication Engineering, Kyushu University
Hakozaki Higashi-ku Fukuoka, 812-81 Japan Email: sakurai@csce.kyushu-u.ac.jp

Abstract. Transformability is a property of a digital signature such that one valid signature can be transformed into another valid signature of the same signature scheme. Usually digital signatures should not be forged so that the transformability is regarded as an unfavorable property. Contrarily we show that the transformability can be positively utilized for solving the oracle problem. The oracle problem is the following problem existing in some cryptographic protocols. An entity following a protocol receives a message from an adversary, and returns a certain value computed by a procedure specified in the protocol. In this process the adversary may obtain useful information by interacting with the oracle entity. The blind signature scheme and the blind decoding scheme are examples of such a protocol. Since these blinding techniques are very important in cryptographic applications, e.g. electronic money and digital pay magazine, a method to prevent illegal information leakage should be found. In this paper an oracle problem in the blind decoding scheme based on the ElGamal cryptosystem is solved with the use of a transformable digital signature. As in the original blind decoding scheme, the proposed blind decoding protocol offers users perfect untraceability. We also discuss the relevance of the transformable signature to the blind signature, the divertible zeroknowledge interactive proof and other schemes.

1 Introduction

Carelessly designed cryptographic protocols are easily exploited by an adversary. Even carefully designed ones sometimes possess pitfalls. Some protocols are proven to be secure under a certain assumption, but at a later time they are analyzed to be insecure due to unexamined assumptions, e.g. [PW91]. In order to avoid building an insecure protocol it is important to shed light on robustness principles which cryptographic protocol designers should keep in mind. Protocols constructed by following these principles become more unlikely to be attacked by the adversary. Such robustness principles are shown in [AN95]. Among 8 principles described in it, the third principle is stated as follows.

Principle 3: Be careful when signing or decrypting data that you never let yourself be used as an oracle by your opponent.

Let us consider a protocol where upon request from a user, an entity performs a signing or decrypting operation by using its own secret, and it returns a computed value. In this protocol an opponent might try to obtain useful information by interacting with the entity, who behaves like an oracle following the procedure specified in the protocol. A careful protocol designer may try to foil the pitfall by making the entity return a value other than a generated signature or a decrypted message. Even in this case, the opponent might prepare a tricky message and transform a returned value into desired information related to the entity's secret, which s/he cannot compute alone. Such an attack performed by interacting with the oracle is called an *oracle attack*, and the above principle alerts us an *oracle problem* caused by the oracle attack.

In [AN95] a key exchange protocol discussed in [TMN89] is shown as an example of the oracle problem. In this key exchange protocol a trusted server intermediate two parties and performs the RSA decryption. As pointed out in [Sim94], colluding third parties can compute a session key of other parties. First they eavesdrop the communication among the target parties in the key exchange protocol. Then they execute the key exchange protocol with the trusted center with the help of a value derived from the eavesdropped communication.

Although these protocol failures are found, playing as an oracle [3] cannot always be avoided. This is because the signing or decrypting operation with one's own secret is an important cryptographic primitive. For example we have the following two cases.

Blind signature: Blind signature is a key technique in most of electronic money systems, e.g. [CFN88, OO91, CP92, Fer93, Bran93, Oka95, SPC95, BGK95]. The notion of the blind signature was first introduced in [Cha82] and it was actually realized in [Cha85] based on the RSA signature scheme [RSA78]. Blind signatures based on the discrete logarithm problem are described in [CP92, CPS94, HMP94-2] and at Appendix B in [Oka92]. In these blind signature schemes a user gives a signer a message with hiding his/her real message inside of it. Without knowing the hidden message the signer signs the given message and returns a created signature. Afterwards a signature for the original message is computed from the returned signature and other known values. Since the original message is kept unknown to the signer, the blind signature scheme is useful for protecting user's privacy.

Blind decoding: Blind decoding (blind decryption) is the concept similar to the blind signature. In contrast to the blind signature scheme in which a signature unknown to a signer is created, a ciphertext unknown to a decrypting person is decrypted in the blind decoding scheme. Concerning the RSA systems the signing

---

[3] We use a phrase "playing as an oracle" for a case such as an entity returns a value as specified in the adopted cryptographic protocol. By interacting with such an oracle an adversary may try to extract information. The adversary can freely select messages s/he sends to the oracle. An oracle in a prudently designed protocol does not allow the adversary to actually get useful information. But an oracle in a carelessly designed protocol releases some useful information. We regard that Principle 3 warns that useful information should not be extracted after the interaction with the oracle.

operation in the RSA signature scheme and the decrypting operation in the RSA cryptosystem are exactly the same if the same secret is used in both systems. Thus the blind signature scheme for the RSA signature scheme also provides the blind decoding scheme for the RSA cryptosystem. The RSA blind decoding scheme was first utilized in fair cryptosystems in order to make trustees oblivious of the name of wiretapped parties [Mic92]. As for ElGamal-type system [ElG85], the techniques for the blind signatures [CPS94, HMP94-2] cannot directly be applied to the blind decoding. Hence a blind decoding scheme for the ElGamal cryptosystem was proposed in [SY96], and a digital pay magazine system was indicated as its application. An subscriber of a pay magazine system can obtain decrypted articles with concealing the name of the article against a provider by conducting the blind decoding protocol. Similar to the blind signature, the blind decoding offers users privacy protection.

In order to make full use of the above cryptographic primitives, we should find a way to prevent an adversary from extracting useful information from the oracle. Depending on the applications we have a method to detect an abuse of these protocols. In electronic money systems random numbers are processed, e.g. signed by a bank, and these values are later regarded as electronic money. Since these values come from random numbers, checking their form does not harm user's privacy. In some electronic money systems using the blind signature scheme, the cut-and-choose method is conducted in the electronic money withdrawal session, and the content of messages randomly picked up from a set of submitted messages is checked by an signer. These checked messages are thrown away, and unrevealed messages and their signatures serve as electronic money.

In case of the blind decoding we cannot take the same approach. Once the content of messages is checked, the privacy of user is not preserved any more. An effective method to solve the oracle problem in the blind decoding should be established. This demand is serious when the same key is used for signing and decrypting operations. In the RSA system an adversary can obtain a signature for a message of his/her own choice by participating in the blind decoding scheme. In the ElGamal-type systems an adversary can obtain a signature for the undeniable signature scheme or a key of the Diffie-Hellman problem. In [AN95] multiple use of a key is warned as follows.

Principle 2: Be careful how entities are distinguished. If possible avoid using the same key for two different purpose (such as signing and decryption), and be sure to distinguish different runs of the same protocol from each other.

A protocol designer should be mindful of this principle. But in the computer network system employing cryptographic technology, e.g. in electronic commerce system, the efficiency of the key management would be improved in case of a single pair of secret and public keys compared with the case of double pairs of secret and public keys. So, fewer number of key pairs is attractive.

As mentioned in [SY96] the blind decoding scheme based on the ElGamal cryptosystem has not overcome the oracle problem, and finding a solution to this problem remains to be an open question.

In this paper we discuss the *transformability* of digital signatures, and show digital signatures with this property, *transformable digital signatures*, are effectively used to defeat the oracle attack in the ElGamal blind decoding scheme.

Transformability is a property of a digital signature such that one valid signature can be transformed into another valid signature of the same signature scheme. Usually digital signatures should not be forged so that the transformability is regarded as an unfavorable property. Contrarily we show that the transformability can be positively utilized for solving the oracle problem.

Following this introduction the blind decoding scheme based on the ElGamal cryptosystem [SY96] and its oracle problem is explained in Sect.2. The notion of transformability of digital signatures and examples of the transformable signature are shown in Sect.3. Then the oracle problem described in Sect.2 is addressed in Sect.4. After discussing the relevance of the transformable signature to the blind signature, the divertible zeroknowledge interactive proof(divertible ZKIP) and other schemes in Sect.5, concluding remarks are given in Sect.6.

2 Blind Decoding and the Oracle Problem

A blind decoding scheme based on the ElGamal cryptosystem was proposed in [SY96]. Let p and q be primes satisfying $p = 2q + 1$. $g \in Z_p^*$ of the prime order q. Public and secret keys of Bob are (y_B, g, p) and x_B, respectively. Alice possesses a ciphertext $(c_1, c_2) = (g^k \bmod p, my_B^k \bmod p)$ of Bob for a message $m \in Z_p^*$ and a randomly selected $k \in_R Z_q$. She stores many such ciphertexts and asks Bob to decode a ciphertext without telling which one is actually decoded.

> Step 1. Alice selects a random number $\alpha \in_R Z_q$, and computes $X = c_1^\alpha \bmod p$. X is sent to Bob.
>
> Step 2. After receiving X, Bob computes $Y = X^{x_B} \bmod p$, and returns Y to Alice.
>
> Step 3. After receiving Y, Alice calculates $Z = X^{\{\alpha^{-1} \bmod q\}} \bmod p$. Since $Z \equiv ((c_1^\alpha)^{x_B})^{\{\alpha^{-1} \bmod q\}} \equiv c_1^{x_B} \bmod p$, Alice can determine m by computing $c_2/Z \bmod p (\equiv c_2/c_1^{x_B} \bmod p)$.

Although the above protocol can be executed for p not satisfying $p = 2q + 1$ and g of the order $p - 1$, p satisfying $p = 2q + 1$ and g of the order q should be adopted. Depending on a randomly selected $k \in_R Z_{p-1}^*$, the set $\{S|S = (g^k)^\alpha \bmod p, \alpha \in Z_{p-1}^*\}$ could become a very small set, and α selected by Alice might be guessed by Bob [SY96]. *Perfect untraceability*, or *perfect undetectability*, against Bob, i.e. all ciphertexts are equally likely to produce a request X, can be achieved by the above parameters without depending on the selected k.

As easily observed in the above protocol, a cheating Alice can obtain $(\overline{X})^{x_B} \bmod p$, which she cannot compute alone, for arbitrarily selected message $\overline{X}$, i.e. Bob may play as an oracle to supply Alice with $\overline{X}$ raised to his secret. Such an oracle problem for a scheme based on the discrete logarithm problem can be addressed by a transformable digital signature explained in the next section.

3   Transformability of Digital Signatures

In this section transformability of digital signatures is discussed. There are digital signatures such that given a message and signature pair $(m, \mathcal{S})$ satisfying a verification equation $\mathcal{V}(m, \mathcal{S}, y)$ with a public key y of some signer, another pair $(\widetilde{m}, \widetilde{\mathcal{S}})$ satisfying $\mathcal{V}(\widetilde{m}, \widetilde{\mathcal{S}}, y)$ can be computed without the help of the signer. We call this property of the digital signature as transformability. Usually the transformability is negatively understood, so that a transformable signature is converted into an untransformable signature by requiring a certain structure in the message, i.e. redundancy, or by applying a one-way function to the message before signing it, and only the untransformable signature has been utilized.

From the viewpoints of keeping a signature scheme secure against any signature forgery, the transformability is an unfavorable property. But as long as a valid signature cannot be computed for a selected message, we can find a way to positively utilize the transformable digital signature.

The ElGamal signature scheme [ElG85]: We use parameters p, q and g same as in the ElGamal cryptosystem in Sect. 2. (y_B, g, p) is a public key of Bob and x_B is his secret key. For a message $m \in Z_q$, the triple (m, r, s) is computed by $r = g^k \bmod p$ for a random number $k \in_R Z_q$ and $s = (m - r x_B)k^{-1} \bmod q$. Verification is executed by checking $g^m \equiv y_B^r r^s \bmod p$.

As pointed out in [ElG85], Bob's ElGamal signature (r, s) for a message m can be transformed into his signature $(\widetilde{r}, \widetilde{s})$ for a random message $\widetilde{m}$.

$$\begin{aligned} \widetilde{r} &= r^a g^b y_B^c \bmod p, \quad \text{where } a, b, c \in_R Z_q, \\ \widetilde{s} &= s\widetilde{r}(ar - cs)^{-1} \bmod q, \text{ and} \\ \widetilde{m} &= \widetilde{r}(am + bs)(ar - cs)^{-1} \bmod q \ . \end{aligned} \tag{1}$$

Since the congruence $g^{\widetilde{m}} \equiv y_B^{\widetilde{r}} \widetilde{r}^{\widetilde{s}} \bmod p$ is satisfied, a generated $(\widetilde{r}, \widetilde{s})$ signs $\widetilde{m}$. Although such a transformation is possible, it is believed to be infeasible to compute a valid signature for a message of one's own choice.

There are variants [AMV90, YL93, NR94, HMP94-1] of the ElGamal signature scheme. Other modifications are found in [Schn91, DSS93]. In Meta-ElGamal signature scheme [HMP94-1] a verification congruence is generally described as $g^{\mathcal{A}} \equiv y_B^{\mathcal{B}} r^{\mathcal{C}} \bmod p$, where $r = g^k \bmod p$ and $k \in_R Z_q$. In order to create a signature s for a message m, a congruence

$$\mathcal{A} \equiv x_B \mathcal{B} + k\mathcal{C} \bmod q$$

is solved for a signature s, where $\mathcal{A}$, $\mathcal{B}$ and $\mathcal{C}$ are selected as a permutation of (m, r, s). Here $-m$, $-r$ and $-s$ are included in (m, r, s).

Suppose (r, s) is a valid signature of the Meta-ElGamal signature scheme for a message m, and $(\widetilde{m}, \widetilde{r}, \widetilde{s})$ is another valid triple of the message and signature transformed from (m, r, s). r and $\widetilde{r}$ are related each other by the equation $\widetilde{r} = r^a g^b y_B^c \bmod p$. Since $(\widetilde{m}, \widetilde{r}, \widetilde{s})$ is a valid triple, the verification congruence $g^{\widetilde{\mathcal{A}}} \equiv y_B^{\widetilde{\mathcal{B}}} \widetilde{r}^{\widetilde{\mathcal{C}}} \bmod p$ should be fulfilled. Then applying an analytic method [HMP94-2] for the Meta-ElGamal blind signature scheme, we have $y_B^{\widetilde{\mathcal{B}}} \widetilde{r}^{\widetilde{\mathcal{C}}} \equiv y_B^{\widetilde{\mathcal{B}}} (r^a g^b y_B^c)^{\widetilde{\mathcal{C}}} \equiv$

$r^{a\widetilde{c}}g^{b\widetilde{C}}y_B^{\widetilde{B}+c\widetilde{C}} \equiv g^{a\widetilde{C}(A-x_BB)C^{-1}}g^{b\widetilde{C}}y_B^{\widetilde{B}+c\widetilde{C}} \equiv y_B^{\widetilde{B}+c\widetilde{C}-aBC^{-1}\widetilde{C}}g^{aAC^{-1}\widetilde{C}+b\widetilde{C}} \bmod p$. This value should be equal to $g^{\widetilde{A}} \bmod p$. Thus the following congruences should be satisfied.

$$\widetilde{r} = r^a g^b y_B^c \bmod p, \quad \text{where } a, b, c \in_R Z_q,$$
$$\widetilde{A} = aAC^{-1}\widetilde{C} + b\widetilde{C} \bmod q, \text{ and} \tag{2}$$
$$\widetilde{B} = aBC^{-1}\widetilde{C} - c\widetilde{C} \bmod q .$$

Any one of 6 possible ElGamal-type signatures has the transformability.

A modified ElGamal signature using hash functions cannot be transformed, and the Schnorr signature is not a transformable signature.

The RSA signature scheme also bears transformability. Let $n = pq$. (e_B, n) is a public key of Bob and (d_B, p, q) is his secret key. (m, S) is a message and signature pair of Bob satisfying $S \equiv m^{d_B} \bmod n$. One can transform (m, S) into $(\widetilde{m}, \widetilde{S})$ by computing $\widetilde{m} = \beta^e m \bmod n$ and $\widetilde{S} = \beta S \bmod n$ with a random number $\beta \in_R Z_n^*$. It is also considered to be infeasible to obtain $\widetilde{S}$ for a target message $\widetilde{m}$.

In the RSA signature one can compute a valid forged signature without possessing any signature in advance. First S is selected and then $S^e \bmod n$ is computed. It is easily observed that $(S^e \bmod n, S)$ passes the verification procedure. Similarly an ElGamal signature can be forged without the knowledge of any single signature [ElG85]. This forgery is led by setting $a = 0$ in (1).

$$\widetilde{r} = g^b y_B^c \bmod p, \quad \text{where } b, c \in_R Z_q,$$
$$\widetilde{s} = -\widetilde{r}c^{-1} \bmod q, \text{ and} \tag{3}$$
$$\widetilde{m} = -\widetilde{r}bc^{-1} \bmod q .$$

Even though the above forgeries are possible, they do not mean that one can obtain a signature for a given message.

4 Defeating an Oracle Attack

In this section we show how to utilize the transformability of digital signatures for defeating an oracle attack in the ElGamal blind decoding scheme in Sect.2.

Proposed blind decoding protocol

Step 0. (Preliminary) When Bob creates a ciphertext $(c_1, c_2) = (g^k \bmod p, my_B^k \bmod p)$, he also computes a signature (s, c_1) for c_2 by the ElGamal signature scheme. p, q and g hold the relation explained in Sect.2.

$$s = (c_2 - c_1 x_B)k^{-1} \bmod q .$$

Then (c_1, c_2, s) is given to Alice. Alice checks its validity, and if it is not a valid ElGamal signature, she requests a valid one. Alice does not proceed to Step 1 until she receives a valid ElGamal signature.

Step 1. (Signature transformation and request) When Alice wants to decrypt (c_1, c_2), she computes

$$\tilde{c}_1 = c_1^a g^b \bmod p, \quad \text{where } a, b \in_R Z_q,$$
$$\tilde{s} = sa^{-1}c_1^{-1}\tilde{c}_1 \bmod q, \text{ and} \tag{4}$$
$$\tilde{c}_2 = (ac_2 + bs)a^{-1}c_1^{-1}\tilde{c}_1 \bmod q .$$

$(X, \tilde{c}_2, \tilde{s})$ is sent to Bob, where $X = \tilde{c}_1$. This message indicates a request for the blind decryption.

Step 2. (Signature check, exponentiation and return) Upon receiving the triple, Bob first checks $g^{\tilde{c}_2} \equiv y_B^X X^{\tilde{s}} \bmod p$. If the congruence is not satisfied, he stops proceeding the step and returns nothing or a warning message.
If the congruence is satisfied, he computes $Y = X^{x_B} \bmod p$, and returns Y to Alice.

Step 3. (Final decryption) Upon receiving Y, Alice calculates $Z = (Y/y_B^b)^{\{a^{-1} \bmod q\}}$ $\bmod p$. Since $Z \equiv ((c_1^a g^b)^{x_B}/y_B^b)^{\{a^{-1} \bmod q\}} \equiv (c_1^{ax_B})^{\{a^{-1} \bmod q\}} \equiv c_1^{x_B} \bmod p$, Alice can determine m by computing $c_2/Z \bmod p \; (\equiv c_2/c_1^{x_B} \bmod p)$.

Concerning (4), a signature $(\tilde{c}_1, \tilde{c}_2, \tilde{s})$ correctly transformed from a valid signature (c_1, c_2, s) satisfies

$$g^{\tilde{c}_2} \equiv g^{(ac_2+bs)a^{-1}c_1^{-1}\tilde{c}_1} \equiv (y_B^{c_1} c_1^s)^{c_1^{-1}\tilde{c}_1} g^{bsa^{-1}c_1^{-1}\tilde{c}_1} \equiv y_B^{\tilde{c}_1}(c_1^a g^b)^{sa^{-1}c_1^{-1}\tilde{c}_1}$$
$$\equiv y_B^{\tilde{c}_1} \tilde{c}_1^{\tilde{s}} \bmod p .$$

In the proposed protocol the secret x_B in one cryptosystem is also used for the signature creation, and Principle 2 mentioned in Sect. 1 is not fulfilled. If a protocol designer wants to avoid using the same secret for different purposes, Bob should restrict the use of x_B only for decrypting ciphertexts requested and for signing c_2 of the proposed blind decoding protocol.

Security consideration: Due to transformability of adopted digital signature any adversary that has observed the communication between Alice and Bob can compute a valid forged signature. In addition, as mentioned in Sect.3, the adversary can create a forgery even without obtaining a valid signature. Whatever values an adversary knows, as long as the verification in Step 2 is passed, Bob sends back a value exponentiated by his secret. In this sense, our approach does not guarantee that the adversary gets any information at all.

Even so, it is considered to be hard to find a triple $(X, \tilde{c}_2, \tilde{s})$ for X selected by an adversary. Because the adversary who knows $g, X, Const(= y_B^X \bmod p)$ has to solve $g^{\tilde{c}_2} X^{-\tilde{s}} \equiv Const \bmod p$ for variables $\tilde{c}_2$ and $\tilde{s}$. This problem is estimated as one of cryptographic primitive hard problems and has appeared in the literature, e.g. [CEG87, HP92, Oka92, Bran93, BGK95].

The adversary may execute the above blind decoding protocol for many triples $(X^{(i)}, c_2^{(i)}, s^{(i)})$, $i \in \{1, 2, \ldots\}$, generated either by the transformation (4) or by the procedure (3). Then a constructed database $(X^{(i)}, (X^{(i)})^{x_B})$ is used for finding a set $\mathcal{I} = \{i | \prod_i X^{(i)} \equiv m \bmod p\}$ for a target m. $m^{x_B} \bmod p$ is obtained by computing $\prod_{i \in I}(X^{(i)})^{x_B}$ mod p. From this viewpoint the proposed blind decoding scheme is not existentially unforgeable. But the adversary needs to prepare very large database since each $X^{(i)}$ generated by the transformation (4) or by the procedure (3) randomly varies in Z_p^*.

(Perfect untraceability) The original blind decoding scheme in Sect.2 ensures perfect untraceability against Bob. Even combined with the transformable ElGamal signature scheme employing transformation (4), the blind decoding scheme keeps Alice not to be traced by Bob in a perfect sense. The following is the proof.

From the second and the third equations in the transformation (4) one can compute (a, b) such that

$$a = s\widetilde{s}^{-1}c_1^{-1}\widetilde{c_1} \bmod q, \text{ and} \tag{5}$$
$$b = as^{-1}(c_1\widetilde{c_1}^{-1}\widetilde{c_2} - c_2) \bmod q .$$

These values are uniquely determined only from (c_1, c_2, s) and $(\widetilde{c_1}, \widetilde{c_2}, \widetilde{s})$.

$$c_1^a g^b \equiv c_1^a g^{as^{-1}(c_1\widetilde{c_1}^{-1}\widetilde{c_2}-c_2)} \equiv c_1^a (y_B^{\widetilde{c_1}}\widetilde{c_1}^{\widetilde{s}})^{as^{-1}c_1\widetilde{c_1}^{-1}}(y_B^{c_1}c_1^s)^{as^{-1}}$$
$$\equiv \widetilde{c_1}^{s^{-1}\widetilde{s}ac_1\widetilde{c_1}^{-1}} \equiv \widetilde{c_1}^{s^{-1}\widetilde{s}(s\widetilde{s}^{-1}c_1^{-1}\widetilde{c_1})c_1\widetilde{c_1}^{-1}} \equiv \widetilde{c_1} \bmod p .$$

Hence the probability that an original signature is transformed into a given signature is equal for any original signature among the whole group of signatures.

5 Transformable Signatures, Blind signatures, Divertible ZKIPs and Other Schemes

Transformable signatures are closely related to blind signatures. In the transformable signature a message is signed at first, and then a created signature is transformed. In the blind signature a message is transformed at first, and then transformed message is signed. We study this relation in the following variant of the ElGamal signature scheme.

A variant of ElGamal signature scheme: We use parameters p, q and g as the same as in the ElGamal cryptosystem in Sect. 2. (y_B, g, p) is a public key of Bob and x_B is his secret key. For a message $m \in Z_q$, (r, s) is computed by $r = g^k \bmod p$ for a random number $k \in_R Z_q$ and $s = (rx_B + km) \bmod q$. Verification is executed by checking $g^s \equiv y_B^r r^m \bmod p$.

Note that this variant ElGamal signature can be further changed into a modified version [CPS94] of the DSA [DSS93]. In the modified DSA, $(r, s) = ((g^k \bmod p) \bmod q, rx_B + km \bmod q)$ is a signature for a message m, and $r \equiv ((g^s y_B^{-r})^{\{m^{-1} \bmod q\}} \bmod p) \bmod q$ is the verification congruence.

Since the above variant ElGamal signature scheme and the modified DSA is related each other, the blind signature scheme for the above variant of the ElGamal signature scheme is relatively easily obtained from the method in [CPS94, HMP94-2]. In the following protocol Bob signs a blinded message $\widetilde{m}$ selected by Alice.

Step 1. Bob selects a random number $k \in_R Z_q^*$, and computes $r = g^k \bmod p$. He continues this procedure until $q \nmid r$, and when this relation is satisfied, he sends r to Alice.

Step 2. Alice checks $q \nmid r$, and when it is passed, she computes $\tilde{r}$ and m such that $\tilde{r} = r^a g^b \bmod p$ and $m = \tilde{m} a r \tilde{r}^{-1} \bmod q$ for $a, b \in_R Z_q$. m is sent to Bob.

Step 3. Bob signs m by $s = r x_B + km \bmod q$, and s is returned to Alice.

Step 4. Alice derives a signature $(\tilde{r}, \tilde{s})$ for $\tilde{m}$ by computing $\tilde{s} = sr^{-1}\tilde{r} + b\tilde{m} \bmod q$.

Blindness of the signatures is proven in [CPS94]. Based on the operations in the above blind signature scheme, the signature form of the above variant of the ElGamal signature scheme is transformed as follows.

$$\tilde{r} = r^a g^b \bmod p, \quad \text{where } a, b \in_R Z_q, \quad \text{(From Step 2)}$$
$$\tilde{m} = ma^{-1}r^{-1}\tilde{r} \bmod q, \text{ and} \quad \text{(From Step 2)} \qquad (6)$$
$$\tilde{s} = sr^{-1}\tilde{r} + b\tilde{m} \bmod q . \quad \text{(From Step 3)}$$

Since the operation used in this transformation is equivalent to the operation in the blind signature described above, proof of perfect untraceability is straightforward.

Not all variants of the ElGamal signature scheme have a blind signature scheme. For example it is not known how to construct a blind signature scheme for the original ElGamal signature scheme. Even if a blind signature scheme is not known, a signature may be transformable. As shown in Sect.3, the original ElGamal signature scheme satisfies transformability.

Operations of the most of the blind signatures based on the discrete logarithm problem can be converted into the transformation of digital signatures. In case of the Meta-ElGamal blind signatures [HMP94-2], (2) is changed into

$$\tilde{r} = r^a g^b \bmod p,$$
$$\tilde{A} = a A C^{-1} \tilde{C} + b\tilde{C} \bmod q, \quad \text{and} \qquad (7)$$
$$\tilde{B} = a B C^{-1} \tilde{C} \bmod q .$$

In the blind signature $\tilde{s}$ is not allowed to be included in the congruence for $\tilde{m}$ because $\tilde{s}$ is a value computed just after receiving an answer to a signing request for $\tilde{m}$. So, we cannot have a blind signature scheme for the ordered triple (m, r, s) and (r, m, s) of the parameter (A, B, C). To the contrary, any permutation is allowed for the signature transformation. For the ordered triples (m, r, s) and (s, r, m) the last congruence of (7) is solved at first. For the triple (r, s, m) and (r, m, s) the second congruence of (7) is solved at first. Variables a, b, r and m have to meet the condition $\gcd(arm^{-1} + b, q) = 1$ for the triple (r, s, m), and variables a, b, r and s have to meet the condition $\gcd(ars^{-1} + b, q) = 1$ for the triple (r, m, s). For each case q pairs of (a, b) do not satisfy the condition. Hence perfect untraceability is slightly destroyed in case of the triples (r, s, m) and (r, m, s). But this condition is not too serious condition to cause Bob to find a relation of signatures. The above condition is met only with the probability $1/q(= q/q^2)$ for each of them.

Meanwhile, there are untransformable signature schemes, e.g. the Schnorr signature scheme and the modified DSA, for which a blind signature scheme, i.e. [Oka92] and [CPS94], is constructed. In case of the modified DSA, the operation of the blind signature can be converted into the signature transformation if a longer form of signature $(g^k \bmod p, s)$ is adopted in place of $((g^k \bmod p) \bmod q, s)$.

In [OO89] a blind digital signature scheme based on divertible zeroknowledge interactive proofs(divertible ZKIPs) is presented. A pair of a communication sequence between Alice and Bob and its resultant signature and a pair of a communication sequence between Bob and Cindy and its resultant signature are polynomially indistinguishable or equivalent in the divertible ZKIP. Hence one cannot relate an original signature to a diverted signature as in the transformable signature. On the other hand, the divertibility of a protocol [CP92] for proving $\log_g h \equiv \log_m z$ of the quadruple (g, h, m, z) is utilized for constructing oblivious signatures in [Che94] and for converting a credential issued to a person with a pseudonym into an untraceable credential for a distinct pseudonym of the same person in [Che95]. By the latter procedure, a user possessing a credential issued from one organization can show other organization the possession of the credential without allowing it to link these credentials. The untraceability preserved in these schemes offers users privacy protection as in the transformable signature. The relevance of the transformable signatures to these schemes will be discussed further in the journal version of this paper.

6 Concluding Remarks

We have discussed the transformability of digital signatures, and showed that a digital signature possessing this property can be positively applied to solving the oracle problem in the blind decoding scheme based on the ElGamal cryptosystem. Although the transformable signature itself does not ensure the authenticity of a message, great effect can be expected when it is adequately combined with a process for return messages. The proposed blind decoding protocol utilizing the transformable signature keeps decrypted messages perfectly untraceable, and it offers users high level of privacy protection. We have also shown the relevance of the transformable signature to the blind signature, the divertible ZKIP and other schemes. It is not known until now how to defeat an oracle attack in the blind decoding scheme based on the RSA cryptosystem. We would like to continue to examine the availability of the transformability of the RSA signature scheme for solving this problem.

References

[AMV90]   Agnew, G.B., Mullin, B.C. and Vanstone, S.A.: "Improved Digital Signature Scheme Based on Discrete Exponentiation," Electronics Letters, Vol.26, No.14, pp.1024-1025 (Jul. 1990).

[AN95]   Anderson, R. and Needham,R.: "Robustness Principles for Public Key Pro-
           tocols," Lecture Notes in Computer Science 963, Advances in Cryptology
           -Crypto '95, Spring-Verlag, pp.236-247 (1995).
[Bran93]   Brands, S.: "Untraceable Off-Line Cash in Wallet with Observers," Lec-
           ture Notes in Computer Science 773, Advances in Cryptology -Crypto '93,
           Spring-Verlag, pp.302-318 (1994).
[BGK95]   Brickell, E., Gemmell, P. and Kravitz, D.: "Trustee-Based Tracing Exten-
           sions to Anonymous Cash and the Making of Anonymous Change," Proc.
           of 6th ACM-SIAM Symposium on Discrete Algorithms, pp.457-466 (1995).
[CPS94]   Camenisch, J., Piveteau, J.M. and Stadler, M.: "Blind Signatures Based on
           the Discrete Logarithm Problem," Lecture Notes in Computer Science 950,
           Advances in Cryptology -Eurocrypt '94, Spring-Verlag, pp.428-432 (1995).
[Cha82]   Chaum, D.: "Blind Signatures for Untraceable Payments," Advances in
           Cryptology, Proceedings of Crypto '82 Plenum Press, pp.199-203 (1983).
[Cha85]   Chaum, D.: "Security without Identification: Transaction System to make
           Big Brother Obsolete," Communications of the ACM, Vol.28, No.10,
           pp.1030-1044 (Oct. 1985).
[CEG87]   Chaum, D., Evertse, J.H. and van de Graaf, J.: "An Improved Protocol
           for Demonstrating Possession of Discrete Logarithms and Some General-
           izations," Lecture Notes in Computer Science 340, Advances in Cryptology
           -Eurocrypt '87, Spring-Verlag, pp.127-141 (1988).
[CFN88]   Chaum, D., Fiat, A. and Naor, M.: "Untraceable Electronic Cash," Lec-
           ture Notes in Computer Science 403, Advances in Cryptology -Crypto '88,
           Spring-Verlag, pp.319-327 (1990).
[CP92]   Chaum, D. and Pedersen, T.: "Wallet Databases with Observers," Lec-
           ture Notes in Computer Science 740, Advances in Cryptology -Crypto '92,
           Spring-Verlag, pp.89-105 (1993).
[Che94]   Chen, L.: "Oblivious Signatures," Lecture Notes in Computer Science 875,
           Computer Security -ESORICS '94, Spring-Verlag, pp.161-172 (1994).
[Che95]   Chen, L.: "Access with Pseudonyms," Lecture Notes in Computer Sci-
           ence 1029, Cryptography: Policy and Algorithms, Spring-Verlag, pp.232-243
           (1996).
[ElG85]   ElGamal, T.: "A Public-Key Cryptosystem and a Signature Scheme Based
           on Discrete Logarithm," IEEE Trans. on Information Theory, Vol.IT-31,
           No.4, pp.469-472 (Jul. 1985).
[DSS93]   Digital Signature Standard, FIPS PUB XX (Feb. 1993).
[Fer93]   Ferguson, N.: "Single Term Off-Line Coins," Lecture Notes in Computer
           Science 765, Advances in Cryptology -Eurocrypt '93, Spring-Verlag, pp.318-
           328 (1994).
[HP92]   van Heyst, E. and Pedersen, T.: "How to Make Efficient Fail-Stop Signa-
           tures," Lecture Notes in Computer Science 658, Advances in Cryptology
           -Eurocrypt '92, Spring-Verlag, pp.366-377 (1993).
[HMP94-1] Horster, P., Michels, M. and Petersen, H.: "Meta-ElGamal Signature
           Schemes," Proc. of the 2nd ACM Conference on Computer and Communi-
           cations Security, pp.96-107 (Nov. 1994).
[HMP94-2] Horster, P., Michels, M. and Petersen, H.: "Meta-Message Recovery and
           Meta-Blind Signature Schemes Based on the Discrete Logarithm Problem
           and Their Applications," Lecture Notes in Computer Science 917, Advances
           in Cryptology -Asiacrypt '94, Spring-Verlag, pp.224-237 (1995).

[Mic92]   Micali, S.: "Fair Public Key Cryptosystems," Lecture Notes in Computer
           Science 740, Advances in Cryptology -Crypto '92, Spring-Verlag, pp.113-
           138 (1993).

[NR94]   Nyberg, K. and Rueppel, R.A.: "Message Recovery for Signature Schemes
           Based on the Discrete Logarithm Problem," Lecture Notes in Computer
           Science 950, Advances in Cryptology -Eurocrypt '94, Spring-Verlag, pp.182-
           193 (1995).

[Oka92]   Okamoto, T.: "Provably Secure and Practical Identification Schemes and
           Corresponding Signature Schemes," Lecture Notes in Computer Science
           740, Advances in Cryptology -Crypto '92, Spring-Verlag, pp.31-53 (1993).

[Oka95]   Okamoto, T.: "An Efficient Divisible Electronic Cash Scheme," Lecture
           Notes in Computer Science 963, Advances in Cryptology -Crypto '95,
           Spring-Verlag, pp.438-451 (1995).

[OO89]   Okamoto, T. and Ohta, K.: "Divertible Zero Knowledge Interactive Proofs
           and Commutative Random Self-Reducibility," Lecture Notes in Computer
           Science 434, Advances in Cryptology -Eurocrypt '89, Spring-Verlag, pp.134-
           149 (1990).

[OO91]   Okamoto, T. and Ohta, K.: "Universal Electronic Cash," Lecture Notes in
           Computer Science 576, Advances in Cryptology -Crypto '91, Spring-Verlag,
           pp.324-337 (1992).

[PW91]   Pfitzmann, B. and Waidner, M.: "How to Break and Repair a "Provably
           Secure" Untraceable Payment System," Lecture Notes in Computer Science
           576, Advances in Cryptology -Crypto '91, Spring-Verlag, pp.338-350 (1992).

[RSA78]   Rivest, R., Shamir, A. and Adleman, L.: "A Method for Obtaining Digital
           Signatures and Public Key Cryptosystems," Communication of the ACM,
           Vol.21, pp.120-126 (1978).

[SY96]   Sakurai, K. and Yamane, Y.: "Blind Decoding, Blind Undeniable Signa-
           tures, and their Applications to Privacy Protection," Extended Abstract
           for Preproceedings of Information Hiding Workshop (1996).

[Schn91]   Schnorr, C.P.: "Efficient Signature Generation by Smart Cards," Journal
           of Cryptology, Vol.4, No.3, pp.161-174 (1991).

[Sim94]   Simmons, G.J.: "Cryptanalysis and Protocol Failures," Communications of
           the ACM, Vol.37, No.11, pp.56-65 (Nov. 1994).

[SPC95]   Stadler, M., Piveteau, J.M. and Camenisch, J.: "Fair Blind Signatures,"
           Lecture Notes in Computer Science 921, Advances in Cryptology -
           Eurocrypt '95, Spring-Verlag, pp.209-219 (1995).

[TMN89]   Tatebayashi, M., Matsuzaki, N. and Newman, D.B.: "Key Distribution
           Protocol for Digital Mobile Communication systems," Lecture Notes in
           Computer Science 435, Advances in Cryptology -Crypto '89, Spring-Verlag,
           pp.324-333 (1990).

[YL93]   Yen, S.M. and Laih, C.S.: "New Digital Signature Scheme Based on Discrete
           Logarithm," Electronics Letters, Vol.29, No.12, pp.1120-1121 (Jun. 1993).

On the Risk of Disruption in Several Multiparty Signature Schemes

Markus Michels · Patrick Horster

Theoretical Computer Science and Information Security
University of Technology Chemnitz-Zwickau,
Straße der Nationen 62, D-09111 Chemnitz, Germany
E-mail: {mmi,pho}@informatik.tu-chemnitz.de

Abstract. Multiparty cryptography is an important topic in contemporary cryptography. In this paper we examine the security of some multiparty signature schemes. In particular, we point out that a multisignature scheme is vulnerable to universal forgery by an insider attacker under reasonable assumptions. This attack can be applied to some generalizations as well. Then we present a universal forgery attack on two threshold group signature schemes with anonymous signers. Furthermore, we show that in two threshold multisignature schemes it can't be guaranteed that a signer can decide with whom he is going to sign a message. All attacks have in common that the protocol is disrupted. Thus they are not undetectable. However, as they can only be detected afterwards and knowledge leaked by protocol disruptions must be useless, such attacks are not acceptable in general and must be avoided. Finally, we suggest some heuristic fixes.

1 Introduction

In the well known conventional digital signature concept by Diffie and Hellman [DiHe76] one signer is sufficient to sign a message known to him and one verifier is sufficient to check the validity of any given signature. In other concepts, we may call them *multiparty* signature concepts, it is required that only several signers should be able to sign or that only several verifiers should be able to verify a signature. A lot of schemes for slightly different concepts have been suggested, for an overview see [Desm94]. In this paper we focus on three different multiparty signature concepts, namely

- multisignatures,
- threshold group signatures with anonymous signers and
- threshold multisignatures.

In a *multisignature scheme* [ItNa83] some signers can generate a signature on a message together, one verifier is sufficient to verify a given signature and the verifier needs the identity of the signers for verification. In particular, the signers are not anonymous.

In a *threshold group signature scheme with anonymous signers* [DeFr91] t out of a group of n signers are able to generate a signature on a message together and one verifier is sufficient to verify a given signature. It's not possible to find out from a given signature whose of the n signers generated this signature. Thus the signers are anonymous.

Finally, in a *threshold multisignature scheme* [LiHL94], t out of a group of n signers are able to generate a signature on a message together, one verifier is sufficient to verify a given signature and the verifier needs the identity of the signers for verification. In particular, the signers are not anonymous.

In this paper, we will point out that signature schemes to each of these concepts are vulnerable to some active attacks, which have in common that the attacker is an insider and the protocol will be disrupted. Therefore the attacks are not undetectable. On the other hand, protocol disruptions shouldn't be a threat for a scheme and the attack can only be detected *afterwards*. Further, it should be emphasized that during the signature generation the attacker may choose his value after receiving some values from his co-signers and victims in the broadcast phase, that is we allow *rushing*. We are of the opinion that this assumption is reasonable. Furthermore, this assumption is *not* excluded in the description of the attacked schemes in [Har94a, Har94b, HoMP95, LiHL94].

In the sections 2,3 and 4 it will be shown that

- a multisignature scheme and some generalizations [Har94a, Har94b, HoMP95] can be forged universally,
- two threshold signature schemes with anonymous signers [Har94b] can be forged universally
- and in two proposals for a threshold multisignature scheme [LiHL94] dishonest signers can force their victims to sign a document together although the victims are not aware of all of their co-signers.

In section 5 it is pointed out how to repair the schemes using heuristic methods.

2 Multisignature schemes

The new attack can be applied to Harn's multisignature scheme, which is based on a conventional signature scheme [Har94a]. In this multisignature scheme a *clerk* is needed as an additional participant, who is not necessarily trustworthy.

2.1 Underlying signature scheme

A trusted authority chooses a large prime p and a generator $\alpha \in \mathbf{Z}_p^*$. These values are published as system parameters. The signer *Alice* chooses a random number $x \in \mathbf{Z}_{p-1}$ and computes $y := \alpha^x \pmod p$. She publishes y and keeps x secret. These values are constant for all messages to be signed. To sign a message $m \in \mathbf{Z}_{p-1}$, Alice chooses a random number $k \in \mathbf{Z}_{p-1}$, computes $r := \alpha^k \pmod p$ and solves the equation

$$s := x \cdot (m + r) - k \pmod{p - 1}.$$

The triple (m, r, s) is the signed message. It can be verified by checking the congruence

$$r \cdot \alpha^s \equiv y^{m+r} \pmod{p}.$$

Clearly, to avoid existential forgery m must satisfy a redundancy scheme or its hash value $h(m)$ is signed. We assume that this countermeasure will be used in the following although it will not be mentioned explicitly.

2.2 Multisignature scheme

In a multisignature scheme there are t different signers $1, \ldots, t$ and each of them has a secret key $x_i \in \mathbf{Z}_q^*$ and a related public key $y_i := \alpha^{x_i} \pmod{p}$. Each signer i chooses a random number $k_i \in \mathbf{Z}_q^*$ and computes $r_i := \alpha^{k_i} \pmod{p}$. Then he broadcasts r_i to all other signers and the clerk, such that every signer and the clerk can compute $r := \prod_{i=1}^t r_i \pmod{p}$ himself. Now each signer i computes his signature parameter s_i by

$$s_i := x_i \cdot (m + r) - k_i \pmod{p}.$$

He transmits s_i to a clerk whose task is to check each individual signature by verifying the congruence

$$r_i \cdot \alpha^{s_i} \equiv y_i^{m+r} \pmod{p}.$$

He also generates the multisignature of the message m by computing $s := \sum_{i=1}^t s_i \pmod{p-1}$. Now the triple (m, r, s) is the multisignature of the message m which can be verified by checking the congruence

$$r \cdot \alpha^s \equiv y^{m+r} \pmod{p},$$

where $y := \prod_{i=1}^t y_i \pmod{p}$.

2.3 Known attacks

It was already pointed out that the scheme is vulnerable to two different attacks [HoMP95]. In the first attack, an insider attacker chooses his public key as product of the public keys of his victims. Therefore, if the victims (and some other signers) generate a multisignature on a message, then he can claim that he (and the other signers) have generated it. This attack can easily be prevented by checking, if each signer has chosen his public key correctly, e.g. using a zero-knowledge proof. The second attack is more subtle and the result is similar to the result of the cryptanalysis in the section 4. If several signers collude, it is possible, that these signers choose their random numbers k_i such that the sum is equal to zero modulo $p-1$. As a result, the verification equation also holds if their part of the multisignature is not considered. Clearly, this must be avoided as a signer might agree to sign a message only if other signers known to him sign the message as well. The attack can be prevented by adding the identity of the signers into the signed message.

2.4 New attack

First the possible attacker models are described. In this multisignature environment we can distinguish between an *insider-*, an *outsider-* and a *clerk* attack. The outsider does not play an active role in a protocol, while the insider does. The *clerk* attack can be *active* (he does not follow the protocol) or *passive* (he just reveals some parameters). Furthermore, the strength of the insider attack depends on the *number* of the attacker. *In the following, our attack assumes that one insider attacker and the passive clerk collude*, while the overwhelming majority of signers, more precisely all except the insider attacker, can be assumed to be honest. Furthermore, we assume that in the broadcast phase during the signature generation the attacker can choose him parameters *after* he has received the parameters from the other signers, that is we allow *rushing*.

The *aim* of the attack is universal forgery, that is the attacker obtains a multisignature on any message $\tilde{m}$ chosen by him.

Assume that an insider attacker 1, say Charley, wants his victims $2, \ldots, t$ to sign a message $\tilde{m}$ with him. They reject, but agree to sign the innocent message m with him.

Therefore, signer (and victim) i (for all $i \in \{2, \ldots, t\}$) chooses a random number $k_i \in \mathbf{Z}_{p-1}^*$, computes $r_i := \alpha^{k_i} \pmod{p}$ and sends r_i all other signers and the clerk. Charley waits until he received $r_2, \ldots, r_t$. Then he picks a random $k_1 \in \mathbf{Z}_{p-1}^*$, computes $r_1 := \alpha^{k_1} \pmod{p}$, $r := \prod_{i=1}^{t} r_i \pmod{p}$, $\tilde{r} := \tilde{m} + r - m \pmod{p-1}$ and $\tilde{r}_1 := \tilde{r} \cdot \prod_{i=2}^{t} r_i^{-1} \pmod{p}$. He sends $\tilde{r}_1$ instead of r_1 to all co-signers and the clerk. Now each signer i (for all $i \in \{2, \ldots, t\}$) computes $\tilde{r} := \tilde{r}_1 \cdot \prod_{i=2}^{t} r_i \pmod{p}$ (although he thinks that r is computed), calculates

$$s_i := x_i \cdot (m + \tilde{r}) - k_i \pmod{p-1}$$

and sends s_i to the clerk. As Charley is not aware of $\tilde{k}_1$, he can't compute a valid individual signature to message m.

He disrupts the protocol by telling all signers that he losts the parameter (e.g. by a crash). Then, possibly, the protocol will be repeated and this time Charley behaves honestly. As the new signature is not needed in the further attack, it doesn't matter, if the signers refuse to repeat the protocol. Therefore, this attack doesn't necessarily assume *rejoining* (that is a faulty processor – here Charley – can continue later), if the old signatures co-signed by Charley remain valid. Clearly, it would be unreasonable to assume that all old signatures of a signer are invalid, only because he erroneously broadcasts a wrong value.

The clerk, who colludes with Charley, reveals $s_2, \ldots, s_t$ and Charley computes

$$s_1 := x_1 \cdot (m + \tilde{r}) - k_1 \pmod{p-1}$$

using the known parameter k_1. Charley computes $s := \sum_{i=1}^{t} s_i \pmod{p-1}$. Then $(\tilde{m}, r, s)$ is a valid signature, as

$$\alpha^s \equiv \alpha^{\sum_{i=1}^{t} s_i} \equiv \alpha^{\sum_{i=1}^{t} x_i \cdot (m+\tilde{r}) - k_i} \equiv \alpha^{\sum_{i=1}^{t} x_i \cdot (\tilde{m}+r) - k_i} \equiv y^{(\tilde{m}+r)} \cdot r^{-1} \pmod{p}.$$

Again, the main assumption of this attack is that Charley can choose his $\tilde{r}_1$ according to his wishes and the parts $r_2, \ldots, r_t$ of the victims are already known to him, that is rushing is allowed.

2.5 Extensions

The attack can also be applied to the multisignature scheme given by Harn in [Har94b] and some generalizations of Harn's schemes given in [HoMP95].

3 Threshold group signature schemes with anonymous signers

The attack also works in the threshold group signature scheme with anonymous signers suggested by Harn [Har94b]. In fact, the attack can be regarded as an improvement of the clerk's attack discussed in section 3.4.iv) in [Har94b].

3.1 Underlying signature scheme

A trusted authority chooses two large primes p, q with $q|(p-1)$, a generator $\alpha \in \mathbf{Z}_p^*$ of order q and publishes them as system parameters. The signer *Alice* chooses a random number $x \in \mathbf{Z}_q$ and computes $y := \alpha^x \pmod{p}$. She publishes y and keeps x secret. These values are constant for all messages to be signed. To sign a message $m \in \mathbf{Z}_{p-1}$, Alice chooses a random number $k \in \mathbf{Z}_q$, computes $r := \alpha^k \pmod{p}$ and solves the equation

$$s := x \cdot m - k \cdot r \pmod{q}.$$

The triple (m, r, s) is the signed message. It can be verified by checking the congruence

$$r^r \cdot \alpha^s \equiv y^m \pmod{p}.$$

3.2 First threshold group signature scheme with anonymous signers

In the first threshold group signature scheme with anonymous signers a trusted authority is assumed. The authority picks two large primes p, q with $q|(p-1)$, a generator $\alpha \in \mathbf{Z}_{p-1}$ of order q and a polynomial $f(x) := \sum_{i=0}^{t-1} a_i \cdot x^i$ with $a_0, \ldots, a_{t-1} \in \mathbf{Z}_q^*$. Then the authority determines $x := f(0) = a_0$ as the secret group key and computes $y := \alpha^x \pmod{p}$ as the public group key. The secret share of each user i $(1 \le i \le n)$ with identity ID_i is $x_i := f(ID_i) \pmod{q}$ and the related public key is $y_i := \alpha^{x_i} \pmod{p}$. It should be noted that for all $B \subseteq \{1, \ldots, n\}$ with $|B| = t$ the equation $x \equiv f(0) \equiv \sum_{i \in B} x_i \cdot \prod_{j \in B, i \neq j} \frac{0 - ID_j}{ID_i - ID_j} \pmod{q}$ holds.

If t different signers, say $1, \ldots, t$ without loss of generality, want to sign a message m, each signer i chooses a random number $k_i \in \mathbf{Z}_q^*$ and computes $r_i := \alpha^{k_i} \pmod{p}$. Then he broadcasts r_i to all other signers and the clerk, such that every signer and the clerk can compute $r := \prod_{i=1}^{t} r_i \pmod{p}$. Now each signer i computes his signature parameter s_i by

$$s_i := x_i \cdot \left(\prod_{j=1, i \neq j}^{t} \frac{-ID_j}{ID_i - ID_j} \right) \cdot m - k_i \cdot r \pmod{q}.$$

He transmits s_i to a clerk whose task is to check each individual signature by verifying the congruence

$$r_i^r \cdot \alpha^{s_i} \equiv y_i^{m \cdot \prod_{j=1, i \neq j}^{t} \frac{-ID_j}{ID_i - ID_j}} \pmod{p}.$$

He also generates the signature of the message m by computing $s := \sum_{i=1}^{t} s_i \pmod{q}$. Now the triple (m, r, s) is the signature of the message m which can be verified by checking the congruence

$$r^r \cdot \alpha^s \equiv y^m \pmod{p}.$$

3.3 Cryptanalysis of the first scheme

It's possible for one insider attacker to forge this scheme universally in a similar manner and with the same assumed attacker model as described in section 2. Assume that an insider attacker 1, say Charley, wants his victims, the signers $2, \ldots, t$, to sign a message $\tilde{m}$ with him. They reject, but agree to sign the innocent message m with him. It should be stressed that only one signer must be dishonest.

Therefore, signer i with $2 \leq i \leq t$ chooses a random number $k_i \in \mathbf{Z}_q^*$, computes $r_i := \alpha^{k_i} \pmod{p}$ and sends r_i to the other signers. Insider attacker Charley waits until he received all $r_2, \ldots, r_t$. Charley picks a random $k_1 \in \mathbf{Z}_{p-1}^*$, computes $r_1 := \alpha^{k_1} \pmod{p}$, $r := \prod_{i=1}^{t} r_i \pmod{p}$, $d := \tilde{m} \cdot m^{-1} \pmod{q}$, $\tilde{r} := r^d \pmod{p}$ and $\tilde{r}_1 := \tilde{r} \cdot \prod_{j=2}^{t} r_j^{-1} \pmod{p}$. He sends $\tilde{r}_1$ instead of r_1 to the other signers. Now signer i computes $\tilde{r} := \tilde{r}_1 \cdot \prod_{j=2}^{t} r_j \pmod{p}$ (although he thinks that r is computed), calculates

$$s_i := x_i \cdot \left(\prod_{j=1, i \neq j}^{t} \frac{-ID_j}{ID_i - ID_j} \right) \cdot m - k_i \cdot \tilde{r} \pmod{q}$$

and sends s_i to the clerk. As Charley is not aware of $\tilde{k}_1$, he can't compute a valid s_1 to message m. He disrupts the protocol by finding a suitable excuse. Then the protocol might be repeated and this time Charley behaves honestly. It's worth noting that the result of this repetition is not needed in the following. Therefore, if the victims refuse to repeat the protocol, this doesn't matter. Hence, it's not necessary to assume rejoining. Anyway, the re-start of the protocol can be done by another dishonest insider-signer as well. But then we have to assume that two signers are dishonest.

The clerk, who colludes with Charley, reveals $s_2, \ldots, s_t$ to Charley. Charley computes

$$s_1 := x_1 \cdot \left(\prod_{j=1, j \neq 1}^{t} \frac{-ID_j}{ID_1 - ID_j} \right) \cdot m - k_1 \cdot \tilde{r} \pmod{q}$$

as the other signers by using k_1. Now Charley is able to compute $s := d \cdot \sum_{i=1}^{t} s_i \pmod{q}$. Then the triple $(\tilde{m}, \tilde{r}, s)$ is a valid signature for the message $\tilde{m}$, as

$$\tilde{r} \equiv r^d \equiv \alpha^{d \cdot \sum_{i=1}^{t} k_i} \pmod{p} \tag{1}$$

and

$$\alpha^s \equiv \alpha^{d \cdot \sum_{i=1}^{t} s_i} \equiv \alpha^{d \cdot \left(\sum_{i=1}^{t} x_i \cdot \left(\prod_{j=1, j \neq i}^{t} \frac{-ID_j}{ID_i - ID_j} \right) \cdot m - k_i \cdot \tilde{r} \right)}$$

$$\equiv \alpha^{\sum_{i=1}^{t} x_i \cdot \left(\prod_{j=1, j \neq i}^{t} \frac{-ID_j}{ID_i - ID_j} \right) \cdot m \cdot d - k_i \cdot \tilde{r} \cdot d}$$

$$\equiv \alpha^{\sum_{i=1}^{t} x_i \cdot \left(\prod_{j=1, j \neq i}^{t} \frac{-ID_j}{ID_i - ID_j} \right) \cdot \tilde{m} - k_i \cdot \tilde{r} \cdot d} \overset{(1)}{\equiv} y^{\tilde{m}} \cdot \tilde{r}^{-\tilde{r}} \pmod{p}.$$

Again, the main assumption of this attack is that Charley can choose his r_1 according to his wishes and the parts $r_2, \ldots, r_t$ of the victims are already known to him, that means we allow rushing.

3.4 Second threshold group signature scheme with anonymous signers

In the second threshold group signature scheme with anonymous signers no trusted authority is assumed. Every user is an authority, but all users choose two large primes p, q with $q | (p-1)$, a generator $\alpha \in Z_{p-1}$ of order q together. Each user i $(1 \leq i \leq n)$ chooses a polynomial $f_i(x) := \sum_{j=0}^{t-1} a_{i,j} \cdot x^j$ with $a_{i,0}, \ldots, a_{i,t-1} \in Z_q^*$. Then $x_i := f_i(0) = a_{i,0}$ is the user i's (main) secret key and his related (main) public key is $y_i := \alpha^{x_i} \pmod{p}$. Furthermore, $y := \prod_{i=1}^{n} y_i \pmod{p}$ is the public group key, each user i with identity ID_i gets $x_{i,j} := f_j(ID_i)$ from all other users j as additional secret keys and the related public keys are $y_{i,j} := \alpha^{x_{i,j}} \pmod{p}$.

If t different signers, say $1, \ldots, t$ without loss of generality, want to sign a message m, each signer i chooses a random number $k_i \in Z_q^*$ and computes $r_i := \alpha^{k_i} \pmod{p}$. Then he broadcasts r_i to all other signers and the clerk, such that every signer and the clerk can compute $r := \prod_{i=1}^{t} r_i \pmod{p}$ himself. Now each signer i computes his signature parameter s_i by

$$s_i := \left(x_i + \sum_{j=t+1}^{n} x_{i,j} \cdot \prod_{e=1, e \neq i}^{t} \frac{-ID_e}{ID_i - ID_e} \right) \cdot m - k_i \cdot r \pmod{q}.$$

He transmits s_i to a clerk whose task is to check each individual signature by verifying the congruence

$$r_i^r \cdot \alpha^{s_i} \equiv \left(y_i \cdot \left(\prod_{j=t+1}^n y_{i,j} \right)^{\prod_{e=1, e \neq i}^t \frac{-ID_e}{ID_i - ID_e}} \right)^m \pmod{p}.$$

He also generates the signature of the message m by computing $s := \sum_{i=1}^t s_i \pmod{q}$. Now the triple (m, r, s) is the signature of the message m which can be verified by checking the congruence

$$r^r \cdot \alpha^s \equiv y^m \pmod{p}.$$

3.5 Cryptanalysis of the second scheme

Now the attack can be applied in the same manner as described above.

4 Threshold multisignature schemes

In this section we point out that in a slightly modified way it's possible to show that in two threshold multisignature schemes by Li, Hwang and Lee [LiHL94], the signer can't be sure who his co-signers are. There are situations where this property might be important in a *non-anonymous* setting, e.g. a signer Alice agrees to sign a special message together with Bob and Charley but not with Charley and Donald (with $t = 3$). Note that in contrary to the schemes of the last section, the verifier needs to know whose signers have generated the signature. Therefore, in this concept it might be a difference if, say Alice, Bob and Charley or Alice, Charley and Donald sign the same message m. It should be explicitly stressed that the schemes given by Li, Hwang and Lee can still be used in those situations in which this property is not important.

4.1 First threshold multisignature scheme

Now we review the first scheme by Li, Hwang and Lee [LiHL94]. In this scheme a trusted dealer is assumed. The dealer picks two large primes p, q with $q|(p-1)$, a generator $\alpha \in Z_{p-1}$ of order q and a polynomial $f(x) := \sum_{i=0}^{t-1} a_i \cdot x^i$ with $a_0, \ldots, a_{t-1} \in Z_q^*$. Then the dealer determines $x := f(0) = a_0$ as the group secret key and computes $y := \alpha^x \pmod{p}$ as the public group key. The secret share of each user i ($1 \leq i \leq n$) with identity ID_i is $u_i := g_i + f(ID_i) \pmod{p}$ using a random value $g_i \in Z_q^*$ and the public keys are $y_i := \alpha^{u_i} \pmod{p}$ and $z_i := \alpha^{g_i} \pmod{p}$.

If a group B with $|B| = t$ of signers would like to generate a signature of a message m, then each signer $i \in B$ picks $k_i \in Z_q^*$ and computes $r_i := \alpha^{k_i} \pmod{p}$. The parameter r_i is sent to all other signers and the clerk using a broadcast channel. If all r_i are available, then each signer and the clerk computes

$$R := \prod_{i \in B} r_i \ (\text{mod } p) \text{ and } E := H(m, R) \ (\text{mod } q)$$

using a suitable hash function H. Then each signer i computes

$$s_i := u_i \cdot \left(\prod_{j \in B, i \neq j} \frac{0 - ID_j}{ID_i - ID_j} \right) + k_i \cdot E \ (\text{mod } q).$$

Each signer i sends the values m and s_i to a clerk who can check the validity of the individual signature by

$$\alpha^{s_i} \equiv y_i^{\left(\prod_{j \in B, i \neq j} \frac{0 - ID_j}{ID_i - ID_j} \right)} \cdot r_i^E \ (\text{mod } p).$$

The clerk combines the individual signature by

$$S := \sum_{i \in B} s_i \ (\text{mod } q).$$

Then (m, B, R, S) is the group signature of the signers in B to message m. This signature can be checked by computing

$$T := \prod_{i \in B} z_i^{\left(\prod_{j \in B, i \neq j} \frac{0 - ID_j}{ID_i - ID_j} \right)} \ (\text{mod } p), E := H(m, R) \ (\text{mod } q)$$

and checking, whether the equation

$$\alpha^S \equiv y \cdot T \cdot R^E \ (\text{mod } p)$$

holds.

4.2 Security analysis

Here we point out that the above mentioned property can't be gained. We assume that signer 1, say Charley, is an insider attacker. He is a member of the set of signers $B = \{1, \ldots, t\}$ and $\tilde{B} = \{1, \cdots, t-1, t+1\}$. All signers $2, \ldots, t-1$ agree to sign the message m with all co-signers in B, but not with co-signer $t + 1$ instead of t, that is all co-signers in $\tilde{B}$. We assume that co-signer $t + 1$ is aware of the attack and colludes.

Now the protocols with the signers in B will be proceeded according to the protocol: Let

$$b_i := \prod_{j \in B, j \neq i} \frac{0 - ID_j}{ID_i - ID_j} \ (\text{mod } q) \text{ and } \tilde{b}_i := \prod_{j \in \tilde{B}, j \neq i} \frac{0 - ID_j}{ID_i - ID_j} \ (\text{mod } q).$$

Each signer i with $i \in B - \{1\}$ picks k_i, computes $r_i := \alpha^{k_i} \pmod{p}$ and broadcasts r_i to all other co-signers in B. Charley waits until he knows $r_2, \ldots, r_t$ and gets $r_{t+1} := \alpha^{k_{t+1}} \pmod{p}$ from co-signer $t + 1$. Then he picks a random k_1 and computes $r_1 := \alpha^{k_1} \pmod{p}$,

$$R := \prod_{i=1}^{t} r_i \pmod{p}, \tilde{r}_i := r_i^{b_i^{-1} \cdot \tilde{b}_i} \pmod{p}$$

and

$$\tilde{R} := r_{t+1} \cdot \prod_{i=1}^{t-1} \tilde{r}_i \pmod{p}.$$

He reveals $\tilde{r}_1 := \tilde{R} \cdot R^{-1} \cdot r_1 \pmod{p}$ to all co-signers in B. Therefore, all signers in B computes $\tilde{R}$ instead of R, as

$$\tilde{R} \equiv \tilde{r}_1 \cdot \prod_{i=2}^{t} r_i \pmod{p},$$

although the honest signers $2, \ldots, t$ are not aware of it. Signer i with $i \in B$ computes $E := H(m, \tilde{R})$,

$$s_i := u_i \cdot b_i + k_i \cdot E \pmod{q}.$$

and sends s_i to the clerk. Then the protocol for signing the message m by the group B will be disrupted by Charley. The protocol for group B will be repeated and this time Charley behaves honestly. If the signers in B refuse that, this doesn't matter.

The clerk, who colludes with Charley, reveals the parameter $s_2, \ldots, s_{t-1}$ to Charley. Furthermore, signer $t + 1$ computes

$$s_{t+1} := u_{t+1} \cdot \tilde{b}_{t+1} + k_{t+1} \cdot E \pmod{q}.$$

and sends s_{t+1} to Charley. Charley computes

$$s_1 := u_1 \cdot b_1 + k_1 \cdot E \pmod{q}$$

and $S := s_{t+1} + \sum_{i \in \tilde{B} \cap B} \tilde{b}_i \cdot b_i^{-1} \cdot s_i \pmod{q}$. Then $(m, \tilde{B}, S, \tilde{R})$ is a valid signature of group $\tilde{B}$ for message m, as

$$E = H(m, \tilde{R}), \tilde{R} \equiv r_{t+1} \cdot \prod_{i \in B \cap \tilde{B}} \tilde{r}_i \equiv \alpha^{k_{t+1} + \sum_{i \in B \cap B} k_i \cdot (b_i^{-1} \cdot \tilde{b}_i)} \pmod{p}$$

and

$$\alpha^S \equiv \alpha^{s_{t+1} + \sum_{i \in B \cap B} \tilde{b}_i \cdot b_i^{-1} \cdot s_i} \equiv \alpha^{s_{t+1} + \sum_{i \in B \cap B} u_i \cdot b_i \cdot \tilde{b}_i \cdot b_i^{-1} + \tilde{b}_i \cdot b_i^{-1} \cdot k_i \cdot E}$$

$$\equiv \alpha^{\left(\sum_{i \in B} u_i \cdot \tilde{b}_i\right) + k_{t+1} \cdot E + \sum_{i \in B \cap B} \tilde{b}_i \cdot b_i^{-1} \cdot k_i \cdot E} \equiv y \cdot T \cdot \tilde{R}^E \pmod{p}.$$

4.3 Extensions

The attack can also be applied to the second threshold multisignature scheme given in [LiHL94] in a slightly modified way. However, in this attack an even stronger attacker model is needed, as the signers $t, \ldots, n$ must collude with signer 1 and the clerk as well.

5 Heuristic countermeasures

It's possible to countermeasure all described attacks in a heuristic way. However, the security of the repaired schemes can't be guaranteed.

The attack in the multisignature schemes and the threshold group signature schemes with anonymous signers can be countermeasured by using a simultaneous broadcast channel. Then the attack can't be applied, as $\tilde{r}_1$ is chosen dependent on the parameters $r_2, \ldots, r_t$. A further countermeasure is that every co-signer i proves the knowledge of the discrete logarithm of r_i to base α without revealing it (e.g. by a zero-knowledge proof or a signature on a fixed message with key pair (k_i, r_i)). Then the insider attacker can't broadcast $\tilde{r}_1$ as he is not aware of the discrete logarithm to base α. The disadvantage of both countermeasures is the additional amount of computations. A more elegant countermeasure is to prevent the attacker to compute $\tilde{r}$. For example, if in the signature equation of the signature scheme in section 2.1 the expression $m + r$ is substituted by $h(r, m)$ with a suitable hash function h, then $\tilde{r}$ can't be computed anymore and the attack fails. Then the multisignature scheme based on a variant of Schnorr's signature scheme [Schn91] is obtained In fact, the underlying conventional signature scheme is equivalent to Schnorr's scheme.

In both schemes by Li, Hwang and Lee it seems to be sufficient to compute $E := H(m, R, B)$ instead of $E := H(m, R)$, to use a simultaneous channel for the distribution of the r_i or to require that all signers prove knowledge of the discrete logarithm of r_i without revealing it, e.g. by a proof in which no useful knowledge is revealed [Schn91].

6 Conclusion

We have pointed out some serious flaws in several multiparty signature schemes under reasonable assumptions. Although the attacks are not undetectable as the insider attacker has to cause a disruption during a signature generation, the success of such attacks is not acceptable, as the attacks can only be detected afterwards and the knowledge obtained by protocol disruptions must be useless. We further suggested heuristic countermeasures to overcome the weaknesses.

7 Acknowledgments

The authors would like to thank Markus Jakobsson and Moti Yung for helpful comments.

References

[Desm94] Y.Desmedt, "Threshold cryptosystems", ETT, 5 (4), August, (1994), pp. 449–457.

[DeFr91] Y.Desmedt, Y.Frankel, "Shared generation of authenticators and signatures", Lecture Notes in Computer Science 576, Proc. Crypto '91, Springer Verlag, (1992), pp. 457–469.

[DiHe76] W.Diffie, M.Hellmann, "New directions in cryptography", IEEE Transactions on Information Theory, Vol. IT-22, No. 6, (1976), pp. 644–654.

[Har94a] L.Harn, "New digital signature scheme based on discrete logarithm", Electronics Letters, Vol. 30, No. 5, (1994), pp. 396–398.

[Har94b] L.Harn, "Group-oriented (t,n) threshold digital signature scheme and digital multisignature", IEE Proc.-Comput. Digit. Tech., Vol. 141, No. 5, September, (1994), pp. 307–313.

[HoMP95] P.Horster, M.Michels, H.Petersen, "Meta-Multisignature schemes based on the discrete logarithm problem", Proc. of IFIP/SEC '95, Chapman & Hall, (1995), pp. 128–142.

[ItNa83] K.Itakura, K.Nakamura, "A public key cryptosystem suitable for digital multisignatures", NEC Research and Development, Vol. 71, (1983).

[LiHL94] C.-M.Li, T.Hwang, N.-Y.Lee, "Threshold multisignature schemes where suspected forgery implies traceability of adversarial shareholders", Lecture Notes in Computer Science 950, Proc. Eurocrypt'94, Springer Verlag, (1995), pp. 194–204.

[Schn91] C.P.Schnorr, "Efficient signature generation by smart cards", Journal of Cryptology, Vol. 4, (1991), pp. 161–174.

Correlation Attacks on Cascades of Clock Controlled Shift Registers

Willi Geiselmann[1] and Dieter Gollmann[2]

[1] Institute for Algorithms and Cognitive Systems, University of Karlsruhe,
76128 Karlsruhe, Germany
email: geiselma@ira.uka.de

[2] Department of Computer Science, Royal Holloway, University of London,
Egham, Surrey TW20 0EX, United Kingdom
email: dieter@dcs.rhbnc.ac.uk

Abstract. Recently, short cascades of stop and go registers have been demonstrated to be susceptible to correlation attacks. This paper examines the correlation coefficients which serve as the basis for such attacks and proves that they converge to 0.5 exponentially fast when the number of stages in the cascade is increased. We use two alternative technical approaches, a transformation matrix describing the input/output behaviour of a cascade and a Markov model describing its state transitions, to derive closed expressions for these coefficients for some special cases, and to find an efficient way to compute them explicitly.

1 Introduction

Since the early days of machine ciphers, cryptographic devices built from rotors (shift registers) clocked at different speed have attracted considerable interest. The clock rates of the individual components can be independent of their input, as in the Enigma, but it is also possible to use the input sequence to control the clocks, as in the Lorenz SZ40 cipher [4]. The latter approach also has some merits when applied in the construction of pseudo random generators built from shift registers. In this case, the shift registers are relatively simple linear systems and clock control constitutes the non-linear element in the design. The input to the clock is usually a binary signal and, from the point of implementation, a stop and go clocking scheme where no change occurs at input 0 is particularly attractive. However, with stop and go generators the input sequence and the changes in the output are correlated to some extent. This fact has been used in a number of correlation attacks proposed in recent years [9, 10, 12].

In this paper, we briefly review the history of clock controlled generators and examine the scope and consequences of these recent correlation attacks.

2 History

We have already mentioned the Lorenz SZ40 cipher as an early electro-mechanic device using clock control. In his talk at Eurocrypt'93 [13], Selmer mentioned a scheme proposed by Cato Seeberg, consisting of a directed graph of flip-flops, where the 'first' element is triggered always by ones. Otherwise the input to a flip-flop is the exclusive or of the outputs of other components. This proposal started a series of investigations into the properties of clock controlled generators. Their periodicity was analysed in [5], the randomness of their output sequences in [6], and first results on their linear complexity were given in [11].

The cascaded sequences examined in [6] are generated by a cascade of stop and go registers, where each stage is clocked by the output of the previous register. In such a design, increasing the length of the cascade will decrease the probability for changes between two positions in the output sequence. To get a cascade with more desirable cryptographic properties, we can follow Seeberg's proposal and clock each stage with the exclusive or of the outputs of the previous stages in the cascade [3]. An example for such a cascade is given in Figure 1. The next Section will summarise some of their cryptographic properties. Thereafter, we investigate the scope for correlation attacks.

3 Clock-controlled shift registers

Consider a shift register with cyclic feedback and a variable clock input, which can be 0 or 1. A step$_{lm}$-register steps l positions on input 0 and m positions on input 1. The state of a register of length p is a binary vector of length p. In the following, we exclude the trivial states $0\ldots0$ (all-zero) and $1\ldots1$ (all-one). If p is prime, the remaining $2^p - 2$ states lie on disjoint cycles of length p.

Denote the clocking sequence by (c_i), the output of the register if clocked regularly by (b_i), and the output sequence by (y_i). The function $\sigma(i)$ counts the number of clock pulses up to time i. For stop and go we have

$$\sigma(i) = \sigma(i-1) + c_i \bmod p.$$

We define the output of the clock controlled shift register to be the exclusive or of the clock input and the output bit of the register before stepping, i.e.

$$y_i = c_i \oplus b_{\sigma(i-1)}.$$

Cascades of clock-controlled shift registers can be assembled simply by clocking stage $n+1$ with the output of stage n. These cascades can serve as autonomous pseudo-random generators by always applying input 1 to the first stage.

3.1 Transformation Matrices

For the moment, assume some arbitrary probability distribution on the states of the register. Identify integers $i, j, 0 \le i, j < 2^k$, with the corresponding binary strings of length k. (The most significant bit is the leftmost bit.) The transformation matrix for k-tuples, T_k, is a $2^k \times 2^k$-matrix where the entries $(T_k)_{ij}$ give

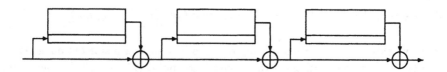

Fig. 1. A cascade of clock controlled shift registers.

the probability that there exists an initial state so that input i generates output j. Strings are processed from left to right, i.e. the leftmost bit of i is applied first. Obviously, each input can be applied to each state, so the sum of entries in each row is 1. Moreover, clock-controlled shift registers are invertible, i.e. for each output and each initial state there exists a corresponding input. Thus, also the entries in each column add up to 1.

3.2 Periodicity

A cascade of n registers of length p, $p \geq 3$ prime, with an appropriate stepping function, e.g. $step_{0,1}$, has period p^n [3, 4]. This is the maximal period achievable.

3.3 Linear complexity

A first partial result for the linear complexity of clock controlled registers is given in [11]. Later, a number of authors independently arrived at more general results [3, 14, 15], all based on the following argument. When a clocking sequence of period p controls a register with output sequence (b_i) and feedback polynomial $f(x)$, then the feedback polynomial of the sequence $(b_{\sigma(i)})$ is a factor of $f(x^p)$. There exist general results for the factorisation of $f(x^p)$, see e.g. Theorem 3.35 in [8]. In particular, if $f(x)$ is irreducible with period p and $p^2 \nmid 2^{p-1} - 1$, then $f(x^p)$ is again irreducible.

Thus, building cascades of registers of the same prime length p guarantees that the linear complexity of the output is at least dp^{n-1}, where d is the smallest linear complexity of a sequence with minimal period p [3].

3.4 Statistical Properties

The distribution of k-tuples in the output of a cascade of clock controlled shift registers with maximal period is given by the product of the transformation matrices of the individual stages. Let $T_k(\underline{q}, n)$ be the transformation matrix for k-tuples for a cascade of length n with initial state $\underline{q}$. The 2^k-vector $\delta = (0, \dots, 0, 1)$ gives the distribution of k-tuples in the all-one input. The probability to observe the k-tuple j in the output of the cascade is given by $\left(\delta \cdot T_k(\underline{q}, n)\right)_j$.

Theorem 1. *For all j, $0 \leq j < 2^k$, and for all $\underline{q}$, $\lim_{n \to \infty} \left(\delta \cdot T_k(\underline{q}, n) \right)_j = 2^{-k}$.*

To prove this theorem, observe that any product of k transformation matrices for k-tuples is a contracting operator with fixed point $(2^{-k}, \ldots, 2^{-k})$. Increasing the length of the cascade results in repeated application of these contracting operators [3]. Bounds on the speed of convergence can be obtained from an analysis of the spectra of eigenvalues of the transformation matrices. For details on the spectral theory of linear operators, the reader is referred e.g. to [7].

4 Cascades of binary random generators

In this section, we examine cascades of binary random generators (BRGs). Each binary random generator on its own produces statistically independent bits (b_i) with $\text{prob}(b_i = 0) = \text{prob}(b_i = 1) = \frac{1}{2}$. The entries in the transformation matrix T_k are now the probabilities for observing given combinations of input and output tuples of length k in the output of a clock-controlled BRG.

We denote the i-th clock input by c_i, the i-th output by y_i, and the bit available from the BRG at time i by $b_{\sigma(i)}$. We have $y_i = c_i \oplus b_{\sigma(i)}$. The transition matrices T_k for $k \leq 3$ are given in Appendix A.

4.1 Construction of T_k

To find general results for T_k, we first show how to construct T_k from T_{k-1} by replacing entries in T_{k-1} by 2×2-matrices. For i even, entries $(T_{k-1})_{ij}$ correspond to input strings of length $k-1$ ending with a 0. Odd row indices correspond to input strings of length $k-1$ ending with a 1. The same holds for output strings and we obtain the following rules:

$$i \text{ even, } j \text{ even} : a \to a \cdot \begin{bmatrix} 1 & 0 \\ 0 & 1 \end{bmatrix},$$

$$i \text{ even, } j \text{ odd} : a \to a \cdot \begin{bmatrix} 0 & 1 \\ 1 & 0 \end{bmatrix},$$

$$i \text{ odd} : a \to \frac{a}{2} \cdot \begin{bmatrix} 1 & 1 \\ 1 & 1 \end{bmatrix}.$$

These replacement rules can be justified as follows. Let $i0$, $i1$, $j0$, $j1$, be the strings i, j appended by 0 or 1. Rows $i0$ and $i1$ are adjacent in matrix T_k as are columns $j0$ and $j1$. If i was even, then the BRG did not generate a new bit after the last symbol of i, i.e. $b_{\sigma(k)} = b_{\sigma(k-1)}$. Thus, $y_k = c_k \oplus b_{\sigma(k-1)}$ with probability 1. This gives our first two rules. If i was odd, then the BRG did generate a new bit after the last symbol of i and in the calculation of the next output, the BRG contributes 0 or 1 with equal probability. These rules impose the following structure on the transformation matrices.

Lemma 2. *For $k \geq 2$, partition $T_k = \begin{bmatrix} A_k & B_k \\ C_k & D_k \end{bmatrix}$ into $2^{k-1} \times 2^{k-1}$ matrices. Then*

$$A_k + B_k = T_{k-1}, \quad C_k = D_k = \frac{1}{2} \cdot T_{k-1}, \quad D_k - B_k = \frac{1}{2} \cdot \begin{bmatrix} A_{k-1} & -B_{k-1} \\ -C_{k-1} & D_{k-1} \end{bmatrix}.$$

Proof: $(A_k + B_k)_{ij}$ counts the transformations $0i \to 0j$ and $0i \to 1j$, where i, j are strings of length $k - 1$. Therefore we are counting exactly the tranformations $i \to j$ and $(A_k + B_k)_{ij} = (T_{k-1})_{ij}$.

C_k and D_k count the transformations $1i \to 0j$ and $1i \to 1j$ respectively. In both cases, the first input bit is 1 so the BRG generates a new bit b_2. Hence, the subsequent output sequence is statistically independent of x_1 and y_1.

For $k = 2$, we get by inspection

$$B_2 = \frac{1}{4} \begin{bmatrix} 0 & 2 \\ 2 & 0 \end{bmatrix}, \quad D_2 = \frac{1}{4} \begin{bmatrix} 1 & 1 \\ 1 & 1 \end{bmatrix}, \quad D_2 - B_2 = \frac{1}{4} \begin{bmatrix} 1 & -1 \\ -1 & 1 \end{bmatrix}.$$

For $k > 2$, we proceed by induction. Assume we know

$$(D_{k-1} - B_{k-1})_{ij} = \pm\frac{1}{2}(T_{k-2})_{ij},$$

where the sign depends on the quadrant in T_{k-2}. Split the matrices B_k and D_k into 2×2-squares corresponding to our recursive construction process. The same rules were applied in corresponding positions of the two matrices and the difference of two squares can be written as

$$[(D_{k-1})_{ij} - (B_{k-1})_{ij}] \cdot M = \pm\frac{1}{2}(T_{k-2})_{ij} \cdot M,$$

where M is the 2×2-matrix given by the rule applicable for i, j. The right hand side of this equation gives entries in T_{k-1} with the appropriate sign. ∎

4.2 Eigenvalues of T_k

The eigenvalues of T_k are the roots of its characteristic polynomial $\chi_k(\lambda)$, which is the determinant of the matrix $(T_k - \lambda I)$, where I is the identity matrix of the appropriate dimension.

Theorem 3. *The transformation matrix T_1 has the eigenvalues 0 and 1. For $k \geq 2$, the following holds.*

1. *The eigenvalues of T_k are the eigenvalues of T_{k-1} and of $\frac{1}{2}T_{k-1}$.*
2. *The eigenvalues of T_k are 0 with multiplicity 2^{k-1}, and $\frac{1}{2^i}$ with multiplicity $\binom{k-1}{i}$, for $0 \leq i < k$.*

Proof: The claim for T_1 can be verified by direct inspection. To prove the first part of the theorem, consider the determinant of $T_k - \lambda I$:

$$|T_k - \lambda I| = \begin{vmatrix} A_k - \lambda I & B_k \\ C_k & D_k - \lambda I \end{vmatrix} = \begin{vmatrix} T_{k-1} - \lambda I & B_k \\ 0 & D_k - B_k - \lambda I \end{vmatrix}$$

$$= \begin{vmatrix} T_{k-1} - \lambda I & \pm B_k \\ 0 & \frac{1}{2} T_{k-1} - \lambda I \end{vmatrix}$$

In the last transformation, we multiply rows and columns by -1 exactly 2^{k-1} times. The second claim follows immediately from Part 1. ∎

5 A Markov Model

In the previous section, we have analyzed the relation between inputs and outputs of length k for a single stop and go generator. The n-th power of the corresponding transformation matrix then modelled the behaviour of a cascade of n stop and go generators. Next, we derive a state model for cascades of length n. The k-th power of the transition matrix of this state model will describe the behaviour of a cascade of length n for strings of length $k + 1$.

In our Markov model for cascades of length n, the states are vectors of length n where the i-th component indicates the output bit of register i. Each state transition is indexed with its conditional probability given that ouptut 0 was observed. The following diagramm gives the state model for $n = 2$.

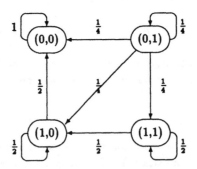

We arrange these probabilities in transition matrices M_n according to the following recursion. Assume we have an ordering of the indices of M_{n-1} so that the indices (states) with even parity come first. We now take first the states of M_n where the first component has output 0 and the remaining $n - 1$ registers have even parity, then the states of M_n where the first component has output 1 and the remaining $n - 1$ registers have odd parity, then the states of M_n where the first component has output 1 and the remaining $n - 1$ registers have even parity, and finally the states of M_n where the first component has output 0 and the remaining $n - 1$ registers have odd parity. Within each quarter, we retain the ordering used in M_{n-1}. The entry in position (i, j) gives the probability to move from state j to state i given that output 0 was observed. For $n = 2$, we get the ordering $(0,0)$, $(1,1)$, $(1,0)$, $(0,1)$. The transition matrices M_n for $n \leq 3$ are given in Appendix B. With our ordering, we get the following construction.

Lemma 4. *Partition M_n into four $2^{n-1} \times 2^{n-1}$ matrices, $M_n = \begin{bmatrix} \tilde{A}_n & \tilde{B}_n \\ \tilde{C}_n & \tilde{D}_n \end{bmatrix}$. For $n \geq 2$ we have*

$$
M_{n+1} = \left[\begin{array}{cc|c} \tilde{A}_n & 0 & \frac{1}{2} \cdot M_n \\ 0 & \tilde{D}_n & \\ \hline 0 & \tilde{B}_n & \frac{1}{2} \cdot M_n \\ \tilde{C}_n & 0 & \end{array}\right].
$$

Proof: Consider a state with even parity of a cascade of $n + 1$ stages. The input bit has to be 0 and the first register will not switch. If the first register has output 0, then the remaining n registers have even parity. The input to those registers is 0 and they will behave as specified in $\tilde{A}_n$ and $\tilde{C}_n$. If the first register has output 1, then the remaining n registers have odd parity. The input to those registers is 1 and they will behave as specified in $\tilde{B}_n$ and $\tilde{D}_n$. For a state with odd parity, the input bit is 1 and the first register will switch. The same argument as above implies that the remaining n registers behave as specified in M_n. ∎

Lemma 5. *The transition matrix M_n and the transformation matrix T_{n+1} are related by $(M_n)_{ji} = 2 \cdot (T_{n+1})_{2i,2j}$. Furthermore, for all values of n, we have*

$$
(1\ldots10\ldots0)M_n = \frac{1}{2} \cdot (10\ldots0) + \frac{1}{2} \cdot (1\ldots1).
$$

Proof: The first part of the Lemma follows immediately from the previous construction and Lemma 2. For the second part, we proceed by induction on n. The proposition holds for $n = 1$ and $n = 2$. The construction of M_{n+1} implies

$$
(1\ldots10\ldots0)M_{n+1} = \left((1\ldots1)\begin{pmatrix} \tilde{A}_n \\ 0 \end{pmatrix}, (1\ldots1)\begin{pmatrix} 0 \\ \tilde{D}_n \end{pmatrix}, \frac{1}{2}(1\ldots1)M_n\right).
$$

We have first

$$
(1\ldots1)\begin{pmatrix} \tilde{A}_n \\ 0 \end{pmatrix} = (1\ldots10\ldots0)\begin{pmatrix} \tilde{A}_n \\ \tilde{C}_n \end{pmatrix} = \frac{1}{2} \cdot (10\ldots0) + \frac{1}{2} \cdot (1\ldots1).
$$

Finally, note that the entries in each column of M_n add up to 1 and that we have $\tilde{D}_n = \frac{1}{2}M_{n-1}$. So

$$
(1\ldots1)\tilde{D}_n = \frac{1}{2} \cdot (1\ldots1)M_{n-1} = \frac{1}{2} \cdot (1\ldots1) \text{ and } \frac{1}{2} \cdot (1\ldots1)M_n = \frac{1}{2} \cdot (1\ldots1).
$$

∎

6 Correlation Attacks

Correlation attacks against stop and go generators exploit the fact that clock input 0 does not change the state of the register. Hence, there is some correlation between the input sequence and changes in the output of the cascade, even when we XOR the output of the register with the clock input. This correlation is most pronounced when we have observed a long run of zeros or ones. The conditional probability that the last input bit was 0 after having observed a run of length k is the sum of the entries in the even rows of the first column of T_k. In a cascade of length n, we consider the entries in the even rows of the first column of T_k^n. A correlation attack is possible as long as this sum is not too close to $\frac{1}{2}$.

Definition 6. Let $\underline{v}$ be a vector of length 2^k and let $(T_k^n)_0$ denote the first column of T_k^n. The advantages of $\underline{v}$ and $(T_k^n)_0$ are given as

$$\Delta(\underline{v}) := \sum_{i=0}^{2^{k-1}-1} v_{2i} - \frac{1}{2} \quad \text{and} \quad \Delta_k^n := \Delta((T_k^n)_0).$$

When we observe a change after a run of length $k - 1$, then the conditional probability that the last input bit was 1 is the same as the conditional probability for input bit 0 after having observed a run of length k. We now endeavour to to derive explicit expressions or at least upper bounds for Δ_k^n.

6.1 Closed Expressions for the Correlation Advantage

Theorem 7. *Let n be the length of the cascade and k the length of the run observed. The advantages are*

1. $\Delta_2^n = \dfrac{1}{2^{n+1}}$, *(see also [10])*
2. $\Delta_3^n = \dfrac{1}{2^n} - \dfrac{1}{2} \cdot \dfrac{1}{4^n}$,
3. $\Delta_4^n = \dfrac{1}{2^{n-1}} - \dfrac{n+1}{4^n} - \dfrac{1}{2} \cdot \dfrac{1}{8^n}$,

Proof. We only prove the first two cases. We have of course for $n \geq 2$, $(T_k^n)_0 = T_k^{n-1}(T_k)_0$. We represent $(T_2)_0$ as the combination of an eigenvector with eigenvalue 1 and an eigenvector with eigenvalue $\frac{1}{2}$,

$$\frac{1}{4} \begin{pmatrix} 2 \\ 0 \\ 1 \\ 1 \end{pmatrix} = \frac{1}{4} \begin{pmatrix} 1 \\ 1 \\ 1 \\ 1 \end{pmatrix} + \frac{1}{4} \begin{pmatrix} 1 \\ -1 \\ 0 \\ 0 \end{pmatrix}, \quad \text{and} \quad \Delta_2^n = \frac{1}{4} \cdot \frac{1}{2^{n-1}} = \frac{1}{2^{n+1}}.$$

Similarly, we represent $(T_3)_0$ in a basis of eigenvectors with non-zero eigenvalues:

$$\frac{1}{8}\begin{pmatrix}4\\0\\0\\0\\2\\0\\1\\1\end{pmatrix}=\frac{1}{8}\begin{pmatrix}1\\1\\1\\1\\1\\1\\1\\1\end{pmatrix}+\frac{1}{4}\begin{pmatrix}1\\-1\\0\\0\\1\\-1\\0\\0\end{pmatrix}+\frac{1}{8}\begin{pmatrix}1\\1\\-1\\-1\\0\\0\\0\\0\end{pmatrix}-\frac{1}{8}\begin{pmatrix}0\\0\\0\\0\\1\\-1\\0\\0\end{pmatrix}.$$

The corresponding eigenvalues are 1, $\frac{1}{2}$, 0, and $\frac{1}{4}$ respectively and we have

$$\Delta_3^n=\frac{1}{2}\cdot\left(\frac{1}{2}\right)^{n-1}-\frac{1}{8}\cdot\left(\frac{1}{4}\right)^{n-1}=\frac{1}{2^n}-\frac{1}{2}\cdot\frac{1}{4^n}.$$

∎

Theorem 8. *Let n be the length of the cascade and k the length of the run observed. The advantages are*

1. $\Delta_k^1=\dfrac{1}{2}-\dfrac{1}{2^k}$,

2. $\Delta_k^2=\dfrac{1}{2}-\dfrac{k-1}{2^k}-\dfrac{2}{4^k}$.

Proof: ad 1: We use the Markov matrix M_1 and assume that initially all two states occur with equal probability. We have

$$\Delta_k^1=\frac{1}{2}\cdot(1\ 0)\,M_1^{k-1}\begin{pmatrix}1\\1\end{pmatrix}-\frac{1}{2}=\frac{1}{2^k}\cdot(1\ 0)\cdot\begin{pmatrix}2^k-1\\1\end{pmatrix}-\frac{1}{2}=\frac{1}{2}-\frac{1}{2^k}.$$

ad 2: Using the Markov matrix M_2 and assuming that initially all four states occur with equal probability, we get by induction

$$\frac{1}{4}\cdot M_2^{k-1}\cdot\begin{pmatrix}1\\1\\1\\1\end{pmatrix}=\frac{1}{4^k}\cdot\begin{pmatrix}4^k-k2^k-1\\2^k-1\\(k-1)2^k+1\\1\end{pmatrix}.$$

The conditional probability that the last input bit was zero given that k zeros had been observed, is the sum of the probabilities for the states $(0,0)$ and $(1,1)$ so

$$\Delta_k^2=\frac{1}{4}\cdot(1\ 1\ 0\ 0)\,M_2^{k-1}\begin{pmatrix}1\\1\\1\\1\end{pmatrix}-\frac{1}{2}=\frac{1}{2}-\frac{k-1}{2^k}-\frac{2}{4^k}.$$

∎

6.2 Bounds on the Correlation Advantage

For larger k and n, it becomes increasingly difficult to obtain a closed expression for Δ_k^n and we settle for an upper bound on the advantage. For that purpose, we express $(T_k)_0$ as the linear combination of an eigenvector and a remainder, which guarantees a negative contribution to the advantage for every value of n. In particular, we will show that this remainder is a *pseudo-eigenvector* of T_k.

Definition 9. A vector $\underline{r}$ of length 2^k, $k \geq 2$, is a *pseudo-eigenvector* of T_k if $r_i \geq 0$ for $i \equiv 0 \bmod 4$, $r_i = -r_{i-1}$ for $i \equiv 1 \bmod 4$, and $r_i = 0$ otherwise.

Lemma 10. Let $\underline{r}$ be a pseudo-eigenvector of T_k, then $\Delta(T_k^n \underline{r}) \geq 0$ for all $n \geq 1$.

Proof: We have

$$(T_k)_{ij} r_j + (T_k)_{i,j+1} r_{j+1} = \begin{cases} (T_k)_{ij} r_j & \text{for } i \equiv 0 \bmod 4, j \equiv 0 \bmod 4, \\ 0 & \text{for } j \equiv 2 \bmod 4, \\ -(T_k)_{ij} r_j & \text{for } i \equiv 1 \bmod 4, j \equiv 0 \bmod 4, \\ 0 & \text{for } i \equiv 2, 3 \bmod 4. \end{cases}$$

Hence, $(T_k \underline{r})_i = 0$ for $i \equiv 2, 3 \bmod 4$, and $(T_k \underline{r})_i \geq 0$, $(T_k \underline{r})_i = -(T_k \underline{r})_{i+1}$ for $i \equiv 0 \bmod 4$. Thus $T_k \underline{r}$ is again a pseudo-eigenvector and $\Delta(T_k^n \underline{r}) \geq 0$. ∎

Definition 11. A vector $\underline{b}$ of length 2^k, $k \geq 2$, is in the Δ-kernel of T_k if $b_i = b_{i+1}$ for all $i \equiv 0 \bmod 2$ and $\sum_i b_{2i} = 0$.

Lemma 12. Let $\underline{b}$ be in the Δ-kernel of T_k. Then $\Delta(T_k^n \underline{b}) = 0$.

Proof:
$$\Delta(T_k^n \underline{b}) = \sum_{i=0}^{2^{k-1}-1} (T_k^n \underline{b})_{2i} = \sum_{i=0}^{2^{k-1}-1} \sum_{j=0}^{2^{k-1}-1} \left((T_k^n)_{2i,2j} + (T_k^n)_{2i,2j+1} \right) b_{2j}$$
$$= \sum_{j=0}^{2^{k-1}-1} b_{2j} \sum_{i=0}^{2^{k-1}-1} (T_{k-1}^n)_{i,j} = 0.$$
∎

To calculate $\Delta_k^n = T_k^n \cdot e_1$, we write the vector e_1 of length 2^k as

$$\begin{pmatrix} 1 \\ 0 \\ 0 \\ \vdots \\ 0 \end{pmatrix} = \frac{1}{2^k} \cdot \begin{pmatrix} 1 \\ 1 \\ 1 \\ \vdots \\ 1 \end{pmatrix} + \begin{pmatrix} \frac{1}{2} - 2^{-k} \\ \frac{1}{2} - 2^{-k} \\ -2^{-k} \\ \vdots \\ -2^{-k} \end{pmatrix} + \frac{1}{2} \cdot \begin{pmatrix} 1 \\ -1 \\ 0 \\ \vdots \\ 0 \end{pmatrix}.$$

This is a sum of an eigenvector with eigenvalue 1, a vector in the Δ-kernel and a pseudo-eigenvector $h_k := {}^t(1, -1, 0, \ldots, 0)$. The all 2^{-k} vector contributes $\frac{1}{2}$ to the calculation of Δ_k^n for all n, thus

$$\Delta_k^n = \frac{1}{2} \cdot \sum_{i=0}^{2^{k-1}-1} T_k^n \cdot h_k.$$

In each row of T_k the entries with even and odd indices are balanced and add up to 1. Let v be a vector with maximal entry a. Then

$$(T_k \cdot v)_i = \sum_{j=0}^{2^k-1} (T_k)_{i,j}\, v_j < \sum_{j=0}^{2^{k-1}-1} (T_k)_{i,2j}\, a < \frac{a}{2}$$

Thus the maximal entry in the vector $T_k^n \cdot e_1$ is at most $\frac{1}{2^{n+1}}$. Only one fourth of the entries of a pseudo-eigenvector are positive and we get:

Theorem 13. *The advantage after observing a run of length k in a cascade of n stages is bounded by $\Delta_k^n \leq 2^{k-n-3}$.*

6.3 Calculating Δ_k^n

When calculating $T_k \cdot v$ for some vector v, it is feasible only for small k to construct the $2^k \times 2^k$-matrix T_k. However, the recursive definition of T_k implies an algorithm for this multiplication that needs $O(2^k \cdot k)$ steps:

$$T_1 \begin{pmatrix} a \\ b \end{pmatrix} := \frac{1}{2} \begin{pmatrix} a+b \\ a+b \end{pmatrix}; \qquad T_k \begin{pmatrix} v_1 \\ v_2 \end{pmatrix} := \begin{pmatrix} A_k(v_1 + rev(v_2)) \\ \frac{1}{2} T_{k-1}(v_1 + v_2) \end{pmatrix};$$

$$A_2 \begin{pmatrix} a \\ b \end{pmatrix} := \frac{1}{2} \begin{pmatrix} a \\ b \end{pmatrix}; \qquad A_k \begin{pmatrix} v_1 \\ v_2 \end{pmatrix} := \begin{pmatrix} A_{k-1} v_1 \\ \frac{1}{2} T_{k-2} v_2 \end{pmatrix}.$$

Here $v_1 + v_2$ means the componentwise sum of the vectors, and $rev(v_2)$ denotes the reverse vector. The values of Δ_k^n for $k, n \leq 20$ are given in Appendix C.

For our final result, we need the following operator ρ that maps a (row) vector v of length 2^k to a pseudo-eigenvectors of T_{k+2} by $\rho(v)_{4j} = v_j$, $\rho(v)_{4j+1} = -v_j$, and $\rho(v)_{4j+2} = \rho(v)_{4j+3} = 0$, for $0 \leq j < 2^k$.

Lemma 14. *Let v be a (row) vector of length 2^k. Then $\rho(v \cdot M_k) = 2 \cdot T_{k+2} \cdot \rho(v)$.*

Proof: As $\rho(v)$ is a pseudo-eigenvector of T_{k+2}, we only have to examine the coefficients $(T_{k+2} \cdot \rho(v))_{4i}$ due to Lemma 10. From Lemma 5, we have further $(M_k)_{ji} = 2 \cdot (T_{k+1})_{2i,2j} = 2 \cdot (T_{k+2})_{4i,4j}$. We thus get

$$(T_{k+2} \cdot \rho(v))_{4i} = \sum_{j=0}^{2^k-1} (T_{k+2})_{4i,4j} v_j = \frac{1}{2} \cdot \sum_{j=0}^{2^k-1} (M_k)_{ji} v_j.$$

∎

When computing the advantage Δ_n^k from M_n, we assume that all states have the same initial probability $\frac{1}{2^n}$ and add up the probabilities for all states with even parity after $k-1$ state transitions. With Lemma 5, we get

$$\Delta_k^n = \frac{1}{2^n} \cdot (1\ldots10\ldots0) M_n^{k-1} \begin{pmatrix} 1 \\ \vdots \\ 1 \end{pmatrix} - \frac{1}{2} = \frac{1}{2^{n+1}} \cdot (10\ldots0) M_n^{k-2} \begin{pmatrix} 1 \\ \vdots \\ 1 \end{pmatrix}.$$

Repeated application of Lemma 14 gives

$$\rho\left((10\dots0)M_n^{k-2}\right) = 2^{k-2} \cdot T_{n+2}^{k-2} h_{k+2}.$$

We have $\Delta_{n+2}^{k-2} = \frac{1}{2} \cdot (10\dots10)T_{n+2}^{k-2}h_{k+2}$ and observing that the sum of all even entries in $\rho\left((10\dots0)M_n^{k-2}\right)$ is just the sum of all entries in $(10\dots0)M_n^{k-2}$ gives

Theorem 15. *For $k \geq 3$, $n \geq 2$, advantages are related by $2^{n+2-k}\Delta_k^n = \Delta_{n+2}^{k-2}$.*

7 On the Merits of Stop & Go

The crucial parameters in the design of cascades of clock controlled shift registers are the period p of the individual stages and the length n of the casacade. As summarised in Section 3, the period and the linear complexity of such a cascade are exponential in the length of the cascade when we fix the period of the stages, but only polynomial in the period of the stages when we fix the length of the cascade.

The correlation coefficients for cascades of BRGs converge towards 0 when the length of the cascade is increased. It was already shown in [3] that this result holds even for cascades of cyclic registers of prime length. Again, the length of the cascade is the essential parameter controlling security properties. Indeed, we could claim that cascades of stop and go generators are 'provably correlation immune' because the size of correlation coefficients decreases exponentially in n. To illustrate this point, compare the security parameters of a cascade built from 10 m-LFSR of length 100, i.e. $p = 2^{100} - 1$ and $n = 10$, a target proposed in [12], with a cascade built from 100 m-LFSR of length 10, i.e. $p = 2^{10} - 1$ and $n = 100$. For a correlation attack, we again follow [12] and observe runs up to length $k = 20$. Both cascades use the same number of register cells.

1. In the first case, the period of the cascade is approximately 2^{1000}, the linear complexity not larger than 2^{907}, and $\Delta_{20}^{10} = 0.39$ so it is not unreasonable to expect that a correlation attack will succeed as suggested in [12].
2. In the second case, the period of the cascade is at least 2^{990}, the linear complexity at least 2^{984}, and $\Delta_{20}^{100} \leq \frac{1}{2^{45}}$. A successful correlation attack is now out of question.

We could of course avoid any potential correlation weakness of stop and go alltogether by using a different clocking scheme. We could, for example, adopt step$_{1,2}$-clocking. However, this turns out to be the most favourable situation for generalised correlation attacks as proposed in [2]. There, the distance between the original sequence and the noisy sequence is no longer measured by the Hamming distance but by an *edit distance* which also allows for the insertion and deletion of bits. With step$_{1,2}$, there is no duplication and the observer misses at most one bit. An algorithm for a correlation attack against two-stage step$_{1,2}$-generators was presented in [16]. In this respect, stop and go is a stronger clocking scheme because the number of duplications is bounded only by the length of the longest 0-run in the clocking sequence. We could then interpret stop and go as the dual of the Shrinking Generator [1], where there number of deletions is bounded by the length of the longest 0-run in the clocking sequence.

References

1. Don Coppersmith, Hugo Krawczyk, and Yshay Mansour. The shrinking generator. In *Proceedings of Crypto'93, D.R. Stinson (ed), LNCS 773*, pages 22–39. Springer Verlag, 1994.
2. Jovan Dj. Golić and M.J. Mihaljević. A generalized correlation attack on a class of stream ciphers based on the Levenshtein distance. *Journal of Cryptology*, 3(3):201–12, 1991.
3. Dieter Gollmann. Pseudo-random properties of cascade connections of clock-controlled shift registers. In *Proceedings of Eurocrypt'84, T. Beth, N. Cot, I. Ingemarsson (eds), LNCS 209*, pages 93–8. Springer Verlag, 1985.
4. Dieter Gollmann and William G. Chambers. Clock-controlled shift registers: a review. *IEEE JSAC*, 7(4):525–33, 1989.
5. V.B. Johnsen and Kjell Kjeldsen. Loop-free composition of certain finite automata. *Information & Control*, 22:303–319, 1973.
6. Kjell Kjeldsen and Einar Andresen. Some randomness properties of cascaded sequences. *IEEE Transactions on Information Theory*, 26(2):227–232, 1980.
7. Erwin Kreyszig. *Introductory Functional Analysis with Applications*. Wiley & Sons, New York, 1978.
8. Rudolf Lidl and Harald Niederreiter. *Introduction to finite fields and their applications*. Cambridge University Press, Cambridge, 1986.
9. Renato Menicocci. Cryptanalysis of a two-stage Gollmann cascade generator. In *Proceedings of SPRC'93, W.Wolfowicz (ed)*, pages 62–69. Rome, 1993.
10. Renato Menicocci. Short Gollmann cascade generators may be insecure. In *Proceedings of the 4th IMA Conference on Cryptography and Coding, P.G.Farrell (ed)*, pages 281–297. IMA, 1995.
11. Peter Nyffeler. *Binäre Automaten und ihre linearen Rekursionen*. Dissertation, Universität Bern, 1975.
12. Sang-Joon Park, Sang-Jin Lee, and Seung-Cheol Goh. On the security of the Gollmann cascades. In *Proceedings of Crypto'95, D. Coppersmith (ed), LNCS 963*, pages 148–156. Springer Verlag, 1995.
13. Ernst S. Selmer. From the memoirs of a Norwegian cryptologist. In *Proceedings of Eurocrypt'93, T. Helleseth (ed), LNCS 765*, pages 142–50. Springer Verlag, 1994.
14. Bernard Smeets. A note on sequences generated by clock controlled shift registers. In *Proceedings of Eurocrypt'85, F. Pichler (ed), LNCS 219*, pages 142–148. Springer Verlag, 1986.
15. Rainer Vogel. On the linear complexity of cascaded sequences. In *Proceedings of Eurocrypt'84, T. Beth, N. Cot, I.Ingemarsson (eds), LNCS 209*, pages 99–109. Springer Verlag, 1985.
16. Miodrag V. Živković. An algorithm for the initial state reconstruction of the clock-controlled shift register. *IEEE Transactions on Information Theory*, 37(5):1488–1490, 1991.

A Transformation Matrices for $k \leq 3$:

$$T_1 = \frac{1}{2}\begin{bmatrix} 1 & 1 \\ 1 & 1 \end{bmatrix}, \quad T_2 = \frac{1}{4}\cdot\begin{bmatrix} 2 & 0 & 0 & 2 \\ 0 & 2 & 2 & 0 \\ 1 & 1 & 1 & 1 \\ 1 & 1 & 1 & 1 \end{bmatrix}, \quad \text{and} \quad T_3 = \frac{1}{8}\cdot\begin{bmatrix} 4 & 0 & 0 & 0 & 0 & 0 & 0 & 4 \\ 0 & 4 & 0 & 0 & 0 & 0 & 4 & 0 \\ 0 & 0 & 2 & 2 & 2 & 2 & 0 & 0 \\ 0 & 0 & 2 & 2 & 2 & 2 & 0 & 0 \\ 2 & 0 & 0 & 2 & 2 & 0 & 0 & 2 \\ 0 & 2 & 2 & 0 & 0 & 2 & 2 & 0 \\ 1 & 1 & 1 & 1 & 1 & 1 & 1 & 1 \\ 1 & 1 & 1 & 1 & 1 & 1 & 1 & 1 \end{bmatrix}.$$

B Markov Matrices for $n \leq 3$:

$$M_1 = \frac{1}{2}\cdot\begin{bmatrix} 2 & 1 \\ 0 & 1 \end{bmatrix}, \quad M_2 = \frac{1}{4}\begin{bmatrix} 4 & 0 & 2 & 1 \\ 0 & 2 & 0 & 1 \\ 0 & 2 & 2 & 1 \\ 0 & 0 & 0 & 1 \end{bmatrix}, \quad \text{and} \quad M_3 = \frac{1}{8}\cdot\begin{bmatrix} 8 & 0 & 0 & 0 & 4 & 0 & 2 & 1 \\ 0 & 4 & 0 & 0 & 0 & 2 & 0 & 1 \\ 0 & 0 & 4 & 2 & 0 & 2 & 2 & 1 \\ 0 & 0 & 0 & 2 & 0 & 0 & 0 & 1 \\ 0 & 0 & 4 & 2 & 4 & 0 & 2 & 1 \\ 0 & 0 & 0 & 2 & 0 & 2 & 0 & 1 \\ 0 & 4 & 0 & 0 & 0 & 2 & 2 & 1 \\ 0 & 0 & 0 & 0 & 0 & 0 & 0 & 1 \end{bmatrix}.$$

C Values of Δ_k^n for $k, n \leq 20$:

k	$n=1$	$n=2$	$n=3$	$n=4$	$n=5$	$n=6$	$n=7$	$n=8$	$n=9$	$n=10$
3	0.375	0.21875	0.11719	0.06055	0.03076	0.01550	0.00778	0.00390	0.00195	0.00098
4	0.4375	0.30469	0.18652	0.10535	0.05663	0.02954	0.01514	0.00768	0.00387	0.00194
5	0.46875	0.37305	0.25964	0.16283	0.09479	0.05241	0.02798	0.01459	0.00749	0.00381
6	0.48438	0.42139	0.32567	0.22584	0.14350	0.08526	0.04819	0.02625	0.01392	0.00725
7	0.49219	0.45300	0.37915	0.28699	0.19844	0.12723	0.07676	0.04415	0.02447	0.01319
8	0.49609	0.47263	0.41925	0.34105	0.25445	0.17558	0.11332	0.06919	0.04037	0.02271
9	0.49805	0.48437	0.44765	0.38550	0.30703	0.22664	0.15615	0.10130	0.06244	0.03687
10	0.49902	0.49121	0.46691	0.42000	0.35319	0.27674	0.20261	0.13943	0.09083	0.05643
11	0.49951	0.49512	0.47953	0.44558	0.39153	0.32295	0.24977	0.18167	0.12490	0.08165
12	0.49976	0.49731	0.48756	0.46383	0.42194	0.36338	0.29498	0.22572	0.16330	0.11218
13	0.49988	0.49854	0.49256	0.47644	0.44513	0.39720	0.33621	0.26929	0.20424	0.14710
14	0.49994	0.49921	0.49561	0.48493	0.46224	0.42441	0.37222	0.31039	0.24578	0.18502
15	0.49997	0.49957	0.49744	0.49052	0.47450	0.44558	0.40249	0.34759	0.28610	0.22433
16	0.49998	0.49977	0.49852	0.49411	0.48308	0.46157	0.42712	0.38005	0.32371	0.26342
17	0.49999	0.49988	0.49915	0.49639	0.48894	0.47334	0.44655	0.40745	0.35757	0.30083
18	0.50000	0.49994	0.49952	0.49782	0.49288	0.48180	0.46149	0.42991	0.38709	0.33543
19	0.50000	0.49997	0.49973	0.49869	0.49547	0.48776	0.47271	0.44784	0.41208	0.36645
20	0.50000	0.49998	0.49985	0.49922	0.49715	0.49188	0.48095	0.46181	0.43271	0.39348

Conditional Correlation Attack on Nonlinear Filter Generators

Sangjin Lee, Seongtaek Chee, Sangjoon Park, Sungmo Park

Section 0710, Yusong P.O. Box 106
Electronics and Telecommunications Research Institute
Taejon, 305-600, KOREA
E-mail : {sjlee,chee,sjpark,smp}@dingo.etri.re.kr

Abstract. In this paper, the optimum correlation attack recently introduced by R. Anderson is improved to be applicable to most of the nonlinear filter generators. We propose a conditional correlation attack by introducing a novel notion of the conditional linear approximation. It is shown that there are always strong correlations between key stream sequences and their corresponding input bits or their linear combinations. Finally, we suggest a practical attacking method that can be applied to most of the nonlinear filter generators.

1 Introduction

A common type of running key generator employed in stream ciphers consists of (maximal length) linear feedback shift register(LFSR) and a nonlinear filter function whose inputs are taken from some shift register stages to produce an output[9]. Such a generator is called the nonlinear filter generator, and it can be used in producing key stream sequence[5, 8, 9].

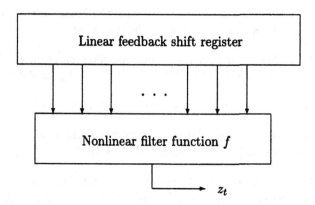

Fig. 1. Structure of the nonlinear filter generator

In this paper, we denote the length of LFSR as k, and the number of input variables of filter function as n. Since the security of a stream cipher totally depends on that of a key stream sequence, the large period and linear complexity of the key stream sequence are needed first. In order to achieve these requirements, one can choose the stages to be equidistant[8, 9]. We assume, without loss of generality, that the input stages of the nonlinear filter function are adjacent.

The first cryptanalysis for the filter generator was suggested by T. Siegenthaler [11]. The analysis can be used to reconstruct the initial state and the filter function of the same or equivalent generator that produces the same key stream sequence. But, this can be applied to the LFSR of length less than 50. R. Forré suggested a fast correlation attack method[3] that applied the correlation attack in [6] to the T. Sigenthaler's method. However, it can not be applied to the LFSRs with 10 or more feedback taps or length greater than 100. Recently, R. Anderson introduced a new cryptanalytic method for nonlinear filter generators, called optimum correlation attack[1]. The main idea is to look at how the filter function reacts with shifted copies of itself. He examined that many functions such as bent functions and correlation immune functions react badly, which were believed robust against several correlation attacks. But, there exists no mentions about the theoretical side and the practical attacking algorithm for the filter generator. Recently, J. Golic studied on the security of the nonlinear filter generator[4]. He discussed the optimum correlation attack from the cryptographic points of view and suggested some requirements for filter generators.

In this paper, we improve the R. Anderson's method by introducing the concept of the conditional linear approximation of filter function and discuss its behaviors. We suggest a practical attacking algorithm for filter generators. Using our attacking method, most of the nonlinear filter generators can be broken eventually.

2 The conditional linear approximation

Let $\mathbb{Z}_2^n$ be the n-dimensional vector space with the binary n-tuples of elements $\mathbf{x} = (x_1, \cdots, x_n)$. For $\mathbf{x} \in \mathbb{Z}_2^n$, $\mathbf{x}^t$ denotes the transpose of $\mathbf{x}$.

Definition 1 *[1] For an n-th degree nonlinear filter function $f : \mathbb{Z}_2^n \longrightarrow \mathbb{Z}_2$, the m-th augmented function of f, $\mathcal{F}^m : \mathbb{Z}_2^{n+m-1} \longrightarrow \mathbb{Z}_2^m$ is defined as*

$$\mathcal{F}^m(x_1, \cdots, x_{n+m-1}) = (f(x_1, \cdots, x_n), f(x_2, \cdots, x_{n+1}), \cdots, f(x_m, \cdots, x_{n+m-1})).$$

In this paper, we only consider the augmented function with its input size $n + m - 1$ is less or equal to the length of the LFSR k.

Definition 2 *Let f be an n-th degree nonlinear filter function and $\mathcal{F}^m$ be its m-th augmented function. For $\mathbf{y} \in \mathbb{Z}_2^m$ and $\mathbf{c} \in \mathbb{Z}_2^{n+m-1}$, define the conditional linear approximation of the function by*

$$\lambda_f^m(\mathbf{y}, \mathbf{c}) = \mid Pr(\mathbf{x} \cdot \mathbf{c} = 0 \mid \mathcal{F}^m(\mathbf{x}) = \mathbf{y}) - 0.5 \mid,$$

where $\mathbf{x} \in \mathbb{Z}_2^{n+m-1}$. And, we define the maximal conditional linear approximation of f by

$$\Lambda^m(f) = \max\{\lambda_f^m(\mathbf{y}, \mathbf{c}) \mid \mathbf{y} \in \mathbb{Z}_2^m, \mathbf{c} \in \mathbb{Z}_2^{n+m-1}\}.$$

Suppose that $\lambda_f^m(\mathbf{y}, \mathbf{c}) = p$. Let $\mathbf{x} = (x_1, x_2, \cdots, x_{n+m-1})$ and $\mathbf{c} = (c_1, c_2, \cdots, c_{n+m-1})$, then the equation

$$\sum_{i=1}^{n+m-1} c_i x_i = 0 \tag{1}$$

holds with conditional probability $p + 0.5$. Since each x_i can be represented by a linear sum of the initial values, we can build the following linear equation with conditional probability $p+0.5$, whose initial values $(\alpha_1, \alpha_2, \cdots, \alpha_k)$ are unknown.

$$\sum_{i=1}^{k} a_i \alpha_i = 0, \tag{2}$$

where each a_i is determined by the connection polynomial of LFSR. These facts will be used in the next section.

Proposition 3 *For* $\mathbf{y} \in \mathbb{Z}_2^m, \mathbf{c} \in \mathbb{Z}_2^{n+m-1}$, *let* $\mathbf{y}_0^* = (\mathbf{y}, 0)$, $\mathbf{y}_1^* = (\mathbf{y}, 1) \in \mathbb{Z}_2^{m+1}$ *and* $\mathbf{c}^* = (\mathbf{c}, 0) \in \mathbb{Z}_2^{n+m}$, *then for any* $f : \mathbb{Z}_2^n \longrightarrow \mathbb{Z}_2$, *we have*

$$\lambda_f^m(\mathbf{y}, \mathbf{c}) \leq \max\{\lambda_f^{m+1}(\mathbf{y}_0^*, \mathbf{c}^*), \lambda_f^{m+1}(\mathbf{y}_1^*, \mathbf{c}^*)\}.$$

Proof. For $\mathbf{x} \in \mathbb{Z}_2^{n+m-1}$, let $\mathbf{x}^* = (\mathbf{x}, x_{n+m}) \in \mathbb{Z}_2^{n+m}$. Let

$$A = \{\mathbf{x}^* \in \mathbb{Z}_2^{n+m} \mid \mathcal{F}^{m+1}(\mathbf{x}^*) = \mathbf{y}_0^*\},$$
$$B = \{\mathbf{x}^* \in \mathbb{Z}_2^{n+m} \mid \mathcal{F}^{m+1}(\mathbf{x}^*) = \mathbf{y}_1^*\},$$
$$U = \{\mathbf{x}^* \in \mathbb{Z}_2^{n+m} \mid \mathcal{F}^m(\mathbf{x}) = \mathbf{y}\}.$$

Then

$$U = A \cup B.$$

Let

$$S = \{\mathbf{x}^* \in \mathbb{Z}_2^{n+m} \mid \mathbf{x}^* \cdot \mathbf{c}^* = 0, \mathcal{F}^{m+1}(\mathbf{x}^*) = \mathbf{y}_0^*\},$$
$$T = \{\mathbf{x}^* \in \mathbb{Z}_2^{n+m} \mid \mathbf{x}^* \cdot \mathbf{c}^* = 0, \mathcal{F}^{m+1}(\mathbf{x}^*) = \mathbf{y}_1^*\}$$

and

$$u = Pr(\mathbf{x} \cdot \mathbf{c} = 0 \mid \mathcal{F}^m(\mathbf{x}) = \mathbf{y}),$$
$$s = Pr(\mathbf{x}^* \cdot \mathbf{c}^* = 0 \mid \mathcal{F}^m(\mathbf{x}^*) = \mathbf{y}_0^*),$$
$$t = Pr(\mathbf{x}^* \cdot \mathbf{c}^* = 0 \mid \mathcal{F}^m(\mathbf{x}^*) = \mathbf{y}_1^*).$$

Then

$$u = \frac{|S| + |T|}{|U|}, \quad s = \frac{|S|}{|A|}, \quad t = \frac{|T|}{|B|}.$$

and

$$u = s \cdot \frac{|A|}{|U|} + t \cdot \frac{|B|}{|U|} = s \cdot p + t \cdot (1-p).$$

Thus we have

$$\min\{s,t\} \le u \le \max\{s,t\}.$$

□

As a consequence of Proposition 3, we have the following

Corollary 4 *For any filter function f, we have*

$$\Lambda^m(f) \le \Lambda^{m+1}(f), \quad m \ge 1.$$

Corollary 4 means that $\Lambda^m(f)$ increases as m does. To guarantee the fact that $\Lambda^m(f)$ converges to $1/2$, we define the following

Definition 5 *Let $f : \mathbb{Z}_2^n \longrightarrow \mathbb{Z}_2$ be an n-th degree nonlinear filter function and $\mathcal{F}^m : \mathbb{Z}_2^{n+m-1} \longrightarrow \mathbb{Z}_2^m$ be its m-th augmented function. For $\mathbf{y} \in \mathbb{Z}_2^m$, let r be the number of inputs of $\mathcal{F}^m$ that produces $\mathbf{y}$ via f, and we let the following $r \times (n+m-1)$ augmented matrix $A\mathbf{y}$ by*

$$A\mathbf{y} = \begin{bmatrix} x_{1,1} & x_{1,2} & \cdots & x_{1,n+m-1} \\ x_{2,1} & x_{2,2} & \cdots & x_{2,n+m-1} \\ \vdots & \vdots & \vdots & \vdots \\ x_{r,1} & x_{r,2} & \cdots & x_{r,n+m-1} \end{bmatrix},$$

where

$$\mathcal{F}^m(x_{i,1}, x_{i,2}, \cdots, x_{i,n+m-1}) = \mathbf{y}, \quad 1 \le i \le r.$$

Let

$$C_j^t = (x_{1,j}, x_{2,j}, \cdots, x_{r,j}) \in \mathbb{Z}_2^r, \quad 1 \le j \le n+m-1.$$

Finally, we let the $r \times (n+m)$ matrix

$$A_{\mathbf{y}}^* = [\ C_1 \quad C_2 \quad \cdots \quad C_{n+m-1} \quad I\ ],$$

where $I^t = (1, 1, \cdots, 1) \in \mathbb{Z}_2^r$.

The following Propositions are immediate consequences of Definition 2 and 5.

Proposition 6 *If $\mathrm{rank}(A_{\mathbf{y}}^*) < n+m$ for some $\mathbf{y} \in \mathbb{Z}_2^m$, then*

$$\Lambda^m(f) = \frac{1}{2}.$$

If the function f produces a binary random sequence, the average value of r in the Definition 5 is 2^{n-1}, and does not exceed 2^n. Thus we obtain

Proposition 7 *For any filter function f that produces a binary random sequence, we have*

$$\Lambda^m(f) = \frac{1}{2} \quad \text{for some } m.$$

From Proposition 7, we can see that there are always strong correlations between the key stream sequences and their corresponding input bits or their linear combinations.

Example 8 *Consider the following 5 filter functions:*

Function 1 : $1 \oplus x_1 \oplus x_3 \oplus x_1 x_s \oplus x_2 x_4 \oplus x_3 x_4 \oplus x_5 \oplus x_2 x_5 \oplus x_3 x_5$
Function 2 : $x_1 x_2 \oplus x_3 x_4 \oplus x_5$
Function 3 : $x_1 \oplus x_2 \oplus (x_1 \oplus x_3)(x_2 \oplus x_4 \oplus x_5) \oplus (x_1 \oplus x_4)(x_2 \oplus x_3)x_5$
Function 4 : $x_1 x_3 x_4 x_5 \oplus x_1 x_2 x_5 \oplus x_5 \oplus x_6 \oplus 1$
Function 5 : $(1 \oplus x_6 x_7 \oplus x_5 x_6 x_7)x_1 \oplus (1 \oplus x_6 \oplus x_6 x_7 \oplus x_5 x_6 x_7)x_2$
$\qquad\qquad \oplus (1 \oplus x_7 \oplus x_6 x_7)x_3 \oplus (x_6 \oplus x_7 \oplus x_6 x_7)x_4$
Function 6 : $x_1 x_2 \oplus x_3 x_4 \oplus x_5 x_6 \oplus x_7$

Function 1, Function 2 and Function 6 are semi-bent functions[2], and Function 3 is the 1st order correlation immune function described in [1], and Function 4 is a de Brujin function used as a nonlinear filter function in [5]. Function 5 is the 2nd order correlation immune function described in [10].

Table 1. The conditional linear approximation of each function

$\Lambda^m(f)$	n	m							
		1	2	3	4	5	6	7	8
Function 1	5	0.17	0.50	0.50	0.50	0.50	0.50	0.50	0.50
Function 2	5	0.13	0.25	0.38	0.44	0.44	0.50	0.50	0.50
Function 3	5	0.27	0.40	0.50	0.50	0.50	0.50	0.50	0.50
Function 4	6	0.38	0.44	0.44	0.50	0.50	0.50	0.50	0.50
Function 5	7	0.19	0.19	0.24	0.30	0.38	0.39	0.47	0.50
Function 6	7	0.06	0.13	0.19	0.28	0.28	0.33	0.38	0.41

All of the functions have been considered to be applicable to the nonlinear filter functions. In nonlinear filter generator, however, there are strong correlations between the fixed output and the linear combinations of each input that produce the output via the nonlinear filter function.

Table 1 shows the conditional linear approximation of each function. Each $\Lambda^m(f)$ approaches 0.5 as m increases and reaches 0.5 rapidly. As in the Table 1, the growth of conditional linear approximation seems to depend on the algebraic normal form of each function not on the cryptographic properties, for example algebraic degree, nonlinearity, correlation immunity etc, of each function.

3   Attacking method

In section 2, we have observed that if the equation (1) holds with probability $0.5 + p$(near to 1) in the case that the filter function generates a certain pattern of outputs, then we can construct the corresponding linear equation (2) that may be used to find the initial values of the LFSR. In this section, we propose a practical attacking algorithm for a nonlinear filter generator using the facts described in Section 2.

[Attacking algorithm for nonlinear filter generator]

Prec.	Compute $D = \{\mathbf{y} \in \mathbb{Z}_2^m \mid \lambda_f^m(\mathbf{y}, \mathbf{c_y}) > p$ for some $\mathbf{c_y} \in \mathbb{Z}_2^{n+m-1}\}$.
Step 1.	To find $\mathbf{y} \in D$, scan the key stream sequence.
Step 2.	Using $\mathbf{c_y}$, obtain a linear equation (2).
Step 3.	Repeat Step 1 and Step 2 l times.
Step 4.	Randomly choose k out of l linear equations and solve the resulting system of linear sequences for the k unknowns.
Step 5.	Test possible solutions obtained in Step 4 to see whether they produce the correct key stream. If there is a correct solution, terminate, else go to Step 4.

In usual cases, l in Step 3 is between $2k$ and $3k$, and the most time consuming job in the above algorithm is the iteration of Step 4 and Step 5. The iteration complexity depends on the probability $q = p + 0.5$. By the similar method in [6, 7], the expected number of trials is r^{-1} where

$$r = \left(\frac{ql}{l}\right)\left(\frac{ql-1}{l-1}\right)\cdots\left(\frac{ql-k+1}{l-k+1}\right) \geq \left(\frac{ql-k+1}{l-k+1}\right)^k.$$

The length of key stream sequence needed to attack depends on the number of elements of D, say s. That is, if the output sequence is uniform, then the length of key stream sequences to succeed in attack is

$$2^m \times \frac{l}{s}.$$

Since the average value of $|\{\mathbf{x} \mid \mathcal{F}^m(\mathbf{x}) = \mathbf{y}\}|$ is 2^{n-1}, the complexity of Prec will be $2^{n+m-1} \times 2^m \times 2^{n-1} = 2^{2n+2m-2}$. On the other hand, most filter functions have conditional linear approximations near to 0.45 whenever $n-2 \leq m \leq n+2$. So, the complexity of Prec will be 2^{4n-2}. And, since the length of the LFSR is normally larger than twice n, so the condition $n + m - 1 \leq k$ is not too strict.

4   Concluding Remarks

The optimal correlation attack suggested by R. Anderson was improved in this paper. We have given a practical method for breaking nonlinear filter generators. Our attack is based on the concept of the conditional linear approximation, which makes it possible to cryptanalyze most nonlinear filter generators.

The possibility of our attacking method for a fixed nonlinear generator depends on the number of input variables and output variables of the augmented function which has high conditional linear approximation. If n is too large, then it is infeasible to compute Prec. So, we recommend a way of taking the vector c with its Hamming weight small enough. In that way, we can cryptanalyze most filter generators. For example, if we consider the nonlinear filter generator suggested in [5], then we can see that $\Lambda^4(f) = \frac{1}{2}$(see Example 8). In the case that the maximal conditional approximation is $\frac{1}{2}$, the Step 4 and Step 5 are performed only once. This means that such a generator can be easily broken.

If we consider a filter generator whose input stages are not equidistant[4], the complexity of our attack will be increased.

Acknowledgement: The authors would like to thank anonymous refrees for their suggesting important and interesting comments.

References

1. R. Anderson, "Searching for the Optimum Correlation Attack", *Fast Software Encryption - Leuven'94*, LNCS 1008, Springer-Verlag, pp. 137-143, 1995.
2. S. Chee, S. Lee, and K. Kim, "Semi-bent Functions", *Advances in Cryptology - ASIACRYPT'94*, LNCS 914, Springer-Verlag, pp. 107-118, 1995.
3. R. Forré, "A Fast Correlation Attack on Nonlinearly Feedforward Filtered Shift-Register Sequences", *Advances in Cryptology - EUROCRYPT'89*, LNCS 434, Springer-Verlag, pp. 586–595, 1990.
4. J. Dj. Golic, "On Security of Nonlinear Filter Generators", *Fast Software Encryption - Cambridge'96*, LNCS 1039, Springer-Verlag, pp. 173-188, 1996.
5. G. L. Mayhew, "A Low Cost, High Speed Encryption System and Method", Proc. of the 1994 IEEE Computer Society Symposium on Research and Security and Privacy, pp. 147-154, 1994.
6. W. Meier and O. Staffelbach, "Fast Correlation Attacks on Stream Ciphers", *Advances in Cryptology - EUROCRYPT'88*, LNCS 330, Springer-Verlag, pp. 301–314, 1989.
7. S. Park, S. Lee, and S.-C. Goh, "On the Security of the Gollmann Cascades", *Advances in Cryptology - CRYPTO'95*, LNCS 963, Springer-Verlag, pp. 148-156, 1995.
8. R. A. Rueppel, *Analysis and Design of Stream Ciphers*, Springer-Verlag, 1986.
9. R. A. Rueppel, "Stream ciphers," in *Contemporary Cryptography: the Science of Information Integrity*, ch. 2, pp. 65–134, IEEE Press, 1992.
10. J. Seberry, X.-M. Zhang, and Y. Zheng, "On Constructions and Nonlinearity of Correlation immune Functions", *Advances in Cryptology - EUROCRYPT'93*, LNCS 765, Springer-Verlag, pp. 181–199, 1994.

11. T. Siegenthaler, "Cryptanalysts Representation of Nonlinearly Filtered ML-Sequences", *Advances in Cryptology - EUROCRYPT'85*, LNCS 219, Springer-Verlag, pp. 103–110, 1986.

The Cryptographic Security of the Syndrome Decoding Problem for Rank Distance Codes

F. Chabaud*   J. Stern
Florent.Chabaud@ens.fr   Jacques.Stern@ens.fr

Laboratoire d'Informatique
de l'École Normale Supérieure**
45, rue d'Ulm
F-75230 Paris cedex 05

Abstract. We present an algorithm that achieves general syndrome decoding of a (n, k, r) linear rank distance code over $GF(q^m)$ in $O((nr + m)^3 q^{(m-r)(r-1)})$ elementary operations. As a consequence, the cryptographical schemes [Che94, Che96] which rely on this problem are not secure with the proposed parameters. We also derive from our algorithm a bound on the minimal rank distance of a linear code which shows that the parameters from [Che94] are inconsistent.

1 Introduction

It is known that the problem of finding a codeword of given weight in a linear binary code is $\mathcal{NP}$-complete [BMT78]. Furthermore, the problem remains difficult when the code is chosen at random and the weight is close to the Gilbert-Varshamov bound (see the discussion in [Ste, FS96]). Recently, several cryptographic schemes aimed at entity identification and based on this property [Gir90, Har89, Ste90, Ste94, Vér95b] have been proposed[1]. They have low computational requirements and high speed. The counterpart is that the communication complexity is significant.

In an attempt to improve the performances of the above systems, Kefei Chen has suggested the idea of using rank metric codes [Gab85] instead of Hamming metric codes in cryptographic schemes. He has designed two authentication schemes [Che94, Che96] with claimed better performances than the above systems. The security of these protocols relies on the following informal assumption:

---

* On leave from *Délégation Générale de l'Armement*
** *Unité de Recherche Associée n° 1327 du Centre National de la Recherche Scientifique*
[1] The authentication scheme [Har89] was broken by P. Véron [Vér95a].

The syndrome decoding problem for rank distance codes appears even more difficult than for Hamming distance codes.

In this paper, we first recall the definition of rank distance codes and how they are used in K. Chen's protocols. Then we present our attack on these protocols. Accordingly, we modify their parameters to achieve security. It is debatable whether or not the original schemes proposed by K. Chen achieve better performances than their analogues based on standard error-correcting codes. But taking into account the loss in the efficiency of the protocols resulting from underestimating the necessary sizes, it appears that rank distance codes are not better than usual codes.

2 Background

2.1 Rank Distance Codes

The rank distance codes were introduced by E.M. Gabidulin [Gab85] and rely on the following observation.

Let $\bar{x} = (x_1, \ldots, x_n)$ be a n-dimensional vector over $GF(q^m)$, where q is the power of a prime. Let $b_1, \ldots, b_m$ be a basis of $GF(q^m)$. Write each element $x_j \in GF(q^m)$ as $x_j = \beta_{1,j} b_1 + \cdots + \beta_{m,j} b_m$, where $\beta_{i,j} \in GF(q)$ for all i. Then the rank of

$$A(\bar{x}) = \begin{pmatrix} \beta_{1,1} & \cdots & \beta_{1,n} \\ \vdots & & \vdots \\ \beta_{m,1} & \cdots & \beta_{m,n} \end{pmatrix}$$

is uniquely determined by $\bar{x}$, and defines a metric on the n-dimensional vector space V over $GF(q^m)$. Following [Gab85], we will denote this metric by $r(\bar{x}, q)$. Generally speaking, given a linear code over $GF(q^m)$, that is to say a k-dimensional subspace of V, the rank distance decoding problem can be stated as follows:

Rank Distance Decoding Problem Let H be a parity check matrix over $GF(q^m)$ of the code C (*i.e.* $\bar{x} \in C \Leftrightarrow H\bar{x}^t = 0$), given a $(n-k)$-vector $\bar{\sigma}$ over $GF(q^m)$, find a n-vector $\bar{s} \in V$ of smallest rank $r(\bar{s}, q)$ such that

$$H\bar{s}^t = \bar{\sigma}^t. \tag{1}$$

In coding theory, vector $\bar{\sigma}$ is called the *syndrome* of the *error vector* $\bar{s}$.

Mutatis mutandis, as for Hamming distance codes, if the error vector has rank r smaller than half the minimum rank distance d of the code, then equation (1) has a unique solution of rank less than $\frac{d}{2}$.

2.2   Minimum Rank Distance Codes

The above metric can be used to formulate a theory analogous to the theory of Minimum Distance Separable codes [MS83]. In particular, if H is a $(n - k) \times n$ parity check matrix of a linear code over a finite field, the minimum rank distance d of the code, *i.e.* the minimum of the non-zero ranks of the codewords, verifies

$$d \leq n - k + 1. \qquad (2)$$

This bound is called the Singleton bound [MS83] in the theory of linear Hamming distance codes and a code that achieves equality is called *Minimum Distance Separable (MDS)*. Following [Gab85], we similarly call *Minimum Rank Distance (MRD)*-code a linear rank distance code that achieves equality

$$d = n - k + 1.$$

Such codes exist. Some of them are constructed in [Gab85] together with coding and decoding algorithms.

2.3   K. Chen's Authentication Schemes

Prover	Verifier
Chooses a random n-vector $\bar{x}$ over $GF(q^m)$, a random $n \times n$ permutation matrix P, and computes the products $\bar{c} = HP\bar{x}$ and $\bar{c}' = H\bar{x}$. $\quad \bar{c}, \bar{c}'$ $\xrightarrow{\hspace{2cm}}$	
	Chooses randomly $\lambda \in GF(q^m)$
Computes the $(n - k)$-vector $\bar{w} = \bar{x} + \lambda P^{-1}\bar{s}$ $\quad \xleftarrow{\lambda}$	
$\quad \xrightarrow{\bar{w}}$	
	$\xleftarrow{b}$ Chooses $b \in \{0, 1\}$
If $b = 0$ sends P, otherwise sends $\bar{x}$. $\quad \xrightarrow{P \text{ or } \bar{x}}$	If $b = 0$, checks if $HP\bar{w} = \bar{c} + \lambda\bar{s}$ and $H\bar{x} = \bar{c}'$. Otherwise checks the rank: $r(\bar{w} - \bar{x}, q) = \begin{cases} r, & \text{if } \lambda \neq 0; \\ 0, & \text{if } \lambda = 0. \end{cases}$

Fig. 1. Kefei Chen's authentication protocol [Che96].

We now briefly describe the identification scheme [Che96] which is an improvement of [Che94]. Both schemes use as public data a $(n - k) \times n$ parity check matrix H of a rank-distance code over $GF(q^m)$ with error-capacity t (Every error vector of rank less than t can be successfully corrected) and an integer $r \leq t$.

Each user chooses a random n-vector $\bar{s}$ over $GF(q^m)$ of rank r and computes the syndrome $\bar{\sigma} = H\bar{s}^t$. The $(n - k)$-vector $\bar{\sigma}$ over $GF(q^m)$ is the public key for authentication. The interactive protocol of figure 1 can now be repeated a certain number of times to achieve "security". This protocol is zero-knowledge. The proposed parameters are

$$q = 2, n = 32, k = m = 16 \text{ and } r = 4.$$

We now show that the underlying problem is too weak for this set of parameters.

3   Algorithm A

3.1   Principle

We now present an algorithm which solves the following problem:

Fixed Rank Codeword Search Problem   Given an integer r and a parity check matrix H of a linear rank-distance code over $GF(q^m)$, find a n-vector $\bar{s}$ over $GF(q^m)$ of rank less than r such that

$$H\bar{s}^t = 0. \tag{3}$$

First we see how such an algorithm can solve the *rank distance decoding problem* described by equation (1). Given H and $\bar{\sigma}$, we can add a column to matrix H and form the matrix

$$H' = (\, H \quad | \quad \bar{\sigma}^t \,).$$

Every solution of the equation

$$H'\bar{s}'^t = 0 \tag{4}$$

can be split into two parts $\bar{s}'^t = (\, \bar{s}_0 \quad | \quad s_1 \,)$, with $\bar{s}_0$ a n-vector over $GF(q^m)$ and s_1 an element of $GF(q^m)$. For every solution $\bar{s}'$ of equation (4), either $H\bar{s}_0{}^t = s_1\bar{\sigma}^t$ or $\bar{s}_0$ is a solution of equation (3) and $s_1 = 0$.

But, if we know *a priori* that the error vector $\bar{s}$, such that $H\bar{s}^t = \bar{\sigma}^t$, has rank r smaller than half the minimum rank distance d of the code H, which is the case for the rank distance decoding problem, then we know that a solution of equation (4) of rank less than $r+1$ cannot be a codeword of matrix H. Hence, we can obtain a solution for equation (1) which is $s_1^{-1} \times \bar{\sigma}$. Therefore, if we have an algorithm that solves problem described by equation (4), it will solve the rank distance decoding problem of equation (1).

We note that this adaptation is made at the cost of increasing the rank parameter of the problem by one. If we want to solve an instance of the problem (1) with a searched rank r, we will have to solve a derived instance of problem (4) with a searched rank $r + 1$. In the very special case of $s_1 = 1$, the rank remains unchanged, but this is of no importance as we will see later.

3.2 Brute Force Algorithm

Assume there exists a solution $\bar{s} = (s_1, \ldots, s_n)$ of equation (3) of rank r. Then, there exists r elements $\theta_0, \ldots, \theta_{r-1}$ of $GF(q^m)$, linearly independent over $GF(q)$, and nr coefficients $\alpha_{j,k} \in GF(q)$, such that for all j, $1 \le j \le n$,

$$s_j = \sum_{k=0}^{r-1} \alpha_{j,k} \theta_k.$$

We denote by $(h_{i,j})_{\substack{1 \le i \le n-k \\ 1 \le j \le n}}$ the coefficients of matrix H. We can then rewrite equation (3), and obtain a system of $(n-k)$ relations over $GF(q^m)$.

$$\forall i,\ 1 \le i \le n-k,\quad \sum_{j=1}^{n} \sum_{k=0}^{r-1} h_{i,j} \alpha_{j,k} \theta_k = 0. \tag{5}$$

As soon as $(\theta_0, \ldots, \theta_{r-1})$ are known, the above system gives a redundant linear system over $GF(q)$, with nr unknowns $(\alpha_{j,k})_{\substack{1 \le j \le n \\ 0 \le k \le r-1}}$ and at most $(n-k)m$ independent equations.

Therefore, our brute force algorithm enumerates all bases $(\theta_0, \ldots, \theta_{r-1})$ over $GF(q^m)$ and tries to solve the linear system over $GF(q)$ resulting from system (5).

There are at most q^{mr} different bases $(\theta_0, \ldots, \theta_{r-1})$ over $GF(q^m)$. The resulting complexity is too high for the proposed parameters of K. Chen's authentication scheme, but note that this exhaustive search is not even mentioned in [Che96]. The rest of the paper is devoted to the study of a better search algorithm.

3.3 Bound for Minimal Rank-Distance Codes

We now fix for this subsection the r elements $(\theta_0, \theta_1, \ldots, \theta_{r-1})$ of $GF(q^m)$. System (5) can give us solutions to equation (3) as soon as it has more unknowns than equations, that is to say if $nr > (n-k)m$. In all (n, k) linear code, this inequality implies that we can find a codeword of rank r if $r \ge \frac{(n-k)m+1}{n}$.

Hence, we obtain a bound on the minimal rank-distance of a (n, k, d) linear rank distance code

$$d \leq \left\lceil \frac{(n-k)m+1}{n} \right\rceil \tag{6}$$

Theorem 1. *No MRD code can exist for $m < n$.*

Proof. An MRD code achieves $d = n - k + 1$. But we can obtain a codeword for $r = n - k$ as soon as $n(n - k) > (n - k)m$.

Note 2. Speaking in terms of coding theory, that means that our bound (6) is better than the Singleton bound for the case $m < n$. One should note that all the MRD codes of Gabidulin's paper are given for $n \geq m$. Therefore, there is no contradiction between the above result and [Gab85].

3.4 Selective Enumeration

We now show how to decrease the cost of our enumerative search. The principle of the following algorithm remain the same. We just want to reduce the number of bases $(\theta_0, \theta_1, \ldots, \theta_{r-1})$ over $GF(q^m)$ for which we have to solve a linear system over $GF(q)$.

First, we can notice that for all $\theta \in GF(q^m)$, if $(s_1, \ldots, s_n)$ is a solution of equation (3), then $(\theta s_1, \ldots, \theta s_n)$ is also a solution. We can therefore only enumerate the bases of the form $(1, \theta_1, \ldots, \theta_{r-1})$.

Let $(b_1, \ldots, b_m)$ be a basis of $GF(q^m)$ over $GF(q)$. For every element B in $GF(q^m)$, there exists m elements $\beta_1, \ldots, \beta_m$ of $GF(q)$ such that

$$B = \sum_{\ell=1}^{m} \beta_\ell b_\ell.$$

Such a basis can for instance be the canonical polynomial representation of $GF(q^m)$, in which case we have $b_\ell = X^{\ell-1}$. For simplicity we symbolize this particular representation by the notation

$$B = [\beta_m \cdots \beta_1] = \beta_m X^{m-1} + \cdots + \beta_2 X + \beta_1,$$

and we call *digits* the particular coefficients of this representation.

As $\theta_0 = 1$, we have $\theta_0 = [0 \cdots 01]$. Therefore, the last digit of every θ_i can be arbitrarily set to zero without loss of generality as

$$[\theta_{i,1} \cdots \theta_{i,m-1} \theta_{i,m}] = [\theta_{i,1} \cdots \theta_{i,m-1} 0] + \theta_{i,m}[0 \cdots 01].$$

We now formalize these ideas and estimate the number of bases to enumerate.

Lemma 3 [LN83, page 455]. *The number of $m \times r$ matrices of rank r over $GF(q)$ is*

$$N_q(m, r) = q^{\frac{r(r-1)}{2}} \prod_{i=0}^{r-1} (q^{m-i} - 1).$$

Corollary 4. *The number $C_q(r)$ of invertible matrices or size r over $GF(q)$ is*

$$C_q(r) = q^{\frac{r(r-1)}{2}} \prod_{i=1}^{r} (q^i - 1).$$

Definition 5. A *strict basis* of rank r, is a basis $\Theta = (1, \theta_1, \ldots, \theta_{r-1})$ for which the last digits of the θ_i are all zeros.

Definition 6. Two strict bases Θ and Θ' are *equivalent* if there exists an invertible matrix T over $GF(q)$ of size r such that

$$\Theta' = \begin{pmatrix} 1 \\ \theta'_1 \\ \vdots \\ \theta'_{r-1} \end{pmatrix} = T \begin{pmatrix} 1 \\ \theta_1 \\ \vdots \\ \theta_{r-1} \end{pmatrix} = T\Theta.$$

It is clear that we only have to enumerate one element in each equivalence class. We now count the number of elements to enumerate.

Lemma 7. *The number of bases in a class is*

$$C_q(r-1) = q^{\frac{(r-1)(r-2)}{2}} \prod_{i=1}^{r-1} (q^i - 1).$$

The proof of this lemma uses a block-wise representation of transition matrix T and is given in A. We set

$$D_q(m, r) = \frac{N_q(m, r)}{C_q(r)} = \frac{\prod_{i=m-(r-1)}^{m} (q^i - 1)}{\prod_{i=1}^{r} (q^i - 1)}. \tag{7}$$

Lemma 7 means that using for instance lexicographic order, we only need to enumerate $D_q(m-1, r-1)$ strict bases in order to find a solution of equation (5). Appendix B gives a way to enumerate such bases.

The following theorem means that this solution is unique. Therefore, we have essentially no better strategy than enumerating one basis in every class and check if the corresponding linear system over $GF(q)$ resulting from system (5) has a solution.

Theorem 8. *Let n be an integer greater than r. Let Θ and Θ' be two bases such that there exists two $n \times r$ matrices over $GF(q)$ A and A' of maximal rank r for which $A\Theta = A'\Theta'$. Then Θ and Θ' are equivalent.*

Proof. As A and A' are of maximal rank, by Gaussian elimination there exists two invertible matrices S and S' of size n over $GF(q)$ and two permutation matrices P and P' of size r such that, using a block-wise representation for S and S' we have $A = \begin{pmatrix} S_1 & S_2 \\ S_3 & S_4 \end{pmatrix} \begin{pmatrix} Id_r \\ 0 \end{pmatrix} P = \begin{pmatrix} S_1 \\ S_3 \end{pmatrix} P$, and $A' =$

$\begin{pmatrix} S_1' & S_2' \\ S_3' & S_4' \end{pmatrix} \begin{pmatrix} Id_r \\ 0 \end{pmatrix} P' = \begin{pmatrix} S_1' \\ S_3' \end{pmatrix} P'$. As A and A' are of rank r, these relations imply in particular that the two $r \times r$ matrices over $GF(q)$ S_1 and S_1' are invertible.

These relations are also true over $GF(q^m)$. Hence, we have

$$S \begin{pmatrix} Id_r \\ 0 \end{pmatrix} P\Theta = S' \begin{pmatrix} Id_r \\ 0 \end{pmatrix} P'\Theta',$$

from which we can extract $S_1 P\Theta = S_1' P'\Theta'$. This completes the proof.

3.5 Implementation

We have implemented our algorithm using the ZEN C-library [CL96]. We enumerate the strict bases as described in appendix B and for each of these bases, we solve the linear system over $GF(q)$ of $(n-k)m$ equations and $n(r+1)$ unknowns resulting from system (5). This second step can be optimized using a kind of parallelization of successive Gaussian eliminations resulting in an improvement by a factor 2.

The above algorithm was successfully tested and the results are summarized in figure 2. The parameters are chosen to match with those proposed in Kefei Chen's schemes. We now discuss the security of these schemes.

r	Number of basis	$(nr)^3$	CPU time by iteration (ms)	Estimated CPU max.
2	$2^{15} = 32767$	2^{18}	6.5	200 s
3	$2^{27.4} = 178940587$	$2^{19.8}$	8.5	18 days
4	$2^{37.6} = 209386049731$	$2^{21.0}$	10.5	70 years
5	$2^{45.7} = 57162391576563$	$2^{22.0}$	12.5	22,400 years

Fig. 2. Finding a codeword of given rank for $q = 2$, $n = 32$, $k = 16$, $m = 16$ on PC-486 100MHz

4 Application to K. Chen's Schemes for Authentication

At this point, let's recall the parameters of K. Chen's protocols. The first one [Che94] used the parameters

$$q = 2, n = 32, k = 16, m = 8 \text{ and } r \geq 4.$$

These parameters are inconsistent. System (5) is not redundant with these parameters. We obtain $(n-k)m = 128$ equations with $n(r+1) \geq 160$ unknowns over $GF(q)$. Therefore, given a public key syndrome, one can easily find a secret key for these parameters. This means that the minimal rank distance of this code is smaller than r. Indeed, bound (6) gives in this case $d \leq 5$. Hence, as we should have $r < \frac{d}{2}$, possible parameters are

$$q = 2, n = 32, k = 16, m = 8 \text{ and } r = 2.$$

With these parameters, there will be no two secret keys with the same public key. But, given a public key, our algorithm need at most $D_q(m-1,r) = 2^{11.4}$ Gaussian eliminations each with $(n(r+1))^3 = 2^{20}$ further elementary operations. This clearly defeats the scheme.

The second scheme [Che96] uses the following parameters:

$$q = 2, n = 32, k = m = 16 \text{ and } r = 4.$$

In this case, our bound (6) gives $d \leq 9$. Codes necessary for this scheme can therefore exist.

Our algorithm leads to at most $2^{45.7}$ Gaussian eliminations each with about 2^{15} operations.

We can estimate the overall complexity of our algorithm A for solving fixed rank codeword search problem (3). On one hand, the number of strict bases grows asymptotically as $O(q^{(m-r)(r-1)})$. On the other hand, it is well known that the number of elementary operations in a Gaussian elimination over $GF(q)$ is $O((nr)^3)$. We therefore obtain for the complexity of our algorithm

$$O\left((nr)^3 q^{(m-r)(r-1)}\right).$$

This first approach has the disadvantage to increase by one the rank of the word to find for solving problem (1). This is necessary to convert the problem in the form of equation (3). Hence, the overall complexity of our algorithm A for solving problem 1 is

$$O\left((n(r+1))^3 q^{(m-r-1)r}\right).$$

In table 2, for instance, one can see that the Kefei Chen's authentication scheme with proposed parameters [Che96] is solved by algorithm A in about 22,000 years. It would be better to avoid this increase in the rank, because we would then obtain a more realistic search in about 70 years.

We now present a modification of the above algorithm that solves directly the initial problem (1) without increasing the search ranked. This results in a better algorithm for solving the initial rank distance decoding problem.

5 General Syndrome Decoding Problem for Linear Rank-Distance Codes

5.1 Algorithm B

We now suppose given a non null syndrome $\bar{\sigma} = (\sigma_1, \ldots, \sigma_{n-k})$ over $GF(q^m)$. In this case, system (5) is replaced by:

$$\forall i, 1 \leq i \leq n - k, \quad \sum_{j=1}^{n} \sum_{k=0}^{r-1} h_{i,j} \alpha_{j,k} \theta_k = \sigma_i,$$

$$h_{i,j} \alpha_{j,0} + \sum_{j=1}^{n} \sum_{k=1}^{r-1} h_{i,j} \alpha_{j,k} \theta'_k = \sigma_i \theta_0^{-1}, \tag{8}$$

with $\theta'_k = \theta_k/\theta_0$. Let $(b_1, \ldots, b_m)$ be a basis of $GF(q^m)$ over $GF(q)$. There exists m elements $\beta_1, \ldots, \beta_m$ of $GF(q)$ such that

$$\frac{-1}{\theta_0} = \sum_{\ell=1}^{m} \beta_\ell b_\ell.$$

Hence, we obtain

$$h_{i,j} \alpha_{j,0} + \sum_{j=1}^{n} \sum_{k=1}^{r-1} h_{i,j} \alpha_{j,k} \theta'_k + \sum_{\ell=1}^{m} \beta_\ell b_\ell \sigma_i = 0. \tag{9}$$

This system of $n - k$ relations over $GF(q^m)$ gives over $GF(q)$ a system of at most $(n - k)m$ independent equations with $nr + m$ unknowns. The remaining of our discussion is the same, and our algorithm B will therefore consist in enumerating the same strict bases and solving for each one a linear system over $GF(q)$. The resulting system has only a little more unknowns than before, but the important point is that there is no more need to increase by one the searched rank, that is to say the number of elements in each basis.

Hence the number of bases to enumerate remains the same. In particular, asymptotically algorithm B performs $O(q^{(m-r)(r-1)})$ Gaussian eliminations. As a Gaussian elimination takes $O((nr + m)^3)$ operations, we eventually obtained the claimed complexity

$$O\left((nr + m)^3 q^{(m-r)(r-1)}\right).$$

Using this algorithm, we obtain for the second scheme proposed by K.Chen an exhaustive search of $D_q(m - 1, r - 1) = 2^{37.6}$ Gaussian eliminations. With the same trick as before that parallelizes Gaussian eliminations, we need on average 2^{15} operations to perform a Gaussian elimination. Thus, we can obtain an exhaustive attack of K. Chen's protocol that discloses a secret key from a public one, in less than 2^{53} elementary operations.

This is less than the time needed for an exhaustive search of a DES-key, and the scheme should therefore be considered unsecure according to current standards.

5.2 Implementation

Algorithm B was also implemented using the ZEN C-library [CL96] and successfully tested. We present in figure 3 our experimentations on same dimensions as in figure 2. One should note that the estimated maximal CPU times are increased by relatively small values which confirms our estimation.

The estimated time of computation to break an instance of Kefei Chen's authentication scheme appears to be 78 years. This figure may still seem high but we note the following:

1. Using a faster machine like a sparc 20, the estimated time falls to 20 years.

2. Our estimation is made in the worst case. On average, we only need half this time to solve a random instance of the problem.

3. The algorithm can be easily distributed on a network. Suppose we have about a thousand machines (like the RSA-130 breaking project), then a secret key would be found in less than a week.

r	Number of basis	$(nr)^3$	CPU time by iteration (ms)	Estimated CPU max.
2	$2^{15} = 32767$	2^{18}	7.5	250 s.
3	$2^{27.4} = 178940587$	$2^{19.8}$	10	20 days
4	$2^{37.6} = 209386049731$	$2^{21.0}$	12	78 years
5	$2^{45.7} = 57162391576563$	$2^{22.0}$	13	24,000 years

Fig. 3. Solving syndrome decoding problem for $q = 2$, $n = 32$, $k = 16$, $m = 16$ on PC-486 100MHz

6 Conclusion

We have presented an attack against the general syndrome decoding of linear rank distance codes problem, and shown that the authentication schemes described in [Che94, Che96] are unsecure with the proposed parameters. Besides, the attack can be easily distributed on a network of stations. Thus, one should be very careful in choices for K. Chen's protocols parameters.

References

[BMT78] E.R. Berlekamp, R.J. McEliece, and H.C.A. Van Tilborg. On the inherent intractability of certain coding problems. *IEEE Trans. Inform. Theory*, IT-24(3):384–386, May 1978.

[Che94] K. Chen. Improved Girault identification scheme. *IEE Electronic Letters*, 30(19):1590–1591, sep 1994.

[Che96] K. Chen. A new identification algorithm. In *Cryptography Policy and Algorithms conference*, volume 1029, pages 244–249. LNCS, 1996.

[CL96] F. Chabaud and R. Lercier. Zen: A new toolbox for finite extensions in finite fields. Rapport de recherche, Laboratoire d'Informatique de l'Ecole Polytechnique, 91128 Palaiseau Cedex, France, 1996. in preparation.

[FS96] J.-B. Fischer and J. Stern. An efficient pseudo-random generator provably as secure as syndrome decoding. In *Advances in Cryptology – EUROCRYPT '96*, volume to appear. LNCS, 1996.

[Gab85] E.M. Gabidulin. Theory of codes with maximum rank distance. *Problems of Information Transmission*, 21:1–12, 1985.

[Gir90] M. Girault. A (non practical) three-pass identification protocol using coding theory. In *Proc. Auscrypt'90*, volume 453, pages 265–272. LNCS, 1990.

[Har89] S. Harari. A new authentication algorithm. In *Coding Theory and Applications*, volume 388, pages 204–211. LNCS, 1989.

[LN83] R. Lidl and H. Niederreiter. Finite fields. In Gian-Carlo Rota, editor, *Encyclopedia of Mathematics and its applications*. Addison-Wesley Publishing Company, 1983.

[MS83] F.J. MacWilliams and N.J.A. Sloane. *The Theory of Error-correcting Codes*. North-Holland, 1983.

[Ste] J. Stern. A new paradigm for public key identification. *IEEE Trans. Inform. Theory*. to be published.

[Ste90] J. Stern. An alternative to the Fiat-Shamir protocol. In *Advances in Cryptology – EUROCRYPT '89*, pages 173–180. LNCS, 1990.

[Ste94] J. Stern. A new identification scheme based on syndrome decoding. In *Advances in Cryptology – CRYPTO '93*, volume 773. LNCS, 1994.

[Vér95a] P. Véron. Cryptanalysis of Harari's identification scheme. In *Cryptography and Coding*, volume 1025, pages 264–269. LNCS, 1995.

[Vér95b] P. Véron. *Problème SD, Opérateur Trace, Schémas d'identification et Codes de Goppa*. PhD thesis, Université de Toulon et du Var, juillet 1995.

A Proof of Lemma 7

We use a block-wise representation of the transition matrix T between two strict bases Θ and Θ'.

$$T = \begin{pmatrix} \Delta & D \\ C & B \end{pmatrix}$$

with

$$B = \begin{pmatrix} \beta_{1,1} & \cdots & \beta_{1,r-1} \\ \vdots & & \vdots \\ \beta_{r-1,1} & \cdots & \beta_{r-1,r-1} \end{pmatrix}, C = \begin{pmatrix} \gamma_1 \\ \vdots \\ \gamma_{r-1} \end{pmatrix}, D = \begin{pmatrix} \delta_1 & \cdots & \delta_{r-1} \end{pmatrix},$$

and $\Delta \in GF(q)$. Matrices B, C and D have coefficients over $GF(q)$.
As Θ' is a strict basis, we must have $\theta'_0 = 1$. Therefore

$$\theta'_0 = [0 \cdots 01] = [0 \cdots 0\Delta] + \sum_{i=1}^{r-1} \delta_i [\theta_{i,m} \cdots \theta_{i,2} 0].$$

That gives a redundant linear system of m equations over $GF(q)$ with $r \leq m$ unknowns $\Delta, \delta_1, \ldots, \delta_{r-1}$. This system implies $\Delta = 1$ and $D = 0$.
We also have $\theta'_j = \gamma_j + \sum_{k=1}^{r-1} \beta_{j,k} \theta_k$. As the last digit of every θ'_i is zero, we have

$$[\theta'_{j,m} \cdots \theta'_{j,2} 0] = [0 \cdots 0\gamma_j] + \sum_{k=1}^{r-1} \beta_{j,k} [\theta_{k,m} \cdots \theta_{k,2} 0],$$

from which we deduce that vector C is all-zeros. Hence, $\theta'_j = \sum_{k=1}^{r-1} \beta_{j,k} \theta_k$ and B must be an invertible matrix over $GF(q)$.
Clearly, matrix T is invertible and we have

$$T = \begin{pmatrix} 1 & 0 \\ 0 & B \end{pmatrix} \text{ and } T^{-1} = \begin{pmatrix} 1 & 0 \\ 0 & B^{-1} \end{pmatrix}.$$

We can deduce from corollary 4 the number of invertible matrices B which is the number of transition matrices T between strict bases:

$$C_q(r-1) = q^{\frac{(r-1)(r-2)}{2}} \prod_{i=1}^{r-1} (q^i - 1).$$

This complete the proof.

B Selective Bases Enumeration

We can uniquely represent a strict basis $\Theta = (1, \theta_1, \ldots, \theta_{r-1})$ by a $(r-1) \times (m-1)$ matrix over $GF(q)$ using the digits of the θ_i

$$\Theta = \begin{pmatrix} \theta_{1,m} & \cdots & \theta_{1,2} \\ \vdots & & \vdots \\ \theta_{r-1,m} & \cdots & \theta_{r-1,2} \end{pmatrix}.$$

In the following, we denote $\succ$ the lexicographic order that one can define on $GF(q^m)$ using a polynomial representation of this set over $GF(q)$.

Our problem is to enumerate all represent-ants $(\theta_1, \ldots, \theta_{r-1})$ of classes of section 3.4. Without loss of generality we can impose

$$\theta_1 \succ \ldots \succ \theta_{r-1}, \tag{10}$$

and every most significant digit of the θ_i can be set to one.

First, let's consider the matrix

$$\Theta_{0,0} = (\, Id_{r-1} \quad 0 \,).$$

This matrix respects condition 10. Besides, for all $(m-r) \times (r-1)$ matrix A_0 over $GF(q)$, the bases

$$\Theta_{0,A} = (\, Id_{r-1} \quad A_0 \,)$$

are all of distinct classes.

Our enumeration will therefore take as radix R all the matrices that are permutations of $\Theta_{0,0}$ with respect to condition 10, and enumerate for every radix the possible completion matrices A_R [2].

---

[2] Let's take as a small example the parameters $q = 3$, $m - 1 = 3$ and $r - 1 = 2$. We first have

$$R_0 = \begin{pmatrix} 1 & 0 & x \\ 0 & 1 & y \end{pmatrix}.$$

For this radix, we enumerate the completion matrices $\begin{pmatrix} x \\ y \end{pmatrix}$. This gives $3^2 = 9$ matrices:

$$\Theta_{0,0} = \begin{pmatrix} 1 & 0 & 0 \\ 0 & 1 & 0 \end{pmatrix}.$$

$$\Theta_{0,1} = \begin{pmatrix} 1 & 0 & 1 \\ 0 & 1 & 0 \end{pmatrix}, \Theta_{0,2} = \begin{pmatrix} 1 & 0 & 2 \\ 0 & 1 & 0 \end{pmatrix}, \Theta_{0,3} = \begin{pmatrix} 1 & 0 & 0 \\ 0 & 1 & 1 \end{pmatrix}, \Theta_{0,4} = \begin{pmatrix} 1 & 0 & 1 \\ 0 & 1 & 1 \end{pmatrix},$$

$$\Theta_{0,5} = \begin{pmatrix} 1 & 0 & 2 \\ 0 & 1 & 1 \end{pmatrix}, \Theta_{0,6} = \begin{pmatrix} 1 & 0 & 0 \\ 0 & 1 & 2 \end{pmatrix}, \Theta_{0,7} = \begin{pmatrix} 1 & 0 & 1 \\ 0 & 1 & 2 \end{pmatrix}, \Theta_{0,8} = \begin{pmatrix} 1 & 0 & 2 \\ 0 & 1 & 2 \end{pmatrix}.$$

The second radix obtained according to the lexicographic order is

$$R_1 = \begin{pmatrix} 1 & x & 0 \\ 0 & y & 1 \end{pmatrix}.$$

This second radix only gives 3 more matrices, because lexicographic order implies $y = 0$:

$$\Theta_{1,0} = \begin{pmatrix} 1 & 0 & 0 \\ 0 & 0 & 1 \end{pmatrix}, \Theta_{1,1} = \begin{pmatrix} 1 & 1 & 0 \\ 0 & 0 & 1 \end{pmatrix}, \Theta_{1,2} = \begin{pmatrix} 1 & 2 & 0 \\ 0 & 0 & 1 \end{pmatrix}.$$

We then obtain a last radix

$$\Theta_{2,0} = \begin{pmatrix} x & 1 & 0 \\ y & 0 & 1 \end{pmatrix},$$

that gives no more matrix because lexicographic order implies $x = y = 0$. One can check that the number of classes in this case is indeed

$$\frac{N_3(3,2)}{C_3(2)} = 13.$$

A World Wide Number Field Sieve Factoring Record: On to 512 Bits

James Cowie[1], Bruce Dodson[2], R. Marije Elkenbracht-Huizing[3],
Arjen K. Lenstra[4], Peter L. Montgomery[5], Jörg Zayer[6]

[1] Cooperating Systems Corporation, 12 Hollywood Drive, Chestnut Hill, MA 02167,
U. S. A. E-mail: cowie@mumonkan.cooperate.com
[2] Department of Mathematics, Lehigh University, Bethlehem, PA 18015-3174, U. S. A.
E-mail: bad0@lehigh.edu
[3] Centrum voor Wiskunde en Informatica, Kruislaan 413, 1098 SJ Amsterdam,
The Netherlands. E-mail: marije@cwi.nl
[4] Citibank, N.A., 4 Sylvan Way, Parsippany, NJ 07054, U. S. A.
E-mail: arjen.lenstra@citicorp.com
[5] 780 Las Colindas Road, San Rafael, CA 94903-2346, U. S. A.
E-mail: pmontgom@cwi.nl
[6] Gartenstrasse 13, 66352 Dorf im Warndt, Germany.
E-mail: j.zayer@ids-scheer.de

Abstract. We present data concerning the factorization of the 130-digit number RSA130 which we factored on April 10, 1996, using the Number Field Sieve factoring method. This factorization beats the 129-digit record that was set on April 2, 1994, by the Quadratic Sieve method. The amount of computer time spent on our new record factorization is only a fraction of what was spent on the previous record. We also discuss a World Wide Web interface to our sieving program that we have developed to facilitate contributing to the sieving stage of future large scale factoring efforts. These developments have a serious impact on the security of RSA public key cryptosystems with small moduli. We present a conservative extrapolation to estimate the difficulty of factoring 512-bit numbers.

1 Introduction

Over the past years several new record integer factorizations have been reported at cryptology conferences. At Eurocrypt'89 a record 100-digit factorization was announced; the result was obtained by running an existing factoring algorithm, the *Quadratic Sieve* method (QS), using a novel *factoring by email* approach (cf. [13]). At Eurocrypt'90 that approach was improved by a new *double large prime* variation of QS (cf. [14]): at the conference a record 107-digit factorization was reported, but the same approach led to a record 116-digit factorization in the journal version of the conference paper, later to a record 120-digit factorization at Crypto'93 (cf. [4]) and ultimately to a record 129-digit factorization at Asiacrypt'94 (cf. [1]).

In this paper we present a new 130-digit integer factoring record. Although our result may seem a marginal improvement over the previous record, the new record is in fact a dramatic step forward. In the first place, the record has been achieved by the *Number Field Sieve* factoring method (NFS) in only a fraction of the amount of computer time spent on the previous record. This shows that NFS is superior to QS for numbers of approximately 130 digits and larger, as far as current implementations are concerned. This had been suspected for a while (cf. [2]); experiments described in [6] suggest, however, that the crossover point between QS and NFS lies considerably lower than 130 digits.

In the second place, part of the work was carried out using a novel *World Wide Web interface* to our NFS implementation. Compared to the old factoring by email approach, the new interface makes it much easier to contribute to large factoring tasks: anybody with access to the World Wide Web is only a few mouse clicks away from becoming a factoring contributor. Because many processors on the World Wide Web have only limited memory, this required a new, more flexible NFS implementation, on top of the design and implementation of some necessary *Common Gateway Interface* scripts.

By using their Web browsers to complete fill-out forms, users invoke simple server-side CGI scripts written in Perl. A registration script, for example, creates appropriate entries in a distributed database of contributors, including a "privacy level" that allows contributors to request partial or total anonymity within the sieving effort. "Status" scripts allowed users to glimpse the latest snapshot of the sieving progress, and determine their standing within the "Hall of Fame" of major contributors. Still other Web pages and CGI scripts offered password-protected administrative services, input range checkout, relation set checkin, online tutorial information, and so forth.

Internet-distributed computing efforts are especially prone to transient connectivity failures; it is not uncommon for sites to disappear from view for minutes or hours at a time. A Web-based sieving effort centered around a central Web server would have imposed severe performance bottlenecks, as well as making the global sieving process prone to single-point failure. To promote scalability and fault-tolerance, additional CGI scripts made it possible to "check out" personalized copies of the Web server software, hyperlinked back to the originating server. These derivative subservers came complete with a large initial subrange of inputs, plus hierarchical protocols for refreshing the server's pool of inputs. As a result, only a prolonged failure (on the order of tens of hours) of the root of the server tree—the primary Web server at Cooperating Systems—would have brought the global sieving process to a halt.

We feel confident that a global Web-based computational environment, guaranteeing the anonymity of participants and based on "best-effort" coordination of contributed resources, can easily scale to hundreds of thousands of globally distributed participants. The practical consequences of these developments for the security of 512-bit RSA-moduli are interesting, as we show in Section 2. Section 3 gives background information on the 130-digit factorization. We conclude with a description of the Web-interface in Section 4.

2 On the security of 512-bit RSA-moduli

Both QS and NFS consist of three major steps: a *sieving step* to collect a set of data, a *matrix step* to find dependencies among the data, and a *final step* where the dependencies are used to derive a factorization. The final step of neither QS nor NFS is considered to be problematic: for QS because it is an entirely straightforward computation, for NFS because of the method developed by Peter L. Montgomery (cf. [15]). In this section we therefore restrict our attention to the sieving and matrix steps.

Let

$$L_x[u, v] = \exp(v(\ln x)^u (\ln \ln x)^{1-u}).$$

It is well known that the sieving and the matrix step of QS both run in heuristic expected time $L_n[1/2, 1 + o(1)]$, for $n \to \infty$, with n the number to be factored (cf. [11]). For numbers in our current range of interest, however, the sieving step takes considerably more time than the matrix step: for the factorization reported in [1] for instance less than 0.3% of the total effort was spent on the matrix step. Large scale QS factoring efforts have shown that the run time estimate $L_n[1/2, 1 + o(1)]$ with $o(1) = 0$ can be used for limited range extrapolations (cf. [1, 4, 14]). Thus, we may expect that the sieving step for the QS-factorization of a 512-bit RSA-modulus would require about one hundred times the effort spent on the 129-digit QS record.

The sieving and the matrix step of NFS both run in heuristic expected time $L_n[1/3, (64/9)^{1/3} + o(1)]$, for $n \to \infty$ (cf. [12]). Asymptotically this is substantially faster than QS. Although the sieving step is still the most time consuming part of the computation, for NFS the difference is much smaller than for QS: for a 119-digit NFS factorization reported in [6], the matrix step took about 7% of the entire computation. Assuming that the run time estimate $L_n[1/3, (64/9)^{1/3} + o(1)]$ can again, with $o(1) = 0$, be used for limited range extrapolations (our results combined with the ones from [6] support this assumption), we find that the sieving step for the NFS-factorization of a 512-bit RSA-modulus would require only about thirty times the effort spent on our current 130-digit NFS record. Since the sieving effort spent on our 130-digit record could have been less than 15% (as shown below) of the effort spent on the previous 129-digit record, we conclude that NFS-sieving for a 512-bit number could take less than 5 times the effort spent on the old 129-digit record, and less than one twentieth of the time required for QS. We stress that these comparisons only hold for current QS and NFS implementations—both might be improved in the future.

This is a disturbingly small security margin for 512-bit RSA-moduli. Several things have to be kept in mind, however. In the first place, this estimate addresses only the sieving step. Although we passed the crossover point between the sieving steps of QS and NFS, we have not reached it yet for the matrix steps—the NFS matrix for our 130-digit number had about seven times as many rows and columns as the QS matrix for the 129-digit record. The matrix step for a 512-bit NFS-factorization would without any doubt pose an interesting new challenge.

Right now this challenge looks hard, but certainly not unsurmountable. Secondly, the estimate does not incorporate possible improvements in the NFS-sieving step that are currently under consideration, and that could have a substantial impact on the sieving time. Finally, we want to reiterate that it is unwise to make predictions about the difficulty of factoring (cf. [1,9]).

3 Factoring RSA130

RSA130. Until April 10, 1996, RSA130 was the smallest unfactored number on the 'RSA challenge list' of d-digit composite numbers, for $d = 100, 110, 120, \ldots$, 490, 500. This list was compiled by RSA Data Security Corporation Inc. in the following manner (cf. [18]):

> Each RSA number is the product of two randomly chosen primes of approximately the same length. These primes were both chosen to be congruent to 2, modulo 3, so that the product could be used in an RSA public-key cryptosystem with public exponent 3. The primes were tested for primality using a probabilistic primality testing routine. After each product was computed, the primes were discarded, so no one—not even the employees of RSA Data Security—knows any product's factors.

RSA100 was factored in April 1991, RSA110 in April 1992 (cf. [5]), and RSA120 in June 1993 (cf. [4]). All these factorizations were achieved using the Quadratic Sieve factoring method. In this section we discuss our Number Field Sieve factorization of RSA130:

$$RSA130 = 18070\,82088\,68740\,48059\,51656\,16440\,59055\,66278\,10251\,67694\,01349\,17012\,70214$$

$$50056\,66254\,02440\,48387\,34112\,75908\,12303\,37178\,18879\,66563\,18201\,32148\,80557.$$

We assume that the reader is familiar with NFS (cf. [12]).

Polynomial selection. Let $n = $ RSA130. The first step of NFS is to select at least two irreducible polynomials with integer coefficients and a common root modulo n, the number to be factored. Although using more than two polynomials may turn out to be more efficient (cf. [8]), we used only two, as in [6,10,12]. In those references the choice of polynomials is restricted to the case where the common root m is an integer close to $n^{1/(d+1)}$ for some small integer d (such as 4 or 5); the polynomials can then be chosen as $f_1(X) = X - m$ and $f_2(X) = \sum_{i=0}^{d} c_i X^i$, where $n = \sum_{i=0}^{d} c_i m^i$ with $-m/2 \leq c_i \leq m/2$ is a base m representation of n.

For $j = 1, 2$ and integers a, b, let $N_j(a, b) = f_j(a/b) b^{\text{degree}(f_j)} \in \mathbf{Z}$. Relations, the type of data we collect during the sieving, are defined as pairs of coprime integers a, b, with $b > 0$, such that $N_j(a, b)$ has only prime factors $\leq B_j$, for $j = 1, 2$, and for appropriately chosen bounds B_1 and B_2. Thus, f_1 and f_2 should be chosen such that the N_j's have a relatively high probability to yield relations. At the moment only ad hoc strategies are known, which are not proven to construct and select the best polynomials possible. For RSA130 we did the following. Scott Huddleston from Oregon State University provided us with a

Table 1

#	yield	norm	B: 25	10^2	10^3	10^4	10^5
			9	25	168	1229	9592
14	100.0%	299.1%(14)	9(3)	25(3)	174(2)	1246(3)	9714(2)
4	99.1%	231.1%(10)	11(1)	25(4)	192(1)	1287(2)	9751(1)
1	93.7%	100.0%(1)	7(7)	19(12)	174(3)	1187(10)	9595(7)
12	87.5%	320.2%(15)	5(10)	24(5)	158(10)	1214(6)	9496(14)
8	82.2%	262.5%(11)	8(4)	24(6)	156(11)	1205(7)	9531(11)
3	80.0%	104.7%(2)	7(8)	21(9)	170(4)	1172(14)	9520(12)
10	77.8%	222.1%(9)	6(9)	27(1)	162(7)	1225(5)	9689(4)
2	76.8%	122.7%(3)	8(5)	21(10)	163(5)	1177(13)	9603(6)
11	76.6%	275.2%(13)	5(11)	23(8)	163(6)	1318(1)	9573(8)
15	75.9%	183.7%(7)	8(6)	26(2)	159(9)	1146(15)	9535(9)
9	75.4%	274.2%(12)	10(2)	20(11)	143(13)	1186(11)	9417(15)
5	70.1%	159.8%(5)	4(12)	18(13)	160(8)	1195(8)	9511(13)
7	64.9%	152.0%(4)	3(13)	18(14)	132(15)	1185(12)	9708(3)
13	64.2%	183.2%(6)	3(14)	24(7)	139(14)	1242(4)	9605(5)
6	57.8%	221.4%(8)	3(15)	14(15)	151(12)	1191(9)	9534(10)

list of 15 pairs of polynomials as above with $d = 5$ (i.e., each pair consisting of one linear and one degree 5 polynomial), ranked from 1 (best) to 15 (worst) depending on his experimental "goodness" measure that depends on the average size of the N_j's over some sieving rectangle.

The ranking that is most relevant for practical purposes is the actual yield in the sieving step. This is however rather expensive to compute. We did sieving experiments with all 15 pairs (using 500 *special q*'s, see below), and found that the pair that was the second worst (number 14) in Huddleston's ranking was most productive. In Table 1 the yields of all pairs are given in the second column, sorted by their relative yield compared to pair number 14. The number in the first column refers to the ranking given by Huddleston. For 7 of the 15 we did more sieving (a total of 800 special q's), confirming the earlier ordering, but giving slightly different relative percentages.

Assuming that a ranking is a randomly chosen permutation of $\{1, 2, \ldots, 15\}$, we define the *correlation coefficient* of two rankings x and y as $(E(xy) - E(x)E(y))/(\sigma(x)\sigma(y))$, with E denoting the expected value, and

$$\sigma(x) = \sqrt{E(x^2) - E(x)^2}.$$

Note that for all rankings x we have that $E(x) = 8$ and $\sigma(x) = \sqrt{56/3}$. The correlation coefficient of Huddleston's and the sieving rank is 0.1. This indicates that Huddleston's goodness measure does not effectively predict the sieving yield. It might be interesting to have a closer look at some of the polynomials he rejected.

In Table 1 we give several other rankings that are easy to compute and that might be useful to predict the sieving yield. The *norm* of a pair $(X - m, \sum_{i=0}^{5} c_i X^i)$ is defined as $m \sum_{i=0}^{5} |c_i|$. In the past rankings based on the norm have often been used. For the 15 candidates the norms relative to the pair with smallest norm are given in column 3, with the resulting norm rank in parentheses. The correlation coefficient of this norm rank and the sieving rank is -0.26. We conclude that the norm does not lead to a useful ranking. Columns 4 through 8 give the number of roots of the second polynomial of each pair modulo all primes $< B$, for $B = 25$, 10^2, 10^3, 10^4, and 10^5, with the resulting ranking between parentheses: more roots are supposedly better and therefore give a lower ranking (the second row contains the values of $\pi(B)$). The resulting correlation coefficients with the sieving rank are: 0.69, 0.54, 0.77, 0.29, and 0.24. Some of these rankings are well correlated with the sieving rank, but they are not reliable predictors: polynomial number 11, ranked 9th for sieving, ranks first for $B = 10^4$. The ranking induced by the average root ranking has correlation coefficient 0.75 with the sieving ranking.

We also found the much better ranking 2, 1, 5, 7, 10, 3, 4, 6, 11, 8, 9, 13, 14, 12, 15 (i.e., Huddleston's number 14 got ranked second, his number 4 got ranked first, etc., until his number 6 which got ranked last) with correlation coefficient 0.86 with the sieving rank. This ranking was obtained by combining the integral of $f_1 \cdot f_2$ over the sieving region with information about the number of real roots and roots modulo primes $< 10^4$, and by considering extreme residual values after sieving instead of average values. Details may be published at a later occasion. We leave the problem of polynomial selection for NFS as a subject for further study.

As a result of the sieving experiments, we decided to use the polynomial that ranked as number 14 on Huddleston's list: $d = 5$, $m = 125\,74411\,16841\,80059\,80468$, $f_1(X) = X - m$, and

$$
\begin{aligned}
f_2(X) =\ & 5748\,30224\,87384\,05200\,X^5 +\ \ 9882\,26191\,74822\,86102\,X^4 \\
& -13392\,49938\,91281\,76685\,X^3 + 16875\,25245\,88776\,84989\,X^2 \\
& +\ 3759\,90017\,48552\,08738\,X\ -\ 46769\,93055\,39319\,05995.
\end{aligned}
$$

Sieving. To find relations we mostly [7] used *lattice sieving with sieving by vectors* as introduced in [17]. We followed the approach sketched and used in [10] and [6], with three important modifications. In the first place, unlike [17], but like [7] we allowed *special q*'s in $N_2(a, b)$ that are larger than B_2. As usual, disjoint ranges of special q's were assigned to different processors, and for efficiency reasons the sizes of the q's depended on the amount of available memory. For implementation technical reasons the q's were bounded from above by $2 \cdot 36^5 \approx 1.2 \cdot 10^8$. Secondly, unlike [10] we allowed processors to use lower values for B_1 and B_2, depending on memory restrictions. In the third place, the physical size of the lattice sieving array depended on the size of the available memory. As a consequence of these changes, the sieving program could be distributed much easier over a variety of machines than the program from [10].

---

[7] We also did a relatively small amount of traditional line-by-line sieving.

Table 2

Memory	$q < B_2$ $q/10^6 \in$	$q \geq B_2$ $q/10^6 \geq$
4M		86
6M		43
8M	$[0.5, 1.9]$	29
10M	$[1.9, 3.8]$	21
12M	$[3.8, 5.8]$	17
14M	$[5.8, 7.9]$	14
16M	$[7.9, 10.0]$	12
$\geq$ 18M	$[2, 11.4]$	2

We describe this set-up in more detail. Let $B_1 = 3497867$ and $B_2 = 11380951$. The number of roots of f_j modulo the primes $\leq B_j$ is 250001 for $j = 1$ and 750001 for $j = 2$. All processors that have at least 18 megabytes available to the siever used this B_1 and B_2; all available memory that remained after storing all relevant factor base data for these B_1 and B_2 was used for the sieving array. As a result 18 megabyte machines used a sieve of at least 2 megabytes: about 2 megabytes if the special q is $> B_2$, more than 2 megabytes if $q < B_2$, because in that case only the (prime, root) pairs from the second factor base for which the prime is at most q need to be stored (so that any remaining memory could be assigned to the sieve array as well).

If less than 18 megabytes was available, we did the following. At least 2 megabytes was used for the sieve. If the special q is $< B_2$, the complete first factor base was used, and all (prime, root) pairs from the second factor base with the prime $\leq q$. This meant that not all $q < B_2$ could be used; Table 2 gives the ranges of q's less than B_2 that we used (and that fit) on machines of various sizes; the q's were also bounded from below to make sure that at least some q's were available for smaller machines. Special q's less than B_2 were not used on machines with at most 6 megabytes. If the special q is $\geq B_2$, only $[x \cdot 250001]$ pairs from the first factor base and $[x \cdot 750001]$ pairs from the second factor base were used, for the largest positive $x \leq 1$ such that all relevant data fit in memory. So, processors with small memories used rather small factor bases, and were therefore not very productive. We therefore reserved the smaller (and better) special q's ($\geq B_2$) for the larger machines; Table 2 gives the lower bounds that we used for $q \geq B_2$ on machines of various sizes. In both cases any remaining memory was used for the sieve as well. Using this set-up the more than 6 million special q's that were available could be distributed over the available processors (and memory) without running out of sieving tasks and without wasting good q's on small machines.

Sieving time. Because sieving was done on machines of many different sizes, and because the number of relations found per second strongly depends on the memory size, it is hard to estimate how much time was spent on the sieving step. We can say, however, that the first $\approx 25 \cdot 10^5$ special q's would have generated about $7 \cdot 10^7$ relations, with at most 20% duplicates (and therefore at least $56 \cdot 10^6$

unique relations, which sufficed; see below). Since we sieved over the rectangle $[-4096, 4095] \times [1, 4000]$ not including the 'even,even' locations, inspecting a total of $\approx 6 \cdot 10^{13}$ sieve locations would have sufficed, with approximately one of every 860000 locations producing a relation. On a Sparc 10 workstation with 24 megabytes available for the sieving process, this would have taken 16.5 years. For 32, 40, and 48 megabytes these timings improve to 15.4, 14.7, and 14.5 years, respectively, but for 20, 16, and 12 megabytes it deteriorates to 18.5, 25, and 32 years, respectively. On the same workstation sieving for the 129-digit QS record would have taken approximately 120 years (cf. [1]). All these timings are $\approx 24\%$ better on a 90Mhz Pentium PC. It is therefore fair to say that sieving for RSA130 could have been done in less than 15% of the time spent on the 129-digit number.

Cycles. As usual we refer to the relations introduced above as *full relations* and the relations with one or more *large primes* $> B_j$ in the factorization of $N_j(a,b)$ as *partial relations*. With $B_1 = 3497867$ and $B_2 = 11380951$ the number of full relations combined with the number of *cycles* (cf. [6]) among the partial relations should be comfortably more than $250001 + 750001 \approx 10^6$ before the factorization can be completed (cf. [12]). The number of cycles can be counted by finding the *useful* partial relations (i.e., the largest subset of the partials in which each large prime occurs at least twice), and by subtracting the resulting number of large primes from the number of usefuls. In Table 3 it can be seen how the number of usefuls and cycles at first slowly increases as a function of the number of partials (after all duplicates had been removed), and how first the number of usefuls and then the number of cycles suddenly grows quite rapidly, as illustrated by the average cycle length (#usefuls/#cycles) in the last column. This was expected based on the data from [6]. The number in row labeled i and column labeled j of Table 4 gives the number of relations with i large primes in $N_1(a,b)$ and j large primes in $N_2(a,b)$, in the final collection of 56515672 relations. The relations referred to in columns labeled 4, 5, and 6, and those in rows labeled 4 and 5 were found early in the sieving stage when one of the authors was using slightly larger B_1 and B_2 than given above. In uncompressed format, listing only the primes $> 2 \cdot 10^6$ per $N_i(a,b)$, the final collection took about 3.5 gigabytes of disk space.

To make the amounts of data more manageable, we first extracted 8426508 partial relations leading to the shortest 968737 cycles (note that $48400 + 968737 = 1017137 > 10^6$ as required). These data could have been used to build a matrix of 1017137 rows (corresponding to the fulls and the cycles) and 1000002 columns (corresponding to the primes $\leq B_i$ in $N_i(a,b)$). As shown in [6: Section 5], however, removing all large primes from the matrix makes it relatively dense and thus expensive to process the matrix. We therefore also included columns in the matrix for large primes that occur at least 4 times in the collection of 8426508 relations. This led to 826592 and 1678272 additional columns for large primes in $N_1(a,b)$ and $N_2(a,b)$, respectively, 1527391 new 'full relations' (i.e., partial relations with only large primes corresponding to the new columns), and 1946210 cycles among the remaining partial relations. The resulting matrix has

Table 3

Date	#fulls	#partials	#usefuls	#cycles	length
95 08 30	4427	2524973	365	179	2.0
95 09 20	21407	8288179	4021	1880	2.1
95 10 14	36434	16756214	14202	6365	2.2
95 11 05	41248	26872640	26450	10553	2.5
95 11 24	44031	35016001	37969	14177	2.7
95 12 10	45653	41319347	47660	16914	2.8
95 12 19	46648	45431262	8214349	224865	36.5
96 01 06	48211	53282421	11960120	972121	12.3
96 01 14	48400	56467272	18830237	2844859	6.6

Table 4

	0	1	2	3	4	5	6
0	48400	479737	1701253	1995537	6836	403	9
1	272793	2728107	9617073	11313254	39755	2212	44
2	336850	3328437	11520120	13030845	56146	3214	71
3	1056	9022	24455	0	0	0	0
4	3	9	31	0	0	0	0

$1000002 + 826592 + 1678272 = 3504866$ columns and $48400 + 1527391 + 1946210 = 3522001$ rows. Note that $3522001 - 3504866 = 1017137 - 1000002$, i.e., the larger matrix is over-square by the same amount as the original matrix, as expected.

A matrix with more than $3.5 \cdot 10^6$ rows and columns is rather large, which makes the matrix step difficult. Also, we may expect $\approx (8426508 + 48400)/2$ relations per dependency, which makes the final step quite expensive too. It is likely that if we had collected more relations, far fewer than 8426508 partial relations would have sufficed to generate the required $> 10^6 - 48400$ cycles, thus making the matrix and final steps easier. In future factorizations this strategy should probably be used to keep the matrix size within reasonable bounds. Also one could try the filtering strategy described in [7], which might give better results than the approach followed here.

The matrix step. After substituting *free relations* (cf. [12]) for the 7000 heaviest rows, and removing some of the excess heavy rows, the above 3522001×3504866 matrix resulted in a 3516502×3504823 bit matrix of total weight 138690744 (on average 39.4 entries per row). To find dependencies modulo 2 among the rows of this matrix we used the *blocked Lanczos* method from [16] on a Cray C-90 supercomputer. Blocked Lanczos consists of a sequence of multiplications of the matrix and its transpose with a *blocked vector*, i.e., b bit-vectors simultaneously, where b is an implementation dependent *blocking factor*. The number of multiplications needed is, approximately, $m/(b - 0.76)$ for an $m \times m$ bit matrix. The best configuration we managed to find on the Cray C-90 was $b = 64$ which resulted in 4.37 seconds per iteration.

As a result it took 67.5 CPU-hours (using a single processor) and 700 megabytes central memory to find 18 dependencies. Each dependency consisted

Table 5

	0	1	2	3	4	5	6
0	24242	154099	330738	255742	1054	52	1
1	75789	443647	885136	648148	2734	164	2
2	56326	300369	565605	389046	1923	131	4
3	182	776	1105	0	0	0	0
4	2	4	7	0	0	0	0

of ≈ 4140000 relations (≈ 3500 of which are free). For one of the dependencies, the breakdown of the large primes amongst its 4140328 (non-free) relations is given in Table 5; this dependency also contained 3506 free relations.

The final step. Let S be the set of relations in a dependency, let α_2 be such that $f_2(\alpha_2) = 0$, and let φ be the homomorphism from $\mathbf{Z}[\alpha_2]$ to $\mathbf{Z}/n\mathbf{Z}$ that maps α_2 to m modulo n. From the matrix step we know that $\gamma_1 = \prod_{(a,b) \in S}(a - bm)$ is a square in $\mathbf{Z}$, say β_1^2, and that $\gamma_2 = \prod_{(a,b) \in S}(a - b\alpha_2)$ is a square in $\mathbf{Z}[\alpha_2]$, say β_2^2. Furthermore, we have that $\gamma_1 \equiv \varphi(\gamma_2) \bmod n$. In the final step we compute $\beta_1 \bmod n$ and $\varphi(\beta_2)$ and attempt to factor n by computing $\gcd(\beta_1 \bmod n - \varphi(\beta_2), n)$.

Computing $\beta_1 \bmod n$ is straightforward, because the prime factorization of all $a - bm$'s is known. To compute $\varphi(\beta_2)$ we used the method from [15]. Instead of γ_2, we work with $\prod_{(a,b) \in S}(a - b\alpha_2)^{\pm 1}$, where the exponents are chosen as 1 or -1 in an attempt to maximize the amount of cancellation between the numerator and the denominator. Note that the -1's can easily be incorporated in the previous argument. The resulting fraction for the product would, when written out, have approximately 9.7 million decimal digits. After about 10^5 iterations, each of which reduced the numerator or denominator of the product by about 200 decimal digits, the algebraic square root was reduced to the trivial square root of 1. This took 49.5 CPU-hours on a single 150 MHz R4400SC processor of an SGI Challenge. The first two dependencies resulted in the trivial factorization. The third one produced:

RSA130 = 39685 99945 95974 54290 16112 61628 83786 06757 64491 12810 06483 25551 57243

· 45534 49864 67359 72188 40368 68972 74408 86435 63012 63205 06960 09990 44599.

4   The Web-interface

Previous factoring efforts used electronic mail as a medium for simple sieving task distribution and relation collection. Since the 129-digit factorization reported at Asiacrypt'94 (cf. [1]), however, Web browser technology has achieved universal penetration of the desktop. Using the Common Gateway Interface (CGI) for providing simple scripted executable content, we constructed a package of Perl scripts that automated most of the work involved in constructing an ad hoc, global-scale sieving workgroup.

Web-factoring volunteers commonly located our Web server by way of a commercial search engine. From one set of Web pages, they could then access a wide range of support services for the sieving step of the factorization: NFS software distribution, project documentation, anonymous user registration, dissemination of sieving tasks, collection of relations, relation archival services, and real-time sieving status reports. We also constructed CGI scripts to support cluster management, directing individual sieving workstations through appropriate day/night sleep cycles to minimize the impact on their owners. Once volunteers downloaded and built the GNFSD sieving software daemon, the daemon automatically became a Web client, using the HTTP protocol to GET q-values from, and POST the resulting relations back to, a CGI script on the Web server.

Three factors combined to make this approach succeed. First, the flexibility of our NFS implementation allowed even single workstations with 4 megabytes to perform useful work using small bounds B_1 and B_2 and a small sieve. Second, we supported anonymous registration—users could contribute their hardware resources to the sieving effort without revealing their identity to anyone other than the local server administrator. Anonymity is a critical prerequisite for altruism, in order to protect contributors from having their donated resources attacked or misused as their reward.

Finally, we recruited other sites to run the CGI script package locally, forming a hierarchical network of RSA130 Web servers. The root server, located at Cooperating Systems, was fed large consecutive ranges of q's by hand; automated scripts then managed the fragmentation and distribution of these large tasks to sieving clients and other Web servers at Boston University and the Northeastern Parallel Architecture Center at Syracuse University. Those remote servers in turn partitioned the incoming q-ranges into manageable tasks for their local single-workstation sievers. These NFS sieving processes interacted directly with CGI scripts on the remote Web server to return their relations and receive a new task to work on; this automated dialog between NFS sieving clients and their host Web server allowed sieving to proceed around the clock with minimal human intervention.

Next Steps. Since we began the Web-based factoring project, Web technologies have taken another major step forward: the widespread availability of Java as a tool for donation and coordination of globally distributed resources. Existing CGI scripts, written in Perl, invented cumbersome protocols for preserving state between successive CGI invocations. By contrast, a Java-based HTTP server can offer integrated Java services, route successive service requests to previous invocations, and dynamically extend its functionality by loading new services at runtime. CGI performance is vastly improved, since instead of forking a new process per CGI request and loading the appropriate interpreter executable, the Java interpreter is already in core and executing when requests for service arrive. As a result, we are currently working on a new revision of the factoring software framework, combining Java-based Web servers, extensible applet interfaces, and NFS sieving code integrated via Java's native method interface.

This software framework will provide many additional management services that are common to globally coordinated volunteer computations, cutting the time required to ramp up and field future factoring projects. These services will include hooks to public-key encryption for interserver communication (authenticating tasks, results, and software upgrades), anonymous user database management, scalable implementations of general-purpose hierarchical multiserver task queues, improved fault-tolerance via distributed persistent state, and Web-based cluster management tools.

Global Implications. We made no formal announcement of the availability of our early prototype Web software. Nonetheless, by virtual word-of-mouth we attracted the interest of browsers from over 500 different Internet hosts; 20 percent of those hosts later participated in the sieving stage. These ranged from SLIP-connected home computers to high-performance corporate workstation clusters, and literally covered the globe. Browsers from 28 countries, from AT (Austria) to ZA (South Africa), left their prints on the RSA130 project.

In future large scale factoring efforts, therefore, we predict that Web technologies will allow us to easily recruit the spare cycles and aggregate memory of individual computers world-wide. We have already demonstrated that using the Internet to provide anonymous point-and-click accessibility to large computational problems is an effective mechanism for tackling problems of communal significance. Meanwhile, steady algorithmic improvements are making our sieving algorithms more flexible and amenable to global participation. As we have seen in Section 2, these developments seriously affect the security of 512-bit RSA-moduli.

Acknowledgments. Acknowledgments are due to to Scott Huddleston and Oregon State University for providing us with 15 candidate pairs of polynomials, and to the contributors to the World Wide Web sieving project. We especially thank our partners at Boston University and the Northeastern Parallel Architecture Center at Syracuse University for their help debugging several prereleases of the Web software, and for useful feedback. This work was sponsored by the Stichting Nationale Computerfaciliteiten (National Computing Facilities Foundation, NCF) for the use of supercomputer facilities, with financial support from the Nederlandse Organisatie voor Wetenschappelijk Onderzoek (Netherlands Organization for Scientific Research, NWO). The fourth author's work on this paper was done at Bellcore.

References

1. D. Atkins, M. Graff, A.K. Lenstra, and P.C. Leyland, *THE MAGIC WORDS ARE SQUEAMISH OSSIFRAGE*, Advances in Cryptology, Asiacrypt'94, Lecture Notes in Comput. Sci. **917** (1995), 265–277.
2. D. J. Bernstein, A. K. Lenstra, A general number field sieve implementation, 103–126 in: [12]

3. J. Buchmann, J. Loho, J. Zayer, *An implementation of the general number field sieve*, Advances in Cryptology, Crypto '93, Lecture Notes in Comput. Sci. **773** (1994) 159–165.

4. T. Denny, B. Dodson, A. K. Lenstra, M. S. Manasse, *On the factorization of RSA-120*, Advances in Cryptology, Crypto '93, Lecture Notes in Comput. Sci. **773** (1994) 166–174.

5. B. Dixon, A. K. Lenstra, *Factoring integers using SIMD sieves*, Advances in Cryptology, Eurocrypt '93, Lecture Notes in Comput. Sci. **765** (1994) 28–39.

6. B. Dodson, A. K. Lenstra, *NFS with four large primes: an explosive experiment*, Advances in Cryptology, Crypto '95, Lecture Notes in Comput. Sci. **963** (1995) 372–385.

7. R. M. Elkenbracht-Huizing, *An implementation of the number field sieve*, Technical Report NM-R9511, Centrum voor Wiskunde en Informatica, Amsterdam, 1995; to appear in Experimental Mathematics.

8. R. M. Elkenbracht-Huizing, *A multiple polynomial general number field sieve*, Proceedings ANTS II, to appear.

9. M. Gardner, *Mathematical games, A new kind of cipher that would take millions of years to break*, Scientific American, August 1977, 120–124.

10. R. Golliver, A. K. Lenstra, K. McCurley, *Lattice sieving and trial division*, ANTS '94, Lecture Notes in Comput. Sci. **877** (1994) 18–27.

11. A. K. Lenstra, H. W. Lenstra, Jr., *Algorithms in number theory*, Chapter 12 in: J. van Leeuwen (ed.), *Handbook of theoretical computer science*, Volume A, *Algorithms and complexity*, Elsevier, Amsterdam, 1990.

12. A. K. Lenstra, H. W. Lenstra, Jr. (eds), The development of the number field sieve, Lecture Notes in Math. **1554**, Springer-Verlag, Berlin, 1993.

13. A. K. Lenstra, M. S. Manasse, *Factoring by electronic mail*, Advances in Cryptology, Eurocrypt '89, Lecture Notes in Comput. Sci. **434** (1990) 355–371.

14. A. K. Lenstra, M. S. Manasse, *Factoring with two large primes*, Advances in Cryptology, Eurocrypt '90, Lecture Notes in Comput. Sci. **473** (1991) 72–82; Math. Comp., **63** (1994) 785–798.

15. P. L. Montgomery, *Square roots of products of algebraic numbers*, Proceedings of Symposia in Applied Mathematics, Mathematics of Computation 1943-1993, Vancouver, 1993, Walter Gautschi, ed.

16. P. L. Montgomery, *A block Lanczos algorithm for finding dependencies over GF(2)*, Advances in Cryptology, Eurocrypt'95, Lecture Notes in Comput. Sci. **921** (1995) 106–120.

17. J. M. Pollard, The lattice sieve, 43–49 in: [12].

18. RSA Data Security Corporation Inc., sci.crypt, May 18, 1991; information available by sending electronic mail to challenge-rsa-list@rsa.com.

Author Index

Abe, M. 244
Anderson, R. 26
Biehl, I. 15
Bleichenbacher, D. 145
Bosselaers, A. 65
Chabaud, F. 368
Chan, A. 276
Chee, S. T. 232, 360
Cowie, J. 382
De Gersem, P. 65
De Win, E. 65
Dodson, B. 382
Elkenbracht-Huizing, R. M. 382
Fan, C.-I. 116
Frankel, Y. 276, 286
Fujisaki, E. 244
Geiselmann, W. 346
Gollmann, D. 133, 346
Hawkes, P. 105
Horster, P. 125, 334
Imai, H. 185
Just, M. 36
Kim, S. J. 311
Knudsen, L. 77
Kobara, K. 185
Korjik, V. 210
Kurosawa, K. 218
Kushnir, D. 210
Lenstra, A. K. 57, 382
Lee, D. K. 232
Lee, S. J. 232, 360
Lei, C.-L. 116

MacKenzie, P. 276
Mambo, M. 322
Maurer, U. 145, 196
McCurley, K. S. 50
Meyer, B. 15
Michels, M. 125, 334
Miyaji, A. 1
Montgomery, P. L. 382
M'Raïhi, D. 266
Nyberg, K. 91
O'Connor, L. 105
Okamoto, E. 322
Park, S. J. 311
Park, S. J. 360
Park, S. M. 360
Pointcheval, D. 252
Preneel, B. 77
Sakurai, K. 159, 322
Satoh, T. 218
Stern, J. 252, 301, 368
Sung, S. H. 232
Thiel, C. 15
Tsiounis, Y. 276, 286
Tsujii, S. 173
Vandenberghe, S. 65
Vandewalle, J. 65
Vaudenay, S. 26, 36
Wolf, S. 196
Won, D. H. 311
Yung, M. 286
Zayer, J. 382
Zhou, J. Y. 133

Lecture Notes in Computer Science

For information about Vols. 1–1083

please contact your bookseller or Springer-Verlag

Vol. 1086: C. Frasson, G. Gauthier, A. Lesgold (Eds.), Intelligent Tutoring Systems. Proceedings, 1996. XVII, 688 pages. 1996.

Vol. 1087: C. Zhang, D. Lukose (Eds.), Distributed Artificial Intelliegence. Proceedings, 1995. VIII, 232 pages. 1996. (Subseries LNAI).

Vol. 1088: A. Strohmeier (Ed.), Reliable Software Technologies – Ada-Europe '96. Proceedings, 1996. XI, 513 pages. 1996.

Vol. 1089: G. Ramalingam, Bounded Incremental Computation. XI, 190 pages. 1996.

Vol. 1090: J.-Y. Cai, C.K. Wong (Eds.), Computing and Combinatorics. Proceedings, 1996. X, 421 pages. 1996.

Vol. 1091: J. Billington, W. Reisig (Eds.), Application and Theory of Petri Nets 1996. Proceedings, 1996. VIII, 549 pages. 1996.

Vol. 1092: H. Kleine Büning (Ed.), Computer Science Logic. Proceedings, 1995. VIII, 487 pages. 1996.

Vol. 1093: L. Dorst, M. van Lambalgen, F. Voorbraak (Eds.), Reasoning with Uncertainty in Robotics. Proceedings, 1995. VIII, 387 pages. 1996. (Subseries LNAI).

Vol. 1094: R. Morrison, J. Kennedy (Eds.), Advances in Databases. Proceedings, 1996. XI, 234 pages. 1996.

Vol. 1095: W. McCune, R. Padmanabhan, Automated Deduction in Equational Logic and Cubic Curves. X, 231 pages. 1996. (Subseries LNAI).

Vol. 1096: T. Schäl, Workflow Management Systems for Process Organisations. XII, 200 pages. 1996.

Vol. 1097: R. Karlsson, A. Lingas (Eds.), Algorithm Theory – SWAT '96. Proceedings, 1996. IX, 453 pages. 1996.

Vol. 1098: P. Cointe (Ed.), ECOOP '96 – Object-Oriented Programming. Proceedings, 1996. XI, 502 pages. 1996.

Vol. 1099: F. Meyer auf der Heide, B. Monien (Eds.), Automata, Languages and Programming. Proceedings, 1996. XII, 681 pages. 1996.

Vol. 1100: B. Pfitzmann, Digital Signature Schemes. XVI, 396 pages. 1996.

Vol. 1101: M. Wirsing, M. Nivat (Eds.), Algebraic Methodology and Software Technology. Proceedings, 1996. XII, 641 pages. 1996.

Vol. 1102: R. Alur, T.A. Henzinger (Eds.), Computer Aided Verification. Proceedings, 1996. XII, 472 pages. 1996.

Vol. 1103: H. Ganzinger (Ed.), Rewriting Techniques and Applications. Proceedings, 1996. XI, 437 pages. 1996.

Vol. 1104: M.A. McRobbie, J.K. Slaney (Eds.), Automated Deduction – CADE-13. Proceedings, 1996. XV, 764 pages. 1996. (Subseries LNAI).

Vol. 1105: T.I. Ören, G.J. Klir (Eds.), Computer Aided Systems Theory – CAST '94. Proceedings, 1994. IX, 439 pages. 1996.

Vol. 1106: M. Jampel, E. Freuder, M. Maher (Eds.), Over-Constrained Systems. X, 309 pages. 1996.

Vol. 1107: J.-P. Briot, J.-M. Geib, A. Yonezawa (Eds.), Object-Based Parallel and Distributed Computation. Proceedings, 1995. X, 349 pages. 1996.

Vol. 1108: A. Díaz de Ilarraza Sánchez, I. Fernández de Castro (Eds.), Computer Aided Learning and Instruction in Science and Engineering. Proceedings, 1996. XIV, 480 pages. 1996.

Vol. 1109: N. Koblitz (Ed.), Advances in Cryptology – Crypto '96. Proceedings, 1996. XII, 417 pages. 1996.

Vol. 1110: O. Danvy, R. Glück, P. Thiemann (Eds.), Partial Evaluation. Proceedings, 1996. XII, 514 pages. 1996.

Vol. 1111: J.J. Alferes, L. Moniz Pereira, Reasoning with Logic Programming. XXI, 326 pages. 1996. (Subseries LNAI).

Vol. 1112: C. von der Malsburg, W. von Seelen, J.C. Vorbrüggen, B. Sendhoff (Eds.), Artificial Neural Networks – ICANN 96. Proceedings, 1996. XXV, 922 pages. 1996.

Vol. 1113: W. Penczek, A. Szałas (Eds.), Mathematical Foundations of Computer Science 1996. Proceedings, 1996. X, 592 pages. 1996.

Vol. 1114: N. Foo, R. Goebel (Eds.), PRICAI'96: Topics in Artificial Intelligence. Proceedings, 1996. XXI, 658 pages. 1996. (Subseries LNAI).

Vol. 1115: P.W. Eklund, G. Ellis, G. Mann (Eds.), Conceptual Structures: Knowledge Representation as Interlingua. Proceedings, 1996. XIII, 321 pages. 1996. (Subseries LNAI).

Vol. 1116: J. Hall (Ed.), Management of Telecommunication Systems and Services. XXI, 229 pages. 1996.

Vol. 1117: A. Ferreira, J. Rolim, Y. Saad, T. Yang (Eds.), Parallel Algorithms for Irregularly Structured Problems. Proceedings, 1996. IX, 358 pages. 1996.

Vol. 1118: E.C. Freuder (Ed.), Principles and Practice of Constraint Programming — CP 96. Proceedings, 1996. XIX, 574 pages. 1996.

Vol. 1119: U. Montanari, V. Sassone (Eds.), CONCUR '96: Concurrency Theory. Proceedings, 1996. XII, 751 pages. 1996.

Vol. 1120: M. Deza. R. Euler, I. Manoussakis (Eds.), Combinatorics and Computer Science. Proceedings, 1995. IX, 415 pages. 1996.

Vol. 1121: P. Perner, P. Wang, A. Rosenfeld (Eds.), Advances in Structural and Syntactical Pattern Recognition. Proceedings, 1996. X, 393 pages. 1996.

Vol. 1122: H. Cohen (Ed.), Algorithmic Number Theory. Proceedings, 1996. IX, 405 pages. 1996.

Vol. 1123: L. Bougé, P. Fraigniaud, A. Mignotte, Y. Robert (Eds.), Euro-Par'96. Parallel Processing. Proceedings, 1996, Vol. I. XXXIII, 842 pages. 1996.

Vol. 1124: L. Bougé, P. Fraigniaud, A. Mignotte, Y. Robert (Eds.), Euro-Par'96. Parallel Processing. Proceedings, 1996, Vol. II. XXXIII, 926 pages. 1996.

Vol. 1125: J. von Wright, J. Grundy, J. Harrison (Eds.), Theorem Proving in Higher Order Logics. Proceedings, 1996. VIII, 447 pages. 1996.

Vol. 1126: J.J. Alferes, L. Moniz Pereira, E. Orlowska (Eds.), Logics in Artificial Intelligence. Proceedings, 1996. IX, 417 pages. 1996. (Subseries LNAI).

Vol. 1127: L. Böszörményi (Ed.), Parallel Computation. Proceedings, 1996. XI, 235 pages. 1996.

Vol. 1128: J. Calmet, C. Limongelli (Eds.), Design and Implementation of Symbolic Computation Systems. Proceedings, 1996. IX, 356 pages. 1996.

Vol. 1129: J. Launchbury, E. Meijer, T. Sheard (Eds.), Advanced Functional Programming. Proceedings, 1996. VII, 238 pages. 1996.

Vol. 1130: M. Haveraaen, O. Owe, O.-J. Dahl (Eds.), Recent Trends in Data Type Specification. Proceedings, 1995. VIII, 551 pages. 1996.

Vol. 1131: K.H. Höhne, R. Kikinis (Eds.), Visualization in Biomedical Computing. Proceedings, 1996. XII, 610 pages. 1996.

Vol. 1132: G.-R. Perrin, A. Darte (Eds.), The Data Parallel Programming Model. XV, 284 pages. 1996.

Vol. 1133: J.-Y. Chouinard, P. Fortier, T.A. Gulliver (Eds.), Information Theory and Applications II. Proceedings, 1995. XII, 309 pages. 1996.

Vol. 1134: R. Wagner, H. Thoma (Eds.), Database and Expert Systems Applications. Proceedings, 1996. XV, 921 pages. 1996.

Vol. 1135: B. Jonsson, J. Parrow (Eds.), Formal Techniques in Real-Time and Fault-Tolerant Systems. Proceedings, 1996. X, 479 pages. 1996.

Vol. 1136: J. Diaz, M. Serna (Eds.), Algorithms – ESA '96. Proceedings, 1996. XII, 566 pages. 1996.

Vol. 1137: G. Görz, S. Hölldobler (Eds.), KI-96: Advances in Artificial Intelligence. Proceedings, 1996. XI, 387 pages. 1996. (Subseries LNAI).

Vol. 1138: J. Calmet, J.A. Campbell, J. Pfalzgraf (Eds.), Artificial Intelligence and Symbolic Mathematical Computation. Proceedings, 1996. VIII, 381 pages. 1996.

Vol. 1139: M. Hanus, M. Rogriguez-Artalejo (Eds.), Algebraic and Logic Programming. Proceedings, 1996. VIII, 345 pages. 1996.

Vol. 1140: H. Kuchen, S. Doaitse Swierstra (Eds.), Programming Languages: Implementations, Logics, and Programs. Proceedings, 1996. XI, 479 pages. 1996.

Vol. 1141: H.-M. Voigt, W. Ebeling, I. Rechenberg, H.-P. Schwefel (Eds.), Parallel Problem Solving from Nature – PPSN IV. Proceedings, 1996. XVII, 1.050 pages. 1996.

Vol. 1142: R.W. Hartenstein, M. Glesner (Eds.), Field-Programmable Logic. Proceedings, 1996. X, 432 pages. 1996.

Vol. 1143: T.C. Fogarty (Ed.), Evolutionary Computing. Proceedings, 1996. VIII, 305 pages. 1996.

Vol. 1144: J. Ponce, A. Zisserman, M. Hebert (Eds.), Object Representation in Computer Vision. Proceedings, 1996. VIII, 403 pages. 1996.

Vol. 1145: R. Cousot, D.A. Schmidt (Eds.), Static Analysis. Proceedings, 1996. IX, 389 pages. 1996.

Vol. 1146: E. Bertino, H. Kurth, G. Martella, E. Montolivo (Eds.), Computer Security – ESORICS 96. Proceedings, 1996. X, 365 pages. 1996.

Vol. 1147: L. Miclet, C. de la Higuera (Eds.), Grammatical Inference: Learning Syntax from Sentences. Proceedings, 1996. VIII, 327 pages. 1996. (Subseries LNAI).

Vol. 1148: M.C. Lin, D. Manocha (Eds.), Applied Computational Geometry. Proceedings, 1996. VIII, 223 pages. 1996.

Vol. 1149: C. Montangero (Ed.), Software Process Technology. Proceedings, 1996. IX, 291 pages. 1996.

Vol. 1150: A. Hlawiczka, J.G. Silva, L. Simoncini (Eds.), Dependable Computing – EDCC-2. Proceedings, 1996. XVI, 440 pages. 1996.

Vol. 1151: Ö. Babaoglu, K. Marzullo (Eds.), Distributed Algorithms. Proceedings, 1996. VIII, 381 pages. 1996.

Vol. 1153: E. Burke, P. Ross (Eds.), Practice and Theory of Automated Timetabling. Proceedings, 1995. XIII, 381 pages. 1996.

Vol. 1154: D. Pedreschi, C. Zaniolo (Eds.), Logic in Databases. Proceedings, 1996. X, 497 pages. 1996.

Vol. 1155: J. Roberts, U. Mocci, J. Virtamo (Eds.), Broadbank Network Teletraffic. XXII, 584 pages. 1996.

Vol. 1156: A. Bode, J. Dongarra, T. Ludwig, V. Sunderam (Eds.), Parallel Virtual Machine – EuroPVM '96. Proceedings, 1996. XIV, 362 pages. 1996.

Vol. 1157: B. Thalheim (Ed.), Conceptual Modeling – ER '96. Proceedings, 1996. XII, 489 pages. 1996.

Vol. 1158: S. Berardi, M. Coppo (Eds.), Types for Proofs and Programs. Proceedings, 1995. X, 296 pages. 1996.

Vol. 1159: D.L. Borges, C.A.A. Kaestner (Eds.), Advances in Artificial Intelligence. Proceedings, 1996. XI, 243 pages. (Subseries LNAI).

Vol. 1160: S. Arikawa, A.K. Sharma (Eds.), Algorithmic Learning Theory. Proceedings, 1996. XVII, 337 pages. 1996. (Subseries LNAI).

Vol. 1161: O. Spaniol, C. Linnhoff-Popien, B. Meyer (Eds.), Trends in Distributed Systems. Proceedings, 1996. VIII, 289 pages. 1996.

Vol. 1162: D.G. Feitelson, L. Rudolph (Eds.), Job Scheduling Strategies for Parallel Processing. Proceedings, 1996. VIII, 291 pages. 1996.

Vol. 1163: K. Kim, T. Matsumoto (Eds.), Advances in Cryptology – ASIACRYPT '96. Proceedings, 1996. XII, 395 pages. 1996.

Vol. 1165: J.-R. Abrial, E. Börger, H. Langmaack (Eds.), Formal Methods for Industrial Applications. VIII, 511 pages. 1996.

Vol. 1166: M. Srivas, A. Camilleri (Eds.), Formal Methods in Computer-Aided Design. Proceedings, 1996. IX, 470 pages. 1996.

Springer
and the
environment

At Springer we firmly believe that an
international science publisher has a
special obligation to the environment,
and our corporate policies consistently
reflect this conviction.
We also expect our business partners –
paper mills, printers, packaging
manufacturers, etc. – to commit
themselves to using materials and
production processes that do not harm
the environment. The paper in this
book is made from low- or no-chlorine
pulp and is acid free, in conformance
with international standards for paper
permanency.

 Springer